Social Work Research and Evaluation

SOCIAL WORK RESEARCH *and* EVALUATION

Foundations of Evidence-Based Practice

EIGHTH EDITION

Edited by RICHARD M. GRINNELL, JR., and YVONNE A. UNRAU

OXFORD
UNIVERSITY PRESS

2008

OXFORD
UNIVERSITY PRESS

Oxford University Press, Inc., publishes works that further
Oxford University's objective of excellence
in research, scholarship, and education.

Oxford   New York
Auckland   Cape Town   Dar es Salaam   Hong Kong   Karachi
Kuala Lumpur   Madrid   Melbourne   Mexico City   Nairobi
New Delhi   Shanghai   Taipei   Toronto

With offices in
Argentina   Austria   Brazil   Chile   Czech Republic   France   Greece
Guatemala   Hungary   Italy   Japan   Poland   Portugal   Singapore
South Korea   Switzerland   Thailand   Turkey   Ukraine   Vietnam

Published by Oxford University Press, Inc.
198 Madison Avenue, New York, New York 10016

www.oup.com

Oxford is a registered trademark of Oxford University Press

Library of Congress Cataloging-in-Publication Data
Social work research and evaluation : foundations of evidence-based practice /
edited by Richard M. Grinnell, Jr. and Yvonne A. Unrau.—8th ed.
    p. cm.
Includes bibliographical references and index.
ISBN 978-0-19-530152-6
1. Social service—Research.   2. Evaluation research (Social action programs)
3. Evidence-based social work.   I. Grinnell, Richard M.   II. Unrau, Yvonne A.
HV11.S589 2007
361.3072—dc22   2007005044

9 8 7 6 5 4 3 2 1

Printed in the United States of America
on acid-free paper

With the input from students like yourself and instructors who used the previous seven editions of this book, we have further refined this edition with their comments in mind. Nevertheless, the audience for this edition remains the same as for the previous ones—advanced undergraduate and beginning graduate social work students who are taking a one-semester research methods course. The book is exceptionally informative and practical for MSW foundation research courses.

EVIDENCE-BASED PRACTICE

As before, our emphasis continues to be on how the goal of evidence-based practice is furthered by the understanding of the two research approaches—quantitative and qualitative (the old subtitle of our book). In a nutshell, the understanding of the research process is absolutely essential for you to become an evidence-based practitioner—as reflected in the book's new subtitle, *Foundations of Evidence-Based Practice*. It is our belief that you must know the basics of research methodology to even begin to use the concept of evidence-based practice effectively.

Thus, research in social work is presented as more than just a way to solve human problems, or to add to our knowledge base, or to guide evidence-based practice—though it is all of these. Since 1981, this book has symbolized tradition and change; it has applied timeless issues of research design and measurement to changing methodologies and social con-

cerns. It has broken some traditions and has taught students to try new research methods without losing sight of the old.

Many beginning social work research courses first cover basic research methodology and then apply this content to more advanced research courses that specialize in single-system designs (case-level evaluation) or program evaluation. Accordingly, we have designed this book to provide you with the basic methodological foundation you will need in order to obtain the advanced knowledge and skills presented in these two specialized advanced research courses.

We have made an extraordinary effort to make this edition less expensive, more aesthetically pleasing, and much more useful than ever before. We have strived to produce a "user-friendly," straightforward introduction to social work research methods couched within the positivist and interpretive traditions—the two approaches most commonly used to generate relevant social work knowledge. Within this spirit:

- We have written this book that emphasizes generalist social work practice. It fully complies with the Council on Social Work Education's (CSWE's) research requirements in this respect.
- We provide you with an extensive background on why social work research does not take place in a vacuum and explain how to be on guard for how your own ethnocentric perspectives influence how you will do research studies, participate in research studies, interpret the results from

research studies, or integrate the studies' findings into your daily practices.

- We discuss the rationale of why the quantitative and qualitative approaches to knowledge development have value, in addition to showing you that the greatest benefit that research can bring to our profession is combining both approaches in any given research study.
- We have included four new chapters (Part VII) on evidence-based practice.
- We have use numerous examples throughout the text in an effort to emphasize the link between practice and research in generalist social work settings.
- We discuss the application of research methods in real-life social service programs rather than in artificial settings.
- We stress numerous ethical issues that crop up when doing research throughout this book and a complete chapter (Chapter 2) is devoted to research ethics.
- We have heavily included human diversity content throughout the chapters. Many of our examples center around women and minorities, in recognition of the need for social workers to be knowledgeable of their special needs and problems. For example, Chapter 16 (Research With Minority and Disadvantaged Groups) gives special consideration to the application of research methods to the study of questions concerning these groups.
- We included only the core material that is realistically needed in order for you to appreciate and understand the role of research in social work. Our guiding philosophy has been to include only research material that you realistically need to know to function adequately as a social work practitioner; information overload was avoided at all costs.
- This book prepares you to become beginning critical consumers of the professional research literature. Thus, it does not prepare you with the necessary knowledge and skills to actually carry out a research study—no introductory research methods text can accomplish this formidable task.

- We explain terms with social work examples that you will appreciate. We have written this book in a crisp style using direct language.
- This book is easy to teach with and from.
- Numerous boxes are inserted throughout the book to complement and expand on the chapters; these boxes present interesting research examples, provide additional aids to learning, and offer historical, social, and political contexts of social work research.
- Numerous tables and figures have been used to provide visual representations of the concepts presented in the book.
- An extensive student-oriented Web site complements the book's contents.

NEW CONTENT

New content has been added to this edition in an effort to keep current, while retaining material that has stood the test of time. For example, a complete part, Part VII, contains four chapters that you need to know to engage in evidence-based practice.

This edition contains six new chapters that were not included in the seventh edition:

- Chapter 5, Conceptualization and Measurement
- Chapter 16, Research With Minority and Disadvantaged Groups
- Chapter 22, Finding Existing Knowledge
- Chapter 23, Evaluating Evidence
- Chapter 24, Meta-Analysis
- Chapter 25, Evidence-Based Practice

Six of the chapters contained in the previous edition have been rewritten by new authors:

- Chapter 2, The Ethical Conduct of Research
- Chapter 9, Structured Observation
- Chapter 14, Content Analysis
- Chapter 19, Writing Reports From Research Studies
- Chapter 20, Evaluating Quantitative Research Studies
- Chapter 21, Evaluating Qualitative Research Studies

NEW ORGANIZATION

Over the years, we have received hundreds of comments from users of the previous seven editions. With these comments, and with the CSWE's new research curriculum requirements in mind, we determined the specific topics to cover, the depth of the topics covered, and the sequencing of chapters within the book.

As in the preceding seven editions, this one is neither a brief primer in social work research nor a book intended for use as a reference manual. With a tremendous amount of input from both instructors and students, this edition has been reorganized into eight parts and 26 chapters. The new organization is an attempt to make the book more functional, realistic, and manageable for students and instructors alike.

Part I: The Contexts of Research

Part I consists of four chapters that lay the necessary background for the remaining parts within this book. More specifically, it examines the basic tenets that make the research method different from the other ways of knowing (Chapter 1), taking into account social work ethics (Chapter 2). The remaining two chapters present how the research method of knowing is composed of two research approaches—the quantitative research approach (Chapter 3) and the qualitative research approach (Chapter 4).

Part II: Designing Research Studies

Part II contains four chapters that build upon the chapters in Part I. They all center around how research studies are designed, from the study's initial conceptualization (Chapter 5) to the measurement of its variables (Chapter 5). Chapter 6 describes how to form a sample of research participants for a research study where the sample can be an individual person (or case) (Chapter 7) or a group of people (Chapter 8).

Part III: Collecting Data

Part III consists of six chapters that detail how to collect data via the most widely utilized social work data collection methods: observations (Chapters 9 and 10),

interviews (Chapter 11), surveys (Chapter 12), secondary analyses (Chapter 13), and content analyses (Chapter 14). Chapter 15, the final chapter in this part, details how to select a data collection strategy for any given research study.

Part IV: Becoming a Culturally Sensitive Researcher

Part IV contains one comprehensive chapter (Chapter 16) that describes how to do social work research with minority and disadvantaged groups of people.

Part V: Data Analysis

Part V consists of two introductory data analysis chapters: Chapter 17 discusses how to analyze quantitative data, and Chapter 18 describes how to do qualitative analyses.

Part VI: Writing and Evaluating Research Reports

Part VI contains a chapter that discusses how to write up a research report that is derived from a research study (Chapter 19). The remaining two chapters are geared toward evaluating quantitatively oriented studies (Chapter 20) and qualitatively oriented ones (Chapter 21).

Part VII: Becoming an Evidence-Based Practitioner

The four chapters in Part VII provide the basic building blocks for the evidence-based social work practitioner. More specifically, Chapter 22 discusses how to find existing information (literature), and the following chapter, Chapter 23, describes how to evaluate the information that is found. Chapter 24 details how meta-analyses are conducted and how they can be used within the evidence-based practitioner model. The final chapter of Part VII provides an introduction on how to do evidence-based practice utilizing the contents from the previous three chapters.

Part VIII: From Research to Evaluation

Part VIII contains one chapter, Chapter 26, on program evaluation. Program evaluation overlaps heavily with social work research. Since most of the research methods contained in this book are used in program evaluations in some form or another, this chapter deals less with the methods of program evaluation—methods contained in the previous 25 chapters—and focuses on four simple ways a social service program can be evaluated.

BOOK'S COMPANION WEB SITE

Our book offers a comprehensive Web site that you can access free of charge. For example, you can use the site when you:

- want to electronically look up a definition of a research concept
- want to click on relevant and important chapter-related links
- want to take short Web-based tutorials

CONTENT MEETS ACCREDITATION STANDARDS

As with the previous editions, we have written this one to comply with the Council on Social Work Education's research requirements for accredited schools and departments of social work at the undergraduate and graduate levels (see Box 1.1). In addition, the book is written with the 16 research principles contained in the National Association of Social Workers' Code of Ethics in mind (see Box 1.2).

LOGICAL AND FLEXIBLE TEACHING PLAN

The book is organized in a way that makes good sense in teaching fundamental research methods. Many other sequences that could be followed would make just as much sense, however. The chapters (and parts) in this book were consciously planned to be independent of one another. They can be read out of the order in which they are presented, or they can be selectively omitted. However, they will probably make the most sense to you if they are read in the sequence as presented, because each builds upon the preceding one.

In general, this edition is organized to help you master eight basic research-related skills that will help you to become an evidence-based practitioner:

Skill 1: Understand the Contexts of Research in Social Work
—Chapters 1 through 4

Skill 2: Understand How to Design a Research Study
—Chapters 5 through 8

Skill 3: Understand How to Collect Data and Select a Data Collection Method
—Chapters 9 through 15

Skill 4: Understand How to Become a Culturally Sensitive Researcher
—Chapter 16

Skill 5: Understand How to Analyze Data
—Chapters 17 and 18

Skill 6: Understand How to Write and Evaluate Research Reports and Proposals
—Chapters 19 through 21

Skill 7: Understand the Concept of Evidence-Based Practice
—Chapters 22 through 25

Skill 8: Understand How Social Work Programs Can Be Evaluated
—Chapter 26

A FINAL WORD

The field of research in our profession is continuing to grow and develop. We believe this edition will contribute to that growth. A ninth edition is anticipated, and suggestions for it are more than welcome. Please send your comments directly to Richard M. Grinnell, Jr., and Yvonne A. Unrau, School of Social Work, Western Michigan University, Kalamazoo, Michigan 49008.

Richard M. Grinnell, Jr.
Yvonne A. Unrau

Contents in Brief

Contents in Detail

Contributors

Jennifer L. Bellamy, PhD, is a postdoctoral fellow within the George Warren Brown School of Social Work at Washington University, Saint Louis, Missouri.

Sarah E. Bledsoe, PhD, is an assistant professor within the School of Social Work at the University of North Carolina at Chapel Hill, Chapel Hill, North Carolina.

Betty Blythe, PhD, is a professor within the Graduate School of Social Work at Boston College, Boston, Massachusetts.

Elaine Bouey, MEd, is a human resource consultant within the University of Calgary, Calgary, Alberta, Canada.

Heather Coleman, PhD, is a professor within the Faculty of Social Work at the University of Calgary, Calgary, Alberta, Canada.

Donald Collins, PhD, is a professor within the Faculty of Social Work at the University of Calgary, Calgary, Alberta, Canada.

Rafael J. Engel, PhD, is an associate professor within the School of Social Work at the University of Pittsburgh, Pittsburgh, Pennsylvania.

Lin Fang, PhD, is an adjunct associate research scholar and an adjunct assistant professor within the School of Social Work at Columbia University, New York, New York.

Peter A. Gabor, PhD, is a professor within the Faculty of Social Work at the University of Calgary, Calgary, Alberta, Canada.

Harvey Gochros, PhD, is an emeritus professor within the School of Social Work at the University of Hawaii at Manoa, Honolulu, Hawaii.

Richard M. Grinnell, Jr., PhD, is a professor and holds the Clair and Clarice Platt Jones/Helen Frays Endowed Chair of Social Work Research within the School of Social Work at Western Michigan University, Kalamazoo, Michigan.

Michael J. Holosko, PhD, is the Pauline M. Berger Professor of Family and Child Welfare within the School of Social Work at the University of Georgia, Athens, Georgia.

André Ivanoff, PhD, is an associate professor within the School of Social Work at Columbia University, New York, New York.

Johnny S. Kim, PhD, is an assistant professor within the School of Social Welfare at the University of Kansas, Lawrence, Kansas.

Judy L. Krysik, Ph.D., is an associate professor within the School of Social Work at Arizona State University, Tempe, Arizona.

Craig W. LeCroy, PhD, is a professor within the School of Social Work at Arizona State University, Tempe, Arizona.

Alice A. Lieberman, PhD, is a professor within the School of Social Welfare at the University of Kansas, Lawrence, Kansas.

Jennifer Manuel, MSW, is a doctoral candidate within the School of Social Work at Columbia University, New York, New York.

Thomas P. McDonald, PhD, is a professor within the School of Social Welfare at the University of Kansas, Lawrence, Kansas.

Robin McKinney, PhD, is an associate professor within the School of Social Work at Western Michigan University, Kalamazoo, Michigan.

Edward J. Mullen, PhD, is the Wilma and Albert Musher Professor for Life Betterment Through Science and Technology within the School of Social Work at Columbia University, New York, New York.

James C. Raines, PhD, is an associate professor within the School of Social Work at Illinois State University, Normal, Illinois.

Richard A. Polster, PhD, currently resides in Denver Colorado.

Allan N. Press, PhD, is a professor emeritus within the School of Social Welfare at the University of Kansas, Lawrence, Kansas.

William J. Reid, PhD, was a distinguished professor within the School of Social Welfare at the State University of New York, Albany, New York.

Gayla Rogers, PhD, is a professor within the Faculty of Social Work at the University of Calgary, Calgary, Alberta, Canada.

Allen Rubin, PhD, is the Bert Kruger Smith Centennial Professor in Social Work within the School of Social Work at the University of Texas at Austin, Austin, Texas.

Russell K. Schutt, PhD, is a professor within the Department of Sociology at the University of Massachusetts, Boston, Massachusetts.

Gary Solomon, M.S.W., currently resides in Portland Oregon.

Leslie Tutty, PhD, is professor within the Faculty of Social Work at the University of Calgary, Calgary, Alberta, Canada.

Yvonne A. Unrau, PhD, is an associate professor within the School of Social Work at Western Michigan University, Kalamazoo, Michigan.

Barbara Walters, PhD, is an assistant professor within the School of Social Work at Eastern Michigan University, Ypsilanti, Michigan.

Margaret Williams, PhD, is a professor within the Faculty of Social Work at the University of Calgary, Calgary, Alberta, Canada.

PART

The Contexts of Research

Part I consists of four chapters that lay the necessary background for the remaining parts within this book. More specifically, it examines the basic tenets that make the research method different from other ways of knowing (Chapter 1), taking into account social work ethics (Chapter 2). The remaining two chapters present how the research method of knowing is composed of two research approaches—the quantitative research approach (Chapter 3) and the qualitative research approach (Chapter 4).

Introduction

Richard M. Grinnell, Jr.
Yvonne A. Unrau
Margaret Williams

1

Basic Steps in the Research Process

You Are Here

Step 1   Choose a problem

2   Review the literature

3   Evaluate the literature

4   Be aware of all ethical issues

5   Be aware of all cultural issues

6   State the research question or hypothesis

7   Select the research approach

8   Determine how the variables are going to be measured

9   Select a sample

10   Select a data collection method

11   Collect and code the data

12   Analyze and interpret the data

13   Write the report

14   Disseminate the report

Madame Cleo is an astrological consultant. She advertises widely on television, promising that her astounding insights into love, business, health, and relationships will help her viewers to achieve more fulfilling and gratifying lives. Hah! you think. I bet she can't do this for me! I bet she's just out for the money! But if she could, but if she could only tell me . . . ! How do I know if she's for real or if I'm just getting taken for a ride? Perhaps the Enron Corporation could have used her services.

There is a parallel here between the people who receive social services—sometimes called clients—and you, the future social worker. Most people who we help—in common with all those people who are never seen by social workers—would like more fulfilling and rewarding lives. Like Madame Cleo's naive clientele who get suckered into calling her, many of our clients also have personal issues, money issues, relationship issues, or health issues. Unlike Madame Cleo, however, who has to be accountable only to her checkbook, we, as a profession, are required to be accountable to society and must be able to provide answers to three basic accountability questions:

1. How do our *clients* know that we can help them?
2. How does our *profession* know that we have helped our clients?
3. How do the *funding bodies* that fund the social service programs (that employ us) know how effectively their dollars are being spent?

RESEARCH AND ACCOUNTABILITY

What is the role that research plays in answering these three accountability questions? In one word, *significant!* That is the position of both the Council on Social Work Education (CSWE) and the National Association of Social Workers (NASW). These two prestigious national accountability organizations have a tremendous amount of jurisdiction over what curriculum content is required to be taught to all social work students (CSWE) and how the students, after they graduate, practice their trade (NASW).

The Council on Social Work Education

The CSWE is the official "educational organization" that sets minimum curriculum standards for BSW and MSW programs throughout the United States. This accreditation organization firmly believes that all social work students should know the basic principles of research. The council mandates that all social work programs have a research curriculum of some sort that addresses the research areas contained in Box 1.1.

The National Association of Social Workers

Just like CSWE, NASW is a parallel "practice organization" that works to enhance the professional growth and development of practicing social workers. Like CSWE's view of social work students, NASW believes that social work practitioners should also know the basics of research that are contained in Box 1.2.

This book provides the beginning research content to comply with the research standards set out by CSWE and NASW. Unlike Madame Cleo, however, social work students and practitioners are expected to have a substantial research knowledge base to guide and support their interventions. This knowledge base is generally derived from your social work education.

Of course, we, as a profession, tend to have more credibility than astrological consultants like Madame Cleo. We have graduated from accredited social work programs (CSWE) and have recognized practice qualifications (NASW). You are expected to have not only good intentions but the skills and knowledge to convert your good intentions into desired practical results that will help your clients. It all boils down to the fact that we have to be accountable to society, and to do so we need to acquire the knowledge and skills to help our clients in an effective and efficient manner.

HOW DO WE ACQUIRE KNOWLEDGE?

Our discussion so far automatically leads us to the question of "where do we acquire the necessary knowledge base to help our clients?" As can be seen in Figure 1.1,

you will acquire your knowledge base to help others through five highly interrelated sources: (1) authority, (2) tradition, (3) experience, (4) intuition, and (5) the research method. All of these "ways of knowing" overlap to some degree, but it greatly simplifies things to discuss them separately.

BOX 1.1

Council on Social Work Education's BSW and MSW Curriculum Research Content

B6.0—BSW Curriculum Content

- The research curriculum must provide an understanding and appreciation of a scientific, analytic approach to building knowledge for practice and to evaluating service delivery in all areas of practice. Ethical standards of scientific inquiry must be included in the research content.
- The research content must include quantitative and qualitative research methodologies; analysis of data, including statistical procedures; systematic evaluation of practice; analysis and evaluation of theoretical bases, research questions, methodologies, statistical procedures, and conclusions of research reports; and relevant technological advances.
- Each program must identify how the research curriculum contributes to the student's use of scientific knowledge for practice.

M6.0—MSW Curriculum Content

- The foundation research curriculum must provide an understanding and appreciation of a scientific, analytic approach to building knowledge for practice and for evaluating service delivery in all areas of practice. Ethical standards of scientific inquiry must be included in the research content.
- The research content must include qualitative and quantitative research methodologies; analysis of data, including statistical procedures; systematic evaluation of practice; analysis and evaluation of theoretical bases, research questions, methodologies, statistical procedures, and conclusions of research reports; and relevant technological advances.
- Each program must identify how the research curriculum contributes to the student's use of scientific knowledge for practice.

BOX 1.2

Ethical Standards for Evaluation Research; Excerpts From the National Association of Social Workers' *Code of Ethics*

(a) Social workers should monitor and evaluate policies, the implementation of programs, and practice interventions.

(b) Social workers should promote and facilitate evaluation and research to contribute to the development of knowledge.

(c) Social workers should critically examine and keep current with emerging knowledge relevant to social work and fully use evaluation and research evidence in their professional practice.

(d) Social workers engaged in evaluation or research should carefully consider possible consequences and should follow guidelines developed for the protection of evaluation and research participants. Appropriate institutional review boards should be consulted.

(e) Social workers engaged in evaluation or research should obtain voluntary and written informed consent from participants, when appropriate, without any implied or actual deprivation or penalty for refusal to participate; without undue inducement to participate; and with due regard for participants' well-being, privacy, and dignity. Informed consent should include information about the nature, extent, and duration of the participation requested and disclosure of the risks and benefits of participation in the research.

(f) When evaluation or research participants are incapable of giving informed consent, social workers should provide an appropriate explanation to the participants, obtain the participants' assent to the extent they are able, and obtain written consent from an appropriate proxy.

(g) Social workers should never design or conduct evaluation or research that does not use consent procedures, such as certain forms of naturalistic observation and archival research, unless rigorous and responsible review of the research has found it to be justified because of its prospective scientific, educational, or applied value and unless equally effective alternative procedures that do not involve waiver of consent are not feasible.

(h) Social workers should inform participants of their right to withdraw from evaluation and research at any time without penalty.

(i) Social workers should take appropriate steps to ensure that participants in evaluation and research have access to appropriate supportive services.

(j) Social workers engaged in evaluation or research should protect participants from unwarranted physical or mental distress, harm, danger, or deprivation.

(k) Social workers engaged in the evaluation of services should discuss collected information only for professional purposes and only with people professionally concerned with this information.

(l) Social workers engaged in the evaluation or research should ensure the anonymity or confidentiality of participants and of the data obtained from them. Social workers should inform participants of any limits of confidentiality, the measures that will be taken to ensure confidentiality, and when any records containing research data will be destroyed.

(m) Social workers who report evaluation and research results should protect participants' confidentiality by omitting identifying information unless proper consent has been obtained authorizing disclosure.

(n) Social workers should report evaluation and research findings accurately. They should not fabricate or falsify results and should take steps to correct any errors later found in published data using standard publication methods.

(o) Social workers engaged in evaluation or research should be alert to and avoid conflicts of interest and dual relationships with participants, should inform participants when a real or potential conflict of interest arises, and should take steps to resolve the issue in a manner that makes participants' interests primary.

(p) Social workers should educate themselves, their students, and their colleagues about responsible research practices.

Authority

Some things you "know" because someone in authority told you they were true. Had you lived in Galileo's time, for example, you would have "known" that there were seven heavenly bodies: the sun, the moon, and five planets. Since "seven" was a sacred number in the seventeenth century, the correctness of this belief was "self-evident" and was proclaimed by professors of philosophy. But Galileo peeked through his

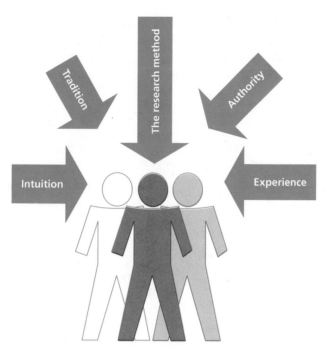

Figure 1.1
How Do You Know Something?

telescope in 1610 and saw four satellites circling Jupiter. Nevertheless, it was clear to those in authority that Galileo was wrong. Not only was he wrong, he had blasphemed against the accepted order. They denounced Galileo and his telescope and continued to comfortably believe in the sacredness of the number "seven."

But the "authorities" could have looked through Galileo's telescope! They could have seen for themselves that the number of heavenly bodies had risen to eleven! In fact, they refused to look because it wasn't worth their while to look because they "knew" that they were right. They had to be right because, in Galileo's time, the primary source of "how you knew something" was by authority—not by reason, and certainly not by observation. Today, this may seem a bit strange, and we may feel a trifle smug about the fact that, in *our* time, we also rely on our own observations in addition to authority. Even today, entrenched opinions are very difficult to change, and facts are more often than not disregarded if they conflict with cherished beliefs.

*Questioning the Accuracy
of Authority Figures*

Fortunately and unfortunately, you have little choice but to believe authority figures. You wouldn't progress very fast in your social work program if you felt it necessary to personally verify everything your professors said. Similarly, practicing social workers lack the time to evaluate the practice recommendations that were derived from research studies; they have no choice but to trust statements made by researchers—the authority figures—who conducted the research studies.

Experts can be wrong, however, and the consequences can sometimes be disastrous. A few decades ago, for example, authority figures in family therapy believed that children who were schizophrenic came from parents who had poor parenting skills. Researchers emphasized such causative factors as parental discord, excessive familial interdependency, and mothers whose overprotective and domineering behaviors did not allow their children to develop individual identities. In accordance with these "research findings," many social workers assumed that all families that had a child with schizophrenia were dysfunctional. Because the social workers focused their interventions on changing the family system, they often inadvertently instilled guilt in the parents and increased tensions, rather than helping the parents to cope with their child's situation.

However, recent research studies show that schizophrenia is caused largely by genetic and other biological factors, not by bad parenting. According to *these* findings, the most effective social work intervention is to support the family system by providing a nonstressful environment. This is what social workers *currently* do, again relying on *current* authority figures. More than likely, the authorities are correct this time— however, not as quite as exact as they will be when our knowledge of schizophrenia has progressed a little bit more over time.

So what are we to do when we need to trust the experts but the experts might be wrong? Put simply, we need to evaluate the soundness of the research study that produced the evidence which the experts utilized to make their pronouncements. This means that we must be able to distinguish good research studies from bad and from, well, quite frankly, the awful ones. The main purpose of this book is to enable you, the future social worker, to evaluate research articles, which were written from research studies, with a more discerning eye. You need to decide for yourself which research findings you will clutch to your heart and use to help your clients and which research findings you will disregard until more information is forthcoming.

There is no doubt about it, you will need to know research methodology if you plan on integrating findings derived from research studies into your daily practice. You will need to evaluate the study's rigor before you can accept the findings as the gospel. This is known as evidence-based social work.

Sources of "Evidence"

The "kind of evidence" on which a practice statement is based that was derived from a research study includes the source(s) of the evidence that supports the finding. For example, we obtain knowledge by watching television shows and movies, in addition to reading newspapers, journals, and magazine articles. These forms of communication provide rich information (right and wrong) about the social life of individuals and society in general. Most people, for example, who have had absolutely no contact with criminals learn about crime by these forms of communications. However, as we all know too well, the media can easily perpetuate the myths of any given culture (Neuman, 2007):

> The media show that most people who receive welfare are African American (most are actually non–African American), that most people who are mentally ill are violent and dangerous (only a small percentage actually are), and that most people who are elderly are senile and in nursing homes (a tiny minority are).
>
> Also, a selected emphasis on an issue by the media can change public thinking about it. For example, television repeatedly shows low-income, inner-city African American youth using illegal drugs. Eventually, most people "know" that urban African Americans use illegal drugs at a much higher rate than other groups in the United States, even though this notion is false. (p. 4)

Tradition

The second way of adding to your social work knowledge base is through tradition. Obviously, authority and tradition are highly related. For example, some things you "know" because your mother "knew" them and her mother before her, and they are a part of your cultural tradition. Your mother was also an authority figure who learned her bits and pieces through tradition and authority.

More often than not, people tend to accept cultural beliefs without much question. They may doubt some of them and test others for themselves, but, for the most part, they behave and believe as tradition dictates. To be sure, such conformity is useful, as our society could not function if each custom and belief were reexamined by each individual in every generation. On the other hand, unquestioning acceptance of "traditional dictates" easily leads to stagnation and to the perpetuation of wrongs.

It would be unfortunate, for example, if women were never allowed to vote because women had never traditionally voted, or if racial segregation were perpetuated because traditionally that's just the way it was.

Some traditional beliefs are based on the dictates of authority, carried on through time. The origins of other beliefs are lost in history. Even in social service programs, where history is relatively brief, things tend to be done in certain ways because they have always been done in these ways. When you first enter a social service program as a practicum student, your colleagues will show you how the program runs. You may be given a manual detailing program policies and procedures that contains everything from staff holidays to rules about locking up client files at night, to standard interviewing techniques with children who have been physically and emotionally abused. Informally, you will be told other things such as how much it costs to join the coffee club, whom to ask when you want a favor, whom to phone for certain kinds of information, and what form to complete to be put on the waiting list for a parking space.

In addition to this practical information, you may also receive advice about how to help your future clients. Colleagues may offer you a few of their opinions about the most effective treatment intervention strategies that are used within your practicum setting. If your practicum is a child sexual abuse treatment program, for example, it may be suggested to you that the nonoffending mother of a child who has been sexually abused does not need to address her own sexual abuse history in therapy in order to empathize with and protect her daughter.

Such a view would support the belief that the best interventive approach is a behavioral/learning one, perhaps helping the mother learn better communication skills in her relationship with her daughter. Conversely, the suggestion may be that the mother's personal exploration into her psyche (whatever that is) is essential and, therefore, the intervention should be of a psychodynamic nature.

Whatever the suggestion, it is likely that you, as a beginning social work student, will accept it, along with the information about the coffee club and the parking space. To be sure, you will want to fit in and be a valued member of the team. If the nonoffending mother is the first client for whom you have really been responsible, you may also be privately relieved that the intervention decision has been made for you. You may believe that your colleagues, after all, have more professional experience than you and they should surely know best.

In all likelihood, they probably do know best. At the same time, they also were once beginning social work students like yourself, and they probably formed their opinions in the same way as you are presently forming yours. They too once trusted their supervisors' knowledge bases and experiences. In other words, much of what you will initially be told is based upon the way that your practicum site has traditionally worked.

This might be a good moment to use your newfound skills to evaluate the research literature on the best way to intervene with children who have been sexually abused (see Chapters 22–25). But if you do happen to find a different and more effective way, you may discover that your colleagues are unreceptive or even hostile. They "know" what they do already works with clients—they "know it works" because it has worked for years.

Thus, on one hand, tradition is useful. It allows you to learn from the achievements and mistakes of those who have tried to do your job before you. You don't have to reinvent the wheel because you've been given a head start. On the other hand, tradition can become much too comfortable. It can blind you to better ways of doing things, and it dies extremely hard.

Knowledge Versus Beliefs

At this point, it is useful to differentiate between knowledge and beliefs (or faith). Knowledge is an accepted body of facts or ideas acquired through the use of the senses or reason. Beliefs are similarly a body of facts or ideas that are acquired through reliance on tradition and/or authority. We now have *knowledge* that the earth is round because we have been into space and observed the earth from above. A few centuries ago, we would have *believed* that it was flat, because someone "in authority" said it was or because tradition had always held it to be flat.

Knowledge is never final or certain. It is always changing as new facts come to our attention and new theories to explain the facts are developed, tested, and accepted or rejected. For example, the planet Pluto was demoted from full-planet status to dwarf-planet status in 2006. Things based on objective evidence just change as time goes along—hopefully for the better.

Belief systems, on the other hand, have remarkable staying power. Various beliefs about life after death, for example, have been held since the beginning of time by large numbers of people and will doubtless continue to be held, without much change, because there is nothing to change them. For example, there is no "evidence" that we survive death and none that we do not, nor is there likely to be—for the moment, that is. A position on the matter must therefore be based on authority and tradition—and authority and tradition change very slowly, more through political maneuverings than through the consideration of emerging facts. As George Bernard Shaw once said, "The moment we want to believe something, we suddenly see all the arguments for it, and become blind to the arguments against it."

Beliefs are often institutionalized through religion and involve not just articles of faith but a set of values that determines how people live their lives. The Manichaean sect, for example, founded in Persia in the third century, believed that sex was wicked, even for the purpose of procreation. They relied on the natural wickedness of men to keep them supplied with disciples. More recently, the belief that one acquires worth through work is strongly held in North American society. The harder you work, the more virtue you acquire by doing the work. At the same time, it is believed that people will avoid work if at all possible—presumably they value ease over virtue—so the social service programs we have in place are designed to punish our clients' "idleness" and reward their "productivity."

Experience

The third way of acquiring knowledge is through experience. You "know" that buttered bread falls when you drop it—buttered side down, of course. You "know" that knives cut and fire burns. You "know," as you gain experience in social work, that certain interven-

tive approaches tend to work better than others with certain types of clients in particular situations. Such experience is of enormous benefit to clients, and it is unfortunate that the knowledge gained by individual social workers over the years is rarely documented and evaluated in a way that would make it available to others.

However, as with anything else, experience has its advantages and disadvantages. Experience in one area, for example, can blind you to the issues in another. Health planners from mental health backgrounds, for example, may see mental illness as the most compelling community health problem because of their experiences with the mentally ill. Mental health issues may therefore command more dollars and attention than other public health issues that are equally deserving. Awareness of your own biases will allow you to make the most of your own experience while taking due account of the experiences of others.

Intuition

Intuition is fourth on our countdown of the ways of knowing. It can be described in a number of ways: revelation through insight, conviction without reason, and immediate apprehension without rational thought. In short, you "know" something without having the faintest clue of how you "know" it. It has been suggested that intuition springs from a rational process at the subconscious level. For example, you may see something out of the corner of your eye that maybe is too small, or happens too quickly, to register at the conscious level, but your subconscious takes it in, combines it with a sound you didn't know you heard, facts that you've forgotten, a familiar scent, and/or an unfelt touch. And now you have it! Knowledge sprung from intuition!

Intuition and Professional Judgment

Perhaps intuition works that way. Perhaps it doesn't. Some of us trust it. Some of us don't. Whatever it is, intuition should not be confused with an experienced social worker's professional judgment. Professional judgment is a *conscious* process whereby facts, as far as they are known, are supplemented with the knowledge derived from experience to form the basis for rational decisions. In this eminently reasonable process, you know what facts you have and how reliable they are, you know what facts are missing, and you know what experiences you're using to fill in the gaps. You are thus in a position to gauge whether your judgment is almost certainly right (you have all the facts), probably right (you have most of the facts), or possibly out to lunch (you know you are almost entirely guessing).

A reasoned professional judgment on your part, no matter how uncertain you may be, is far more beneficial to your client than your intuitive hunch.

The Research Method

We have now come to the fifth and last way of knowing. This way of acquiring knowledge is through the use of the research method—the main focus of this book. It is sometimes called the problem-solving method, the scientific method (scientific inquiry), or the research process.

The research method is a relatively new invention. For example, Aristotle was of the opinion that women had fewer teeth than men. Although he was twice married and the number of teeth possessed by women and men was a contentious issue in his day, it never occurred to him to ask both of his wives to open their mouths so that he could observe and count the number of teeth each had. This is a solution that would occur to anyone born in the twentieth century because we are accustomed to evaluating our assumptions in the light of our observations.

The social work profession—and modern society—is enamored of knowledge development through the use of the research method. Acquiring knowledge through the use of research findings that were derived from the research method is the most objective way of "knowing something." For example, as can be seen in Figure 1.2, when researchers do research studies they must (1) be value aware, (2) be skeptics, (3) share their findings with others, and (4) be honest.

Value Awareness

You must be aware of and be able to set aside your values when you do a research study; you must be unbiased and impartial to the degree it is possible—like a judge. This means that you, as a social work researcher, should be able to put aside your personal values both when you are conducting research studies and when you are evaluating research results obtained by other researchers.

If your personal value system dictates, for example, that health care should be publicly funded and equally available to everyone, you should still be able to use the research method to acquire knowledge about the advantages and disadvantages of a privatized system. If the evidence from your own or someone else's study shows that privatized health care is superior in some respects to your own beliefs, you should

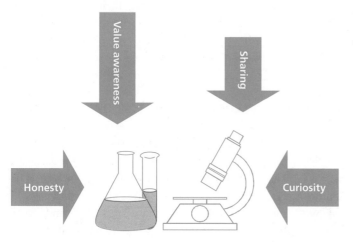

Figure 1.2
Characteristics of the Research Method

be able to weigh this evidence objectively, even though it may conflict with your personal value system.

Skeptical Curiosity

Now that you are valueless, you must become insatiably curious. We now know that knowledge acquired using the research method is never certain. Scientific "truth" remains true only until new evidence comes along to show that it is not true, or only partly true. Skeptical curiosity means that all findings derived from the research method should be—and, most important, must be—questioned. Wherever possible, new studies should be conducted by different researchers to see if the same results are obtained again. In other words, research studies, whenever possible, should be replicated.

Replication of the same study, with the same results, by another researcher makes it less likely that the results of the first study were affected by bias, dishonesty, or just plain old error. Thus, the findings are more likely to be "true" in the sense that they are more likely to reflect a reality external to the researchers. We will come back to this business of "external reality" later on.

For now, it is enough to say that the continual replication of research studies is a routine practice in the physical sciences but is far more rare in the social sciences, especially in the social work profession, for two main reasons. First, it is much more difficult to replicate a study of people than a study of physical objects. Second, researchers in the social sciences have a harder time finding money to do research studies than do researchers in the physical sciences.

Sharing

Like your mother said, "you must share your stuff with others." The results of a research study and the methods used to conduct it should be available to everyone so that the study's findings can be critiqued (Chapters 20 and 21) and the study replicated. It is worth noting that sharing findings from a research study is a modern value. It is not so long ago that illiteracy among peasants and women were valued by those who were neither. Knowledge has always been a weapon as well as a tool. Those who know little may be less likely to question the wisdom and authority of those who are above them in the social hierarchy. Public education is thus an enormously powerful social force that allows people to access and question the evidence upon which their leaders make decisions on their behalf.

Honesty

Not only must you share your research findings with others; you must be honest in what you share. Honesty means, of course, that you are not supposed to fiddle with the results obtained from your study. This may sound fairly straightforward, but, in fact, the results of research studies are rarely as clear-cut as we would like them to be. Quite often, and in the most respectable of scientific laboratories, theories are formulated on the basis of whether one wiggle on a graph is slightly longer than the corresponding woggle.

If "dishonesty" means a deliberate intention to deceive, then probably very few researchers are dishonest. If it means that researchers allow their value systems and their preconceived ideas to influence their methods of data collection, analysis, and interpretation, then there are probably a few guilty ones in the bunch.

In this sense, the term *honesty* includes an obligation on the part of researchers to be explicit about what their values and ideas are. They need to be sufficiently self-aware to both identify their value systems and perceive the effects of these upon their work; then, they need to be sufficiently honest to make an explicit statement about where they stand so that others can evaluate the conclusions drawn from the research studies.

AN INTRODUCTION TO SCIENTIFIC INQUIRY

On a very general level, and in the simplest of terms, the process of scientific inquiry has four generic interrelated phases as illustrated in Figure 1.3. As can be seen, it begins with Phase 1—some kind of an observation and/or measurement. Suppose, for example, we find in the garage an unidentified bag of seeds and we don't know what kind of seeds they are. We plant a random seed from the bag into the ground, and it grows into a petunia. This might be a coincidence, but, if we plant 37 more seeds from the same bag and all of them grow into petunias, we might assume that all the seeds in our bag have something to do with the petunias. We have now reached the second phase in our scientific inquiry process; we have made an assumption based on our observations.

The third phase is to test our assumption. This is done by planting yet another seed (the 38th) in the same way as before. If the 38th seed, too, becomes a petunia, we will be more certain that all the seeds in our bag will grow into petunias.

On the other hand, if the 38th seed grows into a cabbage, we will begin to wonder if our original assumption—the bag contains all petunia seeds—was wrong, the fourth phase of the process. In a nutshell, the four phases of the scientific inquiry process are not just something we are taught at school; they permeate the entire structure of our modern-day thinking.

Example 1: Nothing Is Forever

It is possible, of course, that we are quite mad and we only imagined those petunias in the first place. We would be more certain of the real existence of those petunias if someone else had seen them, as well. The more people who had observed them, the surer we would become. The process of scientific inquiry holds that, in most cases, something exists if we can observe *and* measure it.

To guard against objects that are seen without existing, such as cool pools of water observed by people dying of thirst in deserts, the research method has taken the premise one step further. A thing exists if, and only if, we can measure it. The cool pools of water that we observed, for example, probably could not be measured by a thermometer and a depth gauge. Things that have always occurred in sequence, such as summer and fall, probably will continue to occur in sequence. In all likelihood, rivers will flow downhill, water will freeze at zero degrees centigrade, and crops will grow if planted in the spring.

But nothing is certain, nothing is absolute. It is a matter of slowly acquiring knowledge by making observations and measurements, deriving assumptions from those observations, and testing the assumptions by making more observations and measurements. Even the best-tested assumption is held to be true only until another observation comes along to disprove it. Nothing is forever. It is all a matter of probabilities.

Let's say you have lived your whole life all alone in a log cabin in the middle of a large forest. You have never ventured as much as a hundred yards from your

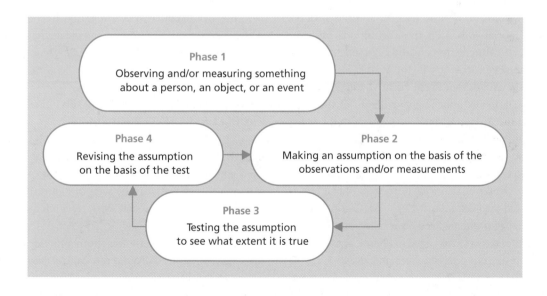

Figure 1.3   Phases of Scientific Inquiry

cabin and have had no access to the outside world. You have observed for your entire life that all of the ducks that flew over your land were white. You have never seen a different-colored duck. Thus, you assume, and rightfully so, that all ducks are white. You would have only to see one nonwhite duck fly over your land to disprove your white-duck assumption. Nothing is certain, no matter how long you "objectively observed" it.

Example 2: Children's Social Skills and Attachment to Their Mothers

Suppose, for a moment, you are interested in determining whether the strength of a child's attachment to his or her mother affects the social skills of the child. In order to test your assumption (hypothesis, if you will), you must now decide on what you mean by "child" (say, under age 6), and you need to find some young children and their respective mothers.

Next, you need to decide what you mean by "attachment" and you need to observe how attached the children are to their mothers. Because you need to measure your observations, you will also need to come up with some system whereby certain observed behaviors mean "strong attachment," other behaviors mean "medium attachment," and still other behaviors mean "weak attachment." Then you need to decide what you mean by "social skills," and you need to observe and measure the children's social skills. All of these definitions, observations, and measurements constitute Phase 1 of the scientific inquiry process (see Figure 1.3).

On the basis of your Phase 1 data, you might formulate an assumption, hunch, or hypothesis, to the effect (say) that the stronger a child's attachment to his or her mother, the higher the child's social skills. Or, to put it another way, children who have stronger attachments to their mothers will have better social skills than children who have weaker attachments to their mothers. This is Phase 2 and involves *inductive* logic (see Figure 1.4). In short, you begin with detailed observations and/or measurements of the world obtained in Phase 1 and move toward more abstract generalizations and ideas.

If your assumption is correct, you can use it to predict that a particular child with a strong attachment to his or her mother will also demonstrate strong social skills. This is an example of *deductive* logic, where you are deducing from the general to the particular (see Figure 1.4). In Phase 3, you set about testing your assumption, observing and measuring the attachment levels and social skills of as many other children as you can manage.

Data from this phase may confirm or cast doubt upon your assumption. The data might also cause you to realize that "attachment" is not as simple a concept as you had imagined. It is not just a matter of the *strength* of the attachment; the *type* of the attachment is also a factor (e.g., secure, insecure, disorganized). If you have tested enough children from diverse cultural backgrounds, you might also wonder if your assumption holds up better in some cultures than it does in others. Is it more relevant, say, for children raised in nuclear families than for children raised in a more communal environment such as a First Nations reserve or an Israeli kibbutz?

These considerations will lead you to Phase 4, where you revise your conjecture in the light of your observations (inductive logic) and begin to test your revised hunch all over again (deductive logic). Probably, this will not be a lonely effort on your part. Other researchers interested in attachment will also examine your assumption and the evidence you formulated it from and will conduct their own studies to see how right you really were. This combined work, conducted with honesty, skepticism, sharing, and freedom from entrenched beliefs, allows our knowledge base in the area of attachment to increase.

RESEARCH AND PRACTICE: BOTH PROBLEM-SOLVING PROCESSES

Believe it or not, social work research and practice have much in common. They are both problem-solving processes. As can be seen in Figure 1.5, there are parallels between social work research and social work practice.

All social work activities, both practice and research, are organized around one central assumption: There is a preferred order of thinking and action which, when rigorously and consciously followed, will

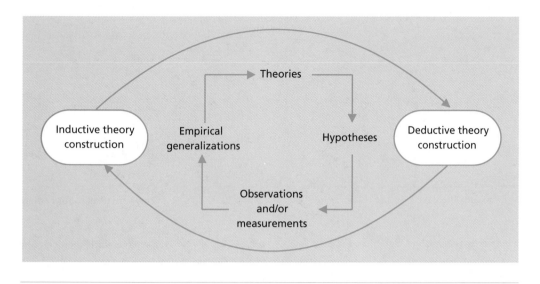

Figure 1.4 Inductive/Deductive Cycle of Theory Construction

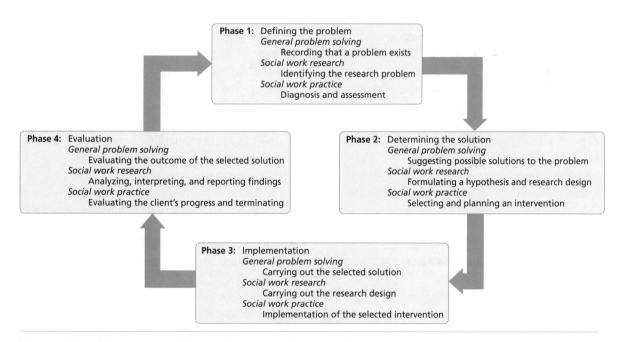

Figure 1.5 Parallels Between Problem Solving in Research and Social Work Intervention

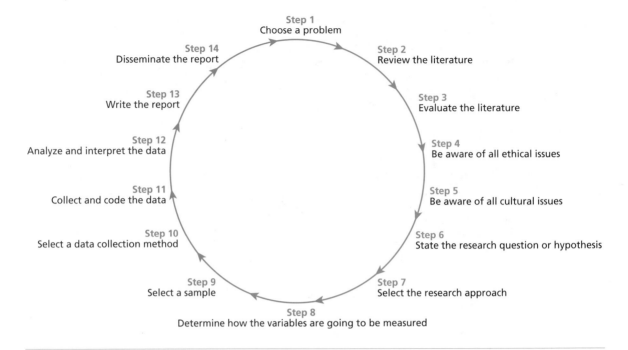

Figure 1.6   Basic Steps Within the Research Process

increase the likelihood of achieving our objectives. This way of looking at our practice and research activities is not new. Social work practitioners and researchers base their conclusions on careful observation, systematic trial, and intelligent analysis. Both observe, reflect, conclude, try, monitor results, and continuously reapply the same problem-solving process until the problem at hand is addressed. Figure 1.6 presents a brief glimpse of what the research process looks like broken down into distinct steps. Figure 1.7 provides a very simple pictorial example of how the research process is an application of the problem-solving model.

APPROACHES TO THE RESEARCH METHOD

The research method of knowing contains two complementary research approaches—the quantitative approach and the qualitative approach. Simply put, the quantitative portion of a research study relies on quan-

tification in collecting and analyzing data and uses descriptive and inferential statistical analyses. If data obtained within a research study are represented in the form of numbers, then this portion of the study is considered "quantitative." On the other hand, a qualitative portion of a research study relies on qualitative and descriptive methods of data collection. If data are presented in the form of words, diagrams, or drawings—not as numbers, as in the quantitative approach—then this portion of the study is considered "qualitative."

It should be pointed out, however, that a research study can be solely quantitative in nature. It can also be exclusively qualitative. As we will see throughout this book, a good research study uses both approaches in an effort to generate useful knowledge for our profession.

The unique characteristics and contributions of the quantitative approach and qualitative approach to knowledge building are examined in Chapters 3 and 4, respectively. The quantitative and qualitative research

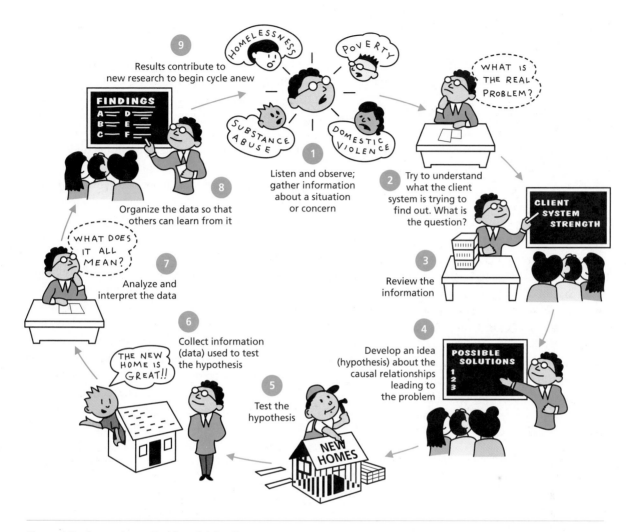

Figure 1.7   Research as a Problem-Solving Process

approaches complement each other and are equally important in the generation and testing of social work knowledge.

Skills Needed to Do Research Studies

As we know from Figure 1.3, there are four highly inter-related phases of scientific inquiry process. With these generic phases in mind, we now turn our attention to the skills (and the chapters within this book that discuss these skills) that the research method follows in order to obtain knowledge that is as "error free" and "objec-tive" as possible. Thus, when you do any research study, you will need to have the following skills:

Skill 1:   Understand the Contexts of Research in So-cial Work (Chapters 1 through 4)

Skill 2:   Understand How to Design a Research Study (Chapters 5 through 8)

Skill 3:   Understand How to Collect Data and Select a Data Collection Method (Chapters 9 through 15)

Skill 4:   Understand How to Become a Culturally Sensitive Researcher (Chapter 16)

Skill 5:   Understand How to Analyze Data (Chapters 17 and 18)

Skill 6:   Understand How to Write and Evaluate Research Reports and Proposals (Chapters 19 through 21)

Skill 7:   Understand the Concept of Evidence-Based Practice (Chapters 22 through 25)

Skill 8:   Understand How Social Work Programs Can Be Evaluated (Chapter 26)

The Research Attitude

The research method, or "scientific method," if you will, refers to the many ideas, rules, techniques, and approaches that we—the research community—use. The research attitude, on the other hand, is simply a way that we view the world. It is an attitude that highly values craftsmanship, with pride in creativity, high-quality standards, and hard work. These traits must be incorporated into both approaches to knowledge building (i.e., quantitative approach, qualitative approach) in order for the findings generated from research studies to be appropriately utilized within our profession's knowledge base. As Grinnell (1987) states:

> Most people learn about the "scientific method" rather than about the "scientific attitude." While the "scientific method" is an ideal construct, the "scientific attitude" is the way people have of looking at the world. Doing science includes many methods: what makes them scientific is their acceptance by the scientific collective. (p. 125)

THE KNOWLEDGE-LEVEL CONTINUUM

We now turn our attention to how the quantitative and qualitative research approaches answer various types of research questions. Any research study falls somewhere along the knowledge-level continuum, depending on how much is already known about the topic (see Figure 1.8). How much is known about the research topic determines the purpose of the study.

If you don't know anything, for example, you will merely want to explore the topic area, gathering basic data. Studies like this, conducted for the purpose of exploration, are known, logically enough, as *exploratory* studies and fall at the bottom of the knowledge-level continuum, as can be seen in Figure 1.8. Usually exploratory studies adopt a qualitative research approach.

When you have gained some knowledge of the research topic area through exploratory studies, the next task is to describe a specific aspect of the topic area in greater detail, using words and/or numbers. These studies, whose purpose is description, are known as *descriptive* studies and fall in the middle of the knowledge-level continuum, as presented in Figure 1.8. As can be seen, they can adopt a quantitative and/or qualitative research approach.

After descriptive studies have provided a substantial knowledge base in the research topic area, you will be in a position to ask very specific and more complex research questions—causality questions. These kinds of studies are known as *explanatory* studies.

The division of the knowledge continuum into three parts—exploratory, descriptive, and explanatory—is a useful way of categorizing research studies in terms of their purpose, the kinds of questions they can answer, and the research approach(es) they can take in answering the questions. However, as in all categorization systems, the three divisions are totally arbitrary, and some social work research studies defy categorization, falling nastily somewhere between exploratory and descriptive, or between descriptive and explanatory. This defiance is only to be expected, since the knowledge-level continuum is essentially that—a *continuum,* not a neat collection of categories. Let's take a moment here to look at exploratory, descriptive, and explanatory studies in more detail and the kinds of questions each type of study can answer.

Exploratory Research Studies

Exploratory studies are most useful when the research topic area is relatively new. In the United States, during the 1970s, for example, the development of new drugs to control the symptoms of mental illness, together with new federal funding for small, community-based mental health centers, resulted in a massive discharge of people from large, state-based mental health institutions.

Some folks applauded this move as restoring the civil liberties of the mentally ill. Others were concerned that current community facilities would prove inadequate to meet the needs of the people being discharged and their families. Social workers active in the 1970s were anxious to explore the situation, both with an eye on influencing social policy and in order to develop programs to meet the perceived needs of this group of people.

The topic area here is very broad. What are the consequences of a massive discharge of people who are psychiatrically challenged and were recently institutionalized? Many different questions pertaining to the topic can be asked. Where are these people living now? Alone? In halfway houses? With their families? On the street? Are they receiving proper medication and nutrition? What income do they have? How do they spend their time? What stresses do they suffer? What impact have

they had on their family members and the communities in which they now reside? What services are available to them? How do they feel about being discharged?

No single study can answer all these questions. It is a matter of devising a sievelike procedure where the first sieve, with the biggest holes, identifies general themes. Each general theme is then put through successively finer sieves until more specific research questions can be asked (Figure 1.9).

For example, you might begin to explore the consequences of the massive discharge by gathering together a group of these discharged people and asking them basic exploratory questions: What have been your experiences since you were discharged? What are the components that make up the discharge experience? These questions will be answered using qualitative data. Individual answers will generate common themes. You may find, for example, that the patients

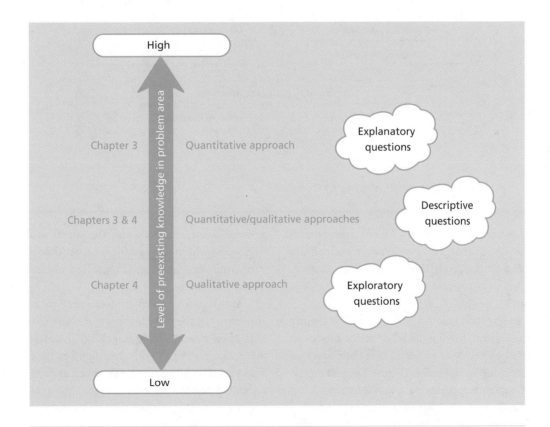

Figure 1.8   The Knowledge-Level Continuum and Approaches to the Research Method

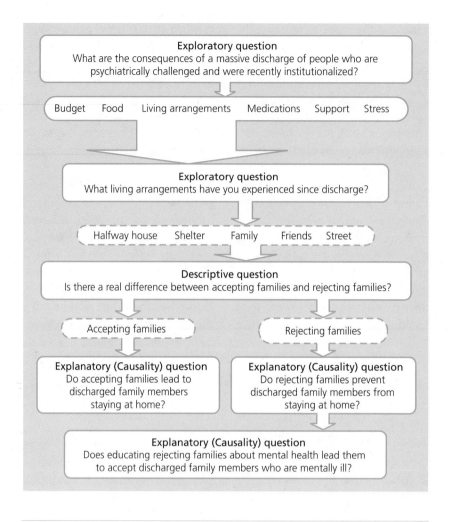

Figure 1.9   Example of a Sieving Procedure

have had a number of different living arrangements since they were discharged, vary greatly in their ability to manage their budget, leisure, food, and medication, feel rejected or supported, suffer less or more stress, and so forth.

You might then take one of these major themes and try to refine it, leaving the other major themes to be explored by someone else at a later date. Suppose you choose living arrangements (Figure 1.9) and mount a second exploratory study to ask respondents what living arrangements they have experienced since discharge. You may find now that those who were institutionalized for a long time have tended to move among halfway houses, shelters, and the street, while those who were institutionalized for a shorter time moved in with family first and stayed regardless of how accepting the family was.

At this point, you might feel a need for numbers. How many of them are living where? How many times have they moved on average? What percentage of those who moved in with their families stayed there? These are *descriptive* questions, aimed at describing or providing an accurate profile of this group of people. You are now moving up the knowledge continuum from the exploratory to the descriptive category, but, before we go there, let's summarize the general goals of exploratory research studies. These are to (Neuman, 2007):

- Become familiar with the basic facts, people, and concerns involved
- Develop a well-grounded mental picture of what is occurring
- Generate many ideas and develop tentative theories and conjectures
- Determine the feasibility of doing additional research studies
- Formulate questions and refine issues for more systematic inquiry
- Develop techniques and a sense of direction for future research

Descriptive Research Studies

At the descriptive level, suppose you have decided to focus on those people who moved in with their families. You have a tentative idea, based on your previous exploratory study, that there might be a relationship between the length of time spent in the institution and whether this group of people moved in with their families after discharge. You would like to confirm or refute this relationship, using a much larger group of respondents than you used in your exploratory study.

Another tentative relationship that emerged at the exploratory level was the relationship between staying in the family home and the level of acceptance shown by the family. You would like to know if this relationship holds with a larger group. You would also like to know if there is a real difference between accepting and rejecting families: Is Group *A* different from Group *B*? What factors contribute to acceptance or rejection of the discharged family member? Eventually, you would like to know if there is anything social workers can do to facilitate acceptance, but you don't have enough data yet to be able to usefully ask that question. In general, the goals of descriptive research studies are to (Neuman, 2007):

- Provide an accurate profile of a group
- Describe a process, mechanism, or relationship
- Give a verbal or numerical picture (e.g., percentages)

- Find information to stimulate new explanations
- Create a set of categories or classify types
- Clarify a sequence, set of stages, or steps
- Document information that confirms or contradicts prior beliefs about a subject

Explanatory Research Studies

Suppose you have learned from your descriptive studies that there are real differences between accepting and rejecting families and that these differences seem to have a major impact on whether the discharged person stays at home. Now you would like to ask two related causality questions: Does an accepting family lead to the discharged person's staying at home, and does a rejecting family prevent the discharged person from staying at home? In both cases, the answers will probably be yes, to some extent. Perhaps 30% of the decision to stay at home is explained by an accepting family and the other 70% remains to be explained by other factors: the severity of the discharged person's symptoms, for example, or the degree of acceptance shown by community members outside the family.

Now, you might want to know whether acceptance on the part of the family carries more weight in the staying-at-home decision than acceptance on the part of the community. The answer to this question will provide a direction for possible intervention strategies; you will know whether to focus your attention on individual families or on entire communities.

Suppose you decide, for example, on the basis of your own and other explanatory studies, to focus on families, and the intervention you choose to increase their acceptance is education around mental illness. In order to evaluate the effectiveness of your intervention, you will eventually need to ask another explanatory (or causality) question: Does education around mental illness lead to increased acceptance by families of their discharged family members? With the answer to this question, you have concluded your sieving procedures as outlined in Figure 1.9, moving from a broad exploratory question about discharge experiences to a tested intervention designed to serve the discharged people and their families. In general, the goals of explanatory research studies are to (Neuman, 2007):

- Determine the accuracy of a principle or theory
- Find out which competing explanation is better
- Link different issues or topics under a common general statement
- Build and elaborate a theory so that it becomes more complete
- Extend a theory or principle into new areas or issues
- Provide evidence to support or refute an explanation

We have concluded our discussion of the three major classifications of the knowledge-level continuum; exploratory, descriptive, and explanatory. We will now take a quick look at the wide range of research questions that can be answered within the various knowledge levels.

THE RANGE OF RESEARCH QUESTIONS

Figure 1.10 is a modification of Figure 1.8 in that it shows how research questions can be placed on a continuum from simple (exploratory studies) to complex

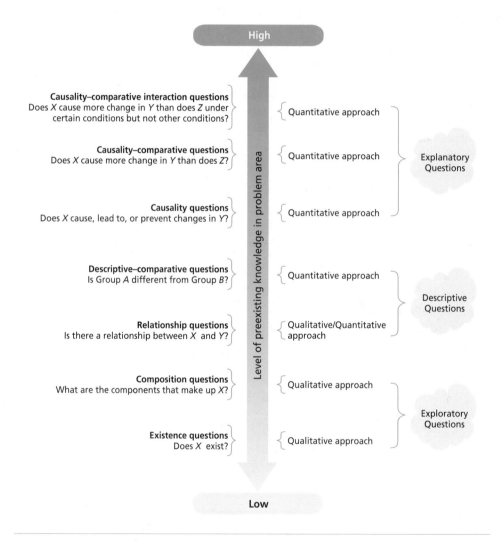

Figure 1.10   Types of Research Questions, the Knowledge-Level Continuum, and Approaches to the Research Method

(explanatory studies). Not surprisingly, we need to ask the simple questions first. When we have the answers to these simple questions, we then proceed to ask more complex ones. We are thus moving from "little knowledge about our research question" to "more knowledge about our research question."

Figure 1.10 presents the knowledge continuum (from high to low—middle arrow), seven general classifications that research questions can take (left side), and the research approach (right side) that is most appropriate to answer each question classification.

On a very general level, there are seven types of questions that research studies can answer: (1) existence questions, (2) composition questions, (3) relationship questions, (4) descriptive-comparative questions, (5) causality questions, (6) causality-comparative questions, and (7) causality-comparative interaction questions.

Existence Questions

Suppose for a moment you have an assumption that there is an association between low self-esteem in women and spousal abuse. You are going to study this topic—over a number of studies—starting at the beginning. The beginning, at the bottom of the knowledge continuum, is an *existence question*—in fact, two existence questions, since your assumption involves two concepts: (1) self-esteem and (2) spousal abuse.

First, knowing nothing whatsoever about either self-esteem or spousal abuse, let alone whether there is an association between them, you want to know if self-esteem and spousal abuse actually exist in the first place. Self-esteem and spousal abuse are concepts—they are nothing more than ideas, human inventions if you like—that have become very familiar to social workers, and it is tempting just to say, "Of course they exist. I know they exist."

But there must have been a time when self-esteem was no more than a vague idea among students of human nature that some people seem to feel better about themselves than other people do. It would then have been just a matter of contacting

Ms. Smith—and Ms. Jones, and Ms. Tasmania—and asking them, "Do you feel good about yourself? What is it that makes you feel good about yourself?" This qualitative study—and many others like it, conducted by different researchers over time—would have provided an indication that yes, indeed, some people do feel better about themselves than other people do. Self-esteem, if that is what you want to call (or label) the feeling, does in fact exist.

The same process can be done to determine if spousal abuse exists. However, spousal abuse can be more easily observed and measured than self-esteem.

Composition Questions

The second question, "What is it that makes you feel good about yourself?," is an attempt to find out what particular personal attributes contribute to self-esteem. That is, it answers the *composition question* next on the knowledge continuum. Qualitative studies exploring this dimension may have discovered that people who feel good about themselves in general also specifically feel that they are liked by others, that they are competent, intelligent, caring, and physically attractive and have a host of other attributes that together make up the concept "self-esteem." Thus, qualitative studies provide *descriptive*, or *qualitative*, *data*, indicating that self-esteem exists and what it is. Similarly, these studies indicate that women are in fact sometimes abused by their partners and what particular forms such abuse can take.

Relationship Questions

Going up one more notch on the list, you next come to *relationship questions*. What, if any, is the relationship between women's self-esteem and spousal abuse? Here, you might begin with another qualitative study, trying to determine, on an individual basis, whether there seems to be any connection between having low self-esteem and being abused. If there does seem to be enough evidence to theorize that such a relationship may exist, you might then use the quantitative approach to see if the relationship holds for a larger number of women rather than just the small number you interviewed in your qualitative study.

Descriptive-Comparative Questions

Next on the continuum you come to *descriptive-comparative questions*: Is Group *A* different from Group *B*? Here, you might go in a number of different directions. You might wonder, for example, whether there is any difference in self-esteem levels between women in heterosexual relationships and women in lesbian relationships. Does self-esteem differ between First Nations women and non–First Nations women? Do women with different sexual orientations or from different cultural groups also differ in how often they are abused, or how severely, or in what particular way? Because you are asking about differences between social groups, which involve large numbers of people, you will need quantitative methods to address these questions.

Causality Questions

Third from the top of the continuum are the *causality questions*. Does low self-esteem actually cause women to be abused? Or, for that matter, does being abused cause low self-esteem? Most complex behaviors don't have single causes. Being abused might certainly contribute to having low self-esteem, but it is highly unlikely to be the sole cause. Similarly, it is unlikely that having low self-esteem leads inevitably to being abused. Quantitative studies here, with their use of impressive statistics, can tell us what percentage of the abuse can be explained by low self-esteem and what percentage remains to be explained by other factors. This will be discussed further in Chapter 17.

Causality-Comparative Questions

If there are factors other than low self-esteem that cause abuse, it would be helpful to know what they are and how much weight they have. Perhaps heavy drinking on the part of the abuser is a factor. Perhaps poverty is, or the battering suffered by the abuser as a child. Once these possible factors have been explored, using the same process you used in your exploration of self-esteem and spousal abuse, quantitative methods can again tell us what percentage of abuse is explained by each factor. If low self-esteem accounts for only 2%, say, and heavy drinking accounts for 8%, you will have answered the *causality-comparative question*. You will know, on the average, that heavy drinking on the abuser's part has more effect on spousal abuse than does the woman's self-esteem level.

Causality-Comparative Interaction Questions

At the tip-top of the continuum are the *causality-comparative interaction questions*. They ask whether your research findings hold up only under certain conditions. For example, if it is true that heavy drinking contributes more to spousal abuse than does the woman's level of self-esteem, perhaps that is only true for couples who are living in poverty. Or, it is only true for couples with children, or it is only true if the abuser himself was abused. This final type of question, again answered through quantitative methods, reflects the highest aim of social work research—explanation. If we are to give our clients the best possible service, we need to know about causes and effects. What action or attribute on the part of whom causes how much of what effect, and under what conditions? What type of treatment will cause most change in a particular type of client in a particular situation?

Phrasing of Research Questions

As we will see in Chapter 16, all research questions should be phrased with attention to the following cultural, gender, and sexual orientation considerations:

- Avoid ethnocentrism (the tendency to judge other cultures by the standards and practices of one's own culture).
- Avoid defining difference as deviance or pathology.
- Assess the question for androcentricity (a view of the world from a male perspective) or gynecocentricity (a view of the world from a female perspective).
- Assess whether expected differences to be uncovered by the question may be due to the gender, ethnic background, or sexual orientation of the participants.

- When research questions pertain to specific groups, consult with group members and invest the time needed to learn about the group culture.
- Explore the meanings of the words contained in the question with respect to group culture.
- Examine the relevance of the research question to the group being studied. (It is not ethical, for example, to involve ethnic-minority people in a research study if they do not see the relevance of the questions and they are unlikely to derive any benefit from the study.)
- Avoid studying women only in the context of family or child rearing. (This does not mean that women should not be studied at all in the context of family or child rearing, only that recognition should be given to other aspects of their lives.)

PURE AND APPLIED RESEARCH STUDIES

Social work research studies can be described as pure or applied. The goal of pure research studies is to develop theory and expand the social work knowledge base. The goal of applied studies is to develop solutions for problems and applications in practice. The distinction between theoretical results and practical results marks the principal difference between pure and applied research studies.

DEFINITION OF SOCIAL WORK RESEARCH

So far, we have discussed the various ways of obtaining knowledge and briefly looked at the characteristics and phases of the research method. Armed with this knowledge, we now need a definition of research, which is composed of two syllables, *re* and *search*. Dictionaries define the former syllable as a prefix meaning "again," "anew," or "over again," and the latter as a verb meaning "to examine closely and carefully," "to test and try," or "to probe" (Duehn, 1985).

Together, these syllables form a noun that describes a careful and systematic study in some field of knowledge, undertaken to establish facts or principles. Social work research therefore can be defined as:

> a systematic and objective inquiry that utilizes the research method to solve human problems and creates new knowledge that is generally applicable.

We obtain much of our knowledge base from the findings derived from research studies that utilize the research method. However, all research studies have built-in biases and limitations that create errors and keep us from being absolutely certain about the studies' outcomes.

This book helps you to understand these limitations and to take them into account in the interpretation of research findings and also helps you to avoid making errors or obtaining wrong answers. One of the principal products of a research study is "objective and systematic" data—via the research method—about reality as it is, "unbiased" and "error-free."

RESEARCH ROLES

We have looked at the reasons why social workers need to engage in research. Since there are many different ways of actually engaging within the research method, it is useful to look at the three research-related roles that social workers might play. These are (1) the research consumer, (2) the creator and disseminator of knowledge, and (3) the contributing partner.

The Research Consumer

If you go to your doctor to discuss your arthritis, you expect the doc to be aware of the most recent advances in the management and treatment of arthritis. All professionals, in all disciplines, are expected by their clients to keep up with the latest developments in their fields. They do this by attending conferences, reading books and journals, and paying attention to the results derived from research studies. In other words, these professionals—which include you as a social worker—are *research consumers*, and, as previously noted, they need to know enough about the research method to consume it wisely, separating the nutritious wheat from the dubious chaff.

The Creator and Disseminator of Knowledge

You may be quite determined that you will never yourself conduct a research study. Never ever! you say, and then you find that you are the only staff person in a small voluntary social service program that desperately requires a needs assessment if the program is to serve its clients and keep its funding base. You look up "needs assessment" in forgotten research texts, and sweat, and stumble through them because someone has to do the study and there is no one there but you.

This may seem like an unlikely scenario, but in fact many social service programs are very small and are run on a wing and a prayer by a few paid staff and a large volunteer contingent. They rise and flourish for a time and die; and death is often hastened along by their inability to demonstrate, in research terms, how much good they are doing on their clients' behalf, how little it is costing, and what the dreadful social consequences would be if they weren't there to do it.

You may escape being the sole social worker in a program that needs research know-how. But even if you are a mere cog in a immense machine of interlocking social workers, the time may come when you want to try something new. Most social workers do. Most of them, however, don't try the something in any structured way. They don't write down exactly what the something was (perhaps a new intervention for raising Jody's self-esteem), they don't say why they needed it (nothing else was working), how they tested it (they measured Jody's self-esteem before and after doing it), or how effective it was (Jody's self-esteem score rose triumphantly, from X to Y and was still at its higher level 3 months later).

Worse, they don't tell anyone else they did it, except for a few murmurs, rapidly forgotten, to a colleague over coffee. One consequence of this is that other Jody-types, who might benefit from the same intervention, never have the opportunity to do so because their social workers don't know that it exists. Another consequence is that the program cannot use this newly founded innovation as evidence of its effectiveness to place before its funders.

The Contributing Partner

In reality, many social service programs conduct some kind of research studies from time to time, particularly evaluative studies. Many more agree to host studies conducted by researchers external to the program, such as university professors and graduate students. Unlike studies conducted by psychologists, social work research rarely takes place in a laboratory but, instead, is usually conducted in field settings. Data may be drawn from program clients or their records and may be collected in the program or in the clients' homes.

Since social workers are usually employed by social service programs, they are often drawn into the program's research activities by default. Such activities are normally conducted by a team, consisting of researchers and program staff members. Today, the solitary social work researcher, like the solitary mad scientist, is very much a thing of the past. Staff members who contribute to research inquiry may have specific skills to offer that they never imagined were research-related.

One may be particularly acute and accurate when it comes to observing client behaviors. A second worker, on the other hand, may work well as a liaison between clients and researcher or between one program and another. Some social workers are cooperative in research endeavors, and others are less so, depending on their attitudes toward knowledge development through the use of the research method. Those of us who know most about research methods tend to be the most cooperative and also the most useful. Hence, the greater the number of social workers who understand research principles, the more likely it is that relevant studies will be successfully completed and that social work knowledge will be increased.

Integrating the Three Research Roles

Just about everything in life is interdependent on everything else. Chaos theory comes readily to mind concerning the idea of interdependence. The same holds true with the three research roles noted earlier—they are not independent of one another. They must be integrated if research is to accomplish its goals of increasing our profession's knowledge base and improving the effectiveness of our interventions with clients.

The issue is not whether we should consume research findings, produce and disseminate research results, or become contributing partners in research studies. Rather, it is whether we can engage the full spectrum of available knowledge and skills in the continual improvement of our practices. Social workers who adopt only one or two research roles are shortchanging themselves and their clients (Reid & Smith, 1989):

> If research is to be used to full advantage to advance the goals of social work, the profession needs to develop a climate in which both doing and consuming research are normal professional activities. By this we do not mean that all social workers should necessarily do research or that all practice should be based on the results of research, but rather that an ability to carry out studies at some level and the facility in using scientifically based knowledge should be an integral part of the skills that social workers have and use. (p. xi)

A research base within our profession will not guarantee its public acceptance, but there is no doubt that the absence of such a base and the lack of vigorous research efforts to expand it will, in the long run, erode our credibility and be harmful to our clients.

SUMMARY

Knowledge is essential to human survival. Over the course of history, there have been many ways of knowing, from divine revelation to tradition and the authority of elders. By the beginning of the seventeenth century, people began to rely on a different way of knowing—the research method.

Social workers derive their knowledge from authority, tradition, professional experience, and personal intuition, as well as from findings derived from research studies.

Social workers engage in three research roles. They can consume research findings by using the findings of others in their day-to-day practices, they can produce and disseminate research results for others to use, and they can participate in research studies in a variety of ways.

Now that we have briefly explored the place of research in social work, the following chapter discusses the various ethical issues we must be aware of before we begin a research study.

The Ethical Conduct of Research

André Ivanoff
Betty Blythe
Barbara Walters

Step 1	Choose a problem
2	Review the literature
3	Evaluate the literature
4	Be aware of all ethical issues
5	Be aware of all cultural issues
6	State the research question or hypothesis
7	Select the research approach
8	Determine how the variables are going to be measured
9	Select a sample
10	Select a data collection method
11	Collect and code the data
12	Analyze and interpret the data
13	Write the report
14	Disseminate the report

You Are Here

As we know from the previous chapter, social workers have an ethical responsibility to engage in research activities. In addition, we also have ethical responsibilities to apply current research findings within our practices to enhance our effectiveness with various client systems—the essence of evidence-based practice. Examples from actual social work research—past and current—are presented throughout this chapter to illustrate the types of ethical oversights and conflicts raised in conducting contemporary social work research.

HISTORY OF ETHICAL PROTECTIONS

The need to protect individuals participating in research studies can be traced back to 1947 with the Nuremberg *Code*. This code was developed by a military tribunal in order to provide standards for judging the horrific and inhumane medical experiments conducted on humans by the Nazi regime during World War II. The Nuremberg *Code* laid the groundwork for the principles underlying our practices today regarding the ethical conduct of research.

The first tenet of the *Code* stipulates that voluntary consent of potential research participants is essential and details the conditions under which consent should be obtained. The second tenet dictates that the potential research study must be expected to be of some benefit to society. Several tenets of the *Code* relate to avoiding unnecessary risk or harm, including physical and mental suffering or injury. Another point in the *Code* speaks to the quality of the study and stipulates that the study should be carried out by qualified researchers. Finally, the *Code* demands that participants be allowed to withdraw from the study at any time without any form of reprisal whatsoever.

The development of guidelines and regulations for the protection of human research participants has matched the significant development and increase in research being conducted around the world. Today, in the United States, the Office for Human Research Protections (OHRP) is located within the U.S. Department of Health and Human Services (HHS; http://www.hhs.gov/ohrp). Since its formation as a separate entity in 2000, OHRP has been charged with providing leadership in the protection of research volunteers and guidance and clarification concerning federal regulations to research institutions, with developing educational programming, and with encouraging innovation to enhance human subjects' protections.

More than 10,000 research institutions, including agencies, hospitals, colleges, and universities, have formal agreements with OHRP, called Federal Wide Assurances, (FWAs), indicating their compliance with human subjects protections regulations. Administering local human subjects' protections is the responsibility of institutional review boards (IRBs), which also will be discussed in this chapter.

Most universities, research institutions, and social service agencies conducting research now require that all individuals involved in carrying out any research activity with humans complete training in human subjects protections before beginning their research projects. Many require retraining on a regular basis as well. Are you aware of your university's human subjects review processes? We encourage you to complete its online training after reading this chapter.

Do We All Abide by IRBs?

It is very difficult to know how many social workers who engage in research do not go through either human subjects review processes or informed consent processes with their potential research participants. Also, it is difficult to know how many of our social service agencies, especially smaller ones, do not have committees to review potential research studies conducted by their staff. We do not know how many agencies ask clients to sign "blanket" consent forms which indicate that the clients' information can be used for evaluation purposes. More importantly, many of these clients do not ask questions about consent forms because they may believe they are just another form to be signed at intake so they can receive the services they are requesting.

Moreover, some agencies may undertake routine evaluation activities to inform the delivery of their services that could raise ethical issues (Unrau, Gabor, & Grinnell, 2007). For example, a focus group conducted by agency staff with certain client groups, such as rape survivors, may uncover personal or confidential information about the participants in the focus group discussion. Or, clients who complete "client satisfaction with service questionnaires" might inadvertently disclose personal information that could be damaging to the client or significant others, or even to agency staff.

HEART'S IN THE RIGHT PLACE BUT HEAD ISN'T

We have yet to describe the various ethical issues that are involved in actually conducting a social work research study—the purpose of this chapter. Let's begin our venture into research ethics with a short vignette that illustrates how a beginning graduate-level social work student, Margaret, wanted to recruit clients (research participants) for a research study.

In her field practicum, Margaret is helping her professor recruit families for a research study that is aimed at providing an intervention to improve the parenting skills of pregnant and parenting teenagers. She recruits potential research participants at the local public social services office (her practicum setting), where the pregnant teenagers meet weekly with their child protection workers. According to the research study's recruitment protocol, recruitment takes place via colorful flyers handed out to clients by the receptionist as they enter the agency. The clients are asked by the receptionist to talk with Margaret to get further information on an "important" study in which they may wish to participate.

One day, Margaret notices a young pregnant teenager crying in the waiting room and asks her if she can do anything to help. Listening to her story, Margaret unwittingly finds herself strongly encouraging the teenager to participate in the research project (a new intervention, yet to be tested) by telling her how much the intervention would improve her parenting skills. She also suggests that her participation in the research study would reflect favorably on the child protection worker's evaluation of the teen.

At this point, do you see anything wrong with Margaret's behaviors? We will return to Margaret and her actions later, but, for now, let's take a look at ethical social work practice and ethical social work research.

ETHICAL PRACTICE AND ETHICAL RESEARCH

Margaret was engaging in both practice and research; that is, she wanted to help the client by enrolling her in the research study (practice), and she wanted to recruit the client to be in the study. Let's now take a look at what ethical practice and ethical research are all about.

Ethical Practice

The ethical conduct of social work practice has much in common with the ethical conduct of social work research. According to the National Association of Social Workers' (NASW) *Code of Ethics* (NASW, 1999), the six primary tenets of social work practice (core values) are:

1. Value: Service
   Ethical Principle: Social workers' primary goal is to help people in need and to address social problems.

   Social workers elevate service to others above self-interest. Social workers draw on their knowledge, values, and skills to help people in need and to address social problems. Social workers are encouraged to volunteer some portion of their professional skills with no expectation of significant financial return (pro bono service).

2. Value: Social Justice
   Ethical Principle: Social workers challenge social injustice.

   Social workers pursue social change, particularly with and on behalf of vulnerable and oppressed individuals and groups of people. Social workers' social change efforts are focused primarily on issues of poverty, unemployment, discrimination, and other forms of social injustice. These activities seek to promote sensitivity to and knowledge about oppression and cultural and ethnic diversity. Social workers strive to ensure access to needed information, services, and resources; equality of opportunity; and meaningful participation in decision making for all people.

3. Value: Dignity and Worth of the Person
   Ethical Principle: Social workers respect the inherent dignity and worth of the person.

   Social workers treat each person in a caring and respectful fashion, mindful of individual differences and cultural and ethnic diversity. Social workers promote clients' socially responsible self-determination. Social workers seek to enhance clients' capacity and opportunity to change and to address their own needs. Social workers are cognizant of their dual responsibility to clients and to the broader society. They seek to resolve conflicts between clients' interests and the broader society's interests in a socially responsible manner consistent with the values and ethical principles of the profession.

4. Value: Importance of Human Relationships
   Ethical Principle: Social workers recognize the central importance of human relationships in the helping process.

   Social workers understand that relationships between and among people are an important vehicle for change. Social workers engage people as partners in the helping process. Social workers seek to strengthen relationships among people in a purposeful effort to promote, restore, maintain, and enhance the well-being of individuals, families, social groups, organizations, and communities.

5. Value: Integrity
   Ethical Principle: Social workers behave in a trustworthy manner.

   Social workers are continually aware of the profession's mission, values, ethical principles, and ethical standards and practice in a manner consistent with them. Social workers act honestly and responsibly and promote ethical practices on the part of the organizations with which they are affiliated.

6. Value: Competence

Ethical Principle: Social workers practice within their areas of competence and develop and enhance their professional expertise.

Social workers continually strive to increase their professional knowledge and skills and to apply both in practice. Social workers aspire to contribute to the knowledge base of the profession.

With these six core values of social work practice in mind, do you think that Margaret practiced ethically? Why, or why not? Let's now examine ethical research.

Ethical Research

The U.S. National Institute of Health released policies to protect human participants in research studies in 1966. These policies did not have regulatory status, however, until 1974, when the U.S. Department of Health, Education, and Welfare (now known as the Department of Health and Human Services) formally adopted them. They also established the IRB as an instrument to protect human participants in research studies. In 1974, Congress passed the National Research Act, which mandated that all research funded by the Department of Health, Education, and Welfare be reviewed by an IRB and required that potential study participants go through informed consent procedures (Dunn & Chadwick, 2002).

This legislation also established the National Commission for the Protection of Human Subjects of Biomedical and Behavioral Research. In 1978, the commission issued *The Belmont Report: Ethical Principles and Guidelines for the Protection of Human Subjects of Research*. This document is significant because it spells out the ethical principles for protecting human participants in research studies. The report's three main principles are respect for persons, beneficence, and justice. Box 2.1 contains a detailed summary of the *Belmont Report*. It is important for you to read this report summary before going further in this chapter.

While the overlap between ethical social work practice and research may not be immediately apparent, it is our hope that by the end of this chapter you will understand the similarities between the concerns and the activities of the ethical conduct of social work practice *and* research.

In the brief vignette introduced earlier, Margaret responded to the client's sad story based on what she believed to be in the client's best interests, that is, participating in the research study. Margaret increases the client's motivation to participate by telling her it will improve her parenting skills. In addition, Margaret asserts that the client's participation would favorably impact the child protection worker's assessment of the teen. While Margaret's intentions may be understandable to the novice, she has in fact violated ethical principles of both practice and research in one brief 3-minute conversation. More specifically, and in no particular order, Margaret:

1. assumed she understood the client's problem without conducting an adequate assessment
2. did not fully disclose the purpose of the research study
3. exerted coercive influence over the client to participate by telling her the intervention will work for her without actually knowing if it would
4. suggested that the client's participation in the study would favorably affect the agency's perception of her
5. did not realize that the young woman may have felt that she had to participate in the research study to receive the services she was asking for by coming into the agency in the first place
6. did not tell the client that she may be randomly assigned to a control group (those who do not receive the treatment) and, thus, may receive no intervention whatsoever (at this time, that is)
7. did not obtain the consent of the teen's parents or legal guardian.

After reading the summary of the *Belmont Report* contained in Box 2.1, can you identify any additional violations of research ethics that Margaret may have committed?

BOX 2.1

The Belmont Report: Ethical Principles and Guidelines for Research Involving Human Subjects

AGENCY: Department of Health, Education, and Welfare.

ACTION: Notice of Report for Public Comment.

SUMMARY: On July 12, 1974, the National Research Act (Pub. L. 93–348) was signed into law, thereby creating the National Commission for the Protection of Human Subjects of Biomedical and Behavioral Research. One of the charges to the Commission was to identify the basic ethical principles that should underlie the conduct of biomedical and behavioral research involving human subjects and to develop guidelines which should be followed to assure that such research is conducted in accordance with those principles. In carrying out the above, the Commission was directed to consider:

- the boundaries between biomedical and behavioral research and the accepted and routine practice of medicine
- the role of assessment of risk-benefit criteria in the determination of the appropriateness of research involving human subjects
- appropriate guidelines for the selection of human subjects for participation in such research
- the nature and definition of informed consent in various research settings.

The Belmont Report attempts to summarize the basic ethical principles identified by the Commission in the course of its deliberations. It is the outgrowth of an intensive 4-day period of discussions that were held in February 1976 at the Smithsonian Institution's Belmont Conference Center supplemented by the monthly deliberations of the Commission that were held over a period of nearly 4 years. It is a statement of basic ethical principles and guidelines that should assist in resolving the ethical problems that surround the conduct of research with human subjects.

By publishing the Report in the *Federal Register* and providing reprints upon request, the Secretary intends that it may be made readily available to scientists, members of Institutional Review Boards, and Federal employees. The two-volume Appendix, containing the lengthy reports of experts and specialists who assisted the Commission in fulfilling this part of its charge, is available as DHEW Publication No. (OS) 78–0013 and No. (OS) 78–0014, for sale by the Superintendent of Documents, U.S. Government Printing Office, Washington, D.C. 20402.

Unlike most other reports of the Commission, the Belmont Report does not make specific recommendations for administrative action by the Secretary of Health, Education, and Welfare. Rather, the Commission recommended that the Belmont Report be adopted in its entirety, as a statement of the Department's policy. The Department requests public comment on this recommendation.

National Commission for the Protection of Human Subjects of Biomedical and Behavioral Research

Scientific research has produced substantial social benefits. It has also posed some troubling ethical questions. Public attention was drawn to these questions by reported abuses of human subjects in biomedical experiments, especially during the Second World War. During the Nuremberg War Crime Trials, the Nuremberg code was drafted as a set of standards for judging physicians and scientists who had conducted biomedical experiments on concentration camp prisoners. This code became the prototype of many later codes[1] intended to assure that research involving human subjects would be carried out in an ethical manner.

The codes consist of rules, some general, others specific, that guide the investigators or the reviewers of research in their work. Such rules often are inadequate to cover complex situations; at times they come into conflict, and they are frequently difficult to interpret or apply. Broader ethical principles will provide a basis on which specific rules may be formulated, criticized and interpreted.

Three principles, or general prescriptive judgments, that are relevant to research involving human subjects are identified in this statement. Other principles may also be relevant. These three are comprehensive, however, and are stated at a level of generalization that should assist scientists, subjects, reviewers and interested citizens to understand the ethical issues inherent in research involving human subjects. These principles cannot always be applied so as to resolve beyond dispute particular ethical problems. The objective is to provide an analytical framework that will guide the resolution of ethical problems arising from research involving human subjects.

(continued)

BOX 2.1 *(continued)*

This statement consists of a distinction between research and practice, a discussion of the three basic ethical principles, and remarks about the application of these principles.

Part A: Boundaries Between Practice & Research

It is important to distinguish between biomedical and behavioral research, on the one hand, and the practice of accepted therapy, on the other, in order to know what activities ought to undergo review for the protection of human subjects of research. The distinction between research and practice is blurred partly because both often occur together (as in research designed to evaluate a therapy) and partly because notable departures from standard practice are often called "experimental" when the terms "experimental" and "research" are not carefully defined.

For the most part, the term "practice" refers to interventions that are designed solely to enhance the well-being of an individual patient or client and that have a reasonable expectation of success. The purpose of medical or behavioral practice is to provide diagnosis, preventive treatment or therapy to particular individuals.[2] By contrast, the term "research" designates an activity designed to test an hypothesis, permit conclusions to be drawn, and thereby to develop or contribute to generalizable knowledge (expressed, for example, in theories, principles, and statements of relationships). Research is usually described in a formal protocol that sets forth an objective and a set of procedures designed to reach that objective.

When a clinician departs in a significant way from standard or accepted practice, the innovation does not, in and of itself, constitute research. The fact that a procedure is "experimental," in the sense of new, untested or different, does not automatically place it in the category of research. Radically new procedures of this description should, however, be made the object of formal research at an early stage in order to determine whether they are safe and effective. Thus, it is the responsibility of medical practice committees, for example, to insist that a major innovation be incorporated into a formal research project.[3]

Research and practice may be carried on together when research is designed to evaluate the safety and efficacy of a therapy. This need not cause any confusion regarding whether or not the activity requires review; the general rule is that if there is any element of research in an activity, that activity should undergo review for the protection of human subjects.

Part B: Basic Ethical Principles

The expression "basic ethical principles" refers to those general judgments that serve as a basic justification for the many particular ethical prescriptions and evaluations of human actions. Three basic principles, among those generally accepted in our cultural tradition, are particularly relevant to the ethics of research involving human subjects: the principles of respect of persons, beneficence, and justice.

Respect for Persons

Respect for persons incorporates at least two ethical convictions: first, that individuals should be treated as autonomous agents, and second, that persons with diminished autonomy are entitled to protection. The principle of respect for persons thus divides into two separate moral requirements: the requirement to acknowledge autonomy and the requirement to protect those with diminished autonomy.

An autonomous person is an individual capable of deliberation about personal goals and of acting under the direction of such deliberation. To respect autonomy is to give weight to autonomous persons' considered opinions and choices while refraining from obstructing their actions unless they are clearly detrimental to others. To show lack of respect for an autonomous agent is to repudiate that person's considered judgments, to deny an individual the freedom to act on those considered judgments, or to withhold information necessary to make a considered judgment, when there are no compelling reasons to do so.

However, not every human being is capable of self-determination. The capacity for self-determination matures during an individual's life, and some individuals lose this capacity wholly or in part because of illness, mental disability, or circumstances that severely restrict liberty. Respect for the immature and the incapacitated may require protecting them as they mature or while they are incapacitated.

Some persons are in need of extensive protection, even to the point of excluding them from activities which may harm them; other persons require little protection beyond making sure they undertake activities freely and with

(continued)

BOX 2.1   *(continued)*

awareness of possible adverse consequence. The extent of protection afforded should depend upon the risk of harm and the likelihood of benefit. The judgment that any individual lacks autonomy should be periodically reevaluated and will vary in different situations.

In most cases of research involving human subjects, respect for persons demands that subjects enter into the research voluntarily and with adequate information. In some situations, however, application of the principle is not obvious. The involvement of prisoners as subjects of research provides an instructive example. On the one hand, it would seem that the principle of respect for persons requires that prisoners not be deprived of the opportunity to volunteer for research.

On the other hand, under prison conditions they may be subtly coerced or unduly influenced to engage in research activities for which they would not otherwise volunteer. Respect for persons would then dictate that prisoners be protected. Whether to allow prisoners to "volunteer" or to "protect" them presents a dilemma. Respecting persons, in most hard cases, is often a matter of balancing competing claims urged by the principle of respect itself.

Beneficence

Persons are treated in an ethical manner not only by respecting their decisions and protecting them from harm, but also by making efforts to secure their well-being. Such treatment falls under the principle of beneficence. The term "beneficence" is often understood to cover acts of kindness or charity that go beyond strict obligation. In this document, beneficence is understood in a stronger sense, as an obligation. Two general rules have been formulated as complementary expressions of beneficent actions in this sense: (1) do not harm and (2) maximize possible benefits and minimize possible harms.

The Hippocratic maxim "do no harm" has long been a fundamental principle of medical ethics. Claude Bernard extended it to the realm of research, saying that one should not injure one person regardless of the benefits that might come to others. However, even avoiding harm requires learning what is harmful; and, in the process of obtaining this information, persons may be exposed to risk of harm. Further, the Hippocratic Oath requires physicians to benefit their patients "according to their best judgment." Learning what will in fact benefit may require exposing persons to risk. The problem posed by these imperatives is to decide when it is justifiable to seek certain

benefits despite the risks involved, and when the benefits should be foregone because of the risks.

The obligations of beneficence affect individual investigators and society at large, because they extend both to particular research projects and to the entire enterprise of research. In the case of particular projects, investigators and members of their institutions are obliged to give forethought to the maximization of benefits and the reduction of risk that might occur from the research investigation. In the case of scientific research in general, members of the larger society are obliged to recognize the longer term benefits and risks that may result from the improvement of knowledge and from the development of novel medical, psychotherapeutic, and social procedures.

The principle of beneficence often occupies a well-defined justifying role in many areas of research involving human subjects. An example is found in research involving children. Effective ways of treating childhood diseases and fostering healthy development are benefits that serve to justify research involving children—even when individual research subjects are not direct beneficiaries. Research also makes it possible to avoid the harm that may result from the application of previously accepted routine practices that on closer investigation turn out to be dangerous.

But the role of the principle of beneficence is not always so unambiguous. A difficult ethical problem remains, for example, about research that presents more than minimal risk without immediate prospect of direct benefit to the children involved. Some have argued that such research is inadmissible, while others have pointed out that this limit would rule out much research promising great benefit to children in the future. Here again, as with all hard cases, the different claims covered by the principle of beneficence may come into conflict and force difficult choices.

Justice

Who ought to receive the benefits of research and bear its burdens? This is a question of justice, in the sense of "fairness in distribution" or "what is deserved." An injustice occurs when some benefit to which a person is entitled is denied without good reason or when some burden is imposed unduly. Another way of conceiving the principle of justice is that equals ought to be treated equally. However, this statement requires explication. Who is equal and who is unequal? What considerations justify departure from equal distribution? Almost all

(continued)

BOX 2.1 *(continued)*

commentators allow that distinctions based on experience, age, deprivation, competence, merit and position do sometimes constitute criteria justifying differential treatment for certain purposes.

It is necessary, then, to explain in what respects people should be treated equally. There are several widely accepted formulations of just ways to distribute burdens and benefits. Each formulation mentions some relevant property on the basis of which burdens and benefits should be distributed. These formulations are (1) to each person an equal share, (2) to each person according to individual need, (3) to each person according to individual effort, (4) to each person according to societal contribution, and (5) to each person according to merit.

Questions of justice have long been associated with social practices such as punishment, taxation and political representation. Until recently these questions have not been associated with scientific research. However, they are foreshadowed even in the earliest reflections on the ethics of research involving human subjects. For example, during the 19th and early 20th centuries the burdens of serving as research subjects fell largely upon poor ward patients, while the benefits of improved medical care flowed primarily to private patients.

Subsequently, the exploitation of unwilling prisoners as research subjects in Nazi concentration camps was condemned as a particularly flagrant injustice. In this country, in the 1940's, the Tuskegee syphilis study used disadvantaged, rural black men to study the untreated course of a disease that is by no means confined to that population. These subjects were deprived of demonstrably effective treatment in order not to interrupt the project, long after such treatment became generally available.

Against this historical background, it can be seen how conceptions of justice are relevant to research involving human subjects. For example, the selection of research subjects needs to be scrutinized in order to determine whether some classes (e.g., welfare patients, particular racial and ethnic minorities, or persons confined to institutions) are being systematically selected simply because of their easy availability, their compromised position, or their manipulability, rather than for reasons directly related to the problem being studied.

Finally, whenever research supported by public funds leads to the development of therapeutic devices and procedures, justice demands both that these not provide advantages only to those who can afford them and that

such research should not unduly involve persons from groups unlikely to be among the beneficiaries of subsequent applications of the research.

Part C: Applications

Applications of the general principles to the conduct of research lead to consideration of the following requirements: informed consent, risk/benefit assessment, and the selection of subjects of research.

Informed Consent

Respect for persons requires that subjects, to the degree that they are capable, be given the opportunity to choose what shall or shall not happen to them. This opportunity is provided when adequate standards for informed consent are satisfied.

While the importance of informed consent is not questioned, controversy prevails over the nature and possibility of an informed consent. Nonetheless, there is widespread agreement that the consent process can be analyzed as containing three elements: information, comprehension and voluntariness.

Information

Most codes of research establish specific items for disclosure intended to assure that subjects are given sufficient information. These items generally include: the research procedure, their purposes, risks and anticipated benefits, alternative procedures (where therapy is involved), and a statement offering the subject the opportunity to ask questions and to withdraw at any time from the research. Additional items have been proposed, including how subjects are selected, the person responsible for the research, etc.

However, a simple listing of items does not answer the question of what the standard should be for judging how much and what sort of information should be provided. One standard frequently invoked in medical practice, namely the information commonly provided by practitioners in the field or in the locale, is inadequate since research takes place precisely when a common understanding does not exist.

Another standard, currently popular in malpractice law, requires the practitioner to reveal the information that reasonable persons would wish to know in order to make a decision regarding their care. This, too, seems insufficient since the research subject, being in essence a volunteer, may wish to know considerably more about risks

(continued)

BOX 2.1   *(continued)*

gratuitously undertaken than do patients who deliver themselves into the hand of a clinician for needed care.

It may be that a standard of "the reasonable volunteer" should be proposed: the extent and nature of information should be such that persons, knowing that the procedure is neither necessary for their care nor perhaps fully understood, can decide whether they wish to participate in the furthering of knowledge. Even when some direct benefit to them is anticipated, the subjects should understand clearly the range of risk and the voluntary nature of participation.

A special problem of consent arises where informing subjects of some pertinent aspect of the research is likely to impair the validity of the research. In many cases, it is sufficient to indicate to subjects that they are being invited to participate in research of which some features will not be revealed until the research is concluded. In all cases of research involving incomplete disclosure, such research is justified only if it is clear that (1) incomplete disclosure is truly necessary to accomplish the goals of the research, (2) there are no undisclosed risks to subjects that are more than minimal, and (3) there is an adequate plan for debriefing subjects, when appropriate, and for dissemination of research results to them.

Information about risks should never be withheld for the purpose of eliciting the cooperation of subjects, and truthful answers should always be given to direct questions about the research. Care should be taken to distinguish cases in which disclosure would destroy or invalidate the research from cases in which disclosure would simply inconvenience the investigator.

Comprehension

The manner and context in which information is conveyed is as important as the information itself. For example, presenting information in a disorganized and rapid fashion, allowing too little time for consideration or curtailing opportunities for questioning, all may adversely affect a subject's ability to make an informed choice.

Because the subject's ability to understand is a function of intelligence, rationality, maturity and language, it is necessary to adapt the presentation of the information to the subject's capacities. Investigators are responsible for ascertaining that the subject has comprehended the information. While there is always an obligation to ascertain that the information about risk to subjects is complete and adequately comprehended, when the risks are more serious,

that obligation increases. On occasion, it may be suitable to give some oral or written tests of comprehension.

Special provision may need to be made when comprehension is severely limited—for example, by conditions of immaturity or mental disability. Each class of subjects that one might consider as incompetent (e.g., infants and young children, mentally disabled patients, the terminally ill and the comatose) should be considered on its own terms. Even for these persons, however, respect requires giving them the opportunity to choose to the extent they are able, whether or not to participate in research.

The objections of these subjects to involvement should be honored, unless the research entails providing them a therapy unavailable elsewhere. Respect for persons also requires seeking the permission of other parties in order to protect the subjects from harm. Such persons are thus respected both by acknowledging their own wishes and by the use of third parties to protect them from harm.

The third parties chosen should be those who are most likely to understand the incompetent subject's situation and to act in that person's best interest. The person authorized to act on behalf of the subject should be given an opportunity to observe the research as it proceeds in order to be able to withdraw the subject from the research, if such action appears in the subject's best interest.

Voluntariness

An agreement to participate in research constitutes a valid consent only if voluntarily given. This element of informed consent requires conditions free of coercion and undue influence. Coercion occurs when an overt threat of harm is intentionally presented by one person to another in order to obtain compliance. Undue influence, by contrast, occurs through an offer of an excessive, unwarranted, inappropriate or improper reward or other overture in order to obtain compliance. Also, inducements that would ordinarily be acceptable may become undue influences if the subject is especially vulnerable.

Unjustifiable pressures usually occur when persons in positions of authority or commanding influence—especially where possible sanctions are involved—urge a course of action for a subject. A continuum of such influencing factors exists, however, and it is impossible to state precisely where justifiable persuasion ends and undue influence begins. But undue influence would include actions such as manipulating a person's choice through

(continued)

BOX 2.1 *(continued)*

the controlling influence of a close relative and threatening to withdraw health services to which an individual would otherwise be entitled.

Assessment of Risks and Benefits

The assessment of risks and benefits requires a careful arrayal of relevant data, including, in some cases, alternative ways of obtaining the benefits sought in the research. Thus, the assessment presents both an opportunity and a responsibility to gather systematic and comprehensive information about proposed research. For the investigator, it is a means to examine whether the proposed research is properly designed. For a review committee, it is a method for determining whether the risks that will be presented to subjects are justified. For prospective subjects, the assessment helps them to determine whether or not to participate.

The Nature and Scope of Risks and Benefits

The requirement that research be justified on the basis of a favorable risk/benefit assessment bears a close relation to the principle of beneficence, just as the moral requirement that informed consent be obtained is derived primarily from the principle of respect for persons. The term "risk" refers to a possibility that harm may occur. However, when expressions such as "small risk" or "high risk" are used, they usually refer (often ambiguously) both to the chance (probability) of experiencing a harm and the severity (magnitude) of the envisioned harm.

The term "benefit" is used in the research context to refer to something of positive value related to health or welfare. Unlike "risk," "benefit" is not a term that expresses probabilities. Risk is properly contrasted to probability of benefits, and benefits are properly contrasted with harms rather than risks of harm. Accordingly, so-called risk/benefit assessments are concerned with the probabilities and magnitudes of possible harm and anticipated benefits.

Many kinds of possible harms and benefits need to be taken into account. There are, for example, risks of psychological harm, physical harm, legal harm, social harm and economic harm and the corresponding benefits. While the most likely types of harms to research subjects are those of psychological or physical pain or injury, other possible kinds should not be overlooked.

Risks and benefits of research may affect the individual subjects, the families of the individual subjects, and society at large (or special groups of subjects in society). Pre-

vious codes and Federal regulations have required that risks to subjects be outweighed by the sum of both the anticipated benefit to the subject, if any, and the anticipated benefit to society in the form of knowledge to be gained from the research. In balancing these different elements, the risks and benefits affecting the immediate research subject will normally carry special weight.

On the other hand, interests other than those of the subject may on some occasions be sufficient by themselves to justify the risks involved in the research, so long as the subjects' rights have been protected. Beneficence thus requires that we protect against risk of harm to subjects and also that we be concerned about the loss of the substantial benefits that might be gained from research.

The Systematic Assessment of Risks and Benefits

It is commonly said that benefits and risks must be "balanced" and shown to be "in a favorable ratio." The metaphorical character of these terms draws attention to the difficulty of making precise judgments. Only on rare occasions will quantitative techniques be available for the scrutiny of research protocols. However, the idea of systematic, nonarbitrary analysis of risks and benefits should be emulated insofar as possible.

This ideal requires those making decisions about the justifiability of research to be thorough in the accumulation and assessment of information about all aspects of the research, and to consider alternatives systematically. This procedure renders the assessment of research more rigorous and precise, while making communication between review board members and investigators less subject to misinterpretation, misinformation and conflicting judgments.

Thus, there should first be a determination of the validity of the presuppositions of the research; then the nature, probability and magnitude of risk should be distinguished with as much clarity as possible. The method of ascertaining risks should be explicit, especially where there is no alternative to the use of such vague categories as small or slight risk. It should also be determined whether an investigator's estimates of the probability of harm or benefits are reasonable, as judged by known facts or other available studies.

Finally, assessment of the justifiability of research should reflect at least the following considerations: (i) Brutal or inhumane treatment of human subjects is never morally justified. (ii) Risks should be reduced to those necessary to achieve the research objective. It should be determined

(continued)

BOX 2.1 *(continued)*

whether it is in fact necessary to use human subjects at all. Risk can perhaps never be entirely eliminated, but it can often be reduced by careful attention to alternative procedures. (iii) When research involves significant risk of serious impairment, review committees should be extraordinarily insistent on the justification of the risk (looking usually to the likelihood of benefit to the subject—or, in some rare cases, to the manifest voluntariness of the participation). (iv) When vulnerable populations are involved in research, the appropriateness of involving them should itself be demonstrated. A number of variables go into such judgments, including the nature and degree of risk, the condition of the particular population involved, and the nature and level of the anticipated benefits. (v) Relevant risks and benefits must be thoroughly arrayed in documents and procedures used in the informed consent process.

Selection of Subjects

Just as the principle of respect for persons finds expression in the requirements for consent, and the principle of beneficence in risk/benefit assessment, the principle of justice gives rise to moral requirements that there be fair procedures and outcomes in the selection of research subjects.

Justice is relevant to the selection of subjects of research at two levels: the social and the individual. Individual justice in the selection of subjects would require that researchers exhibit fairness: thus, they should not offer potentially beneficial research only to some patients who are in their favor or select only "undesirable" persons for risky research. Social justice requires that distinction be drawn between classes of subjects that ought, and ought not, to participate in any particular kind of research, based on the ability of members of that class to bear burdens and on the appropriateness of placing further burdens on already burdened persons.

Thus, it can be considered a matter of social justice that there is an order of preference in the selection of classes of subjects (e.g., adults before children) and that some classes of potential subjects (e.g., the institutionalized mentally infirm or prisoners) may be involved as research subjects, if at all, only on certain conditions.

Injustice may appear in the selection of subjects, even if individual subjects are selected fairly by investigators and treated fairly in the course of research. Thus injustice arises from social, racial, sexual and cultural biases institutionalized in society. Thus, even if individual researchers are

treating their research subjects fairly, and even if IRBs are taking care to assure that subjects are selected fairly within a particular institution, unjust social patterns may nevertheless appear in the overall distribution of the burdens and benefits of research. Although individual institutions or investigators may not be able to resolve a problem that is pervasive in their social setting, they can consider distributive justice in selecting research subjects.

Some populations, especially institutionalized ones, are already burdened in many ways by their infirmities and environments. When research is proposed that involves risks and does not include a therapeutic component, other less burdened classes of persons should be called upon first to accept these risks of research, except where the research is directly related to the specific conditions of the class involved. Also, even though public funds for research may often flow in the same directions as public funds for health care, it seems unfair that populations dependent on public health care constitute a pool of preferred research subjects if more advantaged populations are likely to be the recipients of the benefits.

One special instance of injustice results from the involvement of vulnerable subjects. Certain groups, such as racial minorities, the economically disadvantaged, the very sick, and the institutionalized may continually be sought as research subjects, owing to their ready availability in settings where research is conducted. Given their dependent status and their frequently compromised capacity for free consent, they should be protected against the danger of being involved in research solely for administrative convenience, or because they are easy to manipulate as a result of their illness or socioeconomic condition.

Notes

1. Since 1945, various codes for the proper and responsible conduct of human experimentation in medical research have been adopted by different organizations. The best known of these codes are the Nuremberg Code of 1947, the Helsinki Declaration of 1964 (revised in 1975), and the 1971 Guidelines (codified into Federal Regulations in 1974) issued by the U.S. Department of Health, Education, and Welfare. Codes for the conduct of social and behavioral research have also been adopted, the best known being that of the American Psychological Association, published in 1973.

(continued)

BOX 2.1 *(continued)*

2. Although practice usually involves interventions designed solely to enhance the well-being of a particular individual, interventions are sometimes applied to one individual for the enhancement of the well-being of another (e.g., blood donation, skin grafts, organ transplants) or an intervention may have the dual purpose of enhancing the well-being of a particular individual, and, at the same time, providing some benefit to others (e.g., vaccination, which protects both the person who is vaccinated and society generally). The fact that some forms of practice have elements other than immediate benefit to the individual receiving an intervention, however, should not confuse the general dis-

tinction between research and practice. Even when a procedure applied in practice may benefit some other person, it remains an intervention designed to enhance the well-being of a particular individual or groups of individuals; thus, it is practice and need not be reviewed as research.

3. Because the problems related to social experimentation may differ substantially from those of biomedical and behavioral research, the Commission specifically declines to make any policy determination regarding such research at this time. Rather, the Commission believes that the problem ought to be addressed by one of its successor bodies.

EXAMPLES OF ETHICAL ISSUES

Informed Consent, Privacy, and Confidentiality Issues

Social work research has the possibility of causing unintentional harm to people. Let's illustrate this point with an example. Isa was a graduate-level social work student. She surveyed, via mailed questionnaires, 160 family practice physicians about their attitudes toward providing abortion services to minors. She asked for details about the pregnant young women who received abortion services from these physicians including names, addresses, and other identifying information, as well as incriminating details about the fathers of their children. All this was done without the minors' parental consent.

Isa soon received angry comments from numerous physicians who found the content of her survey, and possibly the implication that they provided abortion services, to be very offensive. Her findings inadvertently identified physicians who provided abortion services and those who did not. Some physicians were concerned about legal reprisal. The only people to review her study were her academic adviser and one of his colleagues, who "eyeballed" the proposed methods and survey questionnaire. Although Isa did not believe that anyone was harmed by her study, it is clear that

there was a potential to harm the participating physicians, their pregnant patients, and others.

Clearly, Isa's study violated the rights to privacy and confidentiality of female minors who obtained—or attempted to obtain—abortion services. Her study provided a potential for real harm to these vulnerable young women and their physicians alike.

Informed Consent Issues

A well-known ethical breach contributing to the call for oversight protection of human research participants was the U.S. Public Health Service syphilis study carried out in Tuskegee, Alabama. Beginning in 1932 in rural Alabama, poor, illiterate black men with syphilis were recruited through community physicians to join a research study. The men were not told that they had syphilis but rather that they were being treated for "bad blood" (Jones, 1993). They were given no actual treatment aside from aspirin and received free medical exams and transportation to the clinic, free meals when they went to the clinic, and some money to pay for their burial.

In many instances, the wives and children of the men in the study also became infected with syphilis. Even after penicillin was recognized as a cure for syphilis in 1947, it was withheld from the study's participants so that the researchers could examine the spread of the disease and its effects, including death.

The study was stopped in 1970 when news of its existence was leaked to the press by public health workers. President Bill Clinton formally apologized to the remaining survivors on behalf of the entire country in a ceremony announcing the formation of OHRP and increased protections for human research participants.

Deception Issues

Shortly after the close of the Tuskegee syphilis study, Milgram (1974) launched another research study that raised ethical issues. His study highlights the need to provide protection for human research participants and illustrates the use of deception in research. Intrigued by the apparent ability of members of the Nazi regime to carry out atrocious acts of punishment, including death, because they were simply obeying orders, Milgram studied the extent to which individuals would obey an authority figure and presumably inflict pain on other people.

Milgram's research participants were volunteers who were led to believe that his study was examining the role of punishment in learning. They were told that they had the role of teacher and were to administer increasingly higher voltages of electric shock to "learners" when they gave incorrect answers to questions. They also were led to believe that the voltages ranged from 15 to 450 volts. In fact, the learners were nothing more than actors who were employed by Milgram. They did not actually receive electric shocks, however, but pretended they did while orally displaying signs of discomfort.

Eventually, the learners (actors) became silent and did not provide answers to questions, but the study participants were told that they should treat their silence as incorrect responses. When some of the participants asked if they could stop giving the shocks, they were told that it was important to continue for the "sake of science." Just over 60% of the study participants "administered" shocks at the highest levels.

After the study was concluded, the research participants were debriefed about the deceptive practices and the actual purpose of the study. While this study may have caused physical or mental harm to some of the research participants, and although its effects were probably not permanent, it still underscores the need

to consider the ethical implications of research (Dunn & Chadwick, 2002).

CURRENT ETHICAL PROTECTIONS

Earlier we noted that IRBs hold FWAs of compliance with federal regulations concerning the protection of human research participants in research studies. While these federal regulations directly apply only to federally funded research projects, most research institutions apply these standards to *all* research studies conducted by their members regardless of their funding sources. This uniformity of application helps raise standards and expectations about the ethical conduct of research and about the level of protection due to all research participants. This means that privacy and confidentiality, informed consent, and voluntary participation are as important in a study conducted in small social service programs in rural areas as they are in large institutional settings in urban areas.

On a general level, an IRB is composed of representatives of the university's or agency's scientific community, at least one unaffiliated member, and at least one local community representative. The IRB is charged with reviewing all elements of protection, including the study's purpose, research design, data collection methods, measuring instruments, and procedures (this includes the informed consent process), along with plans for data use and storage. In essence, the IRB determines the level of risk to participants and whether the benefits of doing the study outweigh the risks to the research participants. Minimal risk is defined as:

> the probability and magnitude of harm or discomfort . . . not greater . . . than those ordinarily encountered in daily life or during the performance of routine physical or psychological examinations or tests. (Federal Policy for the Protection of Human Subjects, 55 Fed. Reg. 28,003, 1991)

This definition is particularly important when assessing the risks associated with research studies that involve vulnerable populations such as prisoners, children, and the mentally ill. If a proposed study does not meet the standard for minimal risk, a more thorough review by the full IRB is required.

ETHICAL DECISIONS ACROSS THE RESEARCH PROCESS

During each stage of any proposed research activity, the investigator is called upon to make numerous decisions. These decisions have methodological implications, but most also share ethical implications concerning the conduct and outcomes of the project. As we begin any study, several ethical questions arise. These questions include:

1. Do the proposed research methods introduce (rather than reduce) bias?
2. Are the proposed research methods coercive or potentially threatening?
3. What is the risk of harm to person, psyche, or privacy?
4. Does the research process itself respect and safeguard the confidentiality and privacy of all of its participants?

Social work researchers have a range of qualitative and quantitative research designs and data collection methods from which to choose. These designs and methods include, but are not limited to, interviews (Chapter 11), observational studies (Chapter 9), focus groups (Chapter 11), case record reviews (Chapter 14), secondary analyses (Chapter 13), survey research (Chapter 12), case-level designs (Chapter 7), and group-level designs (Chapter 8). Each presents numerous ethical considerations and challenges. Because of the importance of evidence-based practice (Chapters 22–25) and the complexity of evaluating the effectiveness of our social work interventions, we will focus on quasi-experimental and experimental research designs.

As we know from Figures 1.6 and 1.7 contained in the preceding chapter, there are numerous steps that we need to take when conducting research studies. This section covers only four of the steps and discusses ethical issues that need to be addressed in each one: (1) the research question, (2) the research design, (3) sample selection and recruitment, and (4) data collection. It should be noted, however, that all the steps in Figures 1.6 and 1.7 that are not discussed in this section (e.g., dissemination of findings) contain ethical issues that need to be addressed before going on to the next step.

The Research Question

What is the purpose or goal of our research study? Is it likely that our research study will increase our understanding of the problem under investigation? Is the research effort likely to benefit individuals (or groups) in need? Sometimes a research study can directly benefit those who participate in it. In addition, it may indirectly benefit others who also share the same or a similar condition or problem but are not actually participating in the study.

If the study does not directly or indirectly benefit its participants, then it must contribute to our professional social work knowledge base. If the research question posed already has been answered, however, what is the argument for answering it again? Some acceptable answers may include replicating clinical findings and/or generalizing the study's findings to other populations.

Research training is another acceptable reason for conducting research that may not directly benefit participants. In many universities and research institutions, providing opportunities for students to learn how to conduct research is an important function and is judged as outweighing the necessity of benefit from the results of the research activity itself.

Our *Code of Ethics* also contains an ethical standard requiring student education in research (NASW, 1999). In cases where there may be little direct or indirect benefit to the research participants, the level of risk posed by their participation should be minimal; that is, there should be little to no chance that their participation in the research study could *harm* them in any way.

As we will see in Chapter 26, when program evaluations are conducted in social service agencies for quality assurance purposes (rather than to increase general knowledge), the same ethical guidelines and practices described here apply.

The Research Design

The research design that is finally chosen also warrants examination from an ethical perspective (see Chapters 7 and 8). In intervention or evaluation research where participants are randomized to either an intervention group or a control group, concerns often arise about withholding treatment or providing a less potent intervention for control group members. The ability to randomly assign research participants to groups significantly strengthens arguments about whether a particular intervention is responsible for the change that has occurred, if any, for those individuals in this group. This decision, however, must be weighed against the reality of the participant's life or problem situation. The study described in Box 2.2 illustrates how clients can be randomly assigned to two groups: One group receives the intervention (experimental group), and the other one does not receive the intervention (control group).

One important fact that social work researchers may lose sight of is that a new untested intervention may not necessarily be better than no treatment at all. It is, as they say, an empirical question. What is clear is that individuals applying for services or treatment have the right to receive the best known evidence-based intervention at that time. In other words, it is unethical to withhold an intervention that has already been demonstrated to be effective. Protecting clients from deprivation of services and ensuring that they have access to the best interventions also is a mandate of our *Code of Ethics* (NASW, 1999).

Individuals applying for experimental or innovative services or treatments of any type also have the right to know what alternative forms of intervention are available and, as covered later, what are the risks and benefits of each research condition. Exploring the use of different kinds of control conditions and determining which is best both for the clients and for answering the research question is an important ethical task.

Central to the consideration of the ethical issues in experimental designs is the question of beneficence, as outlined in the *Belmont Report*. Researchers and the IRBs that guide them must consider how to maximize benefit and minimize harm to participants when con-

sidering how to best test the effectiveness of a social work intervention. The possibility of other viable treatment methods must be considered as well, as opposed to such other options as no treatment. Again, NASW mandates that we must protect both clients and research participants from deprivation of access to evidence-based services (NASW, 1999).

Equipoise, or the Uncertainty Principle

Related to providing the most effective services possible is the concept of *equipoise*, also called the *uncertainty principle*. This principle maintains that research studies that randomize their research participants to different treatment groups should be conducted only if there is a true uncertainty about which of the treatment alternatives is most likely to benefit them. Some questions are easy to answer, but some are much harder.

For instance, if an intervention being tested is known to be superior to an alternative inferior intervention, it is unethical to assign individuals to the inferior intervention. Similarly, an experimental research study that contains two interventions is unethical if there is a third intervention that is known to be more effective, unless the researchers have questions about the efficacy of the effective intervention with a particular subgroup of clients.

All too often, however, a consideration of beneficence and equipoise raise challenging questions for social work researchers, especially those working in fields where there is relatively little data to support the effectiveness of alternative interventions. Moreover, if the usual intervention has little or no evidence to support its effectiveness, can it be considered an appropriate comparison treatment?

Deception

Deception is another aspect of a study's research design that requires ethical forethought. As the Tuskegee study mentioned earlier illustrates, deception can be quite complicated and result in unforeseen consequences to research participants. Let's consider an example to illustrate this point. Harvey wanted to study racial/ethnic bias in employment practices in family service

BOX 2.2

Explaining an Experimental Study to Potential Adolescent Participants

Project Description: Chatham-Kent Children's Services (CKCS) Help-Seeking Project for Adolescents in Out-of-Home Placement

You are invited to participate in Chatham-Kent Children's Services (CKCS) Help-Seeking Project for Adolescents in Out-of-Home Placement. The project is funded by The Provincial Centre of Excellence for Child and Youth Mental Health. The primary person in charge of the project is Mike Stephens, Chief Executive Officer of CKCS.

This handout describes the project and will help you decide if you want to participate. You are free to choose whether or not you will take part. Before you decide, however, you need to know what will be expected of you if you decide to participate and the risks and benefits of your participation.

Please take time to read this handout. A social worker will explain the project to you and answer any questions you might have. There are no negative consequences for not participating in the project or for dropping out at a later date. The services you receive from CKCS will not be affected by your decision to participate in this project.

If you agree to take part in the project, you will be asked to sign a separate assent form. The assent form is a shorter version of this handout and contains important information about the project. When you sign the assent form, you give your "consent," which means that you give your "OK" to be a participant in the project. You should read this handout and the assent form carefully and be sure to ask any questions before signing.

What is the CKCS Help-Seeking Project for Adolescents in Out-of-Home Placement?

The main purpose of the project is to find out whether a workshop on help-seeking for youth living in out-of-home placement at CKCS will help them become more skilled at asking for help when personal or emotional problems arise.

We don't yet know if our help-seeking workshop works. So, we have designed a project that will involve about 120 youth, ages 12 years and older, who are living at CKCS. Half of the youth who participate in the project will attend a special workshop and the other half will not. The special workshop will give you information and ideas about how to seek help when personal or emotional problems arise. We will then compare the help-seeking skills of youth who attended the workshop with those who did not in order to learn whether the workshop was helpful.

You will be assigned, by chance, to a group of youth who attend the workshop, or to a group of youth who do not attend. That is, you may or may not attend the workshop even though you agree to participate in the project. If we learn that the workshop is helpful in the way we expect, then all youth that did not get to attend the workshop will be offered a chance to attend it at a later date, as long as they are still living at CKCS.

What will you be asked to do if you participate in this project?

If you agree to participate in the project you will be assigned to one of two groups as described above. In total about 120 youth will participate in the project. Everyone will be asked to complete a set of questionnaires at 4 different times: this week, 5 weeks from now, 10 weeks from now and 5 months from now. Step-by-step, this is what will happen if you decide to participate in the project.

- You will be contacted twice by telephone. Sometime this week, and then again 5 months from now, a CKCS staff member will call you by telephone and ask you questions. The phone interview takes about 30 minutes and includes questions about common emotional and behavioral problems experienced by teenagers. You do not have to answer any questions that you don't want to.
- You will be asked to come to CKCS 4 times over the next 5 months and to complete 4 other surveys. These surveys are completed at the CKCS computer lab using a special computer program. Sitting at your own computer and wearing headphones, you will see each question appear on the computer screen and hear the question being read through the headphones. You answer the questions by clicking the computer mouse. The computer surveys should take about 30 to 40 minutes to complete each time. As we said above, you do not have to answer any questions that you don't want to.

(continued)

BOX 2.2 *(continued)*

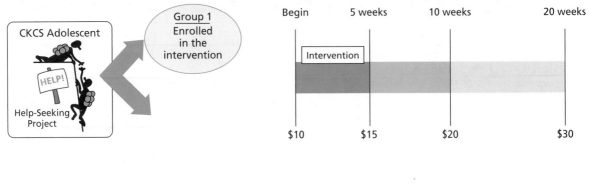

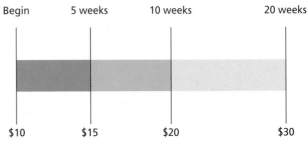

Schedule for CKCS Help-Seeking Project for Adolescents in Out-of-Home Placement

- You will be paid for your participation. You will receive $10 the first time you answer the survey questions, $15 the second time, $20 the third time, and $30 the fourth time. Snacks also will be provided at each meeting and bus fare to CKCS will be available if you need it.

  In addition to the above surveys, if you decide to participate, a project staff member will review your CKCS case file for information such as your placements, services you've received, and family contacts. By chance, half of the youth participating in the project will invited to attend a 2-to-3 hour workshop that will include 6 youth at a time. The workshop will take place at CKCS and be run by a CKCS staff member. The purpose of the workshop is to give you additional information about how you can best get help for your personal or emotional problems while living in a CKCS placement.

Under what circumstances would CKCS end your participation?

If you leave CKCS within 5 weeks of the start of the project, your participation in the project will automatically end at that time.

How will your privacy be protected?

Confidentiality describes what we do to keep information gathered about you completely private. In order to protect your privacy in this project:

- We use numbers instead of names (or other identifiers) on all of the information we get so that no one can connect the information with you.
- The information collected for this project will be sent to researchers at Western Michigan University. The information will not include anything that would individually identify you. The researchers and their staff have been trained in protecting your confidentiality.
- No CKCS staff members will have access to the information that you provide as part of this project. Your information will not be shared with your Children's Service Worker, your foster parent or caregiver, or any other workers at CKCS. Your information will only be used for this project.
- All information is stored in a safe locked area. The computers for this project are protected by a firewall system and all users are required to use passwords.

(continued)

BOX 2.2 *(continued)*

- All of your answers will be kept private unless a staff member thinks you might be in danger of hurting yourself. If you tell us that you are using illegal drugs, or are thinking of harming your self or someone else, project staff are obligated to inform your CKCS Children's Service Worker.
- The information from the project will be used to write papers, make presentations, and work with other education or research centers to improve out-of-home services for youth. Please remember that your name, or information that could identify you, will never be used. We study the survey answers "as a group" and not for any one individual. You or your family will not be identified (for example, by name or social insurance number) in any reports or publications of this project.

Are there any times when we must share your information with others?

Yes. If we know or think we know that a child is being abused, under law we must take action to protect that child. We also must report if we hear you intend to harm yourself or someone else. We will inform your CKCS Children's Service Worker if this is the case.

What are your rights as a participant in our project?

As a participant in our project, you have certain rights that help protect you:

- It is up to you to decide if you want to be in our project. That means your participation is completely voluntary.
- You have the right to change your mind at any time about being in the project. If you decide to leave the project, there will be no penalty of any kind.
- You have the right to refuse to answer any question(s). Some questions might be personal or sensitive to you. These questions are important to our project and we would like you to answer them honestly. However, if there are questions you do not want to answer, you may skip them and move on to other questions.
- You will be given copies of this Project Description as well as the Consent Form.
- This Project Description and Consent Form will also be explained verbally to you. If you have any difficulty in reading these forms, a staff person will read them to you.

- At any time you can ask any staff member questions about our project. You may also call collect Mike Stephens (1-xxx-xxx-xxxx, extension xxx), the Chief Executive Officer at CKCS.
- If you would like to contact someone outside the project staff with questions or concerns, please feel free to call Yvonne Unrau at xxx-xxx-xxxx or Rick Grinnell at xxx-xxx-xxxx, who are the two Western Michigan University researchers involved with the project. You may also contact the Chair, Human Subjects Institutional Review Board (xxx-xxx-xxxx) or the Vice President for Research (xxx-xxx-xxxx) at Western Michigan University if questions or problems arise during the course of the study. You may call collect.

Risks associated with participating in this project.

- There are very few risks in this project. You may, however, feel a little embarrassed or uncomfortable because of the personal nature of some questions on the surveys or due to certain project activities such as role plays in the workshop. Remember, you do not have to answer any questions or take part in any activities at any time.

What are the benefits to you as a participant?

Many people find it helpful to think and talk about personal information about themselves and their families. Being in the project gives you a chance to do this.

The project may improve our knowledge about how youth in care can better seek help when they need it. The information gained may help us understand more about how parents, foster parents, and CKCS can work together to help teenagers who are placed in foster or group care. This information might be used to prevent problems for teenagers in the future and to help those that are having trouble. As a participant, you will be part of a valuable project that might help other people in the future.

Please sign below to show that you have reviewed this Project Description and that you have had all your questions answered.

_____   _____
Participant Signature   Date

_____
Project Staff Signature

agencies in Chicago. He mailed out numerous fake application letters to all family service agencies in Chicago that had current openings for full-time clinicians. He sent the exact same qualifications but changed his name to reflect four different groups of people: African American, Hispanic, Asian, and Irish heritages. In short, everything was the same except his name. He planned to monitor the number of interview requests he received broken down by each group. Sounds harmless, you say. Read on.

In no way in his cover letter for employment did Harvey indicate he was conducting a research study. To Harvey's surprise, Chicago's executive directors of family service agencies met at a local conference and started talking about good job candidates they were going to follow up on. Harvey's name came up several times in the conversation. The executive directors soon became angry when they found out they had been duped by Harvey. Several had not interviewed other qualified individuals because they were holding slots open so they could interview Harvey when time permitted.

Harvey, his school, his dean, and the federal government all became involved in addressing the consequences of his unethical use of deception. Harvey's actions ignored a key concept of NASW's *Code of Ethics*: Whether acting as a practitioner or a researcher, social workers are mandated to act with integrity and in a trustworthy manner (NASW, 1999).

Generally it is good practice to avoid deception whenever possible. While it sounds reasonable to say that good social work researchers should *never* lie to their potential research participants or provide them with less than a full disclosure about the methods of their studies, in reality this is not always desirable (Slone & Hull, 2002).

Let's take an example to illustrate this principle. A social worker assessing bias toward developmentally delayed clients by custodial staff who are employed in juvenile institutions understandably might not want to initially disclose the entire purpose of the study because it might affect how the custodial staff respond. We need to ask the ethical question: Is deception absolutely necessary to carry out the study? In other words, is deception necessary to prevent participants from trying to respond in a contrived and/or socially desirable manner?

Next, we need to ask whether there is a possibility that the deception will harm potential research participants, in either the short or long term. If the deception causes or encourages participants to react in ways they might not otherwise, or is at odds with important self-attributes (such as kindness to others), the research might be psychologically harmful to participants. Our *Code of Ethics* mandates not only that we protect research participants from mental distress but also that we protect our clients from all harm to the fullest extent possible (NASW, 1999).

The majority of deception that is approved in research studies is of minimal risk to research participants and is far less dramatic than Harvey's study of racial/ethnic bias in hiring practices. For example, Sjan would have been wiser if she had used *more* deception in her study that monitored children's seat belt use on school buses. Climbing onto a school bus after the young children had boarded, she announced, "I am doing a research study for your principal, and I'm counting the number of safe and smart children on this bus who buckle up!" In this one simple, very honest sentence, she immediately gave away the purpose of her study, which resulted in an immediate flurry of seat belt buckling—defeating her ability to get an accurate and realistic count of those children who would not have buckled up if it weren't for her disclosure of the study. On another topic: Do you think Sjan would have had to obtain permission from the children's parents to do her simple head count? Why, or why not? After all, the children were minors.

Debriefing.   One of the ways we can rationalize the use of deception is by using debriefing procedures after the study is over. Debriefing involves explaining the true purpose of the research study to the participants after the study is completed, along with *why* the deception was necessary. If there is a concern about psychological distress as a result of having been deceived by the study, then adequate means of addressing this distress must be offered to the research participants (Slone & Hull, 2002).

In some cases, experienced mental health professionals might disagree on whether distressing self-knowledge can be mitigated effectively, and how this should best be done. Some IRBs might argue that the study should not be conducted given the psychological risks to participants. One possible way that the *Code of Ethics* offers to mitigate the situation is to offer participants "appropriate supportive services" after the study (NASW, 1999).

Sample Selection and Recruitment

Who is asked to participate in a research study? How are they selected for participation? While they primarily are driven by the study's purpose and sampling methods, these decisions also are influenced by our own personal values and convenience. Ethical concerns include whether the potential participants are representative of the target population to be studied. In other words, is this the group most affected by the problem we are trying to answer via the research study? As we will see in Chapter 16, it is important to ask whether the group is diverse enough to represent those who are affected by the problem.

As outlined in Chapter 6, research studies with samples lacking cultural diversity limit generalization to the broader population under study, but they also compromise social work ethical tenets that address social justice and increase inclusion. Excluding certain individuals or groups from participating can markedly affect the data one gathers and the conclusions drawn about the phenomena under study. For instance, the methodology of a study of immigrants that excludes non-English-speaking individuals, nonreaders, and agency clients who come in before or after regular hours for the convenience of the researchers introduces several types of sampling biases that will affect the study's results. This example also ignores the mandate that all social workers should engage in culturally competent practice that respects client diversity (NASW, 1999).

How potential research participants are recruited also requires an ethical lens. Four areas of concern, when it comes to recruitment, include:

- the consent and assent processes (ongoing or continuing)
- the possibility of coercion (of both medium and message)

- confidentiality and privacy
- completeness (accuracy as well as truthfulness).

Assessing all possible ways that a potential research participant might feel coerced to participate—such as a personal appeal, a financial incentive, the status of being part of a special group, other tangible or intangible benefits, or fear—can be a daunting task to say the least. Who is actually recruiting the participants? Does the gatekeeper—or the process of the recruitment effort itself—exert pressure, subtle or direct, to participate or not to participate (Khin-Maung-Gyi & Whalen, 2002)? Social workers hold an ethical obligation to examine the fairness or *equity* of recruitment strategies within target populations and the representativeness (or diversity) of the sample selected.

The *Code of Ethics* includes standards which mandate that researchers obtain participants without threatening to penalize anyone who refuses to participate and without offering inappropriate rewards for participation (NASW, 1999). Just as clients have the right to self-determination in the therapeutic process, so too do participants who volunteer for research projects. Take a quick look at Boxes 2.2 and 2.3. Do you see any possibility that the foster children were coerced to participate and/or would not receive services if they did not participate? Why, or why not?

Data Collection

This step of the research process, data collection, contains the ethical issues that surround (1) how data are collected, (2) who is going to collect the data, and (3) frequency and timing of data collection.

How Data Are Collected

As we will see in Chapter 15, a researcher's choice of how to collect the data that answer the research question can introduce unintended bias, coercing some and potentially excluding other desired participants. Awareness is key to understanding the ethical implications of data collection.

For example, Kecia wants to do a follow-up study with juveniles released from custody in her

BOX 2.3

Example of an Assent Form for Adolescents in Foster Care (to be signed after explanation provided in Box 2.2)

Assent Form: Youth in CKCS Care

I have been invited to be part of an evaluation study entitled "Chatham-Kent Children's Services (CKCS) Help-Seeking Project for Adolescents in Out-of-Home Placement." The main purpose of the study is to see if a workshop and additional support given to youth living at CKCS will make youth more skilled at asking for help with personal or emotional problems. In this study:

- I will be phoned by a CKCS staff member twice over 20 weeks and be asked to answer questions on the phone. This will take about 15 minutes each time.
- I will be invited to come to CKCS four times over the next 20 weeks to answer questions from four other survey questionnaires about my help seeking behaviors using a special computer program at CKCS.
  - After the first testing, CKCS will pay me $10 (or equivalent).
  - After the second testing point, CKCS will pay me $15 (or equivalent).
  - After the third testing point, CKCS will pay me $20 (or equivalent).
  - After the fourth (and final) time CKCS will pay me $30 (or equivalent).
- CKCS will provide food snacks at each testing time.
- A project staff member will look at my case file to obtain basic information about me such as my age, sex, time in care, etc.
- My name will not be recorded; instead of recording my name a number code will be used.
- I also may be invited to participate in a 2 to 3 hour workshop with a small group of about 5 other youth in care. The workshop will take place at CKCS and be run by a CKCS mental health worker, and possibly someone who formerly lived in out-of-home placement. At the workshop I will get information and ideas about asking for help related to personal or emotional problems that are common with teenagers.
- If I don't want to participate at this time, the service I receive from CKCS will not be affected.

- Even if I agree today to participate by signing this form, I can change my mind at any time and withdraw from the study and there will be no effect on the service I receive from CKCS.
- If I choose to complete any or all of the questionnaires for the study, then my scores will be sent to researchers at Western Michigan Univesity in Kalamazoo, Michigan.
- As mentioned previously, my name will not be on any of the surveys that are sent to Kalamazoo, Michigan. The researchers will use a code number instead of my name. The researchers will keep a list of names and code numbers that will be destroyed once the researchers have looked at all of the questionnaires.
- All of my answers will be kept private which means even my Children's Service Worker or caregivers won't know what I say unless project staff members think I might be in danger of hurting myself or others. Then project staff will need to tell my Children's Service Worker.
- Your signature below indicates that you agree to be interviewed by phone and surveyed on the computer.

Your signature also indicates that you agree:

- to have your case file at CKCS reviewed for information it contains.
- to be assigned to participate in a special help-seeking workshop for this project if selected.
- to allow CKCS to give the researchers your survey results and case file information (Your name will not be sent to the researchers).
- that you have had a chance to ask any questions you may have.

_____

Print your name on above line

_____   (Date _____)

Sign your name on above line and put in today's date

Assent obtained by: _____

---

state's detention facilities. She goes about conducting a phone survey during the hours she is at work (standard business hours) and calls the youths' "home" phone numbers. She is unaware that she is missing youths who (1) do not have phones, (2) have phones but simply do not answer them, (3) do not hang out at home during the day, and (4) operate primarily from cell phones.

One of Kecia's colleagues, Cheryl, is using an "anonymous" Internet-based survey to examine educational aspirations of young adults. As part of her study she asks participants about their recreational drug use and about any knowledge they might have about their parents' recreational use of illegal substances. Although she does not ask for names or other identifying information, it is possible to trace respondents by their computers' Internet protocol (IP) addresses. Cheryl forgot that all researchers must protect their participants' identities just as practitioners must protect clients' privacy, according to our *Code of Ethics* (NASW, 1999).

Further, although the youths have agreed to consent to participate via completion of the Internet survey itself, Cheryl also was gathering information about the youths' parents. The parents have *not* consented to have their children give Cheryl information about them. Collecting data about parental substance abuse, via their children, without the parents' consent is not a good idea, to say the least. A situation not dissimilar to this one resulted in the temporary shutdown of all federal research at one eastern university after an irate parent contacted the OHRP.

Who Is Going to Collect the Data?

Who is actually going to collect the data that will answer the research question constitutes yet another ethical decision to be made. Having teachers, social workers, administrators, or anyone who might be influential over the research participants collect data introduces the potential for coercion. Coercion can easily result in less than willing participation. It also may influence the quality of the data collected because the participants may respond differently than they normally would if they believe that individuals who have authority over them may see their responses. The *Code of Ethics* also asserts that the presence of coercion violates the tenets of voluntary participation in both therapeutic and research activities (NASW, 1999).

Frequency and Timing of Data Collection

Finally, the choice a researcher makes about the frequency and the timing of data collection activities also may raise privacy issues. Some research designs call for collecting data at additional intervals after the main part of the study has been completed with all research participants (e.g., in the study described in Box 2.2). In situations such as these, the consent process must inform potential research participants that they will be contacted in the future.

THE INFORMED CONSENT PROCESS

Safeguarding the individual's right to freely participate— or to not participate—in a research study is critical to ethical research conduct in addition to the validity and generalizability of the data collected. As we will see in Chapter 16, social work research with vulnerable clients can pose heightened threats to adequate informed consent procedures.

Let's take an example of a social work researcher who is collecting data from young women who are in the waiting room of a family service agency. The researcher distributes survey questionnaires that ask about their beliefs and attitudes regarding parenting practices. These young women are asked to complete the survey questionnaires prior to their initial appointments with social workers.

There are two ethical concerns that come to mind here. First, a potential respondent might believe that she is required to complete the survey in order to obtain the agency's services; that is, she may rightfully believe that she has no other choice but to comply. Second, and more importantly, she might believe she has to provide "correct" responses to certain questions on the survey to receive the services; that is, she might believe that the questionnaire is some sort of screening device to weed out those who are "not qualified for the services." Again, even the unintended suggestion of service deprivation is considered coercive and unethical according to the NASW *Code of Ethics* (NASW, 1999). Let's elaborate a bit on this via the use of questions:

• Do students participating in a simple survey distributed by their classroom instructor believe that choosing not to participate will result in a less favorable grade?

- Does a patient undergoing treatment for breast cancer believe she can say "no" to a request to participate in her social worker's cancer support group research project and still receive good services from her?
- Does a client mandated to receive services for child abuse believe she can freely refuse to participate in an agency-based research study and still have her children returned to her care?
- Does the suicidal client receiving services from a university-based clinic feel she has the right to withdraw from the study without being seen as "paranoid" about privacy concerns?

All of these are examples from real-life social work research projects that pose many issues around the informed and voluntary nature of participation. These examples also illustrate how research projects may undermine the spirit of client/participant self-determination, a key standard in both clinical practice and research activity (NASW, 1999).

Determining Competency to Provide Consent

Who is competent or has the capacity to give consent to participate in a research study? Capacity for consent involves both the legal and mental competency to give permission for activities that may affect the individuals' rights and welfare (Andrews, 1984). Normal, healthy, and not-at-risk adults are capable of providing consent. Children under the age of majority (generally 18 in the United States but younger in some other countries or cultures) may not legally provide informed consent to participate in research studies. Children should be asked to give their assent, or agreement, to participate, but consent itself is reserved for the parent or custodial body.

In residential treatment facilities, for example, this may be the biological parents or a guardian appointed by the state. The importance of seeking both adult consent and youth assent is also clearly specified in the *Code of Ethics* (NASW, 1999). In some states, consent is advisably obtained from as many parties as possible, including parents or other custodial adults, relevant agencies, and courts. Emancipated minors who are independent and not under any form of legal guardianship may provide their own consent in many research and clinical circumstances.

Box 2.2 contains a description of a study involving foster children. The university's IRB required that this description be read out loud to the child by his or her case worker even though it was to obtain the consent of the case worker. This description also acted as a consent form that was signed by the worker, acting as the child's legal guardian. In this study, the children's biological parents were not involved because the children were wards of the state. If the child wanted to participate in the study after hearing the description, he or she would then be given an assent form to sign (Box 2.3). Children who did not want to participate in the study were not contacted again regarding their potential participation.

In this particular study, the IRB required the researchers to obtain the consent of the workers (children's legal guardians), via reading a summary of the study to the children (e.g., Box 2.2). Then, 2 weeks later, if the children wanted to participate in the study, the workers read the assent form to them (e.g., Box 2.3). Thus, the children had two chances to decide if they wanted to participate in the study—once when the worker's consent form was read to them, and once when the worker read the assent form to them.

Identifying adults as unable to provide consent is controversial in areas such as mental disorder, where much work has been done demonstrating that these individuals can appropriately and adequately participate in an informed consent process (Appelbaum & Roth, 1982). Other cognitive incapacitation such as significant developmental delay or unconsciousness also may affect a potential research participant's ability to provide consent. Individuals residing in institutions are at particular risk of being judged incapable of providing informed consent, even in the absence of other supporting information (Grisso, 1996).

Providing Adequate Information

Researchers hold an ethical responsibility to provide information in such a way that potential research participants fully *understand* the study and their involvement in it. Here again, individuals residing in institutional settings are particularly at risk. Institutional staff may be unclear, paternalistic, or insensitive when disclosing risks, thereby failing to provide adequate information (Andrews, 1984), and it often is difficult to make accurate assessments of an individual's competence to make important decisions about participation in institutional settings (Appelbaum & Roth, 1982; Grisso, 1996). Freedom to choose to participate in a research study is significantly diminished in highly restricted settings such as prisons. What about the foster care children who participated in the research study contained in Box 2.2? Could they be described as "residing in a restrictive setting," since they were wards of the state?

Voluntary consent prohibits deception, coercion, or fraud in the recruitment of research participants. This is difficult when compensation or valued services are being offered in exchange for participation. Clients who lack access to these benefits may feel they must participate in order to gain access. For low-income individuals, even small amounts of money may be too great for them to refuse to participate.

For example, the foster children received money at each data-gathering point interval. Was this amount so high that they "just had to participate"? In studies involving more than minimal risk, which may be highly invasive or risky, students or other economically challenged groups may feel the opportunity to earn money is too great and will participate for monetary reasons alone. On the other hand, some children may feel they must do anything an adult asks them to do, and so they participate for obedience purposes only. Could this be the case for the foster children described in Boxes 2.2 and 2.3? Could they have believed they had to participate, since authority figures were requesting that they do so?

As noted earlier, the timing of a request to participate (such as just before services are provided) also may create extra pressure, acting as a coercive inducement to participate. The context, setting, and social milieu in which the potential research participants are recruited and their consent or assent are obtained (such as in a clinic or school, or in front of an adolescent's parents) must always be considered in reference to reducing coercion (Grisso, 1996; Khin-Maung-Gyi & Whalen,

2002). NASW's ethical standards also speak to the necessity of ensuring that consent and assent are freely given in both practice and research without fear, coercion, or deception. These protections apply to both voluntary and involuntary (mandated) clients alike.

Fully informed consent necessitates that participants completely understand what their participation involves, including the purpose of the study, the activities involved, the amount of time required, and the disclosure of personal information. The risks and any benefits of the research study to the individual participant must be made clear. This mandate is echoed in the *Code of Ethics* in terms of requiring that clinicians discuss with clients the possible risks associated with practice interventions prior to providing services to the client (NASW, 1999). Do you feel that these issues were addressed in Boxes 2.2 and 2.3?

In cases where there may be no direct benefit to the individual for participating, both research ethics and practice ethics dictate that this possibility must be clearly addressed with the individual prior to obtaining consent. Obtaining informed consent is now referred to as a "process." Table 2.1 lists the standard elements of a consent form. Did the consent and assent forms in Boxes 2.2 and 2.3 contain these standard elements? Box 2.4 is an example of a "boilerplate" assent form that is recommended by a large research-extensive university for obtaining assent from children.

Anonymity and Confidentiality

Just as in social work practice, social work researchers may ask for or come across highly personal information about a study participant in the course of collecting data. Two ethical issues—confidentiality and anonymity—are critical to assess in this regard. When data are collected anonymously, there is no way for researchers to connect any piece of information in a study to any given study participant. In practice, this means that the participants' names, social security numbers, or other identifying information are not collected. To illustrate, a survey conducted on one university campus about safe sex practices was distributed in residence halls and did not collect identifying information in order to obtain more honest and accurate information

TABLE 2.1

Minimum Basic Elements of Informed Consent

1. Statement of intent to conduct research
2. Purpose of research study
3. Description of research purpose
4. Expected duration of participation
5. Identification of research procedures
6. Risks and discomforts
7. Potential benefits (if any)
8. Alternative treatments or procedures (if any)
9. Provisions for confidentiality
10. Compensation for research-related injury if greater than minimal risk
11. Contact information
12. Research questions
13. Rights questions
14. Voluntary participation and the right to discontinue participation without penalty
15. Additional elements as needed

In contrast, when participants are guaranteed the confidentiality of their responses in a study, the researcher can associate responses with the names of respondents, typically through an identification number. Many research designs call for the use of identification numbers. For example, in a mailed survey, identification numbers allow the researcher to determine who has not responded to the survey and to send follow-up reminders. Or, in an experimental study of an intervention where data are collected at multiple intervals, the identification numbers allow the researcher to connect data from each interval to a given participant, such as in the research study outlined in Boxes 2.2 and 2.3.

In the informed consent process, the researcher explains that the "master key" linking respondents' names and identification numbers is stored separately from the data in a secure, locked location, and also specifies who will have access to the data and when the files will be destroyed. NASW's ethical standards contain similar expectations and protections in regard to handling client records. Clients have the right to know, prior to consenting to services, what type of information about them

will be maintained, how the information is documented, where the records will be stored, who will have access to the information, and when the files will be destroyed (NASW, 1999).

While there are many reasons that social work researchers may prefer confidentiality over anonymity, there are other considerations that must be addressed as well. When asking questions about very private behaviors (such as the earlier example about sexual practices) or about behaviors that have legal implications (such as domestic violence or substance abuse), anonymity is more of an issue. Respondents will be more likely to answer questions and to provide honest answers if they know that their responses are anonymous and cannot be linked directly to them.

Despite the best efforts of researchers and IRBs to think through and anticipate issues related to receiving anonymous or confidential data, ethical issues related to privacy still arise in the conduct of social work research. As an example, Fay conducted a survey of middle and high school students that posed an ethical dilemma. The survey questionnaire covered a variety of general risk and protective factors, including several questions about sexual behavior. One female respondent from a smaller school wrote, "I was forced to have sex" on the questionnaire. As social workers, we are considered mandated reporters in most states if we receive such information. Fay consulted an attorney, however, who indicated that, as a researcher, Fay was not considered a mandated reporter in this situation. Fay, however, was still left with the ethical dilemma. On the one hand, the only way to address this issue was to involve the school and other individuals, which violated their pledge of confidentiality. Moreover, would such actions make the situation more difficult for the student? Or, should Fay attempt to provide services related to this issue to the school in the hopes that the respondent in question would seek help without associating herself with the study?

As is common when asking for highly personal information that may be discomforting or even distressing to discuss, Fay's survey included a statement (often recommended by IRBs) that provided the telephone number of an agency, or clinic, that research

BOX 2.4

Example of a Template Consent Document

[Principal Investigator NAME]
[Title of Study]

Template Consent Document for "Minimal Risk" Behavioral Science Research

Background

A statement that the study involves research and the purpose of the research. Briefly tell the subject the background of the research problem, i.e., why this research is being done, and how this study will address the problem. Explain who is conducting the study.

> Ex: *You are being invited to take part in a research study. Before you decide it is important for you to understand why the research is being done and what it will involve. Please take time to read the following information carefully. Ask us if there is anything that is not clear or if you would like more information. Take time to decide whether or not you volunteer to take part in this research study.*

If you are conducting research where providing complete background information will invalidate the study (e.g., studies that require deception to create a particular psychological state), clearly state this in your IRB proposal and provide justification. In addition, provide the actual debriefing script that will be used to inform participants of the need for deception and the procedures you will follow to address any possible adverse effects of the deception.

Study Procedure

A description of the study procedures which will be followed, and the duration of the subjects' participation. This should allow the subject to see exactly what they will have to do and what they will experience in the study. Ex: *Your expected time in this study will be _____*. Tell the subject what to expect. Describe all procedures in lay language, using simple terms and short sentences.

Risks

A description of any reasonably foreseeable risks or discomforts to the subject (e.g., emotional distress, discomfort, psychological trauma from remembering past experiences, invasion of privacy, embarrassment, loss of social status, potential adverse economic or employment conse-

quences, etc.). If the risks are minimal, describe what these minimal risks are.

> Ex: *The risks of this study are minimal. You may feel upset thinking about or talking about personal information related to problems in your family. These risks are similar to those you experience when disclosing personal information to others. If you feel upset from this experience, you can tell the researchers and they will let you know of resources available to help.*

Benefits

A description of any benefits to the subject or to others that may reasonably be expected from the research. The description of benefits to the subject should be clear and not overstated. If no direct benefit is anticipated, that should be stated.

> Ex: *We cannot promise any benefits from your being in the study. However, possible benefits include_____.*

> Ex: *There are no direct benefits to you from your taking part in this study.*

It is important not to exaggerate the possible benefits to the participant during the course of the study. It would be reasonable to say something similar to: *"There is no direct benefit to you for your participation. However, we hope that the information we get from this study may help _____ in the future."*

DO NOT include any compensation language or amounts in this section. Please refer to the Costs and Compensation section.

Alternative Procedures

A disclosure of appropriate alternative procedures, if any, that might be advantageous to the subject and their attendant risks and benefits. To enable a rational choice about participating in the research study, subjects should be aware of the full range of options available to them.

> Ex: *If you do not want to take part in the study, you may earn research participation credit by . . . ; If you do not want to take part in the study, there are other choices such as . . . ; If you do not want to be in the study, there are no other choices.*

(continued)

BOX 2.4 *(continued)*

Confidentiality

A statement describing the extent and procedures used to maintain the confidentiality of the records and data pertaining to the subject, how the subject's privacy will be protected and notes about who may view the collected data. Statements about when confidentiality will not be maintained are also necessary in some cases (e.g., if data could reveal instances of child abuse, elder abuse, abuse of the disabled, or suicide risk).

> Ex: *Your data will be kept confidential except in cases where the researcher is legally obligated to report specific incidents. These include, but may not be limited to, incidents of abuse and suicide risk. All other information will be kept confidential by* _____.

If you are collecting social security numbers, inform subjects of this fact. Tell subjects whether they can withhold their social security number and still participate.

Person to Contact

An explanation of whom to contact for answers to any questions the subject (or legal representative) may have about the research or related matters. This must include the name of the P.I. and a telephone number where a message can be left. (Names of co-investigators can be included as well.)

If the research involves potential risks to participants that can be minimized by easy contact with the investigator, a 24-hour contact number should be considered. If a 24-hour contact number is provided, state this

> Ex: *You can leave a message for the researcher 24-hours a day at* _____

Institutional Review Board

The following statement must be included verbatim:

> "If you have questions regarding your rights as a research subject, or if problems arise which you do not feel you can discuss with the Investigator, please contact the Institutional Review Board Office at (212) 870–358.

Voluntary Participation

A statement that participation is voluntary, that refusal to participate will involve no penalty or loss of benefits to which the subject is otherwise entitled, and that the subject may discontinue participation at any time and still receive the same standard of care that he or she would otherwise have received.

> Ex: *It is up to you to decide whether or not to take part. If you do decide to take part you will be asked to sign a consent form. If you decide to take part you are still free to withdraw at any time and without giving a reason. This will not affect the relationship you have with the investigator or staff.*

Unforeseeable Risks

A statement that the particular treatment or procedure may involve risks to the subject that are currently unforeseeable. For most minimal risk research, it will be appropriate to state that there may be unanticipated risks.

> Ex: *There may be risks that we do not anticipate. However, every effort will be made to minimize any risks.*

Costs to Subjects and Compensation

Any additional costs to the subject that may result from the research and any compensation to be offered to subjects. If there are no additional costs, say so.

New Information

For most Minimal Risk Behavioral Science research, this section is not necessary. However, if participants are going to be involved in more than one experimental session over time (e.g., longitudinal designs), there should be a statement that significant new findings developed during the course of the research that may relate to willingness to continue participation will be provided to the subject.

Consent

By signing this consent form, I confirm that I have read and understood the information and have had the opportunity to ask questions. I understand that my participation is voluntary and that I am free to withdraw at any time, without giving a reason and without cost. I understand that I will be given a copy of this consent form. I voluntarily agree to take part in this study.

(continued)

Signature Block (Please do not include the following paragraphs in the consent document. This information serves for the PI only)

If the subject is competent to give consent, the form must be signed and dated. The investigator must keep a signed copy of the IRB approved consent form with the IRB stamp showing the approved date and expiration date. If the subject is not competent to give consent, the form must be signed and dated by the subject's legal representative/next of kin.

Note that there may be situations in which the IRB deems that protection of subjects will be enhanced by the addition of a witness to the informed consent process. This is rarely needed for minimal risk behavioral science research. However, prior to submitting your Informed

Consent document to the IRB, it would be useful to consider whether or not a witness would provide additional protections. If so, a witness line should be added to the signature block.

_____
Printed Name of Participant

_____   _____
Signature of Participant   Date

_____
Printed Name of Researcher or Staff

_____   _____
Signature of Researcher or Staff   Date

participants could call if they wanted to discuss a problem they might be experiencing. The *Code of Ethics* directs social work researchers to secure participant access to poststudy supportive services (NASW, 1999). Sometimes simply asking study participants questions may make them more aware of the problems in their lives or may otherwise cause more discomfort or stress. Of course, there is no way to know if the student in this situation took advantage of this potential resource.

Even when there is face-to-face admission of problematic behaviors in a research setting, it may be difficult to take action to protect individuals. Kip described an experience he had as a research counselor in a study with HIV-positive men. The purpose of the study was to examine the effectiveness of a counseling program to reduce the risk of transmitting HIV. In this instance, two men in a relationship, Bill and Ted, both of whom were HIV positive, were enrolled in the research study and were being seen by two different social workers—Bill was being seen by Kip, and Ted was being seen by another social worker.

Kip knew that his client/study participant, Bill, had been arguing with his partner, Ted. During the course of a session, Bill suggested that Ted was having sex with boys. Before Kip could clarify whether "boys"

referred to young adult gay men or actual children, Bill grew angry and left the session early. Because Bill had been promised confidentiality, it was not possible to ask his partner, Ted, about Bill's allegation. Unfortunately, when Kip turned to the principal investigators of the research study for guidance on how to handle the situation, they too were unclear about how to proceed. How would you have proceeded if you were Kip?

SPECIAL CONSIDERATIONS

As communication becomes easier and the world a smaller place in many ways, more research needs and opportunities present themselves. For example, social workers may work with political and criminal prisoners, individuals with serious and persistent mental disorders or impaired cognitive functioning, refugees and internally displaced persons, and women and children who have been trafficked. Social workers assessing needs and developing practice methods in global arenas require accurate information about the problems and the contexts in which these problems occur.

This section addresses only a few of the ethical issues that surround three special considerations: (1) international research, (2) computer- and Internet-based research guidance, and (3) students as subjects/students as researchers.

International Research

Many social workers engage in international research. Our colleague Naselle, for example, is carrying out an HIV/AIDS risk reduction program in Kazakhstan with multiple-risk women. In order to do her research study, Naselle had to obtain permission from her own university, as well as from the minister of health in Kazakhstan and the national research ethics board there. In her home university's IRB application, Naselle was required to provide evidence that her research methods were culturally sensitive and appropriate and had been approved locally.

Depending on the level of risk associated with an international study, a researcher may need to demonstrate a sophisticated understanding of the country, culture, and customs before approval is granted to conduct the study. Our *Code of Ethics* reinforces this notion by mandating that social workers engage in culturally competent practice that respects diversity (NASW, 1999).

Computer- and Internet-Based Research Guidance

Research with human subjects using Web-based methods is a fast-developing data collection method used in social and behavioral sciences. The Internet provides efficient access and the ability to collect widely distributed information. Internet-based research must address the same risks—including violation of privacy, legal risks, and psychosocial stress—and must provide the same level of protection as other types of research involving human research participants.

Recruitment procedures should follow institutional guidelines (usually found in IRB guidance) for recruiting research participants from traditional media such as newspapers and bulletin boards. Unsolicited e-mail messages to multiple users may be prohibited, and accurate disclosure of message origin and author is required in most cases.

Researchers are advised to authenticate respondents, taking steps to assign participants personal identification numbers (PINs) to be used in any follow-up data collection endeavors. Data encryption is important for transmission, and acceptable software varies across countries. Whenever possible, using a professionally administered server is encouraged. Finally, storing and destroying data also involve dual focus on privacy and technological methods. The goal is to provide the same level of protection to human subjects as with more traditional data collection methodologies (Dewhurst, 2005).

Students as Subjects/Students as Researchers

The final special situations we wish to briefly address are students as participants or subjects in research studies, and then students as researchers themselves. Students who participate in agency or university research are a vulnerable group, subject to coercion and influence by faculty, their peers, their field instructors, and agency administrators alike. Students should be particularly well informed about the limits of privacy and confidentiality and should have a thorough understanding of the research goals and procedures prior to giving consent to participate (Tickle & Heatherton, 2002).

As with any research participant, students must be given the right to freely refuse participation without fear of adverse consequences in order for consent to be considered voluntary and informed. Without such assurances, the research study does not meet the standards in the *Code of Ethics* (NASW, 1999). Research studies carried out by one's own classroom instructor or field instructor may violate ethical research guidelines. According to the *Code of Ethics*, this situation may create a conflict of interest and fail to protect the best interests of the student/participant.

Carrying out your own research project as a student can be extremely exciting. As a student, however, you are entitled to guidance and protection from your university and faculty in the ethical as well as methodological conduct of research. A faculty member should carefully review any student research proposal involving human subjects prior to its submission to the IRB. At many universities, students are considered "protected" within the university structure. Therefore, the signing faculty sponsor ultimately is responsible for the ethical conduct of the student's research project. As a student, you have the right to receive education about how to ethically conduct your research (NASW, 1999).

SUMMARY

Social work research has the potential to contribute significantly to our profession's knowledge development. As we have illustrated throughout this chapter, ethical social work practice includes ethical research conduct. Mindful concern for the safety and informed protection of our potential research participants is not enough. In ethical research this concern must be partnered with knowledge of best research practices and skill in methodological implementation.

The Quantitative
Research Approach

Yvonne A. Unrau
Richard M. Grinnell, Jr.
Margaret Williams

3

Basic Steps in the Research Process

Step 1	Choose a problem
2	Review the literature
3	Evaluate the literature
4	Be aware of all ethical issues
5	Be aware of all cultural issues
6	State the research question or hypothesis
7	Select the research approach
8	Determine how the variables are going to be measured
9	Select a sample
10	Select a data collection method
11	Collect and code the data
12	Analyze and interpret the data
13	Write the report
14	Disseminate the report

You Are Here →

You Are Here →

The two previous chapters presented a brief discussion of why the generation of knowledge is best acquired through the use of the research method and the contexts and ethics contained within the research process. As we now know, the research method contains two complementary approaches—the quantitative approach, which is the topic of this chapter—and the qualitative approach—the topic of the following chapter. No matter which approach we use to obtain our professional knowledge base, "knowing" something that resulted from either approach is much more objective than "knowing" that exact same something that was derived from the other ways of knowing.

Before we discuss the quantitative approach to knowledge development you need to understand how this approach is embedded within the "positivist way of thinking" as illustrated in Figure 3.1 and Box 3.1.

RESEARCH STEPS WITHIN THE QUANTITATIVE APPROACH

The preceding discussion encompasses only the philosophy behind the quantitative research approach to knowledge building. With this philosophy in mind, we now turn our attention to the general sequential steps (in a more or less straightforward manner) that all quantitative researchers follow, as outlined on the left side of this page and in Figure 1.6. These steps yield a very useful format for obtaining knowledge in our profession.

The quantitative research approach as illustrated in Figure 1.6 is a "tried and tested" method of scientific inquiry. It has been used for centuries. As we now know, if data obtained within a research study are represented in the form of numbers, then this portion of the study is considered "quantitative." The numbers are then analyzed by descriptive and inferential statistics.

In a nutshell, most of the critical decisions to be made in a quantitative research study occur *before* the study is ever started. This means that the researcher is well aware of all the study's limitations before the study actually begins. It is possible, therefore, for a researcher to decide that a quantitative study has simply too many limitations (ethical and/or procedural) and eventually decide not to carry it out. Regardless of whether or not a proposed study is ever carried out, the process always

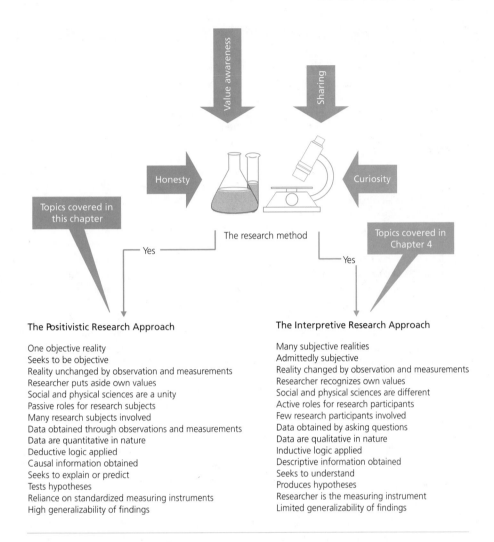

Figure 3.1   The Quantitative (Positivistic) and Qualitative (Interpretive) Research Approaches Within the Research Method

begins with choosing a research topic and focusing the research question.

DEVELOPING THE RESEARCH QUESTION

As can be seen in Figure 1.6, the first steps of the quantitative approach to knowledge development are to identify a general problem area to study and then to refine this general area into a research question that can be answered or a hypothesis that can be tested. These studies are usually deductive processes; that is, they usually begin with a broad and general query about a general social problem and then pare it down to a specific research question or hypothesis. For instance, your general research problem may have started out with a curiosity about racial discrimination within public social service agencies. It could be written simply as:

General Problem Area:

Racial discrimination within public social service agencies

BOX 3.1

What is the Positivist Way of Thinking?

The positivist way of thinking strives toward measurability, objectivity, the reducing of uncertainty, duplication, and the use of standardized procedures (see, for example, the left side of Figure 3.1).

Striving Toward Measurability

The positivist way of thinking tries to study only those things that can be objectively measured, that is, knowledge gained through this belief is based on "objective measurements" of the real world, not on someone's opinions, beliefs, or past experiences. Conversely, and as you know from Chapter 1, knowledge gained through tradition or authority depends on people's opinions and beliefs and not on measurements of some kind. Entities that cannot be measured, or even seen, such as id, ego, or superego, are not amenable to a positivistic-oriented research study but rather rely on tradition and authority.

In short, a positivist principle is that the things you believe to exist must be measureable. However, at this point in our discussion, it is useful to remember that researchers doing studies within a positivistic framework believe that practically everything in life is measurable.

Striving Toward Objectivity

The second ideal of the positivist belief is that research studies must be as "objective" as possible. The things that are being observed and/or measured must not be affected in any way by the person doing the observing or measuring. Physical scientists have observed inanimate matter for centuries, confident in the belief that objects do not change as a result of being observed. In the subworld of the atom, however, physicists are beginning to learn what social workers have always known. Things do change when they are observed. People think, feel, and behave very differently as a result of being observed. Not only do they change; they change in different ways depending on who is doing the observing and/or measuring.

There is yet another problem. Observed behavior is open to interpretation by the observer. To illustrate this point, let's take a simple example of a client you are seeing, named Ron, who is severely withdrawn. He may behave in one way in your office in individual treatment sessions, and in quite another way when his mother joins the interviews. You may think that Ron is unduly silent, while his mother remarks on how much he is talking. If his mother wants him to talk, perhaps as a sign that he is emerging from his withdrawal, she may perceive him to be talking more than he really is.

All folks who do research studies with the positivistic framework go to great lengths to ensure that their own hopes, fears, beliefs, and biases do not affect their research results and that the biases of others do not affect them, either. Nevertheless, as discussed in later chapters, complete "objectivity" is rarely possible in social work, despite the many strategies that have been developed over the years to achieve it.

Suppose, for example, that a social worker is trying to help a mother interact more positively with her child. The worker, together with a colleague, may first observe the child and mother in a playroom setting, recording how many times the mother makes eye contact with the child, hugs the child, criticizes the child, makes encouraging comments, and so forth on a three-point scale (i.e., discouraging, neutral, encouraging). The social worker may perceive a remark that the mother has made to the child as "neutral," while the colleague thinks it was "encouraging."

As you will see throughout this book, in such a situation it is impossible to resolve the disagreement. If there were six objective observers, for example, five opting for "neutral" and only one for "encouraging," the one "encouraging observer" is more likely to be wrong than the five, and it is very likely that the mother's remark was "neutral." As you know from Chapter 1, as more people agree on what they have observed, the less likely it becomes that the observation was distorted by bias, and the more likely it is that the agreement reached is "objectively true."

As should be obvious by now, objectivity is largely a matter of agreement. There are some things—usually physical phenomena—about which most people agree. Most people agree, for example, that objects fall when dropped, water turns to steam at a certain temperature, sea water contains salt, and so forth. However, there are other things—mostly to do with values, attitudes, and feelings—about which agreement is far more rare.

An argument about whether Beethoven is a better composer than Bach, for example, cannot be "objectively" resolved. Neither can a dispute about the rightness of capital punishment, euthanasia, or abortion. It is not surprising, therefore, that physical researchers, who work with physical phenomena, are able to be more "objective" than social work researchers, who work with human beings.

(continued)

BOX 3.1 *(continued)*

Striving Toward Reducing Uncertainty

Positivistic-oriented research studies try to totally rule out uncertainty. Since all observations and/or measurements in the social sciences are made by human beings, personal bias cannot be entirely eliminated, and there is always the possibility that an observation and/or measurement is in error, no matter how many people agree about what they saw or measured. There is also the possibility that the conclusions drawn from even an accurate observation or measurement will be wrong. A number of people may agree, for example, that an object in the sky is a UFO when in fact it is a meteor. Even if they agree that it is a meteor, they may come to the conclusion—probably erroneously—that the meteor is a warning from an angry extraterrestrial person.

In the twentieth century, most people do not believe that natural phenomena have anything to do with extraterrestrial people. They prefer the explanations that modern researchers have proposed. Nevertheless, no researcher would say—or at least be quoted as saying—that meteors and extraterrestrial beings are not related for certain. When utilizing the research method of knowledge development, nothing is certain. Even the best-tested theory is only tentative and accepted as true until newly discovered evidence shows it to be untrue or only partly true. All knowledge gained through the research method is thus provisional. Everything presently accepted as true is true only with varying degrees of probability.

Striving Toward Duplication

Positivistic researchers try to do research studies in such a way that the studies can be duplicated. Suppose, for a moment, you are running a 12-week intervention program to help fathers who have abused their children to manage their anger without resorting to physical violence. You have put a great deal of effort into designing your program and believe that your intervention (the program) is more effective than other interventions currently used in other anger-management programs. You develop a method of measuring the degree to which the fathers in your group have learned to dissipate their anger in nondamaging ways, and you find that, indeed, the group of fathers shows marked improvement.

Improvement shown by one group of fathers, however, is not convincing evidence for the effectiveness of your program. Perhaps your measurements were in error and the improvement was not as great as you hoped for. Per-

haps the improvement was a coincidence, and the fathers' behaviors changed because they had joined a health club and each had vented his fury on a punching bag in order to be more certain, you duplicate your program and measuring procedures with a second group of fathers. In other words, you replicate your study.

After you have used the same procedures with a number of groups and obtained similar results each time, you might expect that other social workers will eagerly adopt your methods. As presented in Chapter 1, tradition dies hard. Other social workers have a vested interest in their interventions, and they may suggest that you found the results you did only because you wanted to find them.

In order to counter any suggestion of bias, you ask another, independent social worker to use your same anger-management program and measuring methods with other groups of fathers. If the results are the same as before, your colleagues in the field of anger management may choose to adopt your intervention method (the program). Whatever your colleagues decide, you are excited about your new found program. You wonder if your methods would work as well with women as they do with men, with adolescents as well as with adults, with Native Americans, Asians, or African Americans as well as with Caucasians, with mixed groups, larger groups, or groups in different settings. In fact, you have identified a lifetime project, since you will have to apply your program and measuring procedures repeatedly to all these different groups of people.

Striving Toward the Use of Standardized Procedures

Finally, a true-to-the-bone positivist researcher tries to use well-accepted standardized procedures. For a positivistic-oriented research study to be creditable, and before others can accept its results, they must be satisfied that your study was conducted according to accepted scientific standardized procedures. The allegation that your work lacks "objectivity" is only one of the criticisms they might bring. In addition, they might suggest that the group of fathers you worked with was not typical of abusive fathers in general and that your results are not therefore applicable to other groups of abusive fathers. It might be alleged that you did not make proper measurements, or that you measured the wrong thing, or that you did not take enough measurements, or that you did not analyze your data correctly, and so on.

(continued)

In order to negate these kinds of criticisms, over the years social work researchers have agreed on a set of standard procedures and techniques that are thought most likely to produce "true and unbiased" knowledge—which is what this book is all about. Certain steps must be performed in a certain order. Fore-seeable errors must be guarded against. Ethical behavior with research participants and colleagues must be maintained, as outlined in Chapter 2. These procedures must be followed if your study is both to generate usable results and to be accepted as useful by other social workers.

You may have noticed through your professional practice as a medical social worker in a local hospital, for example, that many of the patients within your hospital are from ethnic minority backgrounds, have high unemployment rates, have a large proportion of their members living under the poverty level, and have low levels of educational attainment. You believe that these four conditions alone should increase the likelihood of their utilizing the hospital's social service department where you work.

Conversely, and at the same time, you have also observed that there are more ethnic majorities than ethnic minorities who are seen in your hospital's social service department. Your personal observations may then lead you to question whether discrimination against ethic minorities exists when it comes to their having access to your hospital's social service department. You can easily test the possibility of such a relationship by using the quantitative research approach.

The next step in focusing your research question would be to visit the library and review the literature related to your two concepts:

- Racial discrimination within social service agencies (Concept 1)
- Access to social service (Concept 2)

You would want to read the literature related to the two main concepts within the general research question—racial discrimination within social service agencies and access to social services. You would want to learn about how various theories explain both of your main concepts in order to arrive at a meaningful research question. It may be, for example, that many ethnic minority cultures are unlikely to ask "strangers" for help with life's personal difficulties.

Furthermore, you may learn that most social service programs are organized using bureaucratic structures, which require new potential clients to talk to several strangers (e.g., telephone receptionist, waiting-room clerk, intake worker) before they are able to access social services. Given that you know, via the literature, that ethnic minorities do not like talking with strangers about their personal problems and that social services are set up for people to deal with a series of strangers, you could develop a very simple quantitative research question:

Quantitative Research Question:
Do patients who come from ethnic minority backgrounds have difficulty accessing my hospital's social service department?

Your simple straightforward general problem area has become much more specific via the construction of a research question. In your research question, for example, you have identified a person's ethnicity and access to your hospital's social services as your two concepts of interest.

Developing Concepts

What are concepts, anyway? They are nothing more than ideas. When you speak of a client's ethnic background, for example, you have in mind the concept of *ethnicity*. When you use the word *ethnicity*, you are referring to the underlying idea that certain groups of people can be differentiated from other groups on the basis of physical characteristics, customs, beliefs, language, and so on.

Take a female patient in your hospital, for example, who has just been referred to your social service department. She is a patient in the hospital, she is a woman, and she is now also your client. If she is married, she is a wife. If she has children, she is a mother. She may be a home owner, a committee member, an Asian, or a Catholic. She may be hostile, demanding, or compassionate. All of her characteristics are concepts. They are simply ideas that all members of a society share—to a greater or lesser degree, of course.

Some concepts are perceived the same way by all of us. On the other hand, some concepts give rise to huge disagreements. The concept of being a mother, for example, involves the concept of children and, specifically, the concept of having given birth to a child. Today, however, most people would agree that having given birth to a child is only *one* definition of a mother.

The idea of motherhood in Western society involves more than simply giving birth, however. Also involved in motherhood are the concepts of loving, of caring for the child's physical needs, of offering the child emotional support, of advocating for the child with others, of accepting legal and financial responsibility for the child, and of being there for the child in all circumstances and at all times. Some of us could easily argue that a woman who does all of these things is a mother, whether she has given birth or not. Others would say that the biological mother is the *only* real mother even if she abandoned her child at birth.

Like many other qualities of interest to social workers, ethnicity is a highly complex concept with many possible dimensions. Intelligence is another such concept, as are alienation, morale, conformity, cohesion, motivation, delinquency, prejudice, social status, and a host of others.

Identifying Variables Within Concepts

You can now relate the concept of "the existence of different ethnic groups" to the patients who seek out your hospital's social service department. Some patients will belong to one ethnic group, some to another, some to a third, and so on. In other words, these folks *vary* with respect to which ethnic group they belong to. Any characteristic that can vary, logically enough, is called a *variable*.

Putting Value Labels on Variables

You now have a concept, ethnicity—and a related variable, ethnic group. Finally, you need to think about which particular ethnic groups will be useful for your study. Perhaps you know that Asians are patients within your hospital, and so are Caucasians, Hispanics, African Americans, and Native Americans. This gives you five categories, or *value labels,* of your ethnic group variable:

Value Labels for Ethnicity Variable:
Asian
Caucasian
Hispanic
African American
Native American

During your quantitative study, you will ask all of the hospital's patients which of the five ethnic groups they belong to; or perhaps these data will be recorded on the hospital's intake forms and you will not need to ask for them. In any case, the resulting data will be in the form of numbers or percentages for each value label. You will have succeeded in measuring the variable *ethnic group* by describing it in terms of five value labels, or categories.

Value labels do nothing more than describe a variable. You will note that these five categories only provide one possible description. You could also have included Pacific Islanders, for example, if there were any receiving medical treatment in your hospital, and then you would have had six value labels of your ethnic group variable instead of only five. If you were afraid that not all clients receiving medical treatment would fit into one of these categories, then you could include a miscellaneous category, *other*, to be sure you had accounted for everyone.

By reviewing the literature and your knowledge of your social service unit, you have more or less devised a direction for your study in relation to your ethnicity concept. You have come up with a concept, a variable, and five value labels for your variable, which are related as follows:

Concept: Ethnicity
Variable: Ethnic group
Variable Labels: Asian
                       Caucasian
                       Hispanic
                       African American
                       Native American

As you know, ethnicity is not the only concept of interest in your study. There is also *access to social work services*, which is the idea that some people, or groups of people, are able to access social work services more readily than other people or groups.

You might think of access simply in terms of how many of the patients receiving medical treatment within your hospital actually saw a social worker. Clients will *vary* with respect to whether they saw a social worker or not and so you have the variable—*saw social worker*—and two value labels of that variable:

- *yes*, the patient saw a social worker
- *no*, the patient did not see a social worker

You could, for example, ask each patient upon leaving the hospital a very simple question, such as:

Did you see a social worker while you were in the hospital?
- Yes
- No

If you wish to explore access in more depth, you might be interested in the factors affecting access. For example, perhaps your review of the literature has led you to believe that some ethnic groups tend to receive fewer referrals to social work services than other groups. If this is the case in your hospital, clients will vary with respect to whether or not they received a referral, and you immediately have a second variable—*referral*—and two value labels of that variable:

- *yes*, the patient was referred
- *no*, the patient was not referred

Once again, this variable can take the form of a very simple question, such as:

When you were a patient within the hospital, were you at any time referred to the hospital's social services department?
- Yes
- No

However, there is more to accessing hospital social work services than just being referred. Perhaps, according to the literature, certain ethnic groups are more likely to follow up on a referral than other groups because of cultural beliefs around the appropriateness of asking nonfamily members for help. In that case, you have a third variable, *follow-up of referral*, with two value labels of its own:

- *yes*, the client followed up
- *no*, the client did not follow up

This also can be put into a question form, such as:

If you were referred to social work services while you were a patient in the hospital, did you follow up on the referral and actually see a social worker?
- Yes
- No

In addition, folks who do try to follow up on referrals may meet circumstances within the referral process that are more intimidating for some than for others. Perhaps they are obliged to fill out a large number of forms or to tell their stories to many unfamiliar people before they actually succeed in achieving an appointment with a social worker.

If this is the case, they *vary* with respect to how intimidating they find the process, and you have a fourth variable, *feelings of intimidation around the referral process*. The value labels here are not so immediately apparent, but you might decide on just three:

- not at all intimidated
- somewhat intimidated
- very intimidated

BOX 3.2

Rival Hypotheses

Hypotheses that compete with one- and two-tailed research hypotheses are known as *rival hypotheses.* To be simplistic, rival hypotheses use other extraneous independent variables that may affect the dependent variable. In some cases, the best way to show that a research hypothesis is true is to show that other, or rival, hypotheses are *not* true. For example, if it can be shown that social workers' attitudes toward our profession (dependent variable) are *not* affected by their socioeconomic background (independent variable), it becomes more likely that their attitudes toward our profession are determined solely by whether they value a social institutional change model or an individual client change model of practice.

If we wished to verify the above research hypothesis, we could hypothesize that the social workers' socioeconomic backgrounds were also related to their attitudes in the hope that this rival hypothesis would be untrue.

In order to test the initial research hypothesis, we need to (1) select a sample of social workers, (2) measure their attitudes toward the social work profession, (3) determine which model of practice each values most, and (4) perform a statistical analysis to discover whether the workers who value a social institutional change model have more negative attitudes toward our profession than social workers who value an individual client change model. The possibility that socioeconomic background might be an extraneous variable can be controlled by making it an independent variable in the following rival hypothesis:

Rival Hypothesis:
Social workers who have high socioeconomic backgrounds (a second potential independent variable) will evidence more negative attitudes toward the social work profession (the same dependent variable) than social workers who have low socioeconomic backgrounds.

Obviously, there are other extraneous variables that could invalidate the results, such as gender, age, personality, type of job, educational level, parents' occupations, or length of work experience. We could formulate further rival hypotheses to deal with these, a potentially confusing procedure. An alternative is to declare that these extraneous variables might have affected the study's results but were not addressed in the current study. Others interested in the area may choose to address these extraneous variables in future studies.

Steps in Formulating Hypotheses

It may be helpful at this point to summarize the process by which a general research problem becomes a specific research question and finally a testable hypothesis. Essentially, there are five interrelated steps: (1) identifying the general problem area, (2) gathering information and categorizing ideas, (3) formulating the research question, (4) conceptualizing and operationalizing the variables, and (5) formulating the hypothesis. The final steps, of course, will be, first, to test the hypothesis by implementing the research design and, second, to disseminate the results in the form of journal papers or reports so that knowledge in the problem area is increased. Let us now turn to the first step in hypothesis formulation.

Step 1: Identifying the Problem Area

As previously discussed, we need to select a general problem area based on our own interests and value systems, as well as on the professional and agency considerations. It is a good idea right from the beginning of any research study to keep a research logbook, which is like a diary where ideas, comments, actions, and decisions can be chronologically recorded. When it is time to write the final research report, perhaps 1 or 2 years after the study was initially started, the logbook will be an invaluable aid to our memory of both what was done, when, how, and why, and what difficulties were encountered and what progress resulted.

Step 2: Gathering Information and Categorizing Ideas

Throughout the study, we will spend long hours reviewing the literature on the problem area and discussing ideas with colleagues who are particularly knowledgeable about one aspect or the other. During the process of reading and discussion, vague ideas about the problem area will gradually come together, and we will become more certain about what aspects need to be explored and how the knowledge gained might be of use.

For example, suppose we are interested in the professional career patterns of social workers, and particularly in why some social workers continue to enjoy their work while others become increasingly frustrated and finally resign. Knowledge in this area might be useful to those responsible for selecting social work students, educating them, and initiating them into the workplace.

(continued)

BOX 3.2 *(continued)*

We might want to explore not only the social work literature but also the literature of other allied disciplines, particularly sociology and psychology. Ideas and questions will emerge. The literature may have identified two time periods as being of particular importance in the molding of social workers' attitudes toward our profession: the educational period itself; and the first experience in the workplace, often termed *reality shock*. But suppose students enter social work education already inclined to one of two opposing beliefs: either that the environment is largely to blame for clients' problems (social institutional change model), or that the fault lies with the clients themselves (individual client change model).

For the sake of simplicity, let us suppose that social work students fall into only one of these two camps, depending on such factors as their age, gender, ethnic origin, socioeconomic background, and previous life experience. Suppose that some of them believe they can change the client or the client's environment or both, and they grow frustrated when they find that people and organizations are not so easily changed. Suppose that older students, or minority or female students, have discovered this already and are better able to cope with reality shock. Suppose that reality shock is softened or reinforced depending on the career choice the graduating student makes.

As a result of all this supposing, we will emerge with a large number of concepts that may be related to each other in numerous and different ways. Concepts so far include social workers, the characteristics of social work students, social work education, work experience, career choices, reality shock, the coping capacities of social workers, the two different professional models preferred by social workers, and the degree of frustration felt by social workers at various points in their careers.

Our next task is to examine all the possible relationships between these concepts, perhaps by writing each concept on a plain card and moving the cards around to show diagrammatically the different relationships. Some of the possible relationships will seem more interesting or important than others, and it is from these relationships that research questions and hypotheses will emerge.

Step 3: Formulating the Research Question

Perhaps we have decided that the most interesting relationship is the one between the social workers' preferred professional model and their attitudes toward our profession. There may be evidence to suggest that the individual client change model is still the paramount ideology in social work. We may wish to explore the possibility that social workers, whose personal value systems conflict with this paramount ideology, will develop negative attitudes toward our profession; conversely, we may speculate that social workers who concur with the ideology will show positive attitudes toward our profession.

Research questions follow quite logically from this: For example, "Do social workers who value a social institutional change model of practice exhibit more negative attitudes toward our profession than social workers who value an individual client change model of practice?"

Once tentatively formulated, the adequacy of the research question must be judged according to the same criteria used to assess the research problem—relevancy, researchability, feasibility, and ethical acceptability. In addition, the research question must be specific. The reader must be able to understand precisely what we are asking, without needing to speculate about the meanings of words or the nature of the relationships proposed.

Step 4: Conceptualizing and Operationalizing Variables

When the research question has been tentatively formulated, we need to conceptualize and operationalize the variables contained within the study's concepts (Step 3). For example, what is meant by a social worker in the context of this study? Perhaps we could conceptually and operationally define social workers as:

> All people who hold an MSW degree from an accredited graduate school of social work and who have been employed on a full-time basis for the last 24 months within Agency A.

A person who defines social workers in this way must have sensible reasons for excluding people with other qualifications, as well as people who work part-time, or in other agencies, or have worked for less than 24 months.

In a similar manner, we need to conceptualize and operationally define attitudes toward the social work profession. There will have to be some way of measuring social workers' attitudes. This could be done by looking at some observable indicator(s) such as frequent absenteeism,

(continued)

BOX 3.2   *(continued)*

a larger-than-average number of canceled appointments with clients, lateness, client dissatisfaction as recorded on client evaluation forms, refusal to work with certain types of clients, habitual silence at staff meetings, or, probably most appropriately, the use of some standardized instrument that measures attitudes toward the social work profession (or some similar helping profession).

Whatever indicators or variables are chosen to conceptualize the concept of "attitudes," there must be sensible reasons for selecting these rather than others—some evidence that lateness, for example, does indicate a negative attitude and not just an unfortunate bus connection. In addition, we must be sure that the attitudes expressed are attitudes toward the social work profession as a whole, not just dissatisfaction with Agency A.

While considering the subject of measurement, we need to ensure that all the needed data will be available. If one variable is to be client satisfaction, for example, will Agency A permit access to client evaluation forms? Does Agency A even have client evaluation forms? In the absence of evaluation forms, will we be able to interview clients? What proportion of clients have terminated with the agency and can no longer be traced?

If we find that some variables included in the research question cannot be feasibly measured, it will be necessary to revise it or, in an extreme case, to go back to the beginning and formulate another question. Once the question has been decided, a specific hypothesis or set of hypotheses can be derived.

Step 5: Formulating the Final Hypothesis

The last step before undertaking an explanatory study is to construct the hypothesis. For example, let us take the following hypothesis:

> Social workers who value an individual client change model of practice will exhibit more negative attitudes toward the social work profession than will social workers who value a social institutional change model of practice.

The above is the research hypothesis, or the statement that we hope to verify by undertaking the study. An important part of hypothesis construction is to identify extraneous variables; that is, extraneous factors that may effect the dependent variable (their attitudes) and so invalidate the study's results. There are numerous extraneous variables in this particular example. Social workers may have negative attitudes toward the profession for many reasons quite apart from the model of practice they value. As previously mentioned, one way to control for these extraneous variables is to construct a rival hypothesis around each one and design the study so that the rival hypothesis can be tested as well.

The best research hypothesis fits with an existing theory. Preferably, it should be derived from a gap in the body of knowledge, and the answer should contribute to an extension or revision of what was known before. We should be able to explain why the hypothesis is important and in what ways the answer might be used.

This also can be put into the form of a simple question that you would ask all patients who were referred to social services:

> How intimidated were you when you were referred to the social services department within this hospital?
> * Not at all intimidated
> * Somewhat intimidated
> * Very intimidated

By reviewing the literature and your knowledge of your hospital's social service department, you have more or less devised a direction for your study in relation to your access concept. You have come up with a

concept, four variables, and value labels for each one of the four variables, which are as follows:

Concept:	**Access to social work services**
First Variable:	Saw social worker?
Variable Labels:	• Yes
	• No
Second Variable:	Referral?
Variable Labels:	• Yes
	• No
Third Variable:	Follow-up of referral?
Variable Labels:	• Yes
	• No
Fourth Variable:	Feelings of intimidation around the referral process

Variable Labels:
- Not at all intimidated
- Somewhat intimidated
- Very intimidated

Defining Independent and Dependent Variables

A simple quantitative research study may choose to focus on the relationship between only two variables, called a *bivariate relationship*. The study tries to answer, in general terms: Does Variable *X* affect Variable *Y*? Or, how does Variable *X* affect Variable *Y*? If one variable affects the other, the variable that does the affecting is called an *independent variable*, symbolized by *X*. The variable that is affected is called the *dependent variable*, symbolized by *Y*. If enough is known about the topic and you have a good idea of what the effect will be, the question may be phrased: If *X* occurs, will *Y* result? If Variable *X* affects Variable *Y*, whatever happens to *Y* will depend on *X*.

No Independent or Dependent Variables

Some quantitative research studies are not concerned with the effect that one variable might have on another. Perhaps it is not yet known whether two variables are even associated, and it is far too soon to postulate what the relationship between them might be. Your study might try to ascertain the answer to a simple question, such as "How intimidated do ethnic minority patients feel when they are referred to my hospital's social service department?" In this question, there is no independent variable; neither is there a dependent variable. There is only one variable—degree of intimidation felt by one group of people, the ethnic minorities. You could even include ethnic majorities as well and ask the question: How intimidated do *all* patients feel when they are referred to my hospital's social service department?

Constructing Hypotheses

There are many types of hypotheses, but we only briefly discuss two: (1) nondirectional, and (2) directional.

Nondirectional Hypotheses

A nondirectional hypothesis (also called a two-tailed hypothesis) is simply a statement that says you expect

to find a relationship between two or more variables. You are not willing, however, to "stick your neck out" as to the specific relationship between them. A nondirectional hypothesis for each one of your access variables could be, for example:

- **Nondirectional Research Hypothesis 1:** *Saw a Social Worker*
  Ethnic minorities and ethnic majorities see hospital social workers differentially.
- **Nondirectional Research Hypothesis 2:** *Referral*
  Ethnic minorities and ethnic majorities are referred to the hospital's social service department differentially.
- **Nondirectional Research Hypothesis 3:** *Follow-up*
  Ethnic minorities and ethnic majorities vary in the degree which they follow up on referrals.
- **Nondirectional Research Hypothesis 4:** *Intimidation*
  Ethnic minorities and ethnic majorities feel differently about how intimidated they were by the referral process.

Directional Hypotheses

Unlike a nondirectional hypothesis, a directional hypothesis (also called a one-tailed hypothesis) specifically indicates the "predicted" direction of the relationship between two or more variables. The direction stated is based on an existing body of knowledge related to the research question. You may have found out through the literature (in addition to your own observations), for example, that you have enough evidence to suggest the following directional research hypotheses:

- **Directional Research Hypothesis 1:** *Saw a Social Worker*
  Ethnic majorities see hospital social workers more than ethnic minorities.
- **Directional Research Hypothesis 2:** *Referral*
  Ethnic majorities are referred to the hospital's social service department more than ethnic minorities.
- **Directional Research Hypothesis 3:** *Follow-up*
  Ethnic majorities follow up with social service referrals more than ethnic minorities.

BOX 3.3

Constructing Good Hypotheses

Hypotheses have to be relevant, complete, specific, and testable.

Relevance

It is hardly necessary to stress that a useful hypothesis is one that contributes to the profession's knowledge base. Nevertheless, some social work problem areas are so enormously complex that it is not uncommon for people to get so sidetracked in reading the professional literature that they develop very interesting hypotheses totally unrelated to the original problem area they wanted to investigate in the first place.

The relevancy criterion is a reminder that, to repeat, the hypothesis must be directly related to the research question, which in turn must be directly related to the general research problem area.

Completeness

A hypothesis should be a complete statement that expresses your intended meaning in its entirety. The reader should not be left with the impression that some word or phrase is missing. "Moral values are declining" is one example of an incomplete hypothesis.

Other examples include a whole range of comparative statements without a reference point. The statement "Males are more aggressive," for example, may be assumed to mean "Men are more aggressive than women," but someone investigating the social life of animals may have meant "Male humans are more aggressive than male gorillas."

Specificity

A hypothesis must be unambiguous. The reader should be able to understand what each variable contained in the hypothesis means and what relationship, if any, is hypothesized to exist between them. Consider, for example, the hypothesis "Badly timed family therapy affects success." Badly timed family therapy may refer to therapy offered too soon or too late for the family to benefit, or to the social worker or family being late for therapy sessions, or to sessions that are too long or too short to be effective. Similarly, "success" may mean resolution of the family's problems as determined by objective measurement, or it may refer to the family's—or the social worker's—degree of satisfaction with therapy, or any combination of these.

With regard to the relationship between the two variables, the reader may assume that you are hypothesizing a negative correlation. That is, the more badly timed the therapy, the less success will be achieved. On the other hand, perhaps you are only hypothesizing an association: Bad timing will invariably coexist with lack of success.

Be that as it may, the reader should not be left to guess at what you mean by a hypothesis. If you are trying to be both complete and specific, you may hypothesize, for example:

> Family therapy that is undertaken after the male perpetrator has accepted responsibility for the sexual abuse of his child is more likely to succeed in reuniting the family than family therapy undertaken before the male perpetrator has accepted responsibility for the sexual abuse.

This hypothesis is complete and specific. It leaves the reader in no doubt as to what you mean, but it is also somewhat wordy and clumsy. One of the difficulties in writing a good hypothesis is that specific statements need more words than unspecific or ambiguous statements.

Potential for Testing

The last criterion for judging whether a hypothesis is good and useful is the ease with which the truth of the hypothesis can be verified. Some statements cannot be verified at all with presently available measurement techniques. "Telepathic communication exists between identical twins" is one such statement. A hypothesis of sufficient importance often generates new data-gathering techniques, which will enable it to be eventually tested. Nevertheless, as a general rule, it is best to limit hypotheses to statements that can be tested immediately by current and available measurement methods.

• **Directional Research Hypothesis 4:** *Intimidation*
Ethnic minorities are more intimidated by the
referral process than ethnic majorities.

DESIGNING THE RESEARCH STUDY

The next step involves designing the research study a
bit more. Having focused your general research question and, if appropriate, developed a hypothesis, you
enter into the next phase of your study—designing the
study. We begin with a word about sampling. One objective of your research study may be to generate findings that can be generalized beyond your study's sample. As you will see in Chapter 6, the "ideal" sample
when this is the goal is one that has been randomly selected from a carefully defined population. The topic
of sampling is discussed much more fully in Chapter 6.

As you shall see in this book, many research questions have at least one independent variable and one dependent variable. You could easily design your quantitative study where you have one independent variable,
ethnicity (i.e., ethnic minority, ethnic majority), and one
dependent variable, difficulty in accessing social services
(i.e., yes or no). You could easily organize your variables
in this way because you are expecting that a person's
ethnicity is somehow related to his or her difficulty in
accessing social services. It would be absurd to say the
opposite—that the degree of difficulty that folks have in
accessing social services influences their ethnicity. You
could write your directional hypothesis as follows:

Directional Hypothesis:
Ethnic minorities have more difficulty than ethnic majorities in accessing my hospital's social
service department.

Having set out your hypothesis in this way, you
can plainly see that your research design will compare
two groups (i.e., ethnic minorities and ethnic majorities) in terms of whether or not (i.e., yes or no) each
group had difficulty accessing your hospital's social
service department. Your research design is the "blueprint" for the study. It is a basic guide to deciding how,
where, and when data will be collected. How data are
collected and where they are collected are determined

by the data collection method you choose (Chapters
9–15). *When* data are collected is dictated by the specific
research design you select (Chapters 7 and 8). Clearly,
there are many things for you to consider when developing your research design.

COLLECTING THE DATA

Data collection is one step within any research design.
Data collection is the part of the study where you truly
test out the operational definitions of your study's variables. There are three features of data collection that
are key to all quantitative research studies:

1. All of your variables must be measurable. This
   means that you must precisely record the variable's
   frequency, and/or its duration, and/or its magnitude (intensity). Think about your ethnic minority
   variable for a minute. As noted earlier, you could
   simply operationalize this variable into two categories: ethnic minority and ethnic majority:

   Are you an ethnic minority?
   • Yes
   • No

   Here you are simply measuring the presence (ethnic
   minority) or absence (ethnic majority) of a trait for
   each research participant within your study. You also
   need to operationalize your difficulty in accessing
   the hospital's social services department variable.
   Once again, you could operationalize this variable in
   a number of ways. You may choose to operationalize
   it so that each person can produce a response to a
   simple question:

   Did you have difficulty in accessing our hospital's
   social services department?
   • Yes
   • No

2. All of your data collection procedures must be
   objective. That is, the data are meant to reflect a
   condition in the real world and should not be
   biased by the person collecting the data in any
   way. In your quantitative study, the research

participants will produce the data—not you, the researcher. That is, you will record only the data that each participant individually provides for both variables:

- "Ethnic Minority" **or** "Ethnic Majority" for the ethnicity variable
- "Yes" **or** "No" for the access to social service variable

3. All of your data collection procedures must be able to be duplicated. In other words, your data collection procedures that you use to measure the variables must be clear and straightforward enough so that other researchers could use them in their research studies.

In reference to Box 3.1, the three features of measurability, objectivity, and duplication within a quantitative research study are accomplished by using a series of standardized uniform steps that are applied consistently throughout a study's implementation. You must ensure that all of your research participants are measured in exactly the same way—in reference to their ethnicity and whether or not they had any difficulty in accessing hospital social services.

ANALYZING AND INTERPRETING THE DATA

There are two major types of quantitative data analyses: (1) descriptive statistics, and (2) inferential statistics.

Descriptive Statistics

As presented in Chapter 17, descriptive statistics describe your study's sample or population. Consider your ethnicity variable for a moment. You can easily describe your research participants in relation to their ethnicity by stating how many of them fall into each category label of the variable. Suppose, for example, that 50% of your sample are in the ethnic minority category and the remaining 50% are in the nonethnic minority category, as illustrated:

Variable Label:
- Ethnic Minority, 50%
- Ethnic Majority, 50%

These two percentages give you a "picture" of what your sample looks like with regard to ethnicity. A different picture could be produced where 10% of your sample were ethnic minorities and 90% were not, as illustrated:

Variable Label:
- Ethnic Minority, 10%
- Ethnic Majority, 90%

These data describe only one variable—ethnicity. A more detailed picture is given when data for two variables are displayed at the same time. Suppose, for example, that 70% of your research participants who were ethnic minorities reported that they had difficulty in accessing your hospital's social services, compared to 20% of those who were ethnic majorities:

Difficulty in Accessing Social Services?

Ethnicity	Yes	No
• Ethnic Minority	70%	30%
• Ethnic Majority	20%	80%

Other descriptive information about your research participants could include variables such as average age, percentages of males and females, average income, and so on. Much more is said about descriptive statistics in Chapter 17 when we discuss how to analyze quantitative data—that is, data that are in the form of numbers.

Inferential Statistics

Inferential statistics determine the probability that a relationship between the two variables within your sample also exists within the population from which the sample was drawn. Suppose that in your quantitative study, for example, you find a statistically significant relationship between your research participants' (your sample) ethnicity and whether they successfully accessed social services within your hospital setting. The use of inferential statistics will permit you to say whether or not the relationship detected in your study's sample exists in the larger population from which it was drawn—and the exact probability that your finding is in error. Much more is also said about inferential statistics in Chapter 17.

PRESENTATION AND DISSEMINATION OF FINDINGS

Quantitative findings are easily summarized in tables, figures, and graphs. When data are disseminated to laypeople, we usually rely on straightforward graphs and charts to illustrate our findings. As discussed in depth in Chapter 19, presentation of statistical findings is typically reserved for professional journals.

AN EXPANDED EXAMPLE OF THE QUANTITATIVE RESEARCH METHOD

Figures 3.2 and 3.3 present the positivistic, or quantitative research, process in detail by delineating 13 steps—7 steps for planning research studies (Figure 3.2) and 6 steps for carrying out research studies (Figure 3.3). The most important thing to remember at this point is that all the steps are intertwined to various degrees, and it is difficult to describe a single step in isolation from the remaining 12 steps. For the sake of instruction, however, we will describe each step in a sequential manner.

Step 1: What's the Problem?

Let's pretend for a moment that you are an MSW-level social worker in a large social service agency. The past 3 years of agency intake data reveal that many clients served experience similar social issues. More specifically, as illustrated at the top of Figures 1.7, 3.2, and 3.3, most clients seeking services from your agency regularly present with one or more of the following problems: (1) poverty, (2) domestic violence, (3) substance abuse, and (4) homelessness.

Your agency's executive director establishes a Practice-Informed-by-Research Committee that is "charged" with the following mandate: to design a study involving agency clientele so that workers at the agency will be better informed about the complex relationship between the issues of poverty, domestic violence, substance abuse, and homelessness. You are asked to chair the Practice-Informed-by-Research Committee. Gladly, you accept and begin

leading your committee through the remaining 12 steps of the research process.

Step 2: Formulating Initial Impressions

As chair of the Practice-Informed-by-Research Committee, your first step is to invite open discussion with your committee members about what they "know" about each of the four presenting problems, or variables, and the relationship between them. Drawing upon your task-group facilitation skills learned in one of your social work practice classes, you help your committee members tease out the source(s) of their collective wisdom (or knowledge) as a group.

Questions about possible relationships among the presenting problems are discussed (see Figure 3.2, Step 2), and efforts are made to determine whether committee "answers" are based on authority, tradition, experience, intuition, or research. During this process of discussion, the committee learns some very important things, such as how much of its present knowledge set is based on empirical knowledge versus other ways of knowing; what biases, values, or beliefs are active among committee members; and how the research method can be used to advance the current knowledge base among workers at the agency.

Step 3: Determining What Others Have Found

Given your superb skills as a group facilitator, you have energized your committee members and stimulated their curiosity such that they are eager to read the latest research about poverty, domestic violence, substance abuse, and homelessness. Each committee member accepts an assignment to search the literature for articles and information that report on the relationship between two or more of the four presenting variables of interest.

Committee members search a variety of sources of information, such as professional journals, credible websites, and books (see Chapter 22). Using quality criteria to evaluate the evidence of information gathered (Chapter 23), the committee synthesizes the knowledge gathered from empirical sources. If so desired, the committee might endeavor to systematically assess the literature gathered through meta-analysis (Chapter 24).

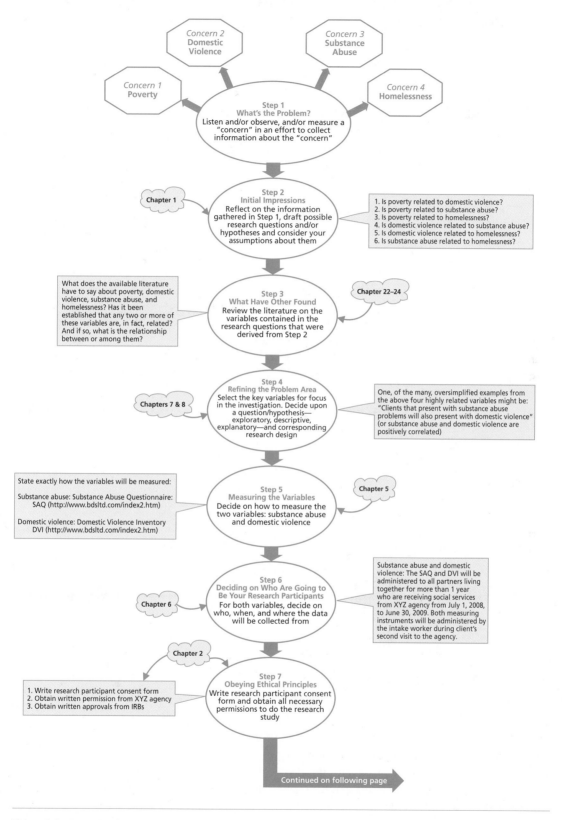

Figure 3.2 Steps in Planning a Research Study

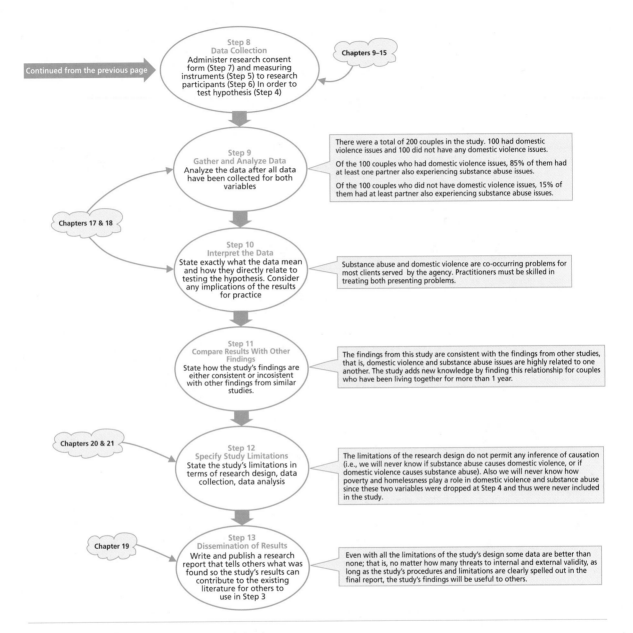

Figure 3.3 Steps in Carrying Out a Research Study

With either a synthesis or a meta-analysis of the literature gathered, the Practice-Informed-by-Research Committee is in an excellent position to make an informed statement about up-to-date knowledge about the relationship between poverty, domestic violence, substance abuse, and homelessness.

Step 4: Refining the General Problem Area

By this point the excitement of your committee members has waned somewhat. As it turned out, the task of reviewing the literature (Step 3) was more onerous than anticipated. Indeed, the number of research studies investigating poverty, domestic violence, substance abuse, and homelessness was overwhelming. Committee members had to agree on the parameters of their search. For example, a search for research on the topic of domestic violence required them to define "partner" in domestic violence and decide whether the research to be reviewed would include gay and lesbian partnerships, as well as heterosexual partners. Moreover, applying criteria to evaluate individual studies was not as straightforward as initially thought. Nevertheless, your committee trudged through and indeed was successful at finding relevant empirical articles.

To re-charge the committee and keep the momentum of the research process going, you work with committee members to set priorities for the remainder of your work together. In short, you decide what research question(s)—exploratory, descriptive, or explanatory—will be the focus of your investigation. In turn, you decide what research design is best suited to investigating the proposed research question. As Figure 3.2 suggests, the committee decides to focus on the descriptive relationship between only two presenting problem areas—domestic violence and substance abuse.

Step 5: Measuring the Variables

At Step 5 you review with committee members the work already accomplished in the previous four steps and note that planning thus far has largely been a conceptual exercise. Beginning with Step 5—defining and deciding how to measure variables—you realize that the tasks for the committee become much more specific, particularly as related to the research process. With respect to measurement, committee members must develop operational definitions for the two presenting problems, or variables (i.e., substance abuse and domestic violence) that will be studied and find measuring instruments for each variable.

What's more, the committee wants to select measuring instruments that are not only valid and reliable but also relevant to their clientele and meaningful to their practice. As chair of the Practice-Informed-by-Research Committee, you suggest that committee members "refresh" themselves on the concepts of measurement by reading Chapter 5 of this book. As identified in Figure

3.2, the end result of this step is the selection of the Domestic Violence Inventory (*DVI*), which will measure domestic violence, and the Substance Abuse Questionnaire (*SAQ*), which will measure substance abuse.

Step 6: Deciding on a Sample

With a clear research hypothesis, a solid understanding of other research, and the selection of measuring instruments for key variables, the next step for the committee is to choose the sampling procedures for the study. At this point, research and practice knowledge come together to decide which parameters for the sample will be most meaningful. For example, it turns out that intake data show that most (but not all) clients presenting with either substance abuse or domestic violence problems at intake report that they have been living together for more than 1 year.

The intake data show that only a handful of coupled clients are in new relationships of less than 1 year. Consequently, this characteristic of clients at the agency becomes a criterion to define the population, and consequently the sample, to be studied. Once all the sampling criteria are established, the committee must decide the particular sampling method to use. The aim is to select a sample that is representative (e.g., similar in age, race, marital status, service history) of *all* clients who fit the eligibility criteria. Much more will be said about sampling in Chapter 6.

Step 7: Obeying Ethical Principles

As an ethical social work practitioner who adheres to the NASW *Code of Ethics*, you are aware that not one speck of data for the study will be collected until proper procedures have been developed and independently reviewed. After reading Chapter 2 of this text and Section 5 of the NASW *Code of Ethics*, the committee gets to work developing proper consent forms and research protocols, as well as getting all necessary ethics approvals.

Step 8: Collecting the Data

As shown in Figure 3.3, data collection is a step that indicates the study is under way. Many different methods of data collection are available, and each has particular advantages and disadvantages. Continuing with our example illustrated in Figure 3.2, data collection involves administering *SAQ* and *DVI* instruments to sampled partners who have been living together for more than 1 year.

Once the study is under way, the protocols established for data collection should be carried out precisely so as to avoid errors. Moreover, data collection procedures should not be changed. If changes are necessary, they must be approved by the ethical oversight bodies involved at Step 7 *before* those changes are implemented. Your committee's, focus at this point is only to monitor that the study is being carried out as planned and to use research principles to troubleshoot any problems that arise. Chapters 9 through 14 present the various data-collection methods that could have been used to collect the data.

Step 9: Gathering and Analyzing the Data

Step 9 is an exciting one in the research process because it is at this step that you and your committee get the "answer" to your stated hypothesis—clients who have substance abuse issues will also have domestic violence issues (and vice versa). Step 9 in Figure 3.3 reveals two key facts or results from your study that indeed support this hypothesis. Before it was possible to produce these results, your committee was hard at work ensuring that data were properly entered into an appropriate computer program and analyzed. Since data analysis (quantitative and qualitative) requires advanced skills, it may be that your committee hired a consultant to complete this step of the research process. Or perhaps you developed such skills (in this example, statistics would be required) in your graduate program and decide to perform this step yourself. Chapters 17 and 18 discuss data analysis in detail: Chapter 17 on quantitative analyses and Chapter 18 on qualitative analyses.

Step 10: Interpreting the Data

Getting an answer to your research question and deciding the usefulness of the answer are two separate steps.

In Step 10, the committee will go beyond the reported "facts" of the study's findings to make a conclusive statement such as the one shown in Step 10 of Figure 3.3.

Step 11: Comparing Results With Other Findings

As chair of the Practice-Informed-by-Research Committee, you are aware that every research study is only a single piece in the puzzle of knowledge development. Consequently, you ask that the committee consider the findings of your study in the context of other research that was reviewed in Step 3, as well as any new research published while your study was under way. By contrasting your findings with what others have found, your committee builds on the existing knowledge base.

Step 12: Specifying the Study's Limitations

Of course, you also realize that no study is perfect, and that includes yours. Many study limitations are predetermined by the particular research design that you used. For example, threats to internal and external validity are limitations commonly discussed in research reports and articles. Acknowledging your study's limitations can be a humbling experience. While you may be better informed at the conclusion of your study, you will not have found the "magic cure" that is sure to alleviate your clients' struggles and suffering in only one research study.

Step 13: Writing and Disseminating the Study's Results

A final and important step in the research process is sharing the new knowledge learned in your study. In the academic world, dissemination most often refers to publication of the study in a peer-reviewed journal (like those reviewed in Steps 2 and 11). While some practitioners also publish in peer-reviewed journals, dissemination in the practice world more commonly refers to sharing findings at conferences or local meetings.

The purpose of dissemination is to make your study results available to others who are working in the same area—whether as practitioners, researchers, policy makers, or educators. As chair of the

Practice-Informed-by-Research Committee, you will want to share your study's results with others in your agency. The knowledge gained might be used to develop new procedures in the agency (e.g., intake, training, referrals). Whatever the route of dissemination, the aim is to have completed Steps 1 through 12 at the highest level of research integrity so that the dissemination of your results will be most useful to others.

SUMMARY

This chapter briefly discussed the process of the quantitative research approach to knowledge development as outlined in Figure 3.2 and 3.3. The following chapter presents how the qualitative research approach can be used within the research method using the same example of this chapter.

The Qualitative
Research Approach

Margaret Williams
Yvonne A. Unrau
Richard M. Grinnell, Jr.

4

Basic Steps in the Research Process

Step 1	Choose a problem
2	Review the literature
3	Evaluate the literature
4	Be aware of all ethical issues
5	Be aware of all cultural issues
6	State the research question or hypothesis
7	Select the research approach
8	Determine how the variables are going to be measured
9	Select a sample
10	Select a data collection method
11	Collect and code the data
12	Analyze and interpret the data
13	Write the report
14	Disseminate the report

You Are Here (pointing to Step 6)

You Are Here (pointing to Step 7)

The preceding chapter presented a brief discussion of how the generation of social work knowledge is acquired through the use of research studies that gather quantitative data. This chapter is a logical extension of that one in that we now focus our attention on how knowledge is developed through the use of qualitative data.

As we know from the preceding chapter, the quantitative approach to knowledge development is embedded within the "positivist way of thinking, or viewing the world." To complement the quantitative approach, the qualitative approach to knowledge development is embedded within the "interpretive way of thinking, or viewing the world." We now turn our attention to the "interpretive way of thinking" in detail.

WHAT IS THE INTERPRETIVE WAY OF THINKING?

The interpretive approach to knowledge development is the second way of obtaining knowledge in our profession (see the right side of Figure 3.1). It basically discards the positivist notion that there is only one external reality waiting to be discovered. Instead, the qualitative research approach is based on the interpretive perspective, which states that reality is defined by the research participants' interpretations of their own realities. In sum, it is the *subjective* reality that is studied via the qualitative research approach, rather than the *objective* one that is studied by the quantitative approach.

As you will see in Chapters 9 through 15, the differences between the philosophy of the quantitative approach and the qualitative approach to knowledge development naturally lead to different data collection methods. Subjective reality, for example, cannot be explored through the data collection method of observation. Empiricism—the belief that science must be founded on observations and measurements, another tenet of positivism—is thus also discarded. The qualitative approach says that the only real way to find out about the subjective reality of our research participants is to ask them, and the answer will come back in words, not in numbers. In a nutshell, qualitative research methods produce *qualitative* data in the form of text. Quantitative research methods produce *quantitative* data in the form of numbers.

Multiple Realities

As you know, from a positivist standpoint, as presented in the preceding chapter, if you do not accept the idea of a single reality, which is not changed by being observed and/or measured, and from which you—the researcher—are "detached," then you are not a "real researcher" doing a "real research study." Thus, because you are a nonresearcher doing a nonresearch study, your findings are not thought to be of much use.

Many of the supposed "nonresearchers" whose views have not been thought to be valid were women and/or people who came from diverse minority groups. Feminists, for example, have argued that there is *not* only one reality—there are many realities. They contend that men and women experience the world differently and so they both exist in different realities, constructed by them from their own perceptions. Similarly, people from various cultural groups view the world from the perspective of their own beliefs and traditions and also experience different realities.

As for the idea that reality is not changed by being observed and/or measured, feminists have argued that a relationship of some kind is always formed between the researcher and the research participant (subject), resulting in yet another mutual reality constructed between the two of them. In any study involving human research participants, there are thus at least three realities:

1. the researcher's reality
2. the research participant's reality
3. the mutual reality they (researcher and research participant) both created and share

Moreover, all three realities are constantly changing as the study proceeds and as further interactions occur. The positivist idea of a single unchanged and unchanging reality, some feminists have argued, was typically a male idea, probably a result of the fact that men view human relationships as being less important than do women.

This is a low blow, which will quite properly be resented by the many men who do in fact ascribe importance to relationships. But, that aside, perhaps the problem lies less with phenomenalism (a single unchanged reality as opposed to multiple changing realities) than it does with scientism (the idea that the physical and social sciences can be approached in the same way).

Data Versus Information

Here, it is worth pausing for a moment to discuss what is meant by *data*. Data are plural; the singular is *datum*, from the Latin *dare*, to give. A datum is thus something that is given, either from a quantitative observation and/or measurement or from a qualitative discussion with Ms. Smith about her experiences in giving birth at her home. A number of observations and/or measurements, in the quantitative approach, or a number of discussions, in the qualitative approach, constitute *data*.

Data are not the same thing as *information*, although the two words are often used interchangeably. The most important thing to remember at this point is that both approaches to the research method produce data. They simply produce different kinds of data.

Information is something you hope to get from the data once you have analyzed them—whether they are words or numbers. You might, for example, collect data about the home-birthing experiences of a number of women, and your analysis might reveal commonalties between them; perhaps all the women felt that their partners had played a more meaningful role in the birthing process at home than would have been possible in a hospital setting. The enhanced role of the partner is *information* that you, as a researcher, have derived from the interview *data*. In other words, data are pieces of evidence, in the form of words (qualitative data) or numbers (quantitative data), that you put together to give you information—which is what the research method is all about.

Subjects Versus Research Participants

Having dealt with what data are (don't ever write "data *is*"), let's go back to the implications of collecting data about people's subjective realities. Because it is the research participant's reality you want to explore, the research participant is a very important data source. The quantitative approach may seem to relegate the research participant to the status of an object or subject. In a study of caesarian births at a hospital during a certain period, for example, Ms. Smith will not be viewed as an individual within the quantitative approach to knowledge development, but only as the 17th woman who experienced such a birth during that period. Details of her medical history may be gathered without any reference to Ms. Smith as a separate person with her own hopes and fears, failings, and strengths. Conversely, a qualitative approach to caesarian births will focus on Ms. Smith's individual experiences. What *was* her experience? More important, what did it mean to her? How did she interpret it in the context of her own reality?

Values

In order to discover the truth of Ms. Smith's reality, however, you must be clear about the nature of your own reality. In Chapter 1 we discussed *value awareness* as one of the characteristics that distinguishes the research method from the other ways of knowledge development. As you know, value awareness is your ability to put aside your own values when you are conducting research studies or when you are evaluating the results obtained by other researchers. This is sometimes called *disinterestedness*. Researchers who are *disinterested* are ones who are able to accept evidence that runs against their own positions.

From a hard-line quantitative perspective, this putting aside of values seems more akin to sweeping them under the carpet and pretending they don't exist. Researchers engaged in quantitative studies will deny that their own values are important. They claim their values have nothing to do with the study. In a nutshell, their values cease to exist.

On the other hand, qualitative researchers take a very different view. Their values are a part of their own realities and a part of the mutual reality that is constructed through their interaction with their research participants. A qualitative researcher's values therefore must be acknowledged and thoroughly explored so

that the mutual shaping of realities that results from the interaction with their research participants may be more completely and honestly understood.

The term *value awareness*, while important to both research approaches, is thus understood in different ways. To quantitative researchers, it means putting values aside so that they don't affect the study. To qualitative researchers, it means an immersion in values so that their inevitable effect is understood and so that their research participants' realities emerge more clearly.

PHASES WITHIN THE QUALITATIVE APPROACH

Like quantitative researchers, qualitative researchers make a major commitment in terms of time, money, and resources when they undertake research studies. As can be seen in Figures 1.6 through 1.9, a quantitative study has basic sequential steps that must be followed to produce useful quantitative data. On the other hand, as can be seen in Figure 4.1, a qualitative study does not have these specific steps—the activities are more phases than steps, since many of the phases highly interact with one another.

As can be seen by comparing Figures 1.6 through 1.9 and 4.1, one of the major differences between the two research approaches is how they utilize the literature. In a quantitative study, for example, the literature is utilized mostly within the first steps of the research method. In a qualitative study, the literature is heavily utilized in all of the phases.

The qualitative research approach is akin to exploring a "social problem maze" that has multiple entry points and paths. You have no way of knowing whether the maze will lead you to a place of importance, but you enter into it out of your own curiosity and, perhaps, even conviction. You enter the maze without a map or a guide; you have only yourself to rely on and your notebook to record important events, observations, conversations, and impressions along the way.

You will begin your journey of an interpretive inquiry by stepping into one entrance and forging ahead.

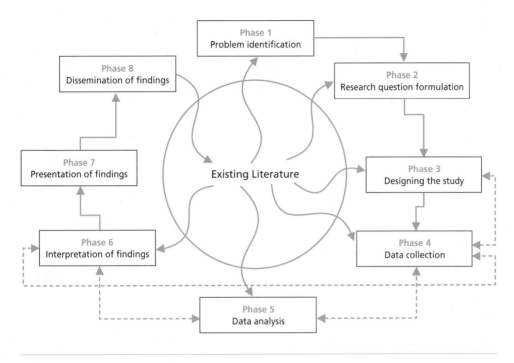

Figure 4.1   Phases of the Qualitative Research Process

You move cautiously forward, using all of your senses in an effort to pinpoint your location and what surrounds you at any one time. You may enter into dead-end rooms within the maze and have to backtrack. You may also encounter paths that you did not think possible. In some cases, you may even find a secret passageway that links you to a completely different maze. Rothery, Tutty, and Grinnell (1996) present a few characteristics that most qualitative research studies have in common:

- They are conducted primarily in the natural settings where the research participants carry out their daily business in a "nonresearch" atmosphere.
- Variables cannot be controlled and experimentally manipulated (though changes in variables and their effect on other variables can certainly be observed).
- The questions to be asked are not always completely conceptualized and operationally defined at the outset (though they can be).

- The data collected are heavily influenced by the experiences and priorities of the research participants, rather than being collected by predetermined and/or highly structured and/or standardized measurement instruments.
- Meanings are drawn from the data (and presented to others) using processes that are more natural and familiar than those used in the quantitative method. The data need not be reduced to numbers and statistically analyzed (though counting and statistics can be employed if they are thought useful).

Phases 1 and 2: Problem Identification and Question Formulation

Qualitative studies are generally inductive and require you to reason in such a way that you move from a part to a whole or from a particular instance to a general conclusion. Let's return to the research problem introduced in the preceding chapter—racial discrimination within a hospital social services department. You begin the qualitative research process, once again, from your observations—ethnic minorities are among the groups with the highest unemployment and poverty rates and the lowest levels of education; however, ethnic majorities outnumber ethnic minorities in seeking assistance from social services.

You can focus your qualitative research question by identifying the key concepts in your question. These key concepts set the parameters of your research study—they are the "outside" boundaries of your maze. As in the quantitative research approach, you will want to visit the library and review the literature related to your key concepts. Your literature review, however, will take on a very different purpose. Rather than pinpointing "exact" variables to study, you will review the literature to see how your key concepts are generally described and defined by previous researchers.

Going with the maze example for the moment, you might learn whether your maze will have rounded or perpendicular corners, or whether it will have multiple levels. The knowledge you glean from the literature assists you with ways of thinking that you hope will help you move through the maze so that you arrive at a meaningful understanding of the problem it represents. Because you may never have been in the maze before, you must also be prepared to abandon what you "think you know" and accept new experiences presented to you along the way.

Let's revisit your research question—Do ethnic minorities have difficulty in accessing social services? In your literature review, you would want to focus on definitions and theories related to discrimination within your social service department. In the quantitative research approach, you reviewed the literature to search for meaningful variables that could be measured. You do not want, however, to rely on the literature to define key variables in your qualitative study. Rather, you will rely upon the qualitative research process itself to identify key variables and how they relate to one another.

On rare occasions, hypotheses can be used in a qualitative research study. They can focus your research question even further. A hypothesis in a qualitative study is less likely to be outright "accepted" or "rejected," as is the case in a quantitative study. Rather, it is a "working hypothesis" and is refined over time as new data are collected. Your hypothesis is changed throughout the qualitative research process on the basis of the reasoning of the researcher—not on a statistical test. So all of this leads us to ask the question "What do qualitative researchers actually do when they carry out a research study?" Neuman (2007) has outlined several activities that a qualitative researcher engages in when carrying out studies:

- Observes ordinary events and activities as they happen in natural settings, in addition to any unusual occurrences
- Is directly involved with the people being studied and personally experiences the process of daily social life in the field
- Acquires an insider's point of view while maintaining the analytic perspective or distance of an outsider
- Uses a variety of techniques and social skills in a flexible manner as the situation demands
- Produces data in the form of extensive written notes, as well as diagrams, maps, or pictures to provide detailed descriptions
- Sees events holistically (e.g., as a whole unit, not in pieces) and individually in their social context
- Understands and develops empathy for members in a field setting and does not just record "cold," objective facts
- Notices both explicit and tacit aspects of culture
- Observes ongoing social processes without upsetting, disrupting, or imposing an outside point of view
- Is capable of coping with high levels of personal stress, uncertainty, ethical dilemmas, and ambiguity

Phase 3: Designing the Research Study

You can enter into a qualitative research study with general research questions or working hypotheses. However, you are far less concerned about honing in on specific variables. Because qualitative research studies are inductive processes, you do not want to constrain yourself with preconceived ideas about how your concepts or variables will relate to one another. Thus, while you will have a list of key concepts, and perhaps loosely defined variables, you want to remain open to the possibilities of how they are defined by your research participants and any relationships that your research participants may perceive.

A qualitative study is aimed at an in-depth understanding of a few cases, rather than a general understanding of many cases, or people. In other words, the number of research participants in a qualitative study is much smaller than in a quantitative one. As we will see in Chapter 6, sampling is a process of selecting the "best-fitting" people to provide data for your study. Nonprobability sampling strategies are designed for this task because they purposely seek out potential research participants. More is said about nonprobability sampling strategies in Chapter 6.

The qualitative research approach is about studying a social phenomenon within its natural context. As such, the "case study" is a major qualitative research design. A case can be a person, a group, a community, an organization, or an event. You can study many different types of social phenomena within any one of these cases.

Any case study design can be guided by different qualitative research methods. *Grounded theory* is a method that guides you in a "back and forth" process between the literature and the data you collect. Using grounded theory, you can look to the literature for new ideas and linkages between ideas that can bring meaning to your data. In turn, your data may nudge you to read in areas that you might not have previously considered.

Ethnography is a branch of interpretive research that emphasizes the study of a culture from the perspective of the people who live the culture. With your research example, you would be interested in studying the culture of social services, particularly with respect to how ethnic minorities experience it.

Phenomenology is another branch of interpretive research. It emphasizes a focus on people's subjective experiences and interpretations of the world. These subjective experiences include those of the researcher, as well as of the research participants. As a researcher in your discrimination study, you would want to keep a careful account of your reactions and questions to the events you observe and the stories you hear. Your task is to search for meaningful patterns within the volumes of data (e.g., text, drawings, pictures, video recordings).

Phase 4: Collecting the Data

Qualitative researchers are the principal instruments of data collection (Franklin & Jordan, 1997). This means that data collected are somehow "processed" through the person collecting them. Interviewing, for example, is a common data collection method that produces text data. Data collection in the interview is interactive; you can check out your understanding and interpretation of your participants' responses as you go along.

To collect meaningful text data, you want to be immersed in the context or setting of the study. You want to have some understanding, for example, of what it is like to be a client of social services before you launch into a dialogue with clients about their experiences of discrimination, if any, within the social services. If you do not have a grasp of the setting in which you are about to participate, then you run the risk of misinterpreting what is told to you.

Given that your general research question evolves in a qualitative study, the data collection process is particularly vulnerable to biases of the data collector. There are several principles to guide you in your data collection efforts:

- First, you want to make every effort to be aware of your own biases. In fact, your own notes on reactions and biases to what you are studying are used as sources of data later on, when you interpret the data (Chapter 18).
- Second, data collection is a two-way street. The research participants tell you their stories and, in turn, you tell them your understanding or interpretation of their stories. It is a process of checks and balances.
- Third, qualitative data collection typically involves multiple data sources and multiple data collection methods. In your study, you may see clients, workers, and supervisors as potential data

sources. You may collect data from each of these groups using interviews, observation, and existing documentation (data collection methods).

Phases 5 and 6: Analyzing and Interpreting the Data

Collecting, analyzing, and interpreting qualitative data are intermingled. Let's say that, in your first round of data collection, you interview a number of ethnic minority clients about their perceptions of racial discrimination in the social services. Suppose they consistently tell you that to be a client of social services, they must give up many of their cultural values. You could then develop more specific research questions for a second round of interviews in an effort to gain more of an in-depth understanding of the relationship between holding certain cultural values and being a social service client.

Overall, the process of analyzing qualitative data is an iterative one. This means that you must read and reread the volumes of data that you collected. You simply look for patterns and themes that help to capture how your research participants are experiencing the social problem you are studying.

The ultimate goal is to interpret data in such a way that the true expressions of research participants are revealed. You want to explain meaning according to the beliefs and experiences of those who provided the data. The aim is to "walk the walk" and "talk the talk" of research participants and not to impose "outside" meaning to the data they provided. Much more is said about analyzing and interpreting qualitative data in Chapter 18.

Phases 7 and 8: Presentation and Dissemination of Findings

Qualitative research reports are generally lengthier than quantitative ones. The reason for this is that it is not possible to strip the context of a qualitative study and present only its findings. The knowledge gained from a qualitative endeavor is nested within the context in which it was derived. Furthermore, text data are more awkward and clumsy to summarize than numerical data. You cannot rely on a simple figure to indicate a finding. Instead, you display text usually in the form of quotes or summary notes to support your conclusions. Much more is said about the presentation and dissemination of qualitative studies in Chapter 19.

COMPARING THE QUANTITATIVE AND QUALITATIVE APPROACHES

Philosophical Differences

By comparing the philosophical underpinnings of quantitative and qualitative research approaches, you can more fully appreciate their important differences. Each approach offers you a unique method to studying a social work–related problem; the same research problem can be studied using either approach. (See Box 4.1.)

Suppose, for example, you are interested in a broad social problem such as racial discrimination. In particular, let's say you are interested in studying the social problem of racial discrimination within public social service programs. Let's now look at the major differences between the two approaches and see how your research problem, racial discrimination, could be studied under both approaches (Jordan & Franklin, 2003).

Perceptions of Reality

Quantitative.   Ethnic minorities share similar experiences within the public social service system. These experiences can be described objectively; that is, a single reality exists outside any one person.

Qualitative.   Individual and ethnic group experiences within the public social service system are unique. Their experiences can be described only subjectively; that is, a single and unique reality exists within each person.

Ways of "Knowing"

Quantitative.   The experience of ethnic minorities within public social services is made known by closely examining specific parts of their experiences. Scientific principles, rules, and tests of sound reasoning are used to guide the research process.

BOX 4.1

Good Research Is Good Research

Fundamental to knowledge acquisition through quantitative and qualitative research studies is the idea that what we think should be rooted in and tested against good evidence and that sound articulated methods—systematic, disciplined inquiry—are necessary to bring this about. A good research study respects these essentials, regardless of the tradition within which it is conducted—quantitative or qualitative.

Bad research can also be found in both approaches. Qualitative case studies that pathologized women, and lower-income people as well, are abundant in the literature into the 1970s and beyond. Often, quantitative methods are now being used to repair the damage. Quantitative studies that evaluated social work interventions without recognizing their complexity or that dismissed the perceptions of the practitioners and their clients as subjective and therefore irrelevant did harm that qualitative researchers are working to correct.

Neither research approach can claim that its adherents have never done harm, and neither can deny that the other has made a genuine contribution. Neither deserves blind faith in its inherent virtues, and neither is innately perverse. As we discussed, however, differences do in fact exist. We now turn to a brief discussion of the implications of those differences as they relate to (1) our profession's knowledge base, (2) the social work practitioner, (3) gender, and (4) culture.

Research and the Profession's Knowledge Base

All approaches to research must generate and test the knowledge we need to be effective with our clients. Quantitative and qualitative approaches alike can contribute significantly in both ways. The main difference between the two is the kinds of knowledge they generate, which overlap but still tend to have different advantages and uses.

The cumulative effect of well-conducted quantitative research methods can be tremendously powerful in establishing client needs and documenting the effectiveness of our interventions. As examples, the steady accumulation in recent decades of evidence about the incidence of child abuse, sexual abuse, and AIDS, as well as about violence against women, has both changed the awareness of the public and professionals and had a wide-ranging impact on services to those populations. Indifference and skepticism about these issues have retreated as increasingly well-designed research has reinforced the message of earlier studies. Quantitative studies have an enviable ability to say, "This is true whether you want to believe it or not."

On the other hand, we need to know more than just the frequencies of the different forms of victimization, or how often a particular social work program produces particular outcomes for traumatized clients. When we want to understand the impacts of trauma in more depth and detail, when we want rich data about the experience of social workers and survivors working to ameliorate the effects of abuse, when we need to describe healing processes in ways that capture this human experience as something highly individual and sensitive to context—when these are our goals, the qualitative research approach is very useful.

The two approaches can contribute differently at different stages in the knowledge-building enterprise. When not much is known about a problem—in the early days of designing social programs for women who have been physically abused by their partners, for example—qualitative methods are well suited to providing exploratory data about possible needs and interventions. Once a reasonable understanding of such variables has been accumulated, quantitative methods can be efficiently used to provide more precise and generalizable data about the impacts that specific interventions have on needs. Qualitative researchers continue to contribute, however, by persisting in exploring issues, adding depth and texture to quantitative findings.

Considerations such as these lead us to believe that our profession would be foolish to reject the contribution to our knowledge base of either research approach. (See Box 4.2 for an extended discussion.)

Research and the Practitioner

In recent years, some educators have suggested that front-line social workers should integrate quantitative research techniques into their practices. This was to be accomplished by educating students to become practitioner/researchers, that is, practitioners who regularly employ quantitative research methods to evaluate the effectiveness and efficiency of their practices.

Arguably, there is little evidence that the researcher/practitioner model has succeeded in winning significant numbers of adherents. One of the many reasons for this is that the quantitative research methods that were offered to practitioners for their consideration

(continued)

BOX 4.1 *(continued)*

were too foreign to practice to be easily integrated into day-to-day activities. The tasks of administering standardized measuring instruments and collating, coding, and statistically analyzing client data are unnatural and intrusive when they are introduced into a practice setting. Additionally, and probably more important, they were too time consuming to use on a regular basis.

It has been hinted within the literature that qualitative research methods may be more promising than quantitative methods when it comes to evaluating the effectiveness of our treatment interventions. Unfortunately, it does not seem to us that this is likely, for reasons of feasibility: qualitative research remains a highly demanding exercise, and the time involved in preparing transcripts and subjecting them to a systematic qualitative analysis is no less formidable than the demands of quantitative research. A somewhat different issue is that of research utilization: Will practitioners find the data generated by either approach more accessible and relevant to their work? Only time will tell.

Research and Gender

There have been rumblings that there are gender issues associated with the quantitative and qualitative research approaches. The suggestion, in brief, is that since the quantitative approach strives for objectivity (read "distance") at all costs, dispassionate logic, and well-engineered and thought-out research designs, it is rooted in male values.

A more extreme extension of this arguments is that quantitative researchers, subjecting the people in their studies to procedures imposed with no consultation or agreement and reducing peoples' experience to numbers, are acting in patriarchal ways. Therefore, some believe that the quantitative research approach is inherently oppressive and morally inferior to the qualitative options. We know of women researchers with clear feminist commitments, however, who have had difficulty getting their work published because its quantitative approach was ideologically unpalatable.

The qualitative research approach, on the other hand, has been said to employ research methods that value relationships, egalitarianism, and empowerment of all research participants, sometimes called co-researchers. With their respect for individual experience, subjectivity, and subtlety, qualitative methods have been said to be more compatible with women's ways of knowing and experiencing the world.

Whatever the general validity of this position, it can easily be seriously overstated. While there appears to be current evidence that women and men are cognitively different, or have "different ways of knowing," the evidence also suggests that these differences are not particularly strong. Differences within the sexes are much greater than differences between them—men and women may experience life somewhat differently, but they do not inhabit separate cognitive worlds. For this reason, it is easy to identify well-known male qualitative researchers as well as female quantitative researchers who do very good research studies—regardless of research approach used.

As well, quantitative research studies and qualitative ones alike have been oppressively used. Practitioners who dismissed women's reports of sexual abuse as wish-fulfilling fantasy, for example, had solid support for their position in an extensive body of qualitative research findings beginning with the case studies of Sigmund Freud. To a large extent, quantitative studies have exposed this falsehood—an example of how this research approach had a liberating and empowering effect of considerable importance.

Research and Culture

Considerable concern has been expressed in recent years about research studies that involve people from diverse cultures. The concerns have indicated difficulties with both quantitative and qualitative approaches. Quantitative researchers have used standardized instruments developed in studies of one culture when studying others, without recognizing the problems this can create. A measure of social support employed with women who have been abused by their partners in a Haitian community in Florida, for example, might be quite inappropriate if it was developed with white college students in New York.

Language, assumptions, and values implicit in an instrument's questions and the way they are interpreted may be foreign to research participants, making the process confusing or difficult and rendering the study's findings invalid. It is also possible that the lack of any meaningful relationship between the researcher and the research participant can be experienced as strange or even intimidating by someone from another culture. Many research studies conducted with diverse cultures have been qualitative in nature (the studies of cultural anthropologists, for example), and these have also been subject to criticism.

(continued)

To the extent that qualitative researchers carry their own cultural assumptions into the field, they risk imposing a foreign frame of reference in interpreting the experience and meanings of the people they study. The problem is severe enough in the eyes of some critics that they have suggested that the only people who should study a culture should be members of that culture.

There are no easy answers to these complex problems. Quantitative researchers are working to develop methods and measures that are sensitive to cultural diversity. At the same time, some qualitative researchers are hopeful that their efforts to develop research approaches that are sensitive to social contexts and different ways of interpreting human experience will help them answer the concerns that have been raised.

In part, the issue will be less of a problem to the extent that members of different cultural groups develop ways of using both research approaches in the service of their own communities' agendas. As we have noted more than once, research in either tradition can be used oppressively. There is truth, however, in the cliché that knowledge is power, and there are certainly examples of culturally disadvantaged groups that are doing good research studies to further their legitimate aims.

Qualitative.   The experience of ethnic minorities within public social services is made known by capturing the whole experiences of a few cases. Parts of their experiences are considered only in relation to the whole of them. Sources of knowledge are illustrated through stories, diagrams, and pictures that are shared by the people with their unique life experiences.

Value Bases

Quantitative.   The researchers suspend all their values related to ethnic minorities and social services from the steps taken within the research study. The research participant "deposits" data, which are screened, organized, and analyzed by the researchers, who do not attribute any personal meaning to the research participants or to the data they provide.

Qualitative.   The researcher *is* the research process, and any personal values, beliefs, and experiences of the researcher will influence the research process. The researcher learns from the research participants, and their interaction is mutual.

Applications

Quantitative.   Research results are generalized to the population from which the sample was drawn (e.g., other minority groups, other social service programs).

The research findings tell us, on average, the experience that ethnic minorities have within the public social service system.

Qualitative.   Research results tell a story of a few individuals' or one group's experience within the public social service system. The research findings provide an in-depth understanding of a few people. The life context of each research participant is key to understanding the stories he or she tells.

Similar Features

So far we have been focusing on the differences between the two research approaches. They also have many similarities. First, they both use careful and diligent research processes in an effort to discover and interpret knowledge. They both are guided by systematic procedures and orderly plans.

Second, both approaches can be used to study any particular social problem. The quantitative approach is more effective than the qualitative approach in reaching a specific and precise understanding of one aspect (or part) of an already well-defined social problem. The quantitative approach seeks to answer research questions that ask about quantity, such as:

- Are women more depressed than men?
- Does low income predict one's level of self-concept?

- Does the use of child sexual abuse investigation teams reduce the number of times an alleged victim is questioned by professionals?
- Is degree of aggression related to severity of crimes committed among inmates?

A qualitative research approach, on the other hand, aims to answer research questions that provide you with a more comprehensive understanding of a social problem from an intensive study of a few people. This approach is usually conducted within the context of the research participants' natural environments (Rubin & Babbie, 2006). Research questions that would be relevant to the qualitative research approach might include:

- How do women experience depression as compared to men?
- How do individuals with low income define their self-concept?
- How do professionals on child sexual abuse investigation teams work together to make decisions?
- How do federal inmates describe their own aggression in relation to the crimes they have committed?

As you will see throughout this book, not only can both approaches be used to study the same social problem, but also they both can be used to study the same research question. Whichever approach is used clearly has an impact on the type of findings produced to answer a research question (or to test a hypothesis).

USING BOTH APPROACHES IN A SINGLE STUDY

Given the seemingly contradictory philosophical beliefs associated with the two research approaches, it is difficult to imagine how they could exist together in a single research study. As is stands, most research studies incorporate only one approach. The reason may, in part, relate to philosophy, but practical considerations of cost, time, and resources are also factors.

It is not unusual, however, to see quantitative data used within a qualitative study or qualitative data in a quantitative study. Just think that, if you were to use a quantitative approach, there is no reason why you could not ask research participants a few open-ended questions to allow them to more fully explain their experiences. In this instance, your quantitative research report would contain some pieces of qualitative data to help bring meaning to the study's quantitative findings.

Let's say you want to proceed with a qualitative research study to examine your research question about discrimination within the public social service system. Surely, you would want to identify how many research participants were included, as well as important defining characteristics such as their average age, the number who had difficulty accessing social services, or the number who were satisfied with the services they received.

While it is possible to incorporate qualitative research activity into a quantitative study (and quantitative research activity into a qualitative study) the approach you finally select must be guided by your purpose for conducting the study in the first place. As seen in Box 4.2, all research studies are about the pursuit of knowledge. Just what kind of knowledge you are after is up to you.

WHAT DO YOU REALLY WANT TO KNOW?

As mentioned previously, both research approaches have their advantages and disadvantages, and both shine in different phases within the research method. Which approach you select for a particular study depends not on whether you are a positivist or an interpretivist but on what particular research question your study is trying to answer. Are you looking for descriptions or explanations? If the former, a qualitative study will be spot on; if the latter, a quantitative one will do the trick.

Human nature being what it is, we are always looking, in the end, for explanation. We want to know not only what reality is like but also what its interconnections are and what we can do to change it to make our lives more comfortable and safer. However, first things first. Description comes before explanation.

BOX 4.2

The Two Research Approaches Complement One Another

As we now know, a fundamental distinction in social work research is that between the use of quantitative and qualitative research approaches. We use quantitative approaches to count and correlate social and psychological phenomena. Likewise, we use qualitative ones to seek the essential character of these social and psychological phenomena. Both approaches attempt to describe and explain reality. The two approaches have been available for our use throughout the history of our profession.

Epistemological Origins

Broadly speaking, *epistemology* refers to the theory of knowledge. Quantitative approaches have epistemological roots in logical positivism. *Logical positivism* refers to a theory of meaning in which a proposition is acceptable only if there are data derived from a quantitative research study that determines whether or not the proposition is true. The theory requires that all meaningful propositions have to be tested by "objective" observation and experiment. Common to these philosophical orientations is the application of the logic and principles of measurement from the physical sciences to the social world, with the goal of prediction and validation of these predictions. In this spirit, the ultimate purpose of such research studies is to generate universal "laws" of social behavior analogous to the laws of the physical sciences.

Qualitative research approaches assume that the subjective dimensions of human experience are continuously changing and cannot be studied using the principles of quantitative research methodologies. Instead, emphasis is placed on fully describing and comprehending the subjective meanings of events to individuals and groups caught up in them.

The two research approaches have existed side by side since the beginnings of contemporary social science. Thus, in discussing the epistemological roots of psychoanalysis, Bettleheim (1982) remarks:

In the German culture within which Freud lived, and which permeated his work, there existed and still exists a definite and important division between two approaches to knowledge. Both disciplines are called Wissenschaften (sciences), and they are accepted as equally legitimate. These two are the Naturwissenschaften (natural sciences) and Geisteswissenschaften (which defies translation into English; its literal meaning is sciences of spirit) and the concept is

deeply rooted in German idealist philosophy. These disciplines represent entirely different approaches to understanding the world.

Attempting to explain some of the distortions that occurred when Freudian theory was translated into English, Bettleheim (1982) notes a division of knowledge between a hermeneutic-spiritual way of knowing and a positivistic-pragmatic way of knowing:

In much of the German world, and particularly in Vienna before and during Freud's life, psychology clearly fell into the realm of the former (Geisteswissenschaften); in much of the English-speaking world, on the other hand, psychology clearly belonged to the Naturwissenschaften.

Despite these philosophical differences and the theoretical distortions that may have occurred, psychology and psychoanalysis have flourished, with significant contributions based on both of the epistemological approaches. Similarly, in describing the origins of organizational theory, Gouldner (1970) contrasts the perspectives of the early French social philosophers Saint-Simon and Comte. Saint-Simon was the first person to recognize the significance of organizations for the modern state; organizational expertise and the "authority of the administrators would rest upon their possession of scientific skills and 'positive' knowledge."

For Comte, on the other hand, organizations and, indeed, all social institutions were best maintained by subjective and spontaneous forms of knowledge and interventions that were indigenous to particular organizations and institutions. Saint-Simon's approach gradually evolved into the "rational model" of organizational analysis, Comte's into the "natural systems" model.

Saint-Simon's approach relies heavily on quantitative measurement and empirical testing of existing theory. In direct contrast, Comte's approach relies heavily on qualitative case studies of single organizations and emphasizes conceptual and theory development. Without both approaches—and their cross-fertilization—our current understanding of organizations would be greatly diminished.

Patterns of Utilization

Given the divergent philosophical underpinnings of the quantitative and qualitative research approaches, how

(continued)

BOX 4.2   *(continued)*

have they been utilized by the social sciences in the study of social reality? To answer this question, let us briefly consider the differences between the quantitative and qualitative approaches in terms of their ultimate purpose, their logic, their point of view, the language they use, the research designs they employ, and their theoretical bases. In emphasizing differences, however, our discussion is not meant to imply that the quantitative and qualitative approaches are incompatible within any given research study or that no exceptions exist in the patterns described.

Ultimate Purpose

In general, we use quantitative research approaches in the testing and validation of predictive, cause-effect hypotheses about social reality. By employing qualitative approaches, on the other hand, we can assemble detailed descriptions of social reality. These descriptions can serve as ends-in-themselves, or they may be useful in generating hypotheses that we can test at a later date by using quantitative approaches.

Logic

As we know, in order to achieve their individual ultimate purposes, each research approach emphasizes a different form of logic. In short, quantitative approaches tend to rely on deductive logic (i.e., applying social science theory to the social reality under investigation). On the other hand, qualitative approaches are used inductively (i.e., deriving concepts and theory from the social reality being studied). This inductive strategy for theory development has been referred to as *grounded theory* and is more suited to the study of relatively uncharted social terrain. The quantitative approach is best suited to studying phenomena that have previously had a high degree of conceptual development, theory construction, and hypothesis testing.

Point of View

Quantitatively oriented research studies attempt to describe social reality from an "objective" standpoint. The adjective (objective) is in quotes because we can never totally eliminate subjectivity from the social judgments that are inevitably involved in all aspects of social science. Still, quantitative approaches place an emphasis on the perceptions that *outside* observers bring to the study of social systems.

Qualitative approaches, on the other hand, are employed most often to describe social reality from the points of view of the research participants within the systems studied. This is based on the assumption that actors in a social situation can tell us most about what they are doing and why.

Language

Another indication of the differences in the two research approaches is the language through which the study's findings are ultimately expressed. Thus, quantitatively oriented studies translate constructs and concepts into operational definitions and finally into numerical indices. Hypotheses are tested and predictions validated through the use of statistical procedures and inferences drawn from them. Qualitative studies, on the other hand, employ the research participants' natural language, and intense attention is given to the argot of system members. Concepts and theories are validated by logical induction and through detailed observation of events and discussion of their meanings with system members.

Research Designs

Quantitative research studies tend to utilize social surveys, structured interviews, self-administered questionnaires, census data, existing statistics, and the like. These approaches, while efficient and systematic, have the disadvantage of being imposed on the systems studied. The data collection approaches themselves may influence and distort the reality that we wish to describe through the measurement process itself. The result may be gross inconsistencies between what system members *tell* us and what they *actually do*.

Qualitative research studies usually rely heavily on observations (Chapter 9), participant observation (Chapter 10), and related methods such as qualitative interviewing (Chapter 11). Quantitative research approaches usually implement descriptive and/or explanatory research designs. Such designs are best suited to testing the causality between two or more variables. Their primary disadvantage has been described as design intrusiveness. So, for example, the implementation of a single-subject experimental design in a social service agency may necessitate incomplete, delayed, or denied service; may impose extraneous requirements on the helping situation; and may result in adverse client reactions. Qualitative research methodologies, on the other hand, more often than not use exploratory research designs.

(continued)

BOX 4.2 *(continued)*

Theoretical Basis

Finally, we can contrast the type of theory used and/or generated by these two divergent research approaches. Although there is no inherent relationship between the theoretical discipline and the approach employed, qualitative studies have been more likely to remain within the disciplinary boundaries of psychology and sociology. Qualitative studies, on the other hand, have generally been social-psychological. It should be stressed that such divisions are historical and arbitrary. They may undergo change in the future as our profession assumes a more scientific base through all types of research studies.

Differences and Similarities

In this discussion we have described and emphasized major differences in the application of the quantitative and qualitative research approaches, ignoring many exceptions to the generalizations. Thus, for example, qualitative studies are sometimes used for descriptive purposes and/or for searching for causal explanations. Similar exceptions could be stated for most of the differentiating dimensions listed. Nevertheless, the discussion captures trends or emphases in the actual application of these two research approaches.

Despite their differences, however, both research approaches are planful, systematic, and empirical. By empirical (often incorrectly used as a synonym for quantitative), we refer to a reliance on practical experience and observation as a source of knowledge verification. In short, both approaches are equally valid methods to social work knowledge generation.

Critiques of Quantitative Approaches

Despite the legitimacy of the two research approaches, the quantitative approach has dominated social work research. This is in part a response to the requisites of the professionalization of our profession. Neo-Marxist critics have alleged that quantitative research approaches are conservative instruments of the social science establishment.

Within social work research, quantitative approaches tend to enjoy greater respectability. And, in a response to this quantitative "emphasis," a few social work researchers have recently begun to question the use of quantitative research approaches in our profession. They are calling for a broader application of qualitative approaches, claiming that the total commitment to measurement and quantitative analyses seems now to have been premature in a field of inquiry still lacking a clear description of how things really happen in the real world.

Taking a similar position, Taylor (1977) suggests that the qualitative research approach, as compared with the quantitative one, is often more in keeping with the internal logic of our profession and more relevant to the problems of day-to-day social work practice. He cites the significant contributions that many qualitative researchers have made to social work knowledge development. He maintains that there is a real conflict between the "proof-oriented," quantitative research approaches and the "discovery-oriented" work that social work practitioners do in their day-to-day practices.

Similarly, DeMaria (1981) argues that quantitative research methodology in particular, and empiricism in general, represent an "impoverished" research paradigm for social work because they fail to question the social structure and dominant values of our society. In other words, quantitative research approaches maintain the institutional status quo. Moreover, DeMaria contends that empirically oriented research studies are incompatible with the reform tradition of social work. Finally, Heineman (1981) goes so far as to declare that the quantitative research approaches are obsolete, outmoded, and overly restrictive.

This critical orientation toward quantitative approaches has expressed itself recently in challenges to particular practice research methodologies. For example, it has been suggested that single-subject methodology in social work practice is scientifically simplistic and overly restricts the mode of treatment interventions. It has also been suggested that a great deal of quantitative research studies are not useful and the types of problems social workers deal with, whether they are working with groups or individuals, often require knowledge that, to date, can be developed only through the qualitative approaches.

Myths Surrounding the Research Approaches

The anti-quantitative ideology that runs through the preceding critiques has been responsible for the creation of four major misconceptions about the quantitative and qualitative research approaches. These four myths are: (1) Quantitative approaches are inherently politically conservative and therefore unsuited to the reform tradition of

(continued)

BOX 4.2 *(continued)*

our profession, (2) qualitative approaches are inherently politically progressive and therefore ideally suited to social work, (3) qualitative approaches are more likely to be utilized by practitioners than are quantitative ones, and (4) quantitative and qualitative approaches are inherently incompatible with one another.

Conservatism

The first myth is that quantitative approaches are inherently conservative. This myth is easily dispelled by considering quantitative social work research studies that have had critical consciousness and that have been change oriented. Consider, for example, Piven and Cloward's classic book, *Regulating the Poor: The Functions of Public Welfare* (1971). Their book is a quantitative study of relief policies in the United States, and the authors used extensive quantitative data to link relief policies to social control and the muting of potential civil disorder. The authors, two of the architects of the welfare rights movement, apparently see no incompatibility between the requisites of social action and quantitative research methodologies.

Progressiveness

The second myth is that qualitative approaches are inherently politically progressive. Much could be written concerning the trivial preoccupations of many of the qualitative research studies that have been conducted and on the scant attention given to social and political influences in much of this literature. Instead, however, let us consider a qualitative research study by a single author well known to social workers. It has been contended that Oscar Lewis's (1966) anthropological-oriented, qualitative research study has been largely responsible for promoting the concept of a "culture of poverty" that separates the poor from other social classes and contributes to their lack of social mobility. Based on participant observation and lengthy in-depth open-ended interviews, Lewis's work has been utilized to indict the poor rather than the social structure that creates and maintains poverty.

In a criticism of Lewis's research approach, data analysis, and interpretation of the data, Valentine (1971) comments:

> The scientific status of the culture of poverty remains essentially a series of un-demonstrated hypotheses. With respect to many or most of these hypotheses, alternative propositions are theoretically more

convincing and are supported by more available evidence. The complex of conceptions, attitudes, and activities that has grown up around the "culture of poverty" has had a predominantly pernicious effect on American society. This complex has been a keystone in the crumbling arch of official policy toward the poor.

Valentine goes on to show how Lewis's central idea has been used to blame poverty on the poor themselves and to justify programs designed to inculcate middle-class values and virtues among the poor and especially their children, rather than changing the conditions of their existence. Hence, Lewis's qualitative methodology did not ensure against the conservative practice of "blaming the victim."

Utilization

The third myth is that qualitative research approaches are more likely to be utilized by social worker practitioners than quantitative ones. Although this has not been true historically, it is difficult to say what the future will bring. In a paper concerning the incorporation of various research approaches into social work practice, Tripodi and Epstein (1978) hypothesize that the utilization of research approaches by social workers will depend on the following four conditions: (1) the availability of research approaches, (2) the compatibility of research approaches to the informational requirements of social workers, (3) the extent to which those approaches can be implemented, and (4) their costs.

Availability

It could be said that the quantitative research approaches are more readily available to social work practitioners than qualitative ones. It could also be argued that the social-psychological perspective that is characteristic of much of contemporary qualitative research is more compatible with the "person-in-environment" perspective of social work practice than the quantitative approaches. Nevertheless, with the advent and development of single-subject designs (see Chapter 7), practice research methodology requires knowledge of quantitative principles as well.

Informational Requirements

Compatibility is the extent to which the knowledge and values necessary to employ the research approaches are compatible with the knowledge and value structures of

(continued)

BOX 4.2 *(continued)*

the social work practitioners themselves. On this dimension, qualitative approaches probably are superior to quantitative ones. Thus, the descriptive, inductive, subjective, and unobtrusive approach to information gathering associated with qualitative approaches is much closer to traditional social work practice than quantitative ones. In addition, social workers are more likely to accept an approach based on natural language than one based on numbers and statistical manipulation. Nevertheless, the implicit logic, specificity, and rigor of quantitative research can still make a significant contribution to social work data gathering and knowledge, even if quantitative approaches, per se, are rejected.

Implementation

Implementation is the degree to which a research approach can be used directly or indirectly. A research approach is directly useful when it can be employed without any modification in format or procedures. In contrast, a research approach that is indirectly useful is one that requires change so that it can be adapted to actual social work practice situations. As we know, the emphasis within the qualitative approaches is on the use of exploratory, or descriptive, unobtrusive research designs and suggests that they would offer fewer problems of direct implementation than would explanatory research designs. Nonetheless, an exploratory, or formative, research design can be used at the program level (see Chapter 26) and at the single-subject level (see Chapter 7). These designs offer greater flexibility for those of us who are interested in the direct implementation of quantitative approaches in social work practice.

As for indirect uses, it could be argued that effective social work practice is based on the extent to which social workers think systematically, test their intuitions with observations, and analyze information through a disciplined use of logic. These elements are part of *both* quantitative and qualitative research approaches.

Costs

Cost considerations are difficult to assess. Doing a qualitative research study is frequently time-consuming and therefore often expensive. These difficulties may render it inaccessible, especially to social workers whose employing agencies expect them to be engaged in client service delivery and in research studies *only* as they relate immediately to client service delivery.

Compatibility

The fourth myth is that the two research approaches are inherently incompatible with one another because they rest on different epistemological assumptions. Although it is true that there are epistemological differences between these two research approaches, some of the most practical and innovative research to be published in recent years makes use of both quantitative and qualitative data. Thus, Maluccio's classic book, *Learning From Clients* (1979), makes use of quantitative and qualitative data collected from clients and social workers to generate ideas about the treatment process and the impact of environmental factors on service delivery in a family service agency.

In a study of classroom structure and teaching style on student compliance, Bossert (1979) skillfully integrated quantitative data concerning teacher and student behavior with narrative descriptions, verbatim accounts of conversation between pupils and teachers, interviews, and so on. A final example is Fabricant's (1982) work on juveniles in the family court system. Here again, we find an effective interplay of quantitative and qualitative research methodologies in a critique of the institutional processing of young offenders. Thus, to imply that we, as professional social workers, must make a choice between one or the other research approach is senseless. Both approaches make meaningful contributions to our understanding of the social world and, when used *together*, can obviously augment it.

Utilization Guidelines

Thus far we have maintained that quantitative and qualitative approaches each have their special uses. As a result, rather than asking which is best, it makes more sense for us to ask under what conditions each approach is better than the other in order to answer a particular research question.

Quantitative approaches are probably most useful when we have extensive prior knowledge of the culture and environment in which our study will take place. Qualitative approaches, on the other hand, are more suitable when we are entering a relatively unfamiliar social system. Quantitative studies often require ease of access and a high level of legitimization because they are generally more intrusive than qualitative approaches. Alternatively, qualitative researchers have given considerable attention to ways of securing access and legitimization in systems that have not as yet been studied. Each of access is facilitated by the employment of their relatively unobtrusive methods of data gathering as well.

(continued)

BOX 4.2   (continued)

Quantitative approaches are probably preferable in those contexts in which we have a high degree of control and authority. If these conditions are not present, the research design, data collection methods, and other essential components of the research process are likely to be subverted. In situations in which we have relatively little control and formal authority, qualitative approaches recommend themselves.

In areas of inquiry in which there has been a considerable amount of conceptual development, theory construction, and testing, quantitative approaches are usually preferable. On the other hand, qualitative approaches are most suitable when there has been a relatively low level of conceptualization and theory building. Here qualitative approaches are appropriately exploratory.

Finally, quantitative approaches are best suited in trying to establish cause-effect relationships between or among variables or to describe relatively straightforward characteristics such as demographic variables. Qualitative approaches lend themselves to the description of complex social processes and the rendering of the subjective implications of these processes by people involved in them. As a result, qualitative approaches are ideal for identifying new concepts and for hypothesis formulation.

This is not to say that occasional departures from these generalizations would not have a positive effect on knowledge development. For example, the literature on social work professionalization is dominated by quantitative research findings. However, it would be interesting to explore the subjective meanings social workers attribute to "professionalization." Alternatively, labeling theory, which is firmly rooted in qualitative methodology, has been uncritically welcomed by social workers despite the paucity of quantitative evidence to support its validity.

Overall, neither quantitative nor qualitative methodology is in any ultimate sense superior to the other. The two approaches exist along a continuum on which neither pole is more "scientific" or more suited to social work knowledge development. As Geismar and Wood (1982) state:

Each research model is needed. But needed also is a more sophisticated awareness of what the questions are that are being posed, and the suitability of each type of research for particular practice problems. To attempt to decide the direction for social work research on any other ground such as those based on emotional faith in any model, subverts the principles of scientific inquiry on which research is based, and on which practice should be based.

Summary

Quantitative and qualitative research approaches have existed side by side since the beginning of contemporary social science. They both attempt to describe and explain social reality. Their main difference lies in the way they do it. Quantitative approaches are based on deductive logic; that is, they proceed from a general theory to a particular instance. Qualitative approaches, on the other hand, are based on inductive logic; that is, they proceed from a particular social reality to a general social theory. Despite their differences, however, both approaches are planful, systematic, and empirical. They are equally valid approaches to social work knowledge generation.

This book contends that neither research approach is clearly more suitable for social work utilization. Instead, we need to consider the context in which our research study is taking place and the question we are attempting to answer.

Before you can know whether poverty is related to child abuse, for example, you must be able to describe both poverty and child abuse as fully as possible. Similarly, if you want to know whether low self-esteem in women contributes to spousal abuse, you must know what self-esteem is and what constitutes spousal abuse.

By now, because you are a social worker interested in people and not numbers, you may be ready to throw the whole quantitative research approach out the window. But let's be sure that you don't throw the baby out with the bath water. Social work values dictate that you make room for different approaches to knowledge development, different opinions, differing views on what reality really is. Believe us, the two different approaches each have value in their own way, depending on what kind of data (quantitative and/or qualitative) you hope to gain from a particular research study.

Example of Using Both Approaches in a Single Study

Suppose, for example, you have an assumption that caesarian operations are being conducted too often and unnecessarily for the convenience of obstetricians rather than for the benefit of mothers and their babies. In order to confirm or refute this hunch (it has yet to be proven), you would need data on the number of caesarian births in a particular time frame and on how many of them were justified on the basis of medical need. Numbers would be required—quantitative data. The questions about how many and how often could not be answered solely by descriptions of Ms. Smith's individual experiences.

On the other hand, Ms. Smith's experiences would certainly lend richness to the part of your study that asked how far the hospital's services took the well-being of mothers into account. Many of the best research studies use quantitative and qualitative methods within the same study. It is important to remember that the former provide the necessary numerical data, while the latter provide the human depth that allows for a richer understanding of the numbers in their particular context.

Sometimes, therefore, depending on the research question (assumption) to be answered, Ms. Smith will be seen as no more than a number. At other times, her individuality will be of paramount importance. If she is seen as a number, for example, her role will be passive. She will be one of a large number of persons. On the other hand, if she is seen as an individual, her part in the research method will be far more active. It is *her* reality that you are now exploring. She will be front and center in a research method that is driven by her and not the researcher. Even the language will change. She is no longer a subject—or possibly an object—but a full and equal *participant*, along with the researcher.

SUMMARY

This chapter briefly discussed the qualitative research approach to knowledge building. We also highlighted a few differences and similarities between the two research approaches. These two complementary and respected research approaches are divergent in terms of their philosophical principles. Yet, they both share the following processes: choosing a general research topic, focusing the topic into a research question, designing the research study, collecting the data, analyzing and interpreting the data, and writing the report.

Designing Research Studies

Part II contains four chapters that build upon

the chapters in Part I. They all center around

how research studies are designed, from the

study's initial conceptualization to the measure-

ment of its variables (Chapter 5). Chapter 6

describes how to form a sample of research par-

ticipants for a research study where the sample

can be an individual person (or case) (Chapter 7)

or a group of people (Chapter 8).

Conceptualization and Measurement

Rafael J. Engel
Russell K. Schutt

5

Basic Steps in the Research Process

Step 1   Choose a problem

2   Review the literature

3   Evaluate the literature

4   Be aware of all ethical issues

5   Be aware of all cultural issues

6   State the research question or hypothesis

7   Select the research approach

You Are Here

8   Determine how the variables are going to be measured

9   Select a sample

10   Select a data collection method

11   Collect and code the data

12   Analyze and interpret the data

13   Write the report

14   Disseminate the report

Substance abuse is a social problem of remarkable proportions. Alcohol is involved in about half of all fatal traffic crashes, and more than 1 million arrests are made annually for driving under the influence. Four in 10 college students binge-drink (Wechsler, Lee, Kuo, & Lee, 2000), and 70% of college presidents consider binge drinking a problem for their school (Wechsler, Nelson, & Weitzman, 2000). Drinking is a factor in as many as two-thirds of on-campus sexual assaults (National Institute of Alcohol Abuse and Alcoholism [NIAA], 1995). All told, the annual costs of prevention and treatment for alcohol and drug abuse exceed $4 billion (Gruenewald, Treno, Taff, & Klitzner, 1997).

Whether your goal is to learn how society works, to deliver useful services, or to design effective social policies, at some point, you will probably need to read the research literature on this topic. If you are reading literature about substance abuse, you will have to answer two questions: What is meant by *substance abuse* in this research? (which concerns conceptualization) and How was substance abuse measured? (which concerns measurement). If you are reading about poverty, you would ask the same two questions.

No matter the topic, we cannot make sense of the results of a study until we know how the concepts were defined and measured. Nor are we ready to begin a research project until we have defined our concepts and constructed valid measures of them. Measurement validity is essential to successful research; in fact, without valid measures, it is fruitless to attempt to achieve the other two aspects of validity, causal validity and generalizability.

Measurement is our attempt to describe an object and is crucial to inform the judgments we make. Measurement means we use a set of rules to assign a value to describe a property of an object. Measurement is not essential just for research, but it is essential for carrying out social work practice at any level, whether it is macro practice or micro practice. The psychosocial assessment some of you complete with a client is a form of measurement.

As you systematically or informally monitor whether a client is improving or not improving, you must have some basis to make this judgment; you must be able to make some assessment to determine whether change has occurred. The evaluation of a program's outcomes requires that the program's broadly stated goals be translated into something that can be measured. When an agency is held accountable for its activities and the director reports to funders information about the program, units of activity have to be defined and calculated.

In this chapter, we describe the process of measurement, from taking an abstract concept and translating the concept to the point that we can assign some value to represent that concept. First, we address the issue of conceptualization, using substance abuse and related concepts as examples. We then focus on the different operations necessary for operationalization. Next, we discuss the levels of measurement reflected in different measures.

In the next section, we will discuss different methods to assess the quality of measures, specifically the techniques used to assess reliability and validity. Finally, we make suggestions about what to consider when choosing an already existing measurement instrument or scale for your practice or your agency. By the chapter's end, you should have a good understanding of measurement and why it is crucial for social work practice and social work research.

CONCEPTS

A May 2000 article in the *New York Times* (Stille, 2000) announced that the "social health" of the United States had risen a bit, after a precipitous decline in the 1970s and 1980s. Should we be relieved? Concerned? What, after all, does "social health" mean? To social scientist Marc Miringoff, it has to do with social and economic inequalities. To political adviser William J. Bennett, it is more a matter of moral values. In fact, the concept (sometimes called a construct) of social health means different things to different people. Most agree that it has to do with "things that are not measured in the gross national product," and it is supposed to be "a more subtle and more meaningful way of measuring what's important to [people]" (Stille, 2000, p. A19). But until we agree on a definition of social health, we cannot decide whether it has to do with child poverty,

trust in government, out-of-wedlock births, alcohol-related traffic deaths, or some combination of these or other phenomena.

Concepts like happiness require an explicit definition before they are used in research because we cannot be certain that all readers will share the same definition. It is especially important to define concepts that are more abstract or unfamiliar. When we refer to concepts like depression or poverty, we cannot count on others knowing exactly what we mean. Even the experts may disagree about the meaning of frequently used concepts if they base their conceptualizations on different theories. That's OK. The point is that there can be only one definition of a concept in a particular research study. We also have to specify clearly what we mean when we use a concept, and we expect others to do the same.

Conceptualization in Practice

Many of the concepts we are interested in are abstract, so a beginning step in measurement is to define the concept. If we are to do an adequate job of conceptualization, we must do more than just think up some definition, any definition, for our concepts. We have to turn to social theory and prior research to review appropriate definitions. We may need to distinguish subconcepts, or dimensions, of the concept. We should understand how the definition we choose fits within the theoretical framework guiding the research and what assumptions underlie this framework.

Researchers start with a nominal definition of the concept. In a nominal definition, the concept is defined in terms of other concepts, such as defining child abuse as occurring when either severe physical or emotional harm is inflicted on a child or there is contact of a sexual nature. The nominal definition of child abuse identifies the different types of abuse and specifies that the harm must be severe, but the definition does not provide the set of rules a researcher uses to identify the abuse or distinguish between severe and not severe harm. Nominal definitions are like those definitions found in dictionaries: You get an understanding of the word and its dimensions, but you still do not have a set of rules to use to measure the concept.

Defining Substance Abuse

What observations or images should we associate with the concept of substance abuse? Someone leaning against a building with a liquor bottle, barely able to speak coherently? College students drinking heavily at a party? Someone in an Alcoholics Anonymous group drinking one beer? A 10-year-old boy drinking a small glass of wine in an alley? A 10-year-old boy drinking a small glass of wine at the dinner table in France? Do all these images share something in common that we should define as substance abuse for the purposes of a particular research study? Do some of them? Should we take into account cultural differences? Gender differences? Age differences? Social situations? Physical tolerance for alcohol?

Many researchers now use the definition of substance abuse contained in the fourth edition of the *Diagnostic and Statistical Manual of Mental Disorders* (*DSM-IV*) of the American Psychiatric Association (Mueser et al., 1990): "repeated use of a substance to the extent that it interferes with adequate social, vocational, or self-care functioning" (p. 33). We cannot judge the *DSM-IV* definition of substance abuse as correct or incorrect. Each researcher has the right to conceptualize as he or she sees fit. However, we can say that the *DSM-IV* definition of substance abuse is useful, in part because it has been widely adopted. If we conceptualize substance abuse the same way that the *DSM-IV* does, many others will share our definition and understand what we are talking about. The definition is stated in clear and precise language that should minimize differences in interpretation and maximize understanding.

This clarity should not prevent us from recognizing that the definition reflects a particular theoretical orientation. *DSM-IV* applies a medical "disease model" to mental illness and substance abuse. This theoretical model emphasizes behavioral and biological criteria instead of the social expectations that are emphasized in a social model of substance abuse. How we conceptualize reflects how we theorize.

Just as we can connect concepts to theory, we can connect them to other concepts. What this means is that the definition of any one concept rests on a shared understanding of the terms used in the definition. So if our audience does not already have a shared understanding of terms like *adequate social functioning, self-care functioning*, and *repeated use,* we must also define these terms before we are finished with the process of defining substance abuse.

Defining Depression

Some concepts have multiple dimensions, bringing together several related concepts under a larger conceptual umbrella. One such concept is depression. Depression is unlike a normal emotional experience leading to sadness, for it includes a range of symptoms such as negative mood (sadness, loneliness, feelings of worthlessness) and somatic symptoms (loss of interest in pleasurable activities, eating and sleeping problems, loss of energy, talking less). Depression, then, is a combination of these different dimensions.

But even when there is agreement about the various dimensions that make up depression, there are still different approaches to measure the presence of depression. One approach, based on the measurement from psychology, assumes that the presence of psychological symptoms is not enough by itself, but these symptoms vary by intensity or severity (Dohrenwend & Dohrenwend, 1982). In the case of depression, it is not sufficient to look at whether the symptoms are present or not; rather, they have to be persistent, lasting for some time period. The symptoms must be so intense that they interfere with an individual's ability to function. So some researchers use scales that measure the intensity of the different items; the Center for Epidemiologic Studies Depression (*CES-D*) scale, for example, asks respondents to rate the intensity (or severity) of each of the items; then the items are summed to represent a range on a continuum of intensity of depression.

The second approach to measure depression is derived from the clinical case identification model used in assessment models such as the *DSM-IV*. In the clinical diagnostic approach, researchers identify the presence of the various dimensions of depression during a specific time period, but they do not assess the intensity of the symptoms. Furthermore, researchers using this method gather additional information to assess whether the responses conform to criteria for a case of depression. Unlike the above model, this approach identifies simply whether depression is present or absent.

Do these different perspectives really matter? Joy Newmann's (1989) analysis found that the relationship between age and depression depended on the type of assessment method. Studies using scales like the *CES-D* scale tended to show that highest depression scores occur among the youngest and oldest age-groups, whereas studies using the clinical case method have found that the younger and older cohorts were less depressed than middle-aged cohorts.

Defining Poverty

Decisions about how to define a concept reflect the theoretical framework that guides the researchers. For example, the concept of poverty has always been somewhat controversial because different theoretical notions of what poverty is shape estimates of how prevalent it is and what can be done about it.

Most of the statistics that you see in the newspaper about the poverty rate reflect a conception of poverty that was formalized by Mollie Orshansky of the Social Security Administration in 1965 and subsequently adopted by the federal government and many researchers (Putnam, 1977). She defined poverty in terms of what is called an *absolute* standard, based on the amount of money required to purchase an emergency diet that is estimated to be nutritionally adequate for about 2 months.

The idea is that people are truly poor if they can barely purchase the food they need and other essential goods. This poverty standard is adjusted for household size and composition (number of children and adults), and the minimal amount needed for food is multiplied by three because a 1955 survey indicated that poor families spend about one-third of their incomes on food (Orshansky, 1977).

Other social scientists reject this way of establishing an absolute standard and suggest an alternative method, the *basic needs budget* approach (Bangs, Kerchis, & Weldon, 1997). This approach suggests that we need to establish the market cost of a basket of goods that each of us needs to meet basic needs. The cost of each category or good is estimated separately. This method also forces us to define what is an "adequate amount" of that particular good. Like the official poverty line, this definition requires adjustments for family size, but it also requires adjustments for the labor status of the parent, ages of the children, and geographic region of residence.

Some social scientists disagree with absolute standards and have instead urged adoption of a *relative* poverty standard. They identify the poor as those in the lowest 5th or 10th of the income distribution or as those having some fraction of the average income. The idea behind this relative conception is that poverty should be defined in terms of what is normal in a given society at a particular time.

Some social scientists prefer yet another conception of poverty. With the *subjective* approach, poverty is defined as what people think would be the minimal income they need to make ends meet. Of course, many have argued that this approach is influenced too much by the different standards that people use to estimate what they "need" (Ruggles, 1990, pp. 20–23).

Which do you think is a more reasonable approach to defining poverty: an absolute standard, a relative standard, or a subjective standard? Which kind of absolute standard—the multiplier approach or the basic needs approach? Our understanding of the concept of poverty is sharpened when we consider the theoretical ramifications of these alternative definitions.

Concepts, Constants, and Variables

After we define the concepts in a theory, we can identify variables (and perhaps constants) that correspond to the concepts in the setting that we will study. Consider the concept of social control, which Donald Black (1984) defines as "all of the practices by which people define and respond to deviant behavior" (p. xi). What variables can represent this conceptualization of social control? Proportion of people in a community who are arrested? Average length of sentences for crimes? Types of bystander reactions to public intoxication? Some combination of these? If we are to study variation in social control, we must identify the variables that we can measure and that are most pertinent to our theoretical concerns.

Not every concept in a particular study is represented by a variable. For example, tolerance of drinking—the presence or absence of rules against drinking—might be an important aspect of the social control of alcoholism in fraternities. However, if we study social life at only those fraternities that prohibit drinking, tolerance of drinking would not be a variable: Because all the fraternities studied have the same level of tolerance, tolerance of drinking is a constant. Of course, the concept of tolerance of drinking would still be important for understanding social life in the "dry" fraternities. If we studied social life in a general sample of fraternities, tolerance of drinking would then be an important variable to measure.

Concepts vary in their level of abstraction, and this in turn affects how readily we can specify the variables pertaining to the concept. We may not think twice before we move from a conceptual definition of *age* as time elapsed since birth to the variable *years since birth*. Binge drinking is also a relatively concrete concept, but it requires a bit more thought. We may define binge drinking conceptually as episodic drinking and select for our research on binge drinking the variable *frequency of five or more drinks in a row*. That is pretty straightforward. A very abstract concept like social status may have a clear role in social theory but a variety of meanings in different social settings. Variables that pertain to social status may include level of esteem in a group, extent of influence over others, level of income and education, or number of friends. It is very important to specify what we mean by an abstract concept like social status in a particular study and to choose appropriate variables to represent this meaning.

How do we know what concepts to consider and then which variables to select in a study? It is very tempting, and all too common, to simply try to "measure everything" by including in a study every variable we can think of that might have something to do with our research question. This haphazard approach will inevitably result in the collection of data that are use-less and the failure to collect some data that are important. Instead, we must take four steps:

1. Examine the theory or theories that are relevant to our research question in order to identify those concepts that would be expected to have some bearing on the phenomena we are investigating.
2. Review the relevant research literature and assess the utility of variables used in prior research.
3. Consider the constraints and opportunities for measurement that are associated with the specific setting(s) we will study. Distinguish constants from variables in this setting.
4. Look ahead to our analysis of the data. Just what role will each variable we have measured play in our analyses?

OPERATIONALIZATION

Once we have defined our concepts in the abstract—that is, we have provided a nominal definition—and we have identified the specific variables we want to measure, we must develop measurement procedures. The goal is to devise an operation that actually measures the concepts we intend to measure—in other words, to achieve measurement validity. Researchers provide an operational definition, which includes what is measured, how the indicators are measured, and the rules used to assign a value to what is observed and to interpret the value.

We will expand on each element of an operational definition, but first, it is useful to look at an example of an operational definition, in this case a possible definition for alcoholism. Previously, we have provided a nominal definition of alcoholism. An operational definition for alcoholism might include the following content.

The Michigan Alcoholism Screening Test (*MAST*) is a 24-item instrument that includes a variety of indicators of symptoms such as seeing drinking as a problem, seeking treatment for problem drinking, delirium tremens, severe shaking, hearing voices, complaints from others about drinking, memory loss from drinking, job loss due to drinking, social problems from drinking, arrests for drunk driving or for drunken behavior, guilt feelings about drinking, and ability to stop drinking. The scale may be administered orally or may be self-administered. Respondents respond yes or no to each item, and each item is given a weighted score ranging from 0 to 5. There are 4 items for which the alcoholic response is "no." The weighted item responses are summed, with a score of 0 to 3 indicating no problem with alcoholism, 4 considered to be suggestive of a problem, and 5 or above an indication of alcoholism.

As you can see from this definition, we are provided with the specific indicators included in the measure, the method(s) for data collection, specific scoring of the information, and the interpretation of scale scores. This detail is often referred to as *operationalization*.

Indicators

Figure 5.1 represents one part of the operationalization process in three studies. The first researcher defines her concept (income) and chooses one variable (annual earnings) to represent it. This variable is then measured with responses to a single question, or an indicator: What was your total income from all sources in 2007?

The second researcher defines her concept (poverty) as having two aspects or dimensions, subjective poverty and absolute poverty. Subjective poverty is measured with responses to a survey question: Do you consider yourself poor? Absolute poverty is measured by comparing family income to the poverty threshold.

The third researcher decides that her concept (social class) is defined by a position on three measured variables: income, education, and occupational prestige.

One consideration is the precision of the information that is necessary. The first researcher in Figure 5.1 is seeking information that is quite precise. She is assuming that respondents will be able to accurately report the information. As an alternative, she might have asked respondents: "Please identify the income category that includes your total income from all sources in 2007." For this question, she will get less exact information. Generally, the decision about precision is based on the information that is needed for the research. It may also be based on what the researcher believes people can recall and the content people may be willing to report.

The variables and particular measurement operations chosen for a study should be consistent with the research question. If we ask an evaluative research question—for example, "Are self-help groups more effective in increasing the likelihood of abstinence among substance abusers than hospital-based treatments?"—we may operationalize *form of treatment* in terms of participation in these two types of treatment. However, if we are attempting to answer an explanatory research

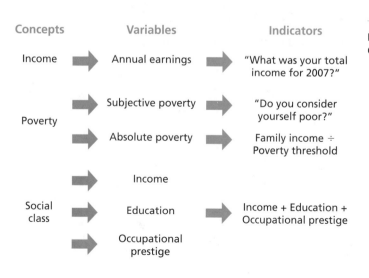

Figure 5.1
Concepts, Variables, and Indicators

question—for example, "What influences the success of substance abuse treatment?"—we should probably consider what it is about these treatment alternatives that is associated with successful abstinence. Prior theory and research suggest that some of the important variables that differ between these treatment approaches are level of peer support, beliefs about the causes of alcoholism, and financial investment in the treatment.

Scales and Indexes

When several questions are used to measure one concept, the responses may be combined by taking the sum or average of responses. A composite measure based on this type of sum or average is termed an *index* or *scale*. The idea is that idiosyncratic variation in response to particular questions will average out, so that the main influence on the combined measure will be the concept on which all the questions focus. In addition, the scale can be considered a more complete measure of the concept than any one of the component questions.

Creating a scale is not just a matter of writing a few questions that seem to focus on a concept. Questions that seem to you to measure a common concept might seem to respondents to concern several different issues. The only way to know that a given set of questions does, in fact, form a scale is to administer the questions to people like those you plan to study. If a common concept is being measured, people's responses to the different questions should display some consistency. Special statistics called *reliability measures* help researchers decide whether responses are consistent.

Scales and indexes have already been developed to measure many concepts, and some of these scales have been demonstrated to be reliable in a range of studies. It usually is much better to use such a scale to measure a concept than it is to try to devise questions to form a new scale. Use of a preexisting scale both simplifies the work involved in designing a study and facilitates comparison of findings to those obtained in other studies.

The six questions in Table 5.1 are taken from the *CES-D*, a scale used to measure the concept of depression. The aspect of depression measured by the scale is the level (the frequency and number combined) of depressive symptoms. Many researchers in different studies have found that these questions form a reliable scale. Note that each question concerns a symptom of depression. People may have idiosyncratic reasons for having a particular symptom without being depressed; for example, people who have been suffering a physical

---

TABLE 5.1

Example of a Scale: The Center for Epidemiologic Studies Depression Scale (CES-D)

At any time during the past week . . . (Circle one response on each line.)	Never	Some of the Time	Most of the Time
1. Was your appetite so poor that you did not feel like eating?	1	2	3
2. Did you feel so tired and worn out that you could not enjoy anything?	1	2	3
3. Did you feel depressed?	1	2	3
4. Did you feel unhappy about the way your life is going?	1	2	3
5. Did you feel discouraged and worried about your future?	1	2	3
6. Did you feel lonely?	1	2	3

ailment may say that they have a poor appetite. But by combining the answers to questions about several symptoms, the scale score reduces the impact of this idiosyncratic variation.

The advantages of using a scale rather than a single question to measure important concepts are very clear, and so surveys and interviews often include sets of multiple-item questions. However, four cautions are in order:

1. Our presupposition that each component question is indeed measuring the same concept may be mistaken. Although we may include multiple questions in a survey to measure one concept, we may find that answers to the questions are not related to one another, and so the scale cannot be created. Alternatively, we may find that answers to just a few of the questions are not related to the answers given to most of the others. We may, therefore, decide to discard these particular questions before computing the average that makes up the scale.

2. Combining responses to specific questions can obscure important differences in meaning among the questions. Schutt et al.'s research on the impact of AIDS prevention education in shelters for the homeless (Schutt, Gunston, & O'Brien, 1992) provides an example. In this study, the researchers asked a series of questions to ascertain respondents' knowledge about HIV risk factors and about methods of preventing exposure to those risk factors. They then combined these responses into an overall knowledge index. The authors were somewhat surprised to find that the knowledge index scores were no higher in a shelter with an AIDS education program than in a shelter without such a program. However, further analysis showed that respondents in the shelter with an AIDS education program were more knowledgeable than the other respondents about the specific ways of preventing AIDS, which were in fact the primary focus of the program. Combining responses to these questions with the others about general knowledge of HIV risk factors obscured an important finding.

3. The questions in a scale may cluster together in subsets. All the questions may be measuring the intended concept, but we may conclude that this concept actually has several different aspects. A multidimensional scale has then been obtained. This conclusion in turn can help us to refine our understanding of the original concept. For example, Schutt and colleagues (Schutt, Goldfinger, & Penk, 1992) included in a survey of homeless mentally ill people a set of questions to measure their residential preferences. When the researchers designed these questions, they sought to measure the continuum of sentiment ranging from a desire to remain in a shelter, to a desire to live in a group home, to a desire to live in an independent apartment.

Their questions ranged from whether people wanted to live with others or by themselves to whether they wanted to have staff in their residence. But statistical analysis indicated that the questions actually formed three subsets, corresponding to three dimensions of residential preference: desire for stable housing, desire for living in a group home with other people, and desire to have staff in the home. Identification of these three dimensions gave the researchers a better understanding of the concept of residential preference.

A scale may be designed explicitly to measure multiple conceptual dimensions, but often the same dimensions do not reappear in a subsequent study. For example, Radloff (1977) and others have found that the *CES-D* scale includes four dimensions, but several studies of different population subgroups have found only three dimensions. The researcher must then try to figure out why: Does the new population studied view issues differently than prior populations surveyed with the scale? Were the dimensions found in previous research really just chance associations among the questions making up the larger scale? Have sentiments changed since the earlier studies when the multidimensional scale was developed? Only after a scale has been used in several studies can we begin to have confidence in the answers to the questions on which it is based.

4. Sometimes particular questions are counted, or weighted, more than others in the calculation of the index. Some questions may be more central than others to the concept being measured and so may be given greater weight in the scale score. It is difficult to justify this approach without extensive testing, but some well-established scales do involve differential weighting. For example, The *MAST* asks questions that are assigned different weights. The question "Have you ever been in a hospital because of your drinking?" is given more points (weighted higher) than the question "Do you feel you are a normal drinker?"

Treatment as a Variable

Frequently, social work researchers will examine the effectiveness of an intervention or compare two different intervention approaches. When an intervention is compared with no intervention, or when two or more interventions are compared, the treatment approach is a variable and, therefore, requires both a conceptual and an operational definition. The treatment or intervention becomes the independent variable that you assume will cause a change in a status or condition.

Therefore, it is important for the researcher to provide a very clear nominal definition of the intervention. For example, it is not enough for the researcher to say that the study is comparing one method to another, such as "traditional" case management to "intensive" case management. Although the general meaning of such an approach may be familiar to you, the researcher must define what each approach involves.

For example, case management may include full support, where the social worker working with the chronically mentally ill provides a variety of services and supports including rehabilitation, social skill building, counseling, links to resources, identification of work and social opportunities, and money management, whereas another social worker may just assess, link the client to other services, and reevaluate periodically.

Nominal definitions of an intervention only provide the characteristics or components of the intervention but fail to fully describe how the intervention was implemented. Researchers provide varying amounts of specificity regarding the actual operationalization of the intervention. For example, Christopher Mitchell (1999) operationalized his cognitive behavioral group therapy approach by designating the length of the groups (8-week program) and the content covered in each of the weekly sessions.

This amount of detail provides a much clearer sense of the nature of the intervention, but it would still not be possible to repeat the research without additional information. Without the actual description of the intervention and how the treatment model was implemented, you cannot adequately evaluate the research or replicate what was done if you want to implement the intervention at your agency.

Gathering Data

Social work researchers and practitioners have many options for operationalizing their concepts. We will briefly mention these options here but go into much greater depth in subsequent chapters.

Measures can be based on a diverse set of activities. One method is to use a direct measure such as visual or recorded observation or a physical measure such as a pulse rate (see Chapter 9). Although these methods are particularly useful for gauging behavior, they are typically *intrusive*. The very act of gathering the information may change people's behavior, thereby altering the accuracy of the obtained information. If a caseworker goes to a client's home to observe the client interacting with a child, the nature of the interactions may change because the parent knows the caseworker is present. The parent is likely to behave in a manner that is more socially acceptable to the caseworker. Similarly, self-monitoring of behavior may have the same effect. If a smoker is asked to monitor the number of cigarettes smoked in a day, the act of such monitoring may reduce the number of cigarettes smoked.

Data may be gathered by interviews or self-administered scales and questionnaires (see Chapter 11). These methods appear to be direct in that we gather the information directly from the respondent or client. Yet, what we are trying to do is infer behavior, attitudes, emotions, or feelings because we cannot observe these directly. These methods may also be quite intrusive, and the quality of the responses can be affected by the nature of the questions or the characteristics of the person asking the questions.

There are other sources of information from which measures can be operationalized. Many large data sets have been collected by the federal government, state governments, and nongovernmental sources (see Chapter 13). Many of these data sets have social indicators that are relevant to social services such as employment, program participation, income, health, crime, mental health, and the like. A drawback to these data is that you are constrained by the way those who collected the data operationalized their measures.

Variables can be operationalized using written information in client records. The quality of these records depends on the recording accuracy of the individual staff. As with data collected by other sources, you are constrained by how variables were operationalized by the staff. Staff may not use common definitions, and these definitions may change over time, leading to inaccuracies in the data.

When we have reason to be skeptical of potential respondents' answers to questions, when we cannot observe the phenomena of interest directly, and when there are no sources of available data, we can use indirect or unobtrusive measures, which allow us to collect data about individuals or groups without their direct knowledge or participation (Webb, Campbell, Schwartz, & Sechrest, 2000). However, the opportunities for using unobtrusive measures are few, and the information they can provide is often limited to crude counts or estimates.

The physical traces of past behavior are one type of unobtrusive measure that is most useful when the behavior of interest cannot be directly observed (perhaps because it is hidden or occurred in the past) and has not been recorded in a source of available data. To measure the prevalence of drinking in college dorms or fraternity houses, we might count the number of empty bottles of alcoholic beverages in the surrounding Dumpsters. Student interest in the college courses they are taking might be measured by counting the number of times that books left on reserve as optional reading are checked out or the number of class handouts left in trash barrels outside a lecture hall.

You can probably see that care must be taken to develop trace measures that are useful for comparative purposes (trace measures are the physical remains of behaviors). For instance, comparison of the number of empty bottles in Dumpsters outside different dorms could be misleading; you would need to take into account, at the least, the number of residents in the dorms, the time since the last trash collection, and the accessibility of each Dumpster to passersby. Counts of usage of books on reserve will be useful only if you take into account how many copies of the books are on reserve for the course, how many students are enrolled in the course, and whether reserve reading is required.

Content analysis, another type of indirect measurement, studies representations of the research topic in such media forms as news articles, TV shows, and radio talk shows (see Chapter 14). An investigation of what motivates child abuse reporting might include a count of the amount of space devoted to newspaper articles in a sample of issues of the local newspaper. Television stories might be coded to indicate the number of times that newscasters reported on the maltreatment of children.

Combining Measurement Operations

Using available data, asking questions, making observations, and using unobtrusive indicators are interrelated measurement tools, each of which may include or be supplemented by the others. From people's answers to survey questions, the U.S. Bureau of the Census develops widely consulted census reports containing available data on people and geographic units in the United States. Data from employee surveys may be supplemented by information available in agency records. Interviewers may record observations about those whom they question. Researchers may use insights gleaned from questioning participants to make sense of the social interaction they have observed. Unobtrusive indicators could be used to evaluate the honesty of survey responses.

The choice of a particular measurement method is often determined by available resources and opportunities, but measurement is improved if this choice also takes into account the particular concept or concepts to be measured. Responses to such questions as "How socially engaged were you at the party?" or "How many days did you use sick leave last year?" are unlikely to provide information as valid, respectively, as direct observation or agency records.

On the other hand, observations at social gatherings may not answer our questions about why some people do not participate; we may just have to ask people. Or if no agency is recording the frequency of job loss in a community, we may have to ask direct questions.

Triangulation—the use of two or more different measures of the same variable—can strengthen measurement considerably (Brewer & Hunter, 1989, p. 17). When we achieve similar results with different measures of the same variable, particularly when the measures are based on such different methods as survey questions and field-based observations, we can be more confident in the validity of each measure. If results diverge with different measures, it may indicate that one or more of these measures are influenced by more measurement error than we can tolerate. Divergence between measures could also indicate that they actually operationalize different concepts.

Measurement in Qualitative Research

As we know from the previous chapter, qualitative research projects approach measurement in a way that tends to be more inductive and holistic. Instead of deciding in advance which concepts are important for a study, what these concepts mean, and how they should be measured, qualitative researchers begin by recording verbatim what they hear in intensive interviews or what they see during observational sessions. This material is then reviewed to identify important concepts and their meaning for participants.

Relevant variables may then be identified and procedures developed for indicating variation between participants and settings or variation over time. As an understanding of the participants and social processes develops, the concepts may be refined and the measures modified. Qualitative research often does not feature the sharp boundaries as found in quantitative research in relation to developing measures, collecting data with those measures, and evaluating the measures.

LEVELS OF MEASUREMENT

The final part of operationalization is to assign a value or symbol to represent the observation. Each variable has categories of some sort, and we need to know how to assign a symbol—typically a number—to represent what has been observed or learned. The symbol may represent a category whereby each separate category represents a different status. In this case, we have a discrete variable. The variable may be a continuous variable for which the number represents a quantity that can be described in terms of order, spread between the numbers, and/or relative amounts.

Part of operationalization, then, is to decide the variable's level of measurement that will be used in the research study. When we know a variable's level of measurement, we can better understand how cases vary on that variable and so understand more fully what we have measured. Level of measurement also has important implications for the type of statistics that can be used with the variable, as you will learn in Chapter 17. There are four levels of measurement: nominal, ordinal, interval, and ratio. Figure 5.2 depicts the differences among these four levels.

Nominal Level of Measurement

The nominal level of measurement (also called the categorical level) identifies variables whose values have no mathematical interpretation; they vary in kind or quality but not in amount. In fact, it is conventional to refer to the values of nominal variables as attributes instead of values. Discrete variables are measured at the nominal level of measurement. Gender is one example. The variable *gender* has two attributes (or categories or qualities): male and female. We might indicate male by the value 1 and female by the value 2, but these numbers do not tell us anything about the difference between male and female except that they are different. Female is not one unit more of "gender" than male, nor is it twice as much "gender." The numbers simply represent a category.

Nominal-level variables are commonplace in social work research. Such variables might include client

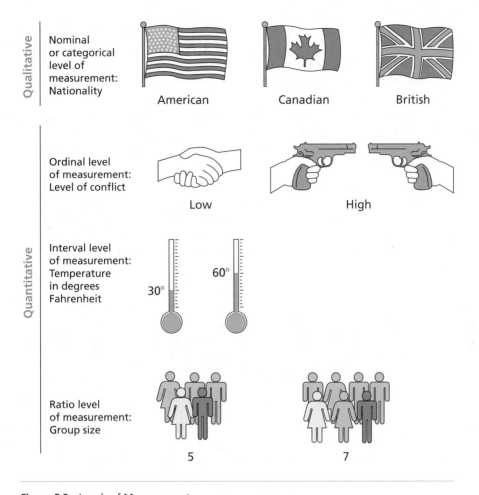

Figure 5.2 Levels of Measurement

characteristics such as ethnicity, marital status, or occupation, or they might include service-related variables such as referral source or services used and the like. A researcher might want to understand the differences between those who use respite care services for the elderly and those who do not use respite services. Another researcher might want to distinguish the characteristics of people who are poor and those people who are not poor. A third researcher might want to know if the decision to place an older parent in a nursing home (placed: yes or no) is based on economic status and use of respite care services. Respite care use, poverty status, and nursing home placement are all nominal-level variables.

Although the attributes of categorical variables do not have a mathematical meaning, they must be assigned to cases with great care. The attributes we use to measure, or categorize, cases must be mutually exclusive and exhaustive:

- A variable's attributes or values are *mutually exclusive* if every case can have only one attribute.
- A variable's attributes or values are *mutually exhaustive* when every case can be classified into one of the categories.

When a variable's attributes are mutually exclusive and exhaustive, every case corresponds to one and only one attribute.

The only mathematical operation we can perform with nominal-level variables is a count. We can count how many clients last month were females and how many were males. From that count, we can calculate the percentage or proportion of females to males among our clients. If the agency served 100 women and 100 men, then we can say that 50% of the clients were female. But we cannot identify an average gender, nor can we add or subtract or compute any other kind of number.

Ordinal Level of Measurement

The first of the three quantitative levels is the ordinal level of measurement. At this level, the numbers assigned to cases specify only the order of the cases, permitting "greater than" and "less than" distinctions. The gaps between the various responses do not have any particular meaning. As with nominal variables, the different values of a variable measured at the ordinal level must be mutually exclusive and exhaustive. They must cover the range of observed values and allow each case to be assigned no more than one value.

The properties of variables measured at the ordinal level are illustrated in Figure 5.2 by the contrast between the levels of conflict in two groups. The first group, symbolized by two people shaking hands, has a low level of conflict. The second group, symbolized by two people pointing guns at each other, has a high level of conflict. To measure conflict, we would put the groups "in order" by assigning the number 1 to the low-conflict group and the number 2 to the high-conflict group. The numbers thus indicate only the relative position or order of the cases. Although *low level of conflict* is represented by the number 1, it is not one unit of conflict less than *high level of conflict*, which is represented by the number 2.

A common ordinal measure used in social service agencies is client satisfaction. Often, agencies will ask a client a global question about satisfaction with the services provided by the agency, using a rating system such as:

4 = *very satisfied*
3 = *satisfied*
2 = *dissatisfied*
1 = *very dissatisfied*

Someone who responds *very satisfied*, coded as 4, is clearly more satisfied than someone who responds *dissatisfied*, coded as 2, but the person responding with a 4 is not twice as satisfied as the person responding with a 2. Nor is the person responding *very satisfied* (4) two units more satisfied than the person responding *dissatisfied* (2). We do know that the first person is more satisfied than the second person, and therefore, the order has meaning. We can count the number of clients who fall into each category. We can also compute an average satisfaction, but the average is not a quantity of satisfaction; rather, the number summarizes the relative position of the group on the given scale.

Many other ordinal measures are used in social services. You might be using a goal attainment scale by which you measure the progress of a client in achieving a particular goal. These scales are usually developed by describing the worst indicators, the best indicators, and several steps in between. The gap between the steps has no meaning, but the scoring represents the progress of the client. Table 5.2 provides an example of a goal attainment scale to measure self-esteem and mother's attitude toward her child. The social worker evaluates the extent to which there is improvement in self-esteem based on the nature of the verbal and nonverbal responses of the client. There is an order to the levels of achievement, and we can describe how many clients fall into each category, but we cannot calculate the average level of achievement using this scale.

Interval Level of Measurement

The numbers indicating the values of a variable at the interval level of measurement represent fixed measurement units but have no absolute or fixed zero point. An interval level of measurement also has mutually exclusive categories, the categories are exhaustive, and there is an order to the responses. This level of measurement is represented in Figure 5.2 by the difference between two Fahrenheit temperatures. Although 60 degrees is 30 degrees hotter than 30 degrees, 60 in this case is not twice as hot as 30. Why not? Because "heat" does not begin at 0 degrees on the Fahrenheit scale.

An interval-level measure is created by a scale that has fixed measurement units but no absolute or fixed

TABLE 5.2

Example of a Goal Attainment Scale

Problem Area	Client Outcome Goal	No Achievement	Some Achievement	Major Achievement
Self-esteem	To develop increased feeling of self-esteem	Makes only negative statements Does not identify strengths No verbal expression of confidence No sense of self-worth	Some positive statements Some negative statements Can identify some strengths but overly critical about self Emerging confidence Emerging self-worth	Makes many positive statements Few to no negative statements Can identify strengths without qualifying statements Is confident Has self-worth
Mother's attitude toward child	Less of a negative attitude toward child	Constantly: Resists child's affection Shows anger verbally and nonverbally Shows frustration Shows hostility Impatient	Occasional: Affection Anger Frustration Hostility Impatience	Accepts child's affection No verbal or nonverbal signs of anger, hostility, frustration Patient

zero point. The numbers can, therefore, be added and subtracted, but ratios are not meaningful. Again, the values must be mutually exclusive and exhaustive.

There are few true interval-level measures in social work, but many social work researchers treat scales created by combining responses to a series of variables measured at the ordinal level as interval-level measures. Frequently, this is done because there are more mathematical operations associated with interval-level variables. For example, an index of this sort could be created with responses to Attkisson's Client Satisfaction Questionnaire (see Figure 5.3 for the CSQ-8).

The questions in this scale have different response categories but the same response numbers. Each question can be used independently of the other questions to provide useful information: an ordinal level of measurement. Or the responses to the eight questions can be summed to reflect overall satisfaction. The scale would then range from 8 to 32, with higher scores representing greater satisfaction. A score of 24 could be treated as if it were 12 more units than a score of 12, but that does not mean that one respondent is twice as satisfied as the other person.

Ratio Level of Measurement

The numbers indicating the values of a variable at the ratio level of measurement represent fixed measuring units and an absolute zero point (zero means absolutely no amount of whatever the variable indicates). On a ratio scale, 10 is two points higher than 8 and is also two times greater than 5. Ratio numbers can be added and subtracted, and because the numbers begin at an absolute zero point, they can be multiplied and divided (so ratios can be formed between the numbers). For example, people's ages can be represented by values ranging from 0 years (or some fraction of a year) to 120 or more. A person who is 30 years old is 15 years older than someone who is 15 years old (30−15=15) and is twice as old as that person (30/15=2). Of course, the numbers also are mutually exclusive and exhaustive, so that every case can be assigned one and only one value.

Figure 5.2 displays an example of a variable measured at the ratio level. The number of people in the first group is 5, and the number in the second group is 7. The ratio of the two groups' sizes is then 1.4, a number that

CLIENT SATISFACTION QUESTIONNAIRE
CSQ-8

Please help us improve our program by answering some questions about the services you have received. We are interested in your honest opinions, whether they are positive or negative. *Please answer all of the questions.* We also welcome your comments and suggestions. Thank you very much. We appreciate your help.

CIRCLE YOUR ANSWERS

1. How would you rate the quality of service you received?

4 *Excellent*	3 *Good*	2 *Fair*	1 *Poor*

2. Did you get the kind of service you wanted?

1 *No, definitely not*	2 *No, not really*	3 *Yes, generally*	4 *Yes, definitely*

3. To what extent has our program met your needs?

4 *Almost all of my needs have been met*	3 *Most of my needs have been met*	2 *Only a few of my needs have been met*	1 *None of my needs have been met*

4. If a friend were in need to similar help, would you recommend our program to him or her?

1 *No, definitely not*	2 *No, I don't think so*	3 *Yes, I think so*	4 *Yes, definitely*

5. How satisfied are you with the amount of help you received?

1 *Quite dissatisfied*	2 *Indifferent or mildly dissatisfied*	3 *Mostly satisfied*	4 *Very satisfied*

6. Have the services you received helped you to deal more effectively with your problems?

4 *Yes, they helped a great deal*	3 *Yes, they helped somewhat*	2 *No, they really didn't help*	1 *No, they seemed to make things worse*

7. In an overall, general sense, how satisfied are you with the service you received?

4 *Very satisfied*	3 *Mostly satisfied*	2 *Indifferent or mildly dissatisfied*	1 *Quite dissatisfied*

8. If you were to seek help again, would you come back to our program?

1 *No, definitely not*	2 *No, I don't think so*	3 *Yes, I think so*	4 *Yes, definitely*

Distributed by Tamalpais Matrix Systems   info@CSQscales.com   www.CSQscales.com

Copyright © 1979, 1989, 1990, 2006 Clifford Attkisson, Ph.D.

Use, transfer, copying, reproduction, merger, translation, modification, or enhancement
(in any format including electronic), in whole or in part is forbidden without written permission.

TMS. 001

Figure 5.3 Example of an Interval-Level Measure: Client Satisfaction Questionnaire (CSQ-8)

mirrors the relationship between the sizes of the groups. Note that there does not actually have to be any group with a size of 0; what is important is that the numbering scheme begins at an absolute zero—in this case, the absence of any people.

As part of your practice, you might use ratio-level variables to describe characteristics of your clients such as their actual income or their actual income from Social Security. You can describe clients based on their level of depressive symptoms because zero means they have no depressive symptoms. Ratio-level variables are often used when reporting to funders or even supervisors, for example, the number of clients seen in the last month, the amount of time spent providing direct casework services, or the number of meals delivered to homebound elderly. The information might be used to describe a community: the number of community organizations or the number of after-school programs in a particular community. For each of these variables, the answer *zero* is meaningful, representing the complete absence of the variable.

The Case of Dichotomies

Dichotomies, variables having only two values, are a special case from the standpoint of levels of measurement. The values or attributes of a variable such as depression clearly vary in kind or quality, not in amount. Thus, the variable is categorical—measured at the nominal level. Yet, in practical terms, we can think of the variable in a slightly different way, as indicating the presence of the attribute *depressed* or *not depressed*.

Viewed in this way, there is an inherent order: A depressed person has more of the attribute (it is present) than a person who is not depressed (the attribute is not present). We are likely to act given the presence or absence of that attribute. We intervene or refer to treatment a depressed client, but we would not do so with a client who was not depressed. Nonetheless, although in practical terms there is an order, empirically, we treat dichotomous variables as a nominal variable.

Comparison of Levels of Measurement

Table 5.3 summarizes the types of comparisons that can be made with different levels of measurement, as well as the mathematical operations that are legitimate. All four levels of measurement allow us to assign different values to different cases. All three quantitative measures allow us to rank cases in order.

Researchers choose levels of measurement in the process of operationalizing the variables; the level of measurement is not inherent in the variable itself. Many variables can be measured at different levels with different procedures. For example, the Core Alcohol and Drug Survey (Core Institute, 1994) identifies binge drinking by asking students, "Think back over the last two weeks. How many times have you had five or more drinks at a sitting?" You might be ready to classify this as a ratio-level measure.

TABLE 5.3

Properties of Measurement Levels

Examples of Comparison Statements	Appropriate Math Operations	Relevant Level of Measurement			
		Nominal	Ordinal	Interval	Radio
A is equal to (not equal to) B	= (≠)	✓	✓	✓	✓
A is greater than (less than) B	> (<)		✓	✓	✓
A is three more than (less than) B	+ (−)			✓	✓
A is twice (half) as large as B	× (÷)				✓

However, this is a closed-ended question, and students are asked to indicate their answer by checking *None, Once, Twice, 3 to 5 times, 6 to 9 times,* or *10 or more times*. Use of these categories makes the level of measurement ordinal. The distance between any two cases cannot be clearly determined. A student with a response in the *6 to 9 times* category could have binged just one more time than a student who responded *3 to 5 times*. You just cannot tell.

It is a good idea to try to measure variables at the highest level of measurement possible. The more information available, the more ways we have to compare cases. We also have more possibilities for statistical analyses with quantitative than with qualitative variables. Furthermore, you can create ordinal or nominal variables from ratio-level variables, but you cannot go in the reverse direction. For example, you can measure age in years rather than in categories. If you know the actual age, you can combine the ages into categories at a later time. When asking people to respond to age by category, you cannot modify that variable to reflect their actual age. Thus, if doing so does not distort the meaning of the concept that is to be measured, measure at the highest level possible.

Be aware, however, that other considerations may preclude measurement at a high level. For example, many people are very reluctant to report their exact incomes, even in anonymous questionnaires. So asking respondents to report their income in categories (such as less than $10,000, $10,000–19,999, or $20,000–29,999) will result in more responses, and thus more valid data, than asking respondents for their income in exact dollar amounts.

MEASUREMENT ERROR

No matter how carefully we operationalize and design our measures, no measure is perfect, and there will be some error. It might be that the measurement instrument itself needs to be corrected or reevaluated. Sometimes people are simply inconsistent in the way that they respond to questions. For example, the U.S. Census Bureau's Survey of Income and Program Participa-

tion 1984 Panel included data collected nine times, with 4 months between interviews. Using this data set, Rafael Engel (1988) completed a study on poverty and aging.

One of the questions dealt with marital status, seemingly an easy question to answer and one that should provide consistent responses. It turned out that a portion of the sample, primarily women, kept moving from divorced to widowed and sometimes back to divorced. On reflection, this made sense because among members of this cohort of older adults (born between 1900 and 1919), divorce was a less acceptable social status than being a widow.

In gathering data, we get a response from the participant, this response being the reported score. The reported score is not necessarily the true score or the true response because of the imperfections of measurement. The true response differs from the reported response because of measurement error, of which there are two types: systematic error and random error.

Systematic Error

Systematic error is generally considered to be predictable error, in that we can predict the direction of the error. Think about weighing yourself on a scale each day. If you put a scale on a particular part of the floor in your house, you will always weigh less (reported score) than you actually do (true score). The direction of the error is predictable: In this case, your scale will always under-report your true weight.

There are different forms of systematic error, some of which we will detail in later chapters, but each of these forms of systematic error reflects some bias. The various forms include:

- Social desirability. Social desirability bias occurs when respondents wish to appear most favorable in the eyes of the interviewer or researcher. For example, in the 1980s, polling information about elections between African American Democratic candidates and white Republican candidates typically showed larger victory margins anticipated for the Democratic candidate than actually occurred in the election. One factor was the un-willingness of white Democrats to admit they were unwilling to vote for an African American, even of the same political party.

• Acquiescence bias. There is a tendency for some respondents to agree or disagree with every statement, whether they actually agree or not.

• Leading questions. Leading questions have language that is designed to influence the direction of a respondent's answer. There are many different ways in which this might be done. You might encounter words that have a negative connotation in society (regardless of the reason). For example, during the 1980s, the use of the words *liberal* and *welfare* began to take on negative connotations. So a question like, Do you support the liberal position on . . . , is meant to lead people to disagree with the position. Another form of a leading question is to use the names of controversial people in the question. A third way of evoking certain responses is simply to include some responses to a question in the actual question but not all responses.

• Differences in subgroup responses according to gender, ethnicity, or age. Differences in cultural beliefs or patterns, socialization processes, or cohort effects may bias findings from what otherwise might seem to be a set of neutral questions. For example, Joy Newmann (1987) has argued that gender differences in levels of depressive symptoms may reflect differences in the socialization process of males and females. She suggests that some scales ask questions about behaviors, such as crying, being lonely, and feeling sad, that are more likely to be admitted by women and not by men, because men are socialized not to express such feelings.

Similarly, Debra Ortega and Cheryl Richey (1998) note that people of color may respond differently to questions used in depression scales. Some ethnic groups report feelings of sadness or hopelessness as physical complaints and, therefore, have high scores on these questions but low scores on emotion-related items. Different ethnic groups respond differently to "how do you feel" questions and "what do you think" questions.

Ortega and Richey also note that some items on depression scales, such as suicidal ideation, are not meaningful to some ethnic groups.

To avoid systematic error requires careful construction of scales and questions and the testing of these questions with different population groups.

Random Error

Unlike systematic error, random error is unpredictable in terms of its effects. Random error may be due to the way respondents are feeling that particular day. On the one hand, respondents may be fatigued, bored, or not in a very cooperative mood. On the other hand, they may be having a great day. Perhaps the lighting or the weather is making them less willing to cooperate. Respondents may also be affected by the conditions of the testing. The lighting may be bad, it may be noisy, the seating may be cramped, the lack of walls in the cubicle may mean other people can hear, there may be other people in the room, or they may not like the looks of the person gathering the information.

Another form of random error is *regression to the mean*. This is the tendency of people who score very high on some measure to score less high the next time, or the reverse, for people who score very low to score higher. What might have influenced the high or low score on the first test may not operate in the second test.

Random error might occur when researchers rating a behavior are not adequately trained to do the rating. For example, two people grading an essay test might come up with different grades if they have not discussed the grading criteria beforehand. A field supervisor and a beginning student might assess a client differently, given the variation in their years of experience.

As we have already said, the effects of random error cannot be predicted: Some responses overestimate the true score, whereas other responses underestimate the true score. Many researchers believe that if the sample size is sufficiently large, the effects of random error cancel each other out. Nonetheless, we want to use measurement scales and questions that are stable to minimize as much as possible the effects of random error.

EVALUATING MEASURES

The issue of measurement error is very important. Do the operations that measure our variables provide stable or consistent responses—are they reliable? Do the operations developed that measure our concepts actually do so—are they valid? When we test the effectiveness of two different interventions or we monitor the progress our client is making, we want the changes we observe to be due to the intervention and not to the measurement instrument.

We also want to know that the measure we use is really a measure of the outcome and not a measure of some other outcome. If we have weighed our measurement options, carefully constructed our questions and observational procedures, and carefully selected from the available data indicators, we should be on the right track. But we cannot have much confidence in a measure until we have empirically evaluated its reliability and validity.

Reliability

Reliability means that a measurement procedure yields consistent or equivalent scores when the phenomenon being measured is not changing (or that the measured scores change in direct correspondence to actual changes in the phenomenon). If a measure is reliable, it is affected less by random error, or chance variation, than if it is unreliable. Reliability is a prerequisite for measurement validity: We cannot really measure a phenomenon if the measure we are using gives inconsistent results. In fact, because it usually is easier to assess reliability than validity, you are more likely to see an evaluation of measurement reliability in a research report than an evaluation of measurement validity.

There are four possible indications of unreliability. For example, a test of your knowledge of research methods would be unreliable if every time you took it, you received a different score, even though your knowledge of research methods had not changed in the interim, not even as a result of taking the test more than once (test-retest reliability). Similarly, a scale composed of questions to measure knowledge of research methods would be unreliable if respondents' answers to each question were totally independent of their answers to the others (internal consistency). A measure also would be unreliable if slightly different versions of it resulted in markedly different responses (alternate forms reliability). Finally, an assessment of the level of conflict in social groups would be unreliable if ratings of the level of conflict by two observers were not related to each other (interrater reliability).

Test-Retest Reliability

When researchers measure a phenomenon that does not change between two points separated by an interval of time, the degree to which the two measurements are related to each other is the test-retest reliability of the measure. If you take a test of your math ability and then retake the test 2 months later, the test is performing reliably if you receive a similar score both times—presuming that nothing happened during the 2 months to change your math ability. We hope to find a correlation between the two tests of about .7 and prefer an even higher correlation, such as .8.

Of course, if events between the test and the retest have changed the variable being measured, then the difference between the test and retest scores should reflect that change. As the gap in time between the two tests increases, there is a greater likelihood that real change did occur. This also presumes you were not affected by the conditions of the testing: a testing effect. The circumstances of the testing, such as how you were given the test, or environmental conditions, such as lighting or room temperature, may impact test scores. The testing effect may extend to how you felt the first time you took the test; because you did not know what to expect the first time, you may have been very nervous, as opposed to the second time, when you knew what to expect.

Radloff's (1977) initial effort to evaluate the test-retest reliability of the *CES-D* highlights the difficulties that may emerge from the testing and that make interpreting the scores problematic. A probability sample of households was taken in one county, and then within each household, one person 18 or older was randomly chosen to participate in an interview. Each person was also asked to complete and mail back a *CES-D* scale either 2, 4, 6, or 8 weeks after the initial interview. Only 419 of the initial 1,089 respondents sent back mail questionnaires. The test-retest correlations were moderately high, ranging from .51 at 2 weeks to .59 at 8 weeks.

Radloff offered a variety of explanations about the moderate correlations, which included such methodological problems as the bias introduced by nonresponse (maybe those who responded differed from those who did not respond), the problem of using an interview at Time 1 and a self-administered questionnaire for the follow-up (perhaps people responded differently to the interviewer than to the questionnaire), and the effects of being tested twice. Furthermore, she noted that the *CES-D* was meant to capture depressive symptoms in a 1-week period, and perhaps there had been real changes. This example illustrates how test-retest reliability scores may potentially be affected by real change or by the effect of testing.

Internal Consistency

When researchers use multiple items to measure a single concept, they are concerned with internal consistency. This is a very common method to demonstrate reliability. For example, if we are to have confidence that a set of questions (like those in Table 5.1) reliably measures depression, the answers to the questions should be highly associated with one another. The stronger the association among the individual items, and the more items that are included, the higher the reliability of the index.

One method to assess internal consistency is to divide the scale into two parts, or split-half reliability. We might take a 20-item scale, such as the *CES-D*, and sum the scores of the first 10 items, then sum the scores of the second 10 items (items 11 through 20), and then correlate the scores for each of the participants. If we have internal consistency, we should have a fairly high correlation, although this correlation typically gets higher the more items there are in the scale. So what may be considered a fairly high split-half reliability score for a 6-item scale might not be considered a high score for a 20-item scale.

As you can imagine, there are countless ways in which you might split the scale, and in practical terms, it is nearly impossible to split the scale by hand into

every possible combination. Fortunately, the speed of computers allows us to calculate a score that indeed splits the scale in every combination. A summary score, such as Cronbach's alpha coefficient, is calculated by the computer program. Cronbach's alpha is the average score of all the possible split-half combinations. In Radloff's study (1977), the alpha coefficients of different samples were quite high, ranging from .85 to .90.

Alternate-Forms Reliability

Researchers are testing alternate-forms reliability or parallel-forms reliability when they compare subjects' answers to slightly different versions of survey questions (Litwin, 1995, pp. 13–21). A researcher may reverse the order of the response choices in a scale, modify the question wording in minor ways, or create a set of different questions. The two forms are then administered to the subjects. If the two sets of responses are not too different, alternate-forms reliability is established.

You might remember taking the SATs or ACTs when you were in high school. When you compared notes with your friends, you found that each of you had taken different tests. The developers had evaluated these tests to ensure there they were equivalent and comparable.

Interobserver Reliability

When researchers use more than one observer to rate the same people, events, or places, interobserver reliability or interrater reliability is their goal. If observers are using the same instrument to rate the same thing, their ratings should be very similar. If they are similar, we can have much more confidence that the ratings reflect the phenomenon being assessed rather than the orientations of the observers.

Assessing interobserver reliability is most important when the rating task is complex. Consider a commonly used measure of mental health, the Global Assessment of Functioning Scale (*GAF*), a bit of which is shown in Figure 5.4. The rating task seems straightforward, with clear descriptions of the subject characteristics that are supposed to lead to high or low *GAF*

Consider psychological, social, and occupational functioning on a hypothetical continuum of mental health-illness. Do not include impairment in functioning due to physical (or environmental) limitations.

Code (**Note:** Use intermediate codes when appropriate, e.g., 45, 68, 72.)

100 91	**Superior functioning in a wide range of activities, life's problems never seem to get out of hand, is sought by others because of his or her many positive qualities. No symptoms.**
90 81	**Absent or minimal symptoms** (e.g., mild anxiety before an exam), **good functioning in all areas, interested and involved in a wide range of activities, socially effective, generally satisfied with life, no more than everyday problems or concerns** (e.g., an occasional argument with family members).
80 71	**If symptoms are present, they are transient and expectable reactions to psychosocial stressors** (e.g., difficulty concentrating after family argument); **no more than slight impairment in social, occupational, or school functioning** (e.g., temporarily falling behind in schoolwork).
70 61	**Some mild symptoms** (e.g., depressive mood and mild insomnia) **OR some difficulty in social, occupational, or school functioning** (e.g., occasional truancy or theft within the household), **but generally functioning pretty well, has some meaningful interpersonal relationships.**
60 51	**Moderate symptoms** (e.g., flat affect and circumstantial speech, occasional panic attacks) **OR moderate difficulty in social, occupational, or school functioning** (e.g., few friends, conflicts with peers or co-workers)
50 41	**Serious symptoms** (e.g., suicidal ideation, severe obsessional rituals, frequent shoplifting) **OR any serious impairment in social, occupational, or school functioning** (e.g., no friends, unable to keep a job).
40 31	**Some impairment in reality testing or communication** (e.g., speech is at times illogical, obscure, or irrelevant) **OR major impairment in several areas, such as work or school, family relations, judgment, thinking, or mood** (e.g., depressed man avoids friends, neglects family, and is unable to work, child frequently beats up younger children, is defiant at home, and is failing at school).
30 21	**Behavior is considerably influenced by delusions or hallucinations OR serious impairment in communication or judgment** (e.g., sometimes incoherent, acts grossly inappropriately, suicidal preoccupation) **OR inability to function in almost all areas** (e.g., stays in bed all day, no job, home, or friends).
20 11	**Some danger of hurting self or others** (e.g., suicide attempts without clear expectation of death, frequently violent, manic excitement) **OR occasionally fails to maintain minimal personal hygiene** (e.g., smears feces) **OR gross impairment in communication** (e.g., largely incoherent or mute).
10 1	**Persistent danger of severely hurting self or others** (e.g., recurrent violence) **OR persistent inability to maintain minimal personal hygiene OR serious suicidal act with clear expectation of death.**
0	Inadequate information.

Figure 5.4   The Challenge of Interobserver Reliability: Excerpt From the Global Assessment of Functioning Scale

scores. But, in fact, the judgments that the rater must make while using this scale are very complex. They are affected by a wide range of subject characteristics, attitudes, and behaviors, as well as by the rater's reactions. As a result, interobserver agreement is often low on the *GAF* unless the raters are trained carefully.

Assessments of interobserver reliability may be based on the correlation of the rating between two raters. Two raters could evaluate the quality of play between five teenage mothers and their children on a 10-point scale. The correlation would show whether the direction of

the raters' scores was similar, as well as how close the agreement was for the relative position for each of the five scores. One rater may judge the five mothers as 1, 2, 3, 4, and 5, while the second rater scores the mothers as 6, 7, 8, 9, and 10. The correlation would be quite high; in fact, the correlation would be perfect. But as demonstrated by this example, the agreement about the quality of the interactions was quite different. So an alternative method is to estimate the percentage of exact agreement between the two raters. In this case, the rater agreement is zero.

Intraobserver Reliability

Intraobserver reliability (intrarater reliability) occurs when a single observer is assessing an individual at two or more points in time. It differs from test-retest reliability in that the ratings are done by the observer as opposed to the subjects. Intraobserver reliability is particularly important when you are evaluating a client's behavior or making judgments about the client's progress. While the *GAF* has been found to have low interobserver reliability, it has been found to have pretty high intraobserver reliability. It turns out that although different raters disagree, a single rater tends to provide consistent reports about an individual.

Measurement Validity

As you know, *measurement validity* refers to the extent to which measures indicate what they are intended to measure. More technically, a valid measure of a concept is one that is closely related to other apparently valid measures of the concept and to the known or supposed correlates of that concept, but that is not related to measures of unrelated concepts, irrespective of the methods used for the other different measures (adapted from Brewer & Hunter, 1989, p. 134). The extent to which measurement validity has been achieved can be assessed with four different approaches: face validation, content validation, criterion validation, and construct validation. The methods of criterion and construct validation also include subtypes.

Face Validity

Researchers apply the term *face validity* to the confidence gained from careful inspection of a concept to see if it is appropriate "on its face." More precisely, we can say that a measure is face valid if it obviously pertains to the meaning of the concept being measured more than to other concepts (Brewer & Hunter, 1989, p. 131). For example, a count of how many drinks people consumed in the past week would be a face-valid measure of their alcohol consumption. Political party preference is unlikely on its face to tell us about alcohol consumption, although it would be related to political beliefs and social class.

Although every measure should be inspected in this way, face validation in itself does not provide very convincing evidence of measurement validity. The question, How much beer or wine did you have to drink last week? may look valid on its face as a measure of frequency of drinking, but people who drink heavily tend to underreport the amount they drink. So the question would be an invalid measure in a study that includes heavy drinkers.

Content Validity

Content validity establishes that the measure covers the full range of the concept's meaning. To determine that range of meaning, the researcher may solicit the opinions of experts and review literature that identifies the different aspects or dimensions of the concept.

An example of an alcoholism measure that covers a wide range of meaning is the *MAST*. The *MAST* includes 24 questions representing the following subscales: recognition of alcohol problems by self and others; legal, social, and work problems; help seeking; marital and family difficulties; and liver pathology (Skinner & Sheu, 1982). Many experts familiar with the direct consequences of substance abuse agree that these dimensions capture the full range of possibilities. Thus, the *MAST* is believed to be valid from the standpoint of content validity.

On the other hand, experts may disagree with the range of content provided in a scale. The *CES-D* depression scale includes various dimensions of somatic symptoms and negative feelings. Some experts (e.g., Liang, Tran, Krause, & Markides, 1989) have questioned the presence of some items such as "feeling fearful" or "people dislike me," suggesting that these items are not reflective of the dimensions of depression. Other experts have suggested that perhaps the dimensions in the scale are not appropriate for how different population subgroups, such as the elderly (Weiss, Nagel, & Aronson, 1986) or African Americans (Barbee, 1992), manifest depression.

This example illustrates one of the difficulties in relying solely on face or content validity. Although face and content validity are important to establish, in the end, they are still subjective assessments of validity.

The next two forms of validity, criterion validity and construct validity, provide empirical evidence about the validity of a measure.

Criterion Validity

Criterion validity is established when the scores obtained on one measure can be accurately compared with those obtained with a more direct or already validated measure of the same phenomenon (the criterion). A measure of blood-alcohol concentration or a urine test could serve as the criterion for validating a self-report measure of drinking, as long as the questions we ask about drinking refer to the same period. A measure of depression could be compared with another accepted self-administered depression scale. A scale measuring job satisfaction could be compared with staying on the job. SAT or ACT scores could be compared with academic success in college. In each of these cases, the measure is being compared with some criterion believed to measure the same construct.

The criterion that researchers select can itself be measured either at the same time as the variable to be validated or after that time. Concurrent validity exists when a measure yields scores that are closely related to scores on a criterion measured at the same time. A store might validate its test of sales ability by administering the test to sales personnel who are already employed and then comparing their test scores with their sales performance. Or a measure of walking speed based on mental counting might be validated concurrently with a stopwatch.

Predictive validity is the ability of a measure to predict scores on a criterion measured in the future. For example, a store might administer a test of sales ability to new sales personnel and then validate the measure by comparing these test scores with the criterion—the subsequent sales performance of the new personnel.

An attempt at criterion validation is well worth the effort because it greatly increases confidence that the measure is measuring what was intended. However, for many concepts of interest to social work researchers, no other variable might reasonably be considered a criterion. If we are measuring feelings or beliefs or other subjective states, such as feelings of loneliness, what direct indicator could serve as a criterion? Even with variables for which a reasonable criterion exists, the researcher may not be able to gain access to the criterion—as would be the case with a tax return or employer document as a criterion for self-reported income.

Construct Validity

Measurement validity can also be established by showing that a measure is related to a variety of other measures as specified in a theory. This validation approach, known as *construct validity*, is commonly used in social research when no clear criterion exists for validation purposes. Koeske (1994) suggests that this theoretical construct validation process relies on using a deductive theory with hypothesized relationships among the constructs. The measure has construct validity (or theoretical construct validity) if it "behaves" as it should relative to the other constructs in the theory.

For example, Danette Hann, Kristen Winter, and Paul Jacobsen (1999) compared subject scores on the *CES-D* to a number of indicators that they felt from previous research and theory should be related to depression: fatigue, anxiety, and global mental health. The researchers found that individuals with higher *CES-D* scores tended to have more problems in each of these areas, giving us more confidence in the *CES-D*'s validity as a measure.

A somewhat different approach to construct validation is termed *discriminant validity*. In this approach, scores on the measure to be validated are compared with scores on another measure of the same variable and with scores on variables that measure different but related concepts. Discriminant validity is achieved if the measure to be validated is related most strongly to its comparison measure and less so to the measures of other concepts.

For example, if we were testing the discriminant validity of the *CES-D*, we might compare it with another measure of depression, such as the Beck Depression Inventory (*BDI*), and with related concepts such as a measure of anxiety and a measure of self-esteem. If the *CES-D* has good discriminant validity, it will correlate strongest with the *BDI* and have lower correlations with the anxiety and self-esteem measures.

Convergent validity is demonstrated when you can show a relationship between two measures of the same construct that are assessed using different methods (Koeske, 1994). For example, we might compare the *CES-D* scale scores to clinical judgments made by practitioners who have used a clinical protocol. The *CES-D* scores should correlate with the scores obtained from the clinical protocol.

Another approach to construct validity is referred to as *known-groups validity*. In this method, we might have two groups with known characteristics, and we compare our measure across these two groups. We would expect that our measure should score higher with the group that it is related to and lower with the unrelated group. For example, we might give the *CES-D* to a group of people who have been clinically diagnosed as depressed and to a group that does not have a clinical diagnosis of depression. We would expect the *CES-D* scores to be higher among those clinically depressed than those who have no clinical diagnosis.

Finally, another method that has become associated with construct validity is *factoral validity*. This approach relies on factor analysis and, in many ways, is simply an empirical extension of content analysis. This procedure is usually applied when the construct of interest has different dimensions. In the analysis, we look to see if the items thought to be measuring the same dimension are more highly related to each other than to items measuring other dimensions. The *CES-D* scale has been hypothesized to have four dimensions: negative affect, positive affect (lack), somatic symptoms, and interpersonal. Several items are associated with each dimension.

Therefore, a factor analysis would test whether the items measuring negative affect are more highly related to each other than to items measuring somatic symptoms. Negative affect items such as *feeling blue, sad, depressed*, and the like should have stronger relationships to each other than to items measuring somatic symptoms such as *overeating, sleeping too much*, or *difficulty concentrating*. A test of factoral validity

would assess the expected internal theoretical relationships of the construct.

The distinction between criterion and construct validation is not always clear. Opinions can differ about whether a particular indicator is indeed a criterion for the concept that is to be measured. For example, if you need to validate a question-based measure of the sales ability of people applying for a sales position, few would object to using actual sales performance as a criterion. But what if you want to validate a question-based measure of the amount of social support that people receive from their friends? Should you just ask people about the social support they have received? Could friends' reports of the amount of support they provided serve as a criterion? Are verbal accounts of the amount of support provided adequate? What about observations of social support that people receive? Even if you could observe people in the act of counseling or otherwise supporting their friends, can an observer be sure that the interaction is indeed supportive? There isn't really a criterion here, just related concepts that could be used in a construct validation strategy.

Even biochemical measures of substance abuse are questionable as criteria for validating self-reported substance use. Urine test results can be altered by ingesting certain substances, and blood tests vary in their sensitivity to the presence of drugs over a particular period. Koeske (1994) suggests that a key difference is simply that with criterion validity, "the researcher's primary concern is with the criterion in a practical context, rather than with the theoretical properties of the construct measure" (p. 50).

What both construct and criterion validation have in common is the comparison of scores on one measure with scores on other measures that are predicted to be related. It is not so important that researchers agree that a particular comparison measure is a criterion rather than a related construct. But it is very important to think critically about the quality of the comparison measure and whether it actually represents a different view of the same phenomenon. For example, it is only a weak indication of measurement validity to find that scores on a new self-report measure of alcohol use are associated with scores on a previously used self-report measure of alcohol use.

Ways to Improve Reliability and Validity of Existing Measures

At this point, we will discuss ways to improve reliability and validity of existing measures. Whether we are working with a new measure or an existing measure, we must always assess the reliability of a measure if we hope to be able to establish its validity. In fact, because it usually is easier to assess reliability than validity, you will see more evaluations of measurement reliability in research reports than evaluations of measurement validity.

Remember that a reliable measure is not necessarily a valid measure, as Figure 5.5 illustrates. This discrepancy is a common flaw of self-report measures of substance abuse. The multiple questions in self-report indexes of substance abuse are answered by most respondents in a consistent way, so the indexes are reli-able. However, a number of respondents may not admit to drinking, even though they drink a lot. Their answers to the questions are consistent, but they are consistently misleading. So the indexes based on self-report are reliable but invalid. Such indexes are not useful and should be improved or discarded. Unfortunately, many measures are judged to be worthwhile on the basis only of a reliability test.

The reliability and validity of measures in any study must be tested after the fact to assess the quality of the data obtained. But then, if it turns out that a measure cannot be considered reliable and valid, little can be done to save the study. Hence, it is supremely important to select in the first place measures that are likely to be reliable and valid. Don't just choose the first measure you find or can think of: Consider the different strengths of different measures and their appropriateness to your study. Conduct a pretest in which you use the measure with a small sample and check its reliability. Provide careful training to ensure a consistent approach if interviewers or observers will administer the

Figure 5.5
The Difference Between Reliability and Validity: Drinking Behavior

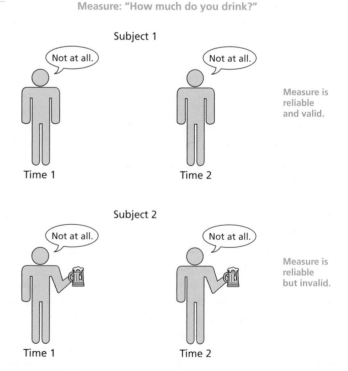

measure. In most cases, however, the best strategy is to use measures that have been used before and whose reliability and validity have been established in other contexts. But the selection of "tried-and-true" measures still does not absolve researchers from the responsibility of testing the reliability and validity of the measures in their own studies.

When the population studied or the measurement context differs from that in previous research, instrument reliability and validity may be affected. So the researchers must take pains with the design of their study. For example, test-retest reliability has proved to be better for several standard measures used to assess substance use among homeless people when the interview was conducted in a protected setting and when the measures focused on factual information and referred to a recent time interval (Drake, McHugo, & Biesanz, 1995). Subjects who were younger, female, recently homeless, and less severely afflicted with psychiatric problems were also more likely to give reliable answers.

It may be possible to improve the reliability and validity of measures in a study that already has been conducted if multiple measures were used. For example, in the 1966 Goldfinger and Schutt study of housing for homeless mentally ill people, the researchers assessed substance abuse with several different sets of direct questions, as well as with reports from subjects' case managers and others. They found that the observational reports were often inconsistent with self-reports and that different self-report measures were not always in agreement—hence, they were unreliable.

A more reliable measure was initial reports of lifetime substance abuse problems, which identified all those who subsequently abused substances during the project. The researchers concluded that the lifetime measure was a valid way to identify people at risk for substance abuse problems. No single measure was adequate to identify substance abusers at a particular point in time during the project. Instead, the researchers constructed a composite of observer and self-report measures that seemed to be a valid indicator of substance abuse over 6-month periods.

If the research focuses on previously unmeasured concepts, new measures will have to be devised. Researchers can use one of three strategies to improve the likelihood that new question-based measures will be reliable and valid (Fowler, 1995):

* Engage potential respondents in group discussions about the questions to be included in the survey. This strategy allows researchers to check for consistent understanding of terms and to hear the range of events or experiences that people will report.
* Conduct cognitive interviews. Ask people a test question, then probe with follow-up questions about how they understood the question and what their answer meant.
* Audiotape test interviews during the pretest phase of a survey. The researchers then review these audiotapes and systematically code them to identify problems in question wording or delivery.

CHOOSING AN INSTRUMENT FOR RESEARCH, EVALUATION, AND PRACTICE

As we have suggested throughout this chapter, measurement has relevancy beyond just research; it touches on every level of social work practice. The issues associated with measurement are crucial, both to research and to practice. Hudson (1978) goes so far as stating: "If you cannot measure the client's problem, it does not exist. If you cannot measure the client's problem, you cannot treat it" (p. 65). Although these are extreme statements, they point to the importance of measurement in understanding whether clients have improved.

The following, then, are suggestions for choosing an instrument when one is available. We believe these suggestions to be relevant whether you are doing research or assessing need and monitoring client progress. These suggestions come from other research and evaluation texts (e.g., Posavac & Carey, 2007; Royse, Thyer, Padgett, & Logan, 2001; Weiss, 1998) and from our own experiences in conducting research and evaluation studies.

* Reliability and validity. We have already tried to convince you of the importance of reliability and validity. At a minimum, there should be evidence of measurement reliability and validity. You want

to actually measure what you are trying to study. Your goal is to be able to say that the changes that occurred were due to the intervention and not the instability of the measurement instrument. When using agency-developed instruments rather than standardized scales, training staff in the use of the instrument will enhance consistency, and the measure can be evaluated by staff for face and content validity.

In evaluating the evidence of reliability and validity, focusing on the strength of the correlations or alpha coefficients is not enough. When you review the research, you need to look at the samples that were used in the studies. Too often, these studies are done without consideration of gender, race, ethnicity, or age. It may be that the samples used in the study or studies look nothing like the population you are serving. If that is the case, the instrument may not be appropriate for your agency or setting. You cannot assume cross-population generalizability (see Chapter 16).

- Cutoff scores. The same concerns regarding reliability and validity studies are true for research on the accuracy of cutoff scores. Just as with reliability and validity, we must be concerned about the cross-population generalizability of this research. Earlier, we described the *CES-D* as a commonly used scale with a more or less acceptable cutoff score of 16. On further inspection, researchers found that this score was too low to be useful with the elderly. Some item reports in the *CES-D* can be due to physical conditions that are common among the elderly. As a result, an appropriate cutoff score for elderly people with physical ailments has been determined to be 25 (Schulberg, Saul, McClelland, Ganguli, & Frank, 1985). The bottom line is to take nothing for granted about cutoff scores unless you believe that there is evidence of cross-population generalizability.

- Feasibility of administration. As we have indicated, there are various methods to collect data, and different measures require different methods. Different methods of administration require different amounts of time to complete. If you choose a measure that requires observation, then you must be able to actually observe the behavior—you must have the time to observe the behavior, and you must be able to arrange to observe the behavior.

Different methods of administration also require skills on the part of the respondent. If you choose a scale that is self-administered, then you are assuming that the respondents can read and understand the instrument. Rafael Engel, Richard Welsh, and Laura Lewis (2000) conducted a study where the available scales are typically self-administered, but the vision level of the respondents was so poor that they could not read the scales. These instruments had to be read to the respondents, which was an imposition on staff already busy with their primary responsibilities.

- Sensitivity. If you are testing an intervention or evaluating the impact of an intervention on a group of clients or a single client, you will need a measure that is sufficiently sensitive to pick up changes in the outcome measures. The scale should have a sufficient number of items that you are able to identify changes. In addition, you want a measure that will provide a spread of responses, rather than having most or nearly all respondents provide the same response. This is a problem with client satisfaction measures because most people report that they are satisfied with services. The skewing of responses limits the analysis.

- Reactivity. To the extent possible, you want measures that do not influence the responses that people provide. We have already suggested that most measures are susceptible to reactivity: The presence of an observer or self-monitoring may change behavior, or an interview may be influenced by the characteristics of the interviewer. You may need to take reactivity into account when reviewing your results.

There are times when reactivity may be useful. Shapiro and Mangelsdorf (1994) designed a parenting skills intervention for teenage moms. The researchers wanted to identify the mothers' "best" parenting skills and felt that if they video-taped the students, the latter would perform at what they considered to be the best interaction level. Reactivity in this case helped the researchers to identify what the teenagers knew, and from that, the effectiveness of the intervention could be tested.

- Cost. The measure should be affordable. Many useful measures and scales can be found in the public domain, but many other scales have to be purchased, and sometimes you must also pay for their scoring.
- Acceptability to staff. The measures have to be accepted by staff as measures that will provide valid data. Staff may disagree about the content of the measure, questioning the validity of the instrument in comparison to the agency's definition of the concept. If this is the case, they are less likely to use it. If the instrument provides useful data to staff as they work with clients, it is likely to be accepted.

SUMMARY

Remember always that measurement validity is a necessary foundation for social work research study. Gathering data without careful conceptualization or conscientious efforts to operationalize key concepts often is a wasted effort. The difficulties of achieving valid measurement vary with the concept being operationalized and the circumstances of the particular study.

Planning ahead is the key to achieving valid measurement in your own research; careful evaluation is the key to sound decisions about the validity of measures in others' research. Statistical tests can help to determine whether a given measure is valid after data have been collected, but if it appears after the fact that a measure is invalid, little can be done to correct the situation. If you cannot tell how key concepts were operationalized when you read a research report, don't trust the findings. If a researcher does not indicate the results of tests used to establish the reliability and validity of key measures, remain skeptical.

Sampling

Russell K. Schutt

6

Basic Steps in the Research Process

Step 1 Choose a problem

2 Review the literature

3 Evaluate the literature

4 Be aware of all ethical issues

5 Be aware of all cultural issues

6 State the research question or hypothesis

7 Select the research approach

8 Determine how the variables are going to be measured

You Are Here ➡

9 Select a sample

10 Select a data collection method

11 Collect and code the data

12 Analyze and interpret the data

13 Write the report

14 Disseminate the report

common technique in journalism is to put a "human face" on a story. A reporter for the *New York Times,* for example, went to an emergency assistance unit near Yankee Stadium to ask homeless mothers about new welfare policies that required recipients to work. One woman with three children suggested, "If you work a minimum wage job, that's nothing . . . . Think about paying rent, with a family." In contrast, another mother with three children remarked, "It's important to do it for my kids, to set an example."

A story about deportations of homeless persons in Moscow focused on the case of one 47-year-old Russian laborer temporarily imprisoned in Social Rehabilitation Center Number 2. He complained that in the town to which he would have to return, "I have no job, no family, no home" (Swarns, 1996, p. A1).

These are interesting comments in effective articles, but we do not know whether they represent the opinions of most homeless persons in the United States and Russia, of most homeless persons in New York City and Moscow, of only persons found in the emergency assistance unit near Yankee Stadium and in Social Rehabilitation Center Number 2—or of just a few people in these locations who caught the eye of these specific reporters.

In other words, we don't know how generalizable these comments are, and if we don't have confidence in their generalizability, their validity is suspect. Because we have no idea whether these opinions are widely shared or quite unique, we cannot really judge what they tell us about the real social world.

DESIGNING A SAMPLING STRATEGY

Whether we are designing a sampling strategy for a particular research study or are evaluating the generalizability of the findings from someone else's research study, we have to understand how and why social work researchers decide to sample in the first place. Sampling is very common in research studies, but sometimes it isn't necessary.

Defining the Sample Components and the Population

Let's say we are designing a research study on a topic that requires us to involve a lot of people (or other entities). These people are called *elements*. Also, we don't have the time or resources to study the entire population of all these people, so we take a subset of the population, which is called a *sample*.

We may collect our data directly from the people in our sample. Some research studies, however, are not so simple. The entities we can easily reach to gather data may not be the same as the entities from whom we really want the data. So we may collect data about the elements from another set of entities, which is called the *sampling units*. For example, if we interview mothers to learn about their families, the families are the elements and the mothers are the sampling units. If we survey department chairpersons

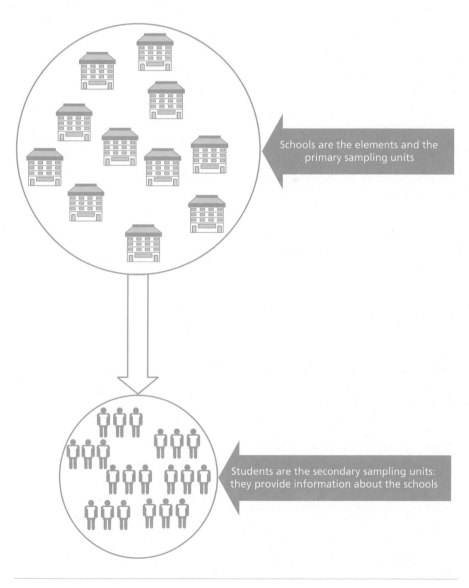

Figure 6.1   Sampling Components in a Two-Stage Study

to learn about college departments, for example, the departments are the elements and the chairpersons are the sampling units. In a study in which individual people are sampled and are the focus of the study, the sampling units are the same as the elements. (See Figure 6.1.)

One key issue with selecting or evaluating a sample's components is understanding exactly what population the sample is supposed to represent. In a survey of "adult Americans," for example, the general population may reasonably be construed as all residents of the United States who are at least 21 years of age. But always be alert to ways in which the population may have been narrowed by the sample selection procedures. Perhaps only English-speaking adult residents of the continental United States were actually sampled. The population for a study is the aggregation of elements that we actually focus on and sample from, not some larger aggregation that we really wish we could have studied.

Some populations, such as the homeless, are not identified by a simple criterion such as a geographic boundary or an organizational membership. A clear definition of such a population is difficult but quite necessary. Anyone should be able to determine just what population was actually studied. However, studies of homeless persons in the early 1980s "did not propose definitions, did not use screening questions to be sure that the people they interviewed were indeed homeless, and did not make major efforts to cover the universe of homeless people." (Perhaps just homeless persons in one shelter were studied.) The result was "a collection of studies that could not be compared" (Burt, 1996, p. 15).

Several studies of homeless persons in urban areas addressed the problem by employing a more explicit definition of the population (Burt, 1996):

> People are homeless if they have no home or permanent place to stay of their own (renting or owning) and no regular arrangement to stay at someone else's place. (15)

Even this more explicit definition still leaves some questions unanswered: What is a "regular arrangement"? How permanent does a "permanent place" have to be? In a study of homeless persons in Chicago, for example, Michael Sosin and his colleagues (1988) answered these questions in their definition of the population of interest:

> We define the homeless as: those current[ly] residing for at least one day but for less than fourteen with a friend or relative, not paying rent, and not sure that the length of stay will surpass fourteen days; those currently residing in a shelter, whether overnight or transitional; those currently without normal, acceptable shelter arrangements and thus sleeping on the street, in doorways, in abandoned buildings, in cars, in subway or bus stations, in alleys, and so forth; those residing in a treatment center for the indigent who have lived at the facility for less than 90 days and who claim that they have no place to go, when released. (22)

This definition reflects accurately Sosin et al.'s concept of homelessness and allows researchers in other locations or at other times to develop procedures for studying a comparable population. The more complete and explicit the definition of the population from which a sample is drawn, the more precise the generalizations of the study's findings can be.

Evaluating the Sample's Generalizability

Once we have clearly defined the population from which a sample will be drawn, we need to determine the scope of the generalizations we wish to make from our sample; that is, can the findings from a sample be generalized to the population from which the sample was drawn? This is really the most basic question to ask about a sample, and social work research methods provide many tools with which to address it.

Sample generalizability depends on sample quality, which is determined by the amount of sampling error. Sampling error is the difference between the characteristics of a sample and the characteristics of the population from which the sample was selected. The larger the sampling error, the less representative the sample—and thus the less generalizable are the study's findings. To assess sample quality when you are planning or evaluating a research study, ask yourself three questions:

1. From what population were the cases selected?
2. What sampling method was used to select cases from this population?

3. Do the cases that were selected—and thus studied—represent, in the aggregate, the population from which they were drawn?

But researchers often project their study's findings onto groups or populations much larger than, or simply different from, those they have actually studied. The population to which generalizations are made in this way is called a *target population*. A target population is a set of elements larger than, or different from, the population that was sampled and to which the researcher would like to generalize the study's findings. When we generalize a study's findings to a target population, for example, we must be somewhat speculative. We must carefully consider the validity of the claim that a study's findings can be applied to other groups, to other geographic areas, to other cultures, and to other times.

Assessing the Diversity of the Population

Sampling is unnecessary if all the units in the population are identical. Physicists don't need to select a representative sample of atomic particles to learn about basic physical processes. They can study a single atomic particle, since it is identical to every other particle of its type. Similarly, biologists don't need to sample a particular type of plant to determine whether a given chemical has a toxic effect on it. The idea is, "If you've seen one, you've seen 'em all."

What about people? Certainly all people are not identical (nor are other animals in many respects). Nonetheless, if we are studying physical or psychological processes that are *exactly the same* among all people, sampling is not needed to achieve generalizable findings. Psychologists and social psychologists often conduct experiments on college students to learn about processes that they think are identical across individuals. They believe that most people would have the same reactions as the college students if they were to experience the same experimental conditions. Field researchers who observe group processes in small communities sometimes make the same assumption.

There is a potential problem with this assumption, however: There is no way to know for sure if the processes being studied are identical across all people. In

fact, experiments can give different results depending on the type of people who are studied or the conditions for the experiment. Stanley Milgram's (1965) classic experiments on obedience to authority, among the most replicated (repeated) experiments in the history of social psychological research, illustrate this point very well. The Milgram experiments tested the willingness of male volunteers in New Haven, Connecticut, to comply with the instructions of an authority figure to give "electric shocks" to someone else, even when these shocks seemed to harm the person receiving them. In most cases, the volunteers complied. Milgram concluded that people are very obedient to authority.

Were these results generalizable to all men, to men in the United States, or to men in New Haven? Similar results were obtained in many replications of the Milgram experiments when the experimental conditions and subjects were similar to those studied by Milgram. Other studies, however, showed that some groups were less likely to react so obediently. Given certain conditions, such as another "subject" in the room who refused to administer the shocks, subjects were likely to resist authority.

So what do the experimental results tell us about how people will react to an authoritarian movement in the real world, when conditions are not so carefully controlled? In the real social world, people may be less likely to react obediently, as well. Other individuals may argue against obedience to a particular leader's commands, or people may see on TV the consequences of their actions. Alternatively, people may be even more obedient to authority than the experimental subjects as they get swept up in mobs or are captivated by ideological fervor. Milgram's research gives us insight into human behavior, but there's no guarantee that what he found with particular groups in particular conditions can be generalized to the larger population (or to any particular population) in different settings.

Generalizing the results of experiments and of participant observation is risky, because such types of research studies often involve a small number of people who don't represent any particular population. Researchers may put aside concerns about generalizability when they observe the social dynamics of specific clubs, college dorms, and the like or in a controlled experiment when they test the effect of, say, a violent movie on feelings for others. But we have to be cautious about generalizing the results of such studies.

The larger point is that social scientists rarely can skirt the problem of demonstrating the generalizability of their studies' findings. If a small sample has been studied in an experiment or field research project, the study should be replicated in different settings or, preferably, with a representative sample of the population to which generalizations are sought (see Figure 6.2). The social world and the people in it are just too diverse to be considered "identical units." Social psychological experiments and small field studies have produced good research studies, but they need to be replicated in other settings with other subjects to claim any generalizability. Even when we believe that we have uncovered basic social processes in a laboratory experiment or field observation, we should be very concerned with seeking confirmation in other samples and in other research studies.

In short, a representative sample "looks like" the population from which it was drawn in all respects that are potentially relevant to the study. Thus, the distribution of the characteristics among the elements of a representative sample is the same as the distribution of those characteristics among the total population from which the sample was drawn. As can be seen in Figure 6.2, in an unrepresented sample, some characteristics are overrepresented or underrepresented.

Considering a Census

In some circumstances, it may be feasible to skirt the issue of generalizability by conducting a *census*—studying the entire population of interest—rather than by drawing a sample from the population. This is what the federal government does every 10 years with the U.S. Census. Censuses may include studies of all the employees (or students) in small organizations, studies that compare

Figure 6.2
Representative and Unrepresentative Samples

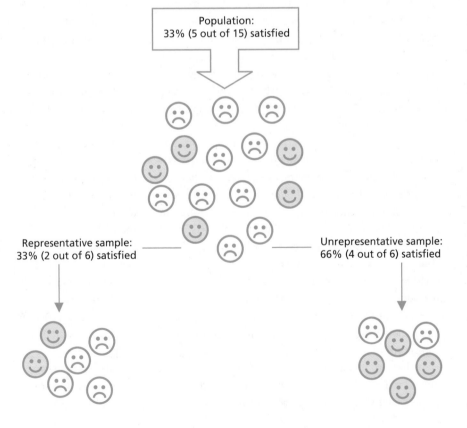

Population:
33% (5 out of 15) satisfied

Representative sample:
33% (2 out of 6) satisfied

Unrepresentative sample:
66% (4 out of 6) satisfied

all 50 states, and studies of the entire population of a particular type of organization in some area. However, in all of these instances, except for the U.S. Census, the population that is studied is relatively small.

The reason that social work researchers don't often attempt to collect data from all the members of some large population is simply that doing so would be too expensive and time-consuming (and they can do almost as well with a sample). Some do, however, conduct research studies with data from the U.S. Census, but it's the government that collects the data, and your tax dollars pay for the effort. For the 1990 census, for example, the Bureau of the Census needed more than 300,000 employees just to follow up on the households that did not return their census forms in the mail (Navarro, 1990). The entire 1990 census effort cost $2.6 billion (Holmes, 1994).

Even if the population of interest for a survey is a small town of 20,000 or students in a university of 10,000, researchers will have to sample. The costs of surveying "just" thousands of individuals exceeds by far the budgets for most research projects. In fact, even the U.S. Bureau of the Census cannot afford to have everyone answer all the questions that should be covered in the census. So it draws a sample. Every household must complete a short version of the census (it had 14 questions in 1990), and a sample consisting of one in six households must complete a long form (it had 45 additional questions in 1990).

Another costly fact is that it is hard to get people to complete a survey. Federal law requires all citizens to complete their census questionnaires, but other researchers have no such authority. So most researchers must make multiple efforts to increase the rate of response to their surveys.

Even the U.S. Bureau of the Census, with all its resources, is failing to count all the nation's households. The U.S. General Accounting Office estimates that almost 10 million people were not included in the 1990 census and 4.4 million were counted twice (Holmes, 1994). Difficulties with the 1990 census included (Gleick, 1990):

too many doors to knock on, and too many people living without doors, [and] a rate of non-

cooperation that exceeded the estimates of even the most severe critics. . . . Those overcounted . . . tend to be wealthier and more rural than those undercounted. In poor urban neighborhoods, field workers are often afraid to enter tenements and housing projects. (22–23, 26)

Because of these problems, many statisticians recommend that the U.S. Census survey a large sample of Americans rather than the complete population, and the Bureau of the Census has tested the feasibility of focusing follow-up efforts on a sample of those who do not return their census form in the mail or respond to phone interview attempts or door-to-door visits (Holmes, 1994). The basic idea is to invest more resources in increasing the rate of response of a representative sample of persons who do not respond easily, rather than spreading even the government's substantial resources thinly over the total respondent pool (Stout, 1997a). These statisticians believe it is "Better to hound 1 in 10 than 10 in 10" (Holmes, 1996, p. A18). Some argue that the U.S. Constitution requires a complete census, but a well-designed sample may still be preferable (Stout, 1997b, p. 31).

One final caution about census studies: Be sure you know exactly what population has been studied. James Wright and Eleanor Weber (1987) undertook a massive study of homeless persons as part of the national Health Care for the Homeless program (HCH). Teams that included doctors, nurses, and social workers filled out a contact form each time they delivered services to a homeless person in a variety of sites in 19 cities. After about a year, the resulting HCH database included data on about 34,035 clients obtained on 90,961 contact forms.

This database is a complete census of persons who receive care from HCH clinics. But the program operated in only 19 large U.S. cities, only 18 of the cities provided usable data, and the number of HCH clients appeared to include only between one-quarter and one-third of the total homeless population in these cities (Wright & Weber, 1987). Thus, the study was a census of the population of HCH clients in 18 cities, not at all a census of the entire homeless population in the nation. We might think it likely that the HCH population is similar to the general homeless population, but we won't know until we figure out how well the HCH population represents all those who are homeless.

SAMPLING METHODS

We now discuss the features of samples that make it more or less likely that they will represent the population from which they are selected. The most important distinction that needs to be made about samples is whether they are based on a probability sampling method or a nonprobability sampling method.

Probability sampling methods allow us to know in advance how likely it is that any element within a population will be selected for the sample. Nonprobability sampling methods do not let us know of this likelihood in advance.

Probability sampling methods rely on random, or chance, selection procedures. This is the same principle as flipping a coin to decide which one of two people "wins" and which one "loses." Heads and tails are equally likely to turn up in a coin toss, so both folks have an equal chance to win. That chance (a person's probability of being selected) is 1 out of 2, or .5.

Flipping a coin is a fair way to select one of two people because the selection process harbors no systematic bias. You might win or lose the coin toss, but you know that the outcome was due simply to chance, not to bias. For the same reason, a roll of a six-sided die is a fair way to choose one of six possible outcomes (the odds of selection are 1 out of 6, or .17). Dealing out a hand after shuffling a deck of cards is a fair way to allocate sets of cards in a card game (the odds of each person getting a particular outcome, such as a full house or a flush, are the same). Similarly, state lotteries use a random process to select winning numbers. Thus, the odds of winning a lottery, the probability of selection, are known, even though they are very much smaller (perhaps 1 out of 1 million) than the odds of winning a coin toss.

There is a natural tendency to confuse the concept of random sampling, in which cases are selected only on the basis of chance, with a haphazard method of sampling. On first impression, "leaving things up to chance" seems to imply not exerting any control over the sampling method. But to ensure that nothing but chance influences the selection of cases, the researcher must proceed very methodically, leaving nothing to chance except the selection of the cases themselves. The researcher must follow carefully controlled procedures if a purely random process is to occur. In fact, when reading about sampling methods, do not assume that a random sample was obtained just because the researcher used a random selection method at some point in the sampling process. Look for these two major particular problems:

1. Selecting a sample from an incomplete list of the total population from which the sample was selected
2. Failing to obtain an adequate response rate

If the sampling frame (the list from which the elements of the population were selected) is incomplete, a sample selected randomly from that list will not really be a random sample of the population from which it was drawn. You should always consider the adequacy of the sampling frame. Even for a simple population like a university's student body, the Registrar's list is likely to be at least a bit out of date at any given time. For example, some students will have dropped out, but their status will not yet be officially recorded. Although you may judge the amount of error introduced in this particular situation to be negligible, the problems are greatly compounded for larger populations. The sampling frame for a city, state, or nation, for example, is always likely to be incomplete because of constant migration into and out of the area. Even unavoidable omissions from the sampling frame can bias a sample against particular groups within a population.

A very inclusive sampling frame may still yield systematic bias if many sample members cannot be contacted or refuse to participate. Nonresponse is a major hazard in survey research because nonrespondents are likely to differ systematically from those who take the time to participate. You should not assume that findings from a randomly selected sample will be generalizable to the population from which the sample was selected if the rate of nonresponse is considerable (certainly not if it is much above 30%).

Probability Sampling Methods

Probability sampling methods are those in which the probability of an element's being selected is known in advance. These methods randomly select elements and therefore have no systematic bias; nothing but chance determines which elements are included in the sample. This feature of probability samples makes them much more desirable than nonprobability samples when the goal of a research study is to generalize its findings to a larger population.

Even though a random sample has no systematic bias, it will certainly have some sampling error due to chance. The probability of selecting a head is .5 in a single toss of a coin and in 20, 30, and however many tosses of a coin you like. But it is perfectly possible to toss a coin twice and get a head both times. The random "sample" of the two sides of the coin is selected in an unbiased fashion, but it still is unrepresentative. Imagine selecting randomly a sample of 10 people from a population comprising 50 men and 50 women. Just by chance, can't you imagine finding that these 10 people include 7 women and only 3 men? Fortunately, we can determine mathematically the likely degree of sampling error in an estimate based on a random sample, assuming that the sample's randomness has not been destroyed by a high rate of nonresponse or by poor control over the selection process.

In general, both the size of the sample and the homogeneity (sameness) of the population from which the sample was drawn affect the degree of error due to chance, the proportion of the population that the sample does not represent. To elaborate:

- The larger the sample, the more confidence we can have in the sample's representativeness. If we randomly pick 5 people to represent the entire population of our city, for example, our sample is unlikely to be very representative of our city's entire population in terms of age, gender, race, attitudes, and so on. But if we randomly pick 100 people, the odds of having a representative sample of our city's entire population are much better; with a random sample of 1,000, the odds become very good indeed.

- The more homogeneous the population, the more confidence we can have in the representativeness of a sample of any particular size. Let's say we plan to draw samples of 50 families from each of two communities to estimate "average family income." One community is very diverse, with family incomes varying from $12,000 to $85,000. In the other, more homogeneous community, family incomes are concentrated in a narrow range, from $41,000 to $64,000. The estimate of average family income based on the sample from the homogeneous community is more likely to be representative than is the estimate based on the sample from the more heterogeneous community. With less variation to represent, fewer cases are needed to represent the homogeneous community.

- The fraction of the total population that a sample contains does not affect the sample's representativeness, unless that fraction is large. We can regard any sampling fraction under 2% with about the same degree of confidence (Sudman, 1976). In fact, sample representativeness is not likely to increase much until the sampling fraction is quite a bit higher. Other things being equal, a sample of *1,000* from a population of 1 million (with a sampling fraction of 0.001, or 0.1%) is much better than a sample of 100 from a population of *10,000* (although the sampling fraction is 0.01, or 1%, which is 10 times higher). The size of a sample is what makes representativeness more likely, not the proportion of the whole that the sample represents.

Polls to predict presidential election outcomes illustrate both the value of random sampling and the problems that it cannot overcome. In most presidential elections, pollsters have predicted accurately the outcomes of the actual final vote by using random sampling and, these days, phone interviewing to learn whom likely voters intend to vote for. Table 6.1 shows how close these sample-based predictions have been in the past. The big exception, however, was the 1980

TABLE 6.1

Election Outcomes: Predicted[1] and Actual

Winner	Year	Polls	Results
Kennedy	1960	49%	50%
Johnson	1964	64%	61%
Nixon	1968[2]	44%	43%
Nixon	1972	59%	61%
Carter	1976	49%	50%
Reagan	1980[2]	42%	51%
Reagan	1984	57%	59%
Bush	1988	50%	53%
Clinton	1992[2]	41%	43%[3]
Clinton	1996[2]	52%[4]	46%[5]
Bush, G. W.	2000[2]	48%	50%
Bush, G. W.	2004[2]	49%	51%

[1] Polls one week prior to election.
[2] There was also a third-party candidate.
[3] Outcome from *Academic American Encyclopedia,* online version.
[4] Source of 1996 poll data: Gallup poll (http://www.gallup.com/poli/data/96prelec.html).
[5] Outcome from Mediacity.com Web pages E6, 8/30/97.
Source: 1960–1992 data, Gallup poll (Loth, 1992).

election, when a third-party candidate had an unpredicted effect. Otherwise, the small discrepancies between the votes predicted through random sampling and the actual votes can be attributed to random error.

But election polls have produced some major errors in prediction. The reasons for these errors illustrate some of the ways in which unintentional systematic bias can influence sample results. In 1936, for example, a *Literary Digest* poll predicted that Alfred M. Landon would defeat President Franklin D. Roosevelt in a landslide, but instead Roosevelt took 63 percent of the popular vote. The problem? The *Digest* mailed out 10 million mock ballots to people listed in telephone directories, automobile registration records, voter lists, and so on.

But in 1936, the middle of the Great Depression, only relatively wealthy people had phones and cars, and they were more likely to be Republican. Furthermore, only 2,376,523 completed ballots were returned, and a response rate of only 24% leaves much room for error. Of course, this poll was not designed as a random sample, so the appearance of systematic bias is not surprising. Unlike the *Literary Digest* poll, George Gallup was able to predict the 1936 election results accurately with a randomly selected sample of just 3,000 (Bainbridge, 1989).

In 1948, pollsters mistakenly predicted that Thomas E. Dewey would beat Harry S. Truman. They relied on the random sampling method that Gallup had used successfully since 1934. The problem? Pollsters stopped collecting data several weeks before the election, and in those weeks many people changed their minds (Kenney, 1987). So the sample was systematically biased by underrepresenting shifts in voter sentiment just before the election.

The year 1980 was the only year in the preceding 32 that pollsters had the wrong prediction in the week prior to the election. With Jimmy Carter ahead of Ronald Reagan in the polls by 45% to 42%, Gallup predicted a race too close to call. The outcome: Reagan 51%, Carter 42%. The problem? A large bloc of undecided voters, an unusually late debate with a strong performance by Reagan, and the failure of many pollsters to call back voters whom interviewers had failed to reach on the first try (these harder-to-reach voters were more likely to be Republican-leaning) (Dolnick, 1984; Loth, 1992). In this case, the sample was systematically biased against voters who were harder to reach and those who were influenced by the final presidential debate. The presence in the sample of many undecided voters was apparently an accurate representation of sentiment in the general population, so the problem would not be considered "sample bias." It did, however, make measuring voting preferences all the more difficult.

Because they do not disproportionately exclude or include particular groups within the population, random samples that are successfully implemented avoid systematic bias. Random error can still be considerable, however, and different types of random samples vary in their ability to minimize it. The four most common methods for drawing random samples are (1) simple random sampling, (2) systematic random sampling, (3) stratified random sampling, and (4) cluster random sampling.

Simple Random Sampling

Simple random sampling requires some procedure that generates numbers or otherwise identifies cases strictly on the basis of chance. As you know, flipping a coin and rolling a die both can be used to identify cases strictly on the basis of chance. These procedures, however, are not very efficient tools for drawing samples. A random numbers table simplifies the process considerably. The researcher numbers all the elements in the sampling frame (the population) and then uses a systematic procedure for picking corresponding numbers from the random numbers table. Alternatively, a researcher may use a lottery procedure. Each case number is written on a small card. Then the cards are mixed up and a sample is selected from the cards.

When a large sample must be generated, these procedures are very cumbersome. Fortunately, a computer program can easily generate a random sample of any size. The researcher must first number all the elements to be sampled (the sampling frame) and then run the computer program to generate a random selection of the numbers within the desired range. The elements represented by these numbers are the sample.

Organizations that conduct phone surveys often draw random samples with another automated procedure, called random digit dialing. A machine dials random numbers within the phone prefixes corresponding to the area in which the survey is to be conducted. Random digit dialing is particularly useful when a sampling frame is not available. The researcher simply replaces any inappropriate telephone numbers (those that are no longer in service or that are for businesses, for example) with the next randomly generated phone number.

The probability of selection in a true simple random sample is equal for each element. If a sample of 500 is selected from a population of 17,000 (that is, a sampling frame of 17,000), then the probability of selection for each element is 500/17,000, or .03. Every element has an equal chance of being selected, just like the odds in a toss of a coin (1/2) or a roll of a die (1/6).

Simple random sampling can be done either with or without replacement sampling. In replacement sampling, each element is returned to the sampling frame after it is selected so that it may be sampled again. In sampling without replacement, each element selected for the sample is then excluded from the sampling frame. In practice, it makes no difference whether sampled elements are replaced after selection, as long as the population is large and the sample is to contain only a small fraction of the population.

In a study involving simple random sampling, for example, Bruce Link and his associates (1996) used random digit dialing to contact adult household members in the continental United States for an investigation of public attitudes and beliefs about homeless people. Sixty-three percent of the potential interviewees responded. The sample actually obtained was not exactly comparable to the population from which his sample was drawn: Compared to U.S. Census figures, his sample overrepresented women, people ages 25 to 54, married people, and those with more than a high school education. It also underrepresented Latinos.

How does this sample strike you? Let's assess sample quality using the questions posed earlier in the chapter:

1. From what population were the cases selected? There is a clearly defined population: the adult residents of the continental United States (who live in households with phones).
2. What method was used to select cases from this population? The case selection method is a random selection procedure, and there are no systematic biases in the sampling.
3. Do the cases that were studied represent, in the aggregate, the population from which they were selected? The findings are very likely to represent the population sampled, because there were no biases in the sampling and a very large number of cases was selected. However, 37% of those selected for interviews could not be contacted or chose not to respond. This rate of nonresponse seems to create a small bias in the sample for several characteristics.

We also must consider the issue of cross-population generalizability: Do findings from this sample have implications for any larger group beyond the population from which the sample was drawn? Because a representative sample of the entire U.S. adult population was drawn, this question has to do with cross-national generalizations. Link and his colleagues don't make any such generalizations. There's no telling what might occur in other countries with different histories of homelessness and different social policies.

Systematic Random Sampling

Systematic random sampling is a variant of simple random sampling. The first element is selected randomly from a list or from sequential files, and then every nth element is selected. This is a convenient method for drawing a random sample when the population elements are arranged sequentially. It is particularly efficient when the elements are not actually printed (that is, there is no sampling frame) but instead are represented by folders in filing cabinets. For example, at a homeless shelter in Boston, a colleague and I drew a systematic random sample of intake records (Garrett & Schutt, 1990).

Systematic random sampling requires three steps:

Step 1.   The total number of cases in the population is divided by the number of cases required for the sample. This division yields the sampling interval, the number of cases from one sampled case to another. If 50 cases are to be selected out of 1,000, for example, the sampling interval is 20 (1000/50); every 20th case is selected.

Step 2.   A number from 1 to 20 (or whatever the sampling interval is) is selected randomly. This number identifies the first case to be sampled, counting from the first case on the list or in the files.

Step 3.   After the first case is selected, every nth case is selected for the sample, where n is the sampling interval. If the sampling interval is not a whole number, the size of the sampling interval is varied systematically to yield the proper number of cases for the sample. For example, if the sampling interval is 30.5, the sampling interval alternates between 30 and 31.

In almost all sampling situations, systematic random sampling yields what is essentially a simple random sample. The exception is a situation in which the sequence of elements is affected by periodicity—that is, the sequence varies in some regular, periodic pattern. For example, the houses in a new development with the same number of houses on each block (eight, for example) may be listed by block, starting with the house in the northwest corner of each block and continuing clockwise. If the sampling interval is 8, the same as the periodic pattern, all the cases selected will be in the same position (see Figure 6.3). But in reality, periodicity and the sampling interval are rarely the same.

Stratified Random Sampling

Although all probability sampling methods use random sampling, some add additional steps to the sampling process in order to make sampling more efficient or easier. A particular sample is more efficient than another when it is easier to obtain without sacrificing confidence that its sample statistics are representative of the population from which it was drawn. Samples are easier to collect when they require less time, less money, and less prior information.

Stratified random sampling uses information known about the total population prior to sampling to make the sampling process more efficient. First, all elements in the population (that is, in the sampling frame) are distinguished according to their value on some relevant characteristic. That characteristic forms the sampling strata. Next, elements are sampled randomly from within these strata. For example, race may be the basis for distinguishing individuals in some population of interest. Within each racial category, individuals are then sampled randomly.

Why is this method more efficient than drawing a simple random sample? Imagine that you plan to draw a sample of 500 from an ethnically diverse neighborhood. The neighborhood's population is as follows:

black	15%
Hispanic	10%
Asian	5%
white	70%

If you drew a simple random sample, you might end up with disproportionate percentages (or numbers) for each group. But if you created sampling strata based

If the sampling interval is 8 for a study in this neighborhood, every element of the sample will be a house on the northwest corner—and thus the sample will be biased.

Figure 6.3
The Effect of Periodicity on Systematic Random Sampling

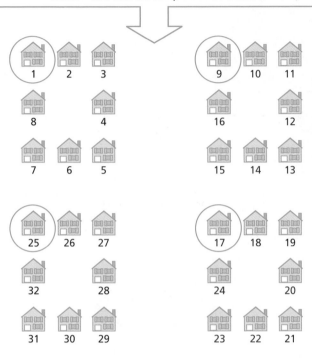

on race and ethnicity, you could randomly select cases from each stratum:

blacks	(15% of the sample)	75 cases selected	(500×.15)
Hispanics	(10% of the sample)	50 cases selected	(500×.10)
Asians	(5% of the sample)	25 cases selected	(500×.05)
whites	(70% of the sample)	350 cases selected	(500×.70)

By using proportionate stratified sampling, you would eliminate any possibility of error in the sample's distribution of ethnicity. Each stratum would be represented exactly in proportion to its size in the population from which the sample was drawn (see Figure 6.4).

In disproportionate stratified sampling, the proportion of each stratum that is included in the sample is intentionally varied from what it is in the population. In the case of the sample stratified by ethnicity, you might select equal numbers of cases from each racial or ethnic group:

125 blacks	(25% of the sample)
125 Hispanics	(25% of the sample)
125 Asians	(25% of the sample)
125 whites	(25% of the sample)

In this type of sample, the probability of selection of every case is known but unequal between strata. You know what the proportions are in the population, and so you can easily adjust your combined sample statistics to reflect these true proportions. For instance, if you want to combine the ethnic groups and estimate the average income of the total population, you have to "weight" each case in the sample. The weight is a number you multiply by the value of each case based on the stratum it is in. For example, you would multiply the incomes of all:

blacks in the sample by 0.6	(75/125)
Hispanics in the sample by 0.4	(50/125)
Asians in the sample by 0.2	(25/125)
whites in the sample by 2.8	(350/125)

Weighting in this way reduces the influence of the oversampled strata and increases the influence of the

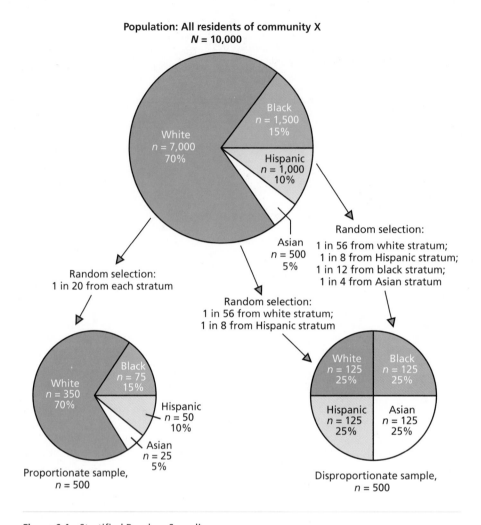

Figure 6.4   Stratified Random Sampling

undersampled strata to just what they would have been if pure probability sampling had been used.

Why would anyone select a sample that is so unrepresentative in the first place? The most common reason is to ensure that cases from smaller strata are included in the sample in sufficient numbers to allow separate statistical estimates and to facilitate comparisons between strata. Remember that one of the determinants of a sample's quality is its size. The same is true for subgroups within samples. If a key concern in a research project is to describe and compare the incomes of people from different racial and ethnic groups, then it is important that the researchers base the average in-

come of each group on enough cases to ensure a valid representation. If few members of a particular minority group are in the population, they need to be oversampled. Such disproportionate sampling may also result in a more efficient sampling design if the costs of data collection differ markedly between strata or if the variability (heterogeneity) of the strata differs.

Cluster Random Sampling

Stratified sampling requires more information than usual prior to sampling (about the size of strata in the population); cluster sampling, on the other hand, requires less prior information. Specifically, cluster sampling can be useful when a sampling frame is not available, as often is the case for large populations spread out across wide geographic areas or among many different organizations.

A cluster is a naturally occurring mixed aggregate of elements of the population, with each element appearing in one and only one cluster. Schools could serve as clusters for sampling students, blocks could serve as clusters for sampling city residents, counties could serve as clusters for sampling the general population, and businesses could serve as clusters for sampling employees.

Drawing a cluster sample is at least a two-stage procedure. First, the researcher draws a random sample of clusters. A list of clusters should be much easier to obtain than a list of all the individuals in each cluster in the population. Next, the researcher draws a random sample of elements within each selected cluster. Because only a fraction of the total clusters are involved, obtaining the sampling frame at this stage should be much easier.

In a cluster sample of city residents, for example, blocks could be the first-stage clusters. A research assistant could walk around each selected block and record the addresses of all occupied dwelling units. Or, in a cluster sample of students, a researcher could contact the schools selected in the first stage and make arrangements with the Registrar to obtain lists of students at each school. Cluster samples often involve multiple stages (see Figure 6.5).

How many clusters and how many individuals within clusters should be selected? As a general rule,

cases in the sample will be closer to the true population value if the researcher maximizes the number of clusters selected and minimizes the number of individuals within each cluster. Unfortunately, this strategy also maximizes the cost of obtaining the sample. The more clusters selected, the higher the travel costs. It also is important to take into account the homogeneity of the individuals within clusters—the more homogeneous the clusters, the fewer cases needed per cluster.

Cluster sampling is a very popular method among survey researchers, but it has one drawback: Sampling error is greater in a cluster sample than in a simple random sample. This error increases as the number of clusters decreases, and it decreases as the homogeneity of cases per cluster increases.

Many professionally designed surveys use multistage cluster samples or even combinations of cluster and stratified probability sampling methods. For example, Peter Rossi (1989) drew a disproportionate stratified cluster sample of shelter users for his Chicago study (see Table 6.2). The shelter sample was stratified by size, with smaller shelters having a smaller likelihood of selection than larger shelters. In fact, the larger shelters were all selected; they had a probability of selection of 1.0. Within the selected shelters, shelter users were then sampled using a systematic random selection procedure (except in the small shelters, in which all persons were interviewed). Homeless persons living on the streets were also sampled randomly. In the first stage, city blocks were classified in strata on the basis of the likely concentration of homeless persons (estimated by several knowledgeable groups). Blocks were then picked randomly

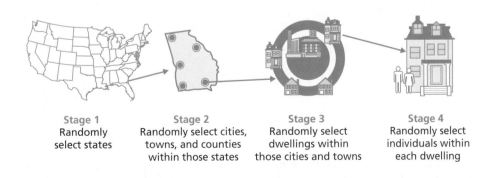

| Stage 1 | Stage 2 | Stage 3 | Stage 4 |
| Randomly select states | Randomly select cities, towns, and counties within those states | Randomly select dwellings within those cities and towns | Randomly select individuals within each dwelling |

Figure 6.5 Cluster Sampling

within these strata and, on the survey night between 1 a.m. and 6 a.m., teams of interviewers screened all people found outside on that block for their homeless status. Persons identified as homeless were then interviewed (and given $5 for their time). The rate of response for two different samples (fall and winter) in the shelters and on the streets was between 73% and 83%.

How would we evaluate the Chicago homeless sample (Table 6.2), using the sample evaluation questions?

1. From what population were the cases selected? The population was clearly defined for each cluster.
2. What method was used to select cases from this population? The random selection method was carefully described.
3. Do the cases that were studied represent, in the aggregate, the population from which they were selected? The unbiased selection procedures make us reasonably confident in the representativeness of the sample, although we know little about the non-respondents and therefore may justifiably worry that some types of homeless persons were missed.

Cross-population generalization seems to be reasonable with this sample, since it seems likely that the findings reflect general processes involving homeless persons. Rossi clearly thought so, because his book's title referred to homelessness in America, not just in Chicago.

Nonprobability Sampling Methods

Four nonprobability sampling methods are used with some frequency: (1) availability sampling, (2) quota sampling, (3) purposive sampling, and (4) snowball sampling. Because they do not use random selection procedures, we cannot expect samples selected with any of these methods to yield representative samples for the populations from which they were drawn. Nonetheless, these methods may be useful when random sampling is not possible, for research questions that do not concern large populations, or for qualitative research studies.

Availability Sampling

Elements are selected for availability sampling because they're available and/or easy to find. Thus, this sampling method is also known as a haphazard, accidental, or convenience sample. News reporters often use person-on-the-street interviews—availability samples—to

---

TABLE 6.2

Chicago Shelter Universe and Shelter Samples, Fall and Winter Surveys

	Fall	Winter
A. Shelter Universe and Samples		
Eligible shelters in universe	28	45
Universe bed capacities	1,573	2,001
Shelters drawn in sample	22	27

B. Details of Winter Shelter Sample

Shelter Size Classification	Number in Universe	Number in Sample	Occupant Sampling Ratio
Large (34 or more beds)	17	17	0.25
Medium (18–33 beds)	12	6	0.50
Small (under 18 beds)	16	4	1.00

Note: Shelters were drawn with probabilities proportionate to size, with residents sampled disproportionately within shelters to form a self-weighting sample. Sampling ratios for the phase two samples are given in Panel B: Details of Winter Shelter Sample.
Source: Rossi, 1989, p. 225.

inject color into a news story and to show what ordinary people think.

An availability sample is often appropriate in social work research, for example, when a field researcher is exploring a new setting and is trying to get some sense of prevailing attitudes, or when a survey researcher conducts a preliminary test of a new set of questions. And there are many ways to select elements for an availability sample: standing on street corners and talking to whoever walks by; asking questions of employees who come to pick up their paychecks at a personnel office and who have time to talk to a researcher; surveying merchants who happen to be at work when the researcher is looking for research participants. For example, when Philippe Bourgois and his colleagues (1997) studied homeless heroin addicts in San Francisco, they immersed themselves in a community of addicts living in a public park. These addicts became their availability sample.

But now I'd like you to answer the three sample evaluation questions with person-on-the-street interviews of the homeless in mind. If your answers are something like "The population was unknown," "The method for selecting cases was haphazard," and "The cases studied do not represent the population," you're right! There is no clearly definable population from which the respondents were drawn, and no systematic technique was used to select the respondents. There certainly is not much likelihood that the interviewees represent the distribution of sentiment among homeless persons in the Boston area or of welfare mothers or of impoverished rural migrants to Moscow or of whatever we imagine the relevant population is. Perhaps person-on-the-street comments to news reporters do suggest something about what homeless persons think. Or maybe they don't; we can't really be sure.

But let's give reporters their due: If they just want to have a few quotes to make their story more appealing, nothing is wrong with their sampling method. However, their approach gives us no basis for thinking that we have an overview of community sentiment. The people who happen to be available in any situation are unlikely to be just like those who are unavailable. We shouldn't kid ourselves into thinking that what we learn can be generalized with any confidence to a larger population of concern.

Availability sampling often masquerades as a more rigorous form of research. Popular magazines periodically survey their readers by printing a questionnaire for readers to fill out and mail in. A follow-up article then appears in the magazine under a title like "What You Think About Intimacy in Marriage." If the magazine's circulation is large, a large sample can be achieved in this way. The problem is that usually only a tiny fraction of readers return the questionnaire, and these respondents are probably unlike other readers who did not have the interest or time to participate. So the survey is based on an availability sample. Even though the follow-up article may be interesting, we have no basis for thinking that the results describe the readership as a whole—much less the population at large.

Quota Sampling

Quota sampling is intended to overcome the most obvious flaw of availability sampling—that the sample will just consist of whomever or whatever is available, without any concern for its similarity to the population of interest. The distinguishing feature of a quota sample is that quotas are set to ensure that the sample represents certain characteristics in proportion to their prevalence in the population from which it is to be drawn.

Suppose, for example, that you wish to sample adult residents of a town to ascertain their support for a tax increase to improve the town's schools. You know from the town's annual report what the proportions of town residents are in terms of gender, race, age, and number of children per family. You think that each of these characteristics might influence support for new school taxes, so you want to be sure that the sample includes men, women, whites, blacks, Hispanics, Asians, older people, younger people, big families, small families, and childless families in proportion to their numbers in the town's population.

This is where quotas come in. Let's say that the town is composed of:

48% men
52% women

60% white
15% black

10% Hispanic

15% Asian

These percentages and the percentages that correspond to the other characteristics become the quotas for the sample. If you plan to include a total of 500 residents in your sample:

240 must be men   (48% of 500)
260 must be women   (52% of 500)

300 must be white   (60% of 500)
75 must be black   (15% of 500)
50 must be Hispanic   (10% of 500)
75 must be Asian   (15% of 500)

You may even set more refined quotas, such as certain numbers of white women, white men, and Asian men.

With the quota list in hand, you (or your research staff) can now go out into the community looking for the right number of people in each quota category. You may go door to door, go bar to bar, or just stand on a street corner until you have surveyed 240 men, 260 women, and so on.

Some features of quota sampling may appear in what are primarily availability sampling strategies. For instance, Doug Timmer and his colleagues (1993) interviewed homeless persons in several cities and other locations for their book on the sources of homelessness. Persons who were available were interviewed, but the researchers paid some attention to generating a diverse sample. They interviewed 20 homeless men who lived on the streets without shelter and 20 mothers who were found in family shelters. About half of those the researchers selected in the street sample were black, and about half were white. Although the researchers did not use quotas to try to match the distribution of characteristics among the total homeless population, their informal quotas helped to ensure some diversity in key characteristics.

Even when we know that a quota sample is representative of the particular characteristics for which quotas have been set, we have no way of knowing whether the sample is representative in terms of any other characteristics. In Figure 6.6, for example, quotas have been set for gender only. Under the circumstances, it's no surprise that the sample is representative

Population
50% male, 50% female
70% white, 30% black

Quota sample
50% male, 50% female

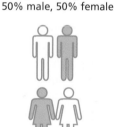

Representative of gender distribution
in population, not representative of
race distribution.

Figure 6.6 Quota Sampling

of the population only in terms of gender, not in terms of race. Interviewers are only human; they may avoid potential respondents with menacing dogs in the front yard, or they could seek out respondents who are physically attractive or who look like they'd be easy to interview. Realistically, researchers can set quotas for only a small fraction of the characteristics relevant to a study, so a quota sample is really not so much better than an availability sample (although following careful, consistent procedures for selecting cases within the quota limits always helps).

This last point leads to another limitation of quota sampling: You must know the characteristics of the entire sample to set the right quotas. In most cases, researchers know what the population looks like in terms of no more than a few of the characteristics relevant to their concerns. And in some cases they have no such information on the entire population.

Purposive Sampling

In purposive sampling, each sample element is selected for a purpose because of the unique position of the sample elements. Purposive sampling may involve studying the entire population of some limited group (directors of shelters for homeless adults) or a subset of a population (mid-level managers with a reputation for efficiency). Or a purposive sample may be a "key informant survey," which targets individuals who are particularly knowledgeable about the issues under investigation.

Herbert Rubin and Irene Rubin (1995) suggest three guidelines for selecting informants when designing any purposive sampling strategy. Informants should be:

- Knowledgeable about the cultural arena or situation or experience being studied
- Willing to talk
- Represent(ative of) the range of points of view

In addition, they suggest continuing to select interviewees until you can pass two tests:

- Completeness. What you hear provides an overall sense of the meaning of a concept, theme, or process.

- Saturation. You gain confidence that you are learning little that is new from subsequent interview(s).

Adhering to these guidelines will help to ensure that a purposive sample adequately represents the setting or issues studied.

Of course, purposive sampling does not produce a sample that represents some larger population, but it can be exactly what is needed in a case study of an organization, a community, or some other clearly defined and relatively limited group. In an intensive organizational case study, for example, a purposive sample of organizational leaders might be complemented with a probability sample of organizational members. Before designing her probability samples of hospital patients and homeless persons, Dee Roth (1990) interviewed a purposive sample of 164 key informants from organizations that had contact with homeless people in each county she studied.

Snowball Sampling

For snowball sampling, you identify one member of the population and speak to him or her, then ask that person to identify others in the population and speak to them, then ask them to identify others, and so on. The sample thus "snowballs" in size. This technique is useful for hard-to-reach or hard-to-identify, interconnected populations (at least some members of the population know each other), such as drug dealers, prostitutes, practicing criminals, participants in Alcoholics Anonymous groups, gang leaders, and informal organizational leaders. It also may be used for charting the relationships among members of some group (a sociometric study), for exploring the population of interest prior to developing a formal sampling plan, and for developing what becomes a census of informal leaders of small organizations or communities. However, researchers who use snowball sampling normally cannot be confident that their samples represent the total populations of interest, so their generalizations must be tentative.

Rob Rosenthal (1994) used snowball sampling to study homeless persons living in Santa Barbara, California:

I began this process by attending a meeting of homeless people I had heard about through my housing advocate contacts . . . . One homeless woman . . . invited me to . . . where she promised to introduce me around. Thus a process of snowballing began. I gained entree to a group through people I knew, came to know others, and through them I gained entree to new circles. (178, 180)

One problem with this technique is that the initial contacts may shape the entire sample and foreclose access to some members of the population of interest (Rosenthal, 1994):

Sat around with [my contact] at the Tree. Other people come by, are friendly, but some regulars, especially the tougher men, don't sit with her. Am I making a mistake by tying myself too closely to her? She lectures them a lot. (181)

More systematic versions of snowball sampling can reduce this potential for bias. The most sophisticated, termed "respondent-driven sampling," gives financial incentives to respondents to recruit peers (Heckathorn, 1997). Limitations on the number of incentives that anyone respondent can receive increase the sample's diversity. Targeted incentives can steer the sample to include specific subgroups. When the sampling is repeated through several waves, with new respondents bringing in more peers, the composition of the sample converges on a more representative mix of characteristics. Figure 6.7 shows how the sample spreads out through successive recruitment waves to an increasingly diverse pool (Heckathorn, 1997).

LESSONS ABOUT SAMPLE QUALITY

Some lessons are implicit in the evaluations of the samples in this chapter:

- We can't evaluate the quality of a sample if we don't know what population it is supposed to represent. If the population is unspecified because the researchers were never clear about just what population they were trying to sample, then we can safely conclude that the sample itself is no good.

- We can't evaluate the quality of a sample if we don't know just how cases in the sample were selected from the population. If the method was specified, we then need to know whether cases were selected in a systematic fashion and on the basis of chance. In any case, we know that a haphazard method of sampling (as in person-on-the-street interviews) undermines the generalizability of the study's findings.

- Sample quality is determined by the sample actually obtained, not just by the sampling method itself. If many of the people selected for our sample are nonrespondents or people (or other entities) who do not participate in the study although they have been selected for the sample, the quality of our sample is undermined—even if we chose the sample in the best possible way.

- We need to be aware that even researchers who obtain very good samples may talk about the implications of their findings for some other groups that are larger than or just different from the population they actually sampled. For example, findings from a representative sample of students in one university often are discussed as if they tell us about university students in general. And maybe they do; we just don't know.

DETERMINING SAMPLE SIZE

Now that you know that more confidence can be placed in the generalizability of statistics from larger samples, you may be eager to work with random samples that are as large as possible. Unfortunately, researchers often cannot afford to sample a very large number of cases. They therefore try to determine during the design phase of their studies how large a sample they must have to achieve their purposes. They have to consider the degree of confidence desired, the homogeneity of the population, the complexity of the analysis they plan, and the expected strength of the relationships they will measure:

- The less sampling error desired, the larger the sample size must be.

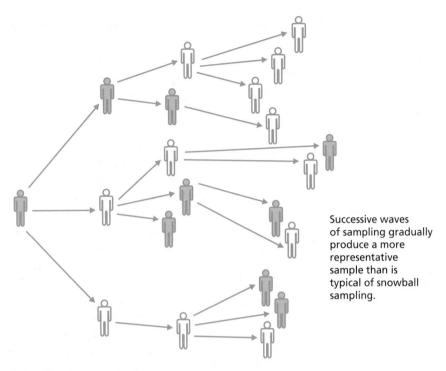

Successive waves of sampling gradually produce a more representative sample than is typical of snowball sampling.

Instructions to respondents:
"We'll pay you $5 each for up to three names, but only one of those names can be somebody from your own town. The others have to be from somewhere else."

Figure 6.7   Respondent-Driven Sampling

- Samples of more homogeneous populations can be smaller than samples of more diverse populations. Stratified sampling uses prior information on the population to create more homogeneous population strata from which the sample can be selected, so the sample can be smaller than if simple random sampling were used.
- If the only analysis planned for a survey sample is to describe the population in terms of a few variables, a smaller sample is required than if a more complex analysis involving sample subgroups is planned.
- When the researchers will be testing hypotheses and expect to find very strong relationships among the variables, they will need smaller samples to detect these relationships than if they expect weaker relationships.

Researchers can make more precise estimates of the sample size required through a method termed *statistical power analysis* (Kraemer & Thiemann, 1987). Statistical power analysis requires a good advance estimate of the strength of the hypothesized relationship in the population. In addition, the math is complicated, so it helps to have some background in mathematics or to be able to consult a statistician. For these reasons, many researchers do not conduct formal power analyses when deciding how many cases to sample.

You can obtain some general guidance about sample sizes from the current practices of social scientists. For professional studies of the national population in which only a simple description is desired, professional social science studies typically have used a sample size of between 1,000 and 1,500, with up to

2,500 being included if detailed analyses are planned. Studies of local or regional populations often sample only a few hundred people, in part because these studies lack sufficient funding to draw larger samples. Of course, the sampling error in these smaller studies is considerably larger than in a typical national study (Sudman, 1976).

SUMMARY

Sampling is a powerful tool for social work research. Probability sampling methods allow a researcher to use the laws of chance, or probability, to draw samples from which population parameters can be estimated with a high degree of confidence. A sample of just 1,000 or 1,500 individuals can be used to estimate reliably the characteristics of the population of a nation comprising millions of individuals.

But researchers do not come by representative samples easily. Well-designed samples require careful planning, some advance knowledge about the population to be sampled, and adherence to systematic selection procedures—all so that the selection procedures are not biased. And even after the sample data are collected, the researcher's ability to generalize from the sample's findings to the population from which it was drawn is not completely certain.

The alternatives to random, or probability-based, sampling methods are almost always much less palatable, even though they typically are much cheaper. Unless the researcher's method of selecting cases is likely to yield a sample that represents the population in which the researcher is interested, research findings will have to be carefully qualified. Unrepresentative samples may help researchers understand which aspects of a social phenomenon are important, but questions about the generalizability of this understanding are left unanswered.

Case-Level Designs

Margaret Williams
Richard M. Grinnell, Jr.
Yvonne A. Unrau

7

Basic Steps in the Research Process

You Are Here →

In the preceding chapter, we discussed how to select research participants for research studies. This chapter is a logical extension of the previous one in that we now look at the different ways of designing or setting up our studies in which research participants are included. On a basic level, a research design is essentially a plan for conducting the entire research study from beginning to end. All research plans—interpretive or positivistic—are formulated in order to answer the following basic questions:

- When, or over what period, should the research study be conducted?
- What variables need to be measured?
- How should the variables be measured?
- What other variables need to be accounted for or controlled?
- From whom should the data be collected?
- How should the data be collected?
- How should the data be analyzed?
- How should the results of the study be disseminated?

As you should know by now, these questions are highly interrelated and are directly related to the question we are trying to answer or the hypothesis we are testing. If you are exploring the concept of bereavement, for example, you will collect data from bereaved people and perhaps involved social workers, and you will need to measure variables related to bereavement, such as grief, anger, depression, and levels of coping. You might need to measure these variables over a period of months or years, and the way you measure them will suggest appropriate methods of how you will analyze your data. Decisions about how best to accomplish these steps depend on how much we already know about the bereavement process: that is, where your bereavement research questions fall on the knowledge level continuum as presented in Figure 1.10.

Over the years, researchers have developed a kind of shorthand, representing research designs in terms of letters and numbers, dividing them into categories, and giving them names. Let us now look at how this research shorthand is applied to research questions that can be loosely classified as case-level designs. They are also called *single-subject designs, single-case experimentations,* or *idiographic research*. They are used to fulfill the major purpose of social work practice: to improve the situation of a client system—*an* individual client, *a* couple, *a* family, *a* group, *an* organization, or *a* community. Any of these client configurations can be studied with a case-level design. In short, they are used to study *one* individual or *one* group intensively.

REQUIREMENTS OF CASE-LEVEL DESIGNS

Our discussion on the requirements of case-level designs has been adapted and modified from three sources: Grinnell and Williams (1990); Grinnell, Williams, and Tutty (1997); and Williams, Tutty, and Grinnell (1995). In order to carry out a single-case study, the client's problem must be identified, the desired objective to be achieved must be decided upon, the intervention that is most likely to eliminate the client's problem must be selected, the intervention must be implemented, and the client's progress must be continually monitored to see if the client's problem has been resolved, or at least reduced. If practitioners are careful to organize, measure, and record what they do, single-case studies will naturally take shape in the clients' files, and the results can be used to guide future interventive efforts. Only three things are required when doing a single-case study:

1. setting client objectives that are measurable
2. selecting valid and reliable outcome measures
3. graphically displaying the results of the outcome measures

Setting Measurable Client Objectives

One of the first tasks a worker does when initially seeing a client is to establish the purpose of why they are together. Why has the client approached the worker? Or, in many nonvoluntary situations, such as in probation and parole or child abuse situations, why has the worker approached the client? The two need to formulate objectives for their mutual working relationship. A specific, measurable, client-desired outcome objective is known as a *client target problem*. Client target

problems are feelings, knowledge levels, or behaviors that need to be changed.

Many times clients do not have just one target problem, they have many. They sometimes have a number of interrelated problems and, even if there is one that is more important than the rest, they may not know what it is. Nevertheless, they may be quite clear about the desired outcome of their involvement with social work services. They may want to "fix" their lives so that "Johnny listens when I ask him to do something," or "My partner pays more attention to me," or "I feel better about myself at work." Unfortunately, many clients express their desired target problems in vague, ambiguous terms, possibly because they themselves do not know exactly what they want to change; they only know that something should be different. If a worker can establish (with the guidance of the client) what should be changed, why it should be changed, how it should be changed, and to what degree it should be changed, the solution to the problem will not be far away.

Consider Heather, for example, who wants her partner, Ben, to pay more attention to her. Heather may mean sexual attention, in which case the couple's sexual relations may be the target problem. On the other hand, Heather may mean that she and Ben do not socialize enough with friends, or that Ben brings work home from the office too often, or has hobbies she does not share, or any of a host of things.

Establishing clearly what the desired change would look like is the first step in developing the target problem. Without this, the worker and client could wander around forever through the problem maze, never knowing what, if anything, needs to be solved. Desired change cannot occur if no one knows what change is desired. It is, therefore, very important that the target problem to be solved be precisely stated as early as possible in the client–social worker relationship.

Continuing with the example of Heather and Ben, and after a great deal of exploration, the worker agrees that Heather and Ben have many target problems to work on, such as improving their child discipline strategies, improving their budgeting skills, improving their communication skills, and many other issues that, when dealt with, can lead to a successful marriage. For now, however, they agree to work on one target problem of increasing the amount of time they spend together with friends. To do this, the worker, Heather, and Ben must conceptualize and operationalize the notion "increasing the amount of time they spend together with friends." As we know, a variable is conceptualized by defining it in a way that is relevant to the situation and operationalized in such a way that its indicators can be measured.

Heather may say that she wishes she and Ben could visit friends together more often. The target problem has now become a little more specific: It has narrowed from "increasing the amount of time they spend together with friends" to "Heather and Ben visiting friends more often." "Visiting friends more often with Ben," however, is still an ambiguous concept. It may mean once a month or every night, and the achievement of the target problem's solution cannot be known until the meaning of "more often" has been clarified.

If Heather agrees that she would be happy to visit friends with Ben once a week, the ambiguous objective may be restated as a specific, measurable objective—"to visit friends with Ben once a week." The social worker may discover later that *friends* is also an ambiguous term. Heather may have meant "her friends," while Ben may have meant "his friends," and the social worker may have imagined that the "friends" were mutual.

The disagreement about who is to be regarded as a friend may not become evident until the worker has monitored Heather and Ben's progress for a month or so and found that no improvement was occurring. In some cases, poor progress may be due to the selection of an inappropriate interventive strategy. In other cases, it may mean that the target problem itself is not as specific, complete, and clear as it should be. Before deciding that the interventive strategy needs to be changed, it is always necessary to clarify with the client exactly what it is that needs to be achieved.

Selecting Valid and Reliable Outcome Measures

A target problem cannot really be said to be measurable until it is decided how it will be operationalized, or measured. Can Heather and Ben, who wanted to visit friends more often, be trusted to report truthfully on whether the friends were visited? Suppose she says they were not visited and he says they were? Social workers must always be very conscious of what measurement methods are both available and feasible when formulating a target problem with a client. It may be quite possible for the social worker to telephone the friends and ask if they were visited; but, if the worker is not prepared to get involved with Heather's and Ben's friends, this measurement method will not be feasible. If this is the case, and if Heather and/or Ben cannot be trusted to report accurately and truthfully, there is little point in setting the target problem.

Heather and Ben's target problem can be easily observed and measured. However, quite often, a client's target problem involves feelings, attitudes, knowledge levels, or events that are known only to the client and cannot be easily observed and/or measured.

Consider Bob, a client who comes to a social worker because he is depressed. The worker's efforts may be simply to lessen Bob's target problem, depression, but how will the worker and/or Bob know when his depression has been alleviated or reduced? Perhaps he will say that he feels better, or his partner may say that Bob cries less, or the worker may note that Bob spends less time in therapy staring at his feet. All these are indicators that his depression is lessening, but they are not very valid and reliable indicators.

What is needed is a more "scientific" method of measuring depression. Fortunately, a number of paper-and-pencil standardized measuring instruments have been developed that can be filled out by the client in a relatively short period of time, can be easily scored, and can provide a fairly accurate picture of the client's condition. One such widely used instrument that measures depression is Hudson's General Contentment Scale (*GCS*). Since higher scores indicate higher levels of depression, and lower scores indicate lower levels of depression, the target problem in Bob's case would be to reduce his score on the *GCS* to a level at which he can adequately function (a score of 30 or lower).

People who are not depressed will still not score zero on the *GCS*. Everyone occasionally feels blue (Item 2) or downhearted (Item 10). There is a clinical cutting score that differentiates a clinically significant problem level from a nonclinically significant problem level, and it will often be this score that the client aims to achieve. If the target problem is "to reduce Bob's score on the *GCS* to or below the clinical cutting score of 30," the worker will know not only what the target problem is but also precisely how Bob's success is to be measured.

Usually, client success, sometimes referred to as *client outcome,* can be measured in a variety of ways. Bob's partner, Maria, for example, may be asked to record the frequency of his crying spells, and the target problem here may be to reduce the frequency of these spells to once a week or less. Again, it would be important to further operationalize the term *crying spell* so that Maria knows exactly what it is she has to measure. Perhaps "crying spell" would be operationally defined as 10 minutes or more of continuous crying, and a gap of at least 10 minutes without crying would define the difference between one "spell" and another.

There are now two independent and complementary indicators of Bob's level of depression: the *GCS* as rated by Bob, and the number of his 10-minute crying spells per day as rated by Maria. If future scores on both indicators display improvement (that is, they both go down), the worker can be reasonably certain that Bob's depression is lessening and the intervention is effective.

If the two indicators do not agree, the worker will need to find out why. Perhaps Bob wishes to appear more depressed than he really is, and this is an area that needs to be explored. Or perhaps Maria is not sufficiently concerned to keep an accurate recording of the number of Bob's 10-minute crying spells per day, and it may be Maria's attitude that has caused Bob's crying in the first place. Accurate measurements made over time can do more than reveal the degree of a client's improvement. They can cast light on the problem itself and suggest new avenues to be explored, possibly resulting in the utilization of different interventive strategies.

Be that as it may, a client's target problem cannot be dealt with until it has been expressed in specific measurable indicators. These indicators cannot be said to be measurable until it has been decided how they will be measured. Specification of the target problem will, therefore, often include mention of an instrument that will be used to measure it. It will also include who is to do the measuring, and under what circumstances.

It may be decided, for example, that Bob will rate himself on the *GCS* daily after dinner, or once a week on Saturday morning, or that Maria will make a daily record of all crying spells that occurred in the late afternoon after Bob returned home from work. The physical record itself is very important, both as an aid to memory and to track Bob's progress. In a single-case study, progress is always monitored by displaying the measurements made in the form of graphs.

Graphically Displaying Data

As we know from Chapter 5, the word *measurement* can be simply defined as the process of assigning a number or value to a variable. If the variable, or target problem, being considered is depression as measured by the *GCS*, and if Bob scores, say 33, then 33 is the number assigned to Bob's initial level of depression. The worker will try to reduce Bob's initial score of 33 to at least 30—the desired *minimum* score. The worker can then select and implement an intervention and ask Bob to complete the *GCS* again, say once a week, until the score of 30 has been reached. Bob's depression levels can be plotted (over a 12-week period) on a graph such as the ones displayed in this chapter.

CASE-LEVEL RESEARCH DESIGNS

Some research studies are conducted in order to study one individual, or case, some to study groups of people (including families, organizations, and communities), and some to study social artifacts (such things as birth practices or divorces). The individual, group, or artifact being studied is called the *unit of analysis*. If you are exploring the advantages and disadvantages of home birth, for example, you might be asking questions from women who have experienced home birth, but the thing you are studying—the *unit of analysis*—is the social artifact, home birth. Conversely, if you are a social work practitioner studying the impact of home birth on a particular client, the unit of analysis is the client or individual; if you are studying the impact on a

BOX 7.1

An In-Depth Look at Case-Level Designs

According to Bloom, Fischer, and Orme (2006), the advantages of case-level designs are as follows:

1. They can be built into every social worker's practice with each and every case/situation without disruption of practice.
2. They provide the tools for evaluating the effectiveness of our practice with each client, group, or system with which we work.
3. They focus on individual clients or systems. If there is any variation in effect from one client or system to another, case-level designs will be able to pick it up.
4. They provide a continuous record of changes in the target problem over the entire course of intervention, not just a pre- and posttest.
5. They are practice-based and practitioner-oriented. Case-level designs provide continuous assessment and outcome data to practitioners so that they can monitor progress and make changes in the nature of the intervention program if so indicated. Unlike traditional group designs and the intervention programs they are used to evaluate, which ordinarily cannot be changed once the study has begun, case-level designs are flexible; the worker can change the intervention and the design depending on the needs of the case.
6. They can be used to test hypotheses or ideas regarding the relationship between specific intervention procedures and client changes, ruling out some alternative explanations and allowing an inference regarding causality: Was the intervention program responsible for the change in the target problem?
7. They can be used to help the worker *assess* the case/situation, leading to selection of a more appropriate program of intervention by clarifying what seem to be the relevant factors involved in the problem.
8. They essentially are theory-free; that is, they can be applied to the practice of any practitioner regardless of the worker's theoretical orientation or approach to practice.
9. They are relatively easy to use and understand. They can be applied within the same time frame the social worker is currently using in seeing clients or others. In fact, use of case-level designs can actually enhance the worker's efficiency by saving time and energy in trying to record and evaluate the social worker's practice.
10. They avoid the problem of outside researchers coming into an agency and imposing a study on the social workers. Case-level designs are established and conducted by practitioners for their benefits and for the benefits of the client/systems.
11. They provide a model for demonstrating our accountability to ourselves, our clients and consumers, our funding sources, and our communities. Systematic, consistent use of case-level designs will allow practitioners, and agencies, to collect a body of data about the effectiveness of practice that provides more or less objective information about the success of our practice.

On the basis of the ongoing measurement of the dependent variable, referred to as the target behavior, the measurements that indicate its status or variability are represented graphically as the frequency of the target behavior over time. Repeated measures of the target behavior prior to the introduction of the intervention serve as a representation of its "normal trends," against which the intervention data can be compared. This phase, referred to as the *baseline*, serves as a control for the experimental phase. A change in the frequency of the behavior which is not consistent with the trends established during the baseline, and which is temporally associated with the systematic introduction of the intervention, strengthens the conclusion that there is a casual relationship between the target behavior change and the intervention.

Characteristics of Case-Level Designs

Case-level designs have several distinguishing characteristics. First, they may be used to evaluate the effects of an intervention on a single individual (the subject). Properties of the designs give validity to their use with a single individual who is able to serve both experimental and control functions.

Second, the designs can be used with both individuals and groups. Group data, however, are derived by combining the individual group members' data and using the mean or total frequency of behavior. The data are then analyzed as if they were representative of a single individual.

Third, they utilize repeated measures to establish trends and analyze change. Multiple data points provide detailed

(continued)

BOX 7.1 *(continued)*

data on how the intervention affects the target behavior over time. This level of information about individual or group behavior produces a fine-grained analysis. Fourth, they base analyses of behavior on comparisons of trends during interventions (experimental condition) with trends established prior to intervention (control or baseline condition). This method highlights changes in the individual's response over time and emphasizes variations in responding between different individuals.

Finally, case-level designs rely on feedback from ongoing data recording to determine when changes in the intervention should take place. The data indicate whether the frequency of the behavior has changed or remained stable in response to the intervention.

As open-ended, responsive approaches to experimental evaluation of intervention effects, case-level designs make it possible to conduct a study (practice or research) that is sensitive to the needs and constraints of applied social work settings. They allow for the generation of new knowledge and techniques while the study is in progress, resulting in a rapid feedback-adjustment-feedback cycle that provides the flexibility and responsiveness needed in social service agencies.

Target Behaviors

The primary emphasis in case-level designs is not on proof or disproof of hypotheses, as in group designs, but on the observations and analyses of the effects of interventions on specific target behaviors. As with group designs (see the following chapter), however, the selection and definition of target behaviors are critical steps in the research process.

Any measurable aspects of the problems social workers are investigating may be selected as target behaviors. Social workers in direct services may select as the dependent variable a problem behavior that has been identified as interfering with the client's functioning, such as parent-child fighting. An administrator of an agency may select a dependent variable that relates to a problem in service provision, such as hours of direct service provided, or a worker behavior such as attendance and completion of paperwork and charting. A social planner or community organizer may choose a target behavior relating to a problem such as utilization of community services. In each of these examples the goal is to alleviate the severity of the problem. The study conducted should evaluate the effectiveness of the interven-

tion in producing the desired change in the target behaviors.

Target behaviors can also be selected to evaluate the relationship between particular behaviors and specific environmental variables. The target behavior need not have been identified as a problem, and the goal may merely be to document that a relationship exists between the behavior and environmental variables. Environmental changes could influence the performance of a particular behavior so that, for example, the relationship between changes in laws or regulations and the number of persons seeking services or the types of services requested might be investigated. Or executive policy changes in response to funding availability could affect staff performance so that, for example, a program director would want to investigate the relationship between the change in policy and staff absenteeism, turnover, and amount of direct service provided.

Since it may not always be possible to measure all aspects of the desired change, the target behaviors selected must be representative of the changes that must occur to indicate successful accomplishment of the intervention goals. The target behavior must also be one that the worker, other cooperative persons (collaterals) in the environment, or the individual (subject) have opportunities to measure. Behaviors that are covert and leave no reliable evidence of having occurred, or that occur in places or at times when no one is available to record them, are not suitable as target behaviors unless the behavior leaves an observable product that can be recorded.

Operationalization of the Dependent Variables

The reliability of data in case-level designs is determined by the ability of two observers (raters) to obtain a high level of agreement on the occurrence or nonoccurrence of the target behavior. Demonstration of the reliability of data recording is basic to the analysis of single-subject designs and is necessary before conclusions can be drawn on the relationship between the intervention and the frequency of behavior. To produce reliable data the target behavior must be operationally defined in terms of its observable characteristics.

Unobservable or private events, such as thoughts or feelings, can be recorded by the individual, but these data cannot be considered reliable due to the inability of an independent observer to observe and record the target behavior. Measurement of observable manifestations of the

(continued)

BOX 7.1 *(continued)*

thoughts and feelings or products of the behavior, however, can produce reliable data. Examples are:

Private Event	Observable Manifestation
Fear	Avoidance of feared objects or places, such as refusing to enter an elevator or a house in which there is a dog.
Anxiety	Stammering, shaking, sweating, or failure to complete tasks.
Depression	Isolable behaviors, such as staying indoors, sleeping, low rate of verbalization.

The first step in developing an operational definition of a target behavior is to gather data about it, either by direct observations or by talking to those who have an opportunity to observe the behavior regularly. Characteristics of the target behavior that distinguish it from all other behaviors should be noted. For example, an administrator may want to study the effects of a policy change on employees' work behavior. Observation of the employees indicates two possibly interrelated problems:

1. Employees spend a high proportion of their time in non-work-related activities, such as personal phone calls, snack breaks, and talking with other employees. They spend little time in their offices alone, working at their desks.
2. Employees are failing to complete paperwork and charting according to defined standards and within expected time limits.

Following the gathering of information, an operational definition of the discrete characteristics of the behavior is developed, along with the specific rules for how the behavior will be recorded. This description, referred to as a *behavioral observation code*, must enable an independent observer to distinguish easily between the target behavior and other behaviors.

What to include in the definition of the target behavior may involve arbitrary decisions, so as much of the problem behavior as possible is recorded, while other behaviors are excluded. The worker should emphasize aspects of the dependent variable that appear to be most closely related to the solution of the problem. The administrator, for example, might develop the following code for work behavior:

1. Employees will be recorded as being "at work" when they are in their assigned offices, sitting on a desk

chair, and facing their desk, which has work-related materials on it. Work materials include charts, reports, note pads, phone messages, journals, or books. Employees can also be facing exposed work materials located on their shelves and in their file cabinets. They will not be recorded as working if other employees are in their offices.
2. Paperwork and charting will be recorded as complete if it is turned in by the assigned date and if the entries are complete according to the instructions in the *Clinical Records Procedures Manual.*

Notice the conscious decision to record only solitary, at-desk, work behavior. Clearly, the definition of work behavior does not include occurrences that necessitate consultation with another employee or completion of work outside the office. Although these aspects of work may be important to overall job functioning, this definition is appropriate if the administrator is primarily concerned with increasing solitary, in-office work behavior and completed paperwork. This operational definition of work behavior avoids the difficulty of distinguishing between work-related and non-work-related conversations among employees. Thus, the likelihood that independent observers would obtain a high level of agreement (reliability) on the occurrence of work and nonwork behavior is increased.

Some clients' problems are initially presented conceptually, so their behaviors are interpreted rather than defined. To measure the problem and evaluate the effects of an intervention, an operational definition specifying the behaviors to be observed must be developed. For example, a client is referred with the problem of having a poor self-concept. Observation and data gathered from the client or collaterals can identify behaviors the client exhibits which result in that label, such as making negative statements about self, refusal to participate in new activities, and failure to initiate inter actions with other persons. The specific behaviors to be recorded may be operationally defined as follows:

1. *Negative statements.* Clients make statements indicating inability to accomplish an activity or goal, listing negative self-attributes, or judging performance as inadequate.
2. *Participation in new activities.* Client engages in new activity within 5 minutes, after only one verbal prompt by the person initiating the activity.

(continued)

BOX 7.1 *(continued)*

3. *Initiation of interactions with others.* Client makes first statement to another person within 30 seconds of coming into contact with the other person.

In this example, desired behaviors are defined as participation in new activities or initiation of interactions, as opposed to refusal to participate or failure to initiate. A decrease in the first behavior and an increase in the second and third behaviors will indicate an improvement in the client's self-concept. The behaviors that originally instigated the referral will be changed.

Operationalization of the Independent Variables

In addition to operationally defining the target behavior, it is crucial to operationalize the intervention, or the modification of the environment, that is expected to produce a change in the target behavior. Failure to operationally define an intervention limits the support for strong conclusions about the study in two ways. First, it allows the worker to be casual about what constitutes the intervention; this makes it difficult to assure uniform application of the intervention with all individuals during all phases of the study. Second, it makes it impossible to provide sufficient detailed data to enable others to replicate the intervention in other settings and with other people.

If the intervention procedures are not clearly defined and measurable, an independent observer could not reliably detect whether the intervention has been correctly applied. To produce the same intervention consistently, the intervention procedures *must* be written, and all persons who are responsible for implementing them *must* be trained and monitored. The operational definition *must* identify the discrete elements or steps of the intervention and describe the criteria for implementing each one. Conceptual descriptions such as family systems therapy or parent training are obviously not precise and need to be operationally defined.

A first step in operationally defining a community education program designed to influence the social behavior of nonhandicapped children toward handicapped individuals, for example, is to describe the elements of the program. A handicap is considered to be any physically disabling condition that manifests itself in uncommon physical characteristics, such as uneven gait, lack of sight or hearing, or contorted limbs. In most situations, artificial or mechanical assistance, such as wheelchairs or hearing aids, is required. Social behavior includes initiat-

ing contact through verbalization or physical means, such as shaking hands or saying "hello."

The community education program includes a 90-minute multimedia presentation to be shown to children in grades 1 through 5. The presentation consists of a 20-minute videotaped documentary on the lives of three handicapped individuals, a 10-minute presentation of a short play by handicapped children depicting common prejudices encountered by handicapped persons, and a 20-minute discussion by handicapped children about what it is like to be handicapped. There also are three exercise designed to allow nonhandicapped children to experiences a handicapping condition:

1. *Blind.* Children are blindfolded and asked to find their way from the classroom to the bathroom.
2. *Deaf.* Children's ears are covered, and they are asked to get directions from another person.
3. *Physically handicapped.* Children are placed in a wheelchair and allowed to navigate through the classroom.

This provides a clearer idea about what is included in the intervention, but there is not yet sufficient information to replicate it. The content of the video presentation and the play must be clearly and specifically defined, and the procedures to be followed in presenting the discussion and the exercises must be specified.

Interventions such as changes in agency policy or procedure must define both the content of the changes and the methods of implementing them. For example, specifics of how the staff or the public will be informed about the changes must be outlined, and new performance expectations that will affect staff compliance must be defined.

Therapeutic interventions may seem difficult to operationalize, since therapy typically involves an ongoing interaction between the client and the social worker. The intervention is defined generally, in terms such as *psychosocial therapy*, *family therapy*, or *behavior therapy*, but the discrete therapeutic techniques that constitute the intervention must be clearly defined. The definitions indicate differences or similarities of the therapeutic intervention with others. In order to study the results of family therapy on a particular problem, for example, the family therapy techniques that will be employed and the conditions under which they will be implemented must be operationally defined. For example, a social worker may want to study the effects of family therapy on the occur-

(continued)

BOX 7.1 *(continued)*

rence of physical and verbal aggression between children and their parents. The intervention might be defined as one 60-minute session per week, for 10 weeks, at which all family members must be present. Communication exercises to be practiced are to consist of the following five components:

1. Presentation of a communication model
2. Guided application of the model to a hypothetical disagreement
3. Application of the model to a real disagreement
4. Videotape replay of the family's performance during the disagreement
5. Discussion of each family member's reactions on:

a. Positive communication by other family members
b. Communication that seemed effective or not effective
c. Own ideas that occurred during the communication practice

This operational definition of the intervention specifies in measurable and observable terms what the worker will be doing, to whom, when, how often, and where. This information constitutes a format that ensures uniform application of the intervention, provides adequate information to compare it to other treatment interventions, and allows the social worker to replicate the intervention or use it with other populations, behaviors, or settings (Mutschler, 1979).

---

group of women, the unit of analysis is the group of women.

Case-level designs can provide information about how well a treatment intervention is working, so that alternative or complementary interventive strategies can be adopted if necessary. They can also indicate when a client's problem has been resolved. Single-case studies can be used to monitor client progress up to, and sometimes beyond, the point of termination.

They can also be used to evaluate the effectiveness of a social work program as a whole by aggregating or compiling the results obtained by numerous social workers serving their individual clients within the program. A family therapy program might be evaluated, for example, by combining family outcomes on a number of families that have been seen by different social workers.

A *case-level* design is represented in terms of the letters *A, B, C,* and *D*. Let us see how this works, first in relation to exploratory research questions.

EXPLORATORY CASE-LEVEL DESIGNS

Suppose you have a client—Celia—whose underlying problem, you believe, is poor self-esteem. She will be the "case" in your case-level design. Before you go ahead with an intervention designed to increase her self-esteem—Celia doesn't need your intervention if

your belief is wrong—you will have to answer the simple question "Does Celia really have a clinically significant problem with self-esteem?" In other words, does the self-esteem problem you think she has in fact really exist in the first place?

In order to answer this question, you select a measuring instrument to measure self-esteem that is valid, reliable, sensitive, nonreactive, and useful in this particular situation. Say you choose Hudson's Index of Self-Esteem, which has a clinical cutting score of 30 (plus or minus 5). You administer it to Celia, and she scores 37. On the Hudson scale, scores above the clinical cutting score indicate a clinically significant problem. You might think, "Ah-hah! She has a problem!" and hurry forward with your intervention.

On the other hand, any social work intervention has the potential to harm as well as help (in the same way that any medication does), and you might first want to be sure that this is a persisting problem and not just a reflection of Celia's poor self-esteem today. You might also want to be sure that her low self-esteem problem will not go away by itself. Doctors usually do not treat conditions that resolve themselves, given time, and the same is true for social workers.

In order to see whether Celia meets these two criteria for treatment—first, the problem is persisting and, second, it is either stable at an unacceptable level or getting worse—you will need to administer the same measuring instrument two or three times more at intervals of, say, a week. You might then graph your results as shown in Figure 7.1. This figure constitutes a baseline measure of Celia's self-esteem and is a very simple example of an *A* design.

A Design

At the risk of sounding a bit ridiculous, the letter *A* simply designates "a research study" where the intention is to establish, via measurement, a baseline for an individual client's problem. Perhaps *research study* is a grandiose term to describe a routine assessment, but the word *re-search* does mean *to look again,* and you are indeed looking again at Celia's potential problem in order to see if her problem exists in the first place.

Figure 7.1 contains four data points. Three is the minimum number needed to show any kind of trend, and some experts maintain that you need no fewer than seven. However, in a clinical situation the client's need for intervention is the primary factor, and you will have to use your judgment to decide how long you ought to continue to gather baseline data before you intervene.

Figure 7.1 indicates a worsening problem that requires intervention, since each score is higher than the last. Remember, higher scores mean higher levels of the problem. Had each score been lower than the preceding one, the problem would have been improving by itself and no intervention would be indicated. If the scores had fallen more or less on a horizontal line, intervention would have been indicated if the line was above the clinical cutting score and not if the line was below it.

Before we proceed from *A* designs to *B* designs, a word is in order about graphs. If math is but a dim and nasty memory for you, the following points might be worthy to note:

- The horizontal line in Figure 7.1 is called the *x*-axis, or abscissa.
- The vertical line is called the *y*-axis, or ordinate.
- The dotted horizontal line indicates the clinical cutting score. It is important to include this, since your objective with Celia when you intervene will be to get her score below the clinical cutting score line.
- Both axes must be labeled. In Figure 7.1 the *y*-axis shows self-esteem level and the *x*-axis shows time

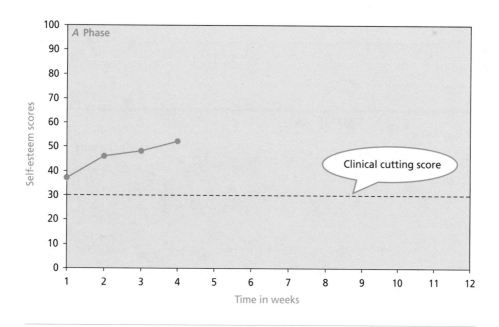

Figure 7.1 *A* Design: Celia's Self-Esteem Scores for the First 4 Weeks Without Intervention

in weeks. By convention, the dependent variable is placed on the *y*-axis and the independent variable on the *x*-axis. In our simple study, there are not yet any dependent and independent variables, but you might hope to show later on that Celia's self-esteem level has been affected by your intervention. If this were the case, self-esteem level would be the dependent variable, since it is the thing being changed, and the intervention over time would be the independent variable, since it is the thing doing the changing

B *Design*

The second type of exploratory single-case research design is the *B* design. As we have seen, an *A* design answers the question "Does the problem exist?" The *A* design also answers another type of exploratory question: "Does the problem exist at different levels over time?" In other words, "Is the problem changing *by itself*?"

A *B* design also addresses the question "Is the problem changing?," but here we want to know whether the problem is changing *while an intervention is being applied*. Let's forget Celia for a moment—we have not

abandoned her; we will return to her in due course—and consider Bob instead.

Bob has come to you complaining that he experiences a great deal of anxiety in social situations. He is nervous when he speaks to his boss or when he meets people for the first time, and the prospect of giving public presentations at work appalls him. You decide that you will measure Bob's anxiety level using a standardized measuring instrument called the Interaction and Audience Anxiousness Scale (*IASS*).

On this particular measuring instrument, higher scores indicate higher anxiety levels, the clinical cutting score for the *IASS* is 40, and Bob scores 62. This one score is more of a base point rather than a baseline, but you decide that it would be inappropriate to collect baseline data over time in Bob's case, as he is experiencing a great deal of discomfort at work, is highly nervous in your presence (you are a stranger, after all), and probably will not be able to bring himself to seek help in the future if he does not receive some kind of intervention now.

You therefore begin your intervention, engaging Bob to the extent that he returns the following week, when you administer the *IASS* again. Now he scores 55. In the third week, he scores 52, as shown in Figure 7.2.

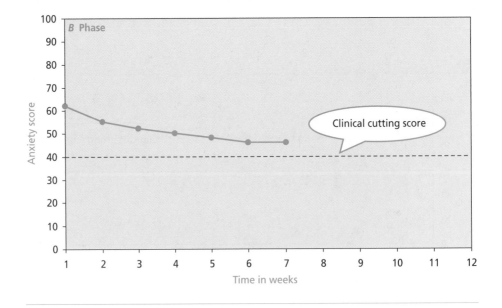

Figure 7.2   *B* Design: Bob's Anxiety Scores for the First 7 Weeks With Intervention

Figure 7.2 is an example of a *B* design, in which you track change in the problem level at the same time as you are intervening. You do not know, from this graph, whether your intervention *caused* the change you see. Anything else could have caused it. Perhaps Bob is having a weekly massage to reduce muscle tension, or his boss has been fired, or the public presentation that he was supposed to do has been postponed. Therefore, you cannot use this design to answer explanatory research questions, which come quite high on the knowledge continuum (refer to Figure 1.10).

BB_1 Design

Figure 7.2 shows that Bob's anxiety level has improved, but it has not fallen below the clinical cutting score. Moreover, it does not look as though it will because it has been relatively stable around 46 for the past three weeks. It may be that Bob is a naturally anxious person and that no intervention, however inspired, will reduce his problem to below significant levels. On the other hand, you might make the clinical decision that it is worth trying a variation on your intervention: You might apply it more *frequently* by having Bob come twice a week instead of once, or you

might apply it more *intensively* by increasing the amount of time Bob is expected to spend each evening on relaxation exercises. You can graph the changes that occur while you are applying the variation, as shown in Figure 7.3.

Figure 7.3 shows two *phases*: the *B* phase and the B_1 phase, separated by the vertical dotted line that runs between Weeks 7 and 8. Week 7 marks the end of your original intervention, designated by the *B* intervention, and all the scores obtained by Bob while you were applying the *B* intervention constitute the *B* phase. (If it seems odd to call the first intervention *B* instead of *A*, remember that *A* has been used already to designate baseline scores.) Week 8 marks the beginning of the variation on your original intervention, designated B_1, and all the scores obtained by Bob while you were applying the variation constitute the B_1 phase. The *B* and B_1 phases together constitute the BB_1 design. You will note that the *B* phase shown in Figure 7.3 has been copied from Figure 7.2. in order to illustrate the BB_1 design.

When you look at the score of 38 that Bob achieved by Week 12, you might be tempted to think, "Hallelujah! My specific intervention *did* work. All Bob needed was a bit more of it." However, the same

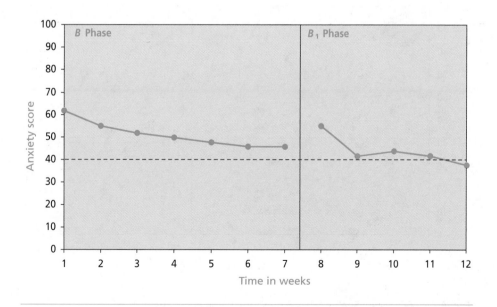

Figure 7.3 BB_1 Design: Bob's Anxiety Scores for *B* Phase and B_1 Phase

considerations apply to the BB_1 design as apply to the B design. You cannot be sure that there is any relationship between your intervention and Bob's decreased anxiety, far less that one was the cause of the other.

BC *Design*

The final exploratory case-level research design is the BC design. Let us go back in time, to the point where you decided that it was worth trying a variation on your B intervention. Suppose you had decided instead to try an entirely different intervention, designated as C because it is a *different* intervention, following immediately after B. Now you implement the C intervention, administering the *IASS* every week, graphing your results, and creating a C phase after the B phase as shown in Figure 7.4.

Again, the B phase in Figure 7.4 is copied from Figure 7.2, and after the C intervention you see that Bob has succeeded in reducing his anxiety level to below the clinical cutting score. Repressing your hallelujahs, you realize that there is still no sure relationship between your intervention and Bob's success. Indeed,

the waters are becoming more murky because even if your intervention were in fact related to Bob's success, you would still not know whether it was the C intervention that did the trick, or a delayed reaction to B, or some combination of B and C.

DESCRIPTIVE CASE-LEVEL DESIGNS

There are two kinds of case-level research designs that center around answering descriptive research questions: (1) AB designs, and (2) ABC and ABCD designs.

AB *Design*

An AB design is simply an A—or baseline phase—followed by a B or intervention phase. Returning to Celia, you have already completed a baseline phase with her, as shown in Figure 7.1, and that phase alone answered the two simple exploratory questions "Does the problem exist?" and "Does the problem exist at different levels over time?" Now you implement a B intervention and find, to your pleasure, that Celia's self-esteem level approaches the clinical cutting score of 30

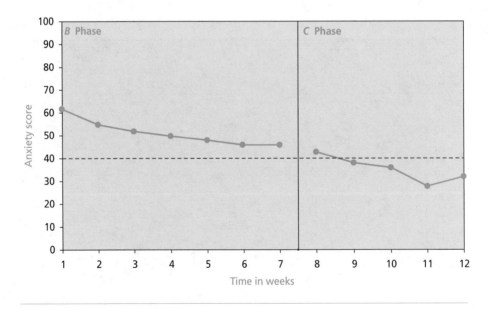

Figure 7.4 *BC* Design: Bob's Anxiety Scores for *B* Phase and *C* Phase

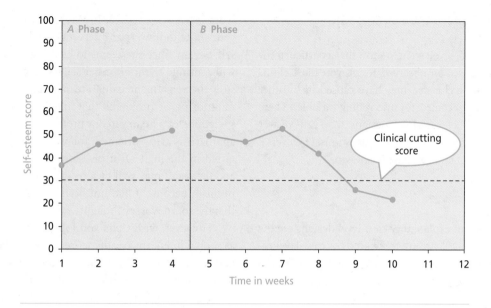

Figure 7.5 *AB* Design: Celia's Self-Esteem Scores for *A* Phase and *B* Phase

and falls below it at Weeks 9 and 10. Celia's progress is illustrated in Figure 7.5.

What you really want to know, of course, is whether there is any relationship between your *B* intervention and Celia's success. You are now in a better position to hypothesize that there is, since you know that Celia was getting worse during the 4 weeks of the baseline phase and began to improve the week after you started your intervention. *Something* happened in Week 5 to set Celia on the road to recovery, and it would be very coincidental if that something were not your intervention.

However, coincidences do happen, and you cannot be certain that your intervention *caused* the change you see unless you can eliminate all the other coincidental happenings that might have caused it. Hence, the *AB* design cannot answer explanatory research questions, but the change between the baseline data (getting worse) and the intervention data (getting better) is enough to indicate that there may be some relationship between your intervention and Celia's improvement. The moral to the story is *always collect baseline data if you can*, since social work ethics requires you to be reasonably sure an intervention is effective before you try it again with another client.

ABC *and* ABCD *Designs*

As discussed earlier, you can always follow a *B* phase with a *C* phase if the *B* intervention does not achieve the desired result. An *A* phase followed by a *B* phase followed by a *C* phase constitutes an *ABC* design, and if there is a *D* intervention as well, you have an *ABCD* design. So long as there is a baseline, you can conclude fairly safely that there is a relationship between the results you see and the intervention you implemented.

However, if you have more than one intervention, you will not know which intervention—or combination of interventions—did the trick, and the more interventions you try the more murky the waters become. Since a single intervention often comprises a package of practice techniques (e.g., active listening plus role play plus relaxation exercises), it is important to write down exactly what you did so that later on you will remember what the *B* or *C* or *D* interventions were.

EXPLANATORY CASE-LEVEL DESIGNS

As we have seen, if you want to show that a particular intervention caused an observed result, you must eliminate everything else that may have caused it: In other words, you must control for intervening variables. There are two types of case-level designs that can answer causality, or explanatory research questions: (1) reversal designs, and (2) multiple baseline designs.

Reversal Designs

The first type of explanatory case-level designs are the reversal designs. There are three kinds of case-level reversal designs: (1) *ABA* and *ABAB* designs, (2) *BAB* designs, and (3) *BCBC* designs.

ABA *and* ABAB *Designs*

Look at Figure 7.5, which illustrates Celia's success in getting her self-esteem score below the clinical cutting

score in Weeks 9 and 10. In Week 11, you decide that you will withdraw your intervention related to Celia's self-esteem since she seems to be doing well, but you will continue to monitor her self-esteem levels to ensure that treatment gains are maintained. Ongoing monitoring of problems that appear to be solved is something of a luxury in our profession. Too often our approach is crisis-oriented; follow-up tends to be ignored in the light of other, more pressing problems, and the result may well be a recurrence of the original problem because it had not been solved to the extent that the social worker thought.

However, with Celia you follow up. In Week 11, as shown in Figure 7.6, the score hovers at the clinical cutting score. In Week 12, it goes up a little; in Week 13, it jumps; and in Weeks 14 and 15, it is no better.

Figure 7.6 illustrates an *ABA* design where the client's scores are displayed first without an intervention (the first *A* phase), then with an intervention (the *B* phase), then without an intervention again (the second *A* phase). The scores are not as high in the second *A*

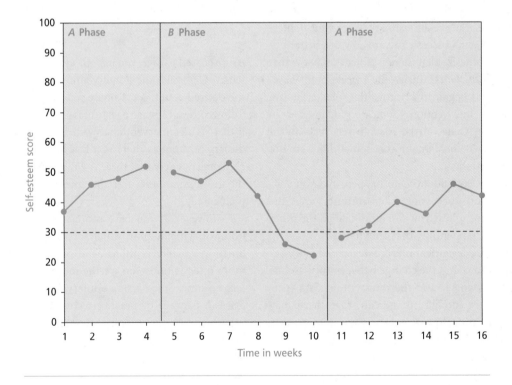

Figure 7.6 *ABA* Design: Celia's Self-Esteem Scores for *A* Phase, *B* Phase, and *A* Phase

phase as they were in the first *A* phase, and this is to be expected, since some of the strategies Celia learned in the *B* phase should remain with her even though the intervention has stopped. However, from a research point of view, the very fact that her scores increased again when you stopped the intervention makes it more certain that it was your intervention that caused the improvement you saw in the *B* phase. Celia's improvement when the intervention started might have been a coincidence, but it is unlikely that her regression when the intervention stopped was also a coincidence.

Your certainty with respect to causality will be increased even further if you reintroduce the *B* intervention in Week 16 and Celia's score begins to drop again as it did in the first *B* phase. Now you have implemented two *AB* designs one after the other with the same client to produce an *ABAB* design. This design is illustrated in Figure 7.7. It is sometimes called a *reversal* design or a *withdrawal* design.

Causality is established with an *ABAB* design because the same intervention has been shown to work twice with the same client and you have baseline data to show the extent of the problem when there was no intervention.

BAB *Design*

Let's now return to Bob, with whom you implemented a *B* intervention to reduce his social anxiety, as shown in Figure 7.2. When Bob's social anxiety level has fallen beneath the clinical cutting score, you might do the same thing with Bob as you did with Celia: withdraw the intervention and continue to monitor the problem, creating an *A* phase after the *B* phase. If the problem level worsens during the *A* phase, you intervene again in the same way as you did before, creating a second *B* phase and an overall design of *BAB*.

We have said that causality is established with an *ABAB* design because the same intervention has worked twice with the same client. We cannot say the same for a *BAB* design, however, as we do not really know that our intervention "worked" the first time. Since there were no initial baseline data (no first *A* phase), we cannot know whether the resolution of the problem on the first occasion had anything to do with the intervention.

The problem may have resolved itself, or some external event (intervening variable) might have resolved it. Nor can we know the degree to which the problem changed during the first *B* phase (intervention), since

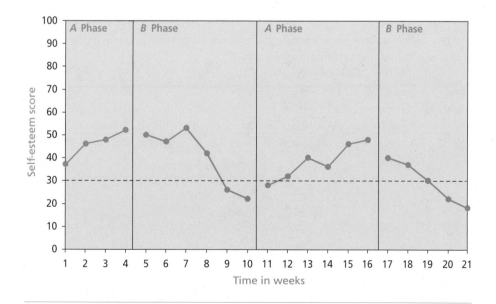

Figure 7.7   *ABAB* Design: Celia's Self-Esteem Scores for Two *A* Phases and Two *B* Phases

there were no baseline data with which to compare the final result. An indication of the amount of change can be obtained by comparing the first and last scores in the B phase, but the first score may have been an unreliable measure of Bob's problem. Bob may have felt less or more anxious that day than usual, and a baseline is necessary to compensate for such day-to-day fluctuations.

Since the effectiveness of the intervention on the first occasion is unknown, there can be no way of knowing whether the intervention was just as effective the second time it was implemented, or less or more effective. All we know is that the problem improved twice, following the same intervention, and this is probably enough to warrant using the intervention again with another client.

BCBC Design

A *BCBC* design, as the name suggests, is a B intervention followed by a C intervention implemented twice in succession. The point of doing this is to compare the effectiveness of two interventions—B and C. It is unlikely that a social worker would implement this design with a client since, if the problem improved sufficiently using B, you would not need C, and, if you did need C, you would hardly return to B whether or not C appeared to do the trick. However, if the problem has nothing to do with a client's welfare but is concerned instead with a social work program's organizational efficiency, say, as affected by organizational structure, you might try one structure B followed by a different structure C and then do the same thing again in order to show that one structure really has proved more effective in increasing efficiency when implemented twice *under the same conditions*.

Multiple Baseline Designs

The second type of explanatory case-level designs are the multiple baseline designs. Multiple baseline designs are like *ABAB* designs in that the *AB* design is implemented more than once. However, whereas *ABAB* designs apply to one case with one problem in one setting, multiple baseline designs can be used with more

than one case, with more than one setting, or with more than one problem.

More Than One Case

Suppose that, instead of Bob with his social anxiety problem, you have three additional clients, Breanne, Warren, and Alison, with anxiety problems. All three are residents in the same nursing home. You use the same measuring instrument to measure anxiety (the *IASS*) in all three cases, and you give all three clients the same intervention. However, you vary the number of weeks over which you collect baseline data, allowing the baseline phase to last for 6 weeks in Breanne's case, 8 weeks in Warren's case, and 9 weeks for Alison. You plot your results as shown in Figure 7.8.

Breanne starts to show improvement in Week 7, the week you began your intervention. Had that improvement been due to some intervening variable—for example, some anxiety-reducing change in the nursing home's routine—you would expect Warren and Alison to also show improvement. The fact that their anxiety levels continue to be high indicates that it was your intervention, not some other factor, that caused the improvement in Breanne. Causality is demonstrated again in Week 9 when you begin to intervene with Warren and Warren improves but Alison does not. Your triumph is complete when Alison, given the same intervention, begins to improve in Week 10.

More Than One Setting

Another way to conduct a multiple baseline study is with one client in a number of settings. Suppose that your objective is to reduce the number of a child's temper tantrums at home, in school, and at the daycare center where the child goes after school. The same intervention is offered by the parents at home, by the teacher in school, and by the worker at the daycare center. They are also responsible for measuring the number of tantrums that occur each day. The baseline phase continues for different lengths of time in each setting as shown in Figure 7.9. If the child improves at home after the intervention begins in Week 7 but continues to throw numerous tantrums in school and at daycare, the indication is that

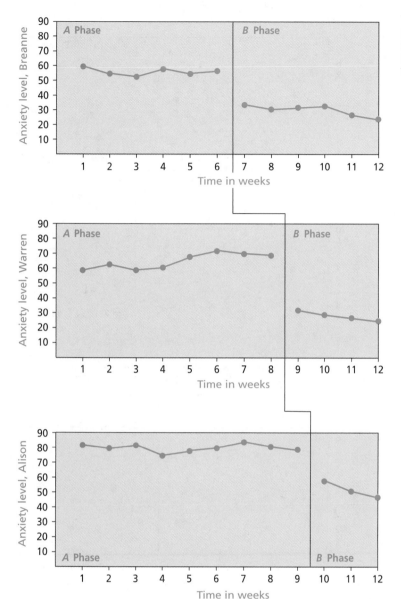

Figure 7.8
Multiple-Baseline Design Across Clients: Magnitude of Anxiety Levels for Three Clients

it was not the intervention that caused the improvement at home. If the intervention was the causal agent, then improvement would occur in all settings.

More Than One Problem

A third way to conduct a multiple-baseline study is to use the same intervention to tackle different target problems. Suppose that Joan is having trouble with her daughter, Anita. In addition, Joan is having trouble with her in-laws and with her boss at work. After exploration, a worker may believe that all these troubles stem from her lack of assertiveness. Thus, the intervention would be assertiveness training. Progress with Anita might be measured by the number of times each day she is flagrantly disobedient. Progress can be measured with Joan's in-laws by the number of times she is able to utter a contrary opinion, and so on. Since the number

Figure 7.9
Multiple-Baseline Design Across Settings:
Number of Temper Tantrums for One
Client in Three Settings

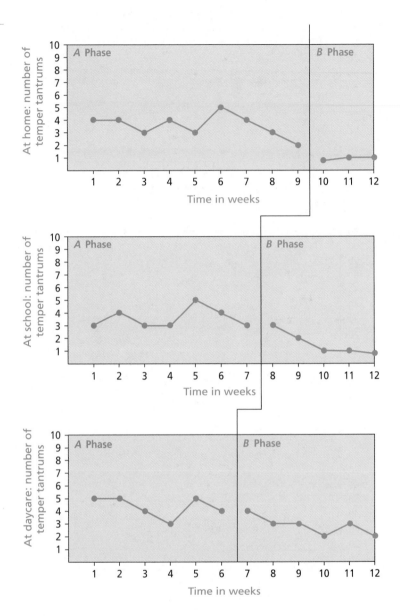

of occasions on which Joan has an opportunity to be assertive will vary, these figures might best be expressed in percentages. Figure 7.10 illustrates an example of a multiple-baseline design that was used to assess the effectiveness of Joan's assertiveness training, which began in Week 3 in three separate problem areas.

Whether it is a reversal design or a multiple-baseline design, an *ABAB* explanatory design involves establishing a baseline level for the client's target prob-lem. This is not possible if the need for intervention is acute, and sometimes the very thought of an *A*-type design has to be abandoned. It is sometimes possible, however, to construct a retrospective baseline—that is, to determine what the level of the problem was before an intervention was implemented.

The best retrospective baselines are those that do not depend on the client's memory. If the target problem occurs rarely, memories may be accurate. For

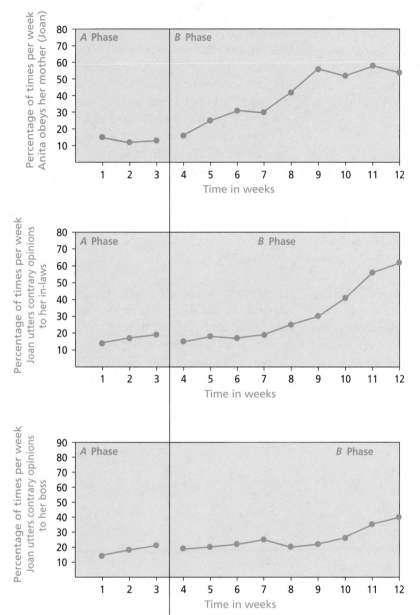

Figure 7.10
Multiple-Baseline Design Across Client Problems: Magnitude of Three Client Target Problem Areas for One Client

example, Tai, a teenager, and his family may remember quite well how many times he ran away from home during the past month. They may not remember nearly so well if the family members were asked how often he behaved defiantly. Depending on the target problem, it may be possible to construct a baseline from archival data: that is, from written records, such as school at-tendance sheets, probation orders, employment inter-view forms, and so forth.

Although establishing a baseline usually involves making at least three measurements before implement-ing an intervention, it is also acceptable to establish a baseline of zero, or no occurrences of a desired event. A target problem, for example, might focus upon the client's reluctance to enter a drug treatment program. The baseline measurement would then be that the client did not go (zero occurrences), and the desired change would be that the client did go (one occurrence). A social worker who has successfully used the same tactics to persuade a number of clients to enter a drug treatment program has conducted a multiple-baseline design across clients.

As previously discussed, a usable baseline should show either that the client's problem level is stable or that it is growing worse. Sometimes an *A*-type design can be used even though the baseline indicates a slight improvement in the target problem. The justification must be that the intervention is expected to lead to an improvement that will exceed the anticipated improvement if the baseline trend continues.

Perhaps a child's temper tantrums are decreasing by one or two a week, for example, but the total number per week is still 18 to 20. If a worker thought the tantrums could be reduced to 4 or 5 a week, or they could be stopped altogether, the worker would be justified in implementing an intervention even though the client's target problem was improving slowly by itself.

In a similar way, a worker may be able to implement an *A*-type design if the client's baseline is unstable, provided that the intervention is expected to exceed the largest of the baseline fluctuations. Perhaps the child's temper tantrums are fluctuating between 12 and 20 per week in the baseline period, and it is hoped to bring them down to fewer than 10 per week.

Nevertheless, there are some occasions when a baseline cannot be established or is not usable, such as when a client's behaviors involve self-injurious ones. Also, sometimes the establishment of a baseline is totally inappropriate.

SUMMARY

Exploratory designs are used when little is known about the field of study and data are gathered in an effort to find out "what's out there." These ideas are then used to generate hypotheses that can be verified using more rigorous designs. No design is inherently inferior or superior to the others. Each has advantages and disadvantages in terms of time, cost, and the data that can be obtained.

Group-Level Designs

Richard M. Grinnell, Jr.
Yvonne A. Unrau
Margaret Williams

8

Basic Steps in the Research Process

Step 1	Choose a problem
2	Review the literature
3	Evaluate the literature
4	Be aware of all ethical issues
5	Be aware of all cultural issues
6	State the research question or hypothesis
7	Select the research approach
8	Determine how the variables are going to be measured
9	Select a sample
10	Select a data collection method
11	Collect and code the data
12	Analyze and interpret the data
13	Write the report
14	Disseminate the report

You Are Here → (Step 7)

Now that we know how to draw samples for qualitative and quantitative research studies, we turn our attention to the various group-level designs that research studies can take. The two most important factors in determining what design to use in a specific study are (1) what the research question is, and (2) how much knowledge about the problem area is available. If there is already a substantial knowledge base in the area, we will be in a position to address very specific research questions, the answers to which could add to the explanation of previously gathered data. If less is known about the problem area, our research questions will have to be of a more general, descriptive nature. If very little is known about the problem area, our questions will have to be even more general, at an exploratory level.

Research knowledge levels are arrayed along a continuum, from exploratory at the lowest end to explanatory at the highest (see Figure 1.10). Because research knowledge levels are viewed this way, the assignment of the level of knowledge accumulated in a problem area prior to a research study, as well as the level that might be attained by the research study, is totally arbitrary. There are, however, specific designs that can be used to provide us with knowledge at a certain level.

At the highest level are the explanatory designs, also called experimental designs or "ideal" experiments. These designs have the largest number of requirements (examined in the following section). They are best used in confirmatory research studies where the area under study is well developed, theories abound, and testable hypotheses can be formulated on the basis of previous work or existing theory. These designs seek to establish causal relationships between the independent and dependent variables.

In the middle range are the descriptive designs, sometimes referred to as quasi-experimental. A quasi experiment resembles an "ideal" experiment in some aspects but lacks at least one of the necessary requirements.

At the lowest level are the exploratory designs, also called pre-experimental or nonexperimental, which explore only the research question or problem area. These designs do not produce statistically sound data or conclusive results; they are not intended to. Their purpose is to build a foundation of general ideas and tentative theories, which can be explored later with more precise and hence more complex research designs and their corresponding data-gathering techniques.

The research designs that allow us to acquire knowledge at each of the three levels are described in a later section of this chapter. Before considering them, however, it is necessary to establish the characteristics that differentiate an "ideal" experiment, which leads to explanatory knowledge, from other studies that lead to lower levels of knowledge.

CHARACTERISTICS OF "IDEAL" EXPERIMENTS

An "ideal" experiment is one in which a research study most closely approaches certainty about the relationship between the independent and dependent variables. The purpose of doing an "ideal" experiment is to ascertain whether it can be concluded from the study's findings that the independent variable is, or is not, the only cause of change in the dependent variable.

As pointed out in previous chapters, some social work research studies have no independent variable—for example, those studies that just want to find out how many people in a certain community wish to establish a community-based halfway house for people who are addicted to drugs.

The concept of an "ideal" experiment is introduced with the word "ideal" in quotation marks because such an experiment is rarely achieved in social work research situations. On a general level, in order to achieve this high degree of certainty and qualify as an "ideal" experiment, an explanatory research design must meet six conditions:

1. The time order of the independent variable must be established.
2. The independent variable must be manipulated.
3. The relationship between the independent and dependent variables must be established.
4. The research design must control for rival hypotheses.
5. At least one control group should be used.
6. Random assignment procedures (and if possible, random sampling from a population) must be employed in assigning research participants (or objects) to groups.

Controlling the Time Order of Variables

In an "ideal" experiment, the independent variable must precede the dependent variable in time. Time order is crucial if our research study is to show that one variable causes another, because something that occurs later cannot be the cause of something that occurred earlier.

Suppose we want to study the relationship between adolescent substance abuse and gang-related behavior. The following hypothesis is formulated after some thought:

Adolescent substance abuse causes gang-related behavior.

In this hypothesis, the independent variable is adolescent substance abuse, and the dependent variable is gang-related behavior. The substance abuse must come *before* gang-related behavior because the hypothesis states that adolescent drug use causes gang-related behavior. We could also come up with the following hypothesis, however:

Adolescent gang-related behavior causes substance abuse.

In this hypothesis, adolescent gang-related behavior is the independent variable, and substance abuse is the dependent variable. According to this hypothesis, gang-related behavior must come *before* the substance abuse.

Manipulating the Independent Variable

Manipulation of the independent variable means that we must do something with the independent variable in terms of at least one of the research participants in the study. In the general form of the hypothesis "if X occurs, then Y will result," the independent variable (X) must be manipulated in order to effect a variation in the dependent variable (Y). There are essentially three ways in which independent variables can be manipulated:

1. X present versus X absent. If the effectiveness of a specific treatment intervention is being evaluated, an experimental group and a control group could be used. The experimental group would be given the intervention; the control group would not.
2. A small amount of X versus a larger amount of X. If the effect of treatment time on client's outcomes is being studied, two experimental groups could be used, one of which would be treated for a longer period of time.
3. X versus something else. If the effectiveness of two different treatment interventions is being studied, Intervention X_1 could be used with Experimental Group 1 and Intervention X_2 with Experimental Group 2.

There are certain variables, such as the gender or race of our research participants, that obviously cannot be manipulated because they are fixed. They do not vary, so they are called constants, not variables, as was pointed out in Chapter 5. Other constants, such as socioeconomic status or IQ, may vary for research participants over their life spans, but they are fixed quantities at the beginning of the study, probably will not change during the study, and are not subject to alteration by the one doing the study.

Any variable we can alter (e.g., treatment time) can be considered an independent variable. At least one independent variable must be manipulated in a research study if it is to be considered an "ideal" experiment.

Establishing Relationships Between Variables

The relationship between the independent and the dependent variables must be established in order to infer a cause-effect relationship at the explanatory knowledge level. If the independent variable is considered to be the cause of the dependent variable, there must be some pattern in the relationship between these two variables. An example is the hypothesis "The more time clients spend in treatment (independent variable), the better their progress (dependent variable)."

Controlling Rival Hypotheses

Rival hypotheses must be identified and eliminated in an "ideal" experiment. The logic of this requirement is extremely important, because this is what makes a cause-effect statement possible.

The prime question to ask when trying to identify a rival hypothesis is "What other extraneous variables might affect the dependent variable?" (What else might affect the client's outcome besides treatment time?) At the risk of sounding redundant, "What else besides X might affect Y?" Perhaps the client's motivation for treatment, in addition to the time spent in treatment, might affect the client's outcome. If so, motivation for treatment is an extraneous variable that could be used as the independent variable in the rival hypothesis "The higher the clients' motivation for treatment, the better their progress."

Perhaps the social worker's attitude toward the client might have an effect on the client's outcome, or the client might win the state lottery and ascend abruptly from depression to ecstasy. These extraneous variables could potentially be independent variables in other rival hypotheses. They must all be considered and eliminated before it can be said with reasonable certainty that a client's outcome resulted from the length of treatment time and not from any other extraneous variables.

Control over rival hypotheses refers to efforts on our part to identify and, if at all possible, to eliminate the extraneous variables in these alternative hypotheses. Of the many ways to deal with rival hypotheses, three of the most frequently used are to keep the extraneous variables constant, use correlated variation, or use analysis of covariance.

Holding Extraneous Variables Constant

The most direct way to deal with rival hypotheses is to keep constant the critical extraneous variables that might affect the dependent variable. As we know, a constant cannot affect or be affected by any other variable. If an extraneous variable can be made into a constant, then it cannot affect either the study's real independent variable or the dependent variable.

Let us take an example to illustrate this point. Suppose, for example, that a social worker who is providing counseling to anxious clients wants to relate client outcome to length of treatment time, but most of the clients are also being treated by a consulting psychiatrist with antidepressant medication. Because medication may also affect the clients' outcomes, it is a potential independent variable that could be used in a rival hypothesis. However, if the study included only clients who have been taking medication for some time before the treatment intervention began, and who continue to take the same medicine in the same way throughout treatment, then medication can be considered a constant (in this study, anyway).

Any change in the clients' anxiety levels after the intervention will, therefore, be a result of the intervention with the help of the medication. The extraneous variable of medication, which might form a rival hypothesis, has been eliminated by holding it constant. In short, this study started out with one independent variable, the intervention, then added the variable of medication to it, so the final independent variable is the intervention plus the medication.

This is all very well in theory. In reality, however, a client's drug regime is usually controlled by the psychiatrist and may well be altered at any time. Even if the regime is not altered, the effects of the drugs might not become apparent until the study is under way. In addition, the client's level of anxiety might be affected by a host of other extraneous variables over which the social worker has no control at all: for example, living arrangements, relationships with other people, the condition of the stock market, or an unexpected visit from an IRS agent. These kinds of pragmatic difficulties tend to occur frequently in social work practice and research. It is often impossible to identify all rival hypotheses, let alone eliminate them by keeping them constant.

Using Correlated Variation

Rival hypotheses can also be controlled with correlated variation of the independent variables. Suppose, for example, that we are concerned that income has an effect on a client's compulsive behavior. The client's income, which in this case is subject to variation due to

seasonal employment, is identified as an independent variable. The client's living conditions—a hotel room rented by the week—are then identified as the second independent variable that might well affect the client's level of compulsive behavior. These two variables, however, are correlated, since living conditions are highly dependent on income.

Correlated variation exists if one potential independent variable can be correlated with another. Then only one of them has to be dealt with in the research study.

Using Analysis of Covariance

In conducting an "ideal" experiment, we must always aim to use two or more groups that are as equivalent as possible on all important variables. Sometimes this goal is not feasible, however. Perhaps we are obliged to use existing groups that are not as equivalent as we would like. Or, perhaps during the course of the study we discover inequivalencies between the groups that were not apparent at the beginning.

A statistical method called *analysis of covariance* can be used to compensate for these differences. The mathematics of the method is far beyond the scope of this text, but an explanation can be found in most advanced statistics texts.

Using a Control Group

An "ideal" experiment should use at least one control group in addition to the experimental group. The experimental group may receive an intervention that is withheld from the control group, or equivalent groups may receive different interventions or no interventions at all.

A social worker who initiates a treatment intervention is often interested in knowing what would have happened had the intervention not been used or had some different intervention been substituted. Would members of a support group for alcoholics have recovered anyway, without the social worker's efforts? Would they have recovered faster or more completely had family counseling been used instead of the support group approach?

The answer to these questions will never be known if only the support group is studied. But, what if another

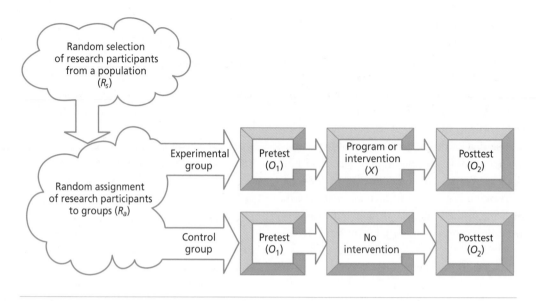

Figure 8.1   True Experimental Research Design

group of alcoholics is included in the research design? In a typical design with a control group, two equivalent groups, 1 and 2, would be formed, and both would be administered the same pretest to determine the initial level of the dependent variable (e.g., degree of alcoholism). Then an intervention would be initiated with Group 1 but not with Group 2. The group treated—Group 1, or the experimental group—would receive the independent variable (the intervention). The group not treated—Group 2, or the control group—would not receive it.

At the conclusion of the intervention, both groups would be given a posttest (the same measure as the pretest). Both the pretest and the posttest consist of the use of some sort of data-gathering procedure, such as a survey or self-report measure, to measure the dependent variable before and after the introduction of the independent variable. There are many types of group research designs and there are many ways to graphically display them. In general, group designs can be written in symbols as shown in Figure 8.1, where

R_s = Random selection from a population
R_a = Random assignment to a group
O_1 = First measurement of the dependent variable

X = Independent variable, or intervention
O_2 = Second measurement of the dependent variable

The R_a in this design indicates that the research participants were randomly assigned to each group. The symbol X, which, as usual, stands for the independent variable, indicates that an intervention is to be given to the experimental group after the pretest (O_1) and before the posttest (O_2). The absence of X for the control group indicates that the intervention is not to be given to the control group. This design is called a classical experimental design because it comes closest to having all the characteristics necessary for an "ideal" experiment.

Randomly Assigning Research Participants to Groups

Once a sample has been selected (see Chapter 6), the individuals (or objects or events) in it are randomly assigned to either an experimental or a control group in such a way that the two groups are equivalent. This procedure is known as *random assignment* or *randomization*. In random assignment, the word "equivalent" means equal in terms of the variables that are important to the

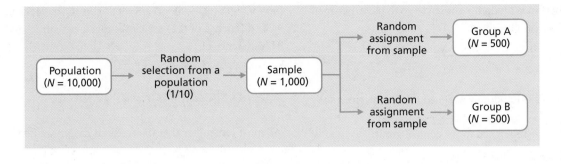

Figure 8.2   Random Sampling From a Population and Random Assignment to Groups

study, such as the clients' motivation for treatment, or problem severity.

If the effect of treatment time on clients' outcomes is being studied, for example, the research design might use one experimental group that is treated for a comparatively longer time, a second experimental group that is treated for a shorter time, and a control group that is not treated at all. If we are concerned that the clients' motivation for treatment might also affect their outcomes, the research participants can be assigned so that all the groups are equivalent (on the average) in terms of their motivation for treatment.

The process of random sampling from a population followed by random assignment of the sample to groups is illustrated in Figure 8.2.

Let us say that the research design calls for a sample size of one-tenth of the population. From a population of 10,000, therefore, a random sampling procedure is used to select a sample of 1,000 individuals.

Then random assignment procedures are used to place the sample of 1,000 into two equivalent groups of 500 individuals each. In theory, Group A will be equivalent to Group B, which will be equivalent to the random sample, which will be equivalent to the population in respect to all important variables contained within the research sample.

Matched Pairs

Another, more deliberate method of assigning people or other units to groups, a subset of randomization, involves matching. The matched-pairs method is suitable when the composition of each group consists of variables with a range of characteristics. One of the disadvantages of matching is that some individuals cannot be matched and so cannot participate in the study.

Suppose a new training program for teaching parenting skills to foster mothers is being evaluated, and it is important that the experimental and control groups have an equal number of highly skilled and less-skilled foster parents before the training program is introduced. The women chosen for the sample would be matched in pairs according to their parenting skill level; the two most skilled foster mothers would be matched, then the next two, and so on. One person in each pair of approximately equally skilled foster parents would then be randomly assigned to the experimental group and the other placed in the control group.

Let us suppose that in order to compare the foster mothers who have been exposed to the new training program with women who have not, a standardized measuring instrument that measures parenting skill level (the dependent variable) is administered to a sample of 10 women. The scores can range from 100 (excellent parenting skills) to zero (poor parenting skills). Then their scores are rank-ordered from the highest to the lowest, and out of the foster mothers with the two highest scores, one is selected to be assigned to either the experimental group or the control group. It does not make any difference to which group our first research participant is randomly assigned, as long as there is an equal chance that she will go to either the control group or the experimental group. In this example, the first person is randomly chosen to go to the experimental group, as illustrated:

Rank Order of Parenting Skills Scores (in parentheses)

First Pair

— (99) Randomly assigned to the experimental group
— (98) Assigned to the control group

Second Pair

— (97) Assigned to the control group
— (96) Assigned to the experimental group

Third Pair

— (95) Assigned to the experimental group
— (94) Assigned to the control group

Fourth Pair

— (93) Assigned to the control group
— (92) Assigned to the experimental group

Fifth Pair

— (91) Assigned to the experimental group
— (90) Assigned to the control group

The foster parent with the highest score (99) is randomly assigned to the experimental group, and this person's "match," with a score of 98, is assigned to the control group. This process is reversed with the next matched pair, where the first person is assigned to the control group and the match is assigned to the experimental group. If the assignment of research participants according to scores is not reversed for every other pair, one group will be higher than the other on the variable being matched.

To illustrate this point, suppose the first participant (highest score) in each match is always assigned to the experimental group. The experimental group's average score would be 95 ($99 + 97 + 95 + 93 + 91 = 475/5 = 95$), and the control group's average score would be 94 ($98 + 96 + 94 + 92 + 90 = 470/5 = 94$). If every other matched pair is reversed, however, as in the example, the average scores of the two groups are closer together; 94.6 for the experimental group ($99 + 96 + 95 + 92 + 91 = 473/5 = 94.6$) and 94.4 for the control group

($98 + 97 + 94 + 93 + 90 = 472/5 = 94.4$). In short, 94.6 and 94.4 (difference of 0.2) are closer together than 95 and 94 (difference of 1).

INTERNAL AND EXTERNAL VALIDITY

We must remember that the research design we finally select should always be evaluated on how close it comes to an "ideal" experiment in reference to the characteristics presented at the beginning of this chapter. As stressed throughout this book, most research designs used in social work do not closely resemble an "ideal" experiment. The research design finally selected needs to be evaluated on how well it meets its primary objective—adequately answering a research question or testing a hypothesis. In short, a research design will be evaluated on how well it controls for:

- Internal validity (Box 8.1)—the ways in which the research design ensures that the introduction of the independent variable (if any) can be identified as the *sole cause* of change in the dependent variable.
- External validity (Box 8.2)—the extent to which the research design allows for generalization of the study's findings to other groups and other situations.

Both internal and external validity are achieved in a research design by taking into account various threats that are inherent in all research efforts. A design for a study with both types of validity will recognize and attempt to control for potential factors that could affect the study's outcome or findings. All research studies try to control as many threats to internal and external validity as possible.

GROUP RESEARCH DESIGNS

While, in some situations, a group research design may need to be complex to accomplish the purpose of the study, a design that is unnecessarily complex costs more, takes more time, and probably will not serve its purpose nearly as well as a simpler one. In choosing

BOX 8.1

Threats to Internal Validity

In any explanatory research study, we should be able to conclude from our findings that the independent variable is, or is not, the only cause of change in the dependent variable. If our study does not have internal validity, such a conclusion is not possible, and the study's findings can be misleading.

Internal validity is concerned with one of the requirements for an "ideal" experiment—the control of rival hypotheses, or alternative explanations for what might bring about a change in the dependent variable. The higher the internal validity of any research study, the greater the extent to which rival hypotheses can be controlled; the lower the internal validity, the less they can be controlled. Thus, we must be prepared to rule out the effects of factors other than the independent variable that could influence the dependent variable.

History

The first threat to internal validity, history, refers to any outside event, either public or private, that may affect the dependent variable and that was not taken into account in our research design. Many times, it refers to events that occur between the first and the second measurement of the dependent variable (the pretest and the posttest). If events occur that have the potential to alter the second measurement, there is no way of knowing how much (if any) of the observed change in the dependent variable is a function of the independent variable and how much is attributable to these events.

Suppose, for example, we are investigating the effects of an educational program on racial tolerance. We may decide to measure the dependent variable, racial tolerance in the community, before introducing the independent variable, the educational program.

The educational program is then implemented. Since it is the independent variable, it is represented by X. Finally, racial tolerance is measured again, after the program has run its course. This final measurement yields a posttest score, represented by O_2. The one-group pretest-posttest study design is presented in Figure 8.12.

The difference between the values O_2 and O_1 represents the difference in racial tolerance in the community before and after the educational program. If the study is internally valid, $O_2 - O_1$ will be a crude measure of the effect of the educational program on racial tolerance, and this is what we were trying to discover. Now suppose that

before the posttest could be administered, an outbreak of racial violence, such as the type that occurred in Los Angeles in the summer of 1992, occurred in the community. Violence can be expected to have a negative effect on racial tolerance, and the posttest scores may, therefore, show a lower level of tolerance than if the violence had not occurred. The effect, $O_2 - O_1$, will now be the combined effects of the educational program *and* the violence, not the effect of the program alone, as we intended.

Racial violence is an extraneous variable that we could not have anticipated and did not control for when designing the study. Other examples might include an earthquake, an election, illness, divorce, or marriage—any event, public or private, that could affect the dependent variable. Any such variable that is unanticipated and uncontrolled for is an example of history.

Maturation

Maturation, the second threat to internal validity, refers to changes, both physical and psychological, that take place in our research participants over time and that can affect the dependent variable. Suppose that we are evaluating an interventive strategy designed to improve the behavior of adolescents who engage in delinquent behavior. Since the behavior of adolescents changes naturally as they mature, the observed changed behavior may have resulted as much from their natural development as from the intervention strategy.

Maturation refers not only to physical or mental growth, however. Over time, people grow older, more or less anxious, more or less bored, and more or less motivated to take part in a research study. All these factors and many more can affect the way in which people respond when the dependent variable is measured a second or third time.

Testing

The third threat to internal validity, testing, is sometimes referred to as the initial measurement effect. Thus, the pretests that are the starting point for many research designs are another potential threat to internal validity. One of the most utilized research designs involves three steps: measuring some dependent variable, such as learning behavior in school or attitudes toward work; initiating a program to change that variable; then measuring the

(continued)

BOX 8.1 *(continued)*

dependent variable again at the conclusion of the program.

The testing effect is the effect that taking a pretest might have on posttest scores. Suppose that Roberto, a research participant, takes a pretest to measure his initial level of racial tolerance before being exposed to a racial tolerance educational program. He might remember some of the questions on the pretest, think about them later, and change his views on racial issues before taking part in the educational program. After the program, his posttest score will reveal his changed opinions, and we may incorrectly assume that the program was responsible, whereas the true cause was his experience with the pretest.

Sometimes, a pretest induces anxiety in a research participant, so that Roberto receives a worse score on the posttest than he should have; or boredom caused by having to respond to the same questions a second time may be a factor. In order to avoid the testing effect, we may wish to use a design that does not require a pretest.

If a pretest is essential, we then must consider the length of time that elapses between the pretest and posttest measurements. A pretest is far more likely to affect the posttest when the time between the two is short. The nature of the pretest is another factor. Questions that deal with factual matters, such as knowledge levels, may have a larger testing effect because they tend to be more easily recalled.

Instrumentation Error

The fourth threat to internal validity is instrumentation error, which refers to all the troubles that can afflict the measurement process. The instrument may be unreliable or invalid, as presented in Chapter 5. It may be a mechanical instrument, such as an electroencephalogram (EEG), that has malfunctioned. Occasionally, the term *instrumentation error* is used to refer to an observer whose observations are inconsistent or to measuring instruments, such as the ones presented in Chapter 5, that are reliable in themselves but that have not been administered properly.

Administration, with respect to a measuring instrument, means the circumstances under which the measurement is made: where, when, how, and by whom. A mother being asked about her attitudes toward her children, for example, may respond in one way in the social worker's office and in a different way at home when her children are screaming around her feet.

A mother's verbal response may differ from her written response, or she may respond differently in the morning than she would in the evening, or differently alone than she would in a group. These variations in situational responses do not indicate a true change in the feelings, attitudes, or behaviors being measured, but are only examples of instrumentation error.

Statistical Regression

The fifth threat to internal validity, statistical regression, refers to the tendency of extremely low and extremely high scores to regress, or move toward the average score for everyone in the research study. Suppose that a student named Maryanna has to take a multiple-choice exam on a subject she knows nothing about. There are many questions, and each question has five possible answers. Since, for each question, Maryanna has a 20% (one in five) chance of guessing correctly, she might expect to score 20% on the exam just by guessing. If she guesses badly, she will score a lot lower; if well, a lot higher. The other members of the class take the same exam, and, since they are all equally uninformed, the average score for the class is 50%.

Now suppose that the instructor separates the low scorers from the high scorers and tries to even out the level of the class by giving the low scorers special instruction. In order to determine whether the special instruction has been effective, the entire class then takes another multiple-choice exam. The result of the exam is that the low scorers (as a group) do better than they did the first time, and the high scorers (as a group) do worse. The instructor believes that this has occurred because the low scorers received special instruction and the high scorers did not.

According to the logic of statistical regression, however, both the average score of the low scorers (as a group) and the average score of the high scorers (as a group) would move toward the total average score for both groups (i.e., high and low).

Even without any special instruction and still in their state of ignorance, the low scorers (as a group) would be expected to have a higher average score than they did before. Likewise, the high scorers (as a group) would be expected to have a lower average score than they did before.

It would be easy for the research instructor to assume that the low scores had increased because of the special instruction and the high scores had decreased because of the lack of it. Not necessarily so, however; the instruction

(continued)

BOX 8.1 *(continued)*

may have had nothing to do with it. It may all be due to statistical regression.

Differential Selection of Research Participants

The sixth threat to internal validity is differential selection of research participants. To some extent, the participants selected for a research study are different from one another to begin with. "Ideal" experiments, however, require random sampling from a population (if at all possible) and random assignment to groups.

This assures that the results of a study will be generalizable to a larger population, thus addressing threats to external validity. In respect to differential selection as a threat to internal validity, "ideal" experiments control for this, since equivalency among the groups at pretest is assumed through the randomization process.

This threat, however, is present when we are working with preformed groups or groups that already exist, such as classes of students, self-help groups, or community groups. In terms of the external validity of such designs, because there is no way of knowing whether the preformed groups are representative of any larger population, it is not possible to generalize the study's results beyond the people (or objects or events) that were actually studied. The use of preformed groups also affects the internal validity of a study, though. It is probable that different preformed groups will not be equivalent with respect to relevant variables and that these initial differences will invalidate the results of the posttest.

A child abuse prevention educational program for children in schools might be evaluated by comparing the prevention skills of one group of children who have experienced the educational program with the skills of a second group who have not. In order to make a valid comparison, the two groups must be as similar as possible with respect to age, gender, intelligence, socioeconomic status, and anything else that might affect the acquisition of child abuse prevention skills.

We would have to make every effort to form or select equivalent groups, but the groups are sometimes not as equivalent as might be hoped—especially if we are obliged to work with preformed groups, such as classes of students or community groups. If the two groups were different before the intervention was introduced, there is not much point in comparing them at the end.

Accordingly, preformed groups should be avoided whenever possible. If it is not feasible to do this, rigorous

pretesting must be done to determine in what ways the groups are (or are not) equivalent, and differences must be compensated for with the use of statistical methods.

Mortality

The seventh threat to internal validity is mortality, which simply means that individual research participants may drop out before the end of the study. Their absence will probably have a significant effect on the study's findings because people who drop out are likely to be different in some ways from the other participants who stay in the study. People who drop out may be less motivated to participate in the intervention than people who stay in, for example.

Since dropouts often have such characteristics in common, it cannot be assumed that the attrition occurred in a random manner. If considerably more people drop out of one group than out of the other, the result will be two groups that are no longer equivalent and cannot be usefully compared. We cannot know at the beginning of the study how many people will drop out, but we can watch to see how many do. Mortality is never problematic if dropout rates are 5% or less *and* if the dropout rates are similar for the various groups.

Reactive Effects of Research Participants

The eighth threat to internal validity is reactive effects. Changes in the behaviors or feelings of research participants may be caused by their reaction to the novelty of the situation or to the knowledge that they are participating in a research study. A mother practicing communication skills with her child, for example, may try especially hard when she knows the social worker is watching. We may wrongly believe that such reactive effects are the result of the intervention.

The classic example of reactive effects was found in a series of studies carried out at the Hawthorne plant of the Western Electric Company, in Chicago, many years ago. Researchers were investigating the relationship between working conditions and productivity. When they increased the level of lighting in one section of the plant, productivity increased; a further increase in the lighting was followed by an additional increase in productivity.

When the lighting was then decreased, however, production levels did not fall accordingly but continued to rise. The conclusion was that the workers were increasing their productivity not because of the lighting level but

(continued)

BOX 8.1 *(continued)*

because of the attention they were receiving as research participants in the study.

The term *Hawthorne effect* is still used to describe any situation in which the research participants' behaviors are influenced not by the intervention but by the knowledge that they are taking part in a research project. Another example of such a reactive effect is the placebo given to patients, which produces beneficial results because the patients believe it is medication.

Reactive effects can be controlled by ensuring that all participants in a research study, in both the experimental and the control groups, appear to be treated equally. If one group is to be shown an educational film, for example, the other group should also be shown a film—some film carefully chosen to bear no relationship to the variable being investigated. If the study involves a change in the participants' routine, this in itself may be enough to change behavior, and care must be taken to continue the study until novelty has ceased to be a factor.

Interaction Effects

Interaction among the various threats to internal validity can have an effect of its own. Any of the factors already described as threats may interact with one another, but the most common interactive effect involves differential selection and maturation.

Let us say we are studying two preformed groups of clients who are being treated for depression. The intention was for these groups to be equivalent, in terms of both their motivation for treatment and their levels of depression. It turns out that Group A is more generally depressed than Group B, however. Whereas both groups may grow less motivated over time, it is likely that Group A, whose members were more depressed to begin with, will lose motivation more completely and more quickly than Group B. Inequivalent preformed groups thus grow less equivalent over time as a result of the interaction between differential selection and maturation.

Relations Between Experimental and Control Groups

The final group of threats to internal validity has to do with the effects of the use of experimental and control groups that receive different interventions. These effects include (1) diffusion of treatments, (2) compensatory equalization, (3) compensatory rivalry, and (4) demoralization.

Diffusion of Treatments

Diffusion, or imitation, of treatments may occur when members of the experimental and control groups talk to each other about the study. Suppose a study is designed that presents a new relaxation exercise to the experimental group and nothing at all to the control group. There is always the possibility that one of the participants in the experimental group will explain the exercise to a friend who happens to be in the control group. The friend explains it to another friend, and so on. This might be beneficial for the control group, but it invalidates the study's findings.

Compensatory Equalization

Compensatory equalization of treatment occurs when the person doing the study and/or the staff member administering the intervention to the experimental group feels sorry for people in the control group who are not receiving it and attempts to compensate them.

A social worker might take a control group member aside and covertly demonstrate the relaxation exercise, for example. On the other hand, if our study has been ethically designed, there should be no need for guilt on the part of the social worker because some people are not being taught to relax. They can be taught to relax when our study is "officially" over.

Compensatory Rivalry

Compensatory rivalry is an effect that occurs when the control group becomes motivated to compete with the experimental group. For example, a control group in a program to encourage parental involvement in school activities might get wind that something is up and make a determined effort to participate, too, on the basis that "anything they can do, we can do better." There is no direct communication between groups, as in the diffusion of treatment effect—only rumors and suggestions of rumors. However, rumors are often enough to threaten the internal validity of a study.

Demoralization

In direct contrast with compensatory rivalry, demoralization refers to feelings of deprivation among the control group that may cause them to give up and drop out of the study, in which case this effect would be referred to as *mortality*. The people in the control group may also get angry.

BOX 8.2

Threats to External Validity

External validity is the degree to which the results of a research study are generalizable to a larger population or to settings outside the research situation or setting.

Pretest-Treatment Interaction

The first threat to external validity, pretest-treatment interaction, is similar to the testing threat to internal validity. The nature of a pretest can alter the way research participants respond to the experimental treatment, as well as to the posttest.

Suppose, for example, that an educational program on racial tolerance is being evaluated. A pretest that measures the level of tolerance could well alert the participants to the fact that they are going to be educated into loving all their neighbors, but many people do not want to be "educated" into anything. They are satisfied with the way they feel and will resist the instruction. This will affect the level of racial tolerance registered on the posttest.

Selection-Treatment Interaction

The second threat to external validity is selection-treatment interaction. This threat commonly occurs when a research design cannot provide for random selection of participants from a population. Suppose we wanted to study the effectiveness of a family service agency staff, for example. If our research proposal was turned down by 50 agencies before it was accepted by the 51st, it is very likely that the accepting agency differs in certain important aspects from the other 50. It may accept the proposal because its social workers are more highly motivated, more secure, more satisfied with their jobs, or more interested in the practical application of the study than the average agency staff member.

As a result, we would be assessing the research participants on the very factors for which they were unwittingly (and by default) selected—motivation, job satisfaction, and so on. The study may be internally valid, but, since it will not be possible to generalize the results to other family service agencies, it will have little external validity.

Specificity of Variables

Specificity of variables has to do with the fact that a research project conducted with a specific group of people at a specific time and in a specific setting may not always be generalizable to other people at different times and in different settings.

For example, a measuring instrument developed to measure the IQ levels of upper-socioeconomic-level Caucasian suburban children does not provide an equally accurate measure of IQ when it is applied to lower-socioeconomic-level children of racial minorities in the inner city.

Reactive Effects

The fourth threat to external validity is reactive effects, which, as with internal validity, occur when the attitudes or behaviors of the research participants are affected to some degree by the very act of taking a pretest. Thus, they are no longer exactly equivalent to the population from which they were randomly selected, and it may not be possible to generalize the study's results to that population. Because pretests affect research participants to some degree, the study results may be valid only for those who were pretested.

Multiple-Treatment Interference

The fifth threat to external validity, multiple-treatment interference, occurs when a research participant is given two or more interventions in succession so that the results of the first intervention may affect the results of the second one. A client who attends treatment sessions, for example, may not seem to benefit from one therapeutic technique, so another is tried. In fact, however, the client may have benefited from the first technique but the benefit may not become apparent until the second technique has been tried. As a result, the effects of both techniques become commingled, or the results may be erroneously ascribed to the second technique alone.

Because of this threat, interventions should be given separately if possible. If the research design does not allow this, sufficient time should be allowed to elapse between the two interventions in an effort to minimize the possibility of multiple-treatment interference.

Researcher Bias

The final threat to external validity is researcher bias. Researchers, like people in general, tend to see what they want to see or expect to see. Unconsciously and without any thought of deceit, they may manipulate a study so that the actual results agree with the anticipated results. A practitioner may favor an intervention so strongly that the research study is structured to support it, or the results may be interpreted favorably.

(continued)

BOX 8.2 *(continued)*

If we know which individuals are in the experimental group and which are in the control group, this knowledge alone might affect the study's results. Students whom an instructor believes to be bright, for example, often are given higher grades than their performance warrants, while students believed to be dull are given lower grades.

The way to control for such researcher bias is to perform a double-blind experiment in which neither the research participants nor the researcher knows who is in the experimental or control group or who is receiving a specific treatment intervention.

a research design (whether a single case [see preceding chapter] or group), therefore, the principle of parsimony must be applied: The simplest and most economical route to the objective is the best choice.

Exploratory Designs

At the lowest level of the continuum of knowledge that can be derived from research studies are exploratory group research designs. An exploratory study explores a research question about which little is already known in order to uncover generalizations and develop hypotheses that can be investigated and tested later with more precise and, hence, more complex designs and data-gathering techniques.

The four examples of exploratory designs given in this section do not use pretests; they simply measure the dependent variable only after the intervention has been introduced. Therefore, they cannot be used to determine whether changes took place in the study's research participants; these designs simply describe the

state of the research participants after they have received the intervention (see Box 8.3).

One-Group Posttest-Only Design

The one-group posttest-only design is sometimes called the *one-shot case study* or *cross-sectional case study design*. Suppose in a particular community, Rome, Wisconsin, there are numerous parents who are physically abusive toward their children. The city decides to hire a school social worker, Antonia, to implement a program that is supposed to reduce the number of parents who physically abuse their children. She conceptualizes a 12-week child abuse prevention program (the intervention) and offers it to parents who have children in her school who wish to participate on a voluntary basis. A simple research study is then conducted to answer the question "Did the parents who completed the program stop physically abusing their children?" The answer to this question will determine the success of the intervention.

BOX 8.3

Treatment: A Variable or a Constant?

For instructional purposes, group designs are displayed using symbols where *X* is the independent variable (treatment) and *O* is the measure of the dependent variable. This presentation is accurate when studies are designed with two or more groups. When one-group designs are used, however, this interpretation does not hold. In one-group designs, the treatment, or program, cannot truly vary because all research participants have experienced the same event; that is, they all have experienced the program. Without a comparison or control group, treatment is considered a constant because it is a quality shared by all members in the research study.

There does not necessarily have to be an independent variable in a study, however; we may just want to measure some variable in a particular population such as the number of people who receive social service assistance over a 4-year period. In this situation, there is no independent or dependent variable.

There are many different ways in which this program can be evaluated. For now, and to make matters as simple as possible, we are going to evaluate it by simply calculating the percentage of parents who stopped physically abusing their children after they attended the program.

At the simplest level, the program could be evaluated with a one-group posttest-only design. The basic elements of this design can be written as shown in Figure 8.3, where:

X = Child Abuse Prevention Program, or the intervention (see Box 8.3)

O_1 = First and only measurement of the dependent variable (percentage of parents who stopped physically abusing their children, the program's outcome, or program objective)

All that this design provides is a single measure (O_1) of what happens when one group of people is subjected to one treatment or experience (X). The program's participants were not randomly selected from any particular population, and, thus, the results of the findings cannot be generalized to any other group or population.

It is safe to assume that all the members within the program had physically abused their children before they enrolled, since people who do not have this problem would not have enrolled in such a program. But, even if the value of O_1 indicates that some of the parents did stop being violent with their children after the pro-

gram, it cannot be determined whether they quit because of the intervention (the program) or because of some other rival hypothesis. Perhaps a law was passed that made it mandatory for the police to arrest anyone who behaves violently toward his or her child, or perhaps the local television station started to report such incidents on the nightly news, complete with pictures of the abusive parent. These or other extraneous variables might have been more important in persuading the parents to cease their abusive behavior toward their children than their voluntary participation in the program.

In sum, this design does not control for many of the threats to either internal or external validity. In terms of internal validity, the threats that are not controlled for in this design are history, maturation, differential selection, and mortality.

Cross-Sectional Survey Design

Let us take another example of a one-group posttest-only design that *does not* have an intervention of some kind. In survey research, this kind of a group research design is called a cross-sectional survey design.

In doing a cross-sectional survey, we survey *only once* a cross section of some particular population. In addition to running her child abuse prevention program geared for abusive parents, Antonia may also want to start another program geared for all the children in the school (whether they come from abusive

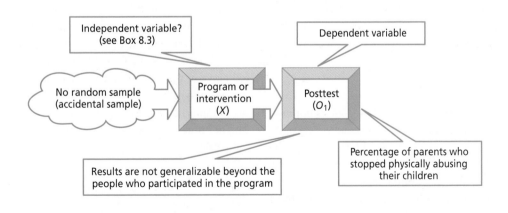

Figure 8.3 One-Group Posttest-Only Design

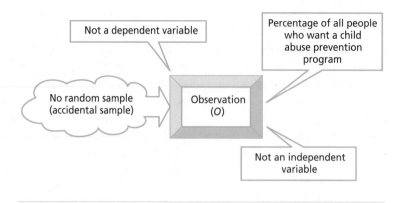

Figure 8.4   Cross-Sectional Survey Design

families or not)—a child abuse educational program taught to children in the school.

Before Antonia starts her educational program geared for the children, however, she wants to know what parents think about the idea. She may send out questionnaires to all the parents, or she may decide to personally telephone every 2nd parent, or every 5th or 10th, depending on how much time and money she has. The results of her survey constitute a single measurement, or observation, of the parents' opinions of her proposed educational program (the one for the children) and may be written as shown in Figure 8.4.

The symbol O represents the entire cross-sectional survey design since such a design involves making only a single observation, or measurement, at one time period. Note that there is no X, since there is really no intervention. Antonia wants only to ascertain the parents' attitudes toward her proposed program—nothing more, nothing less.

Multigroup Posttest-Only Design

The multigroup posttest-only design is an elaboration of the one-group posttest-only design in which more than one group is used. To check a bit further into the effectiveness of Antonia's program for parents who have been physically abusive toward their children, for example, she might decide to locate several more groups of parents who have completed her program and see how many of them have stopped abusing their children—

and so on, with any number of groups. This design can be written in symbols as shown in Figure 8.5, where:

X = Child Abuse Prevention Program, or the intervention (see Box 8.3)

O_1 = First and only measurement of the dependent variable (percentage of parents who stopped physically abusing their children, the program's outcome or program objective)

With the multigroup design it cannot be assumed that all three Xs are equivalent because the three programs might not be exactly the same; one group might have had a different facilitator, the program might have been presented differently, or the material could have varied in important respects.

In addition, nothing is known about whether any of the research participants would have stopped being violent anyway, even without the program. It certainly cannot be assumed that any of the groups were representative of the larger population. Thus, as in the case of the one-group posttest-only design, the same threats to the internal and the external validity of the study might influence the results of the multigroup posttest-only design.

Longitudinal Case Study Design

The longitudinal case study design is exactly like the one-group posttest-only design, except that it provides

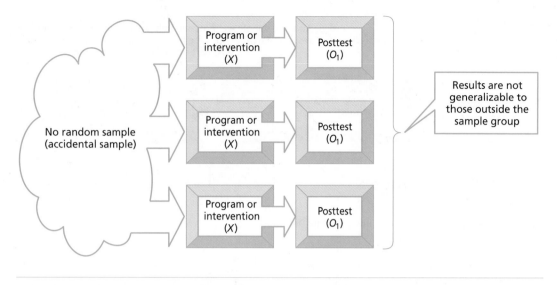

Figure 8.5   Multigroup Posttest-Only Design

for more measurements of the dependent variable (*O*s). This design can be written in symbols as shown in Figure 8.6, where:

X = Child Abuse Prevention Program, or the intervention (see Box 8.3)

O_1 = First measurement of the dependent variable (percentage of parents who stopped physically abusing their children, the program's outcome or program objective)

O_2 = Second measurement of the dependent variable (percentage of parents who stopped physically abusing their children, the program's outcome or program objective)

O_3 = Third measurement of the dependent variable (percentage of parents who stopped physically abusing their children, the program's outcome or program objective)

Suppose that, in our example, Antonia is interested in the long-term effects of the child abuse prevention program. Perhaps the program was effective in helping some people to stop physically abusing their children, but will they continue to refrain from abusing their children? One way to find out is to measure the percentage of parents who physically abuse their children at intervals—say at the end of the program, 3 months after

the program, 3 months after that, and every 3 months for the next 2 years.

This design can be used to monitor the effectiveness of treatment interventions over time and can be applied not just to groups but also to single-client systems, as described in Chapter 7. However, all of the same threats to the internal and external validity that were described in relation to the previous two exploratory designs also apply to this design.

Longitudinal Survey Design

Unlike cross-sectional surveys, where the variable of interest (usually the dependent variable) is measured at one point in time, longitudinal surveys provide data at various points in time so that changes can be monitored over time. They can be broken down into two general types: (1) trend studies and (2) cohort studies.

Trend Studies.   A trend study is used to find out how a population, or sample, changes over time. Antonia, the school social worker mentioned previously, may want to know whether parents of young children enrolled in her school are becoming more receptive to the idea of the school teaching their children child

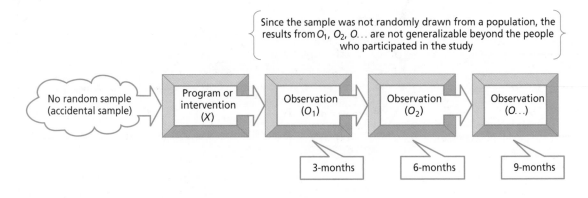

Since the sample was not randomly drawn from a population, the results from O_1, O_2, O... are not generalizable beyond the people who participated in the study

Figure 8.6   Longitudinal One-Group Posttest-Only Design

abuse prevention education in the second grade (Williams, Tutty, & Grinnell, 1995). She may survey all the parents of Grade 2 children this year, all the parents of the new complement of Grade 2 children next year, and so on until she thinks she has sufficient data.

Each year the parents surveyed will be different, but they will all be parents of Grade 2 children. In this way, Antonia will be able to determine whether parents are becoming more receptive to the idea of introducing child abuse prevention material to their children as early as Grade 2. In other words, she will be able to measure any attitudinal trend that is, or is not, occurring. The research design can still be written as shown in Figure 8. 7, where:

$O_1 =$ First measurement of a variable in **Sample 1**

$O_2 =$ Second measurement of a variable in **Sample 2**

$O_3 =$ Third measurement of a variable in **Sample 3**

Cohort Studies.   Cohort studies are used over time to follow a single group of people who have shared a similar experience—for example, AIDS survivors, sexual abuse survivors, or parents of grade-school children. In a cohort study, the *same individuals* are followed over a period of time. Antonia might select one particular sample of parents, for example, and measure their attitudes toward child abuse prevention education in successive years. Again, the design can be written as shown in Figure 8.8, where:

$O_1 =$ First measurement of some variable for a **sample of individuals**

$O_2 =$ Second measurement of some variable **for the same sample of individuals 1 year later**

$O_3 =$ Third measurement of some variable **for the same sample of individuals after 2 years**

Figure 8.7
Trend Research Studies

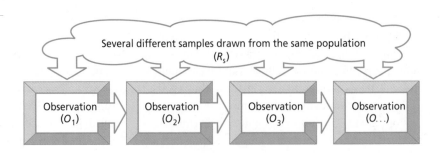

Several different samples drawn from the same population (R_s)

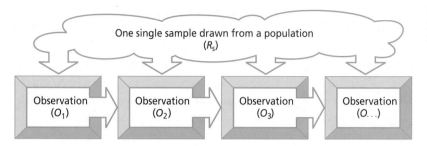

Figure 8.8
Cohort Research Studies

Descriptive Designs

At the midpoint on the knowledge continuum are descriptive designs, which have some but not all of the requirements of an "ideal" experiment. They usually require specification of the time order of variables, manipulation of the independent variable, and establishment of the relationship between the independent and dependent variables.

They may also control for rival hypotheses and use a second group as a comparison (not as a control). The requirement that descriptive designs lack most frequently is the random assignment of research participants to two or more groups.

We are seldom in a position to randomly assign research participants to either an experimental or a control group. Sometimes the groups to be studied are already in existence; sometimes ethical issues are involved. It would be unethical, for example, to assign clients who need immediate help to two random groups, only one of which is to receive the intervention. Since a lack of random assignment affects the internal and external validities of the study, the descriptive research design must try to compensate for this.

Randomized One-Group Posttest-Only Design

The distinguishing feature of the randomized one-group posttest-only design is that members of the group are randomly selected for it. Otherwise, this design is identical to the exploratory one-group posttest-only design. The randomized one-group posttest-only design is written as shown in Figure 8.9, where:

R_s = Random selection from a population
X = Program, or the intervention (see Box 8.3)
O_1 = First and only measurement of the dependent variable

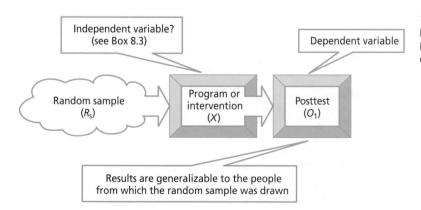

Figure 8.9
Randomized One-Group Posttest-Only Design

In the example of the child abuse prevention program, the difference in this design is that the group does not accidentally assemble itself by including anyone who happens to be interested in volunteering for the program. Instead, group members are randomly selected from a population, say, of all the 400 parents who were reported to child welfare authorities for having physically abused a child in Rome, Wisconsin, in 2005 and who wish to receive voluntary treatment. These 400 parents constitute the population of all the physically abusive parents who wish to receive treatment in Rome, Wisconsin.

The sampling frame of 400 people is used to select a simple random sample of 40 physically abusive parents who voluntarily wish to receive treatment. The program (X) is administered to these 40 people, and the percentage of parents who stop being abusive toward their children after the program is determined (O_1). The design can be written as shown in Figure 8.10, where:

R =   Random selection of 40 people from the population of physically abusive parents who voluntarily wish to receive treatment in Rome, Wisconsin

X =   Child Abuse Prevention Program, or the intervention (see Box 8.3)

O_1 = Percentage of parents in the program who stopped being physically abusive to their children

Say that the program fails to have the desired effect, and 80% of the people continue to physically harm their children after participating in the program. Because the program was ineffective for the sample and the sample was randomly selected, it can be concluded that the program would be ineffective for the physically abusive parent population of Rome, Wisconsin—the other 360 who did not go through the program. In other words, because a representative random sample was selected, it is possible to generalize the program's results to the population from which the sample was drawn.

Since no change in the dependent variable occurred, it is not sensible to consider the control of rival hypotheses. Antonia need not wonder what might have caused the minuscule change—X, her program, or an alternative explanation. If her program had been successful, however, it would not be possible to ascribe her success *solely* to the program.

Randomized Cross-Sectional Survey Design

As discussed earlier, a cross-sectional survey obtains data only once from a sample of a particular population. If the sample is a random sample—that is, if it represents the population from which it was drawn—then the data obtained from the sample can be generalized to the entire population. A cross-sectional survey

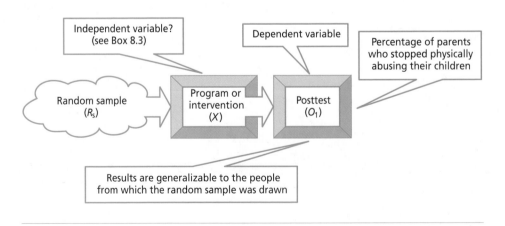

Figure 8.10   Randomized One-Group Posttest-Only Design

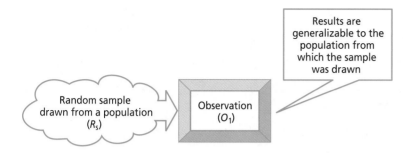

Figure 8.11
Randomized Cross-Sectional Survey Design

design using a random sample can be written as shown in Figure 8.11, where:

R_s = Random sample drawn from a population
O_1 = First and only measurement of the dependent variable (see Box 8.3)

Explanatory surveys look for associations between variables. Often, the suspected reason for the relationship is that one variable caused the other. In Antonia's case, she has two studies going on: the child abuse prevention program for parents who have physically abused their children, and her survey of parental attitudes toward the school that is teaching second-grade children child abuse prevention strategies. The success of the child abuse prevention program (her program) may have caused parents to adopt more positive attitudes toward the school in teaching their children child abuse prevention (her survey). In this situation, the two variables, the program and survey, become commingled. Demonstrating causality is a frustrating business at best because it is so difficult to show that nothing apart from the independent variable could have caused the observed change in the dependent variable.

One-Group Pretest-Posttest Design

The one-group pretest-posttest design is also referred to as a before-after design because it includes a pretest of the dependent variable, which can be used as a basis of comparison with the posttest results. It is written as shown in Figure 8.12, where:

O_1 = First measurement of the dependent variable

X = Program, or the intervention (see Box 8.3)
O_2 = Second measurement of the dependent variable

The one-group pretest-posttest design, in which a pretest precedes the introduction of the intervention and a posttest follows it, can be used to determine precisely how the intervention affects a particular group. The design is used often in social work decision making. It does not control for many rival hypotheses. The difference between O_1 and O_2, on which these decisions are based, could be due to many other factors rather than to the intervention.

Let us take another indicator of how Antonia's child abuse prevention program could be evaluated. Besides counting the number of parents who stopped physically abusing their children as the only indicator of the program's success, she could have a second outcome indicator such as a reduction in the parents' risk for abusive and neglecting parenting behaviors. This dependent variable could be easily measured by an instrument that measures their attitudes toward physical punishment of children.

Let us say that Antonia had the parents complete the instrument *before* participating in the child abuse prevention program (O_1) and *after* completing it (O_2). In this example, history would be a rival hypothesis or threat to internal validity because all kinds of things could have happened between O_1 and O_2 to affect the participants' behaviors and feelings—such as the television station's deciding to publicize the names of parents who are abusive to their children. Testing also could be a problem. Just the experience of taking the pretest could motivate some participants to stop being abusive toward their children. Maturation—in this

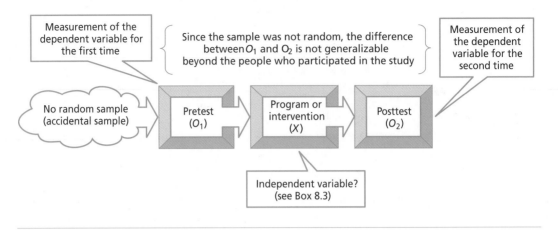

Figure 8.12   One-Group Pretest-Posttest Design

example, the children becoming more mature with age so that they became less difficult to discipline—would be a further threat.

This design controls for the threat of differential selection, since the participants are the same for both pretest and posttest. Second, mortality would not affect the outcome, because it is the differential dropout between groups that causes this threat, and, in this example, there is only one group (Williams, Tutty, & Grinnell, 1995).

Comparison Group Posttest-Only Design

The comparison group posttest-only design improves on the exploratory one-group and multigroup posttest-only designs by introducing a comparison group that does not receive the independent variable but is subject to the same posttest as those who do (the comparison group). The group used for purposes of comparison is usually referred to as a comparison group in an exploratory or descriptive design and as a control group

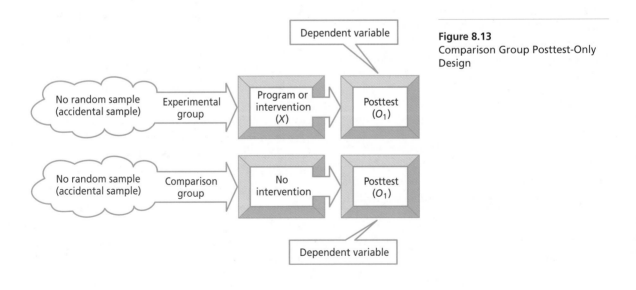

Figure 8.13
Comparison Group Posttest-Only Design

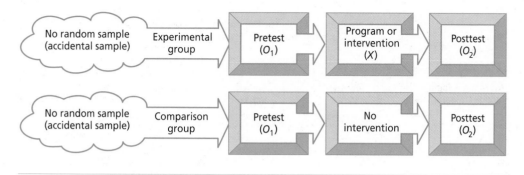

Figure 8.14 Comparison Group Pretest-Posttest Design

in an explanatory design. While a control group is always randomly assigned, a comparison group is not. The basic elements of the comparison group posttest-only design are as shown in Figure 8.13, where:

X = Independent variable, or the intervention
O_1 = First and only measurement of the dependent variable

In Antonia's child abuse prevention program, if the January, April, and August sections are scheduled but the August sessions are canceled for some reason, those who would have been participants in that section could be used as a comparison group. If the values of O_1 on the measuring instrument were similar for the experimental and comparison groups, it could be concluded that the program was of little use, since those who had experienced it (those who had received X) were not much better or worse off than those who had not.

A problem with drawing this conclusion, however, is that there is no evidence that the groups were equivalent to begin with. Selection, mortality, and the interaction of selection and other threats to internal validity are, thus, the major difficulties with this design. The comparison group does, however, control for such threats as history, testing, and instrumentation.

Comparison Group Pretest-Posttest Design

The comparison group pretest-posttest design elaborates on the one-group pretest-posttest design by adding a comparison group. This second group receives both the pretest (O_1) and the posttest (O_2) at the same time as the experimental group, but it does not receive the independent variable. This design is written as shown in Figure 8.14, where:

O_1 = First measurement of the dependent variable, the parents' scores on the measuring instrument
X = Independent variable, or the intervention
O_2 = Second measurement of the dependent variable, the parents' scores on the measuring instrument

The experimental and comparison groups formed under this design will probably not be equivalent, because members are not randomly assigned to them. The pretest scores, however, will indicate the extent of their differences. If the differences are not statistically significant but are still large enough to affect the posttest, the statistical technique of analysis of covariance can be used to compensate for this. As long as the groups are equivalent at pretest, then, this design controls for nearly all of the threats to internal validity. But, because random selection and assignment were not used, the external validity threats remain.

Interrupted Time-Series Design

In the interrupted time-series design, a series of pretests and posttests are conducted on a group of research participants over time, both before and after the

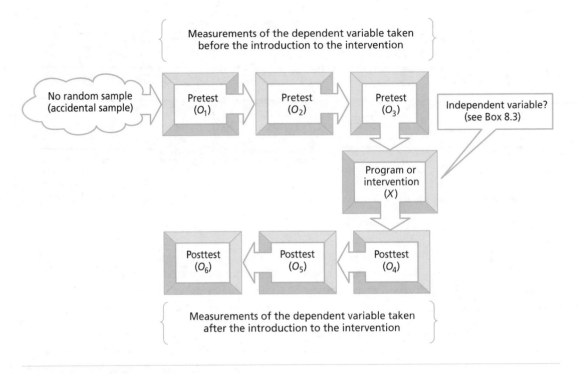

Figure 8.15   Interrupted Time-Series Design

independent variable is introduced. The basic elements of this design are shown in Figure 8.15, where:

O_s = Measurements of the dependent variable
X = The intervention (see Box 8.3)

This design takes care of the major weakness in the descriptive one-group pretest-posttest design, which does not control for many rival hypotheses. Suppose, for example, that a new policy is to be introduced into an agency whereby all promotions and raises are to be tied to the number of educational credits acquired by social workers. Since there is a strong feeling among some workers that years of experience should count for more than educational credits, the agency's management decides to examine the effect of the new policy on morale.

Because agency morale is affected by many things and varies normally from month to month, it is necessary to ensure that these normal fluctuations are not confused with the results of the new policy. Therefore, a baseline is first established for morale by conducting a number of pretests over, say, a 6-month period be-

fore the policy is introduced. Then, a similar number of posttests is conducted over the 6 months following the introduction of the policy.

The same type of time-series design can be used to evaluate the result of a treatment intervention with a client or client system, as in case-level designs described in the previous chapter. Again, without randomization, threats to external validity still could affect the study's generalizability, but most of the threats to internal validity are addressed.

Explanatory Designs

Explanatory group research designs approach the "ideal" experiment most closely. They are at the highest level of the knowledge continuum, have the most rigid requirements, and are most able to produce results that can be generalized to other people and situations. Explanatory designs, therefore, are most able to provide valid and reliable research results that can serve as additions to our professions' knowledge base.

The purpose of an explanatory design is to establish a causal connection between the independent and dependent variable. The value of the dependent variable could always result from chance rather than from the influence of the independent variable, but there are statistical techniques for calculating the probability that this will occur.

Classical Experimental Design

The classical experimental design is the basis for all the experimental designs. It involves an experimental group and a control group, both created by a random assignment method (and, if possible, by random selection from a population). Both groups take a pretest (O_1) at the same time, after which the independent variable (X) is given only to the experimental group, and then both groups take the posttest (O_2). This design is written as shown in Figure 8.16, where:

R = Random selection (R_s) from a population and random assignment (R_a) to group

O_1 = First measurement of the dependent variable

X = Independent variable, or the intervention

O_2 = Second measurement of the dependent variable

Because the experimental and control groups have been randomly assigned, they are equivalent with respect to all important variables. This group equivalence in the design helps control for rival hypotheses, because both groups will be affected by them in the same way.

Randomized Posttest-Only Control Group Design

The randomized posttest-only control group research design is identical to the descriptive comparison group posttest-only design, except that the research participants are randomly assigned to two groups. This design, therefore, has a control group, rather than a comparison group.

The randomized posttest-only control group research design usually involves only two groups, one experimental and one control. There are no pretests. The experimental group receives the independent variable and takes the posttest; the control group only takes the posttest. This design can be written as shown in Figure 8.17, where:

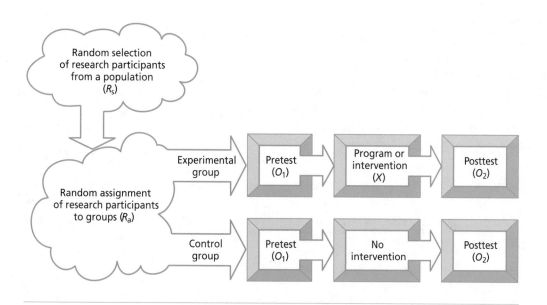

Figure 8.16   Pretest-Posttest Control Group Design (Classical Experimental Design)

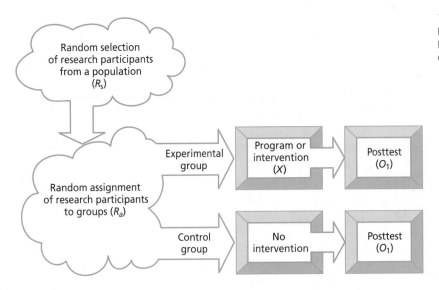

Figure 8.17
Randomized Posttest-Only Control Group Design

R = Random selection (R_s) from a population and random assignment (R_a) to group

X = Independent variable, or the intervention

O_1 = First and only measurement of the dependent variable

In addition to measuring change in a group or groups, a pretest also helps to ensure equivalence between the control and the experimental groups. As you know, this design does not have a pretest. The groups have been randomly assigned, however, as indicated by R, and this, in itself, is theoretically enough to ensure equivalence without the need for a confirmatory pretest. This design is useful in situations where it is not possible to conduct a pretest or where a pretest would be expected to strongly influence the results of the posttest because of the effects of testing. This design also controls for many of the threats to internal validity.

SUMMARY

Group research designs are conducted with groups of cases rather than on a case-by-case basis. They cover the entire range of research questions and provide designs that can be used to gain knowledge on the exploratory, descriptive, and explanatory levels.

Exploratory designs are used when little is known about the field of study and data are gathered in an effort to find out "what's out there." These ideas are then used to generate hypotheses that can be verified using more rigorous research designs. Descriptive designs are one step closer to determining causality. Explanatory designs are useful when considerable preexisting knowledge is available about the research question under study and a testable hypothesis can be formulated on the basis of previous work. They have more internal and external validity than exploratory and descriptive designs, so they can help establish a causal connection between two variables.

No one group research design is inherently inferior or superior to the others. Each has advantages and disadvantages. Those of us who are familiar with all three categories of group research designs will be equipped to select the one that is most appropriate to a particular research question.

PART III

Collecting Data

Part III consists of six chapters that detail how to

collect data via the most widely utilized social

work data collection methods: observations

(Chapters 9 and 10), interviews (Chapter 11), sur-

veys (Chapter 12), secondary analyses (Chapter

13), and content analyses (Chapter 14). Chapter

15, the final chapter in this part, details how to

select a data collection strategy or strategies for

any given research study.

Structured Observation

Richard A. Polster
Donald Collins

You Are Here

The data collection method described in this chapter depends on structured observations in which people are directly observed in their natural environments. Observations are made by trained observers in a specified place and over a specified time period, using specified methods and measurement procedures. This data collection method therefore is highly structured—probably the most highly structured of all the ones that are discussed in this text—and rigid procedures must be followed in order to produce valid and reliable data. In addition, it is the most obtrusive data collection method that can be used in social work research situations. This means that our research participants are aware that we are observing them.

USES IN SOCIAL WORK RESEARCH

The term *target problem*, introduced in Chapter 7 in relation to case-level evaluation designs, is used in this chapter to refer to a measurable behavior, feeling, or cognition (idea, belief, or attitude) that is either a problem in itself or symptomatic of some other problem. In the structured-observation method of data collection, the target problem in the research question or hypothesis is operationally defined, a measuring instrument is selected or constructed for recording the data, direct observations are made of the individuals or groups, and data on the observations are recorded and analyzed.

Structured observation can be used in both case-level evaluations to study client target problems (Chapter 7) and group research designs (Chapter 8) to study research questions or test hypotheses. This method of data collection is generally used when the target problem is not amenable to traditional measurement techniques and survey instruments such as questionnaires, interviews, and self-reports, or when an outside, presumably more objective, assessment seems necessary. Observing participants in their natural environments as well as in clinical or laboratory settings also can provide us with data that are otherwise not obtainable.

In a case-level evaluation, for example, we may directly observe the behavior of clients in order to supplement our assessment of the clients' self-reports.

Both the self-report measuring instruments and our direct observations can provide reliable data on the success of treatment interventions.

In a group research design to study the aggressive behavior of small children, an observer might be asked to watch a children's group through a one-way mirror and record acts of aggression according to a prescribed set of instructions. Or a study by a social service agency to identify the intervention techniques commonly employed by its staff might use trained observers to watch videotapes of social workers' interviews and code the types and frequency of techniques they use. In both instances, the observer would use a measuring instrument and an accompanying set of instructions to make the ratings.

OBSERVATIONAL DATA RECORDING

Each of the various methods used to record data from observations of people in their natural environments provides a different type of data. The method chosen must be consistent with the characteristics of the target problem being observed. We must also take into account who will be making the observations and recording the data and the amount of instruction they will need in order to produce valid and reliable data.

Table 9.1 summarizes six methods that we can use in making direct observations and measuring and recording the data needed to examine a research question or test a hypothesis. These methods described in this section are (1) interval recording, (2) frequency recording, (3) duration recording, (4) magnitude recording, (5) spot-check recording, and (6) permanent-product recording.

Interval Recording

Interval recording involves continuous, direct observation of individuals during specified observation periods divided into equal time intervals. The observations recorded in Figure 9.1 show the number of times a target problem was observed for an individual during a 1-minute period divided into six 10-second intervals. An observer recorded instances of the prob-

lem at least once during the second, third, fourth, and sixth intervals.

Occurrence data are obtained by recording the first occurrence of the target problem in each time interval. Subsequent occurrences during the same interval are not recorded. Nonoccurrence data can be obtained by recording those intervals in which the problem did not occur.

The resulting data will show the number of intervals during which the target problem occurred at least once and the number of intervals during which the target problem did not occur. These data are presented in terms of the percentage of intervals in which the target problem occurred at least once or did not occur. For example, the data in Figure 9.1 indicate that the target problem occurred in 4 out of 6 (two-thirds), or 67%, of the intervals.

If we want to know the duration of the target problem, data should be recorded only when it occurs throughout the entire interval (10 seconds in this example). In this case, a problem that occurs for only a portion of the interval would not be recorded. This procedure might be used, for example, to record the duration of a worker's on-task performance. Occurrence of the target problem (on-task behavior) would be recorded only if the worker was on task for the entire interval. An interval during which both on-task and off-task behavior were exhibited would be recorded as off task. The resulting data would indicate the number of intervals during which the worker sustained on-task activity, but it would not indicate the precise amount of time the worker was on task.

If more than one target problem is to be recorded in the same time intervals, a form like that shown in Figure 9.2 is used. A good procedure is to attach a form, containing the time intervals as shown, to a clipboard with a stopwatch fastened to the top. Audio recorders with earphones also can be used to play back prerecorded tapes that signal intervals as time passes.

Occurrence or nonoccurrence of the target problems is noted by placing a check mark in the space corresponding to each time interval. Ideally, environmental conditions that would affect the occurrence of the target problem or the accuracy of the observation should be controlled for (Bloom, Fischer, & Orme, 2006; Fischer

TABLE 9.1

Characteristics of Data Recording Methods for Structured Observation

Recording Method	Target Problems (Behaviors, Feelings, Cognitions)	Kinds of Information Gained	Formality of Observer Training	Relative Expense
Interval	Appropriate for measuring problems with high frequencies or highly variable frequencies and multiple behaviors, feelings, or cognitions	Fine grained (precise) measures Percent of intervals with occurrence or nonoccurrence of target problem Patterns of behavior, feelings, or cognitions and relationships among them	Extensive Formal training necessary	High due to costs for outside observers and observer training
Frequency	Appropriate for high- or low-frequency problems Interest in how often problem occurs	Gross measures Total occurrences per observation	Informal if observational code is simple Formal if code is complex	Low to high, depending on complexity of code and collateral or self-recording vs. trained observers
Duration	Appropriate for problems with measurable duration Interest in how long occurrence lasts or how long until it appears	Gross measures Length of time per occurrence	Informal if observational code is simple Moderate if code is complex	Low to high, depending on complexity of code and collateral of self-recording vs. trained observers
Magnitude	Appropriate for problems that vary in degree performed	Medium-grained measures Rating on scale per occurrence Profiles problem by frequency or severity of occurrence	Moderate if observational code is simple Formal training if code is complex	Low to high, depending on complexity of code and collateral or self-recording vs. trained observer
Spot check	Appropriate for sustained, ongoing problems	Gross measures Occurrence or nonoccurrence per spot check	Informal if observational code is simple Moderate if code is complex	Low to moderate, depending on complexity of code and collateral or self-recording vs. trained observers
Permanent product	Appropriate for problems that produce lasting effects on the environment or are recorded as part of ongoing process	Gross- to medium-grained measures Frequency or duration or magnitude of occurrence	Informal if product code is simple Moderate if code is complex	Low—requires no direct observation of behavior, feeling, or cognition, only coding of end products

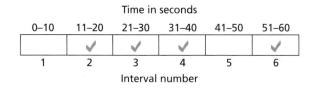

Figure 9.1 Characteristics of Data Recording Methods for Structured Observation

& Corcoran, 2007). If possible, the observer should ignore environmental stimuli such as crying children or other activities taking place and should observe from an unobtrusive location.

The data obtained through interval recording are highly detailed and provide a temporal picture (over time) of the target problem, in addition to information about the frequency or duration of the problem. Because small changes in the rate or pattern of behavior can usually be observed in the data, they provide fine-grained, or precise, measures for use in data analysis. Other data collection methods for structured observation provide gross, or broad, measures, at the other extreme, or medium-grained measures, which are neither too precise nor too broad (see Table 9.1).

Reliability

The reliability of the data collected with interval recording is computed by having at least two independent observers simultaneously record the same target problem or problems. The percentage of agreement in the observations is a measure of the overall reliability of the data. The common formula for computing percentage of agreement in interval recording data is as follows:

$$\text{Percentage of agreement} = \frac{\text{Agreements}}{(\text{Disagreements} + \text{Agreements})}$$

Agreements can be calculated by comparing the two recording forms and counting the intervals for which both observers recorded occurrence or nonoccurrence of the target problem. Disagreements occur

Client's Name		Recorder's Name										
Target Problems to Be Observed: A. _____ B. _____ Time Period: _____ Duration of Each Interval: _____		General Comments:										

		Interval									
Minute	Problem	1	2	3	4	5	6	7	8	9	10
1	A										
	B										
2	A										
	B										
3	A										
	B										

Figure 9.2 Interval Recording Form for Two Target Problems

when one observer records occurrence and the other records nonoccurrence in the same interval.

Applications

We can use the patterns of occurrence of target problems to plan treatment interventions. Since more than one target problem in the same time interval can be recorded, temporal relationships between target problems for an individual can be easily examined. We can determine whether a specific target problem usually follows, precedes, or occurs at the same time as another target problem, for example. Target problems of people interacting in dyadic relationships, such as parent-child, teacher-student, or husband-wife, or in small-group situations also can be studied. The effects of a teacher's use of contingent reinforcement on a student's rate of task completion is one example.

Because interval recording involves continuous, concentrated observation over a relatively short time period, it is more suitable for target problems that occur frequently. Economically, it is not suited to recording problems that occur at low frequencies. The shorter the intervals used, the more precisely can the time at which the target problems occur be determined.

Since this is a complex and time-consuming data recording procedure, observers who record interval data must be highly trained. Before beginning a study, practice recording sessions should be conducted to ensure that observers will be able to produce reliable data. Interval recording is not recommended for use by indigenous observers (those who are part of the environment in which the observations are made) unless the target problem to be recorded is simple and discrete and the intervals are large. Since an observer cannot do anything else while recording data, this procedure cannot be used for self-recording.

Compared with the other data recording methods discussed in this chapter, interval recording is the most rigorous, precise, and expensive. Disregarding cost, the decision to use this method should depend on whether the target problem occurs at a high enough frequency to warrant its use and whether, for practical purposes, the research question requires such detailed data.

Frequency Recording

Like interval recording, frequency recording involves the direct observation of individuals, but the techniques used for recording the data are less complex. Thus, the target problem can be observed over a longer period of time. Frequency recording is appropriate with both high- and low-frequency target problems.

During the specified observation period, each occurrence of a target problem is noted on a data recording form with an X. The X's are totaled for each period and can be expressed as the number of occurrences per the length of the observation period. An example of frequency recording during a 3-hour observation period in which there were 5 recorded occurrences of the target problem is given below:

Observation Period	Number of Occurrences
8 A.M. to 11 A.M.	X X X X X

The rate of the target problem, 5 occurrences in 3 hours, can be expressed as 5/3, or 1.7 occurrences per hour.

Frequency recording forms for a single period of time and for different periods are given in Figures 9.3 and 9.4, respectively.

Reliability

As with interval recording, the reliability of the data collected with frequency recording can be determined by having two observers simultaneously and independently record data on the same target problem. Frequency data, however, provide only a gross measure indicating the total number of times the target problem has occurred during a specific time period. Therefore, comparison of the data recorded by the two observers only shows whether they recorded the same number of occurrences of the target problem.

The common formula for computing reliability in frequency recording (with two observers) is based on the percentage of agreement between the observer with the lower frequency and the observer with the higher frequency. This is written as follows:

$$\text{Percentage of agreement} = \frac{\text{Lower frequency observed}}{\text{Higher frequency observed}} \times 100$$

Client's Name	Recorder's Name
Target Problem to Be Observed: A. _____ Time Period (Hours/Day): _____	General Comments:

Date	Frequency	Additional Comments

Figure 9.3 Frequency Recording Form for One Target Problem for One Time Period

This reliability computation will not indicate whether the two observers recorded the same occurrences of the target problem. Each observer could miss 25% of the occurrences and still arrive at the same number of occurrences. Although this method is not highly accurate, it can allow us to conclude that the data are representative of the frequency of the target problem. Confidence in the reliability of the frequency recording can be increased by having both observers record the actual time the target problem occurred, so it is possible to deter-

Client's Name	Recorder's Name
Target Problem to Be Observed: A. _____	General Comments:

Date	Frequency	Total	Time	Rate	Additional Comments

Figure 9.4 Frequency Recording Form for One Target Problem for Various Periods of Time

mine if the same problem was recorded by both of them at the same time.

Applications

Frequency recording is appropriate when the number of times the target problem occurs is the relevant measure. An administrator, for example, might use frequency recording to calculate the effect of a new policy to evaluate the work performance of social workers by measuring such tasks as the number of referrals processed or the number of clients served. Community organizers might use frequency recording to evaluate the effectiveness of a community action program by recording the number of requests for social services.

Target problem areas such as hitting, arguments, temper tantrums, compliance, communication, and physical affection can easily be measured with frequency recording. The frequency rates of the target problem may vary for different activities, particularly in settings such as homes or schools in which the schedule of activities changes often. Therefore, frequency data should be recorded under standardized conditions as much as possible. The number of arguments a couple has between 6:00 P.M. and 10:00 P.M. might vary according to the activities in which they are involved, for example. An evening at the movies or a party may result in few arguments; an evening at home may include many.

Generally, all three types of observers discussed further in a later section of this chapter can be used for frequency recording. These types are trained outside observers; indigenous observers who are naturally part of the research participant's environment, such as relevant others (family members, peers) and collaterals (caseworkers, other staff members); and self-observers, or research participants who make self-reports. The amount of observer training required to record frequency data depends on the number and complexity of the target problem. If fine discriminations must be made or if many target problems are to be recorded, observers may need extensive training and practice. To facilitate the implementation of frequency recording, the target problem should be clearly defined, especially when collaterals or relevant others are recording the data.

Frequency data recording is relatively inexpensive if the data are recorded by collaterals or research participants. If trained observers are used or extensive training is necessary, however, frequency data recording may be as costly as interval recording.

Duration Recording

Duration data are obtained by directly observing the target problem and recording the length of time taken by each occurrence within the specified observation period. The duration of an occurrence can be measured in seconds or minutes by watching a clock, triggering a stopwatch, or noting the time the target problem begins and ends and calculating the duration later.

In the following simple example of duration recording, the target problem occurred three times in the 1-hour observation period, and the observer noted the duration for each occurrence.

Observation Period (in minutes)	(Number) and Duration
6 P.M. to 7 P.M.	(1) 3: (2) 25: (3) 5

The first occurrence lasted for 3 minutes, the second for 25 minutes, and the third for 5 minutes. A more detailed duration recording form for a single target problem is reproduced in Figure 9.5

Reliability and Applications

In calculating the reliability of the data in duration recording, two observers simultaneously and independently use synchronized timepieces to note the time of onset and completion of the problem. Comparison of the two observers' times indicates whether they were recording the same occurrence of the behavior, feeling, or cognition.

One common use of duration data is in case-level evaluation designs. These data can compare the duration of occurrences of the target problem before and after intervention. These data can also be used to determine the cumulative time engaged in the target problem by an individual during the observation period by totaling the duration data for each occurrence.

Client's Name			Recorder's Name	
_____			_____	

Target Problem to Be Observed:

A. _____

Time Period for Observation:

A. _____

General Comments:

Date	Length of Time Problem Occurred (e.g., minutes)	Total Time (minutes)	Additional Comments

Figure 9.5   Duration Recording Form for One Target Problem for One Time Period

When this sum is divided by the total length of the observation period, the average amount of time engaged in the target problem by the individual is produced.

The duration of each occurrence during the observation period may also be averaged, but this could obscure important variations in the data. For instance, in the example where the occurrences of the target problem lasted from 3 to 25 minutes, with one occurrence of 5 minutes, the average occurrence is 11 minutes. This calculation hides the fact that the longest episode was more than twice as long as the average (Weinbach & Grinnell, 2007).

Duration data can easily be recorded by trained observers, collaterals, or research participants. Unless the target problem is difficult to discriminate, observer training should be minimal. If the problem is highly noticeable and occurs infrequently, other activities can be engaged in until it appears, and there is no need to be preoccupied with waiting for it. If the target problem is subtle at the outset, is of high frequency, or has an extremely long duration, the observer may need to concentrate on recording the data.

Duration recording should be used only when the length of time a target problem persists is the relevant issue. Many target problems can be measured in terms of both their duration and their frequency. The selection of the specific data recording method depends on the target problem to be measured.

Some examples of target problems that can be measured by duration recording are the length of episodes of crying, arguments, work breaks, illness, and time engaged in a task without interruption. It can also be used to measure the length of time between the presentation of a stimulus and the onset of the target problem, such as the elapsed time between a call for emergency services (stimulus) and delivery of the services (target problem), or the time between a parent's request and a child's compliance.

If trained outside observers are used, duration recording will be as expensive as interval recording. However, the training time will most likely be shorter. In many cases, duration data can be recorded by indigenous observers or self-observers at minimum expense.

Magnitude Recording

Magnitude recording involves recording data on the amount, level, or degree of the target problem during each occurrence. A magnitude recording can also be made by rating the target problem at prescribed intervals according to frequency or severity of occurrence. Ratings are made on a scale that shows the most minor level of the problem at one end and the most significant level at the other.

The following example is a 4-point scale to measure the magnitude of a child's temper tantrums:

1. Child cries and whines—low volume.
2. Child screams and shouts—high volume.
3. Child uses body to hit or throw inanimate objects; stamps feet on floor, kicks furniture, throws objects (but not in the direction of a person), hits furniture with hands.
4. Child uses body to strike other persons or self; throws an object in the direction of, or hits, another person.

These points on the scale should be operationally defined whenever possible, but a simple 4-point subjective rating scale could be used by collaterals or relevant others to rate their observations. Research participants can also use this recording method to record their own target problems related to private events such as degree of depression or anxiety.

Reliability

When simultaneous and independent ratings by two observers are used as a reliability check, the data should correspond not only to the number of occurrences but also to the magnitude rating. As in frequency recording, it is not possible to ensure that the observers have recorded and rated the same occurrence of the target problem unless the exact time of occurrence is noted.

An example of a reliability computation for magnitude recording, in which two observers each made three observations, is described as follows:

Observer 1		Observer 2	
Time	Magnitude	Time	Magnitude
10:02	3	10:02	3
10:57	2	10:57	3
11:17	3	11:17	3

Because the observers achieved 100% agreement on the time the target problems occurred, they were able to compare their ratings on each episode. There was agreement on the ratings of two out of three occurrences, for a 67% level of agreement on magnitude.

Applications

Magnitude recording is an appropriate measure for target problems that are characterized by a wide range of responses, provided the degree of the response is the relevant issue. Measures of magnitude can provide data about a problem that would not be reflected in a duration or frequency measure. A community organizer, for example, may want to know if the degree to which school board members use community complaints as an input for planning has improved over the past year. The board's responses to each citizen complaint could be rated according to the following 5-point scale:

1. Refuses to hear complaint.
2. Gives time for complaint but does not respond.
3. Discusses complaint but does not attempt to solve problem.
4. Devises solution to citizen problem.
5. Devises solution, discusses implication for future planning, and implements plan.

Magnitude recording requires more training than frequency or duration recording because observers need to make judgments about the degree of the target problem, in addition to noting its occurrence. Minor distinctions between the levels of the target problem may necessitate the use of trained outside observers. For most target problems with distinct levels and clear operational definitions, however, one practice session is likely to afford sufficient training.

If outside observers are not used, magnitude recording is a relatively inexpensive method of data recording. Recording the magnitude of target problems requires attention to every detail, so it may be time-consuming if the problem is of long duration.

Spot-Check Recording

Spot-check recording occurs when we observe the target problem at specified intervals. Unlike the four methods discussed earlier, spot checks involve our intermittent rather than continuous observations. At the specified observation time, we record whether or not the individual being observed is engaged in the target problem at that moment.

Spot-check recording produces occurrence-nonoccurrence data on the target problem. Figure 9.6 presents an example of spot-check recording in which the target problem was recorded as occurring in the second, third, and fifth spot checks.

To determine the percentage of spot checks in which the target problem occurred, the number of spot checks in which the target problem was observed is divided by the total number of spot checks conducted. If the problem is spot-checked a number of times each day, the percentages can be compared and the daily data averaged to compare data from day to day. Target problems of groups of individuals can be expressed as the percentage of group members who were engaged in the behavior, feeling, or cognition in the observation period.

Reliability and Applications

The reliability of data in spot-check recording is computed with the same formula used to determine reliability in frequency recording, by comparing the data collected by two independent observers. Because observation periods last only a moment, the two observers must be precisely synchronized to record simultaneously.

Spot-checking is a useful method for assessing the target problems of individuals in a group. For instance, the social behavior of nursing home residents could be measured by counting the number who are alone in their rooms at a specific time. Continued spot checks at prescribed intervals would indicate the level of social activity among the residents, and activity programs designed to affect social behavior could also be evaluated using this measure. This method can be used by observers who spend minimal time in the settings or by indigenous observers such as nurses who have little time to record data.

Generally, spot checks are best suited for measuring target problems that occur at a high frequency or are sustained over a long period, such as social interaction, play, and work. Low-frequency target problems may not be accurately represented by this method.

Spot checks can be conducted by observers who are normally part of the environment or by outside observers. Research participants may react more to outside observers; because the observer is present only intermittently for the spot checks, the stimulus may continue to be novel. Participants can record spot-check data on their own target problems by using a timer to signal the instants when they should record whether or not they are engaged in the target problem. Naturally occurring time intervals such as lunch breaks, coffee breaks, and end of work can also be used as signals to record data.

The amount of observer training needed is minimal unless the target problem to be measured is difficult to distinguish from other target problems. Instructions

Spot Check	Behavior Was Occurring	Behavior Was Not Occurring
1.		✓
2.	✓	
3.	✓	
4.		✓
5.	✓	

Figure 9.6   Spot-Check Recording Form

alone may be sufficient, but having a practice session or two is advisable.

Spot checks are typically the least expensive direct-observation method of data collection, since the target problem is observed only intermittently. This also enables collaterals and research participants to record data with minimal interruption of their normal activities.

Permanent-Product Recording

Permanent-product recording does not require direct observation of the occurrences of the target problem. Instead, the occurrence is determined by observing the product of the problem. Examples of permanent-product recording include records of social services provided, teachers' records, and end products of work activity, such as empty wastebaskets and vacuumed carpets for custodial work. Data can be recorded at a convenient time after the occurrence of the target problem but before the product is altered or obliterated by subsequent target problems.

Reliability and Applications

Reliability of the data is determined by comparing the data of two or more independent observers. The reliability measures do not have to be taken simultaneously, however. In most instances, durable records can be stored indefinitely for future reference.

Permanent-product recording is appropriate for measuring target problems that alter the state of the environment or are recorded in a lasting form. Written reports of such matters as school attendance, work completion, and various crimes can be measured by inspecting the records maintained on these problems rather than by observing the problems themselves.

A staff trainer, for example, may want to know if treatment intervention plans improve after staff members take part in a new program that teaches techniques for maintaining clinical records. Frequency of record completion or duration of work on the intervention plans would not reflect an improvement in quality. A frequency count could be made of all intervention plans that meet minimal standards, but those data would indicate only how many intervention plans

do or do not meet these standards. Instead, the records could be compared over time according to a standard of "completeness" or quality that was taught in the training session. The permanent product of the case reports then could be used to demonstrate fine-grained changes in the quality of work over time.

Target problems that produce an observable change in the environment can easily be measured by observing and recording the changes rather than observing the target problem as it occurs. A parent, for example, can record data on a child's completion of assigned chores, such as taking out the garbage, by looking to see if the garbage has been removed after the deadline for completion of the chore. Or the effectiveness of a policy on recruiting and hiring members of racial minority groups can be evaluated by recording the number of minority staff actually hired after the policy was introduced.

Permanent-product recording can also be used to measure a target problem that could not be observed otherwise. An individual, for example, could demonstrate mastery of the cognitive process of learning how to perform a mathematical function such as multiplication by consistently producing the correct answers to multiplication problems. The written answers are permanent products that indicate whether or not learning has occurred. Measuring instruments such as questionnaires or tests can also create permanent products.

Permanent-product data can be recorded by trained observers, collaterals, and relevant others, or self-observers. Since the measure relies on ongoing recording of environmental changes, this type of recording can usually be implemented in the absence of the research participants. Therefore, it is the least intrusive method of recording data. Permanent-product recording, however, provides data only on the end result of the target problem, not on the problem itself. Other data recording methods, such as interval recording, must be used to measure the process of the target problem.

THE ROLE OF THE OBSERVER

Regardless of the data recording method used in direct observations, the data obtained will be only as good as the observers or recorders who collect them. With each method, the reliability of the data is determined by comparing the results obtained by two or more independent observers. To ensure that the data collected will be determined reliable, the target problem should be clearly defined so it can be differentiated from other problems, recording procedures should be made as simple as possible, and observers should be carefully trained so they know precisely what to look for, at what time, and how it should be recorded. Reliability checks should be made as often as possible during the study, using the prescribed formulas and methods to determine the percentage of agreement in the data of two or more observers.

Observer reliability is analogous to the test-retest and alternate-forms methods of establishing the reliability of measuring instruments discussed in Chapter 5. It is concerned with the stability of observations made by a single observer at several points in time (intraobserver reliability) or the equivalence of observations made by two or more observers at one point in time (interobserver reliability).

Interobserver reliability, which is also referred to as interjudge, interrater, or intercoder reliability, has been widely used in social work research. In this approach, the reliability of the observations of two or more observers who use the same instrument to measure the same individuals at a certain point in time is assessed by calculating the percentage of agreement between them. Procedures for doing this for the various types of structured observations were explained in the preceding section.

Selection of Observers

Observers who collect and record data by direct observation may be selected from several categories:

- Outside observers, often professionally trained, who are engaged to record data
- Indigenous observers, including relevant others (such as family members and peers) and collaterals (such as social service staff members), who are naturally a part of the research participants' environment
- Research participants, who provide self-reports

A number of factors need to be taken into consideration in deciding which of these sources to use. These include direct costs; time—both the observer's time and the time frame of the research situation; type of data required; and clinical factors such as intrusion into participants' lives.

Outside Observers

Observers brought in for the purpose of recording data are expensive to use and may not always be available. Since they are not a part of the participants' normal environment, they are likely to intrude into their lives in a way that indigenous observers will not. In some situations, the presence of an outside observer can alter the target problem being measured and produce erroneous results.

Most outside observers, however, have had considerable training and experience and know how to use sophisticated procedures to record data on complex target problems. Because of this, and because outside observers have no vested interest in the results of the study, data obtained by them are generally considered to be more reliable than data from other sources.

Indigenous Observers

Indigenous observers are naturally a part of the research participant's environment. They may be members of the individual's family or staff members in an institution, such as a hospital, school, residential facility, or agency. Such collaterals, however, have their own jobs to do, and a major consideration in employing them as observers must be the amount of time required for data collection. Will it interfere with their other work if they are asked to make a frequency recording of a particular person's target problem? Will they resent the extra burden placed on them and fail to cooperate? A spot-check recording would take less time, but would such data be sufficiently accurate to fulfill the research study's requirements?

A compromise in research methods often is necessary when we find ourselves in a position where the gathering of interval or frequency data by outside observers would be too expensive or intrusive, and the use of indigenous observers would be too time-consuming.

While the way in which a research question is formulated determines what and how data are to be collected, the practical difficulties in the collection of data also affect the formulation of the question. This is one of the factors to take into account when deciding on a hypothesis to be tested. In this case, we would be obligated to adapt our question to fit the data collection methods that are actually open to us.

The problem of time is not so large when members of the research participant's family are asked to gather data and there is no direct cost. There are other difficulties, however. It is far easier for a staff member in an institution to observe a person unobtrusively than it is for a member of the individual's family to do so in the home.

A person who is aware of being watched might well alter the target problem, even subconsciously. Difficulties might also arise over which family members are selected to record the data; jealousies and frictions normally present within the family system might be aggravated. Observation of one family member by others, even with the best of intentions, may not be advisable.

Since family members usually have no training or experience in recording data, they must be carefully trained. Even so, they may only be able to cope with simple recording procedures and straightforward target problems that can be easily differentiated from other problems. The type and reliability of data obtained from family members are often limited.

Self-Observers

Self-recording may be the only possible alternative when data are needed on an individual's thoughts and feelings, or when the act of observation would change the target problem. Moreover, some target problems occur in situations that preclude the presence of an observer. Cost and the observer's time are seldom considerations when the data are self-recorded. Some recording methods, however, such as interval recording, cannot be used in self-recording because it is difficult for the participant to experience the target problem and record it at the same time.

The most important consideration when data are self-recorded is reliability. Even when the research participant is cooperative and truly wishes to record the problem accurately, it is very difficult to prevent the recording process from interfering with the target problem being recorded. Sometimes self-reports can be verified by other observers. People who report feelings of depression, for example, may exhibit behaviors (or target problems) consistent with depression, such as crying spells or unusual sleeping habits, which can be observed by others.

UNSTRUCTURED OBSERVATION

Not every observational method of data collection uses structured observations—as is done in the types that have been discussed in this chapter. In unstructured or nonsystematic observations, one or more observers provide narrative or qualitative accounts of their observations, without using structured, numerical categories to observe and record target problems. As we saw in Chapter 4, unstructured observation is generally used in the qualitative research approach. Social work practitioners make unstructured observations all the time when working with clients, and these observations can be used to generate clinical or research questions to be answered or hypotheses to be tested.

SUMMARY

The six basic methods of data recording—interval, frequency, duration, magnitude, spot-check, and permanent product—obtain data for structured observations. The observations are made in a specified place and over a specified time period; the target problem to be observed is operationally defined, and the data are recorded on an instrument designed for the purpose. In each case, reliability is determined by calculating the level of agreement between the observations or ratings of two or more independent observers.

Which method or combination of methods is selected for a particular study depends on the kind of data required for the study—that is, the formulation of the research question to be investigated and the hypothesis to be tested. The choice is also determined by constraints of time and money and the availability of observers who are willing and able to collect the necessary data. Observers may be outside observers, indigenous observers, or research participants.

As in all research situations, the factors to be considered in formulating a research question or hypothesis and in selecting a data collection procedure are interdependent. The question will determine which data collection method is to be selected, and this, in turn, will determine how the observers are to be selected. The availability and willingness of observers to perform the necessary operations will affect which method is to be used, and this, in turn, will affect the research question. The art of constructing any research hypothesis lies in juggling these factors so that a meaningful hypothesis can be formulated from the research question and data can be collected to test it within the context of the research situation.

Participant Observation

Gayla Rogers
Elaine Bouey

10

You Are Here

The preceding chapter ended with a brief discussion of how participant observation can be used to collect original data. This chapter continues the discussion of participant observation and discusses this data-collection method in much more detail. Like all the other data-collection methods presented in this book, its appropriateness for any particular research study is directly related to the study's research question. This chapter provides a definition and description of participant observation and discusses its practical application to social work research.

DEFINITION

It is difficult to provide an exact definition of participant observation, since there are many different ways of defining it depending on the discipline of the definer and how it has been applied to research situations over the past 80 years. Participant observation as a data-collection method began with early anthropological ethnomethodology studies in the 1920s. Since then, it has undergone a radical transformation as a result of an effort to look for new ways to obtain useful, reliable, and valid data from research participants.

Currently, participant observation is viewed as more of a mind-set (or an orientation) toward research rather than as a set of specific, applied data-collection techniques (Neuman, 2006). Further, the terms *field research*, *ethnographic research*, and *ethnography* are often used interchangeably with *participant observation*.

Distinguishing Features

Participant observation is an obtrusive data-collection method, because it requires the one doing the study, the participant observer, to undertake roles that involve establishing and maintaining ongoing relationships with research participants who are often in field settings.

The passage of time is also an integral part of participant observation. We need to consider, for example, the sequences of events (and to monitor processes) over time so that research participants' relationships and the meanings of what they are experiencing can be discovered. We gather data primarily through direct observation, supplemented with other data-gathering methods such as interviewing (Chapter 11), using existing documents (Chapters 13 and 14), and using our own personal experiences.

Participant observation is an excellent way to gather data for understanding how other people see or interpret their experiences (Spradley, 1980). It represents a unique opportunity to see the world from *other* points of view, often at the sites where the activities or phenomena occur. It is also compatible with the "reflective practitioner" model of social work practice, as part of the process involves examining our personal insights, feelings, and perspectives in order to understand the situations we are studying (Papell & Skolnik, 1992; Schön, 1983).

A key factor in participant observation is its emphasis on the use of *relatively unstructured* data-gathering methods, such as observing everyday events in natural settings in an effort to understand how other people see or interpret their experiences and then stepping outside that perspective to add a "more objective" viewpoint (Neuman, 2006). In practice, however, it is often a back-and-forth (or recursive) process.

Through observations and interactions with research participants over time (e.g., weeks, months, years), we can learn a great deal about them—their histories, habits, and hopes, and their cultures, values, and idiosyncrasies, as well. These observations and interactions can be fascinating and fun as well as time-consuming, costly, and emotionally draining.

As we know, data derived from a participant observation study can easily be augmented with survey research data. In addition, they can be used with both research approaches—quantitative and qualitative. The use of several data-gathering methods, such as participant observation and survey research, in addition to the use of supplemental data sources such as existing documents, as well as the observation of people in different roles, creates the potential for a fuller understanding of the phenomena being studied.

Participant observation is an excellent data-collection method for exploring a wide variety of social settings and subcultures and most aspects of social life. It is valuable, for example, in studying deviant behavior (e.g., prostitution, drug use), unusual or traumatic circumstances (e.g., spinal cord injury, rape), and important life events (e.g., birth, divorce, death). It can be used to study entire communities in a range of settings or relatively small groups that interact on a regular basis in a fixed setting.

Some examples include studies of women's emergency shelters, the workings of social service agencies from the perspective of the members in those settings, or an immigrant group living in a particular neighborhood. Participant observation can also be used to study social experiences that are not fixed in a place but for which in-depth interviewing and direct observation are the only ways to gain access to the experience—for example, the feelings of women who have left violent relationships.

Researchers who participate in these settings can also occupy other roles, including social worker, volunteer, English as a Second Language tutor, program aide, or administrative assistant. The more roles we assume, the better our understanding of the situation because we come to understand different points of view.

When to Use Participant Observation

Participant observation as a data-collection method is well suited to situations where we wish to better understand how people see their own experiences, as well as those where we want to gain an in-depth perspective on people within the contexts and environments in which these events occur. It is exceptionally useful when it is applied to the study of processes, interrelationships among people and their situations, and events that happen over time and the patterns that have developed, as well as the social and cultural contexts in which human experiences occurred (Jorgensen, 1989).

Participant observation allows for the collection of data about phenomena that are not obvious from the viewpoint of the nonparticipant. It provides an opportunity to achieve a comprehensive understanding of human situations, and richly textured perspectives. Furthermore, when conducted in natural settings, it has the potential to elucidate certain nuances of attitude or behaviors that may not be included when data are gathered using other data-collection methods.

Participant observation is often helpful in identifying problem areas that can be the topics for subsequent studies that use other data-collection methodologies. We can then *triangulate*, or compare and contrast, the data gathered via these different methods in order to enhance our study's credibility. We may initially select a role as a volunteer in a women's emergency shelter, for example, find that we would like to learn more about the conditions that led women to the shelter, and subsequently gain permission to both review intake records and conduct structured interviews with a sample of women who enter the shelter. Participant observation is especially appropriate for scholarly problems in the following circumstances (Jorgensen, 1989):

- Little is known about a situation or event (e.g., job satisfaction among workers at a women's emergency shelter).
- There are important differences between the views of one group and those of another (e.g., perspectives on domestic violence among police and medical service professionals versus perspectives of social workers inside a women's emergency shelter).
- The phenomenon is obscured in some way from those outside a setting (e.g., spouse battering within a community of immigrants who do not commonly interact with social service agencies and who do not speak English).
- The phenomenon is hidden from society in general (e.g., drug abuse treatment for those in higher socioeconomic levels).

While participant observation is appropriate for gathering data for almost any aspect of human existence, it is not suited to every scholarly research inquiry that involves humans and their interactions with one another. It is particularly applicable to exploratory and descriptive studies out of which theoretical interpretations and hypotheses emerge. Its primary contribution allows for the creation of in-depth understandings of situations in an effort to support the development of different theoretical viewpoints.

Minimal Conditions for Participant Observation

In using participant observation as a data-collection method, there are minimal conditions that must be present (Jorgensen, 1989):

- The research question is concerned with human meanings and interactions viewed from the insider's perspective.
- The phenomenon is observable within an everyday life setting or situation.
- Gaining access to an appropriate setting is not a problem.
- The phenomenon is sufficiently limited in size and location to be studied as a case.
- The research question is appropriate for a case study.
- The research question can be addressed by qualitative data gathered by direct observation and other means pertinent to the field setting.

Getting Involved and Observing

Participant observation involves a dual purpose: *getting involved* in activities appropriate to the situation and *observing* people, the physical site, and the events happening in a particular context or setting. While a regular member experiences events in a direct and personal manner, the participant observer experiences being both an insider (with a "subjective" viewpoint) and an outsider (with a more "objective" viewpoint). Thus, it requires personal preparation and ongoing mindfulness to maintain an objective perspective even while one is involved in a field setting as a participant. It means being explicitly aware of one's values and assumptions while holding one's judgments in abeyance. This is often challenging and proves to be a very intensive experience for the participant observer.

There is little question that the participant observer's involvement in a setting can have an emotional impact of varying degrees. As Neuman (2006) notes:

Field research can be fun and exciting, but it can also disrupt one's personal life, physical security, or mental well being. More than other types of social research, it reshapes friendships, family life, self identity, or personal values.

Since the researcher is the primary instrument through which data are gathered and interpreted, he or she may have a potential influence on the study. This is why it is crucial to prepare oneself as much as possible in advance for this experience, maintain a separate log of personal notes and reflections, and make arrangements for regular advisory and debriefing sessions.

It is also important to note that some of us may be very well suited to use participant observation as a data-collection method, while others may be advised to use other data-collection methodologies. Thus, a team approach is often appropriate, with one person doing participant observation and another conducting structured interviews and examining existing documentation, for example.

ROLES

This section provides an overview of the various roles for those involved in a participant observation study and describes the tasks associated with each role. Being a *participant-observer* in a field setting is quite different from being a *regular participant* in a field setting. Researchers who use participant observation as a data-collection method often assume a variety of roles. These roles can be placed on a continuum and are classified into four categories as presented in Figure 10.1: (1) complete participant, (2) observer-participant, (3) participant-observer, and (4) complete observer.

We can sit in on staff meetings, for example, and view other operational activities as a *complete observer* to gather data on how the agency staff function in an office setting; or, with varying degrees of involvement

as a *participant-observer* or *observer-participant*, we can be volunteers who come in to help with some aspect of the agency's operation on a regular basis to gather data on how a particular program works; or, as a *complete participant*, we can, at the other end of the continuum, be one of the permanent staff in an agency who also happens to be doing a research study on the day-to-day activities within the program.

Balancing the Roles

In assuming any one of the four roles in doing a participant observation study, we need to be acutely aware of the need to maintain a balance between our participation and our ability to be objective. There may be so many temptations to become totally involved that we can easily lose this balanced perspective. This is often a particular challenge when we are *complete participants* as compared to *complete observers*. Some aids to maintaining this balance include reflective journal writing and regular debriefing sessions with other professionals who are not familiar with our field setting.

When we take on different roles, however, these roles can be overtly revealed, or in some cases they can be undertaken on a covert basis and not revealed. We strongly recommend, whenever possible, that any role played be on an overt or openly explained basis. This helps us with ethical considerations and is in keeping with the way in which participant observation has evolved in relation to social work settings.

If we are going to be studying a women's emergency shelter, with all the appropriate advance clearances for access to that setting, for example, and if we assume a role as a children's playroom assistant so that we can observe the interaction of the children with their mothers and with the shelter's staff, it is absolutely mandatory that we let the parents, the shelter's staff,

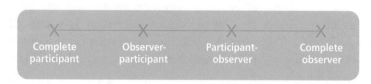

Figure 10.1
Continuum of Participant Observation

and the children know why we are there (our dual role) and what we will be doing with the data collected. These need not be lengthy explanations initially, but they set the stage for trust and acceptance.

We should be ready to answer questions as they surface. On the other hand, sharing of the initial analyses of our raw observational data or of our personal recorded reflections is not appropriate. Yet, it is quite reasonable to provide a summary (or a full copy) of our final research report to interested participants.

In assuming roles in a field setting, we should be aware that the social and physical locations are very important influences on the type of data we will be able to collect. As we note *what* occurs at different points in time and space, we may begin to recognize that *when* something occurs is often important. In a women's emergency shelter, for example, the physical locations at which we observe could include the children's playroom, the outside playground, and the dining room.

The different roles we could take—such as a social worker or a children's playroom aide—affect our interactions with those at the shelter and, in turn, provide us with a rich variety of different perspectives. In some cases, it might be difficult to operate in these different roles in one field setting, so we might choose to select one or two roles at one women's shelter and take on others at another shelter.

NEEDED STRATEGIES AND SKILLS

As previously mentioned, the participant observation experience is intense and demanding. Participant observation is both an art and a science, calling on many aspects of our capabilities. In order to deal with the many situations that come up in a field setting, we can use a few strategies to minimize difficulties and stresses for all those involved, as well as to ensure that a high-quality research study takes place.

- We need to practice observing and making notes that are as detail-rich as possible and that are based on our recall of events (e.g., we might observe people interacting in a busy city recreation center).

- We need to keep a daily personal journal that includes our reflections on events that are occurring in our life; this will help with both the discipline of writing field notes and with enhancing our self-knowledge.
- We need to get help from a knowledgeable adviser in designing, planning, and implementing our research study, as well as in setting up a regular schedule of debriefing and advisory sessions throughout the study.
- We need to tap into supporting systems and services to help us maintain our physical, emotional, and spiritual well-being.
- We need to develop a working knowledge of our topic area by reading the literature and by talking with people who have done research studies in our particular research area.
- We need to identify, record, and, if possible, let go of our assumptions or preconceptions that might influence the study.

The specific skills needed for using participant observation as a data-collection method are:

- The skills of careful looking and listening— paying attention to all possible details
- The skills of remembering things—including verbatim comments, nonverbal cues, and "climatic" conditions
- The skills of disciplined, regular writing— describing events and exchanges as well as personal reactions and reflections
- The skills of tuning into oneself—knowing our vulnerabilities, values, and views and owning our thoughts and feelings, assumptions, and biases

STEPS IN DOING PARTICIPANT OBSERVATION

Our direct participation in, and observation of, events as they occur in their natural field settings is the cornerstone of participant observation as a data-collection method. Thus, it is essential that we be well organized and prepared, but also flexible and adaptable enough to change with the circumstances. The specific steps of using participant observation as a data-collection method cannot be entirely predetermined; however, they can serve as a guide to the overall process.

We need to recognize and seize opportunities and rapidly adjust to these new situations as they occur in the field. In the beginning of our study, we can expect to have little control over our data and not much focus. Once we are socialized into our field setting, however, we can focus our inquiry and gain some control over the data we finally end up gathering.

Notwithstanding that participant observation is characterized by a back-and-forth, nonlinear process, there are six fundamental steps that serve as a guide. These steps are (1) gaining access and entry to a study site, (2) engaging and forming relationships, (3) gathering the data, (4) recording the data, (5) making sense of the data, and (6) reporting the findings.

Step 1: Gaining Access and Entry to a Study Site

A site is the context in which our study occurs, and it need not be a fixed geographic location. A particular group of research participants, for example, may interact across several sites. In addition, our own characteristics may limit access to a site. A white single male, for example, may have a difficult time gaining access to a group of single-parent women of color. Physical access can also be an issue; we may find that we are not allowed on a site(s) or that there are legal or political barriers to access, such as in public schools, hospitals, and prisons.

Access to such settings depends on *gatekeepers*—those with formal or informal authority to control access to sites. Permission is usually required from a gatekeeper and involves bargaining and negotiating. In some cases, permission from gatekeepers may inhibit the cooperation of people whom we want to study. Juvenile offenders, for example, may not want to participate in a study if they know that the director of secure treatment has authorized us to be there. Gaining access and entering a site depends on our personal attributes, prior connections, and social skills.

Entry and access is more analogous to peeling away the layers of an onion than it is to opening a door. We begin at the outermost layer where access is easy. At this stage, as outsiders, we are most likely looking for data more or less in the public domain. The next layer requires an increased degree of access as we become more of a passive, unquestioning observer of events as they occur in the field setting.

Over time, and as trust develops, we peel off another layer and observe more sensitive interactions or activities and ask for clarification of our personal observations. At yet a deeper layer, we can shape or influence the interaction so that particular data or certain behaviors are revealed. This layer is also necessary in order to access highly sensitive material that requires a deep level of trust.

Step 2: Engaging and Forming Relationships

The process of engaging and developing relationships with our research participants requires sensitivity and well-developed communication and interpersonal skills. We must be prepared to explain what we are doing and why, repeatedly, with each research participant. We should be ready to deal with a degree of hostility, rejection, and resistance. These reactions will be more or less intense depending on who we are and the population we are studying.

Gaining entry and access to women with breast cancer, for example, may pose fewer obstacles if the researcher is a woman who has had breast cancer than if the researcher is a white woman who is trying to enter a poor Hispanic neighborhood but is seen as part of the "white establishment."

The participant observer must establish rapport and build relationships. This is not always easy, as field settings can be very uncomfortable and individuals in these settings can behave in frightening ways. Building trust is a complex matter: It develops over time and requires continual reaffirmation. We need to learn the language and the meanings constructed by the research participants we are studying—how to think and act from the perspective of the *insiders*.

In short, we need to empathize and understand their experiences. Thus, it is crucial to monitor how our actions and appearances affect the members so that the data we gather are as rich and reflective as possible. This requires a degree of sharing and disclosure on our part; we cannot remain neutral or distant and expect to be a participant observer.

Our relationships must be characterized by dialogue and partnership, mutual interest and reciprocity, and trust and cooperation, while remaining within the parameters of professional ethics. This means that we must be alert to the dimensions of cultural, ethnic, and other differences, while being sensitive to the dynamics of power and privilege in the relationships we are building. The longer (or more often) we are in a field setting, the more we will be regarded as nonthreatening and our presence taken for granted.

As our relationships evolve and deepen over time, we must be careful about not slipping into roles that may be an aside to being a researcher, which would breach the agreement we made with our research participants. In some circumstances, it may be easier to become a therapist, change agent, advocate, or active member (full participant) than it is to remain a participant observer. Should we undertake such roles, however, we will change the nature of our relationships, which will impact and likely thwart the original purpose of our research study.

Some of the first questions that research participants ask are "Why should I cooperate with your research study?," "What's in it for me/us?," and "What's in it for you?" Our direct and candid answers to these questions are important. Research participants need to know that we seek to understand and describe their reality from their point of view and that ultimately there is value in having their stories told.

But they also need to know that we expect to gain such things as publications, expertise, or an academic degree from the study. The data collected will, we hope, contribute to the knowledge base and may lead to solutions to their problems. Participants also need to know, however, that there are no absolute guarantees; nor is it the intent that our study will change their lives in any meaningful way.

Engaging and forming relationships that are sustained over time with insiders in a field setting is imperative to gathering meaningful, valid, and reliable data. Building these relationships is like being socialized into a way of life. We need to "be there," to "hang out," to "watch, listen, and learn the norms, language, and patterns of interaction." The same skills used to make friends are used to connect with the insiders, our

research participants, in a field setting so that we have the ability to gather meaningful data that will be used to answer our research question.

Step 3: Gathering the Data

Participant observation data are usually gathered in four non–mutually exclusive ways: (1) observing, (2) interviewing, (3) using existing documents and other materials, and (4) reflecting upon our personal experiences.

Observing

Good observers need to use all of their senses to notice what they see, hear, touch, smell, and taste. Start with the physical surroundings of the settings, for example, and pay particular attention to the details that influence human behavior, such as lighting, temperature, colors, odors, and available space.

The next level is to observe people and their actions. Begin by noting observable physical characteristics of individuals and the composition of the group in such areas as gender, ethnicity, age, shape/size, and appearance. Notice what people do in relation to each other, such as who talks, who listens, and who sits or stands next to whom. As our observations become more focused, we pay more attention to such issues as the nature of the gathering and discern whether this is typical or unusual.

At this stage, our observations serve the purpose of familiarizing ourselves with the field setting, helping us to get a "feel for the people and the place." These observations allow the widest possible field of vision. We are, however, limited to learning by looking and listening and will soon need to more sharply focus our attention and move away from passive observation to being a more active participant by asking questions through interviewing.

Interviewing

The data collected at the beginning of a participant observation study are in the form of words, including direct quotes and thick descriptions of particular events. There are general guidelines for asking good questions, but the type and style depend on the purpose and nature of the specific research study.

Questions that ask *what, when, where,* and *how* provide good descriptive data. Questions that ask *why* pressure people, put them on the defensive, and should therefore be used selectively. *Compare-and-contrast* questions constitute another type of inquiry. By asking how things are similar to and different from one another, we can discern what is included or excluded, what is part of or outside the phenomenon, and thus we can start to grasp the multiple meanings and layers involved in understanding the phenomenon we are studying.

Data gathering by engaging in dialogue and asking questions may be undertaken in a variety of situations ranging from casual conversations to formal interviews. Structured interview schedules used in formal interviews, where specific questions are asked in exactly the same way of each research participant, have the advantage of producing a uniform set of data.

On the other hand, as we know from the previous chapter, unstructured interviews have the advantage of producing richly qualitative data at a more in-depth level of disclosure. Both structured and unstructured interviewing contribute useful and meaningful data. Gayla Rogers and Elaine Bouey (1996) present a clear description of how to collect interview data in qualitatively oriented research studies. Figure 10.2 provides a summary of the main differences between survey and participant observation interviewing (Neuman, 2006).

Using Existing Documents and Other Materials

In the course of a participant observation study, it is not unusual to come across existing documents such as files, records, articles, pamphlets, and other materials, such as objects, artwork, videos, and clothing. These data sources are extremely useful in providing support for the findings we derived from our observing and interviewing. They provide a background, in addition to offering alternative points of view or explanations. The use of existing documents is an unobtrusive data-collection method that collects data that already exist.

Reflecting Upon Our Personal Experiences

Our feelings, insights, and perceptions are other sources of data and should be treated as just that—duly documented and reported, however. By participating in the world of those we are studying, we generate the experiences of an insider. Reflecting upon our personal experiences in our field setting gives us access to the standpoint of the insider. It provides us with insights and new understandings of particular ways of life. These data can be used as a source of further questions to be asked of our research participants in order to check out our inner responses, hypotheses, and assumptions.

Through these various methods, high-quality data are gathered. This means that our data are richly varied, detailed descriptions that emerge from our observations and experiences.

Step 4: Recording the Data

Regardless of the type of data collected, their purpose is lost if we fail to adequately record our observations, impressions, and actual words. In addition to our notes, tapes, and transcriptions, we can use visual aids, such as diagrams, flowcharts, eco-maps and genograms, and photographs. Their type, form, and content depend on a number of factors: the field setting, the available and suitable technologies, the purpose of our study, and our personal preferences.

There is a great temptation to postpone systematically recording the gathered data. This is a mistake, as data that are not carefully organized and stored after they have been recorded create many challenges in the data analysis stage. Researchers are strongly encouraged to develop the habit of regularly recording what they see, hear, and experience.

There are many ways to record data when using participant observation as a data-collection method. Three of the more common ones are: (1) using field notes, (2) using taping devices, and (3) using visual aids.

Survey Interview	Participant Observation Interview
1. It has a clear beginning and conclusion.	1. The beginning and end are not clearly defined. The interview can be picked up later.
2. The same standard questions are asked of all research participants in the same order.	2. The questions and the order in which they are asked are tailored to certain people and situations.
3. The interviewer remains neutral at all times.	3. The interviewer shows interest in responses, encourages elaboration.
4. The interviewer asks questions, and the interviewee answers.	4. It is like a friendly conversational exchange, but with more interview-like questions.
5. It is almost always with a single research participant.	5. It can occur in a group setting or with others in the area, but varies.
6. The researcher maintains a professional tone and businesslike focus. Diversions are ignored.	6. It is interspersed with jokes, asides, stories, diversions, and anecdotes, which are recorded.
7. Closed-ended questions are common, with rare probes.	7. Open-ended questions are common, and probes are frequent.
8. The interviewer alone controls the speed and direction of the interview.	8. The interviewer and insider jointly influence the pace and direction of the interview.
9. The social context in which the interview takes place is not considered and is assumed to make little difference.	9. The social context of the interview is noted and seen as essential for interpreting the meaning of responses.
10. The interviewer attempts to shape the communication pattern into a standard framework.	10. The interviewer adjusts to the insider's norms and language usage, following his or her lead.

Figure 10.2   Survey Research Interviews Versus Participant Observation Interviews

Using Field Notes

The majority of gathered data are in the form of field notes. Writing field notes requires self-discipline and the allocation of time for the task. We will save a lot of backtracking (not to mention aggravation) if we organize our notes into categories at the outset of the study. Visualize creating separate containers to hold different types of notes.

Factual observations, for example, are noted separately from personal feelings, impressions, or speculations; notes about our reactions to an interview or extraneous factors affecting the interview are kept separate from transcriptions or direct quotes from an interview. It may be hard to decide, particularly during the initial stages, what constitutes something worth noting. It may also worry us at later stages that, having made all these notes, we have so much data that it seems impossible to decipher any of them. These concerns can be addressed by following the recommendations for making field notes (Neuman, 2006):

- Make notes as soon as possible after each period in the field.
- Begin a record of each field visit with a new page, and note the date and time.
- Use jotted notes only as a temporary memory aid—use key words or terms, or note the first and last things said.
- Use wide margins and double-space everything to make it easy to add to notes at any time. Add to the notes if you remember something later.
- Type notes and store them on disks in separate files so that it will be easy to go back to them later.
- Record events in the order in which they occur, and note how long they last (e.g., a 15-minute wait, a 1-hour ride).
- Make notes as concrete, specific, complete, and comprehensible as possible.
- Use frequent paragraphs and quotation marks. Exact recall of phrases is best, with double quotes; use single quotes for paraphrasing.
- Record small talk or routines that do not appear to be significant at the time; they may become important later.
- "Let your feelings flow," and write quickly without worrying about spelling or "wild ideas." Assume that no one else will see the notes, but use pseudonyms as a precaution to maintain confidentiality.
- Never substitute tape recordings completely for field notes.
- Include diagrams or maps of the setting, and note your own movements and those of others during the period of observation.
- Include your own words and behavior in the notes. Also record emotional feelings and private thoughts in a separate section.
- Avoid evaluative summarizing words. Use nonjudgmental, descriptive words. Instead of "The sink looked disgusting," say, "The sink was rust-stained and looked as if it had not been cleaned in a long time. Pieces of food and dirty dishes that looked several days old were piled into it."
- Reread notes periodically, and record ideas triggered by the rereading.
- Organize materials neatly into types or methods of data collected so that they can be easily accessed.
- Always make one or more backup copies, keep them in a locked location, and store the copies in different places in case of fire.

There are many different types of field notes. We have chosen to describe four that represent different levels of data: (1) direct observation notes, (2) interpretive notes, (3) thematic notes, and (4) personal journal notes.

Using Direct Observation Notes.   The first level of field notes, *direct observation notes*, is usually organized chronologically and contains a detailed description of what was seen and heard. At this level, the notes report the facts—who, what, when, and where—and include verbatim statements, paraphrases, and nonverbal communications. These also include summary notes made after an interview.

Using Interpretive Notes.   The next level of field notes is *interpretive notes*. Our interpretations of events are kept separate from the record of the facts noted as direct observations but should be written in a column adjacent to the direct observations. These notes include our interpretation of the meanings implied by the words and gestures we observed. We can speculate about the social relationships, the emotions, and the influence of culture and context on what actually took place.

By keeping our interpretations separate, we leave room for multiple interpretations (or different interpretations) to arise as our knowledge and experience increase. If we are not vigilant, however, it is quite easy to combine the facts with our interpretation of them, and we run the risk later on of viewing our interpretations as fact, which in turn might narrow our ability to see other versions or meanings as they emerge.

Using Thematic Notes.   The third level of field notes is *thematic notes*. These provide a place to record our emerging ideas, hypotheses, theories, and conjectures. This is the place to speculate and identify themes, make linkages between ideas and events, and articulate our thoughts as they emerge while we are still in the field setting. In these notes, we might expand on some of the ideas that have occurred to us, and develop our theories as we go or as we reread our direct observation notes and interpretive notes.

This is the place to describe the thoughts that emerge in the middle of the night or to elaborate on any "Aha!" connections. It is critical to have a separate container for thoughts at this level, even if they are speculative and in the early stages of development, because we might lose an important seed for later analysis if they are not recorded.

Using Personal Journal Notes.   A journal of *personal notes* provides an outlet for our feelings and emotional reactions, as well as for the personal experiences of being the researcher or the participant-observer. These reactions are a rich source of data. They give voice to our journey over time and provide a place to consider such things as what is going on at any given time during our involvement in the field.

A running record of personal life events, feelings, physical well-being, and our moods, particularly as they relate to events in the field, will facilitate our data analysis. In this way, we can capture any particular intrapersonal or interpersonal experiences that might affect the way we make sense of the data. The process has an effect upon the quality of the content gathered, our interpretation of the content, and what steps we decide to take next. Identifying these effects as they are revealed also facilitates our interpretation and reporting of them later.

The four different levels of field notes are shown below using an example of recording a period of observation in a field setting with a woman named Kay (Neuman, 2006):

Direct Observation. *Sunday, October 4, 2008: Kay's Cafe 3:00 P.M. Large white male in mid-40s, overweight, enters. He wears worn brown suit. He is alone sits at booth #2. Kay comes by,*

asks, *"What'll it be?" Man says, "Coffee, black for now." She leaves and he lights cigarette and reads menu. 3:15 P.M. Kay turns on radio.*

Interpretive. *Kay seems friendly today, humming. She becomes solemn and watchful. I think she puts on the radio when nervous.*

Thematic. *Women are afraid of men who come in alone since the robbery.*

Personal Journal. *It is raining. I am feeling comfortable with Kay but am distracted today by a headache.*

Using Taping Devices

As we participate more actively and purposefully in the field setting and as our interactions with our research participants become less casual and more planned, we conduct interviews that are recorded and later transcribed.

There are three typical approaches to recording the data gathered in qualitative research interviews: (1) taping the interview (either audio or video); (2) taking notes during the interview; and (3) recording notes immediately following the interview.

Taping the Interview.   There are both advantages and disadvantages to tape-recording interviews. The presence of a recorder can be intrusive and a barrier to full disclosure; however, it may be the only way to capture the richness and subtleties of speech. Video recording is the only way to capture the nonverbal language used by our research participants or to accurately identify each speaker in a group situation. Recording devices may also be a means of self-monitoring and self-improvement for the interviewer. Using a tape recorder may provide us with the confidence to focus all our attention on the person being interviewed, knowing that we do not have to worry about remembering all of the details or writing notes. At the same time, however, knowing the tape will record everything that is said, we might be tempted to let our minds wander.

Ultimately, the decision about whether to tape depends on what we want to do with the data gathered. If we want to include many direct quotations, for example, then it is useful to have the verbatim account, which can be transcribed and subjected to editing at a later date. If capturing the exact phrasing of all interview responses is not critical to the study, then note-taking may suffice. If time and money are not an issue, it is clearly best to fully transcribe all interviews from the tape. On the other hand, if time and money are limited, we might listen to the tape and use our notes to help decide what parts to transcribe and paraphrase.

Taking Notes During the Interview.   Many interviewers advocate *taking notes during the interview* as well as tape-recording them. The notes serve as a backup or safeguard against mechanical difficulties. They also serve as guides to the tape in helping decide what to transcribe and what to leave out. In some cases, where tape-recording is not possible, brief notes may be the only way of recording the data. In this case we would try to write down some exact quotations and brief comments, supplemented by notes recorded after the interview.

Recording Notes Immediately Following the Interview.   The third approach to recording interview data is to *make a record of the interview soon after it occurs.* This can be done in a variety of ways, but it is important to allow sufficient time for this. One hour of interviewing may require 4 hours later spent developing the notes, particularly if they will be the only record of the interview.

Writing a process recording of the interview as soon as possible after the interview helps. The same four levels used in making field notes can be used in writing up research interviews—that is, to use a four-column format. In the first column we write as close to a verbatim account of the interview as we can recall. This column includes our questions, probes, and statements, as well as the interviewee's responses.

We use the next column to note our interpretations of the meanings, emotions, and relationships inferred from the words and gestures. In the third column, any insights or themes that occur are noted. The fourth column is for reflections on what we were thinking or feeling at the time and for recording other things that

were occurring that may have caused interference (e.g., the room was too warm or too noisy).

Using Visual Aids

Visual aids record data in a way that supplements and supports our field notes and tapes. Diagrams show how ideas are related, and flowcharts outline sequences, processes, and events. Eco-maps and genograms present relationships and their various dimensions. Photographs capture the field setting or environment. All of these visual aids contain a great deal of data and depict our specific field setting and the people within it in a manner that written words simply cannot convey as effectively or as economically. Visual aids add an additional dimension in combination with other data-collection methods.

Step 5: Making Sense of the Data

Methods for analyzing qualitative data are presented in depth in Chapter 18. It is important to keep in mind at this point, however, that we need to make some sense of our experiences as participant observers. This involves analyzing the data collected. At some point, notwithstanding some initial prior reviews of the data as they are being gathered and organized, there comes a time when a full-scale intensive analysis occurs as the next step in the research process.

This step is marked by a critical shift in how we have been working so far, and it requires the use of a different set of skills and abilities. It also comes at a time when we are overwhelmed by the prospect of wading through masses of data and making sense of them. It may be a particular challenge to move into this step, particularly if our forte has been the developing of social relationships, taking on various participant-observer roles, and being flexible and resourcefully adaptable in our field setting in an effort to ensure that we have good data to analyze.

The analysis step allows our data to be coded, sifted, sorted, and categorized so that themes, theories, and generalizations can be constructed and generated. In this way, meaning can be made of our research endeavor, and our results can be reported.

Step 6: Reporting the Findings

As should be evident by now, participant observation studies allow for the creation of a rich source of data about a situation or phenomenon that involves people. The raw data include such items as our written observation notes and correspondence, audiotapes, videotapes, and personal journals with reflections, as well as notes made after debriefing and consultation sessions with research advisers.

A final report of our study includes an overview of our research question and the methods and techniques used in the study, detailed descriptions of the people and related phenomena, themes or hypotheses that have emerged from all the different data sources, information about our personal process, biases, and assumptions, and recommendations based upon our findings.

Normally, once the data are gathered and analyzed, they are written up as a case study, with quite detailed descriptions about the events or situation being studied. The final report includes themes and theoretical interpretations (or hypotheses) that have emerged from the data. It also includes recommendations for further study or action.

The intended audience of the report affects what and how it is written. The general public requires a different level of explanation from an academic audience. The use of jargon is avoided unless the audience comprises others who work in similar or related areas. Other possible audiences include other researchers or professional practitioners and government departments or agencies. Given the newly emerging view of research participants as having a vital partnership role in the research process, all those who have had a part in our study should have access to, or otherwise be provided with, a summary or a full copy of the final report.

Writing is facilitated by having blocks of uninterrupted time and perseverance. It involves drafting and editing and often includes showing early drafts to some or all of the insiders and consulting with research advisers. Eventually, a unique document is produced that is appropriate for the study undertaken and its intended audience.

ETHICAL CONSIDERATIONS

As we know from Chapter 2, ethical considerations must be taken into account for any research situation. There are additional ethical issues that must be addressed in doing participant observation because of the close and sustained relationships between the researcher and the research participants and the fact that the balance of research activities occurs in a field setting where many other influences may surface and need to be dealt with as the study proceeds. Thus, through proper sponsorship and approvals, plus the informed consent of all those involved, it is crucial to attend to what is required to prevent adverse consequences.

Beyond this, there is the issue of the level of information we provide our research participants in reference to the roles we assumed during the study and the degree to which we disclosed personal information. While there are different views on this, we advise that, wherever possible, research participants be included as copartners in the research study in as open and as equal a way as possible. We have to decide how much to reveal about ourselves and the research project itself. Disclosure ranges on a continuum from fully covert (no one in the field setting is aware of the study) to fully disclosed (everyone knows the specifics of the study).

It is unlikely, however, that a social work research project would get approval from an ethics board either in an academic or in a social-work–related setting unless it was near the fully disclosed end of the spectrum, where research participants give their informed consent and know how the data will be stored and used. Covert research studies are simply not ethical.

SUMMARY

This chapter presented an overview of participant observation as an obtrusive data-collection method. It described its unique characteristics, such as issues of gaining access and entry into a field setting, forming and sustaining relationships (which includes the continuum of roles adopted by the researcher), and data gathering involving the use of relatively unstructured data-gathering approaches.

We included strategies for recording the data and attempted to create an awareness of the fine and delicate balance that exists between the participant-observer and the research participants and of the importance of the researcher's being attuned to this and making the necessary adjustments as the study unfolds to ensure that the perspective of the research participants comes through clearly, accurately, and in considerable detail.

As we know, using participant observation as a form of data collection is obtrusive; that is, the researcher intrudes into the research participants' lives in some form or another. The following chapter continues our discussion of obtrusive data-collection methods by presenting how interviews can be used to collect data for a research study.

Qualitative Interviewing

Harvey L. Gochros

Basic Steps in the Research Process

Step 1 Choose a problem

2 Review the literature

3 Evaluate the literature

4 Be aware of all ethical issues

5 Be aware of all cultural issues

6 State the research question or hypothesis

7 Select the research approach

8 Determine how the variables are going to be measured

9 Select a sample

10 Select a data collection method

11 Collect and code the data

12 Analyze and interpret the data

13 Write the report

14 Disseminate the report

Interviewing is at the core of social work practice and is the most consistently and frequently employed social work technique. Social work education emphasizes the skills and purposes of the interview; therefore, it is not surprising that social workers are most comfortable with interviewing as a method of collecting data for research studies. Indeed, the goal of much of the interviewing social work researchers do is to gather data about clients and their situations or data on which program evaluations can be based. Familiarity with the purposes and techniques of interviewing, therefore, is a necessity in conducting research studies that depend on data elicited from interviews.

The two major sources of self-reported data in research studies are material presented by individuals in written form through questionnaires and data elicited from interviewees through research interviews. This chapter describes the uses of research interviews in the social work researcher's problem-solving process, suggests some procedures for conducting effective research interviews, and considers the advantages and disadvantages of interviews for collecting research data.

ADVANTAGES OF RESEARCH INTERVIEWING

The advantages of interviewing as a data-collection method are related primarily to naturalness and spontaneity, flexibility, and control of the environment. Combined with a high response rate, they provide a good argument for the use of this method when compared to mailed survey questionnaires, which are discussed in the following chapter.

Naturalness and Spontaneity

Interviews usually create a natural situation in which individuals can present information. For most people, it is easier and more natural to respond to questions orally than in writing, and a casual, relaxed setting leads to more spontaneous answers. What people say "off the top of their heads" may be free of the self-censorship often encountered in written responses. Also, it is more difficult in an interview than in a mailed survey questionnaire to "erase" an answer and replace it with a more "appropriate" and perhaps less valid answer.

High Response Rate

As we will see in the following chapter, research participants may leave out answers in mailed survey questionnaires because they lack reading or language skills, do not understand the questions, are unmotivated to answer the instrument, or simply overlook some items. In a research interview, the interviewer is there to see that each item is answered, and the interviewer can interpret or reword the item if necessary without distorting it. Many people not only are more comfortable expressing their ideas in speech than in writing; they may even enjoy talking to an interviewer, whereas they would consider filling out a survey questionnaire a nuisance and toss the form in a wastebasket.

Interviewers also are much harder to avoid than survey questionnaires, particularly survey questionnaires that arrive in the mail. The presence of a trained interviewer allows for a far more detailed and complex set of questions than is possible in a mailed questionnaire. The interviewer can slowly and carefully go over intricate items and make sure every question is covered.

Flexibility

Interviews permit far more flexibility than survey questionnaires. In talking with an interviewee, areas that might be difficult to frame in specific questions can be explored, and probing questions can be used to give responses greater depth. The interviewer can also adapt the sequence and timing of questions, change the way items are phrased, and even decide which questions can be eliminated, according to the characteristics of a particular interviewee (such as age, ethnic group, intelligence, or experience).

In past studies of sexual behavior, for example, researchers soon learned that the areas with which people are most uncomfortable tend to vary with their socioeconomic levels. Thus, the interviewers were instructed to ask people from lower socioeconomic levels about premarital intercourse (a behavior they tended to be comfortable about) early in the interview, while items about masturbation (a behavior they tended to be more uncomfortable about) were to be asked later. The reverse order was used with interviewees of higher socioeconomic levels because of their different relative ease with these two behaviors.

Access to Serendipitous Information

Since interviewers are present, they can make use of any unanticipated data interviewees offer. Content thus "stumbled on" can provide useful data for the study and, perhaps, subsequent investigations. The concept of unexpected events was expanded upon in Chapters 10, on participant observation.

For example, in the pretest of a study conducted on postplacement adoption services by Gochros (1970), an adoptive parent mentioned quite casually the extent to which she and her husband had lied to their social worker during their adoptive study. Her degree of comfort in sharing this information impressed the interviewer, and in subsequent interviews a question about parents' misinforming and withholding information from the social workers was added.

Nonverbal Responses

Skilled social workers are sensitive to their clients' nonverbal responses, which also can supply significant data in research interviews. The tone of the interviewee's voice, an interruption of eye contact, an unexplained smile or frown can all reflect on the verbal response they accompany and can lead the interviewer to probe for explanations.

Observation of and Control Over the Environment

In mailed survey questionnaires, investigators have little or no control over when, where, or how the measuring instruments are answered, or even who answers them. The interviewer can both observe and, to some extent, control these factors. For example, with group-administered survey questionnaires (see Chapter 12), research participants may have little control over who is looking over their shoulders. Indeed, they may choose to have others in their environment help them with their answers. The interviewer can see to it that research participants answer the questions in private and without the prompting or influence of others. Thus, the answers are clearly the interviewees' own answers.

DISADVANTAGES OF RESEARCH INTERVIEWING

There are problems and limitations in any data-collection method that depends on research participants' self-reports, whether the data come from a survey questionnaire or an interview. According to Bailey (1994), there are four major sources of research participant errors and biases in self-reported data. Research participants may:

1. Deliberately lie because they do not know an answer.
2. Make mistakes without realizing it (often because they are not able to admit socially undesirable feelings, attitudes, or traits, even to themselves).
3. Give inaccurate answers by accident simply because they misunderstand or misinterpret the question.
4. Be unable to remember, despite their best efforts. Research participants may even blend truth with fiction to cover up their memory gaps.

In addition to these problems, which are endemic to self-report studies, there are other problems that particularly affect research based on the interview method in comparison to survey research. These are principally related to time and cost constraints, the reactions of research participants, and possible interviewer influence or distortion.

Time and Expense

Perhaps the most obvious limitation of interview research is its high cost and the considerable amount of time involved. The postage involved in mailing questionnaires in surveys is far less expensive than hiring, training, and supervising interviewing staff, let alone paying for the long hours of the interviews, as well as the time and expense involved in getting to and from them. Further, translating data from interview notes and completed instruments adds an extra, often expensive, step in the research process that may not be necessary with the relatively simpler survey questionnaire forms.

Unless an extravagantly large interviewing team is accessible—and affordable—interview research is a slow process. Especially in situations in which it is necessary to go to the interviewees (which is often the case), the number of interviews any one interviewer can cover in a day is quite limited. In contrast, large numbers of mailed survey questionnaires can be accumulated and coded in a relatively short time.

There are also problems in coding responses that are associated with interviewers' having worded items differently. The time problems are aggravated when research participants are hard to reach, fail to keep appointments, or do not complete interviews because of outside distractions. These are old stories to social workers who are experienced with home visits with clients, but the motivation for being a research participant is usually weaker than that for receiving social work services. The number of interviews that may be needed to accumulate a large enough sample for many research studies adds to the difficulty of conducting these interview-based research projects.

Interview Intensity

While many people enjoy the attention and stimulation of being interviewed, others may consider it a nuisance, particularly if the interview comes at a time when they are tired, preoccupied, or uncomfortable. With mailed surveys, research participants can determine when and where they will answer the questionnaire; they may even choose to answer it in dribs and drabs.

When interviewers are seated opposite research participants, urging them on, they have little choice but to stay with the interview until the end, and the resulting fatigue, discomfort, and even anger may well influence their responses. Research participants may provide poor answers in an interview situation merely because the interviewer arrives when the baby is crying, the dog is barking, dinner is burning, or they need to go to the bathroom.

Inaccessibility of Potential Interviewees

An obvious limitation of research interviews is that the investigators may have a hard time getting to the interviewees. Sampling procedures may suggest a group of research participants who are geographically widely distributed or located in areas that are hard to reach, such as the hollows of West Virginia or distant military bases.

Loss of Anonymity

Mailed survey questionnaires, especially those that ask for little identifying data, can provide anonymity for research participants, who can feel relatively sure their participation will have no negative effects. Responding to a research interview can pose greater anticipated and perhaps real threats to interviewees, despite reassurances of confidentiality. The interviewer not only sees the interviewee in person but, if the interview is in the home, may come to know the interviewee's address and observe her home as well as her family, neighbors, and friends.

Some people could consider such "observations" embarrassing or even incriminating. For example, in the postplacement adoption study referred to earlier, interviewees may well have feared the interviewer's impressions of their handling of their adopted children. Furthermore, interviewers may be seen by neighbors and others as they enter or leave research participants' homes, with possibly uncomfortable implications.

Interviewer Distortion

The research interviewer adds a link in the chain from the research participants' responses to the data that does not exist in mailed survey questionnaires (see Chapter 12). In mailed questionnaires, research participants read the questions and place their answers directly on the instrument. In interview research, the interviewer asks items in what may or may not be a standardized format, listens to the answers, and then summarizes or attempts to put the full response into notes that may be later rewritten or reformulated and then put into the data bank.

While the presence of the interviewer can facilitate the gathering of more meaningful data, for reasons stated earlier, there are risks of interviewer distortion or error at several points in the process. Interviewers may misread or badly phrase a question, or they may interpret or hear an interviewee's answer incorrectly.

It is also possible for the interviewer to check an answer on the wrong line or in other ways fail to record responses accurately. Further distortion may occur later if the interviewer misreads or cannot understand the notes taken during interviews.

In general, there are four common interviewer distortions based on various types of errors:

1. Asking errors. Interviewers may change the wording of questions or even fail to ask a particular item.
2. Probing errors. Interviewers may negatively affect their interviewees' answers by asking follow-up questions or probes that are unnecessarily challenging, hostile, biased, or irrelevant.
3. Recording errors. Unless interviewers use tape recorders or have excellent memories, they must record their interviewees' answers either by the cumbersome and time-consuming process of writing exactly what their interviewees have said or by summarizing their responses. Such processes have a high potential for error.
4. Cheating. Interviewers are subject to the same temptations as any other employed mortal. Whatever the motivation, an interviewer may deliberately fill in gaps in interviews or even record a response for an item that was never asked.

Interviewer Influence

Interviewers can influence their interviewees not only by the phrasing of questions and tone of voice but by their own apparent comfort or discomfort with a particular question. This can be demonstrated, for example, by a change in eye contact or in the rapidity with which a question is asked.

Even the words that are emphasized in an item can influence the response. Consider the different implications of these two questions:

Did you *ever* feel like hurting your children?
Did you ever feel like *hurting* your children?

Other characteristics of the interviewer, in addition to specific behaviors in the interview, may have an effect, for better or worse, on the reliability of the data gathered from a research interview. Such variables as the interviewer's age, gender, physical appearance, racial or ethnic group, or language and accent can affect the quality of the interviewees' responses. Moreover, these same variables and other characteristics of the interviewees (such as "apparent intelligence") may well elicit diverse patterns of behavior from interviewers, and this can affect the way they carry out the interviews, which in turn affects the data gathered.

CONSIDERATIONS IN RESEARCH INTERVIEWS

Once an area of study that lends itself to self-reports elicited through research interviews has been selected and the necessary resources for conducting such interviews have been assembled, the researcher is concerned with how to prepare for, conduct, and record the data from such a study.

The remainder of this chapter discusses some of the points to consider in going through these stages in research interviewing. The procedures include determining the degree of structure in content, developing the interviewing schedule, determining the format of interview items, selecting interviewers, gaining access to interviewees, deciding where to conduct the interviews, checking the interviewers' appearance, developing the interviewer-interviewee relationship, formulating and asking questions, and recording the data.

DEGREE OF STRUCTURE

The preparation of the interview instrument or schedule (a written instrument that sets out the overall plan for the interviews and determines the structure, sequence, and content of the specific items to be asked) is crucial to the outcome of the study. Many of the considerations in the development of the instrument, as well as the overall plan for research conducted through interviews, are somewhat similar if not identical to those associated with mailed survey questionnaire construction and group-administered survey research.

An important variable in planning research interviews, however, is the degree to which the interview is to be structured. Structure refers to the extent to which the interview schedule or instrument includes predetermined, specific items. There are three options for structure in research interviews: (1) structured; (2) semistructured, or focused; and (3) unstructured. Each has particular purposes, advantages, and disadvantages.

Structured Interviews

In a structured interview, the instrument prescribes exactly what items will be asked, their sequence, and even their specific wording. Both open- and closed-ended items may be used. This is the easiest type of interview to code, since all interviewees are asked exactly the same items in the same order. Predetermining the exact wording of the items reduces the risk that interviewers may introduce their biases by the way they word questions.

Structured interviews also provide consistency in the nature of the data collected from interview to interview. The investigator can use interviewers with relatively little training, since individual decisions are kept at a minimum and the interviewers need only follow specific instructions.

Structured interviews have a number of limitations, however. Interviewers have little freedom to draw fully on their interviewees' knowledge of the research question or to explore respondents' answers or encourage them to expand on answers by the use of probing questions. They may not even seek clarification of ambiguous or vague answers. Thus, structured interviews provide few of the advantages of interviews over mailed survey questionnaires, yet they are more expensive and time-consuming.

Semistructured, or Focused Interviews

The semistructured interview schedule may include some specific items, but considerable latitude is given to interviewers to explore in their own way matters pertaining to the research question being studied. A form of the semistructured interview called the focused interview centers on selected topics and hypotheses, but the specific items used are not entirely predetermined. Usually this form of interview is used for research participants who have shared a common experience, such as having received a particular type of social work service, been the victim of a particular crime, or suffered a certain illness.

The semistructured interview requires a more skilled and better trained interviewer than does the structured form. Interviewers must learn as much as possible about the particular attribute or experience the interviewees have shared. On the basis of this knowledge, they decide before the interviews what aspects of the interviewees' experience are to be explored, and they may develop hypotheses about these experiences to be tested in the interviews. Thus the general areas to be explored are determined before the interviews, although few, if any, of the questions may be formulated in advance. The process was described many years ago by Merton, Fiske, and Kendall (1956) as follows:

First of all, the persons interviewed are known to have been involved in a particular situation: they have seen a film, heard a radio program, read a pamphlet, article or book, taken part in a psychological experiment or in an uncontrolled, but observed, social situation (for example, a political rally, a ritual, or a riot). Secondly, the hypothetically significant elements, patterns, processes and total structure of this situation have been provisionally analyzed by the social scientist. Through this content or situational analysis, he has arrived at a set of hypotheses concerning the consequences of determinate aspects of the situation for those involved in it. On the basis of this analysis, he takes the third step of developing an interview guide, setting forth the major areas of inquiry and the hypotheses which provide criteria of relevance for the data to be obtained in the interview. Fourth and finally, the interview is focused on the subjective experiences of persons exposed to the pre-analyzed situation in an effort to ascertain their definitions of the situation. The array of reported unanticipated responses gives rise to fresh hypotheses for more systematic and rigorous investigation.

Since the hypotheses may be formulated before a semistructured interview, the interviewer must avoid biasing the items to confirm the hypotheses. Moreover, although research participants have a right to be informed about the general purposes of a study in which they are participating, it may not be advisable to inform them of the specific hypothesis being tested, because knowing this might bias their responses.

Semistructured interviews allow for the introduction of unanticipated answers from interviewees. For example, Gochros had not anticipated before the pretest for the study of postplacement adoption services mentioned earlier that adoptive parents would volunteer that they had misled their adoption study workers and that they were concerned that their postplacement workers would discover their deceptions. As a result, probes in this area were later introduced.

Such exploration in semistructured interviews often is accomplished with "funneling" techniques, in which a general item is followed up with more specific probing questions. An example of this procedure was used in an interview study of 300 mothers whose children had been placed in foster care. The interviewers were all trained social workers who visited the mothers in their homes.

After explaining the purposes of the study and obtaining the mothers' agreement to explore their experiences with foster care, the researchers recorded the responses as accurately as possible following a very detailed semistructured instrument, the opening segment of which is shown in Figure 11.1. The full interview instrument covered 34 pages and required an interview approximately 2 hours long. It included open- and closed-ended questions, checklists, and scales. This obviously long and complicated instrument was necessitated by the quantity and complexity of the data the researchers hoped to gather.

A. MAIN QUESTION: Respondent's Statement of Problem

1. First of all, would you tell me in your own words what brought about the placement of _____ away from home in foster care?

    (Probe if not spontaneously answered)

1a. Who first had the idea to place_____?

    Did anyone oppose it or disagree with it? If yes:
    a. Who?
    b. Why?

1b. Were any attempts made to make other arrangements for_____other than placement? If yes:
    a. What?
    b. Who did this?
    c. Why didn't it work out?

1c. Was there anyone whom you usually depend on who couldn't or didn't help out? If yes:
    a. Who? (relationship)
    b. Why not?

1d. Did all your children who were in your home go into placement at that time? If no:
    a. Which children were not placed at that time (name, age, etc.)?
    b. Why weren't they placed?

1e. Who was caring for _____ just before he/she was placed? If other than natural mother:
    a. For how long had she been caring for_____?
    b. Why was she caring for the child (rather than the child's mother)?

(If sample child 2 years or older, ask if)

1f. Was _____ told that he/she was going into placement? If yes:
    a. By whom? What was he/she told?
    If no:
    b. What was the reason for that?

1g. Was _____ prepared for placement in any (other) way? If yes:
    a. By whom? In what way(s)?
    If no:
    b. What was the reason for that?

1h. Did anyone help you get ready for_____ going into placement away from home? If yes:
    a. Who?
    b. In what way(s)?

1i. Who actually took _____ to the agency the day he/she went into placement?

2. From all you have told me, what would you say was the one main reason for _____ going into foster care?

2a. When would you say this problem first started?

3. And what would you say was the next most important reason for _____ going into foster care?

3a. When would you say this problem first started?

Figure 11.1 Opening Segment of a Semistructured Interview Instrument

Semistructured and focused interviews allow for considerable latitude in the length and detail of the instrument. If only one or two researchers who are intimately familiar with the phenomenon being studied and the goals of the study will be conducting the interviews, the instrument can be comparatively shorter and less detailed. In Gochros's study of postplacement adoption services, for example, he was the sole interviewer.

While there may be a considerable hazard of interviewer bias when the researcher is both the hypothesis formulator and the interviewer, such economy of personnel does allow for a much simpler measuring instrument. The instrument used for the interviews with each of the 114 adoptive parent research participants (and a similar one used with their 18 postplacement social workers) was less than two pages in length. This interview schedule is shown in Figure 11.2.

The brevity of the instrument in Figure 11.2 leads to less disconcerting paper-shuffling during the interview and fuller attention to the folks being interviewed. Extensive use of abbreviations (e.g., AP = adoptive parent, CW = caseworker, SP = supervisory or postplacement period) allows the instrument to be further condensed. The interview schedule (the measuring instrument, if you will) does not need to conform to the strict design and construction methods as presented in Chapter 5 because only the interviewer sees it. The person being interviewed does not see the interview schedule.

To determine the degree of detail that will be necessary in the instrument for the semistructured or focused interview, the researcher must answer three questions:

1. What is it that is to be learned, and how much is already known about it?
2. To what extent are the interviewers trained, prepared, and able to elicit data on their own from their research participants (the interviewees)?
3. To what extent is the simplicity of coding responses (with its implications for validity) to be a determining factor?

Unstructured Interviews

In unstructured interviews, only the general problem area to be studied is determined in advance of the interviews. The interviewers choose the timing, structure, and content of items to be asked, not unlike the procedures used in worker-client fact-gathering interviews.

The main advantage of unstructured interviews is that the interviewer has almost unlimited freedom to ask interviewees wide-ranging items, to seek in-depth clarification of their answers, and to explore any possibly profitable avenues which may emerge in the interview.

The interviewee is clearly at the center of this form of interview. Responses are often elicited from neutral probes provided by the interviewer. This form of research interview is derived from the field of psychotherapy. It often seeks to probe the interviewees' deepest feelings and experiences and may well uncover emotions, attitudes, and beliefs the interviewee was not even aware of prior to the interview.

This type of research interviewing depends heavily on the competence and self-awareness of the interviewer. It requires well-trained interviewers who are skilled in techniques for developing working relationships and eliciting data from research participants. They must be able to make quick decisions about what to ask and when and how to ask productive questions. They must also be knowledgeable about the general subject they are exploring. Further, they must be fully aware of the dangers of leading or biasing interviewees, which are greater because of the nature of the unstructured give-and-take.

One of the most significant limitations of this type of interview is the problems it creates in coding. However, if little is known about the research question being studied or if the question is a sensitive one, unstructured interviews may lead to the acquisition of useful data for more structured future inquiries.

Indeed, unstructured interviews are generally not as useful for testing out hypotheses or for deriving accurate measurements of specific phenomena as they are for developing preliminary data in relatively uncharted areas that may lead to the formulation of hypotheses later down the line. Such research studies usually require very small samples.

For example, Gochros (1978) contacted only six former male clients who were homosexually oriented and heterosexually married. He interviewed them by

1. What were you told about the purposes and content of the SP?
    By whom:
2. What did you expect the visits to be like?
3. How were they different from what you expected?
4. Why do you think there is a SP?
5 How many SP visits were there?
6. Average length?
7. How many AP initiated? Why?
8. How many unexpected? Opinion
9. How many were you present:
10. Ever feel left out?
11. What did you talk about?
12. What do you think CW wanted you to bring up or discuss in SP visits?
13. Subsequent contacts.
14. What sort of problems did you run into during the SP?
    Freedom
    Rel: Husband–Wife
    Rel: Parent–Child
    Depressed
    Neglected
15. Books recommended? Why? Read? Useful?
16. Did you think of CW more as a friend or caseworker?
17. What did you like most about CW?
18. What did you like least about CW?
19. Did CW create the kind of atmosphere where you felt free to talk over your real feelings about things?
20. Did you ever withhold any information or feelings from CW?
21. How much do you think CW knew about child care and development?
22. What did you think about when you knew a visit was scheduled?
23. What did you think about just after the visit was over?
24. Did your feelings change about the visits during the SP?
25. What did you find the most helpful result of the visits?
26. What did you find to be the least helpful or most unpleasant aspect of the visits?
27. Any way agency could have been more helpful during the SP?
28. How helpful was the SP to you, overall?
29. Can you think of any way that the visits may be helpful to you in the future?
30. How did you feel when the decree was finally granted?
31. Do you think there should be a waiting period?
32. If yes, how long?
33. Should there be CW visits? Why?
34. Compulsory? Why?
35. If they had been voluntary, would you have requested any?
36. If adopt again and if voluntary, would you have requested any?
37. Groups for parents of 5-year-olds, interested?
38. Groups for parents of adolescents, interested?
39. If ran into a problem with a child, contact worker?
40. Second child: planning, applied, placed, not planning
41. If worker was different from study, was transition difficult?
42. Comments:

Figure 11.2   Interview Schedule With Adoptive Parents

focusing on their hopes and expectations from treatment and their reactions to it, as well as their subsequent experiences.

While the general purposes of his interviews were clear to both the interviewer and interviewees (i.e., what they wanted and what they got from their social work contact), the interviews were entirely unstructured. The report of the study included hypotheses about counseling gay husbands derived from the interviews, illustrated with extensive direct quotations from his former clients. Such an exploratory study can provide a stepping-stone to larger, more detailed descriptive and explanatory studies.

DEVELOPING THE INTERVIEW SCHEDULE

As noted in Chapter 5, there is no "right" way to construct a measuring instrument, despite advances in research methods and techniques—many of which are reported in this book. Decisions on how to structure and design an instrument must generally be based on informed hunches that are pretested before being used with the actual sample or population.

One of the few generalities that can be drawn from the experience of social work researchers is that usually far more data are elicited from the interviews than will subsequently be used in the research analysis and report. The social work researcher, having the typical limitations of time and money, may be well advised to be parsimonious in deciding what will be covered in a measuring instrument.

In deciding what is to be covered and how the items can best elicit these data, a number of questions must first be answered:

1. What do we want to know that we don't know already?
2. Who can tell us what we don't know and what we want to know?
3. How can we formulate and ask questions that will increase the probability that the interviewees will tell us what we want to know?
4. What would keep the interviewees from telling us what we want to know or would lead them to deceive us or present us with incomplete data?

5. How can we override these sources of withholding and distortion?

The answers to the first three questions have been presented in the previous chapters. To answer the remaining two questions, it is necessary to consider some successful strategies that have been developed to elicit desired data through research interviews.

Sequencing of Questions

Generally, the funneling techniques referred to earlier have been found to be useful in gaining honest and complete answers from research participants. This involves starting the interview with broad, general questions and then moving on to narrower, more specific, and perhaps more difficult and sensitive questions as the interview progresses. The advantage of this approach is that rapport can be established early in the interview with questions that do not make the interviewee particularly uncomfortable. As the folks being interviewed establish more trust and confidence in their interviewers, more challenging questions can be asked.

Bailey (1994) has suggested six guidelines for establishing an order for questions in interviews. These suggestions are the basis for the discussion in this section.

First, open-ended questions, and those that are likely to be sensitive or difficult to answer, should be placed late in the interview. If difficult items come early, the interviewee may become resentful or immobilized and may refuse to continue. What is sensitive to one interviewee, however, may not be sensitive to another. For example, Pomeroy's finding that research participants of low socioeconomic standing tended to be uncomfortable with questions about masturbation but were relatively comfortable with items about premarital sex was noted earlier. The degree of sensitivity was generally reversed among research participants who were at the higher socioeconomic levels.

Thus, interviewers may need some flexibility in the order in which they ask such items. Even if open-ended questions are not sensitive, they should generally be placed last, because answers to this type of question take more time and energy. For example, in studying reactions to group therapy, it may be easier for interviewees to answer such items as "How often did you meet?" and

"Was the group therapist always there?" than a question like "How did you feel when other group members were confronting you?"

Second, easy-to-answer items should be asked first in the interview. Such questions usually ask for facts, rather than feelings, beliefs, or opinions. Thus, interviews usually start with questions about such demographic variables as age, gender, home address, marital status, occupation, and place of employment. (In survey research, demographic variables are asked last; see Chapter 12). Although even such seemingly innocuous items can cause discomfort, they are usually at least clear and nonthreatening (demographic variables about race, income, and religion are more likely to be discomforting). Whenever possible, opening questions should also be interesting and perhaps mildly provocative so as to gain the interviewees' interest and clarify the subject matter of the interview.

Third, answers should be obtained early in the interview to items that may be necessary to guide the remainder. For example, getting the names, gender, and ages of siblings and determining whether they are still living would be a logical, early step in studies of family relationships.

Fourth, items should be asked in a logical order. This provides a flow to the interview that facilitates moving easily from item to item. The most obvious and frequently used organizing theme is time sequence. In describing children, for example, it seems most logical to ask about them in order of birth. Indeed, that is the sequence in which most people usually present these data. The frame of reference of the interview should also be clear and orderly. Each segment should be covered completely before you move on to the next. It is both awkward and confusing to the interviewee to move back and forth between topics.

For example, in Gochros's study of adoptive parents' experiences with postplacement services, the unstructured interview (see Figure 11.2) was constructed in the following sequence:

1. How parents were prepared by the agency for postplacement services (Item 1)
2. What they expected postplacement services to be like (Items 2 through 4)

3. What the postplacement services were like (specific facts, such as number of visits, followed by more difficult questions, including reactions) (Items 5 through 15)
4. Evaluation of the social workers and the usefulness of their services (Items 16 through 28)
5. Suggestions for how services could be improved (Item 29)
6. Reactions to the postplacement period itself (Items 30 through 35)
7. Anticipation of any future problems and whether agency services might be used in the future (Items 36 through 41)
8. Any other comments (Item 42)

Fifth, the creation of a "response set" should be avoided. The suggestion that there should be a logical sequence of questions and the interviewer should avoid skipping around from topic to topic should not be regarded as a rigid requirement. Indeed, if the researcher senses that asking items in a particular order will lead an interviewee to answer in a particular way, that order should probably be changed. This avoids what is called a response set, whereby the interviewers cause their interviewees to reply in ways that do not reflect the questions' content or the interviewees' accurate answers.

As we know from Chapter 5, one of the most common response sets is a function of social desirability, or the tendency to reply to items in a way the research participants perceive as conforming to social norms. The order of items may well encourage such a response set. An exaggerated example would be asking an item such as "Do you think most people love their mothers?" followed by another item such as "Do you love your mother?" When research participants are asked to give their salaries in a succession of jobs, they may well have a response set to report increased salaries from job to job, whether or not such a pattern really existed.

The probability of response sets can be reduced by changing the order of questions or the answer format. This has the disadvantage of possibly confusing the interviewee, but if it is done with moderation, such a procedure may also lessen the boredom of a long series of items. In the postplacement adoption study, for example, items about parents' perceptions of the social worker's activities were interspersed with an activity in which research participants were presented with a deck of index cards on which various worker activities were written and asked to rearrange them in order of what they believed their social workers were trying to do—from "most trying to do" to "least trying to do."

Sixth, reliability-question pairs should be asked at various points in the interview. In this procedure, two questions, one phrased negatively and the other phrased positively, are asked to check the reliability of the research participants' answers. For example, at one point in an interview, the interviewer may ask, "Did you think your social worker generally understood what you were up against?" and at another, "Did you get the feeling that your social worker didn't understand the problems you were facing?"

Such a procedure can be used to double-check the reliability of particularly strategic items either for a particular research participant or for an entire sample. Where there is a disparity in the responses, the interviewer can ask probing items in order to amplify or clarify the interviewees' ideas. This procedure should be used cautiously for a variety of reasons, most conspicuously because the interviewees may perceive the device—accurately—as a trick.

DETERMINING THE FORMAT OF INTERVIEW ITEMS

It is often desirable to vary the format of items in an interview schedule. For example, the interviewee may be asked to read a statement, then be asked some questions about it. The length and type of answers expected can also be varied; at various times, facts, beliefs, opinions, or experiences can be requested. In addition to adding variety to an interview and thus avoiding response sets and maintaining interest in the interview, the use of different types of items can achieve different purposes. The relative merits of the two primary forms of items, open- and closed-ended questions, were discussed in Chapters 5, and we need only summarize some of their advantages and disadvantages in research interviews.

Utilizing Open- and Closed-Ended Questions

In closed-ended questions, the interviewee has a limited, predetermined range of answers, such as "yes–no," and "male–female." With open-ended questions, research participants can give any answer they choose, rather than selecting from a range of options. For example, "Do you get along with your children?" is a closed-ended question that invites a yes or no response, while "How do you get along with your children?" is an open-ended question that allows for a wide range of answers.

Open-ended questions are relatively easy to formulate and to ask, but the answers are difficult to code and categorize. For example, the item "If you had three wishes, what would they be?" can produce data that may be a practitioner's dream but a researcher's nightmare. However, for the price of agonizing over more complex response categories, the interviewer may gain a greater range of responses, many of which may not have been anticipated.

It may seem logical that open-ended questions would elicit answers reflecting greater depth and feelings from research participants, but this is not necessarily the case. There is no evidence that open-ended questions produce answers of greater depth or validity than closed-ended questions do.

Indeed, with situations in which research participants are considered resistant, the closed-ended, "objective" questions often provide more valid results. Additionally, closed-ended questions are most useful when specific categories are available against which the interviewees' replies can be measured and when a clear conceptual framework exists in which the interviewees' replies will logically fit.

Using Probes

Perhaps the most useful type of item in semistructured interviews is the probe, or follow-up question. The intent of such items is to seek greater depth or clarity about answers the interviewee has already given. Often, vague or general replies will be given to open-ended items because the research participants have not completely thought through their replies or are not sure how to answer. They may also be holding back from giving a complete answer for fear of appearing sick, bad, stupid, or worthless. This is when a probe is called for. The intent of such questions is to help interviewees provide more complete and accurate data.

Probes may also be used to increase the probability that all areas of interest to the interviewer have been explored. For this purpose, the need for probes may be anticipated and included in the interview schedule, on the basis of the interviewer's experience with responses to particular areas of questioning in the pretest. These predetermined probes can then be used as "contingency questions" the interviewer can draw upon if the interviewee answers—or fails to answer—questions in certain anticipated ways.

There are a variety of interviewing techniques that can be used as probes to encourage interviewees to amplify, expand, or clarify responses. These probes need not be included in the interview schedule but should become part of the interviewer's standard repertoire, to be called upon when the interviewees' answers suggest their use. Bailey (1994) has described the procedures investigators can use in probing for responses. They are:

1. Repeating the question. This is done whenever the interviewee hesitates or appears not to understand the question.
2. Repeating the answer. This type of neutral probe can be used by an interviewer who is not certain about understanding the interviewee's answer correctly. Repetition of the answer can correct errors and assure both interviewee and interviewer that the answer is recorded carefully. Repetition also gives the interviewee an opportunity to think about elaborating it further.
3. Indicating understanding and interest. The interviewer indicates that the answer has been heard and approved of, thus stimulating the interviewee to continue.
4. Pausing. The interviewer pauses and says nothing if the response is obviously incomplete. This indicates that the interviewer knows the interviewee has begun to answer and is waiting for the rest of the reply.
5. Using a neutral question or comment. "How do you mean that?" or "Tell me more" indicates to the interviewee that an answer is on the right track but that more data are desired.

SELECTING INTERVIEWERS

It would appear logical for social workers to do their own research interviewing, since their training and experience should have made them knowledgeable about human behavior and social problems. This background would seem to equip them for interviewing in sensitive areas. However, there are a number of significant differences between social work practice interviewing and research interviewing. As a result, years of service-oriented practice may, paradoxically, be both a limitation and an asset for the social worker as research interviewer. Moreover, trained social work researchers are expensive to employ and may be hard to recruit for research interviewing positions.

The choice of the particular level of training required for a research interviewing assignment should be determined by a review of the population to be interviewed, the content of the interview, and the availability of supervisory staff and other resources for the study. Interviewers who lack social work training, such as indigenous community residents, graduate students, paraprofessionals, and social work moonlighters, have been used effectively in a wide range of social work research efforts.

Indeed, such classifications of researchers are used more often than full-time trained social workers. Since there is some evidence that the personality of interviewers is more predictive of effectiveness than is education or social status, there is good reason to at least consider alternatives to social work staff. Nevertheless, as Jenkins (1975) suggests, "Where feasible and appropriate filling the role of research interviewer is one way for the practitioner to contribute to social work research."

Indeed, doing so may provide social workers with new and useful perspectives on their practice and is one way to introduce them to the practitioner/researcher concept. Matching other characteristics of the interviewee and interviewer may be more significant for the quality of the data derived from research interviews than the formal, professional training of the interviewer.

Matching Interviewer and Interviewee Characteristics

Social work researchers usually have limited financial resources and thus have little control over which interviewers will interview which research participants, regardless of similar or different characteristics. However, the differences or similarities of interviewers and interviewees can have considerable influence on the usefulness of the data acquired.

Thus, if the luxury of choice is available, deliberately matching interviewers to interviewees may be desirable. But what should be matched to what? Generally, interviewees and interviewers seem to do best when they can identify with each other. However, the means to achieve such empathy is not always simple or clear. This section briefly reviews the effects of a number of physical and social characteristics of interviewers on the answers their interviewees provide. These variables are (1) gender, (2) age, (3) language, (4) socioeconomic level, and (5) race or ethnicity.

Gender

Since rapport is usually (but not always) better when interviewer and interviewee have somewhat similar characteristics, it would seem likely that interviewers who are of the same gender as their interviewees would get better results. Such would certainly seem to be the case in such situations as research studies on rape. Gender-linked patterns of relating may also affect perceptions of interviewers.

Mark Benney and his colleagues (1956) asked male and female interviewers who had surveyed political attitudes to rate each of their interviewees in terms of their honesty. The male interviewers rated 68% of their male interviewees and 56% of their female interviewees as "completely frank and honest," while the female interviewers rated 79% of *both* their male and female interviewees this way.

Another study found that both men and women responded to questions about whether they would like to see a particular movie in a way that they thought would please their interviewers on the basis of the interviewer's gender, especially if the interviewer was of the other gender.

Age

Considerable disparity in age between interviewers and interviewees may also contribute to the biases of either. One study, for example, examined the effect of age differences with the hypothesis that the closer in age interviewees and interviewers were, the more rapport there would be.

Although the results of the study were inconclusive, interviewers who were considerably older or younger than their interviewees often rated the respondents as being equally or more frank and honest than did interviewers who were in the same age group as their interviewees. However, when both age and gender were considered together, it was found that young female interviewers rated young male interviewees significantly higher for honesty than they did older males. Older interviewers did not display such a disparity.

Language

Matching interviewer and interviewee in language and accent has been found to be of considerable importance. If interviewees are more comfortable in a language other than English, it would, of course, be desirable to use bilingual interviewers. Obviously, also, translations of items originally composed in English must not distort the meaning of the original item. This might best be accomplished by having a professional with competence in both languages develop the items to be used.

Word use also is important in interviewing research participants who use a particular argot or slang words peculiar to their particular situation. Populations such as drug users, prostitutes, homosexually oriented individuals, and ethnic minorities often develop a unique vocabulary to describe concepts important to them. Terms such as *cracker*, *closet queen*, or *angel dust*, which are a part of some group's everyday vocabulary, may be incomprehensible to the uninitiated.

Interviewers with life situations similar to those of their research participants may be more comfortable and conversant with this language than those who have merely been tutored in the argot. Professionals studying former drug users have successfully involved them in developing the interview schedule and doing the actual interviewing, thus permitting the meaningful, unstilted, and appropriate use of the vernacular of addicts.

Indeed, interviewers who ask questions in simple language compatible with the everyday speech of those who are being interviewed tend to get better results. One study examined low-income families and found that abstract and complex items elicited far fewer responses than items that were simply phrased.

Socioeconomic Level

It is sometimes difficult to separate socioeconomic differences from racial disparity in matching interviewers to potential interviewees. They are often interrelated; one research study, for example, found an inverse relationship between biased data and the social distance between interviewees and interviewers. In the case of white interviewers, there was a stronger bias against lower-socioeconomic-level black interviewees than against those who were in a higher socioeconomic level. Dohrenwend and her colleagues (1968) asked white interviewers what variables (e.g., gender, age, race, and economic level) they preferred in the interviewees they interviewed. She found that those interviewers who preferred not to inter-view older people also rejected poor people and blacks in general.

In a discussion of social work interviewing, Kadushin and Kadushin (1997) introduced the concept of *homophily*, the idea that social workers and clients from similar cultural backgrounds will be more comfortable with each other and thus will work together more effectively. However, it may be dangerous to translate this observation from social work practice to research interviewing. Overidentification, lack of control of bias, and confusion of roles are possible consequences of overemphasis on matching.

As an example, in a study of welfare mothers in which both interviewers and interviewees were black, the social distance between the interviewers and inter-viewees was examined in relation to their rapport and to the validity of the study. Surprisingly, the results indicated that it was similarity in background, rather than difference, that was associated with interviewer bias. Furthermore, the interviewers who had the greatest rapport with their interviewees were the most biased.

There is evidence that interviewers who are socially too close to their interviewees may become too involved with them, rather than relating to the task of the study. It may be that either too little or too much social distance between interviewer and interviewee can create biases that reduce the value of a study.

In the past, most research interviewers in studies of interest to social workers were from the middle socioeconomic levels, white, and well educated, while most of the interviewees were less educated, from a lower socioeconomic level, and often nonwhite.

In a classic study on interview bias in polls, Daniel Katz (1942) demonstrated a lack of rapport between interviewers and lower-socioeconomic-level interviewees that led to a clear bias in the research participants' answers on matters of concern to them. Socioeconomic disparity between interviewees and interviewers continues to be a problem in social work research.

Race or Ethnicity

The effects of racial differences and similarities between interviewers and interviewees are longstanding social research topics. A study conducted during World War II found that blacks interviewed by black interviewers gave significantly more responses indicating the existence of racial protest and discrimination in the army than those interviewed by whites. For another study in Memphis, Tennessee (a southern city during a period of considerable racial tension), 1,000 black research participants were randomly assigned to black and white interviewers, and there were significant differences in the responses to the interviews of the two groups (Hyman, 1954). Black social aspirations and problems were presented in a more passive way to white interviewers than to black interviewers. Further, the white interviewers obtained significantly higher proportions of what might be called "proper" or "acceptable" answers.

Much has changed, of course, in black-white relations today, but differences in blacks' responses to black interviewers and to white ones still are apparent. One research study reported that this difference showed up most clearly when questions were directed at race relation issues and were less significant in questions related to family patterns and other aspects of daily living (Schuman & Converse, 1970).

In terms of social work services, both black and white research interviewers asked blacks' preferences for black or white workers. The study found that blacks preferred receiving their social services from blacks, assuming equal competence for black and white workers, and this preference was expressed more strongly to black interviewers than to whites (Brieland, 1969).

Racial and ethnic bias is not limited to black-white differences. In a study of the effects of Gentile research participants interviewed by Gentile and Jewish interviewers in New York City, for example, research participants were asked whether they believed Jewish people had too much influence, not enough influence, or about the amount of influence they should have in the business world (Hyman, 1954). When the interviewer was also a Gentile, one-half of the interviewees reported that they believed Jewish people had too much influence. However, only 22% stated that they thought Jewish people had too much influence when they were asked the question by a Jewish interviewer.

Many of these studies concerning the impact of ethnic and racial differences between interviewers and their interviewees were conducted when racial, religious, and ethnic biases were socially more acceptable than they are today (Robinson & Rhodes, 1946). There is little doubt, however, that such biases still exist and may be a factor in both interviewee and interviewer behavior. Indeed, growing minority assertiveness among such racial and social groups as women, gays, Latinos, and blacks may maintain biases that can well affect interview behaviors on both sides of the notepad.

In any case, matching interviewers and their interviewees can enhance the value of social work research. The biases of both interviewers and interviewees deriving from gender, race, and social distance must be considered. However, it is important to recognize that women interviewers *can* be sexists, older

people *can* be ageists, gays *can* be homophobic, and blacks *can* be racists. These biases can be minimized by careful selection of interviewers, open exploration of biases, and consideration of how to minimize the impact of any residual biases on the interview process.

GAINING ACCESS TO INTERVIEWEES

As we have seen in Chapter 2, it is often necessary to get permission to approach potential research participants. When an organization is involved, this may entail going through a chain of command. For example, in order to interview prisoners, the investigator may have to ask not only the prisoners but also the warden, who might in turn have to seek permission from the commissioner of corrections, who might have to check with the governor. For most populations or samples social workers study, such official permission will be necessary, and it is not always easy to obtain. Some communities, such as Beverly Hills, California, require a city permit before some forms of interview research can be undertaken.

Governmental and organizational regulations pertaining to access to samples should be examined to determine to what extent the population has already been studied. Many social work studies call for interviews of lower-income groups, ethnic minorities, or other populations that already consider themselves "overstudied."

Their resentment and feelings of being used as guinea pigs for more affluent, mainstream investigators may impair the formal or informal group acceptance of the study. Many African Americans, for example, have suggested that what needs to be studied is white racism, not black family dynamics. Similarly, some gays feel that research studies should explore the homophobia of nonhomosexuals, and some women feel that male investigators should study their own sexism.

Obtaining Organizational Consent

As we have seen in Chapter 2, many procedures have been adopted in recent years to protect people who are asked to participate in research studies. Studies supported by federal or other institutional funds or conducted under university auspices generally must be subjected to review by research committees, which must be satisfied that no harm will be done to the study's research participants. The National Institutes of Health requires that statements to that effect be filed for the studies it funds. Such reviews usually cover the measurement instruments to be used and the methods to be undertaken to safeguard the confidentiality of the research participants. The risks to research participants, as well as the benefits anticipated from the study, must be specified.

It is appropriate that social work researchers protect the rights of research participants as carefully as social work ethics and social service program policies protect the rights of clients. The ethics involved in social work research are discussed in Chapter 2.

Obtaining Potential Research Participants' Cooperation

Once organizational consent has been obtained, the researcher must secure evidence of the potential research participants' willingness to be interviewed. If the sample refuses, the result is nothing but a list of nonrespondents. The two most important elements in achieving a research participant's cooperation are (1) convincing the potential interviewees that their participation is important and that the study is legitimate, and (2) appealing to the potential interviewees' self-interest by showing how the results of their participation will be worthwhile to them.

Demonstrating the Importance and Legitimacy of the Study

Prospective interviewees will be more likely to participate if they are made aware that the proposed study is sponsored, approved by, or conducted under the auspices of a prestigious organization, social service program, or philanthropic association. This information is especially valuable if they are familiar with the organization and have positive experiences and feelings for it.

The endorsement of the organization can be demonstrated in a cover letter written under the organization's letterhead endorsing the project and encouraging the interviewees' cooperation. Such a letter should spell out the purposes of the study and reassure the potential research participant of the legitimacy of the project and the "safety" of their participation. The letter can also prepare the potential interviewees for a direct contact from the interviewer.

In the study of adoption postplacement services, letters to adoptive parents were sent to the sample selected for the study from the social service programs that had placed babies with the parents. The request letter attempted to communicate the following five points to the sample:

1. The program considered research important for improving services, and parents' participation in the present study would be helpful in accomplishing this.
2. The project had been legitimized by the involvement of both the adoption agency and the state division of child welfare.
3. There were reasons why the particular parents had been chosen to participate.
4. The parents were guaranteed confidentiality, and there were ways to safeguard this confidentiality.
5. The interviewer, identified by name, would contact them soon.

Appeal to Research Participants' Self-Interests

The cover letter presented in Figure 11.3 also appealed to the adoptive parents' self-interest. Many parents wished to show their appreciation to the program for having had a baby placed with them, and participating in the study afforded this opportunity. Many also wanted to help in any way they could to improve the quality of the program's services, in view of their hopes of adopting more children. Others wanted a chance to express dissatisfaction with the services they had received.

There are also more general ways in which participating in interviews may appeal to research participants' self-interest. Being "selected" for a study in itself may be valued by those who enjoy the prospect of the attention they will receive. Participating in social work studies

[Agency Letterhead]

Dear _____:

Our agency recognizes research as a basic method for evaluating old ways and developing new ways of providing more effective services for couples adopting children. The State Division of Child Welfare, in cooperation with this and other Twin City adoption agencies, is currently conducting a study of the supervisory period in adoption.

Because you have recently adopted a child through this agency, your experiences and opinions would be of much value. We are therefore asking your cooperation in this study. Your participation will involve an interview between each of you and a researcher from the State Division of Child Welfare.

We wish to emphatically assure you that the information requested in your interview will be treated confidentially by the researcher. Your observations and comments will in no way be identified with your name to this agency. Your information will be known only to the researcher who is conducting this study and will be incorporated anonymously, with that of many other adoptive parents, into the final research report.

Within the next few weeks you will be called by Mr. Smith to arrange an appointment with you. We hope you will be able to participate in this most important study. Thank you for your anticipated cooperation.

Sincerely,

Executive Director

Figure 11.3 Example of a Simple Cover Letter Requesting a Research Interview

may appeal to the altruism of research participants and provide a chance to contribute to the common good, while demanding relatively little. The purposes of a study can often be phrased in a way that conveys the idea that the findings will help improve life, create a better society, aid individuals, or in some other fashion be beneficial to people or organizations.

Other techniques can enhance potential research participants' belief that they will get some benefit from being interviewed. When they are contacted to get their agreement to participate and to arrange for an appointment, for example, they should be told the limits of time and data to be required. The idea that the interview should be interesting—perhaps even fun—can be conveyed, and the interviewees can be offered a summary of the research findings if they request it.

For example, one research study found that when unmarried couples were approached to be interviewed for a student research project that was to study the patterns and problems encountered in such relationships, a number expressed considerable interest in receiving the results of the study. They wanted to be able to compare their relationships to those of other couples who were studied. As perhaps a final resort, research participants may be paid a fee for participating in a research study. Such a procedure has been used in a study of delinquents and their rehabilitation, for example.

Of course, any promises, offers, and incentives given by the interviewer must be honored. Generally, prospective research participants will make themselves available if they feel a study is legitimate, will not demand excessive time, will respect their limits on what they choose to disclose, will protect their confidentiality, and will in some way be advantageous to them.

Another approach to encourage potential interviewee cooperation is to involve representatives, especially acknowledged leaders, of the population to be studied in the development of the research procedures and measurement instruments. This gives such populations greater commitment to the study, since it is not only *about* them but *for* them, and, at least partially, *by* them, as well. The involvement of representatives of the sample also provides useful inputs on such matters as areas to explore, access to the sample or population, and the language and phrasing of items.

DECIDING WHERE TO CONDUCT THE INTERVIEWS

Several locations may be available for conducting the interview: (1) the researchers' offices, (2) the interviewees' homes, or (3) "neutral" settings. The determination of which option to select may boil down to what is available, or where the interviewee is willing to be interviewed. However, if the interviewer has a choice, the advantages and disadvantages of the most common settings should be considered.

Offices

Conducting interviews in the offices of the sponsoring organization (assuming that space is available) is certainly the most economical arrangement in terms of money and time. Furthermore, it provides the researcher with the most control over environmental conditions, such as privacy, temperature, lighting, and seating arrangements.

However, if research participants have to come to the site of the interviews, they are more vulnerable to the vagaries of motivation—they simply may not show up. The formality of the office setting may be intimidating to some research participants, who may make their discomfort evident by withholding or distorting responses.

This distortion is most likely if the office represents an organization whose services the interviewees are evaluating. They may be understandably cautious about giving honest feedback regarding services from a social service program in whose offices they are sitting. Such an arrangement could well call into question any promises of confidentiality.

Interviewees' Homes

Conducting the interview in the interviewee's home poses a number of problems. It takes time and money to get to and from interviewees' homes, and they may not even be there when the interviewer arrives, regardless of previous arrangements. Privacy may be limited if children and other family members and neighbors wander in and out. The physical surroundings (e.g., furniture arrangement) also may not be conducive to interviewing.

The home interview also offers a number of advantages, however. In the postplacement adoption services study, all parents were interviewed in their homes, and the social workers were interviewed in their offices. It was anticipated that the adoptive parents would be more relaxed and would behave and respond more naturally on their own turf. They would be less inhibited at home about evaluating the services they had received than they would have been in a social service program's office. Furthermore, the interviewer would have the opportunity to observe interactions between parents and their children in their natural settings.

A special problem with this setting was that both parents were to be interviewed separately, using the same instrument, and it was preferable that neither parent be biased by hearing the responses of the other. This would have been comparatively easy to arrange in an office by having one parent wait outside while the other was being interviewed.

It was possible, however, to arrange for nearly the same privacy in the parents' home by starting the interview with both parents present and then instructing one parent to fill out some written checklists in another room while the other was being interviewed. Since there was nothing particularly confidential in the interviews, the fact that one parent would occasionally overhear the other was not considered a drawback to the use of the home as the site for the interviews.

Neutral Places

Some research interviews are best conducted on neutral territory—neither the interviewer's office nor the interviewee's home. With such research participants as teenagers or people with deviant lifestyles (e.g., prostitutes), a public setting may be the most acceptable setting for an interview. Although such settings may not be very private in terms of the proximity of strangers, they may be preferable to some interviewees because of the absence of family and acquaintances.

CHECKING THE INTERVIEWERS' APPEARANCE

Most research interviewers spend considerably less time with their research participants than social workers do with their clients. Because rapport must be established relatively quickly, the physical appearance of the interviewer is important.

Few studies have reported the effects of grooming and clothing on interviewers' effectiveness, but, as with other social work roles, an unobtrusive, neat, and conservative appearance that is compatible with the interviewees' standards of proper dress for someone in a researcher's role seems advisable. Interviewers should dress in a fashion fairly similar to that of the people they will be interviewing. A too well-dressed interviewer will probably not get good cooperation and responses from disadvantaged research participants, and a poorly dressed interviewer will have similar difficulties with others.

Too much jewelry, sexually provocative clothes, unorthodox hairstyles, or excessive makeup can all be distracting to those who are being interviewed. In brief contacts such as occur in research interviews, first appearances, including clothing and grooming, are cues that can profoundly affect the way people subsequently relate to each other.

Interviewers must create a climate in which their interviewees will be able and willing to provide clear and complete answers. Therefore, they should appear the way they anticipate the interviewees will expect them to appear.

The University of Michigan Survey Research Center employs interviewers throughout the United States to carry out studies on a wide variety of topics. The center's *Interviewer's Manual* instructs its interviewers to:

> Aim for simplicity and comfort: a simple suit or dress is best. Avoid identification with groups or orders (pins or rings, for instance, of clubs or fraternal orders). The respondent should be led to concentrate on you as a person and the interview you want to take, and not the way you are dressed.

The manual goes on to recommend that the interviewer always carry the "official blue folder." Interviewers may or may not have an official folder to carry with them, but a neat binder carried in a clean, untattered briefcase can enhance the image of a purposeful, well-organized interviewer, while a pile of dogeared papers balanced precariously could shatter it.

DEVELOPING THE INTERVIEWER-INTERVIEWEE RELATIONSHIP

There are both similarities and differences between worker-client and research interviewer–interviewee relationships. Ideally, both are purposeful, goal-directed relationships. Both are, or should be, guided by basic social work values and ethics regarding clients and research participants, such as respect for personal dignity, protection of confidentiality, and acceptance of the right to self-determination, including the right of the interviewee to refuse to answer any question. In both situations, the social worker and the researcher try to create a climate in which the client or the research participant will be able to provide honest and complete data.

But there are differences between the worker-client relationship and the researcher interviewer–interviewee relationship that some social workers may have difficulty adjusting to. The social worker who either conducts or supervises research interviews must understand these differences and accommodate them.

The social work practice interview is generally focused on establishing a helping relationship and eliciting data in order to provide services to clients. In the research interview, however, acquiring data is an end in itself, although the long-range effect of the study may be beneficial to the interviewees.

Again, since the time for research interviews is limited and the parameters for the data to be obtained are predetermined (as opposed to the generally more open-ended goals of social work treatment interviews), research interviews tend to be much more focused. Social work relationships are often ongoing; research relationships are almost always relatively brief.

The goal of social work *practice* interviews is to help a particular client system. The goal of *research* interviews is to obtain data about and from a particular population. The social worker represents help to be offered to the client; the research interviewer cannot make promises or commitments.

These differences in purpose account for the differences between worker-client and research interviewer–interviewee relationships. In the research interview, the interviewer takes the primary (if not entire) responsibility for the direction of the interview, including the topics covered and the sequence of questions asked. In a social work interview, it is often preferable to follow the client's lead. The social work *practice* interview is for the *client*; the social work *research* interview is for the *interviewer*.

There is considerable evidence in research of clinical relationships that the therapists' communication of warmth, empathy, and genuineness to clients is positively associated with effective treatment. Whether similar communication by the research interviewer would enhance research interviews has not been determined; no studies are yet available that compare the effectiveness of research interviewers who have high ratings on any or all of these dimensions with the effectiveness of those who do not.

We could hypothesize that since these attributes in an interviewer seem to be effective because they allow interviewees to be truly themselves, to trust the interviewer, and to explore their feelings and experience more easily, they would be equally useful in enabling the research participant to provide more valid and reliable data. However, a number of the factors that differentiate research from treatment interviewing raise questions about just how much, and what kind of, warmth, empathy, and genuineness should be communicated in research interviews.

While research interviewers who communicate empathy may indeed be brought closer to their interviewees, at the same time this could make them "anticipate" or even prejudice their interviewees' answers. The interviewers might project themselves into their interviewees' feeling and beliefs, rather than objectively eliciting and recording their answers.

The warmth emanating from the interviewers also could delay or inhibit their interviewees from sharing personal data. It is sometimes easier to convey sensitive information to a neutral stranger than to a friend; witness the ease with which people reveal personal details to fellow passengers on an airplane. Objectivity and even professional detachment on the part of the interviewer may be more effective in obtaining valid and reliable answers.

It is neither fair to the interviewee nor an effective use of research time to involve interviewees in a pseudotherapeutic relationship, which the active communication of warmth and empathy may do. If interviewees reveal problems amenable to professional treatment intervention during the course of research interviews and indicate a desire to seek help, it would certainly be appropriate for interviewers to refer them to appropriate resources. But offering professional social work services is not the intent of research interviews.

Since there have been few studies to guide investigation of the interviewer–interviewee relationship, and since worker-client relationship research may be of limited applicability, we can only suggest some attributes of interviewers which may guide research interview relationships. Interviewers should:

1. Clearly communicate to the interviewees the purposes and limits of the interviewer's contact.
2. Be trustworthy, friendly, courteous, and kind to interviewees, yet focus clearly on the goals of the study.
3. Communicate to the interviewees that the interviewer's only interest in their answers is for the purposes of the study and that the interviewer has no personal interest in the responses. In conducting the sexual behavior interviews in Pomeroy's study cited at the beginning of this chapter, for example, the interviewers communicated to their research participants that, personally, they didn't care what sexual behaviors their interviewees reported, other than for the contribution a response could make to the study.

FORMULATING AND ASKING QUESTIONS

Most of the guidelines for formulating and asking questions in interviews are similar to those that have already been suggested for survey measuring instruments. Some of the basic guidelines that are especially applicable to asking questions in interviews are described in this section.

Keeping the Language Simple

The wording of questions should generally be simple, clear, and unobtrusive. Words from the average person's vocabulary, rather than the jargon of graduate social workers, should be used. "Meaningful others" is meaningless to most research participants. Generally, "angry" is better than "hostile," "sad" is better than "depressed," and certainly "brothers and sisters" is better than "siblings."

It has been suggested that the interviewer should use the type of vocabulary usually found in most newspapers and popular magazines (*not* in professional journals). Further, the use of slang expressions such as "getting stoned," "giving head," or "being ripped off" may be unclear to research participants and may also "turn them off" to the interviewer.

Avoiding Double-Barreled Questions

The interviewee should be asked for only one reply at a time. There are three ways in which double-barreled questions can confuse research participants, thereby leaving the interviewer unsure about the intent of their answers. The first is that some double-barreled questions essentially ask two questions at once.

For example, medical students on psychiatric rotation were given an interviewing schedule prepared by the staff psychiatrists to be used in obtaining a brief sexual history. One of the items was clearly double-barreled: "Have you ever masturbated *or* participated in a homosexual activity?" Of course, most patients hurriedly answered "no" (much to the relief of the medical students). What they were saying no to remained obscure.

A second type of double-barreled question starts with a statement of alleged fact that is the premise on which the question is based. For example, parents could be asked: "Of course, you wanted your daughter to finish high school. How did you go about keeping her going?" Such a question has a built-in bias that

may or may not reflect the thinking or feelings of the interviewee.

The third type of double-barreled question is built on a hidden premise, such as the classic "When did you stop beating your child?" Some assumptions may be useful in facilitating questioning, but these must be used cautiously. It's best to assume very little. Assumptions often lead the interviewee to offer socially desirable but inaccurate answers.

Avoiding Double-Negative Questions

Double negatives imply a positive, and such questions can be confusing: "Do you feel that most married women would really prefer not to work if they were not under financial stress?" might better be phrased, "Do you feel most married women prefer to work only if they are under financial stress?"

Discouraging Biased Responses

Questions should be asked in such a way that the interviewees will not feel constrained to give only those answers that they perceive would fit generally accepted social norms. Research participants often choose to provide answers that sound good—whether they're true or not. For example, pupils in a third-grade class were asked to tell the teacher their greatest wish. Most of the children replied with such answers as "to go to Disneyland" or "to get a bicycle," but one boy said "to have peace on earth." The teacher was impressed and sent home a laudatory note to his parents. The student confided a few years later that he knew that answer would get him "strokes" from the teacher and that what he really wanted to answer was "to be able to fly"!

It will help those being interviewed to be more open about sensitive areas if such items are phrased in a way to convey the idea that the interviewer knows there is a wide range of human behaviors, most people have problems, and there is nothing (well, almost nothing) that will shock the interviewer.

One of the most effective ways to encourage research participants to answer questions truthfully, even if the answers might be embarrassing or violate social norms, is the "many people" technique. This approach enabled Pomeroy's investigators to uncover data about sexual behavior that might otherwise have been impossible to obtain.

For example, rather than asking a married adult "Do you masturbate?," which might prompt an immediate and defensive "no," the interviewer might say, "Many married men and women find that stimulating themselves to orgasm is a satisfying supplement to other sexual experiences" and then ask, "Have you found this to be true for you?"

It is unlikely that such a question would lead people to answer "yes" if they did not masturbate at least occasionally, but it does provide support for a yes answer if that is the case. It also could pave the way to subsequent, more detailed items. Note that in the rephrased question the emotionally laden "masturbation" was replaced with the more cumbersome but less emotionally charged euphemism "stimulating yourself to orgasm." As long as a concept is clear in meaning, it is best to use the least emotionally charged word or phrase—even a euphemism—that describes it.

For example, it might be better to ask "How often is your behavior altered by drinking alcoholic beverages?" than "How often do you get drunk?" Similarly, "How often has an employer let you go?" may be a less threatening question than "How often have you been fired?"

Investigators also found that presenting a wide range of options for answers in random order enables research participants to avoid biasing their answers according to what might be expected of them. Thus, after asking the questions "How often do you and your husband have sexual intercourse?," the interviewers would add, "Once a month? Twice a day? Less than once a year? Four times a week? Every 6 months?" This provides interviewees with considerable latitude in answering what might otherwise be an embarrassing item.

It is often difficult for research participants to give negative evaluations of social service programs and the experiences they have had with these programs. A technique that can help them overcome this resistance is to ask paired questions that make it possible to offer both praise and criticism, ideally in that order. For example, "What did you like most about your social worker?" can be followed with "What did you like least about your social worker?" The overall effect of such pairs of questions is to elicit a balanced evaluation that can justify the expression of negative opinions or observations.

Avoiding Interviewer Bias

Research participants may feel, or be made to feel, that the research interview is essentially an examination or trial and that they must somehow please or satisfy the interviewer. Often, therefore, they will try to get the interviewer's opinions or experiences on particular questions before they respond.

Interviewers may bias answers by the way they phrase questions or by the expressions on their faces. They can also bias subsequent answers by their verbal and nonverbal reactions to responses. Asking the questions as consistently as possible, and reviewing tape recordings of interviewer-interviewee interchanges, can reduce this bias.

Reinforcing Interviewees' Answers

Research interviewees, like everyone else, respond to reinforcement. If interviewers demonstrate that they appreciate and value their interviewees' answers, the quality of subsequent answers will generally be enhanced. A previous study on the effects of experimental interviewing techniques used in health interview studies demonstrated that verbal reinforcement by the interviewer increased both the amount and the quality of research participants' recall in interviews.

Without overdoing it, the interviewer can follow interviewees' answers with reactions ranging from a simple head nod and "uh-huh" to "Thanks for giving me such a detailed answer." Comments that do not evaluate the content of the response but do reinforce its completeness need not bias the interviewee.

RECORDING THE DATA

The final consideration in research interviewing is how best to record the interviewees' answers. The conversion of these answers to a pool of valid, useful data challenges the interviewer's skill in avoiding distortion or omission of data.

Generally, the recording procedure chosen should meet the following three criteria:

1. It should accurately record the manifest intent if not the exact wording of the interviewees' answers.
2. It should be as unobtrusive as possible so that it does not inhibit the flow of the interview or distract the interviewee from giving complete, candid answers.
3. It should facilitate transmittal of the data from the recording instrument to the data bank.

Interviews that rely on closed-ended questions are the easiest to record and run the least risk of recording distortion and bias. All the interviewer has to do is check, underline, or circle the appropriate answer on the interview schedule. At most, it is necessary to record a few words per answer.

Semistructured and unstructured interviews pose greater problems in recording. Two alternative methods of recording are available to interviewers: (1) handwritten and (2) mechanical.

Using Handwritten Recording

In the unlikely event that interviewers were skilled at taking shorthand, they would still have difficulty taking down their interviewees' answers verbatim. And, even if that were possible, excessive note taking can be distracting not only to those who are being interviewed but to the interviewers, as well. Furthermore, verbatim responses are rarely necessary for recording useful data.

The interviewer may choose to wait until the interview is over and then try to recall and record answers as completely and accurately as possible. However, this procedure is risky. The interviewer may forget significant answers and nuances. Furthermore, if the researcher has interviewed a number of research participants in a relatively short amount of time, one respondent's answers may blur with another's, seriously distorting the data.

A safer procedure is for the interviewer to record summaries of responses from time to time throughout the interview, supplemented with direct quotations for illustrative purposes. If necessary, the interviewer may interrupt or slow down the interviewee with such comments as "Wait a second, that was an interesting point, I want to get it down in my notes."

Again, the social work research interview is different from a social work practice interview. The purpose of research interviews is clearly defined as data gathering, not service delivery. Therefore, while note taking may be distracting and even inappropriate in a treatment interview, it can be an acceptable and integral part of the research interview.

However, the recording procedures used by research interviewers should be as brief and uncomplicated as possible. This can be achieved by developing a coding procedure and other shortcuts to recording data—as long as the interviewer can remember what the notes and codes mean. Pomeroy's sexual behavior investigators, for example, developed a code by which they could record extensive, detailed sexual life histories on a single index card.

Using Mechanical Recording

The development of compact, reliable cassette recorders makes it possible to record exactly what is said by the interviewees. Furthermore, once the recorder is turned on, it provides none of the distractions that handwritten recording can. Clients generally have no objection to being recorded. A research participant should, of course, be informed that an interview is being recorded. However, no extensive discussion of its use is necessary unless the interviewee initiates such a discussion.

Although there are obvious advantages to the absolute accuracy that mechanical recording can provide, tape-recorded data have their limitations. Machines can break down, tapes can break, and microphones can pick up background noises that obscure the comments of the interviewee.

Occasionally, research participants will object to having their comments recorded. The greatest limitation, however, is the considerable time and expense of either transcribing the recording or listening to the entire recording for research analysis. In some ways, this is a duplication of energy, since the interviewees' answers have already been heard by the interviewer while the interview was being taped.

It is possible, however, that after the taped interviews have been analyzed, the researcher will choose additional variables to study and return to the original tapes for reanalysis. Thus, taped interviews provide more comprehensive and flexible data.

SUMMARY

This overview of interviewing in social work research began with a consideration of the advantages of research interviewing over questionnaires in self-report surveys and of some of the limitations of interviews in research. The tasks in planning and organizing interview-based research were then discussed: determining the content of interviews and developing the interview schedule, phrasing the questions, selecting the interviewers, gaining access to the research participants, deciding where to conduct the interviews, deciding how interviewers should be groomed and dressed, and being aware of the nature of effective interviewer-interviewee relationships. Finally, the manner in which questions should be asked in the interview and procedures for recording answers were explored.

Throughout this discussion, differences and similarities between treatment and research interviews have been described. While there are numerous differences, the significance of social work skills, knowledge, and values for research interviewing must be stressed.

As we know, using interviewing as a form of data collection is obtrusive; that is, the researcher intrudes into the research participants' lives in some form or another. The following chapter continues our discussion of data collection methods by presenting how a social work research study can use another obtrusive data collection method, known as surveys.

Survey Research

12

Rafael J. Engel
Russell K. Schutt

Basic Steps in the Research Process

Step 1	Choose a problem
2	Review the literature
3	Evaluate the literature
4	Be aware of all ethical issues
5	Be aware of all cultural issues
6	State the research question or hypothesis
7	Select the research approach
8	Determine how the variables are going to be measured
9	Select a sample
10	Select a data collection method
11	Collect and code the data
12	Analyze and interpret the data
13	Write the report
14	Disseminate the report

You Are Here → (pointing to Step 10)

The intersection between work and family life has changed considerably during the 20th century. For much of the industrial period, separation of work and family activities and a gender-based division of responsibilities were the norm. But we have seen in recent decades a dramatic increase in the proportion of two-income families, many more single-parent/single-earner families, more telecommuting and other work-at-home arrangements, and some changes in the household division of "labor." Social scientists who seek to understand these changes in the social structure have had plenty to keep themselves busy.

University of Texas sociology professor Catherine Ross (1990) wanted to know how these changes shape people's sense of control and, in turn, how their sense of control affects feelings of depression, anxiety, and distress. To answer these questions, she proposed to the National Science Foundation a survey of adult Americans. In this chapter, we will use her successful project to illustrate some key features of survey research. After an initial review of the reasons for using survey methods, we explain the major steps in questionnaire design and then consider the features of four types of surveys, highlighting the unique problems attending each one and suggesting some possible solutions. We discuss ethics issues in the final section. By the chapter's end, you should be well on your way to becoming an informed consumer of survey reports and a knowledgeable developer of survey designs—as well as a more informed student of the relationships among work, family, and well-being.

SURVEY RESEARCH IN SOCIAL WORK

Survey research involves the collection of information from a sample of individuals through their responses to questions. As you probably have observed, a great many researchers—as well as newspaper editors, political pundits, and marketing gurus—make the same methodological choice. In fact, surveys have become such a vital part of our social fabric that we cannot assess much of what we read in the newspaper or see on TV without having some understanding of this method of data collection (Converse, 1984).

Attractions of Survey Research

Regardless of its scope, survey research owes its continuing popularity to three features: (1) versatility, (2) efficiency, and (3) generalizability.

Versatility

First and foremost is the versatility of survey methods. Although a survey is not the ideal method for testing all hypotheses or learning about every social process, a well-designed survey can enhance our understanding of just about any social issue. Social work researchers have used survey methods to investigate every field of social work practice, including (but not limited to) child welfare, gerontology, health, mental health, income maintenance, community building, and community development. If you have worked in an agency or you are in field practicum, you have probably noticed that the methods of survey research have been adapted by the agency for program evaluation and practice. Surveys are used in agencies to assess the impact of policy changes, identify community needs, track changes in community characteristics, monitor and evaluate program effectiveness, and assess client satisfaction with programs. Your practicum supervisor or the agency executive director has probably responded to surveys sent by the state, accrediting boards, or funding agencies such as the United Way.

Efficiency

Surveys also are popular because data can be collected from many people at relatively low cost and, depending on the survey design, relatively quickly. Catherine Ross contracted with the University of Illinois Survey Research Laboratory (SRL) for her 1990 telephone survey of 2,000 adult Americans. SRL estimated that the survey would incur direct costs of $60,823—only $30.41 per respondent—and take 5 to 6 months to complete. Large mailed surveys cost even less, about $10 to $15 per potential respondent, although the costs can increase greatly when intensive follow-up efforts are made. Surveys of the general population using personal interviews are much more expensive, with costs ranging from about $100 per potential respondent for studies in a limited geographic area to $300 or more when lengthy travel or repeat visits are needed to connect with respondents (Fowler, personal communication, January 7, 1998; see also Dillman, 1982; Groves & Kahn, 1979). As you would expect, phone surveys are the quickest survey method, followed by mail surveys and then interviews.

Surveys also are efficient because many variables can be measured without substantially increasing the time or cost. Mailed questionnaires can include up to 10 pages of questions before respondents begin to balk. In-person interviews can be much longer, taking more than an hour; for example, the 1991 General Social Survey included 196 questions, many with multiple parts, and was 75 pages long. The upper limit for phone surveys seems to be about 45 minutes.

Of course, these efficiencies can be attained only in a place with a reliable communications infrastructure (Labaw, 1980, pp. xiii–xiv). A reliable postal service, which is required for mail surveys, has generally been available in the United States—although residents of the Bronx, New York, have complained that delivery of local first-class mail often takes 2 weeks or more, almost ruling out mail surveys (Purdy, 1994). Phone surveys can be effective in the United States because 95% of households have phones (Czaja & Blair, 1995), and only 4% of people live in households without a phone (Levy & Lemeshow, 1999, p. 456).

Generalizability

Survey methods lend themselves to probability sampling from large populations. Thus, survey research is very appealing when sample generalizability is a central research goal. In fact, survey research is often the only means available for developing a representative picture of the attitudes and characteristics of a large population.

Surveys also are the method of choice when cross-population generalizability is a key concern, because they allow a range of social contexts and subgroups to be sampled. The consistency of relationships can then be examined across the various subgroups.

The Omnibus Survey

An omnibus survey shows just how versatile, efficient, and generalizable a survey can be. An omnibus survey covers a range of topics of interest to different researchers, in contrast to the typical survey, which is directed at a specific research question. The omnibus survey has multiple sponsors or is designed to generate data useful to a broad segment of the social science community rather than to answer a particular research question. It is usually directed to a sample of some general population, so the questions about a range of issues are appropriate to at least some sample members. Communities across the country are developing their own omnibus surveys, designed to document a variety of economic, political, social, health, and demographic trends in the particular communities.

One of the most successful omnibus surveys is the General Social Survey (GSS) of the National Opinion Research Center at the University of Chicago. It is a 90-minute interview administered biennially to a probability sample of almost 3,000 Americans, with a wide range of questions and topic areas chosen by a board of overseers. Some questions are asked of only a randomly selected subset of respondents. This split-ballot design allows more questions without increasing the survey's cost. It also facilitates experiments on the effect of question wording: Different forms of the same question are included in the split-ballot subsets. The GSS is widely available to universities, instructors, and students (Davis & Smith, 1992; National Opinion Research Center, 1992), as are many other survey data sets archived by the Inter-University Consortium for Political and Social Research (ICPSR; more details about the ICPSR appear later in this chapter).

Errors in Survey Research

It might be said that surveys are too easy to conduct. Organizations and individuals often decide that a survey would help to solve some important problem because it seems so easy to prepare a form with some questions and send it out. But without careful attention to sampling, measurement, and overall survey design, the effort is likely to be a flop. Such flops are too common

for comfort, and the responsible survey researcher must take the time to design surveys properly and to convince sponsoring organizations that this time is worth the effort (Turner & Martin, 1984, p. 68).

For a survey to succeed, it must minimize the risk of two types of error: poor measurement of cases that are surveyed (errors of observation), and omission of cases that should be surveyed (errors of nonobservation; Groves, 1989). Measurement error was a key concern in Chapter 5, but there is much more to be learned about how to minimize these errors of observation in the survey process. We will consider in this chapter potential problems with the questions we write, the characteristics of the respondents who answer the questions, the way we present these questions in our questionnaires, and the interviewers we may use to ask the questions. The potential measurement errors that survey researchers confront in designing questions and questionnaires are summarized in Figure 12.1; we will discuss each of these sources of error throughout this chapter.

There are three sources of errors of nonobservation:

- Coverage of the population can be inadequate due to a poor sampling frame.
- The process of random sampling can result in sampling error—differences between the characteristics of the sample members and the population, which arise due to chance.
- Nonresponse can distort the sample when individuals refuse to respond or cannot be contacted. Nonresponse to specific questions can distort the generalizability of the responses to those questions.

We considered the importance of a good sampling frame and the procedures for estimating and reducing sampling error in Chapter 6; we will add only a few more points here. We will give much more attention in this chapter to procedures for reducing nonresponse in surveys. Unfortunately, nonresponse is becoming an increasing concern for survey researchers. For reasons that are not entirely understood, but that may include growing popular cynicism and distrust of government, nonresponse rates have been growing in

Question Wording—Does the question have a consistent meaning to respondents? Problems can occur with:

- *Lengthy wording* — Words talk are unnecessary, long, and complicated
- *Lengthy of question* — The question is unnecessarily long
- *Lack of specificity* — It is not clear from the question what Information is desired
- *Lack of frame of reference* — The question does not specify to what reference comparisons should be made
- *Vague language* — Words and phrases can have different meanings to respondents
- *Double negatives* — Use of two or more negative phrases in the question
- *Double-barreled question* — Question actually asks two or more questions
- *Using jargon and Initials* — Professional or academic discipline specific terms are used
- *Leading questions* — Question phrasing meant to bias the response
- *Cultural differences in meaning* — Phrases or words that have different meaning to different population subgroups

Respondent Characteristics—Characteristics of respondents may produce inaccurate answers. These include:

- *Memory recall* — Problems of remembering events or details about events
- *Telescoping* — Remembering events as happening more recently than when they really occurred
- *Agreement or acquiescence bias* — Tendency for respondents to "agree"
- *Social desirability* — Tendency to want to appear in a positive light and therefore provide the desirable response
- *Floaters* — Respondents who choose a substantive answer when they really don't know
- *Fence-sitters* — People who see themselves as being neutral so as not to give the wrong answer
- *Sensitive questions* — Questions deemed too personal

Presentation of Questions—The structure of questions and the survey instrument may produce error including:

- *Open-ended questions* — Response categories are not provided, left to respondent to provide
- *Closed-ended questions* — Possible response categories are provided
- *Agree-disagree* — Tendency to agree when only two choices are offered
- *Question order* — The context or order of questions can effect subsequent responses are respondents try to remain consistent
- *Response set* — Giving the same response to a series of questions
- *Filter questions* — Questions used to determine if other questions are relevant

Interviewer—The use of an interviewer may produce these errors.

- *Mismatch of interviewer-interviewee demographic characteristics*
- *Unconscious judgmental actions to responses*

Figure 12.1   Measurement Errors Associated With Surveys

the United States and Western Europe since the early 1950s (Groves, 1989, pp. 145–155; Groves & Couper, 1998, pp. 155–189).

We can begin to anticipate problems that lead to survey errors and identify possible solutions if we take enough time to think about the issue theoretically. Survey expert Don Dillman (2000, pp. 14–15) suggests using the framework of social exchange theory, which asserts that behavior is motivated by the return the individual expects for the behavior (Blau, 1964). Expected returns include the social rewards that the individual thinks will be received for the behavior, the costs that will be incurred, and the trust that in the long run the

rewards will exceed the costs. A well-designed survey will maximize the social rewards, minimize the costs for participating in the survey, and establish trust that the rewards will outweigh the costs.

Using clear and interesting questions and presenting them in a well-organized questionnaire go a long way to reducing the cost of responding carefully to a survey. Question writing will be the focus of the next section, and questionnaire design will be discussed in the section that follows. Other steps for increasing rewards, reducing costs, and maximizing trust in order to reduce nonresponse in each type of survey will be the focus of the last section.

CONSTRUCTING QUESTIONS

Questions are the centerpiece of survey research. In the social sciences, asking people questions is the most common method for measuring variables, and social work research (or practice, for that matter) is no different. Some questions may focus on knowledge or what people know or do not know. Some questions focus on attitudes, or what people say they want or how they feel about something. Some questions focus on feelings or symptoms or how they feel about themselves. Some questions focus on behavior, or what people do. And some questions focus on attributes, or what people are like or have experienced (Dillman, 1978, pp. 79–118; Gordon, 1992). Rarely can a single question effectively address more than one of these dimensions at a time. Nor should we try to focus on more than one dimension, lest the question become too complex.

In principle, survey questions can be a straightforward and efficient means to measure different variables, but in practice, survey questions can result in misleading or inappropriate answers. All questions proposed for a survey must be screened carefully for their adherence to basic guidelines and then tested and revised until the researcher feels some confidence that they will be clear to the intended respondents (Fowler, 1995). Some variables may prove to be inappropriate for measurement with any type of question. We have to recognize the limits of people's memories and perceptions of the events about which we might like to ask.

Closed-Ended Questions

Questions can be designed with or without explicit response choices. When explicit response categories are offered, the type of question is a closed-ended question, or fixed-choice question. For example, the following question asked in a survey of clients receiving vision-related services is closed-ended because the desired response categories are provided.

> Overall, how would you rate your health? Would you say your health is excellent, very good, good, fair, or poor?

_____ Excellent
_____ Very good
_____ Good
_____ Fair
_____ Poor

Most surveys of a large number of people contain primarily closed-ended questions, which are easy to process with computers and analyze with statistics. With closed-ended questions, respondents are also more likely to answer the question that the researcher really wants them to answer. Including the response choices reduces ambiguity. However, fixed-response choices can obscure what people really think unless the choices are designed carefully to match the range of possible responses to the question. Respondents can become frustrated when they are not able to find a category to fit their desired answer. Finally, closed-ended questions do not create rapport when conducting an interview.

Most important, response choices should be mutually exclusive and exhaustive, so that every respondent can find one and only one choice that applies to him or her (unless the question is of the "Check all that apply" format). To make response choices exhaustive, researchers may need to offer at least one option with room for ambiguity. For example, older adults were asked to check all social services they had used in the past month. The list included 15 different services but concluded with the following category because the researchers were not sure they had all the possible services on their list:

> Other (please specify_____)

If respondents do not find a response option that corresponds to their answer to the question, they may skip the question entirely or choose a response option that does not indicate what they are really thinking.

Open-Ended Questions

Open-ended questions are questions without explicit response choices, so that respondents provide their own answers in their own words. The following question is an open-ended version of the earlier closed-ended question asked of the older adults.

Please identify the kinds of social services you have used in the past month.

An open-ended format is preferable with questions for which the range of responses cannot adequately be anticipated—namely, questions that have not previously been used in surveys and questions that are asked of new groups.

Open-ended questions provide additional information that may not be available from a closed-ended question. For example, in a questionnaire dealing with psychiatric conditions, respondents were asked a yes-no question,

In the last 2 weeks, have you had thoughts that you would be better off dead or of hurting yourself in some way?

____ Yes
____ No

They were then asked, "Can you tell me about it?"

The purpose of the second question was to expand on the first question and help the analyst to determine whether there was a threat of suicide.

Open-ended questions can be used to explain what a concept means to the respondent. For example, mental illness is a complex concept that tends to have different meanings for different people. In a survey that Schutt (1992) conducted in homeless shelters, staff were asked whether they believed that people at the shelter had become homeless due to mental illness. About 47% chose *Agree* or *Strongly agree* when given fixed-response choices. However, when these same staff members were interviewed in depth using open-ended questions, it became clear that the meaning of these responses varied among staff. Some believed that mental illness caused homelessness by making people vulnerable in the face of bad luck and insufficient resources:

Mental illness [is the cause]. Just watching them, my heart goes out to them. Whatever the circumstances were that were in their lives that led them to the streets and being homeless I see it as very sad. . . . Maybe the resources weren't there for them, or maybe they didn't have the capabilities

to know when the resources were there. It is misfortune. (Schutt, 1992, p. 7)

Other staff believed that mental illness caused people to reject housing opportunities:

I believe because of their mental illness that's why they are homeless. So for them to say I would rather live on the street than live in a house and have to pay rent, I mean that to me indicates that they are mentally ill. (Schutt, 1992, p. 7)

Although open-ended questions provide a wealth of information, they are not always easy to use. Administering, analyzing, and summarizing open-ended questions can be time-consuming and difficult. Some respondents do not like to write a lot and may find open-ended questions taxing. Interviewing is not necessarily the solution: The amount of information provided by a respondent may depend on the respondent's personality—some respondents may provide short or cursory answers, while other respondents may provide extensive answers with a great deal of relevant (and irrelevant) information.

Writing Clear Questions

Because the way questions are worded can have a great effect on the way they are answered, selecting good questions is the single most important concern for survey researchers. All hope of achieving measurement validity is lost unless the questions in a survey are clear and convey the intended meaning to respondents. You may be thinking that you ask people questions all the time and have no trouble understanding the answers you receive, but can't you also think of times when you have been confused in casual conversation by misleading or misunderstood questions? Now consider just a few of the differences between everyday conversations and standardized surveys that make writing survey questions much more difficult:

- Survey questions must be asked of many people, not just one.
- The same survey question must be used with each person, not tailored to the specifics of a given conversation.

- Survey questions must be understood in the same way by people who differ in many ways.
- You will not be able to rephrase a survey question if someone doesn't understand it because that would result in a different question for that person.
- Survey respondents don't know you and so can't be expected to share the nuances of expression that help you and your friends and family to communicate.

Question writing for a particular survey might begin with a brainstorming session or a review of previous surveys. Then, whatever questions are being considered must be systematically evaluated and refined. Although most professionally prepared surveys contain previously used questions as well as some new ones, every question that is considered for inclusion must be reviewed carefully for its clarity and ability to convey the intended meaning. Questions that were clear and meaningful to one population may not be so to another. Nor can you simply assume that a question used in a previously published study was carefully evaluated.

Adherence to a few basic principles will go a long way toward ensuring clear and meaningful questions. Each of these principles summarizes a great deal of the wisdom of experienced survey researchers, although none of them should be viewed as an inflexible mandate. As you will learn in the next section, every question must be considered in terms of its relationship to the other questions in a survey. Moreover, every survey has its own unique requirements and constraints; sometimes, violating one principle is necessary to achieve others.

Avoid Confusing Phrasing

What is a confusing question? Try this question sent by the Planetary Society in its National Priorities Survey, United States Space Program:

> The Moon may be a place for an eventual scientific base, and even for engineering resources. Setting up a base or mining experiment will cost tens of billions of dollars in the next century. Should the United States pursue further manned

and unmanned scientific research projects on the surface of the Moon?

____ Yes
____ No
____ No opinion

Does a *Yes* response mean that you favor spending tens of billions of dollars for a base or mining experiment? In the 20th or 21st centuries (the survey was distributed in the 1980s)? Could you favor further research projects on the Moon but oppose funding a scientific base or engineering resources? Are engineering resources supposed to have something to do with a mining experiment? Does a mining experiment occur "on the surface of the Moon"? How do you answer if you favor unmanned scientific research projects but not manned projects?

There are several ways to avoid such confusing phrasing. In most cases, a simple direct approach to asking a question minimizes confusion. Use shorter rather than longer words: *brave* rather than *courageous, job concerns* rather than *work-related employment issues* (Dillman, 2000, p. 52). Use shorter sentences when you can. The longer the question, the more confusing it will be to the respondent. A lengthy question often forces the respondent to have to "work hard," that is, to have to read and reread the entire question. Lengthy questions may go unanswered or may be given only a cursory reading without much thought to the answer.

On the other hand, questions should not be abbreviated in a way that results in confusion: To ask, "In what city or town do you live?" is to focus attention clearly on a specific geographic unit, a specific time, and a specific person (you). The simple statement does not provide sufficient focus:

Residential location: _____

It is a general question when a specific kind of answer is intended. There are many different reasonable answers to this question, such as Squirrel Hill (a neighborhood), rural, or a busy street. Researchers cannot assume that we have all been trained by past surveys to know what is being asked in this particular question, and the phrasing should provide sufficient specificity to clarify for the respondent the intent of the question.

Researchers can also be confused by the answers respondents give when the question lacks a frame of reference. A frame of reference provides specificity about how respondents should answer a question. Take the question:

Overall, the performance of this caseworker is:

____ Excellent
____ Good
____ Average
____ Poor

The problem with this question is that the researcher does not know the basis of comparison the respondent is using. In formulating an answer, some respondents may compare the caseworker to other caseworkers. On the other hand, some respondents may use their personal "absolute scale" about a caseworker's performance, so that no one may be excellent. To avoid this kind of confusion, the basis of comparison should be specifically stated:

Compared to other caseworkers you have had, the performance of this caseworker is:

____ Excellent
____ Good
____ Average
____ Poor

In addition to questions lacking specificity, another issue arises from the fact that many words have different meanings. It is important to avoid vague language. For example, the question,

How many times in the last year have you talked with a doctor?

has at least two words, *doctor* and *talk*, that create ambiguity. Any kind of doctor (e.g., dentist, medical doctor, chiropractor)? What does talk mean—a conversation about a physical problem or social problem, or a casual conversation? A conversation over the phone, in the doctor's office, at a hospital?

Some words are vague, and their meaning may differ from respondent to respondent. The question,

Do you usually or occasionally attend programs at the community center?

will not provide useful information because the meaning of *usually* or *occasionally* can differ for each respondent. A better alternative is to define the two terms, such as *usually (2–3 times a week)* and *occasionally (2–3 times a month)*. A second option is to ask the respondents how often they attend programs at the community center; the researcher can then classify the responses into categories.

A sure way to muddy the meaning of a question is to use double negatives: "Do you *disagree* that there should *not* be a tax increase?" Respondents have a hard time figuring out which response matches their sentiments. Such errors can easily be avoided with minor wording changes, but even experienced survey researchers can make this mistake unintentionally, perhaps while trying to avoid some other wording problem. For instance, in a survey commissioned by the American Jewish Committee, the Roper polling organization wrote a question about the Holocaust that was carefully worded to be neutral and value-free:

Does it seem possible or does it seem impossible to you that the Nazi extermination of the Jews never happened?

Among a representative sample of adult Americans, 22% answered that it was possible the extermination never happened (Kifner, 1994, p. A12). Many Jewish leaders and politicians were stunned, wondering how one in five Americans could be so misinformed. But a careful reading of the question reveals how confusing it is: Choosing *possible*, the seemingly positive response, means that you do not believe the Holocaust happened. In fact, the question was then rephrased to avoid the double negative; it gave a brief definition of the Holocaust and then asked,

Do you doubt that the Holocaust actually happened or not?

Only 9% responded that they doubted it happened. When a wider range of response choices was given, only 2.9% said that the Holocaust *definitely* or *probably* did not happen.

So-called double-barreled questions are also guaranteed to produce uninterpretable results because they actually ask two questions but allow only one answer.

For example, during the Watergate scandal, Gallup poll results indicated that, when the question was,

> Do you think President Nixon should be impeached and compelled to leave the presidency, or not?

only about a third of Americans supported impeaching President Richard M. Nixon. But when the Gallup organization changed the question to ask respondents if they "think there is enough evidence of possible wrongdoing in the case of President Nixon to bring him to trial before the Senate, or not," over half answered yes. Apparently the first, double-barreled version of the question confused support for impeaching Nixon—putting him on trial before the Senate—with concluding that he was guilty before he had had a chance to defend himself (Kagay & Elder, 1992, p. E5).

You should also avoid the use of jargon or technical language related to a profession or academic discipline. It is easy for each of us to write questions in a language that is specific to our profession. Words like *social justice, empowering,* and *strengths* may appear in social work literature, but they do not necessarily have a shared meaning in the profession, let alone the broader community. Using acronyms to abbreviate phrases is also a form of professional jargon. For example, to some social work students (particularly those students specializing in gerontology), AAA refers to the Area Agency on Aging, but to other social work students and the general population, the acronym is just as likely to refer to the Automobile Association of America.

Minimize the Risk of Bias

Specific words in survey questions should not trigger biases, unless that is the researcher's conscious intent. Such questions are referred to as leading questions because they lead the respondent to a particular answer. Biased or loaded words and phrases tend to produce misleading answers. For example, a 1974 survey found that 18% of respondents supported sending U.S. troops "if a situation like Vietnam were to develop in another part of the world." But when the question was reworded to mention sending troops to "stop a com-

munist takeover"—*communist takeover* being a loaded phrase—favorable responses rose to 33% (Schuman & Presser, 1981, p. 285).

Answers can also be biased by more subtle problems in phrasing that make certain responses more or less attractive to particular groups. There are words, such as *welfare* or *liberal*, that over time have taken on meanings that stir reactions, at least in some people. To minimize biased responses, researchers have to test reactions to the phrasing of a question. When Catherine Ross (1990) was seeking to determine respondents' interests in household work rather than formal employment, she took special care to phrase her questions in a balanced, unbiased way.

For example, she asked, "If you could choose, would you rather do the kind of work people do on jobs or the kind of work that is done around the house?" Her response options were *Jobs, House, Both, Neither, Don't care,* and *Don't know.* She could easily have biased the distribution of responses to this question by referring to housework as "the kind of work that women traditionally have done around the house." The explicit gender typing would probably have made men less likely to choose housework as their preference. Note that if Ross's purpose had been to find out how men respond to explicitly gender-linked roles, this wording would have been appropriate. Bias can only be defined in terms of the concept that the question is designed to measure.

Responses can also be biased when response alternatives do not reflect the full range of possible sentiment on an issue. When people pick a response choice, they seem to be influenced by where they are placing themselves relative to the other response choices. For example, the Detroit Area Study (Turner & Martin, 1984, p. 252) asked the following question: "People feel differently about making changes in the way our country is run. In order to keep America great, which of these statements do you think is best?" When the only response choices were "We should be very cautious of making changes" and "We should be free to make changes," only 37% said that we should be free to make changes.

However, when a response choice was added that suggested we should "constantly" make changes, 24%

picked that response and another 32% chose the "free to make changes" response, for a total of 56% who seemed open to making changes in the way our country is run (Turner & Martin, 1984, p. 252). Including the more extreme positive alternative ("constantly" make changes) made the less extreme positive alternative more attractive.

A similar bias occurs when some but not all possible responses are included in the question. "What do you like about your community, such as the parks and schools?" focuses respondents on those two categories, and other answers may be ignored. It is best left to the respondent to answer the question without such response cues.

When the response alternatives fall on a continuum from positive to negative sentiment of some type, it is important that the number of positive and negative categories be balanced so that one end of the continuum does not seem more attractive (Dillman, 2000, pp. 57–58). If you ask respondents, "How satisfied are you with the child care program here?" and include *Completely satisfied* as the most positive possible response, then *Completely dissatisfied* should be included as the most negative possible response.

Use Specific Memory Questions

Often we ask respondents to try to remember an event. We are assuming that the respondent can actually remember when something happened or that it happened at all. Yet, memory of an event will be affected by the length of time since the event occurred and how important the event was to the respondent. Events important to the respondent are likely to be remembered, even if they happened long ago, whereas events unimportant to the respondent, even if they happened recently, are likely to be forgotten. Even when the event is important, the length of time from the event can affect memory. The actual event may become distorted because we may remember only aspects of what actually happened.

Researchers confront problems with recall loss when a respondent does not remember an event or behavior or can remember only aspects of the event. They also face a second issue, called a *telescoping effect*,

which occurs when an event is thought to have happened during a particular time period when it actually happened before that time period. Some things we remember, "just like they happened yesterday" because they are so meaningful or important. Unfortunately, they can be reported that way, too.

Adding questions may improve memory about specific past events. This is the approach taken in cognitive interviewing, in which a series of questions help to improve memories about the event of real interest (Dillman, 2000, pp. 66–67). Imagine the problem you might have identifying the correct response to the question "How often did you receive help from classmates while preparing for exams or completing assignments during the last month? (*Very often, Somewhat often, Occasionally, Rarely,* or *Never*)." Now imagine a series of questions that asks you to identify the exams and assignments you had in the past month and, for each one, inquires whether you received each of several types of help from classmates: study suggestions, study sessions, related examples, general encouragement, and so on. The more specific focus on particular exams and assignments should result in more complete recall.

Questions about thoughts and feelings will be more reliable if they refer to specific times or events (Turner & Martin, 1984, p. 300). Usually, a question like "On how many days did you read the newspaper in the last week?" produces more reliable answers than one like "How often do you read the newspaper? (*Frequently, Sometimes, Never*)." In her survey, Ross (1990) sensibly asked the question "Do you currently smoke 7 or more cigarettes a week?" rather than the vaguer question "Do you smoke?" Of course, being specific does not help if you end up making unreasonable demands of your respondents' memories. One survey asked, "During the past 12 months, about how many times did you see or talk to a medical doctor?" According to their written health records, respondents forgot 60% of their doctor visits (Goleman, 1993, p. C11). Another method for improving memory about life events is to use a life history calendar (Axinn, Pearce, & Ghimire, 1999).

Life history calendars are used to help sequence the timing of personal events by using standardized visual cues, including years (or months) and other cues related to individual responses such as births, job changes, or moves. Using such cues, the respondent is then asked about the events related to the study. In this way, respondents can focus on less important events using the important events as cues (Axinn et al., 1999). Life history calendars have been used in studies of subjects such as the transition from adolescence to adulthood (Caspi et al., 1996), the effect of stressors on psychological distress over a 15-year period (Ensel, Peek, Lin, & Lai, 1996), and the relationship of the use of child care with behavior and hospitalization of young children (Youngblut & Brooten, 1999).

Take Account of Culture

Although the term *culture* is often linked to ethnicity, shared belief systems may develop among members of different social groups (Stewart & Napoles-Springer, 2000); therefore, when we speak of culture, we are including different subgroups of the population such as gender, ethnicity, age cohort, or socioeconomic class. When developing individual questions, we need to be careful about our choice of language. The goal is to have all survey respondents attach the same meaning to a question; therefore, it is necessary to ensure that the question has the same meaning across different population subgroups. Although it is important that the wording be appropriate for different groups, it is also necessary to show that the concept being examined is equivalent across groups—that questions adequately reflect group values, traditions, and beliefs (Marin & Marin, 1991). Ideally, we want measures that capture not only universal definitions of the concept but also group-specific concerns and issues (Stewart & Napoles-Springer, 2000).

Even when there is evidence that a measure is reliable and valid across groups, the concept may still not be equivalent in meaning. For example, the meaning of a concept such as *family* can differ across subgroups. Various groups may have different concepts about the boundaries of who is included in family or the obligations expected of family (Luna et al., 1996). Therefore, the wording and response categories would need to account for these differences.

Guidelines for Closed-Ended Questions and Response Categories

When writing response categories for closed-ended questions, there are several guidelines that might help improve the questions. We have already mentioned that it is important to ensure that the responses are mutually exclusive and that the list is exhaustive. We offer these additional guidelines to consider when designing questions.

Avoid Making Either Disagreement or Agreement Disagreeable

People often tend to agree with a statement just to avoid seeming disagreeable. This tendency is referred to as *acquiescence* or *agreement bias*. You can see the impact of this human tendency in a 1974 Michigan Survey Research Center survey that asked who was to blame for crime and lawlessness in the United States. When one question stated that individuals were more to blame than social conditions, 60% of the respondents agreed. But when the question was rephrased so respondents were asked, in a balanced fashion, whether individuals or social conditions were more to blame, only 46% chose individuals.

You can take several steps to reduce the likelihood of agreement bias. As a general rule, you should present both sides of attitude scales in the question itself (Dillman, 2000, pp. 61–62): "In general, do you believe that *individuals* or *social conditions* are more to blame for poverty in the United States?" The response choices themselves should be phrased to make each one seem as socially approved, as "agreeable," as the others. You should also consider replacing a range of response alternatives that focus on the word *agree* with others. For example, "To what extent do you support or oppose the new health care plan?" (response choices range from *Strongly support* to *Strongly oppose*) is probably a better approach than the question "To what extent do you agree or disagree with the statement: 'The new health care plan is worthy of support?'" (response choices range from *Strongly agree* to *Strongly disagree*).

Avoid Appeals to Social Desirability

A related problem that often occurs in interviews is social desirability or the tendency for individuals to respond in ways that make them appear in the best light to the interviewer. The error, in this case, is that respondents are not providing their true opinions or answers. Social desirability effects are likely to occur when discussing issues that are controversial or when expressing a view that is not popular. Some surveys include scales to determine if a respondent is providing socially desirable responses.

Minimize Fence-Sitting and Floating

Two related problems in question writing also stem from people's desire to choose an acceptable answer. There is no uniformly correct solution to these problems; researchers have to weigh the alternatives in light of the concept to be measured and whatever they know about the respondents.

Fence sitters, people who see themselves as being neutral, may skew the results if you force them to choose between opposites. In most cases, 10% to 20% of such respondents—those who do not have strong feelings on an issue—will choose an explicit middle, neutral alternative (Schuman & Presser, 1981, pp. 161–178). Adding an explicit neutral response option is appropriate when you want to find out who is a fence-sitter. But adding a neutral response may provide an easy escape for respondents who do not want to reveal their true feelings. Some respondents will choose the neutral response to avoid thinking about the question.

Even more people can be termed *floaters*: respondents who choose a substantive answer when they really don't know. A third of the public will provide an opinion on a proposed law that they know nothing about if they are asked for their opinion in a closed-ended survey question that does not include *don't know* as an explicit response choice. However, 90% of these people will select the *Don't know* response if they are explicitly given that option. On average, offering an explicit response option increases the *Don't know* responses by about one-fifth (Schuman & Presser, 1981, pp. 113–160).

Figure 12.2 depicts the results of one study that tested the effect of giving respondents an explicit *No opinion* option to the question "Are government leaders smart?" Notice how many more people chose *No opinion* when they were given that choice than when their only explicit options were *Smart* and *Not smart*.

Because there are so many floaters in the typical survey sample, the decision to include an explicit *Don't know* option for a question is important. This decision is particularly important with surveys of less-educated populations because *Don't know* responses are offered more often by those with less education—except for questions that are really impossible to decipher, to which more educated people are likely to say they don't know (Schuman & Presser, 1981, pp. 113–146). Unfortunately, the inclusion of an explicit *Don't know* response choice leads some people who do have a preference to take the easy way out and choose *Don't know*.

There are several ways to phrase questions and response choices to reduce the risk of completely missing fence-sitters and floaters. One good idea is to include an explicit *No opinion* category after all the substantive responses; if neutral sentiment is a possibility, also include a neutral category in the middle of the substantive responses (such as *Neither agree nor disagree*; Dillman, 2000, pp. 58–60). Adding an open-ended question in which respondents are asked to discuss their opinions (or reasons for having no opinion) can help by shedding some light on why some choose *Don't know* in response to a particular question (Smith, 1984). Researchers who use in-person or telephone interviews (rather than self-administered questionnaires) may get around the dilemma somewhat by reading the response choices without a middle or *Don't know* alternative but recording a noncommittal response if it is offered.

Use Filter Questions

Often, there are questions that will not apply to all survey respondents. To avoid asking irrelevant questions, researchers use a type of closed-ended question called a filter question. Based on the response to a filter question, respondents will be asked either to skip one or

Figure 12.2
The Effect of Floaters on Public
Opinion Polls

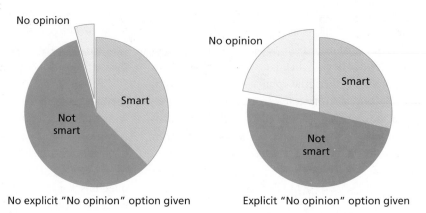

No explicit "No opinion" option given   Explicit "No opinion" option given

more questions or to answer those questions. The questions asked of the more limited group of people are referred to as *contingency questions*. For example, if you were interested in the current employment experiences of women who had participated in a job training program, you would want to ask those questions of women who were currently working and not of women who were no longer working. As you can see in Figure 12.3, the women who answer *Yes*, go on to answer the next question, whereas those women not currently working skip to a subsequent question.

One concern in surveys, particularly lengthy surveys, is that respondents learn during the course of the survey how to answer filter questions so that they can avoid a set of additional questions. While a student, Engel conducted very lengthy interviews during a study of adult children with aging parents. There were many subsections that were asked of people who responded *yes* to particular filter questions. At least some respondents began to answer *no* as a way to avoid increasing the length of the interview. Although this was a problem of the length of the survey, filter questions enabled respondents to skip questions that were nonetheless relevant to them.

Sensitive Questions

There are topics, such as drug use, sexual activity, or the use of mental health services, that respondents may

consider too sensitive or embarrassing to discuss. Some respondents will be reluctant to agree that they have ever done or thought such a thing. In this situation, the goal is to write a question and response choices that will reduce the anxiety or threat of providing an answer. To do so may violate some of the guidelines we have mentioned.

One way is to make agreement seem more acceptable. For example, Dillman (2000, p. 75) suggests that we ask, "Have you ever taken anything from a store without paying for it?" rather than "Have you ever shoplifted something from a store?" Asking about a variety of behaviors or attitudes that range from socially acceptable to socially unacceptable will also soften the impact of agreeing with those that are socially unacceptable. The behavior will also be softened by asking:

How often have you . . .

rather than using a filter and asking,

Have you ever . . .

and having *Never* as one of the response categories.

Single or Multiple Questions

Writing single questions that yield usable answers is always a challenge, whether the response format is fixed-choice or open-ended. Simple though they may seem, single questions are prone to problems due to

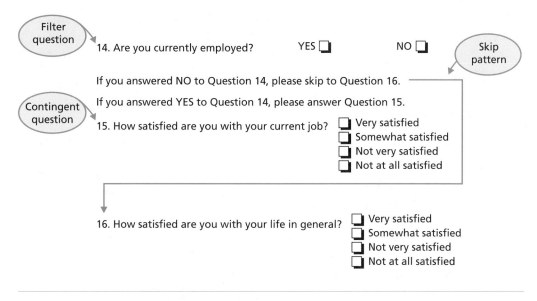

Figure 12.3   Filter Questions and Skip Patterns

idiosyncratic variation, which occurs when individuals' responses vary because of their reactions to particular words or ideas in the question. Differences in respondents' backgrounds, knowledge, and beliefs almost guarantee that they will understand the same question differently. If some respondents do not recognize some of the words in a question, we will not know what their answers mean—if they answer at all. If a question is too complex, respondents may focus on different parts of the question. If prior experiences or culturally based orientations lead different groups to interpret questions differently, answers will not have a consistent meaning.

If just one question is used to measure a variable, the researcher may not realize that respondents had trouble with a particular word or phrase in the question. One solution is to phrase questions more carefully; the guidelines for writing clear questions should help to reduce idiosyncratic variation due to different interpretations of questions. But the best option is to devise multiple rather than single questions to measure concepts, as discussed in Chapter 5. Therefore, you might choose to use a scale or index that includes multiple questions to measure the concept.

Because of the popularity of survey research, scales already have been developed to measure many con-

cepts, and some of these scales have been demonstrated to be reliable in a range of studies. It usually is much better to use such a scale to measure a concept than to try to devise questions to form a new scale. Use of a preexisting scale both simplifies the work involved in designing a study and facilitates comparison of findings to those obtained in other studies. But it is also important to remember that the scale should be appropriate for the population you want to study, and there should be evidence of its reliability and validity for your study population.

You will come across different kinds of scales, but several of the most popular types include the following:

Likert Scale.   Likert-scale responses reflect the extent to which a respondent holds a particular attitude or feeling. Typically, respondents are given a set of alternatives to select the level at which they hold a feeling. For instance, if you were collecting information about client satisfaction with services, you might offer the respondent a list of alternatives reflecting degrees of satisfaction. A statement might look like:

Overall, how satisfied are you with the service you have received?

_____ Very satisfied

_____ Somewhat satisfied

_____ Neither satisfied nor dissatisfied

_____ Somewhat dissatisfied

_____ Very dissatisfied

Similar kinds of responses could be applied to attitudes such as agreement (*Strongly agree* to *Strongly disagree*), opinions (*Strongly support* to *Strongly oppose*), or behaviors (*Very frequently* to *Not at all* or *Almost always* to *Almost never*). Likert scales provide both the sense of what the respondent feels about the question (e.g., satisfied or not satisfied) and how strongly that feeling is held. When the response categories are the same, Likert-scale items can be added to create a summate scale. As with any scale, the reliability and the validity of the measure can be evaluated using the techniques described in Chapter 5.

Semantic Differential.   In a semantic differential scale, the concept of interest is described by a number of opposite pairs of words, with each pair being an adjective that captures some aspect of the concept. If you were interested in measuring mood, one pair, for example, might be *happy-sad*. Respondents then rate themselves on a 5- or 7-point scale for each of the paired opposite words. The scores are then summed to obtain a measure of the attitude. The challenge is to identify a set of adjectives that captures all the dimensions of the concept. Judith Lee and James Twaite (1997) assessed the impact of contact between birth mothers and adoptive mothers on attitudes toward the birth mother and attitudes toward parenting. To measure the adoptive mother's attitude toward the birth mother, they developed a semantic differential scale. They used 30 adjective pairs, such as *grateful-ungrateful, honest-dishonest,* and *successful-unsuccessful,* with respondents using a 7-point rating scale to rate each adjective pair.

Guttman Scale.   Another variation of a scale is a Guttman scale. Guttman scales are meant to be unidimensional so that the scale measures only one concept. They are designed to try to capture different levels of the concept, where the different levels might be differences in the strength of an attitude, different intensity of ser-

vices, or difficulty in answering the question. The assumption is that if you can answer the difficult question, then you are likely to answer the easier question. In a Guttman scale, there is a hierarchy from the easiest to the hardest or the most general to the most specific. Michael Zakour (1994) developed a Guttman scale to describe the use of volunteering as a career development method. The scale appeared to have a hierarchy of five steps, with most respondents endorsing that their experience led them to "develop new interests"; a smaller number agreed with the statement "accept other volunteer jobs," and the fewest endorsed "return to school." Respondents who agreed with the last response typically also agreed with the previous responses.

DESIGNING QUESTIONNAIRES

Survey questions are answered as part of a questionnaire (or interview schedule, as it is often called in interview-based studies), not in isolation from other questions. The context created by the questionnaire has a major impact on how individual questions are interpreted and whether they are even answered. As a result, survey researchers must give very careful attention to the design of the questionnaire, as well as to the individual questions that it includes.

The way a questionnaire should be designed varies with the specific survey method used and with other particulars of a survey project. There can be no precise formula for identifying questionnaire features that reduce error. Nonetheless, some key principles should guide the design of any questionnaire, and some systematic procedures should be considered for refining it. We will use Ross's (1990) questionnaire for studying the psychological effects of changes in household structure to illustrate some of these principles and procedures.

Maintain Consistent Focus

A survey (with the exception of an omnibus survey) should be guided by a clear conception of the research problem under investigation and the population to be sampled. Does the study seek to describe some phenomenon in detail, to explain some behavior, or to explore some type of social relationship? Until the research objective is formulated clearly, survey design cannot begin. Throughout the process of questionnaire design, this objective should be the primary basis for making decisions about what to include and exclude, and what to emphasize or treat in a cursory fashion. Moreover, the questionnaire should be viewed as an integrated whole, in which each section and every question serves a clear purpose related to the study's objective and is a complement to other sections or questions.

Surveys often include too many irrelevant questions and fail to include questions that, the researchers realize later, are crucial. One way to ensure that possibly relevant questions are asked is to use questions suggested by prior research, theory, or experience or by experts (including participants) who are knowledgeable about the setting under investigation. Of course, not even the best researcher can anticipate the relevance of every question. Researchers tend to try to avoid "missing something" by erring on the side of extraneous questions (Labaw, 1980, p. 40).

Build on Existing Instruments

If another researcher already has designed a set of questions to measure a key concept, and evidence from previous surveys indicates that this measure is reliable and valid, then by all means use that instrument. Resources like Delbert Miller's *Handbook of Research Design and Social Measurement* (1991) can give you many ideas about existing instruments; your literature review at the start of a research project should be an even better source. Catherine Ross drew many of her measures from an extensive body of prior research (including her own). She measured feelings of distress with the well-established Center for Epidemiological Studies Depression scale (see Chapter 5), self-esteem with a measure developed by Morris Rosenberg (1965), and "learned helplessness" with Martin Seligman's (1975) scale.

But there is a trade-off here. Questions used previously may not concern quite the right concept or may not be appropriate in some ways to your population. For example, scales developed much earlier may no longer be appropriate for your population—times

change. Ross (1990) used the need to develop new measures for the study of work and family issues as a selling point in her research proposal: "Part of the proposed project will be to refine, modify, and develop measures, in addition to reviewing literature on already developed measures" (p. 8). Together with John Mirowsky (Mirowsky & Ross, 1991), she developed a new measure of the sense of control, the central concept in her 1990 survey.

So even though using a previously designed and well-regarded instrument may reassure other social scientists, it may not be appropriate for your own specific survey. A good rule is to use a previously designed instrument if it measures the concept of concern to you and if you have no clear reason for thinking it is inappropriate for your survey population. You can always solicit the opinions of other researchers before making a final decision.

Refine and Test Questions

Adhering to the preceding question-writing guidelines will go a long way toward producing a useful questionnaire. However, simply asking what appear to you to be clear questions does not ensure that people will have a consistent understanding of what you are asking. You need some external feedback—the more of it the better. This feedback is obtained from some type of pretest (Dillman, 2000, pp. 140–147).

One important form of feedback results from simply discussing the questionnaire content with others. People who should be consulted include expert researchers, key figures in the locale or organization to be surveyed (such as elected representatives, company presidents, and community leaders), and some individuals from the population to be sampled. Run your list of variables and specific questions by such people whenever you have a chance. Reviewing the relevant literature to find results obtained with similar surveys and comparable questions is also an important step to take, if you have not already conducted such a review before writing your questions.

Another increasingly popular form of feedback comes from guided discussions among potential respondents, called *focus groups*, to check for consistent understanding of terms and to identify the range of events or experiences about which people will be asked to report. By listening to and observing the focus group discussions, researchers can validate their assumptions about what level of vocabulary is appropriate and what people are going to be reporting (Fowler, 1995). Focus group techniques are particularly useful for developing questionnaires with different economic and ethnic groups because participants will answer in their own terms and language. Kerth O'Brien (1993) described using focus groups to develop a survey of social relationships and health behavior among gay and bisexual men at risk for AIDS. In part, the groups were conducted to "learn the language the men used to discuss their private emotional and sexual experiences" (p. 106).

Professional survey researchers have also developed a technique for evaluating questions called the *cognitive interview* (Fowler, 1995). Although the specifics vary, the basic approach is to ask people to "think aloud" as they answer questions. The researcher asks a test question, then probes with follow-up questions to learn how the question was understood and whether its meaning varied for different respondents. This method can identify many potential problems, particularly if the individuals interviewed reflect much of the diversity of the population to be surveyed. A different approach to identifying problems is *behavior coding*: A researcher observes several interviews or listens to taped interviews and codes according to strict rules the number of times that difficulties occur with questions. Such difficulties include respondents asking for clarification and interviewers rephrasing questions rather than reading them verbatim (Presser & Blair, 1994, pp. 74–75).

Conducting a pilot study is the final stage of questionnaire preparation. Prepare for the pilot study by completing the questionnaire yourself and then revising it. Next, try it out on some colleagues or other friends, and then revise it. For the actual pilot study, draw a small sample of individuals from the population you are studying or one very similar to it, and carry out the survey procedures with them. This should include as many mailings as you plan for a mailed questionnaire and actual interviews if you are prepar-

ing to conduct in-person interviews. You may include in the pretest version of a written questionnaire some space for individuals to add comments on each key question or, with in-person interviews, audiotape the test interviews for later review (a good idea particularly if you have not conducted cognitive interviews).

Review the distribution of responses to each question, listen to the audiotapes, or read all the comments, and then code what you heard or read to identify problems in question wording or delivery. Revise any questions that respondents do not seem to interpret as you had intended or that are not working well for other reasons. If the response rate is relatively low, consider whether it can be improved by some modifications in procedures.

Ross's (1990) survey of U.S. households included limited pretesting, as Johnny Blair noted in a letter to Ross summarizing the procedure to be used:

> Before being used for data collection, the survey questionnaire will be given a pretest consisting of 30 interviews conducted in Illinois. The pretest will be used to evaluate the adequacy of the questionnaire, to try out systematically all the various procedures in the main survey, to establish and evaluate codes for questionnaire responses, and to gauge the length of the interview. Only upon the basis of the diagnostic information obtained in the pretest interviews will the fully refined version of the survey questionnaire be prepared, ready for administration in the full-scale survey. (Personal communication, April 10, 1989)

Which pretesting method is best? They each have some unique advantages and disadvantages. Behavior coding, with its clearly specified rules, is the most reliable method across interviewers and repetitions, whereas pilot studies are the least reliable. However, behavior coding provides no information about the cause of problems with questions; the other methods are better at this. Review of questions by an expert panel is the least expensive method and identifies the greatest number of problems with questions (Presser & Blair, 1994).

Add Interpretive Questions

A survey researcher can also try to understand what respondents mean by their responses after the fact—that is, by including additional questions in the survey itself. Adding such interpretive questions after key survey questions is always a good idea, but it is of utmost importance when the questions in a survey have not been thoroughly pretested.

An example from a study of people with motor vehicle driving violations illustrates the importance of interpretive questions:

> When asked whether their emotional state affected their driving at all, respondents would reply that their emotions had very little effect on their driving habits. Then, when asked to describe the circumstances surrounding their last traffic violation, respondents typically replied, "I was mad at my girlfriend," or "I had a quarrel with my wife," or "We had a family quarrel," or "I was angry with my boss." (Labaw, 1980, p. 71)

Were these respondents lying in response to the first question? Probably not. More likely, they simply did not interpret their own behavior in terms of general concepts like *emotional state*. But their responses to the first question were likely to be misinterpreted without the further detail provided by answers to the second.

Consider five issues when you develop interpretive questions—or when you review survey results and need to consider what the answers tell you:

- What do the respondents know? Answers to many questions about current events and government policies are almost uninterpretable without also learning what the respondents know. Surveys about social service utilization often find that respondents are aware that a particular social service or a service provider exists, but the respondents do not know that the service applies to their needs or that they are eligible for the service (Krout, 1985).
- What relevant experiences do the respondents have? Such experiences undoubtedly color the responses. For example, the meaning of opinions about crime and punishment may be quite different for those who have been crime victims themselves and those who have not. Ross (1990) had to begin her survey with a question about the respondent's current employment status, which determined whether many of the work-related questions would be relevant. Similarly, her questions about child care were preceded by questions to determine whether the respondent had children.
- How consistent are the respondents' attitudes, and do they express some larger perspective or ideology? An employee who seeks more wages because she believes that all employer's profits result from exploitation is expressing a different sentiment from one who seeks more wages because she really wants a more expensive car with which to impress her neighbors.
- Are respondents' actions consistent with their expressed attitudes? We probably should interpret differently the meaning of expressed support for gender equality from married men who help with household chores and from those who do not. Questions about behavior may also provide a better way to assess orientations than questions about attitudes. Labaw (1980) points out that "the respondent's actual purchase of life insurance is a more accurate representation of what he believes about his life insurance needs than anything he might say in response to a direct question [about whether it is important to carry life insurance]" (p. 100). In her study, Ross eschewed attitudinal questions about household roles altogether, instead focusing on behaviors in such questions as "What percentage [of the housework] do you do?" and "Who makes decisions in your household?"
- How strongly are the attitudes held? The attitudes of those with stronger beliefs are more likely to be translated into action than attitudes that are held less strongly. Just knowing the level of popular support for, say, abortion rights or gun control thus fails to capture the likelihood that people

will march or petition their representatives on be-half of the cause; we also need to know what pro-portion of supporters feel strongly (Schuman & Presser, 1981, chap. 9). Thus, rather than just asking if respondents favored or opposed their spouse having a job, Ross (1990) used the follow-ing question and response choices to measure at-titude strength in her telephone survey:

How do you feel about your (spouse/partner) having a job? (Are you/Would you be)

strongly in favor	1
somewhat in favor	2
somewhat opposed or	3
strongly opposed	4
mixed	5
do not care/up to him/her	6

Order the Questions

The order in which questions are presented will influence how respondents react to the questionnaire as a whole and how they may answer some questions. As a first step, the individual questions should be sorted into broad thematic categories, which then become separate sections in the questionnaire. Ross's (1990) questionnaire contained the following four sections:

1. sociodemographics
2. social-psychological attitudes
3. health and well-being
4. work and employment

Both the sections and the questions within the sec-tions must then be organized in a logical order that would make sense in a conversation. Throughout the design process, the grouping of variables in sections and the ordering of questions within sections should be adjusted to maximize the questionnaire's overall coherence.

The first question deserves special attention, par-ticularly if the questionnaire is to be self-administered. This question signals to the respondent what the sur-vey is about, whether it will be interesting, and how easy it will be to complete it. For these reasons, the first question should be connected to the primary purpose of the survey, it should be interesting, it should be easy, and it should apply to everyone in the sample (Dill-man, 2000, pp. 92–94).

Question order can lead to context effects when one or more questions influence how subsequent ques-tions are interpreted (Schober, 1999, pp. 89–88). For ex-ample, when a sample of the general public was asked, "Do you think it should be possible for a pregnant woman to obtain a legal abortion if she is married and does not want any more children?" 58% of respondents said yes. However, when this question was preceded by a less permissive question that asked whether the re-spondent would allow abortion of a defective fetus, only 40% said yes. Asking the question about a defec-tive fetus altered respondents' frame of reference, per-haps by making abortion simply to avoid having more children seem frivolous by comparison (Turner & Mar-tin, 1984, p. 135). Context effects have also been identi-fied in the measurement of general happiness. Married people tend to report that they are happier "in general" if the general happiness question is preceded by a ques-tion about their happiness with their marriage (Schu-man & Presser, 1981, pp. 23–77).

Prior questions can influence how questions are comprehended, what beliefs shape responses, and whether comparative judgments are made (Tourangeau, 1999). The potential for context effects is greatest when two or more questions concern the same issue or closely related issues, as in the example of the two questions about abortion. The impact of question order also tends to be greater for general, summary-type questions, as with the example about general happiness.

Context effects can be identified empirically if the question order is reversed on a subset of the question-naires (the so-called split-ballot design) and the results compared. However, knowing that a context effect oc-curs does not tell us which order is best. Reviewing the overall survey goals and any other surveys with which comparisons should be made can help to decide on question order. What is most important is to be aware of the potential for problems due to question order and to evaluate carefully the likelihood of context effects in any particular questionnaire. Those who report survey results should mention, at least in a footnote, the order in which key questions were asked when more than one question about a topic was used (Labaw, 1980).

Consider Matrix Questions

Some questions may be presented in a matrix format. Matrix questions are actually a series of questions that concern a common theme and that have the same response choices. The questions are written so that a common initial phrase applies to each one (Question 49 in Figure 12.4). This format shortens the questionnaire by reducing the number of words that must be used for each question. It also emphasizes the common theme among the questions and so invites answering each question in relation to other questions in the matrix. It is very important to provide an explicit instruction to "Circle one response on each line" in a matrix question because some respondents will think that they have completed the entire matrix after they have responded to just a few of the specific questions.

Matrix questions are susceptible to another form of error called a *response set*. When scales are used (or a set of single questions, for that matter) with the same set of response categories, there is the possibility that rather than reading and answering each question, the respondent simply circles the same response down the entire set of questions. If a respondent was to answer each question in Question 49 of Figure 12.4 with 1 (*No difficulty*), the respondent may truly have no difficulty or may have tired and just circled 1 for all the questions without bothering to read them.

To avoid this problem, researchers often phrase some questions in the opposite direction. For example, the developers of the Center for Epidemiological Studies Depression scale (see Chapter 5 to see the questions) wrote 16 questions reflecting negative feelings and 4 questions reflecting positive feelings. The developers assumed that if you answered that you were rarely sad, then you were unlikely to answer that you were rarely happy unless you were just answering the questions in the same way across all the items without reading them, that is, a response set.

Make the Questionnaire Attractive

An attractive questionnaire is more likely to be completed and less likely to confuse either the respondent or, in an interview, the interviewer. An attractive questionnaire also should increase the likelihood that different respondents interpret the same questions in the same way.

Printing a multipage questionnaire in booklet form usually results in the most attractive and simplest-to-use questionnaire. Printing on both sides of folded-over legal size paper (8½ by 14) is a good approach, although pages can be printed on one side only and stapled in the corner if finances are very tight (Dillman, 2000, pp. 80–86). An attractive questionnaire does not look cramped; plenty of white space—more between questions than within question components—makes the questionnaire appear easy to complete. Response choices are distinguished clearly and consistently, perhaps by formatting them with light print (while questions are formatted with dark print) and keeping them in the middle of the pages. Response choices are listed vertically rather than horizontally across the page.

The proper path through the questionnaire for each respondent is identified with arrows or other graphics and judicious use of spacing and other aspects of layout. Respondents should not be confused about "where to go next" after they are told to skip a question. Instructions should help to route respondents through skip patterns, and such skip patterns should be used infrequently. Instructions should also explain how each type of question is to be answered (such as by circling a number or writing a response)—in a neutral way that is not likely to influence responses. Some distinctive type of formatting should be used to identify instructions.

Figure 12.4 contains portions of the questionnaire Ross (1990) used in her phone survey of contemporary families. This page illustrates three of the features that we have just reviewed: numeric designation of response choices, clear instructions, and an attractive open layout. Because this questionnaire was read over the phone rather than self-administered,

45. In the past 12 months about how many times have you gone on a diet to lose weight?

                Never 0

                Once 1

                Twice 2

                Three times or more 3

                Always on a diet 4

46. What is your height without shoes on?   v95

                _____ ft.   _____ in.

47. What is your weight without clothing?   v96

                                        _____ lbs.

48a. Do you currently smoke 7 or more cigarettes a week?   v97

                Yes 1   (SKIP TO Q.49)

                No 2

48b. Have you ever smoked 7 or more cigarettes a week?   v98

                Yes 1

                No 2

49. How much difficulty do you have . . .
    (Circle one response on each line)

		No difficulty,	Some difficulty, or	A great deal of difficulty?	
a.	Going up and down stairs? Would you say	1	2	3	v99
b.	Kneeling or stooping?	1	2	3	v100
c.	Lifting or carrying objects less than 10 pounds, like a bag of groceries?	1	2	3	v101
d.	Using your hands or fingers?	1	2	3	v102
e.	Seeing, even with glasses?	1	2	3	v103
f.	Hearing?	1	2	3	v104
g.	Walking?	1	2	3	v105

Figure 12.4   A Page From Ross's Phone Interview Schedule

there was no need for more explicit instructions about the matrix question (Question 49) or for a more distinctive format for the response choices (Questions 45 and 48).

ORGANIZING SURVEYS

There are five basic social science survey designs: mailed, group-administered, phone, in-person, and electronic. Figure 12.5 summarizes the typical features of the five different survey designs. Each design differs from the others in one or more important features.

Manner of Administration.   The five survey designs differ in the manner in which the questionnaire is administered. Mailed, group, and electronic surveys are completed by the respondents themselves. During phone and in-person interviews, however, the researcher or a staff person asks the questions and records the respondent's answers.

Questionnaire Structure.   Survey designs also differ in the extent to which the content and order of questions are structured in advance by the researcher. Most mailed, group, phone, and electronic surveys are highly structured, fixing in advance the content and order of questions and response choices. Some of these types of surveys, particularly mailed surveys, may include some open-ended questions (respondents write in their answers rather than checking off one of several response choices).

In-person interviews are often highly structured, but they may include many questions without fixed response choices. Moreover, some interviews may proceed from an interview guide rather than a fixed set of questions. In these relatively unstructured interviews, the interviewer covers the same topics with respondents but varies questions according to the respondent's answers to previous questions. Extra questions are added as needed to clarify or explore answers to the most important questions.

Setting.   Most surveys are conducted in settings where only one respondent completes the survey at a time; most mail and electronic questionnaires and phone interviews are intended for completion by only one respondent. The same is usually true of in-person interviews, although sometimes researchers interview several family members at once. On the other hand, a variant of the standard survey is a questionnaire distributed simultaneously to a group of respondents, who complete the survey while the researcher (or assistant) waits. Students in classrooms are typically the group involved, although this type of group distribution also occurs in surveys of employees and members of voluntary groups.

Cost.   As mentioned earlier, in-person interviews are the most expensive type of survey. Phone interviews are much less expensive, but surveying by mail is even cheaper. Electronic surveys are now the least expensive method because there are no interviewer costs, no mailing costs, and, for many designs, almost no costs for data entry. Of course, extra staff time and expertise are required to prepare an electronic questionnaire.

Design	Manner of Administration	Setting	Questionnaire Structure	Cost
1. Mailed survey	Self	Individual	Mostly structured	Low
2. Group survey	Self	Group	Mostly structured	Very low
3. Phone survey	Professional	Individual	Structured	Moderate
4. In-person interview	Professional	Individual	Structured or unstructured	High
5. Electronic survey	Self	Individual	Mostly structured	Very low

Figure 12.5   Typical Features of the Five Survey Designs

Because of their different features, the five designs listed in Figure 12.5 vary in the types of error to which they are most prone and the situations in which they are most appropriate. The rest of this section focuses on their unique advantages and disadvantages and identifies techniques for reducing error with each design.

Mailed Self-Administered Surveys

A mailed survey is conducted by mailing a questionnaire to respondents, who then administer the survey themselves. The central concern in a mailed survey is maximizing the response rate. Even an attractive questionnaire full of clear questions will probably be returned by no more than 30% of a sample unless extra steps are taken to increase the rate of response. It is just too much bother for most potential recipients; in the language of social exchange theory, the costs of responding are perceived to be much higher than any anticipated rewards for doing so. Of course, a response rate of 30% is a disaster; even a response rate of 60% represents so much nonresponse error that it is hard to justify using the resulting data. Fortunately, the conscientious use of a systematic survey design method can be expected to lead to an acceptable 70% or higher rate of response to most mailed surveys (Dillman, 2000).

Sending follow-up mailings to nonrespondents is the single most important requirement for obtaining an adequate response rate to a mailed survey. The follow-up mailings explicitly encourage initial nonrespondents to return a completed questionnaire; implicitly, they convey the importance of the effort. Don Dillman (2000, pp. 155–158, 177–188) has demonstrated the effectiveness of a standard procedure for the mailing process:

1. A few days before the questionnaire is to be mailed, send a brief letter to respondents that notifies them of the importance of the survey they are to receive.
2. Send the questionnaire with a well-designed, personalized cover letter (see the next section), a self-addressed stamped return envelope, and, if possible, a token monetary reward. The materials should be inserted in the mailout envelope so that

they will all be pulled out together when the envelope is opened (Dillman, 2000, pp. 174–175). There should be no chance that the respondent will miss something.
3. Send a reminder postcard, thanking respondents and reminding nonrespondents, to all sample members 2 weeks after the initial mailing. The postcard should be friendly in tone and must include a phone number for those people who may not have received the questionnaire. It is important that this postcard be sent before most nonrespondents have discarded their questionnaires even though this means the postcard will arrive before all those who might have responded to the first mailing have done so.
4. Send a replacement questionnaire with a new cover letter only to nonrespondents 2 to 4 weeks after the initial questionnaire mailing. This cover letter should be a bit shorter and more insistent than the original cover letter. It should note that the recipient has not yet responded and stress the survey's importance. Of course, a self-addressed stamped return envelope must be included.
5. The final step is taken 6 to 8 weeks after the initial survey mailing. This step uses a different mode of delivery—either priority or special delivery—or a different survey design, usually an attempt to administer the questionnaire over the phone. These special procedures emphasize the importance of the survey and encourage people to respond.

The cover letter is critical to the success of a mailed survey. This statement to respondents sets the tone for the entire questionnaire. A carefully prepared cover letter should increase the response rate and result in more honest and complete answers to the survey questions; a poorly prepared cover letter can have the reverse effects.

The cover letter or introductory statement must be:

- Credible. The letter should establish that the research is being conducted by a researcher or organization that the respondent is likely to accept as a credible, unbiased authority. Research conducted by government agencies, university personnel, and recognized research organizations (like Gallup or the RAND Corporation) is usually credible in this sense, with government surveys getting the most attention. On the other hand, a questionnaire from an animal rights group on the topic of animal rights will probably be viewed as biased.

- Personalized. The cover letter should include a personalized salutation (using the respondent's name, not just "Dear Student," for example), close with the researcher's signature (blue ballpoint pen is best because it makes it clear that the researcher has personally signed), and refer to the respondent in the second person ("Your participation . . .").
- Interesting. The statement should interest the respondent in the contents of the questionnaire. Never make the mistake of assuming that what is of interest to you will also interest your respondents. Try to put yourself in their shoes before composing the statement, and then test your appeal with a variety of potential respondents.
- Responsible. Reassure the respondent that the information you obtain will be treated confidentially, and include a phone number to call if the respondent has any questions or would like a summary of the final report. Point out that the respondent's participation is completely voluntary (Dillman, 1978, pp. 165–172)

Figure 12.6 is an example of a cover letter for a questionnaire.

Other steps are necessary to maximize the response rate (Fowler, 1988, pp. 99–106; Mangione, 1995, pp. 79–82; Miller, 1991, p. 144):

- It is particularly important in self-administered surveys that the individual questions are clear and understandable to all the respondents because no interviewers will be on hand to clarify the meaning of the questions or to probe for additional details.
- Use no more than a few open-ended questions because respondents are likely to be put off by the idea of having to write out answers.
- Have a credible research sponsor. According to one investigation, a sponsor known to respondents may increase their rate of response by as much as 17%. Government sponsors also tend to elicit high rates of response. The next most credible sponsors are state headquarters of an organization and then other people in a similar field. Publishing firms, college professors or students, and private associations elicit the lowest response rates.

- Write an identifying numbers on the questionnaires so you can determine who the nonrespondents are. This is essential for follow-up efforts. Of course, the identification must be explained in the cover letter.
- Enclosing a token incentive with the survey can help. Even a coupon or ticket worth $1 can increase the response rate, but a $2 or $5 bill seems to be the best incentive. Such an incentive is both a reward for respondents and an indication of your trust that they will carry out their end of the bargain. Offering a large monetary reward or some type of lottery ticket only for those who return their questionnaire is actually less effective, apparently because it does not indicate trust in the respondent (Dillman, 2000, pp. 167–170).
- Include a stamped, self-addressed return envelope with each copy of the questionnaire. This reduces the cost of responding. The stamp helps to personalize the exchange and is another indication of trust in the respondent (who could use the stamp for something else). Using a stamp rather than metered postage on the mail-out envelope does not seem to influence the response rate, but it is very important to use first-class rather than bulk rate postage (Dillman, 2000, pp. 171–174).
- Consider presurvey publicity efforts. A vigorous advertising campaign increased considerably the response to the 2000 census mailed questionnaire; the results were particularly successful among members of minority groups, who had been targeted due to low response rates in the census (Holmes, 2000).

If Dillman's procedures are followed, and the guidelines for cover letters and questionnaire design also are adopted, the response rate is almost certain to approach 70%. One review of studies using Dillman's method to survey the general population indicates that

---

University of Massachusetts at Boston
Department of Sociology
May 24, 2003

Jane Doe
AIDS Coordinator
Shattuck Shelter

Dear Jane:

AIDS is an increasing concern for homeless people and for homeless shelters. The enclosed survey is about the AIDS problem and related issues confronting shelters. It is sponsored by the Life Lines AIDS Prevention Project for the Homeless—a program of the Massachusetts Department of Public Health.

As an AIDS coordinator/shelter director, you have learned about homeless persons' problems and about implementing programs in response to those problems. The Life Lines Project needs to learn from your experience. Your answers to the questions in the enclosed survey will improve substantially the base of information for improving AIDS prevention programs.

Questions in the survey focus on AIDS prevention activities and on related aspects of shelter operations. It should take about 30 minutes to answer all the questions.

Every shelter AIDS coordinator (or shelter director) in Massachusetts is being asked to complete the survey. And every response is vital to the success of the survey: The survey report must represent the full range of experiences.

You may be assured of complete confidentiality. No one outside of the university will have access to the questionnaire you return. (The ID number on the survey will permit us to check with nonrespondents to see if they need a replacement survey or other information.) All information presented in the report to Life Lines will be in aggregate form, with the exception of a list of the number, gender, and family status of each shelter's guests.

Please mail the survey back to us by Monday, June 4, and feel free to call if you have any questions.

Thank you for your assistance.

Yours sincerely.

Russell K. Schutt

Russell K. Schutt, PhD
Project Director

Stephanie Howard

Stephanie Howard
Project Assistant

Figure 12.6   Sample Questionnaire Cover Letter

---

the average response to a first mailing will be about 24%; the response rate will rise to 42% after the post-card follow-up, to 50% after the first replacement questionnaire, and to 72% after a second replacement questionnaire is sent by certified mail (Dillman, Christenson, Carpenter, & Brooks, 1974).

The response rate may be higher with particular populations surveyed on topics of interest to them, and it may be lower with surveys of populations that do not have much interest in the topic. When a survey has many nonrespondents, getting some ideas about their characteristics by comparing late respondents to early respondents can help to determine the likelihood of bias due to the low rate of response. If those who returned their questionnaires at an early stage are more educated or more interested in the topic of the questionnaire, the sample may be biased; if the respondents are not more educated or more interested than nonrespondents, the sample will be more credible.

If resources did not permit phone calls to all nonrespondents, a random sample of nonrespondents can be selected and contacted by phone or interviewed in person. It should be possible to secure responses from a substantial majority of these nonrespondents in this way. With appropriate weighting, these new respondents can then be added to the sample of respondents to the initial mailed questionnaire, resulting in a more representative total sample (for more details, see Levy and Lemeshow, 1999, pp. 398–402).

Related to the threat of nonresponse in mailed surveys is the hazard of incomplete response. Some respondents may skip some questions or just stop answering questions at some point in the questionnaire. Fortunately, this problem does not occur often with well-designed questionnaires. Potential respondents who have decided to participate in the survey usually complete it. But there are many exceptions to this observation because questions that are poorly written, are too complex, or deal with sensitive personal issues simply turn off some respondents. The revision or elimination of such questions during the design phase should minimize the problem. When it does not, it may make sense to impute values for the missing data. One imputation procedure would be to substitute the mean (arithmetic average) value of a variable for those cases that have a missing value on the variable (Levy & Lemeshow, 1999, pp. 404–416).

Finally, with a mailed questionnaire, there is no control over the manner in which the respondent answers the questions. Despite efforts to create a meaningful order to the questions, the respondent can choose in what order the questions will be answered. Furthermore, the respondent can choose to answer all the questions at once or answer them over several days. The respondent may even discuss the questions with significant others, family, friends, and coworkers.

Group-Administered Surveys

A group-administered survey is completed by individual respondents assembled in a group. The response rate is not usually a major concern in surveys that are distributed and collected in a group setting because most group members will participate. The real difficulty with this method is that it is seldom feasible, for it requires what might be called a captive audience. With the exception of students, employees, members of the armed forces, and some institutionalized populations, most populations cannot be sampled in such a setting.

Whoever is responsible for administering the survey to the group must be careful to minimize comments that might bias answers or that could vary between different groups in the same survey (Dillman, 2000, pp. 253–256). A standard introductory statement should be read to the group that expresses appreciation for their participation, describes the steps of the survey, and emphasizes (in classroom surveys) that the survey is not the same as a test. A cover letter like the one used in mailed surveys also should be distributed with the questionnaires. To emphasize confidentiality, respondents should be given an envelope in which to seal their questionnaire after it is completed.

Another issue of special concern with group-administered surveys is the possibility that respondents will feel coerced to participate and as a result will be less likely to answer questions honestly. Also, because administering a survey in this way requires approval of the powers that be—and this sponsorship is made quite obvious by the fact that the survey is conducted on the organization's premises—respondents may infer that the researcher is not at all independent of the sponsor. No complete solution to this problem exists, but it helps to make an introductory statement emphasizing the researcher's independence and giving participants a chance to ask questions about the survey. The sponsor should also understand the need to keep a low profile and to allow the researcher both control over the data and autonomy in report writing.

Telephone Surveys

In a phone survey, interviewers question respondents over the phone and then record respondents' answers. Phone interviewing has become a very popular method of conducting surveys in the United States because almost all families have phones. But two matters may undermine the validity of a phone survey: not reaching the proper sampling units, and not getting enough complete responses to make the results generalizable.

Reaching Sample Units

There are three different ways of obtaining a sampling frame of telephone exchanges or numbers: (1) Phone directories can provide a useful frame for local studies; (2) a nationwide list of area code numbers can be obtained from a commercial firm (random digit dialing is used to fill in the last four digits); and (3) commercial firms can prepare files based on local directories from around the nation.

There are coverage errors with each of these frames: 10% to 15% of directory listings will turn out to be no longer valid residential numbers; more than 35% of U.S. households with phones have numbers that are unlisted in directories—and the percentage is as high as 60% in some communities; fewer than 25% of the area codes and exchanges in the one national comprehensive list (available from Bell Core Research, Inc.) refer to residential units (Levy & Lemeshow, 1999, pp. 455–460). Survey planning must consider the advantages and disadvantages of these methods for a particular study and develop means for compensating for the weaknesses of the specific method chosen.

Most telephone surveys use random digit dialing at some point in the sampling process (Lavrakas, 1987). A machine calls random phone numbers within the designated exchanges, whether or not the numbers are published. When the machine reaches an inappropriate household (such as a business in a survey that is directed to the general population), the phone number is simply replaced with another. The University of Illinois Survey Research Laboratory used the following procedures to draw a sample for Ross's (1990) study of social structure and well-being:

> The universe for this study will be all persons 18–65 years of age, in the coterminous United States. A national probability sample designed to yield 2,000 interviews will be generated by the random-digit-dialing technique developed

by J. Waksberg. The Waksberg method involves a two-stage sample design in which primary sampling units (PSUs) are selected with probabilities proportionate to size at the first stage and a specified cluster size at the second stage. To achieve 2,000 interviews, approximately 8,400 telephone numbers will be sampled. In order to avoid any potential bias in the sex or age distributions of the sample that might result from simply interviewing the persons who answer the telephone, a further sampling stage is required. For each selected household, one person will be chosen from all adults 18–65 years of age in that household in such a way that each adult has an equal probability of being selected for an interview. (J. E. Blair, personal communication to C. E. Ross, April 10, 1989)

However households are contacted, the interviewers must ask a series of questions at the start of the survey to ensure that they are speaking to the appropriate member of the household. Figure 12.7 displays a phone interview schedule, the instrument containing the questions asked by the interviewer. This example shows how appropriate and inappropriate households can be distinguished in a phone survey, so that the interviewer is guided to the correct respondent.

Maximizing Response to Phone Surveys

Four issues require special attention in phone surveys. First, because people often are not home, multiple callbacks will be needed for many sample members. The failure to call people back was one of the reasons for the discrepancy between poll predictions and actual votes in the 1988 presidential race between George Bush and Michael Dukakis. Andrew Kohut (1988) found that if pollsters in one Gallup poll had stopped attempting to contact unavailable respondents after one call, a 6-percentage-point margin for Bush would have been replaced by a 2-point margin for Dukakis. Those with more money and education are more likely to be away from home, and such people are also more likely to vote Republican.

PATH COMMUNITY SURVEY
CALL RECORD (CR)

Metro Social Services
Nashville-Davidson County, TN
October 1987

Respondent Household (RH)

_____

Case No. [SEE TOP OF
_____ INTERVIEW FORM]

Date Precontact Letter
Mailed

_____

[TRY REACHING RH ON FIVE
DIFFERENT DAYS BEFORE
CLOSING OUT CR]

Call Outcome Codes

CI = Completed interview
PC = Partially completed
RI = Refused interview
II = Impossible: language
      etc.
BN = Business number
OC = Number outside county
NA = No answer
BS = Busy signal
LD = Line disconnected
WN= Wrong number
UL = Unlisted number
ML = Message left on machine
NC = Number changed
CB = Call back [WRITE DATE]
      Date:
      Time:
      R's First Name:

Call Record:	Day/Date	Call No.	Time	Call Outcome

_____ Case No.

Introduction

A. Hello, is this the (*R's* last name) residence?

 *[IF NOT, SAY: The number I was calling is (*R's phone no.*) and
 it was for the (*R's first and last name*) residence. IF WRONG
 NUMBER, CODE OUTCOME IN CR AND TERMINATE WITH: I'm sorry to
 have bothered you. Goodbye.]

Figure 12.7   Phone Interview Procedures for Respondent Designation

B. My name is _____ . I'm calling for Metro Social Services and the Tennessee Department of Human Services. We're conducting a study to find out how local residents feel about the issue of homelessness in our community. Your household has been randomly selected to help us with this important task.

C. I don't know if you've seen it yet, but a letter about the study was mailed to your home several days ago. Just to verify our records, your home is located is Davidson County, isn't it?

   *[IF NOT, ASK: What county are you in? WRITE COUNTY ON RH LABEL, CODE OUTCOME IN CR, AND TERMINATE WITH: I'm sorry but only Davidson County residents are eligible for the study. Thanks anyway. Goodbye.]

D. We need to interview men in some households and women in others so that our results will represent all adults in the county. According to our selection method, I need to interview the . . .

   DESIGNATED R: youngest / oldest / man / woman

   presently living in your houehold who is at least 18 years of age. May I please speak with him/her?

   *[IF PERSON ON PHONE, GO TO E.]

   *[IF NO SUCH PERSON, ASK: As a substitute, then, may I please speak with the . . . SUBSTITUTE R: youngest / oldest / man / woman in your household who is at least 18? IF PERSON ON PHONE, GO TO E. IF NOT AVAILABLE, MAKE ARRANGEMENTS TO CALL BACK AND WRITE DATE, TIME, AND R'S FIRST NAME IN CR. CLOSE WITH: Please tell (R's first name) that I will be calling back on (date and time). Thank you.]

   *[IF DIFFERENT PERSON COMES TO THE PHONE, REPEAT B AND ADD: You are the adult who's been randomly chosen in your household. GO TO E:]

   *[IF NOT AVAILABLE, MAKE ARRANGEMENTS . . . (see above).]

E. The questions I'd like to ask you are easy to answer and should take only about 15 minutes. Everything you tell me will be kept strictly confidential. If you have any questions about the study, I'll be happy to answer them now or later. Okay?

   Time interview started:

   Person actually interviewed:

   1 Designated R
   2 Substitute R

Figure 12.7 (*continued*)

I'll be using the word "homeless" to mean not having a permanent address or place to live. Please think about all types of people who fit that description as we go through the interview.

Here's the first question.

1. Right now, how important is homelessness as a public issue in Nashville? Would you say it's . . . [READ 0–2]

0	Not too important	8	DK
1	Somewhat important, or	9	NR
2	Very important?		

Figure 12.7   (*continued*)

The number of callbacks needed to reach respondents by telephone has increased greatly in the last 20 years, with increasing numbers of single-person households, dual-earner families, and out-of-home activities. Survey research organizations have increased the usual number of phone contact attempts from just 4–8 to 20. The growth of telemarketing has created another problem for telephone survey researchers: Individuals have become more accustomed to "just say no" to calls from unknown individuals and organizations or to simply use their answering machines to screen out unwanted calls (Dillman, 2000, pp. 8, 28).

Phone surveys also must cope with difficulties due to the impersonal nature of phone contact. Visual aids cannot be used, so the interviewer must be able to convey verbally all information about response choices and skip patterns. With phone surveys, then, instructions to the interviewer must clarify how to ask each question, and response choices must be short. The Survey Research Laboratory developed the instructions shown in Figure 12.8 to clarify procedures for asking and coding a series of questions that Ross (1990) used to measure symptoms of stress within households.

In addition, interviewers must be prepared for distractions as the respondent is interrupted by other household members. Sprinkling interesting questions throughout the questionnaire may help to maintain respondent interest. In general, rapport between the interviewer and the respondent is likely to be lower with phone surveys than with in-person interviews, and so respondents may tire and refuse to answer all the questions (Miller, 1991, p. 166).

Careful interviewer training is essential for phone surveys. This is how one polling organization describes its training:

In preparation for data collection, survey interviewers are required to attend a two-part training session. The first part covers general interviewing procedures and techniques as related to the proposed survey. The second entails in-depth training and practice for the survey. This training includes instructions on relevant subject matter, a question-by-question review of the survey instrument, and various forms of role-playing and practice interviewing with supervisors and other interviewers. (J.E. Blair, personal communication to C. E. Ross, April 10, 1989)

Procedures can be standardized more effectively, quality control maintained, and processing speed maximized when phone interviewers are assisted by computers using computer-assisted telephone interviewing (CATIs):

The interviewing will be conducted using "CATI" (Computer-Assisted Telephone Interviewing). . . . The questionnaire is "programmed" into the computer, along with relevant skip patterns throughout

---

Question:

41. On how many of the past 7 days have you . . .

Number of days

    a. Worried a lot about little things?. . . . .   _____

    b. Felt tense or anxious? . . . .   _____

Instructions for interviewers:

Q41 For the series of "On how many of the past 7 days," make sure <u>the respondent</u> gives the numberical answer. If he/she responds with a vague answer like "not too often" or "just a few times, " ask <u>again</u> "On how many of the past 7 days would you say?" Do <u>NOT</u> lead the respondent with a number (e.g., "would that be 2 or 3?"), If R says "all of them," verify that the answer is "7."

Question:

45. In the past 12 months about how many times have you gone on a diet to lose weight?

Never   0

Once   1

Twice   2

Three times or more   3

Always on a diet   4

Instructions for interviewers:

Q45 Notice that this question ends with a question mark. That means that you are <u>not</u> to read the answer categories. Rather, wait for R to respond and circle the appropriate number.

Figure 12.8   Sample Interviewer Instructions

the instrument. Only legal entries are allowed. The system incorporates the tasks of interviewing, data entry, and some data cleaning. (J. E. Blair, personal communication to C. E. Ross, April 10, 1989)

Phone surveying is the method of choice for relatively short surveys of the general population. Response rates in phone surveys traditionally have tended to be very high—often above 80%—because few individuals would hang up on a polite caller or refuse to stop answering questions (at least within the first 30 minutes or so). Ross (1990) achieved a response rate of 82% over a 3-month period at the end of 1990, resulting in a final sample of 2,031 Americans. However, as we have noted, the refusal rate in phone interviews is rising

with the prevalence of telemarketing and answering machines.

In-Person Interviews

What is unique to the in-person interview, compared with the other survey designs, is the face-to-face social interaction between interviewer and respondent. If money is no object, in-person interviewing is often the best survey design.

In-person interviewing has several advantages: Response rates are higher than with any other survey design; questionnaires can be much longer than with mailed or phone surveys; the questionnaire can be complex, with both open-ended and closed-ended questions and frequent branching patterns; the order in which questions are read and answered can be controlled by the interviewer; the physical and social circumstances of the interview can be monitored; and respondents' interpretations of questions can be probed and clarified.

But researchers must be alert to some special hazards due to the presence of an interviewer. Respondents should experience the interview process as a personalized interaction with an interviewer who is very interested in the respondent's experiences and opinions. At the same time, however, every respondent should have the same interview experience—asked the same questions in the same way by the same type of person, who reacts similarly to the answers. Therein lies the researcher's challenge—to plan an interview process that will be personal and engaging and yet consistent and nonreactive (and to hire interviewers who can carry out this plan). Careful training and supervision are essential (Groves, 1989, pp. 404–406). Without a personalized approach, the rate of response will be lower and answers will be less thoughtful—and potentially less valid. Without a consistent approach, information obtained from different respondents will not be comparable—and, thus, less reliable and less valid.

Balancing Rapport and Control

Adherence to some basic guidelines for interacting with respondents can help interviewers to maintain an appropriate balance between personalization and standardization:

- Project a professional image in the interview, that of someone who is sympathetic to the respondent but nonetheless has a job to do.
- Establish rapport at the outset by explaining what the interview is about and how it will work and by reading the consent form. Ask the respondent if he or she has any questions or concerns, and respond to these honestly and fully. Emphasize that everything the respondent says is confidential.
- During the interview, ask questions from a distance that is close but not intimate. Stay focused on the respondent and make sure that your posture

conveys interest. Maintain eye contact, respond with appropriate facial expressions, and speak in a conversational tone of voice.
- Be sure to maintain a consistent approach; deliver each question as written and in the same tone of voice. Listen empathetically, but avoid self-expression or loaded reactions.
- Repeat questions if the respondent is confused. Use nondirective probes—such as "Can you tell me more about that?"—for open-ended questions.

As with phone interviewing, computers can be used to increase control of the in-person interview. In a computer-assisted personal interviewing (CAPI) project, interviewers carry a laptop computer that is programmed to display the interview questions and to process the responses that the interviewer types in, as well as to check that these responses fall within allowed ranges. Interviewers seem to like CAPI, and the quality of data obtained this way is at least as good as data from a noncomputerized interview (Shepherd, Hill, Bristor, & Montalvan, 1996). A CAPI approach also makes it easier for the researcher to develop skip patterns and experiment with different types of questions for different respondents without increasing the risk of interviewer mistakes (Couper et al., 1998).

The presence of an interviewer may make it more difficult for respondents to give honest answers to questions about sensitive personal matters. For this reason, interviewers may hand respondents a separate self-administered questionnaire containing the more sensitive questions. After answering these questions, the respondent then seals the separate questionnaire in an envelope so that the interviewer does not know the answers. When this approach was used for the GSS questions about sexual activity, about 21% of men and 13% of women who were married or had been married admitted to having cheated on a spouse ("Survey on Adultery," 1993, p. A20). You may have heard reports of much higher rates of marital infidelity, but these were from studies using unrepresentative samples.

The degree of rapport becomes a special challenge when survey questions concern issues related to such demographic characteristics as race or gender (Groves,

1989). If the interviewer and respondent are similar on the characteristics at issue, the responses to these questions may differ from those that would be given if the interviewer and respondent differ on these characteristics. For example, a white respondent may not disclose feelings of racial prejudice to an African American interviewer that he or she would admit to a white interviewer.

Although in-person interview procedures are typically designed with the expectation that the interview will involve only the interviewer and the respondent, one or more other household members are often within earshot. In a mental health survey in Los Angeles, for example, almost half the interviews were conducted in the presence of another person (Pollner & Adams, 1994). It is reasonable to worry that this third-party presence will influence responses about sensitive subjects—even more so because the likelihood of a third party being present may correspond to other subject characteristics. For example, in the Los Angeles survey, another person was present in 36% of the interviews with Anglos, in 47% of the interviews with African Americans, and in 59% of the interviews with Hispanics. However, there is no consistent evidence that respondents change their answers because of the presence of another person. Analysis of this problem with the Los Angeles study found very little difference in reports of mental illness symptoms between respondents who were alone and those who were in the presence of others.

Maximizing Response to Interviews

Even if the right balance has been struck between maintaining control over interviews and achieving good rapport with respondents, in-person interviews can still have a problem. Because of the difficulty of catching all the members of a sample, response rates may suffer. Figure 12.9 displays the breakdown of nonrespondents to the 1990 GSS. Of the total original sample of 2,165, only 86% (1,857) were determined to be valid selections of dwelling units with potentially eligible respondents. Among these potentially eligible respondents, the response rate was 74%. The GSS is a well-designed survey using carefully trained and supervised interviewers, so this response rate indicates the difficulty of securing respondents from a sample of the general population even when everything is done "by the book."

Several factors affect the response rate in interview studies. Contact rates tend to be lower in central cities, in part because of difficulties in finding people at home and gaining access to high-rise apartments and in part because of interviewer reluctance to visit some areas at night, when people are more likely to be

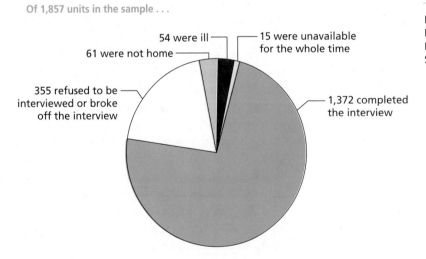

Figure 12.9
Reasons for Nonresponse in Personal Interviews (1990 General Social Survey)

home (Fowler, 1988, pp. 45–60). On the other hand, households with young children or elderly adults tend to be easier to contact, whereas single-person households are more difficult to reach (Groves & Couper, 1998, pp. 119–154).

Refusal rates vary with some respondent characteristics. People with less education participate somewhat less in surveys of political issues. Less education is also associated with higher rates of *don't know* responses (Groves, 1989). High-income people tend to participate less in surveys about income and economic behavior (perhaps because they are suspicious about why others want to know about their situation). Unusual strains and disillusionment in a society can also undermine the general credibility of research efforts and the ability of interviewers to achieve an acceptable response rate. These problems can be lessened with an advance letter introducing the survey project and by multiple contact attempts throughout the day and evening, but they cannot be avoided entirely (Fowler, 1988, pp. 52–53; Groves & Couper, 1998).

Electronic Surveys

The widespread use of personal computers and the growth of the Internet have created new possibilities for survey research. In 1999, 43% of American households had Internet connections, and another 22% had personal computers without Internet connections (Nie & Erbring, 2000). These percentages are growing rapidly; it is not unreasonable to think that use of the Internet will soon become comparable to the use of telephones. Already, some credible surveys have been conducted with the Internet (National Geographic Society, 2000; Nie & Erbring, 2000). As the proportion of the population that is connected increases, the Internet will become the preferred medium for survey research on many topics.

Electronic surveys can be prepared in two ways (Dillman, 2000, pp. 352–354): e-mail and Web.

E-mail surveys can be sent as messages to respondent e-mail addresses. Respondents then mark their answers in the message and send them back to the researcher. This approach is easy for researchers to develop and for respondents to use. However, this approach is cumbersome for surveys that are more than four or five pages in length.

By contrast, Web surveys are designed on a server controlled by the researcher; respondents are then asked to visit the Web site and respond to the Web questionnaire by checking answers. This approach requires more programming by the researcher and in many cases requires more skill on the part of the respondent. However, Web surveys can be quite long, with questions that are inapplicable to a given respondent hidden from them so that the survey may actually seem much shorter than it is.

Web surveys are becoming the more popular form of Internet survey because they are so flexible. The design of the questionnaire can use many types of graphic and typographic features. Respondents can view definitions of words or instructions for answering questions by clicking on linked terms. Lengthy sets of response choices can be presented with pull-down menus. Pictures and audio segments can be added when they are useful. Because answers are recorded directly in the researcher's database, data entry errors are almost eliminated, and results can be reported quickly.

The most important drawback to either Internet survey approach is the large fraction of households that are not yet connected to the Internet. For special populations with high rates of Internet use, however, the technology makes possible fast and effective surveys. Another problem researchers must try their best to avoid is creating survey formats that are so complicated that some computers cannot read them or would display them in a way that differs from what the researcher intended. Access to a Web survey must be limited to sample members, perhaps by requiring use of a personal identification number (PIN) (Dillman, 2000, pp. 353–401).

Computerized interactive voice response (IVR) systems already allow the ease of Internet surveys to be achieved with a telephone-based system. In IVR surveys, respondents receive automated calls and answer questions by pressing numbers on their touchtone phones or speaking numbers that are interpreted by computerized voice recognition software. These surveys can also record verbal responses to open-ended questions for later transcription. Although they present some difficulties when many answer choices must be used or skip patterns must be followed, IVR surveys have been used successfully with short questionnaires and when respondents are highly motivated to participate (Dillman, 2000, pp. 402–411). When these conditions are not met, potential respondents may be put off by the impersonal nature of this computer-driven approach.

Mixed-Mode Surveys

Survey researchers increasingly are combining different survey designs. Mixed-mode surveys allow the strengths of one survey design to compensate for the weaknesses of another and can maximize the likelihood of securing data from different types of respondents. For example, a survey may be sent electronically to sample members who have e-mail addresses and mailed to those who do not. Alternatively, nonrespondents in a mailed survey may be interviewed in person or over the phone. As noted previously, an interviewer may use a self-administered questionnaire to present sensitive questions to a respondent.

Mixing survey designs in this way makes it possible that respondents will give different answers to different questions because of the mode in which they are asked, rather than because they actually have different opinions. However, use of what Dillman (2000, pp. 232–240) calls *unimode design* reduces this possibility substantially. A unimode design uses questions and response choices that are least likely to yield different answers according to the survey mode that is used. Unimode design principles include use of the same question structures, response choices, and skip instructions across modes, as well as using a small number of response choices for each question.

A Comparison of Survey Designs

Which survey design should be used when? Group-administered surveys are similar in most respects to mailed surveys, except that they require the unusual circumstance of having access to the sample in a group setting. We therefore do not need to consider this survey design by itself; what applies to mailed surveys ap-

plies to group-administered survey designs, with the exception of sampling issues. The features of mixed-mode surveys depend on the survey types that are being combined. Thus, we can focus our comparison on the four survey designs that involve the use of a questionnaire with individuals sampled from a larger population: mailed surveys, phone surveys, in-person surveys, and electronic surveys. Figure 12.10 summarizes the advantages and disadvantages of each survey design.

The most important consideration in comparing the advantages and disadvantages of the four methods is the likely response rate they will generate. Because of the great weakness of mailed surveys in this respect, they must be considered the least preferred survey design from a sampling standpoint. However, researchers may still prefer a mailed survey when they have to reach a widely dispersed population and do not have enough financial resources to hire and train an interview staff or to contract with a survey organization that already has an interview staff available in many locations.

Contracting with an established survey research organization for a phone survey is often the best alternative to a mailed survey. The persistent follow-up attempts that are necessary to secure an adequate response rate are much easier over the phone than in person. But the process is not simple:

> Working phone numbers in the sample are called up to 10 times at different times of the day and on different days of the week before the number is recorded as a noncontact. To facilitate contact with households and individuals, telephoning is done in the evening during the week, and during the day over weekends. A final disposition is obtained and recorded for each sample telephone number, i.e., whether an interview, refusal, noncontact, nonworking number, or other disposition. "Control" reports are issued weekly showing progress of the work through various stages of data collection. (J. E. Blair, personal communication to C. E. Ross, April 10, 1989)

In-person surveys are clearly preferable in terms of the possible length and complexity of the questionnaire itself, as well as the researcher's ability to monitor conditions while the questionnaire is being completed.

Characteristics of Design	Mail Survey	Phone Survey	In-Person Survey	Electronic Survey
Representative sample				
Opportunity for inclusion is known				
For completely listed populations	High	High	High	Medium
For incompletely listed populations	Medium	Medium	High	Low
Selection within sampling units is controlled	Medium	High	High	Low
(e.g., Specific family members must respond)				
Respondents are likely to be located				
If samples are heterogeneous	Medium	High	High	Low
If samples are homogeneous and specialized	High	High	High	High
Questionnaire construction and question design				
Allowable length of questionnaire	Medium	Medium	High	Medium
Ability to include				
Complex questions	Medium	Low	High	High
Open questions	Low	High	High	Medium
Screening questions	Low	High	High	High
Tedious, boring questions	Low	High	High	Low
Ability to control question sequence	Low	High	High	High
Ability to ensure questionnaire completion	Medium	High	High	Low
Distortion of answers				
Odds of avoiding social desirability bias	High	Medium	Low	High
Odds of avoiding interviewer distortion	High	Medium	Low	High
Odds of avoiding contamination by others	Medium	High	Medium	Medium
Administrative goals				
Odds of meeting personnel requirements	High	High	Low	Medium
Odds of implementing quickly	Low	High	Low	High
Odds of keeping costs low	High	Medium	Low	High

Figure 12.10 Advantages and Disadvantages of the Four Survey Designs

Mailed surveys often are preferable for asking sensitive questions, although this problem can be lessened in an interview by giving respondents a separate sheet to fill out on their own. Although interviewers may themselves distort results, either by changing the wording of questions or by failing to record answers properly, this problem can be lessened by careful training interviewers, monitoring conditions, and tape-recording the answers.

A phone survey limits the length and complexity of the questionnaire but offers the possibility of very carefully monitoring interviewers (Dillman, 1978; Fowler, 1988, pp. 61–73):

Supervisors in [one organization's] Telephone Centers work closely with the interviewers, moni-

tor their work, and maintain records of their performance in relation to the time schedule, the quality of their work, and help detect and correct any mistakes in completed interviews prior to data reduction and processing. (J. E. Blair, personal communication to C. E. Ross, April 10, 1989)

The advantages and disadvantages of electronic surveys must be weighed in light of the capabilities at the time that the survey is to be conducted. At this time, too many people lack Internet connections for general use of Internet surveying, and too many people who have computers lack adequate computer capacity for displaying complex Web pages.

These various points about the different survey designs lead to two general conclusions. First, in-person interviews are the strongest design and generally preferable when sufficient resources and a trained interview staff are available; telephone surveys have many of the advantages of in-person interviews at much less cost, but response rates are an increasing problem. Second, a decision about the best survey design for any particular study must take into account the unique features and goals of the study.

SECONDARY DATA SURVEYS

Secondary data (most often the term is used in reference to quantitative data) are data that the researcher did not collect to answer the research question of interest. Instead, secondary data are obtained from publicly available data archives, from another researcher, or even from one's own previous projects, which were designed to address some other research question.

As we will see in Chapter 13, the analysis of secondary data presents several challenges, ranging from uncertainty about the methods of data collection to the lack of maximum fit between the concepts that the primary study measured and each of the concepts that are the focus of the current investigation. Responsible use of secondary data requires a good understanding of the primary data source. The researcher should be able to answer the following questions (most adapted from Riedel, 2000, pp. 55–69; Stewart, 1984, pp. 23–30):

1. What were the agency's goals in collecting the data? If the primary data were obtained in a research project, what were the project's purposes?
2. Who was responsible for data collection, and what were their qualifications? Are they available to answer questions about the data? Each step in the data collection process should be charted and the personnel involved identified.
3. What data were collected, and what were they intended to measure?
4. When were the data collected?
5. What methods were used for data collection? Copies of the forms used for data collection

should be obtained, and the way in which these data are processed by the agency/agencies should be reviewed.
6. How were the data organized (by date, event, etc.)? Are identifiers used to distinguish the different types of data available on the same case? In what form are the data available (computer tapes, disks, paper files)? Answers to these questions can have a major bearing on the work that will be needed to carry out the study.
7. How consistent are the data with data available from other sources?
8. What is known about the success of the data collection effort? How are missing data treated and indicated? What kind of documentation is available?

Answering these questions helps to ensure that the researchers are familiar with the data they will analyze and can help to identify any problems with it.

Data quality is always a concern with secondary data, even when the data are collected by an official government agency. Census counts can be distorted by incorrect answers to census questions, as well as by inadequate coverage of the entire population. For example, the percentage of the U.S. population not counted in the U.S. Census appears to have declined since 1880 from 7% to 1%, but undercounting continues to be more common among poorer urban dwellers and recent immigrants (King & Magnuson, 1995). The relatively successful 2000 U.S. census reduced undercounting (Forero, 2000b) but still suffered from accusations of shoddy data collection procedures in some areas (Forero, 2000a).

Researchers who rely on secondary data analysis inevitably make trade-offs between their ability to use a particular data set and the specific hypotheses they can test. If a concept that is critical to a hypothesis was not measured adequately in a secondary data source, the study may have to be abandoned until a more adequate source of data can be found. Alternatively, hypotheses or even the research question itself may be modified to match the analytic possibilities presented by the available data (Riedel, 2000, p. 53).

Many sources of data and surveys relevant to social work are available on the Internet. The U.S. Bureau of the Census Web site (http://www.census.gov) provides access to a wide variety of surveys in addition to the decennial census. Some of these data sets include *Current Population Survey* (monthly survey of 72,000 households looking at employment and economic status); *National Health Interview Survey* (which looks at acute and chronic illness and health-related services); *National Long Term-Care Survey* (data on elderly individuals, including demographic characteristics and their ability to perform activities of daily living); and the *Survey of Income and Program Participation* (a series of panel studies of households providing data about source and amount of income, labor force participation, program participation, and program eligibility data; U. S. Bureau of the Census, 2003). The ICPSR at the University of Michigan (http://www.icpsr.umich.edu) provides access to a large number of survey data sets that are of interest to social work researchers and students. In addition to the many surveys on economics, business, politics, and social relations, there are special archives related to health, mental health, aging, criminal justice, substance abuse, and child care.

ETHICAL ISSUES IN SURVEY RESEARCH

Survey research usually poses fewer ethical dilemmas than do experimental or field research designs. Potential respondents to a survey can easily decline to participate, and a cover letter or introductory statement that identifies the sponsors of and motivations for the survey gives them the information required to make this decision. The methods of data collection are quite obvious in a survey, so little is concealed from the respondents. Only in group-administered survey designs might the respondents be, in effect, a captive audience (probably of students or employees), and so special attention is required to ensure that participation is truly voluntary. (Those who do not wish to participate may be told they can just hand in a blank form.)

Confidentiality is most often the primary focus of ethical concern in survey research. Many surveys include some essential questions that might in some way prove damaging to the subjects if their answers were disclosed. To prevent any possibility of harm to sub-

jects due to disclosure of such information, it is critical to preserve subject confidentiality. Nobody but research personnel should have access to information that could be used to link respondents to their responses, and even that access should be limited to what is necessary for specific research purposes. Only numbers should be used to identify respondents on their questionnaires, and the researcher should keep the names that correspond to these numbers in a safe, private location, unavailable to staff and others who might otherwise come across them. Follow-up mailings or contact attempts that require linking the ID numbers with names and addresses should be carried out by trustworthy assistants under close supervision. If an electronic survey is used, encryption technology should be used to make information provided over the Internet secure from unauthorized people.

Not many surveys can provide true anonymity, so that no identifying information is ever recorded to link respondents with their responses. The main problem with anonymous surveys is that they preclude follow-up attempts to encourage participation by initial non-respondents, and they prevent panel designs, which measure change through repeated surveys of the same individuals. In-person surveys rarely can be anonymous because an interviewer must in almost all cases know the name and address of the interviewee.

However, phone surveys that are meant only to sample opinion at one point in time, as in political polls, can safely be completely anonymous. When no future follow-up is desired, group-administered surveys also can be anonymous. To provide anonymity in a mail survey, the researcher should omit identifying codes from the questionnaire but could include a self-addressed, stamped postcard so the respondent can notify the researcher that the questionnaire has been returned without creating any linkage to the questionnaire itself (Mangione, 1995, p. 69).

SUMMARY

Survey research is an exceptionally efficient and productive method for investigating a wide array of social research questions. In 6 months, Catherine Ross's

(1990) survey produced a unique, comprehensive data set on work, family, and health issues. These data allowed Ross and her coauthors to investigate the relations among sex stratification, health lifestyle, and perceived health (Ross & Bird, 1994); between education and health (Ross & Wu, 1995); between physical impairment and income (Mirowsky & Hu, 1996); among gender, parenthood, and anger (Ross & Van Willigen, 1996); and among age, the sense of control, and health (Mirowsky, 1995; Mirowsky & Ross, 1992, 1999; Ross & Wu, 1996). As a result, we know much more about how social structure influences health, what might be done to mitigate the negative health consequences of aging and low income, and where social theories of health need to be improved.

In addition to the potential benefits for social science, considerations of time and expense frequently make a survey the preferred data collection method. One or more of the six survey designs reviewed in this chapter (including mixed-mode) can be applied to almost any research question. It is no wonder that surveys have become the most popular research method in social work and that they frequently inform discussion and planning about important social and political questions. As use of the Internet increases, survey research should become even more efficient and popular.

The relative ease of conducting at least some types of survey research leads many people to imagine that no particular training or systematic procedures are required. Nothing could be further from the truth. But as a result of this widespread misconception, you will encounter a great many nearly worthless survey results. You must be prepared to examine carefully the procedures used in any survey before accepting its findings as credible. If you decide to conduct a survey, you must be prepared to invest the time and effort required by proper procedures.

Secondary Analysis

Allen Rubin

Basic Steps in the Research Process

Step 1   Choose a problem

2   Review the literature

3   Evaluate the literature

4   Be aware of all ethical issues

5   Be aware of all cultural issues

6   State the research question or hypothesis

7   Select the research approach

8   Determine how the variables are going to be measured

9   Select a sample

10   Select a data collection method

11   Collect and code the data

12   Analyze and interpret the data

13   Write the report

14   Disseminate the report

You Are Here

As you know by now, data can be collected from research participants or respondents when we use structured observations (Chapter 9), participant observations (Chapter 10), interviewing (Chapter 11), and surveys (Chapter 12). In some research situations, particularly if the costs or time requirements of these data collection methods are a consideration, a sample is difficult to locate, or a low response rate is likely, we have the alternative of using data that have already been collected. The data collection method discussed in this chapter and the one described in the following chapter (content analysis) rely on available data; that is, the data have already been collected.

Secondary analysis is more accurately referred to as a data utilization method rather than a data collection method. This process does not involve the collection of original data; instead, available data relevant to a problem or question are located in records or a computerized database. A research study is then designed to analyze these data with the goal of answering questions, arriving at hypotheses that can be tested, or building theory.

UTILIZATION OF DATA

In secondary analysis, the data must be at hand before the design of the study in which they will be analyzed can be formulated. Moreover, the researcher usually has little control over the original format of the data and must take them as they are presented. This does not relieve the researcher of the responsibility for verifying the validity and reliability of the data, however. As with any research design, studies that rely on secondary analysis must use (or, in this case, reuse) data that accurately measure what they are supposed to measure.

Another consideration in using this method is that the secondary analysis cannot be used for the same purpose as the data were when they were first collected. In situations where researchers participated in or designed the original research study with the intention of doing a secondary analysis later, that analysis could only be described as secondary if it were conducted as a separate, independent investigation. It

306

should not merely inquire further into the implications of the data as an expansion of the preceding study.

For example, suppose a social service agency uses data from a research study of clients and services provided as a basis for designing a system for collecting and storing comprehensive data on this topic. The system is put into operation, and then the researchers who helped develop it are approached with additional practice questions involving the database. To answer these questions, they could formulate a new analysis of the data. This would be a secondary analysis even though the researchers had helped to gather the original data.

Example: Big Brothers/Big Sisters Programs

To demonstrate the secondary analysis method of data utilization, an example will be given that involves a Big Brothers/Big Sisters program. In these programs, youths at risk are matched with volunteers of the same gender. A motherless girl, for example, will be matched with a Big Sister who will act as a role model and try to compensate for the absence of the mother; a fatherless boy will be matched with a Big Brother. There are two major problems that affect both the maintenance of the programs and the quality of the services they provide:

1. premature turnover among volunteers (the Big Brothers and Big Sisters)
2. uncertainty about how the volunteers might affect the psychosocial functioning of the service recipients (the Little Brothers and Little Sisters)

Turnover is a clinical problem in terms of the potentially harmful impact that aborted relationships might have on the boys and girls. It is an administrative problem for the same reason, and it represents a drain on scarce agency resources and can ultimately lower the public's image of the program and its effectiveness. To reduce turnover, social workers and administrators need to know about the variables that distinguish volunteers who leave prematurely from those who do not. They need data they can use as a basis for decisions about modifications in volunteer screening,

the orientation of volunteers, or changes in the ways volunteers and youths are matched.

Program impact or effectiveness also is of concern to both practitioners and administrators. Administrators could use quantitative data about the impact of the program as a selling point with funding sources; indeed, funders are demanding such data. Social workers could use the data to identify the types of volunteers and youths associated with the best outcomes for the service recipients. They could see what dyad matches do best; that is, what type of youth benefits most from association with what type of volunteer. In order to obtain data about the program's effectiveness, however, it is necessary to obtain and analyze data about the psychosocial functioning of the youths the program affects.

The question is, who will collect the data to address these types of questions? Who has the time and money to generate data about volunteers and youths throughout the course of their involvement in the program? Obtaining turnover data could mean waiting several years after the initial data-gathering effort to see when volunteers terminate. Obtaining the program impact data could mean gathering longitudinal data on each child's psychosocial functioning several times over the same period.

In Big Brothers/Big Sisters programs, social workers' efforts are often stretched thin with heavy caseloads, and administrators can be swamped with the resource procurement and public relations activities necessary to keep the program afloat. Collecting original data themselves, in person or by mail or phone, may be out of the question, and limited finances may make it impossible for them to hire outside researchers to do the data collection. Moreover, since the needed data are usually collected with a longitudinal study design, both administrators and social workers may well be working elsewhere by the time a study is completed. Even if they are still with the same program, the agency boards or funding bodies wanting these data may not wait that long. The problems could become irrelevant by the time the studies are completed.

Secondary analyses can be used to study the questions implicit in both the turnover and the program-effectiveness questions. The turnover question can be studied retrospectively by analyzing existing data in the agency's records about volunteers who had participated in the program in the past. The attributes of these volunteers and their Little Brothers or Little Sisters could be examined in relation to how long the volunteer-youth relationship had lasted. This would require considerable time to examine the agency's records and process and analyze data from them, particularly if the files have not been computerized. Nevertheless, using available data could make an otherwise impractical research project feasible. It also could enable agency staff to complete the study before it becomes irrelevant to those who want to utilize the findings.

The same applies to the program-effectiveness question. Assessing effectiveness with a sufficient degree of internal validity would require higher-level research designs such as those discussed in Chapter 8. Suppose one effectiveness measure of the program to be assessed is the school performance of the Little Brothers and Little Sisters. Existing school records on such indicators as grades, tardiness, and number of detentions per report period would be used to conduct a series of studies with single-system or multiple-baseline designs (see Chapter 7). These studies would be based on time-series analyses of each child's school performance before and after the child was matched with a volunteer. Because available data would be used, the study could focus on closed cases, and the analyses could include trends in school performance (e.g., grades, tardiness, detentions) after the intervention had been completed.

Sources of Data

For many secondary analyses conducted by social workers, the principal source of existing data is social service agency records. But available data may be obtained from a variety of other sources. In the United States, many federal agencies, such as the Department of Health and Human Services, the Bureau of Labor Statistics, the Federal Bureau of Investigation, and the National Center for Health Statistics, regularly report current data. The largest secondary database is provided by the U.S. Bureau of the Census, which conducts a national census of the population every 10 years that attempts to

account for every person in the country and to provide data on a variety of variables such as housing, gender, age, income, and family relationships. The bureau also conducts periodic surveys and publishes annual editions of the *Statistical Abstract of the United States*, in which data from numerous federal agencies on a wide variety of topics of interest to social workers are presented in tabular form.

Other good sources of secondary data are national voluntary agencies such as the Council on Social Work Education (CSWE), which annually produces a report of statistics on students and faculty in all accredited undergraduate and graduate schools of social work in the United States. (These data provide a source for a variety of secondary analyses that will be used as examples in this chapter.) On the state and local levels, public agencies such as local housing departments and private agencies such as community councils also make data available.

The use of agency records for secondary analysis, including the case records on file in almost any social service agency, has been stimulated by the adoption in recent years of management information systems (MISs) in which data from agency records are processed, stored, retrieved, and analyzed by computer technology. These systems provide agencies with a computerized database of information that is collected routinely by social workers on such variables as client characteristics, workers' activities, costs and outcomes of agency services, and other aspects of service delivery. They have made secondary analysis a common method of data collection for social workers.

RESEARCH DESIGNS FOR SECONDARY ANALYSIS

Various ways to classify social work research designs apply to studies that use secondary analysis for data collection. One simple classification scheme differentiates among these studies on the basis of reasoning processes, classifying them as either inductive or deductive. Another classification scheme differentiates studies on the basis of levels of knowledge, classifying them as exploratory, descriptive, or explanatory.

Classification by Deductive or Inductive Reasoning

The classification of research designs by deductive or inductive reasoning processes distinguishes between those designs in which hypotheses are deduced from theory and tested in order to further develop theory and those designs in which hypotheses are induced from the results of research studies to formulate theory. According to the principles of these two forms of logic, deductive logic consists of forming a theory, making deductions from the theory, and testing those deductions, or hypotheses, against reality. This is the basis for the hypothetico-deductive approach to hypothesis testing introduced in Chapter1, which represents the positivistic approach to research.

As pointed out in Chapter 3, inductive logic begins with specific observations of actual events, things, or processes, as in naturalistic research, and builds on these observations to make inferences or more general statements. In research, therefore, inductive reasoning is applied to data collection and research results in order to make general statements and see if they fit theory; deductive reasoning is applied to theory in order to arrive at hypotheses that can be empirically tested.

Briefly stated, inductive secondary analyses emphasize the process of accumulating observations to build theories, whereas deductive secondary analyses test the hypotheses derived from theories. As indicated in Chapter 3, the greater the number of hypotheses that are derived from a theory and proved true, the more reason there is to believe in the truth of the theory. Conversely, the greater the number of hypotheses that are derived, tested, and proved false, the greater is the skepticism generated about the theory from which the hypotheses were drawn.

Secondary analyses are typically associated with inductive reasoning, but they also can be employed in a deductive fashion. For example, various research studies have found that when schizophrenics live with their families, relapse rates are higher among patients whose families express high levels of emotionality than among patients whose families are more restrained. Other studies have observed that psychiatric programs that seek to increase cognitive arousal and rely on psychotherapy are less successful than those that seek to develop occupational rehabilitation and de-emphasize psychotherapy.

In inductive fashion, a variety of such studies have been taken together to develop a theory on the vulnerability of schizophrenics to overly stimulating environments. From this theory, hypotheses have been deduced regarding intervention with families and agencies to reduce the level of overstimulation and expressed emotion, which can affect patients. The results of studies to verify the efficacy of the treatment interventions have supported not only the hypotheses derived from the theory but also the plausibility of the theory.

In the Big Brothers/Big Sisters example used earlier in this chapter, problems of volunteer turnover and program effectiveness for service recipients were addressed with two different types of secondary analysis. The first study described dealt with attributes of youths and volunteers that were associated with the length of the youth-volunteer relationship. This study could be termed inductive because data were examined in an effort to discover some plausible pattern that would account for volunteer turnover.

The second study described examined the program's impact on the school performance of the Little Brothers and Little Sisters. This study could be termed deductive because it began with a theory concerning the impact of same-gender role models on the psychosocial functioning of the youths. It then utilized an exploratory research design to verify a hypothesis derived from the theory concerning changes in school performance. In other words, the first study inductively accumulated observations to generate theory, whereas the second study addressed the plausibility of a theory by verifying a hypothesis derived from it.

Classification by Knowledge Levels

Secondary analyses can be used with all three types of designs for research studies based on level of knowledge, as described in Chapter 1. The level of knowledge a secondary analysis is capable of producing is arrayed along a continuum ranging from exploratory at the lowest level, where data are analyzed to build a foundation of general ideas and tentative hypotheses; to descriptive at the middle level, where data are analyzed to describe variables more precisely; to explanatory at the highest level, where data are analyzed as the basis for examining relationships between variables.

Exploratory Secondary Analyses

Secondary analyses are often used for data collection in exploratory studies, which are concerned with the generation of tentative insights and explanations that can then be studied more rigorously at other levels of the knowledge continuum. Many different possible relationships between variables can be discovered in an existing database. For example, if there is no strong basis for explaining a phenomenon by testing hypotheses with a limited set of variables, the procedures of secondary analysis can be utilized to search through a much wider range of independent variables to determine which ones might be associated with a particular dependent variable. An association discovered through secondary analysis might merit further theoretical development and study at the explanatory level.

An example using the Council on Social Work Education data will help illustrate this point. Social work educators have been concerned about the potential consequences of a significant decline in MSW applications to graduate schools of social work in recent years. To find ways to offset this decline and maintain enrollments and the quality of students who do apply, and to ensure the survival of these educational programs, bold and innovative strategies and curriculum revisions have been tried.

One of the first attempts to seek quantitative evidence supporting such proposals was an exploratory secondary analysis of the CSWE database undertaken by a graduate-level social work research class. This class project was essentially a "fishing expedition" to consider every variable in the CSWE data that seemed to have any possibility of explaining why the decline in applications was much greater in some MSW programs than in others. These variables included tuition; provisions for part-time study; provisions for advanced standing, enabling students to graduate sooner; concentrations offered; a BSW or doctoral social work program; length and types of field practicums; pro-

gram auspices (public or private); availability of financial grants to students; student-faculty ratios; and size of the program.

The study's findings indicated that the steepest declines were occurring in schools with doctoral programs, schools with lower (e.g., "better") student-faculty ratios, and schools offering more financial aid. Based on these findings, which at first seemed to defy logic, the class postulated that the schools experiencing the smallest declines in applications were those that had lower academic standards and fewer resources, compared with better-endowed schools with more academic prestige. They suggested that the former schools had more applicants because they took earlier, more aggressive steps to recruit them (Rubin, Conway, Paterson, & Spence, 1983).

This study, being exploratory, utilized secondary analysis to generate hypotheses, not test them. The reasoning was in the form of a postulated explanation of variation in applications decline; it was not an attempt to imply that the true explanation had been found or verified. The ease and speed of analyzing arrays of variables with computers to determine relationships simplifies the task, but it is a method that can be misused. The more pairs of dependent and independent variables that are examined in order to find pairs that are related, or covary, the greater is the likelihood of finding some pairs that covary not for any theoretical reason but merely due to statistical chance. When relationships are found in such fishing expeditions, it makes a great deal of difference whether the findings are interpreted as plausible hypotheses warranting further investigation or as verification of hypotheses. The former would be an acceptable conclusion in an exploratory context; the latter would be misleading and wrong.

To understand the importance of this distinction requires some knowledge of the concept of statistical significance. The level of statistical significance or probability found in a statistical test (usually set at .05) represents the probability of finding relationships by chance. With a .05 significance level, if researchers were to look for covariation among 100 pairs of variables, they could expect to find it for 5 pairs merely due to statistical chance. Therefore, the relationships found for those five pairs of variables need not have any theoretical or practical meaning.

When statistical significance is found with secondary analysis, therefore, the researcher must take into account whether it was found in order to verify a hypothesis or was found for some pairs of variables out of a much larger array that was explored with electronic data processing. Failure to identify the tentative nature of findings that are only postulations for future study represents an abuse of computer technology—massaging the data until something "significant" appears and then misrepresenting that finding as a verified hypothesis.

Descriptive Secondary Analyses

Like other descriptive studies, some secondary analyses are intended only to describe a population's characteristics, not to generate or test explanations of phenomena in the population. In the Big Brothers/Big Sisters program example, the problem of program impact could be addressed with a series of case-level designs naturally occurring in the available database. School records on academic performance for each Big Brother or Big Sister could be examined in relation to measurements taken before and after the beginning of a volunteer relationship, as identified in the agency records.

Another example involves the CSWE statistics, which provide descriptive data useful in educational planning without getting into explanatory or theoretical issues. The council often receives requests from schools of social work for secondary analyses with additional descriptive data that are not included in its annual reports. A dean of a midwestern school of social work in a public university might need to know how the school's student-faculty ratio compares with that of other similar schools in the Midwest, for example. The dean needs these data not to construct or test an explanation about the causes or consequences of variation in student-faculty ratios but merely to help make a case with faculty or administration regarding the adequacy or inadequacy of the school's resources compared with the resources of similar schools.

Descriptive secondary analyses also are used frequently in social service agencies with computerized information systems to make such descriptive data as caseload trends and program costs readily available to administrators and planners.

Explanatory Secondary Analyses

Explanatory designs are used in secondary analyses, as in other types of studies, to verify hypotheses and examine relationships between variables. A cross-sectional secondary analysis could be used in an explanatory study to analyze the existing data to see if a specific hypothesized relationship exists at one point in time. It might also assess whether that relationship holds up when rival hypotheses in the database are controlled for. An example would be a secondary analysis of the CSWE database to assess a postulated disparity between male and female faculty salaries when academic degrees, ranks, and administrative responsibilities are controlled for (held constant).

ISSUES IN METHODOLOGY

There are a number of methodological issues in the analysis of data that have been previously collected, such as the misuse of computer technology, already discussed. These problems concern the adequacy of the database and the reliability, validity, and availability of data relevant to a proposed research question.

An easy mistake researchers can make when using secondary analysis is to assume that since they are using an available database and have not been responsible for gathering the data, they can assume that the validity and reliability of the data they wish to reanalyze have been established. However, it does not follow that because others have collected the data, no matter how prestigious or "official" their auspices may be, researchers doing secondary analyses can accept the data without question.

Measurement Reliability

As we know from Chapter 5, reliability refers to accuracy, precision, or consistency in measurement, and some available databases are riddled with measurement inconsistencies. If social workers who are instructed to collect data for a new computerized management information system in their agency resent the extra work and the time it takes away from direct service to their clients, for example, they may not be careful to complete the measuring instruments accurately, precisely, and consistently.

Inconsistencies in measurement can plague even the most esteemed databases. In the CSWE annual data, for example, one variable is ethnicity. Asking schools to report the ethnicity of their faculty and students seems a relatively straightforward and easy task. A couple of decades ago, the CSWE administration decided that, in order to be more sensitive to Native American constituents, the category of ethnicity formerly labeled American Indian should more correctly read Native American.

Theoretically, this was a proper decision. However, in the year the change was made, the proportion of Native American students and faculty reported on the forms shot up to a level several times higher than it had been previously. In fact, the data reported by some schools in industrial areas of the Northeast and Midwest indicated that all their faculty and students classified as white the previous year had been replaced by Native Americans! Fortunately, it was not too difficult to spot and correct this error. Some of the clerical staff who completed the CSWE forms apparently thought that Native American meant white or born in the United States and overlooked the category of white ethnicity, which appeared lower in the list.

Measurement Validity

As noted in Chapter 5, inconsistent or unreliable measuring instruments cannot produce valid data because they do not accurately measure what they purport to measure. But even if the data are reliable, they still may not be valid. Consistency is a necessary condition for a measuring instrument to be valid, but it is not a sufficient condition.

For example, suppose a database in a probation department contains data on the frequency of criminal acts by probationers, based on their reports to their probation officers. The probationers would undoubtedly underreport such acts. These data would be reliable as a measure of their self-reports, but they would not be valid because they would contain a consistent bias that has more to do with avoiding being returned to prison than with an accurate count of criminal acts.

Example: Interpretation of Impact Data

Before conducting any type of secondary analysis, researchers must carefully investigate what the data they intend to reuse really reflect or are intended to reflect. To assess the impact of a community-based psychiatric rehabilitation center for former patients of state hospitals, for example, the rehospitalization rates of patients discharged to the community in which the center is located could be compared with the rates for patients discharged to a community with a less structured mental health program. State hospital records could be used to identify the patients in both communities who had been rehospitalized after their initial discharge, and for how long.

It can be assumed that a state hospital would be consistent in measuring the number of former patients from various communities who are readmitted to it and the length of each hospitalization. But would this measurement really mean what it is intended to? The administration and staff of community-based psychiatric rehabilitation centers often are dedicated to their belief that such patients are almost always better off in the community than in the hospital. They are unlikely to recommend rehospitalization for patients who experience a relapse; indeed, they may forcefully advocate against it. Mental health professionals in a community with a different type of program might view the state hospital in positive terms, as an acceptable way to provide a temporary, protected environment for patients who need it. They therefore would send comparatively more patients back to the hospital.

A good case could be made that what would really be measured by reliable data that indicate this disparity in rehospitalization rates is largely a difference not in ideology but in the clinical benefits of the different community treatment programs. At least there should be considerable doubt as to how much of the disparity is due to ideological differences and how much really reflects differences in the well-being of the former patients. Before using such available data, therefore, a brief preliminary investigation should be conducted to examine the attitudes, beliefs, and practices of those who influenced or determined what was recorded in the database. A few brief interviews might reveal disparate staff ideologies concerning the value of rehospitalization, which would suggest the dubious validity of these data as a measure of clinical outcome.

An even more likely case, in view of cutbacks in funding for community mental health programs, is that a community with a program for former patients of state hospitals would be found to have significantly higher rehospitalization rates than another community that lacked any sort of program for former patients. Would the higher rates mean the program was harmful? Or would they mean that the community with the program was doing a better job in following up on discharged patients and making sure that some form of service (in this case, rehospitalization) was provided in case of relapse? Conceivably, the community with no program simply neglected these patients, allowing them to go their own way and get along in the community as best they could with the minimal public health and welfare benefits available.

Sources of Error

Problems in the validity and reliability of available data can stem from a variety of sources. Some have been mentioned previously, such as haphazard data recording. There are inconsistencies in how respondents interpret the meaning of questions or response categories on measuring instruments, and their personal response sets may lead them to supply data that present a socially desirable impression or that they think will please the interviewer or observer. There also are inconsistencies in the definition of available data that may be reliably recorded in a certain context but mean something different in another context.

Another source of error is that different agencies or programs contributing to a database may have different operational definitions of the same variables. Because they define the terms differently, their respective counts might not be comparable, and the sum of

all the counts might overestimate or underestimate the true amount. For example, at one time the CSWE database included the full-time enrollment of each undergraduate social work program in the United States. In some schools, however, freshman and sophomore social work majors were included in these counts; other schools could not do so because university policy required students to wait until the junior year to declare their majors. Consequently, the latter schools appeared to be devoting excessive resources to faculty; they had lower student-faculty ratios than the schools that counted freshmen and sophomores.

The CSWE adjusted its reporting procedures to improve the comparability among undergraduate programs by asking them all to include only juniors and seniors in their enrollment counts. This, however, introduced a different problem; the assessment of trends over time became more difficult. In comparing the number of full-time students before and after the CSWE adjusted its reporting procedures, the implications of including freshmen and sophomores before the adjustment but not after it must be taken into account. If this is not done, it would be easy to conclude that full-time enrollments had dropped more than they really had in some schools, simply because freshman and sophomore students no longer were being counted. Before trends can be assessed over time using secondary analyses, therefore, careful inquiries must be made about changes in reporting procedures.

For the same reasons, the possibility of differences in response rates from year to year must also be considered. Each year, a small proportion of social work education programs fail to respond to the annual canvass for the CSWE database. Let's take a simple hypothetical example to illustrate this point. Let's say that in 2008, 19% of CSWE-accredited baccalaureate programs failed to respond; the previous year (2007), 13% failed to do so. The larger proportion of nonrespondents in 2008 than in 2007 must be taken into account in developing trend data from one year to the next. Moreover, changes in the programs that fail to respond can cause distortions regarding some variables. For example, a substantial drop in the proportion of Puerto Rican faculty members and students in a given year may have more to do with the failure of one large program in Puerto Rico to respond to the canvass that year than with any real trend in the ethnicity of faculty and students.

Missing Data

A related problem is missing data. Just because an agency intends to include a particular statistic in its records or database is no guarantee that the statistic will be consistently available. It may be missing or "unknown" for many cases. In the CSWE database, for example, certain schools regularly refuse to supply data on faculty salaries. In social service agencies, some social workers may not conform to expectations that they routinely record data on service goals or client outcomes. There may even be a bias influencing which data are omitted. For example, social workers might be more disposed to record behaviors and events that reflect client progress than those that reflect poor treatment outcomes. They might be more likely to be aware of (and thus record) acting-out behavior than withdrawal behavior.

Consequently, before a great deal of time is invested in a research study, some preliminary spot-checking of the data sources to be used is advisable to get an idea of how consistently the data are available. This provides a basis for deciding whether the extent of missing data will create too great a margin of error in the results of the proposed research study.

SUMMARY

Secondary analysis is a method of data utilization in which existing data collected by others are used to answer questions, test hypotheses, or build theory, so there is no need to collect original data. In some research situations, the time, cost, and other resources saved by avoiding the collection of original data are a distinct advantage of secondary analysis. It also may be the preferable method when it is difficult to find an appropriate sample or a low response rate is anticipated.

Data for secondary analyses may be obtained from a variety of agency sources—public or voluntary and at the national, state, or local levels. Especially when computer technology is used to process, store, retrieve, and analyze data on an ongoing basis, secondary analyses can be done routinely and easily by social work researchers.

Designs for studies using secondary analyses can be classified in several ways. In inductive studies, theories are built from accumulated observations, whereas in deductive studies, the hypotheses derived from these theories are tested. Secondary analyses are typically associated with inductive reasoning, but they can be employed in a deductive fashion as well. They can also be used at all three levels of the research knowledge continuum. In exploratory studies, the utility of secondary analyses is related to the ease with which many different possible relationships between variables can be identified in an existing database. In descriptive studies, social work researchers can use existing data to obtain more precise definitions of variables, without examining or testing relationships between them. In explanatory designs, they can analyze existing data to try to verify research hypotheses about these relationships.

A number of methodological issues are involved in the analysis of data that others have collected. The data researchers propose to analyze must be valid and reliable. Problems in the validity and reliability of available data can stem from haphazard recording of original data, inconsistencies in how respondents interpret requests for information, or the inclination of respondents to report socially desirable information. Data that have been reliably recorded can mean different things in different contexts, and some data may be missing in a database. Researchers must also take care that they do not abuse computer technology by merely massaging data in inappropriate efforts to statistically verify potential hypotheses.

Content Analysis

Craig W. LeCroy
Gary Solomon

14

Basic Steps in the Research Process

Step 1   Choose a problem

2   Review the literature

3   Evaluate the literature

4   Be aware of all ethical issues

5   Be aware of all cultural issues

6   State the research question or hypothesis

7   Select the research approach

8   Determine how the variables are going to be measured

9   Select a sample

10   Select a data collection method

You Are Here

11   Collect and code the data

12   Analyze and interpret the data

13   Write the report

14   Disseminate the report

ontent analysis is similar to secondary analysis (discussed in the preceding chapter) in that both use existing data sets. In content analysis, however, the data are generated by quantifying units of analysis in the content of recorded communications so they can be counted. Because content analysis allows us to investigate research questions without needing to collect original data, we can formulate research questions about anything that has taken place and been recorded. Our research question may involve content describing some historical situation or something that occurred a moment ago. In either case, the content is defined, coded, and tallied to generate new data that may be analyzed immediately or at some future date.

If our research question can be stated in terms that meet the criteria of specificity, relevancy, researchability, feasibility, and ethical acceptability (see Chapter 3), and if recorded communications on the question exist, a content analysis could well be the best method of collecting data to investigate it. Content analyses are well suited to the study of communications because they address the questions of who says what to whom, why, how, and with what effect. The "what" of a research study, or the defining aspect, is found in the content of the text to be studied.

CHARACTERISTICS OF CONTENT ANALYSES

In content analyses, communications are examined in a systematic, objective, and quantitative manner (Holsti, 1969). To be systematic, a content analysis must follow specified procedures. If we want to compare the lyrics in the songs of three different rock groups, for example, we must systematically use the same procedures in examining the content for each group. As we know from Chapter 5, if the same measuring procedures are not used, our results will not be considered reliable; it could be argued that the difference in the way the criteria were applied to the groups is a source of bias or error in our results. This occurs when we structure our data collection procedures to confirm our own predictions or support our own theoretical positions.

Objectivity is another characteristic of content analyses that helps ensure validity and avoid bias. This characteristic is concerned with making the criteria or rules used to categorize the contents of the text impartial and objective. Clearly defining the criteria to be applied and making explicit the rules to be used in classifying the content of a communication help control any special interest or ideology that might influence our research study (Williamson, Karp, Dalphin, & Gray, 1982).

In our study of rock lyrics, for example, the rules to be used in categorizing the lyrics must be specified. Otherwise a conclusion that rock lyrics consist of sexual and violent content, or a conclusion that they are harmless, could be considered invalid. While people interested in the results of our research study might not agree with the categories that we devised, the standards for deciding how to categorize the data and code them for recording would be clear, so others could evaluate how our conclusions had been reached. Objective procedures also allow others to replicate our study; even if they have different biases, if they follow the same rules for categorizing the content, the results should be the same.

A Quantitative Research Approach

Content analyses are ordinarily used in quantitative research approaches because they focus on the operational definitions and quantifications of the dependent variables (and sometimes the independent variables) in research questions or hypotheses. Before the content of any communication can be analyzed it must be possible to quantify it in some manner. In a study to examine the way women are portrayed in children's books, for example, the number of times women are portrayed as mothers and as workers outside the home could be counted. The unit of analysis is women. Each time a unit occurs in a particular category (mother or worker), it is "counted" and recorded in that category.

A common use of content analyses is recording the frequency with which certain symbols or themes appear in a communication. Dodd, Foerch, and Anderson (1988), for example, did a content analysis of

women and racial and ethnic minorities as subjects of newsmagazine covers, an indication of their coverage in the content of a particular issue. The covers of *Time* and *Newsweek* from 1953 through 1987 were studied, and each appearance of a woman or minority member was counted. The researchers then could determine whether these variables were represented in relation to their proportions in the U.S. population and whether there had been changes in the subjects of the covers and cover stories over time.

When quantification is used in this manner, the results are usually presented in terms of simple proportions or percentages. A content analysis of a diary, for example, may reveal that the term *love* made up 5% of the total words used or that it appeared on 61% of the pages. Also, it could show an increase in use of the term between certain dates.

Quantification is not always that easy, however. We must often attempt to examine not just the frequency of a variable but also its intensity or deeper meaning. To compare how liberal two congressional candidates are, a content analysis of their speeches could be done. In addition to counting the number of "liberal" statements each one made, according to some specified criteria, there might be an attempt to evaluate how liberal each statement is. The task of devising adequate categories then would become much more complicated. Perhaps each statement could be rated as extremely liberal, moderately liberal, or minimally liberal. Because the concept of liberalism is becoming increasingly difficult to define in terms of political parties or ideologies, there would be limits to the possible options in using such a content analysis.

STEPS IN DOING A CONTENT ANALYSIS

To illustrate the process of conducting a content analysis, we will use an example involving a problem area of great social concern to social workers: suicide. While the steps in this process closely follow those in the quantitative research process described in Chapter 3, they are collapsed in this section to four distinctive steps that emphasize the nature and characteristics of content analyses: (1) developing a research question, (2) selecting a sample, (3) selecting the unit of analysis, and (4) coding, tallying, and analyzing the data.

Step 1: Developing a Research Question

As in all research studies, content analyses begin with a researcher's interest in a problem area and the development of a specific research question or hypothesis. In our example, we are interested in the problem area of suicide, and the purpose of our study is to contribute to an understanding of why people commit suicide. From this general perspective, a group of research questions could be advanced:

- Are there predictable patterns of behavior in people who commit suicide?
- Are the reasons for suicide different now than they were 20 years ago?
- Can we predict the act of suicide by examining the themes in suicide notes?
- Do people who leave suicide notes use similar words or describe common experiences and feelings?
- Do the suicide notes written by women and men differ?

For this example, our study will focus on the last two questions. The method will be a content analysis of suicide notes written in recent years.

Step 2: Selecting a Sample

Choosing the appropriate sampling strategy in a content analysis can be tedious. Suppose, for example, we are interested in how men and women are portrayed in children's books. Our population is all available children's books, and it is necessary to decide which parameters should be used to limit the sample. A sample from the population of writers might be selected, or the books published in a certain year might be chosen instead. Our sample could be limited to schoolbooks used for second and third graders; if this universe is still too large, the books used by all elementary schools in a specific city might be sampled. Such options must be considered in an attempt to gather a representative sample. The sample selection process also can redefine the specific problem area.

The decisions that must be made in selecting a sample for a research study are discussed in Chapter 6. For our suicide note example, the sampling plan is relatively straightforward. The universe (or population) from which our sample is to be extracted is identified as the suicide notes in the files of the Suicide Prevention Center, which collects and records suicide notes written in various U.S. cities that agree to participate. Although the content analysis for this example will be limited to what is available at the center, that universe is still large, and sampling considerations are necessary.

The Suicide Prevention Center has been in existence for decades and has collected more than 15,500 suicide notes. For our study, therefore, our universe is further limited to suicide notes written in a 2-year period, and only the suicide notes of adult men and women (21 years of age and older) are included. Within these parameters, a total of 1,327 suicide notes is available. From this population, a random sample of 100 suicide notes is selected.

Random sampling thus is chosen as the sampling strategy, but other techniques could also be used. With stratified sampling, for example, the suicide notes would be grouped according to strata such as year written, age category, or gender. After grouping, equal-sized samples of notes would be generated for each stratum and sampled separately, using simple or systematic random sampling techniques.

The limitation of the population parameters to determine the composition of our sample often follows a three-part process: sampling of sources (which suicide notes?), sampling of dates (suicide notes from what years?), and sampling of units (which aspects of the notes are to be analyzed?). When sampling according to units analyzed, our decisions are often based on what characterizes the content best for purposes of our study.

Step 3: Selecting the Unit of Analysis

In all content analyses, the specific unit of analysis, that is, what is to be counted, must be specified. This step is dependent on the quantification, or operational definition, of the dependent variable(s) in our research question. Units of analysis vary considerably, depending on the complexity of the research question and the universe of communications to be sampled. In many studies, recording the unit of analysis is simple, such as counting the number of certain words; in others, recording involves the establishment of complex categorical systems and coding rules and procedures.

In our suicide note example, the word content of suicide notes is chosen as the unit to be counted. To begin, the choice of a single concept, death, as a unit of analysis keeps our coding simple and reliable. We do not have to struggle to make judgments about whether a particular unit fits in the category—all the units do. We simply count the number of words that refer to the variable, death. But because many different words refer to death, there must be coding rules to clarify what to code in the category of death. In our example, any reference to death—words such as *dying, dead, ending,* or *terminating*—is to be used as the unit of analysis and counted.

Step 4: Coding, Tallying, and Analyzing the Data

The coding of data has to do with the categories of the unit of analysis. With a single concept such as death, there is only one category, but the different words that refer to death are defined as belonging in that category. With a concept such as gender, there are two obvious categories, male and female. Thus, coding data is dependent on the way the categories are operationally defined; they should reflect the concepts (the dependent and independent variables) represented in the research question.

To aid in the data collection process, a coding or tally sheet is developed. Figure 14.1 is an example of a coding sheet used to record the data we want to extract from the suicide notes sampled. Three references to death were counted in Note 1, written by a male, and five references to death in Note 2, written by a female. The coder continues to count and tally until all 100 randomly selected suicide notes have been tallied. Then the individual tallies are totaled, and the frequencies of the tallies for men and women are compared.

Suicide Notes	Death Concept Tally	Gender of Writer	
		Male	Female
Note 1	3	✓	
Note 2	5		✓
Note 3			
Note 4			
Note 5			
Note 6			

Figure 14.1 Recording Sheet for Two Subcategories (Death and Gender) in Suicide Notes

If different units of analysis, other than the concepts of death and gender, were used, additional concepts and categories would be included in the tally sheet. For instance, the age of the writer, the city of residence, any reference to a friend, parent, spouse, or relevant other, or a mention of a plan for the suicide might be operationally defined, coded, and tallied.

Categorizing Latent Content

In our example, coding is limited to the tabulation of gender and the frequency of occurrence of words relating to death. This type of information is referred to as *manifest content*—the obvious, clearly evident, visible aspects of the communication. Examples of coding manifest content are counting certain types of words, coding whether men or women appear on the cover of a magazine, and counting the number of times violence occurs in a TV program.

Beyond the manifest content of communications, we often are interested in their *latent content*—content that is present but not evident or active. Latent content is an indicator of the underlying meaning of what is communicated. We may, for example, want to assess the political orientation of a newspaper editorial or the intensity of the violence portrayed on certain television shows. Manifest content is specific, is easy to code, and produces reliable data. Latent content is less specific and more difficult to code because it represents the meaning, depth, and intensity of a communication.

In our example, we may want to understand what people considering suicide think and feel. Because it could be difficult to get these impressions via simple word counts, we attempt to characterize the meanings expressed in the suicide notes, which requires more judgment and interpretation.

As we study the various suicide notes in the sample, we recognize several recurrent themes. We may decide, for example, to code the notes according to four themes identified in suicide notes (Schneidman, 1985): unendurable psychological pain, searching for solutions, helplessness and hopelessness, and constriction of options. Obviously, these themes are difficult to code, but operational definitions could be formulated from types of statements found in the notes. For the first two concepts, for example, *unendurable psychological pain* could be coded from the statements "I feel so desperate" and "This will all be over soon"; *searching for solutions* could be coded from the statements: "I can't face life, there's only one thing to do" and "I've done everything I can, there are no more options for me."

By uncovering such themes, we may develop an interest in discovering in what ways the themes differ in notes written by men and women, or we may want to examine the degree of intensity in each theme. Using such latent content results in a complex coding task because the themes must be identified in the content and then coded or placed in an assigned category, to indicate the intensity with which the theme is being expressed. Once the theme of helplessness and hopelessness has been defined in terms of certain types of statements found in suicide notes, for example, three ordinal categories might be set up to indicate the intensity of particular statements:

1 = Great feelings of helplessness and hopelessness
2 = Average feelings of helplessness and hopelessness
3 = Minimal feelings of helplessness and hopelessness

The coder must identify each statement according to theme and determine in which of the three categories of intensity it belongs.

When such judgments must be made in the coding of data, the reliability of the data produced by the coding system must be established. This is done in terms of interrater reliability, using a process whereby two or more independent coders or judges agree on how a unit of analysis should be categorized. While it is not necessary for them to agree completely on the categorization of every statement, if they can reach no agreement, the study's results will lack reliability and will seriously jeopardize the findings.

Coders, or judges, should agree on their coding results about 80% of the time. To achieve good reliability, coders often go through a training program to teach them how to compare and discuss their decisions about the coding and categorization of data. Codebooks are often developed with operational definitions and rules for how the data should be coded.

Content analysis thus can go beyond simple word counts and manifest content to examine communications more intensively. For some research questions, studies that have great specificity and reliability are required; for others, it is necessary to attempt to grapple with the meaning of the content in depth. When the research study uses latent content to elicit depth and meaning, several considerations emerge: the number of categories increases, the time required to do the coding increases, and the reliability of the coding decreases, because more interpretation by coders is necessary. Nevertheless, the research questions asked often determine the necessity of searching for depth and meaning in order to explore answers for them.

USES IN SOCIAL WORK RESEARCH

Despite the structured process of content analyses, they can be put to a variety of uses in social work research. They serve several distinct purposes and can be used in combination with other data-gathering methods. Developments in methodology, such as the use of computers to analyze communications with both quantitative and qualitative content and the acceptance of less structured forms such as ethnographic analyses, are increasing the range of uses to which content analyses can be put.

Classification of Content Analyses by Purpose

Content analyses can be classified into four broad categories according to the purpose of the analysis: (1) to make inferences to the source of communications, (2) to make inferences to populations, (3) to evaluate the effects of communications, or (4) to make structured observations (Williamson et al., 1982).

Inferences to the Source of Communications

An example of how content analyses are used to make inferences about the source of communications is analysis of the content of messages in an effort to understand the motives, values, or intentions of those who wrote them. Content analyses also may be done in order to understand something about people or institutions through their symbolic communications, which can reveal attitudes or beliefs. To do this, such documents as diaries, speeches, newspapers, or transcriptions of interviews might be examined.

Diaries or personal documents were used in some of the first examples of content analyses. An example is an early study of the psychology of adolescence, for which a collection of more than 100 diaries of adolescent girls was established at the Psychological Institute at the University of Vienna. This made possible a comparison of adolescents at two different time periods, 1873 and 1910, which would have been difficult with other methods of data collection. The results indicated that despite the significant cultural changes that took place between these years, many basic developmental issues such as the need for intimate personal relationships remained the same. Changes were observed, however, in such factors as the girls' relationships with their parents. Analysis of the diaries, particularly the girls' descriptions of rare or significant events, produced unique knowledge and provided a perspective on the inner aspects of life for adolescents in those times.

A much more recent content analysis was done to examine the experience of loneliness, using the accounts of people who were asked to describe in writing their loneliest experience (Rokach, 1988). Analysis of these descriptions enabled the researcher to build a conceptual model to help explain the phenomenon of loneliness.

Other content analyses attempt to build understanding of how political or social issues are reflected in the content of communications such as professional journals, laws, and existing policies (Williamson et al., 1982). To evaluate how social work practice had changed from 1960 to the 1980s, for example, one such study involved a content analysis of social work practice position vacancy descriptions (Billups & Julia, 1987). Job advertisements in the *Journal of Social Casework* and the *NASW News* were randomly sampled to determine how job titles and fields of practice had changed over three consecutive 10-year periods, the 1960s, 1970s, and 1980s. This study helped answer such research questions as: Have there been changes in the way social work practice is conceptualized? What jobs are being advertised most frequently?

In a similar manner, a content analysis of course outlines of social work practice courses was done to discover the extent to which the teaching of these courses reflected current theoretical and ideological issues in social work (LeCroy & Goodwin, 1988). Course units, required textbooks, required outside readings, and types of assignments were used as categories of practice courses (the unit of analysis), and the researchers attempted to make inferences about how these courses were being conceptualized. This study sought to answer such questions as: Is there any commonality among the course units? Do the courses include content on women and ethnic minorities? What textbooks are used most often? The results were used as a basis for characterizing the content and teaching methods currently being used in social work practice courses.

Inferences to Populations

By making inferences to populations, content analyses can be used to ascertain the values of the audiences that are reached by various communications. A well-known content analysis, for example, examined the relationship between economic development and the value a society places on achievement. David C. McClelland (1961) operationalized the definition of achievement as the presence of achievement themes in more than 1,000 children's stories from almost every country in the world and the definition of a society's economic development in terms of such factors as coal and electricity consumption. The results of this study indicated that countries with high achievement values were more likely to have higher rates of economic growth than countries with lower achievement values.

Other content analyses have attempted to make inferences about social change and cultural values. The portrayal of women and men in the content of television commercials (Brett & Cantor, 1988) and the portrayal of violence on prime-time television (Cumberbatch, Jones, & Lee, 1988) have been analyzed, for example. Such studies must be understood in terms of the assumption that the content being analyzed represents society's values.

In the content analysis of the covers of two major newsmagazines described earlier in this chapter (Dodd et al., 1988), it was concluded that society did not see women and minorities as more newsworthy in the 1980s than in the preceding decades, and values about how women and minorities are perceived had not changed. But would it be accurate to say that the covers of two magazines represent how society perceives women and minorities? Such conclusions point to the need for replications of the study using different printed media to see if similar conclusions are reached.

Evaluating the Effects of Communications

In addition to studying themes discerned in communications, content analyses can focus on the effects of items of analysis recorded in communications. One of the earliest uses of content analysis in social work research was in an attempt to measure the effectiveness of social work interventions, using clients' records. John Dollard and O. H. Mowrer (1947), for example, hypothesized that the effectiveness of social work intervention would be revealed in reduced tension in the clients. They evaluated the variable of tension according to a change in the relative proportions of verbal expressions of discomfort (or distress) and expressions of relief from distress recorded in the clients' case records. They then developed a complex coding system to classify emotional tone as a unit of analysis according to categories of distress clauses, relief clauses, or neither.

They also devised a distress quotient, the number of distress clauses divided by the sum of distress and relief clauses, to be used in measurement. Unfortunately, this complex method was found to have little relationship to client change. Later research studies in which similar methods were used to analyze client case records did establish the effectiveness of short-term interventions, however (Reid & Shyne, 1969).

A more recent application of an outcome-oriented content analysis was a single-case study with an emotionally disturbed child. The goal of this study was simply to evaluate the effects of the social worker's behavior (the intervention) on the client's acting-out behavior (Broxmeyer, 1979). Recorded and transcribed interviews were analyzed, and two behaviors the social worker used in working with the child—empathy and limit setting—were coded. These behaviors were then correlated with the child's acting-out behavior.

The results of the content analysis revealed that the social worker had responded to acting out with empathic responses eight times, and on six of those occasions the child stopped; therefore, there was a 75% reduction in the behavior. When the social worker used limit setting, the child discontinued the behavior 45% of the time. When the worker displayed no response, there was only a 25% reduction in the child's acting out.

In these examples the focus of the research studies was to determine whether communications can indicate the cause of certain behaviors. Studies that make such inferences are experimental, and measurement of the dependent and independent variables must be carefully controlled. If this is done, analysis of the relationships between variables indicated in recorded communications can contribute to the knowledge base of social work as much as other experimental studies can.

Making Structured Observations

Content analyses can also be used with other data collection methods. A content analysis of observational data can specify clearly what is being observed and what measurements are to be used. Typically, the frequency, duration, intensity, and effects of various verbal and nonverbal behaviors are coded in the analysis.

Many years ago, Bales (1950) conducted numerous research studies on small-group behavior by developing a coding scheme for group behaviors. He divided small-group interactions into three classes:

1. Positive interactions in the social-emotional area
2. Negative interactions in the social-emotional area
3. Neutral interactions in the task area

Under each category the observational unit could represent various behaviors such as agrees, disagrees, gives suggestions, and asks for opinions. Observers also gathered qualitative data by taking notes on events not covered by the three categories. Much of what is known about small-group behavior is a result of these types of research studies.

By coding various units of verbal and nonverbal behavior observed in marital interactions, John Gottman (1979) developed the elaborate Couples Interaction Scoring System. The system involved transcribing videotaped interactions and breaking them down into thought units for analysis. Each thought unit received a verbal content code and a nonverbal content code. The verbal content code included categories such as agreement, disagreement, mind reading, summarizing self, and feelings about a problem.

In the nonverbal content code were such categories as positive, neutral, or negative ratings, based on nonverbal cues from face, voice, and body movements. It took approximately 28 hours to transcribe and code each hour of videotape—a time-consuming process. But the process made it possible to examine the effects of different interactions; for example, one partner who is mind reading is most likely to cause the other partner to disagree.

Developments in Procedures

A large part of a content analysis involves the tedious process of coding the data. Computers are proving invaluable in counting and synthesizing masses of data, not only from communications such as books and records, in which the units of analysis can be easily defined in quantitative terms, but from communications such as speeches and interviews with extensive qualitative content. A less formal form of analysis that deals with qualitative data sources is ethnographic content analysis, another development that some researchers have found useful.

Computerized Content Analysis

Computer programs are increasingly being used in content analysis (Weber, 1984; Weitzman & Miles, 1995). Analyzing a large body of text very quickly is facilitated by computerized text coding, which requires unambiguous coding rules and classifications. Computerized content analyses are limited to the study of manifest content and typically are used for data reduction and analyses in which words or phrases are the units of analysis.

A number of widely used computer software programs are used in content analyses, such as ATLAS.tiV5, HyperRESEARCHV.2.06, MAXqdaV2,N6, NViv02, NViv07, QDAMiner, Qualrus, General Inquirer, Textpack, and Transana. In general, these software programs code the text according to word groupings, using electronic dictionaries in which specific words have been tagged. The computer is programmed to identify these tag words and put them in previously defined categories. The computerized analysis produces data such as a list of tag words, the frequency of tag words, the proportion of sentences in the text containing certain tag words, and so forth.

There are limitations to the use of electronic data processing in content analysis. Complex or abstract notions cannot be reduced to word groupings, and the communication as a whole may have to be considered. The meaning of a communication comes from sentences, phrases, and paragraphs—not single words. Therefore, computers cannot be used for content analysis when there is an interest in the abstract or thematic meaning of a communication (Weitzman & Miles, 1995). To understand such latent content, interpretive judgments about the meaning of the content must be made before assigning a unit of analysis to a category.

Ethnographic Content Analyses

Ethnographic content analysis, a form developed in the qualitative research approach, is used to document the communication of meaning as well as to verify theoretical relationships. Its distinctive characteristic is the highly reflexive and interactive nature of the relationships between the researcher and the study's concepts, data collection, and analysis.

In an ethnographic content analysis, the researcher is a central figure in evaluating the meaning of the content. This method is less rigid in its research approach, compared with traditional content analyses. Categories and variables guide the study; however, as is the practice in the qualitative research approach, ethnographic content analysis allows for the emergence of new categories and variables during the study.

ADVANTAGES AND DISADVANTAGES

Like all the data collection and utilization methods considered in Part III of this text, a content analysis has its advantages and disadvantages. Perhaps the greatest advantage is its unobtrusive nature. Observations, interviews, self-report surveys, and other data collection methods used in social work research intrude into the research situation and may produce reactive effects that change or disturb the concepts under study in some way. Content analyses do not fall into this trap because what is being studied has already taken place. The measuring instrument is applied to an undisturbed system, allowing content analyses to uncover data without influencing the data collection process.

If we want to find out which candy is most popular at the state fair, for example, we could approach customers and ask, "What is your favorite candy?" We could stand by the candy counter and record the purchases. In either case, our presence may affect the outcome, and it may be difficult to approach each customer or to observe clearly in a crowd what candy is being purchased. So we could go to the trash cans, collect the wrappers, divide them into piles, and draw conclusions from the findings. Or we could get the records of suppliers and determine how many boxes of

each kind of candy were ordered and how many were unsold or returned at the end of the fair. These unobtrusive options are examples of content analyses.

These unobtrusive options also would be the least expensive and time-consuming because observers and interviewers would not have to be trained and paid to be present for a specified period. For many research studies, a content analysis may be the most economical and time-efficient data collection method.

Another advantage is that a content analysis can be used in a historical research study to answer questions about the past that cannot be examined with other research methods (Woodrum, 1984). Communications from any time period can be used, as long as historical documents are available for study. A content analysis therefore allows for the examination of trends in both recent times and the distant past. An example was our study described earlier in this chapter that used the diaries of adolescent females written in 1873 and 1910 to examine how relationships with parents had changed between these periods. Thus, we can use content analyses to bridge the gap in time that separates us from our research participants or respondents.

Content analysis is not without disadvantages, however. By definition, the method is confined to the exploration and examination of previously recorded data. If the data are not part of a permanent record, they cannot be content analyzed.

A distinct disadvantage is the questionable validity of the data provided by some content analyses. Whether what is being measured is really a valid measure of the unit of analysis must be determined, particularly when inferences about populations are to be made. Accurate operational definitions of the units and their categories are essential to ensure validity. The effects of reducing data to categories, as a result of which the true meaning of the data may be lost, must also be taken into account.

The quantification of the data that characterize content analyses can be both an advantage and a disadvantage. It allows for a systematic and objective approach to social work research studies, but the cost may be in terms of limits to the depth of understanding that the analysis can provide. Over time, social work researchers have increasingly become interested in studying the latent content of data in order to get at the underlying meaning.

SUMMARY

A content analysis is a versatile data collection method in which communications are examined in a systematic, objective, and quantitative manner. It can be applied to different types of content, including personal documents such as diaries and suicide notes; mass communications such as magazine covers and television programs; and interviews such as counseling sessions. It is often used to discover themes present in a communication—for example, themes that represent the inner aspects of an individual's life, the values of a society, or the effects of a communication.

The process of conducting a content analysis is straightforward, consisting of four steps. From a problem area, we formulate a research question, which leads to a consideration of how to sample the content of interest. The unit of analysis is operationally defined, and categories are developed for the coding of the data. Findings and conclusions are then drawn from the data gathered.

Content analysis is an unobtrusive data collection method. As long as we develop reliable coding procedures and valid categories for the classification of the data, through content analyses we will be able to build new knowledge for social work practice.

Selecting a Data Collection Method

Yvonne A. Unrau

15

Basic Steps in the Research Process

As we know, Chapters 9 through 14 presented six different ways to collect data. This chapter examines the data collection process from the vantage point of choosing the most appropriate data collection method and data source for any given research study.

Data collection is the heartbeat of a research project. The goal is to have a steady flow of data collected systematically and with the least amount of bias. When the flow of data becomes erratic or stops prematurely, a research study is in grave danger. When data collection goes well, it is characterized by an even pulse and is rather uneventful.

DATA COLLECTION METHODS AND DATA SOURCES

There is a critical distinction between a data collection method and a data source, which must be clearly understood before developing a viable data collection plan. A data collection method consists of a detailed plan of procedures that aims to gather data for a specific purpose—that is, to answer a research question or to test a hypothesis.

As we know, the previous chapters in this book presented six different data collection methods. Each one can be used with a variety of data sources, which are defined by who (or what) supplies the data. Data can be provided by a multitude of sources such as people, existing records, and existing databases.

When data are collected directly from people, data may be firsthand or secondhand. Firsthand data are obtained from people who are closest to the problem we are studying. Male inmates participating in an anger management group, for example, can provide firsthand data about their satisfaction with the program's treatment approach.

Secondhand data may come from other people who are indirectly connected to our primary problem area. The anger management group facilitator or the prison social work director, for example, may be asked for a personal opinion about how satisfied inmates are with treatment. In other instances, secondhand data can be gained from existing reports written about inmates or inmate records that monitor their behavior or other important events.

DATA COLLECTION AND THE RESEARCH PROCESS

Data collection is a critical step in the research process because it is the link between theory and practice. Our research study always begins with an idea that is molded by a conceptual framework, which uses preexisting knowledge about our study's problem area. Once our research problem and question have been refined to a researchable level, data are sought from a selected source and gathered using a systematic collection method. The data collected are then used to support or supplant our original study's conceptions about our research problem under investigation. The role of data collection in connecting theory and practice is understood when looking at the entire research process.

As we have seen throughout this book, choosing a data collection method and data source follows the selection of a problem area, selecting a research question, and developing a sampling plan. It comes before the data analysis phase and writing the research report phase. Although data collection is presented in this text as a distinct phase of the research process, it cannot be tackled separately or in isolation.

All phases of the research process must be considered if we hope to come up with the best strategy to gather the most relevant, reliable, and valid data to answer a research question or to test a hypothesis. This section discusses the role of data collection in relation to four steps of the research process: (1) selecting a problem area and research question, (2) formulating a research design, (3) analyzing the data, and (4) writing the report.

Selecting a Problem Area and Research Question

The specific research question identifies the general problem area and the population to be studied. It tells us what we want to collect data about and alerts us to potential data sources. It does not necessarily specify the exact manner in which our data will be gathered, however. Suppose, for example, a school social worker proposes the following research question: How effective is our Students Against Violence Program (SAVP) within the Forest Lawn High School? One of the many objectives of our program is "To increase student's feelings of safety at school." This simple evaluative research question identifies our problem area of interest (school violence) and our population of focus (students). It does not state how the question will be answered.

Despite the apparent clarity of our research question, it could in fact be answered in numerous ways. One factor that affects how this question is answered depends on how its variables are conceptualized and operationalized. Students' feelings of safety, for example, could be measured in a variety of ways. Another factor that affects how a research question is answered (or a hypothesis is tested) is the source of data—that is, who or what is providing the data. If we want to get firsthand data about the students' school safety, for example, we could target the students as a potential data source.

If such firsthand data sources were not a viable option, secondhand data sources could be sought. Students' parents, for example, can be asked to speculate on whether their children feel safe at school. In other instances, secondhand data can be gained from existing reports written about students (or student records) that monitor any critical danger or safety incidents.

By listing all possible data collection methods and data sources that could provide sound data to answer a research question, we develop a fuller understanding of our initial research problem. It also encourages us to think about our research problem from different perspectives, via the data sources.

Because social work problems are complex, data collection is strengthened when two or more data sources are used. If the students, teachers, and parents rate students' feelings of safety as similar, then we can be more confident that the data (from all these sources) accurately reflect the problem being investigated. Reliability of data can be assessed, or estimated, when collected from multiple sources.

The exercise of generating a list of possible data collection methods and sources can be overwhelming.

With reasonably little effort, however, we can develop a long list of possibilities. We may also end up seeing the problem in a different light than what we had thought of previously. By considering parents as a source of secondhand data, for example, we open up a new dimension of the problem being studied. Suddenly family support factors may seem critical to how safe students feel at school.

We may then want to collect data about the family. This possibility should be considered within the context of our study's conceptual framework. Once we have exhausted all the different ways to collect data for any given study, we need to revisit our original research question. In doing so, we can refocus it by remembering the original purpose of the study.

Formulating a Research Design

As we know, the research design flows from the research question, which flows from the problem area. A research design organizes our research question into a framework that sets the parameters and conditions of the study. As mentioned, the research question directs *what* data are collected and *who* data could be collected from. The research design refines the *what* question by operationalizing variables and the *who* question by developing a sampling strategy. In addition, the research design also dictates *when, where,* and *how* data will be collected.

The research design states how many data collection points our study will have and specifies the data sources. Each discrete data-gathering activity constitutes a data collection point and defines *when* data are to be collected. Thus, using an exploratory one-group, posttest-only design, we will collect data only once from a single group of research participants. On the other hand, if a classical experimental design is used, data will be collected at two separate times with two different groups of research participants—for a total of four discrete data collection points.

The number of times a research participant must be available for data collection is an important consideration when choosing a data collection method. The gathering of useful, valid, and reliable data is enhanced when the data collection activities do not occur too frequently and are straightforward and brief.

Consider the high school students targeted by our SAVP. Already, many of the students live with the fear of avoiding confrontations with hostile peers and wonder whether they should tell someone about being threatened or harmed. Asking students about their feelings of safety too often may inadvertently make them feel less safe; alternatively, they may tire of the whole process of inquiry and refuse to participate in our study.

Where the data are collected is also important to consider. If our research question is too narrow and begs for a broader issue that encompasses individuals living in various geographic locations, then mailed surveys would be more feasible than interviews. If our research question focuses on a specific population where all research participants live in the same geographic location, however, it may be possible to use direct observations or individual or group interviews.

Because most social work studies are applied, the setting of our study usually involves clients in their natural environments where there is little control over extraneous variables. If we want to measure the students' feelings toward school safety, for example, do we observe students as they walk the school halls, observe how they interact with their peer groups, or have them complete a survey form of some kind? In short, we must always consider which method of data collection will lead to the most valid and reliable data to answer a specific research question or to test a specific hypothesis.

The combination of potential data collection methods and potential data sources is another important consideration. A research study can have one data collection source and still use multiple data collection methods. High school students (one data source) in our study, for example, can fill out a standardized questionnaire that measures their feelings of safety (first data collection method) in addition to participating in face-to-face interviews (second data collection method).

In the same vein, another study can have multiple data sources and one data collection method. In this case, we can collect data about how safe a student feels through observation recordings by the students' parents, teachers, or social workers. The combination of data collection methods should not be too taxing on any research participant or any system, such as the school itself. That is, data collection should try not to interfere with the day-to-day activities of the persons providing (or responsible for collecting) the data.

In some studies, there is no research design per se. Instead we can use existing data to answer the research question. Such is the case when a secondary analysis is used. Content analysis may also be used on existing data, as when we gather data from existing client records. When the data already exist, we must then organize them using the best-case scenario, given the data at hand and the details of how they were originally gathered and recorded. In these situations, we give more consideration to the analysis of the data.

Analyzing the Data

Collecting data is a resource-intensive endeavor that can be expensive and time consuming. The truth of this statement is realized in the data analysis phase of our research study. Unless a great deal of forethought is given to what data to collect, data may be thrown out because they cannot be organized or analyzed in any meaningful way.

In short, data analyses should always be considered when choosing a data collection method and data source because the analysis phase must summarize, synthesize, and ultimately organize the data in an effort to have as clear-cut an answer as possible to our research question. When too much (or too little) data have been collected, we can easily become bogged down or stalled by difficult decisions that could have been avoided with a little forethought.

After we have thought through our research problem and research question and have arrived at a few possible data collection methods and data sources, it is worthwhile to list out the details of how the dependent and independent variables will be measured by each data collection method and each data source. We must think about how they will be used in our data analysis. This exercise provides a clearer idea of the type of results we can expect.

One of the dependent variables in our example is the students' feelings of safety. Suppose the school social worker decides to collect data about this variable by giving students (data source) a brief standardized questionnaire (data collection method) about their feelings of safety. Many standardized questionnaires contain several subscales that, when combined, give a quantitative measure of a larger concept.

A questionnaire measuring the concept of feelings of safety, for example, might include three subscales: problem awareness, assertiveness, and self-confidence. We need to decide if each subscale will be defined as three separate subvariables, or if only the total combined scale score will be used.

Alternatively, if data about feelings of safety were to be collected using two different data sources such as parent (source 1) and teacher (source 2) observations, we must think about how the two data types "fit" together. That is, will data from the two sources be treated as two separate variables? If so, will one variable be weighted more heavily in our analysis than the other? Thinking about how the data will be summarized helps us to expose any frivolous data—that is, data that are not suitable to answer our research question.

It is also important to be clear on how our independent variable(s) will be measured and what data collection method would be most appropriate. In our example, we want to know whether our SAVP is effective for helping students feel more safe in the school environment. Because a social service program is being evaluated, it is essential to know what specific intervention approach(es), procedures, and techniques are used within the program. What specific intervention activities are used? Is student participation in our SAVP voluntary? How often do our SAVP's intervention activities occur in the school? Anticipating the type of data analysis that will be used helps to determine which data collection method and data source provide the most meaningful and accurate data to gather.

Besides collecting data about the independent and dependent variables, we must also develop a strategy to collect demographic data about the people who participated in our study. Typical demographic variables include age, gender, education level, and family income. These data are not necessarily used in the analysis of the research question. Rather, they provide a descriptive context for our study. Some data collection methods, such as standardized questionnaires, include these types of data. Often, however, we are responsible for obtaining them as part of the data collection process.

Writing the Report

It is useful to think about our final research report when choosing a data collection method and data source as it forces us to visualize how our study's findings will ultimately be presented. It identifies both who the audience of the study will be and what people will be interested in our findings. Knowing who will read our research report and how it will be disseminated helps us to take more of an objective stance toward our study.

In short, we can take a third-person look at what our study will finally look like. Such objectivity helps us to think about our data collection method and data source with a critical eye. Will consumers of our research study agree that the students in fact were the best data collection source? Were the data collection method and analysis sound? These are some of the practical questions that bring scrutiny to the data collection process.

CRITERIA FOR SELECTING A DATA COLLECTION METHOD

Thinking through the research process from the vantage point of collecting data permits us to refine the conceptualization of our study and the place of data collection within it. It also sets the context within which our data will be gathered. At this point, we should have a sense of what the ideal data collection method and data source would be. Clearly, there are many viable data collection methods and data sources that can be used to answer any research question.

Nevertheless, there are many practical criteria that ultimately refine the final data collection method (and

sources) to fit the conditions of any given research study. These criteria are (1) size, (2) scope, (3) program participation, (4) worker cooperation, (5) intrusion into the lives of research participants, (6) resources, (7) time, and (8) previous research findings. They all interact with one another, but for the sake of clarity each one is presented separately.

Size

The size of our study reflects just how many people, places, or systems are represented in it. As with any planning activity, the more people involved, the more complicated the process and the more difficult it is to arrive at a mutual agreement. Decisions about which data collection method and which data source to use can be stalled when several people, levels, or systems are consulted. This is simply because individuals have different interests and opinions. Administrators, for example, may address issues such as accountability more than do line-level social workers.

Imagine if the effectiveness of our SAVP were examined on a larger scale such that all high schools in the city were included. Our study's complexity is dramatically increased because of such factors as the increased number of students, parents, school principals, teachers, and social workers involved. Individual biases will make it much more difficult to agree upon the best data collection method and data source for our study.

Our study's sample size is also a consideration. The goal of any research study is to have a meaningful sample of the population of interest. With respect to sample size, this means that we should strive for a reasonable representation of the sampling frame. When small-scale studies are conducted, such as a program evaluation in one school, the total sampling frame may be in the hundreds or fewer. Thus, dealing with the random selection of research participants poses no particular problem.

On the other hand, when large-scale studies are conducted, such as when the federal government chooses to examine a social service program that involves hundreds of thousands of people, dealing with a sample is more problematic. If our sample is in the thousands, it is unlikely that we would be able to successfully *observe* all participants in a particular setting. Rather, a more efficient data collection method—say a mailed *survey*—may be more appropriate.

Scope

The scope of our research study is another matter to consider. Scope refers to how much of our problem area will be covered. In our SAVP, if we are interested in gathering data about students' academic standings, family supports, and peer relations, then three different aspects of our problem area will be covered.

In short, we need to consider whether one method of data collection and one data source can be used to collect all the data. It could be that school records are used to collect data about students' academic achievements, interviews with students are conducted to collect data about students' family supports, and observation methods are used to gather data about students' peer relationships.

Program Participation

Many social work research efforts are conducted in actual real-life program settings. Thus, it is essential that we gain the support of program personnel to conduct our study. Program factors that can impact the choice of our data collection methods and data sources include variables such as the program's clarity in its mandate to serve clients, its philosophical stance toward clients, and its flexibility in client record keeping.

First, if a program is not able to clearly articulate a client service delivery plan, it will be difficult to separate out clinical activity from research activity, or to determine when the two overlap.

Second, agencies tend to base themselves on strong beliefs about a client population, which affect who can have access to their clients and in what manner. A child sexual abuse investigation program, for example, may be designed specifically to avoid the problem of using multiple interviewers and multiple interviews of children in the investigation of an allega-

tion of sexual abuse. As a result, the program would hesitate to permit us to conduct interviews with the children to gather data for "research purposes."

Third, to save time and energy there is often considerable overlap between program client records and research data collection. The degree of willingness of a program to change or adapt to new record-keeping techniques will affect how we might go about collecting certain types of data.

Worker Cooperation

On a general level, programs have few resources and an overabundance of clients. Such conditions naturally lead their administrators and social workers to regard clinical activity as a top priority. When our research study requires social workers to collect data as a part of their day-to-day client service delivery, it is highly likely that they will view it as additional work. In short, they may not be likely to view these new data collection activities as a means to expedite their work, at least not in the short term.

Getting cooperation of social workers within a program is a priority in any research study that relies directly or indirectly on their meaningful participation. They will be affected by our study whether they are involved in the data collection process or not. Workers may be asked to schedule additional interviews with families or adjust their intervention plans to ensure that data collection occurs at the optimal time. Given the fiscal constraints faced by programs, the workers themselves often participate as data collectors. They may end up using new client recording forms or administer questionnaires. Whatever the level of their participation, it is important for us to strive to achieve a maximum level of their cooperation.

There are three factors to consider when trying to achieve maximum cooperation from workers. First, we should make every effort to work effectively and efficiently with the program's staff. Cooperation is more likely to be achieved when they participate in the development of our study plan from the beginning. Thus, it is worthwhile to take time to explain the purpose of our study and its intended outcomes at an early stage. Furthermore, administrators and front-line workers can provide valuable information about what data collection method(s) may work best.

Second, we must be sensitive to the workloads of the program's staff. Data collection methods and sources should be designed to enhance the work of professionals. Client recording forms, for example, can be designed to provide focus for supervision meetings as well as summarize facts and worker impressions about a case.

Third, a mechanism should be set up by which workers receive feedback based on the data they have collected. When data are reported back to the program's staff before the completion of our study, we must ensure that the data will not bias later measurements (if any).

Intrusion Into the Lives of Research Participants

When clients are used as a data source, client self-determination takes precedence over research activity. As we know, clients have every right to refuse participation in a research study and cannot be denied services because they are unwilling to participate. For example, it is unethical to use participant observation (Chapter 10) as a data collection method in a group-based treatment intervention when one member of the group has not consented to participate in the study. This is unethical because the nonconsenting group member ends up being observed as part of the group dynamic in the data collection process. The data collection method(s) we finally select must be flexible enough to allow our study to continue even when some clients will not participate.

As you will see in the following chapter, cultural consideration must also be given to the type of data collection method used. One-to-one interviewing with Cambodian refugees, for example, may be extremely terrifying for them, given its resemblance to the interrogation they may have experienced in their own country. If direct observational strategies are used in studies in which we are from a different cultural background than our research participants, it is important to ensure that interpretation of their behaviors, events, or expressions is accurate from their perspectives.

We must also recognize the cultural biases of standardized measuring instruments because most are based on testing with Caucasian groups. The problems here are twofold. First, we cannot be sure if the concept that the instrument is measuring is expressed the same way in different cultures. For instance, a standardized self-report instrument that measures family functioning may include an item such as "We have flexible rules in our household that account for individual differences," which would likely be viewed positively by North American cultures but negatively by many Asian cultures. Second, because standardized measuring instruments are written in English, research participants must have a good grasp of English to ensure that the data collected from them are valid and reliable.

Another consideration comes into play when particular populations have been the subject of a considerable amount of research studies already. Many aboriginal people living on reservations, for example, have been subjected to government surveys, task force inquiries, independent research projects, and perhaps even to the curiosity of social work students learning in a practicum setting. When a population has been extensively researched, it is even more important that we consider how the data collection method will affect those people participating in the study. Has the data collection method been used previously? If so, what was the nature of the data collected? Could the data be collected in other ways, using less obtrusive measures?

Resources

There are various costs associated with collecting data in any given research study. Materials and supplies, equipment rental, transportation costs, and training for data collectors are just a few things to consider when choosing a data collection method. In addition, once the data are collected, additional expenses can arise when they need to be entered into a computer or transcribed.

An effective and efficient data collection method is one that collects the most valid and reliable data to answer a research question or test a hypothesis while requiring the least amount of time and money. In our example, to ask students about their feelings of safety via an open-ended interview may offer rich data, but we take the risk that students will not fully answer our questions in the time allotted for the interview. On the other hand, having them complete a self-report questionnaire on feelings of safety is a quicker and less costly way to collect data, but it gives little sense about how well the students understood the questions being asked of them or whether the data obtained reflect their true feelings.

Time

Time is a consideration when our study has a fixed completion date. Time constraints may be self-imposed or externally imposed. Self-imposed time constraints are personal matters we need to consider. Is our research project a part of a thesis or dissertation? What are our personal time commitments?

Externally imposed time restrictions are set by someone other than the one doing the study. For instance, our SAVP study is limited by the school year. Other external pressures may be political, such as an administrator who wants research results for a funding proposal or annual report.

Previous Research Studies

Having reviewed the professional literature on our problem, we need to be well aware of other data collection methods that have been used in similar studies. We can evaluate earlier studies for the strengths and weaknesses of their data collection methods and thereby make a more informed decision as to the best data collection strategy to use in our specific situation. Further, we need to look for diversity when evaluating other data collection approaches. That is, we can triangulate results from separate studies that used different data collection methods and data sources to answer a research question or test a hypothesis.

SELECTION OF A DATA COLLECTION METHOD

As should be evident by now, choosing a data collection method and data source for a research study is not a simple task. There are numerous conceptual and practical factors that must be thought through if we hope to arrive at the best possible approach to gathering data. How do we appraise all the factors to be considered in picking the best approach? The previous six chapters in this book present six different non-mutually exclusive data collection methods. Theoretically, all of them could be used to evaluate the effectiveness of our SAVP. Each one would offer a different perspective to our research question and would consider different data sources.

Table 15.1 is an example of a grid that can be used to assist us in making an informed decision about which data collection method is best. The grid includes both general and specific considerations for our study question. The first section of the grid highlights the eight criteria for selecting a data collection method discussed earlier. The bottom section of the grid identifies five additional considerations that are specific to our SAVP.

The grid can be used as a decision-making tool by subjectively rating how well each data collection method measures up to the criteria listed in the left column of Table 15.1. We mark a "+" if the data collection method has a favorable rating and a "−" if it has an unfavorable one. When a particular criterion is neutral, in which case it has no positive or negative effect, then a zero is indicated.

Once each data collection method has been assessed on all the criteria, we can simply add the number of pluses and minuses to arrive at a plus or minus total for each method. This information can be used to help us make an informed decision about the best data collection method, given all the issues raised. Based on Table 15.1, where only five of the six data collection methods are illustrated, the survey research method is most appealing for our study if a single method of data collection is used.

TRYING OUT THE SELECTED DATA COLLECTION METHOD

Data collection is a particularly vulnerable time for a research study because it is the point where "talk" turns to "action." So far, all the considerations that have been

| TABLE 15.1 |

Decision-Making Grid for Choosing a Data Collection Method

	Data Collection Methods				
	Survey Research (*Chapter 12*)	Structured Observation (*Chapter 9*)	Secondary Analysis (*Chapter 13*)	Content Analysis (*Chapter 14*)	Qualitative Interviewing (*Chapter 11*)
General Criteria					
1. Size	+	0	+	+	+
2. Scope	+	–	–	–	–
3. Program participation	+	0	+	+	–
4. Worker cooperation	+	–	+	+	–
5. Intrusion into clients' lives	–	–	+	+	–
6. Resources	+	–	+	+	0
7. Time	+	–	+	+	0
8. Previous research	+	0	–	–	+
Specific Criteria					
1. Student availability	+	+	0	0	+
2. Student reading level	+	0	0	0	0
3. School preference	+	–	–	0	–
4. School year end	–	–	+	+	–
5. Access to existing records	0	0	+	+	0
Totals	8	–6	5	6	–3

weighed in the selection of a data collection method have been in theory. All people involved in our research endeavor have cast their suggestions and doubts on the entire process. Once general agreement has been reached about which data collection method and data source to use, it is time to test the waters.

Trying out a data collection method can occur informally by simply testing it out with available, willing research participants or, at the very least, with anyone who has not been involved with the planning of the study. The purpose of this trial run is to ensure that those who are going to provide data understand the questions and procedures in the way that they were intended. Data collection methods might also be tested more formally, such as when a pilot study is conducted.

A pilot study involves carrying out all aspects of the data collection plan on a miniscale. That is, a small portion of our study's actual sample is selected and run through all steps of the data collection process. In a pilot study, we are interested in the process of the data collection as well as the content. In short, we what to

know whether our chosen data collection method produces the expected data. Are there any unanticipated barriers to gathering the desired data? How do research participants (data source) respond to our data collection procedures? Is there enough variability in research participants' responses?

IMPLEMENTATION AND EVALUATION

The data collection phase of a research study can go smoothly if we are proactive. That is, we should guide and monitor the entire data collection process according to the procedures and steps that were set out in the study's planning stage and were tested in the pilot study.

Implementation

The main guiding principle to implementing the selected data collection method is that a systematic approach to data collection must be used. This means that the steps to gathering data should be methodically detailed so that there is no question about the tasks of the person or people collecting the data—the data collectors. This is true whether we are using a quantitative or qualitative research approach.

As we know from Chapters 3 and 4, the difference between these two research approaches is that the structure of the data collection process within a qualitative research study is often documented as the study progresses. On the other hand, in a quantitative research study the data collection process is decided at the study's outset and provides much less flexibility after the study is under way.

It must be very clear from the beginning who is responsible for collecting the data. When we take on the task, there is reasonable assurance that the data collection will remain objective and be guided by our research interests. Data collection left to only one person may be a formidable task. We must determine the amount of resources available to decide what data collection method is most realistic. Regardless of the study size, we must attempt to establish clear roles with those involved in the data collection process.

The clearer our research study is articulated, the less difficulty there will be in moving through all the phases of the study. In particular, it is critical to identify who will and will not be involved in the data collection process. To further avoid mix-ups and complications, specific tasks must be spelled out for all persons involved in our study. Where will the data collection forms be stored? Who will administer them? How will their completion be monitored?

In many social work research studies, front-line social workers are involved in data collection activities as part of their day-to-day activities. They typically gather intake and referral data, write assessment notes, and even use standardized questionnaires as part of their assessments. Data collection in programs can easily be designed to serve the dual purposes of research *and* service delivery.

Thus, it is important to establish data collection protocols to avoid problems of biased data. As mentioned, everyone in a research study must agree *when* data will be collected, *where,* and in *what* manner.

Agreement is more likely to occur when we have fully informed and involved everyone participating in our study.

Evaluation

The process of selecting a chosen data collection method is not complete without evaluating it. Evaluation occurs at two levels. First, the strengths and weakness of a data collection method and data source are evaluated, given the research context in which our study takes place. If, for example, data are gathered about clients' presenting problems by a referring social worker, it must be acknowledged that the obtained data offer a limited (or restricted) point of view about the clients' problems. The strength of this approach may be that it was the only means for collecting the data. Such strengths and weaknesses are summarized in the decision-making grid presented in Table 15.1.

A second level of evaluation is monitoring the implementation of the data collection process itself. When data are gathered using several methods (or from several sources), it is beneficial to develop a checklist of what data have been collected for each research participant. Developing a strategy for monitoring the data collection process is especially important when the data must be collected in a timely fashion. If pretest data are needed before a client enters a treatment program, for example, the data collection must be complete before admission occurs. Once the client has entered the program, the opportunity to collect pretest data is lost forever.

Another strategy for monitoring evaluation is to keep a journal of the data collection process. The journal records any questions or queries that arise in the data-gathering phase. We may find, for example, that several research participants completing a questionnaire have difficulty understanding one particular question. In addition, sometimes research participants have poor reading skills and require assistance with completion of some self-report standardized questionnaires. Documenting these idiosyncratic incidents accumulates important information that can be used to comment on our data's validity and reliability.

TABLE 15.2

Common Data Collection Methods

Data Collection Method	Description	Advantages	Disadvantages
Questionnaire (General)	A paper-and-pencil method for obtaining responses to statements or questions by using a form on which participants provide opinions or factual information	• Relatively inexpensive, quick way to collect large amounts of data from large samples in short amounts of time. • Convenient for respondents to complete. • Anonymity can result in more honest responses. • Questionnaires are available. • Well suited for answering questions related to "What?" "Where?" and "How many?"	• Limited ability to know if one is actually measuring what one intents to measure. • Limited ability to discover measurement errors. • Question length and breadth are limited. • No opportunity to probe or provide clarification. • Relies on participants' ability to recall behavior, events. • Limited capability to measure different kinds of outcomes. • Must rely on self-report. • Not well suited to answering questions related to "How?" and "Why?" • Difficult with low-literacy groups.
One-to-One Interview (General)	An interaction between two people in which information is gathered relative to respondent's knowledge, thoughts, and feelings about different topics.	• Allows greater depth than a questionnaire. • Data are deeper, richer, have more context. • Interviewer can establish rapport with respondent. • Interviewer can clarify questions. • Good method for working with low-literacy respondents. • Higher response and completion rates. • Allows for observation of nonverbal gestures.	• Requires a lot of time and personnel. • Requires highly trained, skilled interviewers. • Limited number of people can be included. • Is open to interviewer's bias. • Prone to respondents giving answers they believe are "expected" (social desirability). • No anonymity. • Potential invasiveness with personal questions.
One-to-One Interview (Unstructured)	Totally free response pattern; allows respondent to express ideas in own way and time.	• Can elicit personal information. • Can gather relevant unanticipated data. • Interviewer can probe for more information.	• Requires great skill on part of interview. • More prone to bias in response interpretation. • Data are time-consuming to analyze. • Cannot do true exploratory research.
One-to-One Interview (Semistructured)	Limited free response, built around a set of basic questions from which interviewer may branch off.	• Combines efficiency of structured interview with ability to probe and investigate interesting responses.	• Predetermined questions limit ability to probe further.
One-to-One Interview (Structured)	Predetermined questions, often with structured responses.	• Easy to administer. • Does not require as much training of interviewer.	• Less ability to probe for additional information. • Unable to clarify ambiguous responses.

Method	Description	Advantages	Disadvantages
Focus Group	Interviews with groups of people (anywhere from 4 to 12) selected because they share certain characteristics relevant to the questions of study. Interviewer encourages discussion and expression of differing opinions and viewpoints.	• Studies participants in natural, real-life atmosphere. • Allows for exploration of unanticipated issues as they are discussed. • Can increase sample size in qualitative evaluation. • Can save time and money. • Can stimulate new ideas among participants • Can gain additional information from observation of group process. • Can promote greater spontaneity and candor.	• Interviewer has less control than in a one-to-one interview. • Data are sometimes difficult to analyze. • Must consider context of comments. • Requires highly trained observer-moderators. • Cannot isolate one individual's train of thought throughout.
Phone Interview	One-to-one conversation over the phone.	• Potentially lower cost. • Anonymity may promote greater candor.	• Not everyone has a phone. • Unlisted numbers may present sampling bias. • No opportunity to observe nonverbal gestures.
Participant Observation (General)	Measures behaviors, interactions, processes by directly watching participants.	• Spontaneous quality of data that can be gathered • Can code behaviors in a natural setting such as a lunchroom or a hallway. • Can provide a check against distorted perceptions of participants. • Works well with a homogeneous group. • Good technique in combination with other methods. • Well suited for study of body language (kinesics) and study of people's use of personal space and its relationship to culture (proexmics).	• Quantification and summary of data are difficult. • Recording of behaviors and events may have to be made from memory. • Difficult to maintain objectives. • Very time-consuming and expensive. • Requires a highly trained observer.
Participant Observation (Participant as Observer)	The evaluator's role as observer is known to the group being studied and is secondary to his or her role as participant.	• Evaluator retains benefits of participant without ethical issues at stake.	• Difficult to maintain two distinct roles. • Other participants may resent observer role. • Observer's presence can change nature of interactions being observed.

(continued)

TABLE 15.2 *(continued)*

Data Collection Method	Description	Advantages	Disadvantages
Participant Observation (Observer as Participant)	Evaluator's observer role is known, and his or her primary role is to assess the program.	• Evaluator can be more focused on observation role while still maintaining connection to other participants.	• Evaluator is clearly an outsider. • Observer's presence can change nature of the interactions being observed.
Participant Observation (Complete Observer)	The evaluator has no formal role as participant; is a silent observer; may also be hidden from the group or in a completely public setting where his or her presence is unnoticed and unobtrusive.	• More objective observations possible. • Evaluator is not distracted by participant role. • Evaluator's observations do not interfere in any way with the group's process if his or her presence is hidden.	• If evaluator's presence is known, it can inhibit or change interactions of participants. • If evaluator's presence is hidden, it raises ethical questions.
Document Analysis	Unobtrusive measure using analysis of diaries, logs, letters, and formal policy statements to learn about the values and beliefs of participants in a setting or group. Can also include class reviews, letters to teachers, letters from parents, and letters from former students to learn about the processes involved in a program and what may be having an impact.	• Diaries reduce problems of memory relating to when, where, with whom. • Provides access to thoughts and feelings that may not otherwise be accessible. • Can be less threatening to participants. • Evaluator can collect and analyze data on own schedule. • Relatively inexpensive.	• Quality of data varies between subjects. • Diaries may cause change in subjects' behaviors. • Not well suited for low-literacy groups. • Can be very selective data. • No opportunities for clarification of data.
Archival Data	Analysis of archival data from a society, community, or organization. Can include birthrates, census data, contraceptive purchase data, and number of visits to hospitals for STDs.	• More accurate than self-report.	• Not all data are available or fully reported. • Difficult to match data geographically or individually.
Historical Data	Analysis of historical data is a method of discovering, from records and personal accounts, what happened in the past. It is especially useful for establishing a baseline or background of a program or of participants prior to measuring outcomes.	• Baseline data can help with interpretation of outcome findings. • Can help answer questions about why a program is or is not successful in meeting its goals. • Provides a picture of the broader context within which a program is operating.	• Can be difficult to obtain data. • Relies on data that may be incomplete, missing, or inaccurate. • May rely on participants selective memory of events and behaviors. • Difficult to verify accuracy.

SUMMARY

As we can see from Table 15.2, there are many possible data collection methods and data sources that can be used in any given research situation. We must weigh the pros and cons of both within the context of a particular research study to arrive at the best data collection method and data source. This process involves both conceptual and practical considerations. On a conceptual level, we review the phases of the research process through a "data collection and data source lens." We think about how various data collection methods and data sources fit with each phase of the research process. At the same time, considering the different data collection methods and data sources helps us to gain a fuller understanding of our problem area and research question.

There are many considerations that need to be addressed when deciding on the best data collection method(s) and data source(s) for a particular study. Factors such as worker cooperation, available resources, and consequences for the clients all influence our final choices. We can map out such decision-making criteria by using a grid system on which all criteria to be considered are listed and evaluated for each potential data collection method and data source.

Part IV contains one comprehensive chapter that

describes how to do social work research with

minority and disadvantaged groups of people.

Research With Minority and Disadvantaged Groups

Robin McKinney

16

Basic Steps in the Research Process

You Are Here

In an ever-shrinking world, awareness, understanding, and interactions with diverse cultures, races, ethnicities, and sexualities are unavoidable. The degree to which we, as professional social workers, are effective in our transactions within and across these diverse groups and individuals is inherently linked to our accurate understanding of them. Without a doubt, our profession has advanced its acknowledgment of diversity over the years. There remain additional opportunities, however, to expand our understanding of and interaction with diversity. This can be done by focusing on the commonalities of a group or groups instead of emphasizing their differences. In addition, exploration of within-group variation will enhance our awareness and understanding of individual differences in the presence of overarching cultural and ethnic influences.

How ethnic, cultural, and racial terminology is used in research has a significant impact on the generalizability of findings between and among research studies.

Because of globalization, we need to clearly define our terms rather than assuming that terminology is interchangeable. There must be recognition that many people belong to multiple groups—and membership may be, by and large, subjective rather than objective (Manuel, 2000). Disadvantages associated with membership in certain groups may foster conflicting private and public acknowledgment of membership. Thus, by carefully conceptualizing and operationalizing terminology, researchers may improve between-study comparisons and further our knowledge regarding ethnic and cultural groups if they follow the guiding principles contained in Box 16.1.

BECOMING A CULTURALLY COMPETENT RESEARCHER

To become culturally competent researchers, we must do the following: (1) We must be sure our operational definitions are meaningful and relevant, (2) we must not treat ethnic and cultural groups as homogeneous, (3) we must be careful of within- and between-group comparisons, (4) we must be aware of socioeconomic

---

BOX 16.1

Guiding Principles for Multicultural Evaluation

Inclusion in Design and Implementation

- Multicultural evaluation is not imposed on diverse communities; communities understand and support the rationale for the research and agree with the methods used to answer key evaluation questions.
- Diverse beneficiary stakeholders are actively involved in all phases of the evaluation, including problem definition, development of research questions, methods chosen, data collection, analysis and reporting.
- To the extent possible, multicultural evaluation empowers diverse communities to do self-evaluation through intentional capacity building in evaluation.

Acknowledgment/Infusion of Multiple World Views

- Evaluators in multicultural evaluations have a genuine respect for communities being studied and seek deep understanding of different cultural contexts, practices and paradigms of thinking.
- "Expert" knowledge does not exclusively reside with the evaluator; the grantee and/or community being studied is assumed to know best their issues, strengths and challenges.
- The diversity of communities studied are represented in multicultural evaluation staffing and expertise whenever possible.

Appropriate Measures of Success

- Measures of success in multicultural evaluations are discussed and/or collaboratively developed with those being evaluated.

- Data collection instruments and outcome measures are tested for multicultural validity across populations that may be non-English speaking, less literate, or from a different culture.
- Multicultural evaluation data collection methods and instruments accommodate different cultural contexts and consider alternative or nontraditional ways of collecting data.

Cultural and Systems Analysis

- Multicultural evaluations take into account how historical and current social systems, institutions and societal norms contribute to power and outcome disparities across different racial and ethnic communities.
- Multicultural evaluations incorporate and trace impacts of factors related to racial, cultural, gender, religious, economic and other differences.
- Multicultural evaluation questions take a multi-level approach to understanding root causes and impact at the individual, interpersonal, institutional, cultural, system and policy level, rather than focusing the analysis solely on individual behavior.

Relevance to Diverse Communities

- Multicultural evaluations inform community decision-making and program design.
- Findings from multicultural evaluations are co-owned with diverse communities and shared in culturally appropriate ways.

---

influences, (5) we must assess sampling strategies carefully, (6) we must know the limitations of measuring variables, (7) we must realize that it is difficult to publish a study's findings, and (8) we must be sensitive to gender, sexual orientation, and race/ethnicity issues.

We Must Be Sure Our Operational Definitions Are Meaningful and Relevant

Cultural, Racial, and Ethnic Groups

What are cultural groups, racial groups, and ethnic groups? The potential use and misuse of terminology is very problematic. In fact, in some cases, terms such as *race, ethnicity,* and *culture* have been used interchangeably. This presents a major conceptual flaw because these terms represent unique—and oftentimes mutually exclusive—categories. For example, the correct use of *race* involves physical characteristics associated with the three races: Negroid, Mongoloid, and Caucasoid. And, sometimes, the concept of race is used interchangeably with ethnicity. This is not correct. Ethnicity addresses the shared heritage, values, beliefs, and attitudes of a group. While ethnicity may overlap with race, they may be distinct entities (Zastrow & Kirst-Ashman, 2007; Manuel, 2000).

Similarly, the use of the term *culture* has produced confusion within the literature. Culture implies a set of shared beliefs, customs, and mores held by a group. However, in defining groups, the criteria may not be as clear as with racial groups. When we use the term *American culture*, what exactly are we describing? There is wide variance in what this term encompasses. In conducting social work research, this vague and nebulous term requires succinct conceptual and operational definitions to render the research study in this area useful.

The term *sexual orientation* succinctly demonstrates this dilemma. As is commonly known, whether an individual is homosexual, bisexual, or heterosexual is independent of an individual's racial origin. However, the two concepts (i.e., sexual orientation, racial origin) can overlap; that is, one is based upon physical attributes associated with race (racial origin), and the other is based upon lifestyle issues (sexual orientation). Thus, an individual can belong to two, or more, groups at the same time. For individuals belonging to multiple groups, it may be advantageous to publicly identify with one group regardless of the private and/or emotional identification with another (Laird, 2003). In the case of sexual orientation, for example, there remains de jure (legal) discrimination on the basis of sexual orientation.

In the United States, and many other jurisdictions as well, same-sex-oriented persons are not afforded legal protections as some other groups are. If individuals belong to a protected group on the basis of race, gender, or another characteristic, for example, they may more readily publicly acknowledge that membership rather than membership in the unprotected group based upon sexual orientation. The public reception of sexual orientation may alter public acknowledgment of strongly held private affiliation in the presence of sanctions associated with the private affiliation. Domination by the majority culture supersedes the minority culture, rendering the minority culture inferior (Curry, Clifford, & Hertz, 2002).

Religion

Religiosity provides an excellent example of the confusion related to the generic use of terminology in research studies when they describe a population. In the Western European culture, for example, there is an effort to separate secular and sacred doctrines. In many Western con-

stitutions, the integration of the two is expressly forbidden. In such cases, religion becomes a private matter, independent of national and civil regulation. However, in some non–Western European cultures, civil and religious doctrines are inherently wedded. The goal of religion becomes consolidation of sacred and secular ideologies, thereby rendering religion a public matter.

In some cases, there may be one recognized "state" religion where sacred and secular doctrines are interwoven. In some Arab nations, for example, the Islamic religion serves as the basis for worship and civil law. The Qur'an has specific commands regarding marriage, family roles, and division of property that are interwoven into civil law (Abudabbeh, 2005). However, the experience of religion may be a private matter if individuals do not accept the "state-sponsored" religion. Identification with other sacred doctrines may not be expressed for fear of civil reprisal. Research studies based upon "religiosity" may be flawed if there is one operational definition of religion in which it is assumed to be equivalent across cultures or that there is a unified view of religion.

Culturally Oriented Operational Definitions

With minority-related concepts there maybe no single universally accepted operational definition. For example, when defining sexual orientation, some folks have emphasized sexual activity while others have emphasized emotional bonding. Other definitions have integrated sexual activity, emotional attachment, and lifestyle issues such as lasting, emotional, and sexual connection with a partner of the same or opposite sex as the defining factor for sexual orientation (Laird, 2003). In such cases, who should develop these operational definitions? This is a controversial issue warranting further investigation.

We Must Not Treat Ethnic and Cultural Groups as Homogeneous

Race

As we have seen previously, the misuse of terminology in social work research is problematic. So, too, is the assumption that cultural, racial, ethnic, and gender-based groups are homogeneous. It has been noted that stereotyping and harmful depictions of groups can be linked to overgeneralizations made from poorly defined populations (sampling frame). In the 1970s, for example, a genre of films known as *blaxploitation* emerged as a major vehicle for the African American entrée into popular media (Robinson, 1998). For the first time, African American actors had leading roles and were no longer relegated to supporting roles as servants or other menial, demeaning characterizations.

However, in the new films, they were tough "gangstas" or police officers fighting against their crime-infested neighborhoods. The central themes of these new films were violence and the sexual prowess of African American males. While media exposure expanded, the quality of African American representation in the media was stigmatized by harsh depictions of the African American underclass—an image that may still today haunt some African American males (Ward, 2004; Constantine & Blackmon, 2002)

Historically, many research studies have treated African Americans as a racially and culturally unified group. This is an inaccurate assumption (McAdoo, 1997a). During slavery, for example, slave owners sometimes had sexual liaisons with their African female slaves. The resulting offspring were, at times, treated differently from other persons of African descent. In some cases the children looked like Caucasians, and they were able to pass as such. When they could "pass" on the basis of having a lighter skin color, they were not assigned hard labor such as working in the fields. Rather, they were domestic servants who cleaned homes, cared for children, and prepared meals for the slave owners. Hence arose the terms *field negro* and *house negro*, denoting status and privilege associated with skin color (Patterson, 1969). This differential treatment on the basis of skin color was, and remains, a source of conflict within the African American community.

The controversial Moynihan Report is a classic example of a well-intentioned effort gone awry. The Report, was a meticulous piece of research, that described the ongoing disintegration of black families, as demonstrated especially by the weakened role of men. It em-phasized the need for public policies that were designed to strengthen the economic role of black men. Its central thesis raised questions about the ability of the black family to continue its important function as socializer of future generations. Armed with erroneous data, Congress enacted legislation to attempt to make African American families more like European American families, that is, families with two-parent households (Johnson, 1997). Not surprisingly, this legislation failed to have any significant influence on the family lives of African Americans. The effects of racism, lack of employment opportunities for African American males, and other social factors influencing mate selection for African Americans were overlooked or dismissed in the Moynihan Report. Despite research to the contrary, there remains an erroneous assumption that two-parent families are superior to single-parent families (Cain & Combs-Orme, 2005).

Gender

Much can also be learned from research on women's issues. Because gender transcends race, ethnicity, and sexual orientation, factors such as race, ethnicity, and sexual orientation alter subjective experience of womanhood within and between groups. Much has been written on oppression and the ill-treatment afforded women in many cultures (Zastrow & Kirst-Ashman, 2007). However, in the United States, a European American female's experience of oppression may differ from that of a Native American female. On the basis of membership in the European American racial group, women from this group may have greater access to advantages associated with this group membership not available to those excluded on the basis of race. This within-group distinction has, in some cases, led to in-group competition and disintegration of solidarity within the group.

Moreover, women, in general, have been criticized for rearing children without a male or father figure within the home. Much of what we know about single-parent mothers pertains to single women in poverty and the poor outcomes of their children (Riciutti, 1999; Duncan, Brooks-Gunn, & Klebanov, 1994). While it is true that children who have interaction with or reside with a father figure can have a richer home life than those who do not, we must be cautious in overstating the importance of family structure alone in determining family functioning. When male presence is destructive (as in the case with a substance-abusing male), family functioning may be diminished by the presence of a male within the home (Cain & Combs-Orme, 2005).

Also, a growing number of female professionals are choosing to be single parents via adoption and/or artificial insemination. Are we to assume that these women are destined to create harmful home environments on the basis of single-parent status (Morell, 2000)? Researchers who believe that family structure alone predicts family functioning and outcomes for children may unwittingly perpetuate the myth of the "two-parent family" superiority (Anderson, 2003; Crosbie-Burnett & Lewis, 1993).

Geography

Another source of within-group variation is geographic location. Recently, we have discovered that rural-urban distinctions exist within cultural groups. Certain values, beliefs, and customs arise as a function of location rather than race, ethnicity, or gender (Brown, 2003). For example, liberal-minded individuals tend to reside in the coastal regions of the United States, while the conservative-minded tend to reside in the southern and midwestern regions. Knowledge of these distinctions has permitted some politicians to target specific regions for national political support. Political support in this case is independent of racial, ethnic, and gender affiliations.

Immigration and Cultural Research

Immigration also influences within-group behavior and customs. In studying Asian and Hispanic groups within the United States, for example, it is prudent to address acculturation—the degree to which immigrant groups have displaced customs from their "homelands" with those of the adopted region or location (Sudarkasa, 1997). Those who have newly migrated to another region may have customs and beliefs more closely aligned with their region of origin as compared with those who have resided in the same region for several generations. In addition, those born in the new region may have greater subjective connection with the new region and feel distantly related to their land of origin.

Marital practices in East Indian communities exemplify this often overlooked source of within-group variance. In some East Indian communities, arranged marriages between children remain the norm (Almeida, 2005). However, for those born in the United States, there may be a rejection of this custom in favor of the self-selection of marital partners. Thus arises potential within-group variation based upon length of exposure to novel and oftentimes conflicting cultural expectations.

Age and Cultural Research

The final area of consideration is age. Within-group variation can arise as a function of generational differences. Periodically, views held by one generation may be rejected by subsequent generations (Zastrow & Kirst-Ashman, 2007). Interracial dating and marriage were highly controversial in the early 20th century. In some regions of the United States, it was illegal to marry outside one's racial group. While there may remain some social stigma associated with interracial dating and marriage, the civil regulation of such unions has ended. Today, multiracial families and children are commonplace in certain regions of the country (Patterson, 1969).

Many factors influence within-group behaviors, customs, attitudes, and beliefs. Researchers who approach ethnicity, race, gender, and sexual orientation as homogeneous groupings do little to further our understanding of these groups. Rather, it is important to determine other factors that may supersede membership in the larger group and be the source(s) of within-group variation. As we saw in Chapter 6, when defining groups, we must precisely define the population that we are studying. Applying identifiers such as age, racial affiliation, urban/rural, first-generation, and political affiliation help to further refine the population under study (Manuel, 2000). This refinement will also assist in dismantling myths and stereotypes that emanate from the overgeneralization of minority groups as being homogeneous.

We Must Be Careful of Within- and Between-Group Comparisons

Ethnocentricism

Varying perspectives have been employed when investigating diversity and culture in social work research studies. In many instances, the "cultural ethnocentric" perspective has dominated the literature (Dodson, 1997; Johnson, 1997). Ethnocentricism is predicated on the notion that one's own culture is superior to the culture of other groups. Research findings emanating from such a perspective proceed from what is now considered a pathology basis. Simply put, groups differing from "the" dominant group are considered to be deficient or deviant. Few attempts are made to determine the origin or the meaning of the difference. The theme of majority group domination remains problematic in culturally sensitive research.

The ethnocentric approach has been criticized by a number of researchers. One important argument is that diversity and cultural experiences and expectations necessitate acceptance of varying perspectives and subjective experiences of the world (Alexander, 2006). For example, some Native Americans have not assimilated into the European culture. Instead, they have maintained their traditional tribal customs, rituals, and value systems, whereas some other Native Americans have adopted the European culture. Are both groups Native American? Also, no one outcome or finding is beneficial to all members of a certain group. Individual needs, wants, and preferences may be more important than the collective or shared needs, wants, and preferences. While understanding differences across cultures is important, recognition of causal factors pertaining to these differences is also important.

At first glance, using an ethnocentric perspective, one could assume that wage differentials between Hispanics and European Americans are a function of a deficiency in Hispanics, since they earn, as a whole, less than European Americans (Zastrow & Kirst-Ashman, 2007). However, upon further investigation, it is recog-

nized that there are wage differentials based upon race; that is, European Americans earn more than Hispanics for similar work with similar educational and professional preparation. The latter is a better explanation of the elevated poverty rates in Hispanics when compared directly with European Americans. Nonetheless, ethnocentric research may describe the predicament without exploring casual factors regarding wage differentials based upon race. Thus, ethnocentric research may adequately highlight differences between groups but not necessarily address causal factors related to the differences (Rankin & Quaine, 2000).

Cultural Equivalency and Research

Another challenge to the ethnocentric paradigm pertains to equivalency of concepts across cultures. Do concepts such as marriage, fidelity, and parenting conjure similar or differing notions across cultures and races? For example, some gays prefer "open" relationships as opposed to monogamous relationships; that is, it is permissible for partners in an open gay relationship to engage in sexual liaisons without jeopardizing the stability of the primary relationship between the partners (LaSalla, 2001). In contrast, some heterosexual couples would consider an "open" relationship as a violation of the sanctity of the primary relationship. From the ethnocentric perspective of monogamous heterosexual couples, the open relationship could be interpreted as dysfunctional on the basis of the presence of extrarelationship liaisons despite both partners agreeing to such an arrangement.

The existence of "open relationships" found in some gay couples can lead researchers with an ethnocentric bias toward monogamous heterosexual relationships to conclude that some gays have problems establishing and maintaining intimate relationships. Indeed, some researchers have found that gays in open relationships have greater satisfaction and relationship longevity than those who have more traditional, monogamous relationships (LaSalla, 2001). The functionality of open relationships could be questioned when compared with relationships in other groups. The expectation of monogamy as the preferred and superior relationship form may stigmatize individuals and bias interpretation of findings as they differ from the expected norm. Cultural and ethnic research has, at times, failed to recognize that there are no cultural equivalents for certain behaviors. It may be more useful to explore the function of differences, if and when they occur, rather than the perceived value of the identified differences.

Ecological Perspective

Out of dissatisfaction with ethnocentric perspectives emphasizing differences without an explanation of the differences, some researchers have adopted an "ecological approach." Ecological theory suggests that to understand individual and group behavior, we must also understand the context in which such behavior arises. Here, there is a greater emphasis on the subjective meaning of behavior of individuals and groups. In some cases, contextual factors may better explain individual and group behavior than do individual and group characteristics alone. In essence, ecological research has been closely aligned with qualitative research methods and their emphasis on the subjective meaning of behavior and attitudes (Bronfenbrenner & Ceci, 1994; Bronfenbrenner, 1989).

Parenting and issues related to parenting have received a great deal of attention of late. It has been well established that disciplinary strategies differ along racial, ethnic, and cultural lines (Baer, 1999). However, only recently have we explored causal factors that explain these differences. One important distinction between African American and European American parents pertains to the function of child discipline. Some African American parents believe that their children may face issues related to race in the future, and they raise children to anticipate and cope with the perceived future difficulties they may face as adults (Pinderhughes, 2000).

However, some researchers have compared African American parents with European American parents and found African American parents deficient soley on the basis of any differences found between the two groups. With further ecological exploration of parenting, it is now understood that the differences in parenting styles across cultures are more a function of the desired out-

come rather than the deficiency or superiority of either group. The false notion of dichotomous parenting has hampered advancement of meaningful explorations of parenting (Cain & Combs-Orme, 2005; Caldwell, Zimmerman, Bernat, Sellers, & Notaro, 2002).

The ecological exploration of social phenomena has enhanced our understanding of diversity. However, it is not without criticism. The primary area of concern pertains to generalization of results between and among research studies. As mentioned previously, some ecological research efforts rely upon qualitative research methodologies. Such methodologies, with their emphasis on the subjective meanings of their research participants, are difficult to replicate. Also, without normative data, it is difficult to interpret findings as valid or idiosyncratic to the participants within a given study.

Mixed Research Methodologies

Adoption of "mixed research methodologies" has offset the limitations of ethnocentric and ecological approaches. In mixed research methodologies, positivistic (more related to quantitative methods) and interpretative (more related to qualitative methods) approaches are combined. Mixed methods allow comparisons between groups using standardized measures (quantitative) and explains between- and within-group variations by gathering subjective data (qualitative) as well. Mixed methods permit robust exploration of social phenomena without negatively impacting upon any one group (Neuman, 2006). The main goal of using mixed research methodologies is to identify similarities and differences between and among groups, thereby rendering the argument of superiority moot.

The preceding discussion illustrated the importance of both qualitative and quantitative data collection methods in research studies that focus on ethnicity, race, gender, and culture. To understand behavior between and within groups, it is necessary to understand normative and subjective meaning of behavior. Normative data collection facilitates recognition and appreciation of behavioral and attitudinal differences between groups. However, qualitative data collection and its interpretation may be more useful in identifying causal factors and functionality of the observed differences. Overreliance on either method can result in the misinterpretation and overgeneralization of a study's findings.

We Must Be Aware of Socioeconomic Influences

Some researchers have argued that racial and ethnic minorities are overrepresented in the literature on poverty and negative life circumstances linked to poverty (Boyd-Franklin, 2003; McLoyd, Cauce, Takeuchi, & Wilson, 2000). Despite the alleged overrepresentation, we may inadvertently continue to pursue differences and negative outcomes associated with poverty and social economic deprivation, thereby perpetuating negative images of ethnic and racial minorities on the basis of income differentials. What is needed are research studies that address oppression and other societal ills that contribute to the lack of financial security and access to financial resources for some members of racial and ethnic-minority groups. The monolithic view of some ethnic and racial groups as poor and uneducated could have the tendency to foster stereotypes of these groups as underachieving.

Class and Caste

Class, based largely on income, is even less discussed in the literature. It is the belief here that class and caste are relevant discussion points regarding socioeconomic status. Caste in this context pertains to a relatively fixed status in life based upon a characteristic such as sexual orientation, race, and/or gender. Class is then a fluid condition based upon one's economic resources (Ogbu, 1997). Both class and caste have distinct values, beliefs, attitudes, and behaviors thought to be the function of membership in a particular class or caste. For some minority groups, for example, class change and mobility may be attainable through educational endeavors, leading to great access to financial resources. Sometimes, for some, class change can lead to their marginalization and isolation. Low-income African Americans adolescents, for example, may move into a new class by virtue of earning a college degree.

The consequences of such mobility can, at times, be destructive. Some affluent African Americans, for example, report feeling ignored by less fortunate members of their own group and by European Americans who do not readily accept entry of African Americans into the middle and upper classes. The resulting sense of isolation can have far-reaching implications. Children reared in upwardly mobile, African American families report confusion and have troubled relationships with their less affluent peers. They also believe that they are not welcomed as equals by similarly affluent European Americans. Absence of affluent African Americans as research participants in many research studies has inadvertently rendered this segment of society invisible and ignored (Tatum, 1997).

Similarly, the drive for advancement and professional achievement for which males are lauded may bring distain and hostility toward women with similar aspirations. This phenomenon is not limited to women, however. Ethnic and racial minorities report similar reception when they seek educational and occupational advancement. Women's and ethnic minorities' contributions to the work setting are oftentimes minimized or devalued when compared with those of European American males. Furthermore, women and ethnic minorities may require additional academic and professional credentials than European American males to receive similar recognition and advancement. Culturally sensitive research should focus upon factors contributing to adjustment difficulties of women and ethnic minorities rather than just the distress these groups report related to upward mobility.

Caste and Cultural Research

If class mobility is not a causal factor in the perceived social isolation of upwardly mobile African Americans, then perhaps caste is. When discussing caste, two negative categories emerge, the *discreditable* and the *discredited*. Discreditable individuals and groups are those who possess qualities that are not acceptable to members of the dominant culture (Martin & Hetrick, 1988). Women who enter male-dominated professions sometimes are "devalued" in these settings. While their presence in tolerated, women are, at times, not allowed status and access to advancement consistent with men in the same setting. Women in male-dominated professions often report double standards. Cultural and ethnic research may need to address the impact of caste on members of ethnic and minority groups.

The discredited are those whose presence is not tolerated on the basis of a particular characteristic or set of characteristics (Martin & Hetrick, 1988). For example, research on families oftentimes excludes families headed by gay/lesbian parents. This omission renders gay/lesbian households virtually invisible to those studying "normal" family processes. While researchers may not intend to ignore gays/lesbians with children, the effect is the proliferation of theories relative to heterosexual parents. Much can be learned by studying children reared in gay/lesbian households.

Developmental research, conducted on children reared in gay/lesbian-headed households, indicates that those children are more tolerant and accepting of differences in others than are children reared in traditional heterosexual households. Despite studies supporting positive outcomes for children reared in gay/lesbian households, there remains a strong public sentiment that it may be undesirable for children to be reared by gay/lesbian parents.

The fact that most states, and many foreign countries as well, preclude gays/lesbians from jointly adopting children is a testament to the widespread undesirable status of the gay/lesbian parent (Berger, 2002; Curry, Clifford, & Hertz, 2001). With a large percentage of children in foster care being racial and ethnic minorities, it makes little sense to deprive these children of stable homes on the basis of adoptive parental sexual orientation. It appears that some believe is it better to have children stagnate in foster homes rather than provide them with emotional and economic support, thereby bettering their odds for successful adulthood. Cultural research addressing discredited groups may need to address factors contributing to the discredited status of some groups and the impact of maintaining their discredited status.

Researcher Characteristics

The ethnic and socioeconomic status of researchers can also exacerbate the misconceptions of ethnic minorities, women, and gays/lesbians in scientific literature. By virtue of advanced educational achievements, researchers are often middle- to upper-class in terms of income and status. As such, the topics chosen for research may be influenced by the values and beliefs consistent with the economic and social status of the researchers themselves. Perhaps nowhere is such bias more pronounced than in research regarding family structure. Until the 1990s, much of what was understood about African American family life was relative to single-parent families headed by females. Some scholars have suggested that African Americans preferred single-parent households (Johnson, 1997).

The professional literature is ripe with descriptions of how American families function. In addition it has identified broken homes as a main cause for them not to function properly. However, upon further investigation, it was discovered that family income, not family structure, was a better predictor of family functioning—in particular, child development and academic performance. Furthermore, two-parent families in poverty have more chaotic family functioning than single-parent families that are not in poverty. Conceptualization of family structure as a conscious moral dilemma has had far-reaching negative implications for the American culture and is largely related to researcher misinterpretation of the characteristics of diverse family structures.

In sum, a variety of social and economic factors impact research studies surrounding ethnicity, race, gender, and sexual orientation. Often overlooked is the background of the researchers. Depending upon the social and economic status of the researchers, studies can be conducted to perpetuate or deconstruct erroneous research involving issues of diversity. Research participants' class and caste can also influence research studies and the interpretation of studies' findings. When disempowered groups are studied, there may be a tendency to overinterpret the data. When more affluent participants are involved, in contrast, researchers may be more cautious in how data are presented and subsequently interpreted.

We Must Assess Sampling Strategies Carefully

As we know from Chapter 6, sampling—how we select people to participate in research studies—has been and remains problematic in culturally based studies (Wendler et al., 2006; Hussain-Gambles, Atkin, & Leese, 2004). In some cases, it is very difficult to define the population to be studied, let alone draw a representative sample from the population. For example, sexual orientation remains ill defined, thereby rendering studies with this population somewhat limited. Given the limited precision with which we define groups, convenience sampling (studying those who are available) is prominent in cultural and ethnic research. Convenience samples can be problematic for a variety of reasons.

It is certain that convenience samples will be biased. For example, the literature on African Americans is focused primarily upon poor and disadvantaged individuals and families. Many poor and disadvantaged African Americans appear at public agencies to seek some type of assistance. While seeking assistance, they may participate in research studies or provide data that then are used to make inferences about all African Americans in general. However, are we certain that data collected from poor and disadvantaged African Americans are applicable to African Americans who are not similarly disadvantaged? Probably not. Nevertheless, generalizations based upon skewed samples have been made with respect to all African Americans.

A similar predicament exists in terms of sexual orientation. The emergence of AIDS and HIV has brought much attention to gays (S.E. Laird, 2003). Sexual activity and other behaviors associated with contracting and transmitting the HIV were scrutinized. Some researchers concluded that some gays have many sexual partners and use illicit substances. This may be true for some, but not all. Recent efforts by gays to gain legal recognition of same-sex unions and marriages suggest that some gays prefer long-term relationships

over casual sexual encounters. Overgeneralizations, based upon research samples of gays with AIDS and their substance-abuse behaviors, have hindered understanding of gays and their relationships.

Research studies that have focused on women's issues are also subject to sampling errors. As mentioned previously, research samples composed of single mothers in poverty have been used to make generalizations for all women. Convenience samples drawn from women living under poverty conditions are insufficient when addressing the needs of women who may not be in poverty.

It is nearly impossible to replicate a research study that uses a convenience sample. As we know, one of the benchmarks of the scientific method is its ability to replicate research studies. Research studies that use convenience samples, however, are susceptible to local and geographic influences. As we saw in Chapter 6, the extent of the generalization of their findings is compromised because of the susceptibility to regional influences.

While convenience samples may be better than no samples at all, recognition of the limitations of convenience samples must be observed when interpreting a study's findings. The dangers of overgeneralizations made from samples that are too small or inadequate can have far-reaching negative consequences for the populations being studied (Neuman, 2006). In a perfect world (and where would that be?), probabilistic sampling techniques are preferable to nonprobabilistic ones. Inadequate definitions of specific population parameters (or sampling frame) of minority and ethnic populations increase the difficulty associated with adequate sample selections. Sampling remains an area requiring further refinement if we are to improve research efforts with women and with ethnic and cultural groups.

We Must Know the Limitations of Measuring Variables

Instrument Bias

Researchers have debated measurement issues with racial/ethnic minorities for decades (Dietal, Herman,

& Kruth, 1991). Prominent among the debates has been the issue of testing the intelligence of ethnic minority children. Some researchers have argued that scores on standardized intelligence tests are underestimates of these children's actual abilities (Tucker, 1994). The primary concern pertains to the standardization of the measuring instruments themselves. It has been suggested that the samples utilized to standardized the instruments did not include enough ethnic minority children to provide the valid interpretation of the instruments' scores when they were used with ethnic minority children (Luster & McAdoo, 1994). Also, to do well on intelligence tests, ethnic minority children must demonstrate proficiency with the European American culture. On the other hand, there is no such requirement for European American children to demonstrate proficiency with ethnic minority cultures. By default, the European American culture is deemed "superior" to the ethnic minority culture.

Measurement Sensitivity

The lack of sensitivity of measuring instruments with ethnic minority populations has been well documented. However, these instruments continue to be used with populations for which they were not designed. The question of validity is apparent. As we know from Chapter 5, validity addresses the extent to which a measuring instrument achieves what it claims to measure. In many cases, we have no means to determine the validity of measuring instruments or procedures with ethnic minorities because ethnic minorities were not included in the development of instruments or procedures. Nevertheless, researchers have attempted to interpret results using culturally insensitive instruments. This undoubtedly has led to the misrepresentation and understanding of ethnic minorities.

Importance of Variables Measured

Of equal concern to the quality of measurement is whether or not the variables being measured are similarly important to all cultures and ethnic groups. The assumption that all groups value variables equally is another potential misuse of measurement and could assert the superiority of one group's values and beliefs over those of another. For example, when spirituality, a variable, is studied, it may be of greater importance for Native Americans than for other groups. For a group that values spirituality, attainment of material possessions may be of lesser importance than spirituality. We know that there are often competing values in research. Thus, we need to study those variables that are important to each group—not only important to the researcher—and attempt to further our understanding of the importance placed on their valued beliefs, attitudes, and lifestyles.

Language

Language also creates measurement issues. Some ethnic minorities lack facility with the English language, yet they are assessed with measuring instruments assuming that English is their primary language. There have been some efforts to translate measuring instruments into other languages, but few studies have been conducted regarding the equivalency of the translations from the original instruments to the newly translated ones (Neuman, 2006). The results of translated versions may be different from those with the English versions. Translators and interpreters have also been used to bridge the language barriers with ethnic minority populations. Some suggest that the presence of interpreters and translators influences participants' responses. The extent to which interpreters and translators influence the research participants' responses remains a contentious issue.

Observations

Qualitative studies using observational data collection methods are subject to misinterpretation as well. In observing nonverbal communication such as body language, for example, a researcher can easily misinterpret research participants' behaviors. In some Native American cultures, for example, direct eye contact of a subordinate with a person in authority would be deemed disrespectful. But in the European American culture, direct eye contact is indicative of respect (Neuman, 2006; Sutton & Broken Nose, 2005). In this case, the unfamiliarity with the culture could easily lead a researcher to incorrectly interpret the eye-contact behavior.

In short, measuring instruments and procedures remain problematic with research studies that focus on ethnic minorities. The validity of studies using instruments insensitive to ethnic minorities has created erroneous and conflicting reports. Refinement of the instruments (and their protocols) is necessary to improve the understanding of ethnic minorities with respect to their own values, beliefs, and behaviors.

We Must Realize That It Is Difficult to Publish a Study's Findings

Disseminating the results of ethnic and cultural research studies can be a challenging endeavor. Some of us have reported difficulties securing publication outlets for our work. This is particularly true if a study's finding challenges current widely held views of ethnic groups. Many ethnic studies have focused on the comparisons between European Americans and other ethnic groups on some pivotal outcome variable(s). Typically, European Americans have superior outcome(s) on the measure(s) of interest than other ethnic groups (Neuman, 2006; Council of National Psychological Associations for the Advancement of Ethnic Minority Interests, 2000).

Other studies have compared men with women and have indicated that men are superior to women on some outcome(s). And, in some cases, heterosexuals are compared with gays/lesbians, with heterosexuals having superior performance than gays/lesbians on targeted outcome(s). What may merely be only differences between two groups studied is sometimes inappropriately interpreted as a "deficiency" in one group. The resulting hierarchy places European American males at the top of the pyramid, with gays/lesbians at the bottom. All others are somewhere between the top and bottom depending on the variable in question.

When hopeful authors challenge the "prescribed hierarchy," there may be resistance from mainstream journals. Ethnic scholars often publish in lesser known journals. The difficulty in getting published may deter them from pursuing ethnic-oriented research (Tucker,

1994). The high rejection rate for ethnic-oriented works challenging the "status quo" provides some deterrents for publication. Also, because ethnic research is reported in second- and third-tier journals, it is much easier to dismiss a study's findings than if it were to appear in top-tier journals.

Limited circulation and exposure adversely impact the audience for second- and third-tier journals as well. Some university libraries subscribe only to top-tier journals. Thus, quality research studies published in lesser known journals may fail to reach target audiences. The notion that "specialty journals" and publications are radical and dogmatic has also been used to justify the lack of mainstream acceptance of some journals within academic circles. There may be some stigma for scholars publishing in journals identified with certain causes. Researchers may avoid publishing in gay/lesbian journals for fear of reprisal from peers. Does one have to be a gay/lesbian to publish in a gay/lesbian journal? The assumption is that researchers have some personal attachment to specialized journals, and their findings are therefore biased. Dismissal on the basis of personal bias and researcher affiliation with a specialty forum may limit mainstream exposure to quality research (Tucker, 1994).

We Must Be Sensitive to Gender, Sexual Orientation, and Race/Ethnicity Issues

Table 16.1 provides a comprehensive summary of the variety of issues related to cultural, gender, and sexual orientation research. As depicted in the table, three broad categories emerge.

Racism, heterosexism/homophobia, and sexism are believed to influence how research studies may have not accurately portrayed a group or groups. Within the broad categories, several specific themes arise. *Domination* refers to an assumption that the dominant culture is superior to nondominant ones, whereas the monolithic theme assumes that all member of a group think, act, or feel the same way regarding a specific issue. With insensitivity, researchers do not address the subtle influence of race, gender, and sexual orientation on outcomes of studies, which can cause misinterpretation of their findings. Omission and invisibility are similar in

TABLE 16.1

Examining Sexism, Racism, and Heterosexism in Research Projects

Nature of Problems*	Sexism	Racism	Heterosexism/Homophobia
Domination	Research question focuses on "problems" of women as compared with men.	Research question focuses on "problems" of minority versus dominant groups.	Research question focuses on "problems" of gays/lesbians as compared with heterosexuals.
Monolithic	All females in the sample are assumed to be homogeneous.	All members of a minority group in the sample are assumed to be homogeneous.	All gays or all lesbians in the sample are assumed to be homogeneous
Insensitivity	Gender insensitivity (Eichler, 1988); gender not included as a salient variable.	Race and ethnicity are not included as salient variables.	Sexual orientation is not included as a salient variable (Herek et al., 1993).
Omission	Variables that might covary with sex are not included, and the effects of sexism are attributed to gender only.	Factors that might covary with race are not included, and the effects of racism are attributed to race only.	Factors that might covary with sexual orientation are not included, and the effects of heterosexism are attributed to sexual orientation only
Invisibility	Androgentricity (Eichler, 1988). Participants assumed to be male.	Participants are assumed to be members of the dominant racial group, or sample of minority persons is inadequate.	Participants are assumed to be heterosexual, or samples of gays or lesbians inadequate (Herek et al., 1993).
Over-generalization	Findings based on male samples are applied to females.	Findings based on white samples are applied to minority groups.	Findings based on heterosexual samples are applied to gays and lesbians.
Double standards	Similar characteristics are interpreted differently in males and females.	Similar characteristics are interpreted differently in whites and minority groups.	Similar characteristics are interpreted differently in heterosexuals and homosexuals.
Dichotomism	Sexual dichotomism (Eichler, 1988). Gender differences are exaggerated and overlapping characteristics overlooked.	Racial differences are exaggerated and overlapping characteristics overlooked, sometimes because of confounding with racism (Engram, 1982).	Sexual orientation differences are exaggerated and overlapping characteristics overlooked.

*Definitions of several of the problem types as applies to sexism were described by Eichler (1988).

that members of minority groups are absent from (or ignored in) research. Overgeneralizations occur when small, underrepresentative samples are used to make broad statements regarding much larger populations. Stereotyping of the larger population is often the result of overgeneralization. Double standards pertain to similar behaviors being interpreted differently across groups. Typically the behavior is interpreted positively for one group and negatively for another.

And, dichotomism results when difference between groups on a particular variable is exaggerated, yielding false interpretation of findings. Racism, heterosexism/homophobia, and sexism, in conjunction with the aforementioned themes, have produced biased and exploitive research on women, gays/lesbians, and ethnic minority groups. To overcome past methodological errors, we must advance our acceptance and appreciation of diversity as a strength rather than as a threat to the "status quo." Through a strengths-based approach we can understand the importance of similarity and difference between and within groups.

TOWARD A STRENGTHS-BASED PERSPECTIVE

The previous section identified eight issues that need to be addressed when doing research studies with ethnic and minority groups. This section presents some practical strategies to deal with these issues in an attempt to produce an accurate portrayal and understanding of these groups.

Diversity Versus Stereotyping

As mentioned in the previous section, convenience sampling has led to faulty interpretations of ethnic and minority groups. Overgeneralizations made from inadequate samples have reinforced the preoccupation with apparent differences between groups rather than factors responsible for the between-group differences, if any. Perhaps the error lies in the questions asked within the research study itself.

As we know from Chapter 8, exploratory and descriptive studies are useful in identifying group variations. However, they do not facilitate the greater comprehension of why the differences exist and the function of those differences. To advance culturally sensitive research studies, the questions of how and why differences emerge require further consideration. To appreciate diversity, three types of research designs are needed: exploratory, descriptive, and explanatory.

Exploratory Studies

First and foremost, we have to ask, "Are there any differences on a particular area of interest based upon ethnicity, gender, or sexual orientation?" This is an example of an exploratory research question. In answering this question, we must be certain that we have adequately defined: the area of concern, the conceptual and operational variables, and the population under consideration.

We must also ensure that our research participants fully understand our conceptual definitions. Inaccuracies in any of these components could compromise the integrity and utility of the study's findings. Are there culturally equivalent terms? For example, when studying dating practices between gays/lesbians and heterosexuals, we will need to develop clear operational definitions for *heterosexuality, gay, lesbian,* and *dating practices*. This must be done in a manner that precisely defines the populations (heterosexual and gays/lesbians) and the outcome in question (dating practices). The assumption that these terms have a shared meaning by all of our research participants could lead to misinterpreting our data.

A simple research question could be, "Is there a relationship between sexual orientation and dating practices?" Recommendations for replication are necessary. The ability to replicate the study with another sample assures that the differences we observe, if any, are not spurious. Replication also increases the confidence with which we can discuss our study's findings. And, replication can reduce stereotyping. If the results remain constant from study to study, the findings may represent "real" differences between the groups studied.

Descriptive Studies

Once the question of *if* there are differences is explored, and there are sufficient replications to support the findings, we can proceed to ask *what* are the differences. In this phase, description of similarities and differences is appropriate. In exploratory studies, small samples and qualitative methods are typically used to collect and interpret the data. In descriptive studies, larger samples and shifts toward quantifying the differences, if any, occur. Highly structured surveys and questionnaires may be developed based upon the findings of the replicated exploratory studies.

The danger with descriptive studies is that they can overstate the importance of between-group differences without addressing functionality and the context of those differences. This can lead to a negative reception and perception of certain groups because they differ from the majority group. For example, some women choose to remain single all their lives and never have children. Some scholars have questioned the validity of this choice and have been vocal and critical of these women (Morell, 2000). Also, care should be taken to avoid causal inferences if questions regarding causality have not been incorporated into the design of the study. Suppositions regarding causality can be made, leading to additional research studies. The fact that substance abuse is often accompanied by marital distress is not indicative of marital stress causing substance abuse or vice versa. They merely co-occur. As we know, co-occurrence is not equivalent to cause and effect.

Explanatory Studies

Why groups are different (explanatory research) is worthy of exploration as well. As noted previously, ethnic and cultural studies may rely too heavily upon exploratory and descriptive designs. In explanatory studies, the aim is to identify causal links between variables and concepts. In the proposed study previously mentioned on sexual orientation and dating practices, it may be found that gays may have more secretive dating practices when compared with heterosexual men. The novice researcher may interpret this difference as a choice or preference and dismiss the social context in which dating occurs. The experienced researcher may want to determine if secretive dating is a choice or a necessity for some gays. It may be discovered that social stigma, to a greater degree than personal preference, determines dating practices for gays.

Other influences that could affect dating practices are age, occupation, race, and community status. Those gays who are at risk of persecution or great financial or social loss may be more secretive about dating than those who have no such risks (Laird, 2003). Explanatory studies can be useful in discovering social inequities that create and maintain social disadvantages for certain minority groups. Recommendations for social and political change can emerge from explanatory studies. Such studies also assist in the understanding of why some differences between groups are necessary and important, thereby furthering tolerance and acceptance of group differences. Rather than focus on the superiority of one group versus another, it is possible to recognize their strength of diversity and that difference, in some respect, maybe desirable (Alexander, 2006).

Increasing Research Participation of Ethnic and Cultural Groups

Several factors impact upon the participation of ethnic and minority groups in research projects. These include time, money, perceived importance of projects, age of participants, and comfort and accessibility to researchers and facilities (Wendler et al. 2006; Brown, 2003). As mentioned previously, convenience samples are often used in ethnic and minority group research endeavors. This is an attractive and popular option because many times the participants are already involved with social service agencies and organizations for other purposes.

While convenient, these samples may be biased and limit the diversity within and between groups. If we study only families receiving services, could we use our study's findings to address the concerns of families not receiving services? It depends on why and what services are provided. If all the families in our sample are poor and our social service program provides food, then we would not necessarily be able to address the needs of families who are not poor. They most likely would not need food if they were not poor. The needs between the two groups simply are not the same.

Respect for People's Time

Time is of great importance for those with few resources. When embarking upon research endeavors, temporal demands need to be considered. Those in distress may perceive participation in studies as a burdensome task, to say the least. To increase ethnic and minority groups' participation, our research projects may need to be brief yet thorough enough to yield meaningful results (Wendler et al., 2006). One strategy is to have short surveys and questionnaires requiring minimal time obligations by participants. Where possible, any follow-up should be conducted by telephone or other correspondence.

Respect for People's Finances

Of equal importance is the issue of cost. One assured method of decreasing ethnic and minority groups' participation is to overlook the monetary value of a potential participant's time. Those in low-income groups may fail to participate in studies if they incur incidental expenses. If data collection requires participants to find child care or miss work, they may decline to participate due to these added costs. Researchers can address this by collecting data at times scheduled by participants or by providing on-site child care to facilitate participation. Monetary incentives consistent with research projects can prove helpful in increasing ethnic and minority groups' participation in research studies (Wendler et al., 2006). This and other facilitative gestures can enhance participant-researcher relationships and yield richer findings.

Promote the Relevance of the Study

The perceived importance and relevance of studies by potential ethnic and minority research participants are possibly the most influential factors surrounding their eventual participation (Neuman, 2006). Overcoming negative stereotypes associated with racist, sexist, and homophobic perspectives of ethnic minorities remains an obstacle in ethnic minority participation in research studies. Instead of focusing on deficits related to minority status, it may be more fruitful to focus on the coping, problem-solving, and adaptive skills demonstrated by some members of ethnic and minority groups. The successful strategies utilized by oppressed and otherwise disadvantaged groups can further the appreciation and understanding of diversity.

Age of Potential Research Participant

The age of potential research participants is also important. For the elderly, it may be difficult to arrange transportation to research sites. Therefore, it may be necessary to provide transportation to increase participation. For children and adolescents, parental consent and support in participation is vital. Young children and some adolescents may rely upon parents for transportation. A good number of ethnic and minority parents may lack transportation or means to access research sites. Mileage reimbursement is useful in assisting them to participate. It may be helpful for researchers to acknowledge this as a legitimate barrier

to participation and to include transportation arrangements in the research design. Otherwise, they may sample only those who can reach sites independent of investigators.

Researcher Relationships With Participants

Perhaps the most important factor in getting stigmatized groups to participate in research studies is the relationship between the researchers and their potential research participants (Neuman, 2006). Stigmatized groups such as gays/lesbians may find it very difficult to openly participate in research projects. Oftentimes, they may conceal membership in stigmatized groups related to social and other status issues. Fear of negative consequences and reception by others is linked to secretive membership. At times, there may be illegal activity related to membership, such as a gang or other organization.

Assurances of anonymity and confidentiality may improve comfort levels for those in the stigmatized groups and researchers alike. Inclusion of members of stigmatized groups on research teams helps legitimize researchers and their projects. Inclusion of ethnic minority leaders and community members can increase their participation. When researchers have support from established members of nonmainstream communities, they may gain access to participants who otherwise would not participate.

In addition to acceptance by participants and community leaders, researchers must be mindful to address how the results will be used and what potential impact the study will have on the lives of the participants. Studies demonstrating the inferiority of certain groups when compared with other groups may not be deemed meaningful. Studies acknowledging inequalities and oppression with corresponding recommendations for remediation may be more welcomed and supported by ethnic minorities.

Use Research Methodologies That Are Culturally Sensitive

It has been well documented that some research studies that have focused on ethnic minorities and other cultural groups were plagued by numerous methodological problems (Neuman, 2006). These included, but are not limited to, overgeneralization, misuse of measuring instruments, misinterpretation of findings, and language barriers. Sampling issues appear to be at the core of methodological issues in ethnic minority research. The monolithic view of ethnic and cultural groups has been perpetuated through the use of convenience samples. The assumption that ethnic and cultural groups are homogeneous undermines expression and acceptance of cultural and ethnic diversity.

Pilot Studies

To overcome the fallacies linked to overgeneralization, we must modify our existing research strategies. Development of pilot projects may be one method of addressing the overgeneralization issue. With pilot studies, it is assumed that all findings are provisional and require further investigation. During the pilot phase, methodological issues can be addressed and refined prior to a wide-scale study. Equipped with a better understanding of what worked and what did not work, we will increase the possibility that we will avoid harmful generalizations resulting from flawed designs. Once research design issues are resolved, conducting replications may be useful in evaluating modifications and determining the necessity of further revision.

Measuring Instruments and Procedures

In addition, pilot studies allow refinement and/or development of adequate measuring instruments. As noted earlier, we sometimes may have used measuring instruments without adequate standardization and norms for cultural and ethnic minority groups. The assumption of one "universal experience" has been, and remains, problematic. Interpreting results of such instruments with ethnic and cultural groups has, at times, further disadvantaged and stigmatized these groups.

The validity of some studies remains in question. When ethnic and cultural groups' performances deviate from the expected performance, it may be a function of the instrument rather than the group. Pilot studies are excellent avenues for evaluating the appropriateness of existing instruments for use with ethnic and cultural

groups. Norms can be established on a particular instrument consistent with ethnic and cultural groups. When such steps are taken, the utility of a study's findings is enhanced (Dietal, Herman, & Kruth, 1991).

Language Issues

Language and vernacular are closely related to measurement. Errors can arise when research participants have primary languages that differ from that of the researchers studying them. Here, it may be helpful to utilize interpreters (Neuman, 2006). The use of interpreters is not without controversy, however. Some have argued that data collected through interpreters are flawed by the interpreters' subjective nuances. Researchers sensitive to potential interpreter influence have opted to translate existing instruments into other languages.

Assuming that there are cultural equivalents for measured variables, this may be useful. However, we must be certain that the original intent, content, and meaning of the instrument is not altered when the instrument is translated. Thus, translated instruments must be tested and piloted to assure alternate-form reliability and validity. Without piloting, the results may not be valid.

Indeed, the misinterpretation of a study's findings can lead to the misunderstanding of cultural and ethnic minority groups. The myth of universality has further hampered research studies with ethnic minorities. The assumption that ethnic minorities will have similar outcomes when compared with European Americans negates the impact of social treatment of ethnic minorities and, at times, competing ethnic and cultural expected outcomes. When ethnic minorities and cultural groups seek outcomes contrasting with those of European Americans, the cultural and ethnic outcomes may be deemed as inferior or deficient. This ethnocentric perspective has the possibility of alienating and marginalizing those in minority ethnic and cultural groups.

To be useful, an ecological research approach must emphasize the influence of minority status and how membership in an ethnic and/or cultural group influences social and personal outcomes (Sudarkasa, 1997).

For example, some immigrants are first-generation residents in this country. They may bring with them their values, beliefs, and customs that were associated with their regions of origin and may raise their children to adhere to those customs despite residing in a different culture. For many immigrants, affiliation with the customs of their "homelands" may be more important than adopting the customs of their "new lands."

Without a contextual framework, it is difficult, if not impossible, to interpret a study's findings. Differences which may emerge may be just that—differences. Difference may demonstrate diversity rather than deficiency. Also, a difference that is not a culturally held preference may be indicative of differential access to resources and other adverse social conditions that lead to differing outcomes. When interpreting a study's results, differentiation between preference and necessity is vital.

Divorced women are excellent examples. It has been well documented that many divorced women and their children experience some financial distress (Anderson, 2003). In some cases, the standard of living for women diminishes greatly after a divorce. Those women who relied upon spousal financial support experience divorce differently than those who were and remain financially independent.

Understand Group Differences and Individual Differences

As mentioned previously, the monolithic view of cultural and ethnic minorities and women can lead to the proliferation of erroneous assumptions regarding these groups. Monolithic views can limit our understanding and appreciation of group and individual differences. Rather, the assumption of homogeneity associated with monolithic views, at times, supersedes the preferences of individuals. When making between-group comparisons, for example, group similarities and differences can become distorted and exaggerated by monolithic views. The assumption that two groups will have differences between them related to a particular variable, for example, may lead us to overinterpret any slight differences that may be found.

Similarly, when making within-group comparisons, the monolithic approach can lead us to underestimate difference when it occurs because there was no expectation of difference. True differences may be dismissed as errors or attributed to factors other than a genuine difference. Much of the difficulty with the monolithic approach is the overreliance on quantitative methodologies (Dodson, 1997).

The monolithic approach, however, is not without merit. However, as it is typically utilized in research studies, it can lead to flawed and inaccurate interpretations of groups. If we use monolithic assumptions as a starting point rather than an ending point, we may enhance our understanding of within- and between-group similarities and differences. This is especially true with some low-income groups, who are often targeted for large-scale social interventions. When an intervention is anchored to an erroneous assumption of similarity or difference, the likelihood of the intervention's failure increases. To increase our understanding of within- and between-group issues, it may be helpful to ask three questions.

1. Are there any differences?
2. If there are differences, how do these differences arise?
3. What are the functions of these differences?

Too often, research studies have focused on some characteristic in relation to gender, ethnicity, or sexual orientation to explain the existence of difference. In some cases, the aforementioned conditions may be responsible for the differences. Religious affiliation can determine how, when, and which holidays are observed. However, in some cases, social, political, and economic factors may be responsible for the differences. Earned income has been related to gender and race, with men earning more than women, and European Americans earning more than other groups. As such, assessing differences without considering their contexts and functions may not adequately explain the existence of the differences.

In short, monolithic approaches are useful as starting points for investigating group norms. However, to fully appreciate the significance of group similarities and differences, we must embark upon quantitative and qualitative approaches to diversity. Only then can we understand both the existence and the function of difference and similarity.

Use Research Findings to Improve the Integration of Cultural and Ethnic Groups

Research studies that have utilized cultural and ethnic groups have many times focused upon the deficiencies associated with them (Johnson, 1997). As noted earlier, both social disadvantage and economic disadvantage occur with greater frequency in ethnic and cultural minority groups than in majority groups. Sometimes, the very members of cultural and ethnic groups are blamed for their social and economic disadvantage. We know that racism, sexism, and heterosexism are responsible for much of the hardship endured by members of minority and disadvantaged groups (Zastrow & Kirst-Ashman, 2007). Yet, many times our interventions remain largely concerned with changing the individuals in these groups rather than changing the social and political factors that created and maintain their socially disadvantaged status.

To be useful, we have to openly acknowledge that oppression creates social and economic disadvantage for some cultural and ethnic groups. Rather than focusing on the plight of oppressed populations, it may be useful to investigate how members of these groups successfully cope with the harsh realities of oppression. In addition, research studies can be useful for enhancing existing coping strategies and developing new ones to facilitate successful coping with members of socially and economically disadvantaged groups (Alston & Turner, 1994). By publishing studies identifying successful coping of members of socially and economically disadvantaged groups, the strategies can be shared with others. Professionals working with socially and economically disadvantaged groups may gain additional knowledge, and consumers may receive better services (Crosbie-Burnett & Lewis, 1993).

Also, recognition of the role of oppression can help challenge existing social and political structures that create, maintain, and exacerbate social and economic disadvantage for some cultural and ethnic groups. To improve the lives of the oppressed, we have

to accurately describe, investigate, and report social and political policies and structures that contribute to social and economic disadvantage in some groups while affording social and economic advantage to other groups (Zastrow & Kirst-Ashman, 2007; Tucker, 1994). A two-pronged research agenda focusing on what disadvantaged groups do to become and remain successful and how society impacts upon these groups is necessary and long overdue. Researchers cannot be content with merely finding fault with disadvantaged groups. We must also examine social policy and impact social change strategies, thereby enhancing the lives of the oppressed (McAdoo, 1997b).

TECHNOLOGY AND ITS APPLICATION TO ETHNIC AND CULTURAL RESEARCH

Technological advances have increased the availability of participants for large-scale research endeavors. The growing popularity of the Internet, personal computing products, and television-based computer services has provided most segments of the population with access to global communities. Indeed, researchers have capitalized on the global market by conducting many studies via online surveys completed by participants in their home settings. Online surveys are cost-effective and are attractive options when considering large samples and diversity (Brown, 2003). While these advances have had positive impact upon response rates and the amount of data compiled, they are not without challenges. Of particular concern is the possibility of forged and/or fictive data. Because the data are entered via computer, it is difficult to determine the identities of those responding to surveys. In the absence of proctoring, anyone could complete an online survey. This is also true of mailed surveys as well.

Historically, cultural research has been plagued by numerous methodological flaws. The potential for technological abuse via fictive data presents an interesting challenge. Do the benefits of large, varied samples warrant the risk of data fabrication? Some would argue that the benefits outweigh the potential abuses. Perhaps the key is devising verification formats that could minimize the potential for abuse while maximizing the

BOX 16.2

Some Important Things to Consider When Doing Cross-Cultural Research

- How ethnic and cultural groups are defined has been a source of confusion and, oftentimes, inaccurate representation of cultural and ethnic groups in research.

- Many factors have adversely influenced cultural research. These include racism, homophobia, and gender bias. Research with cultural groups tends to be pathology-based as a result of cultural biases toward some groups.

- The monolithic perspective, the assumption that cultural groups are homogenous, has hampered research with cultural groups. Overgeneralizations related to the monolithic perspective have led to increased stigma and stereotyping of some ethnic groups.

- Within- and between-group comparisons are difficult when examining ethnic groups. Inadequate definitions of populations render much of what we consider ethnic research, marginally useful.

- The role of socioeconomic factors and ethnic group functioning has not received sufficient attention in research. Members of ethnic and cultural groups experience more economic and social disadvantage than European Americans.

- Obtaining adequate samples remains problematic in cultural and ethnic research. Mistrust of investigators, lack of meaningful incentives for participants, fear of negative reception by researchers, and economic hardship create participant barriers in cultural and ethnic research.

- Faulty research methodology and design has further blurred perception of ethnic groups. Research methods emphasizing the strengths of ethnic groups are rare.

- The use of standardized instruments when evaluating diverse groups is also problematic. Sometimes, findings are invalid because measurement instruments have not been normed for ethnic and cultural groups.

- Publication in mainstream journals can be difficult. When research challenges widely held views of cultural groups, it may be rejected by major journals. Much of the best cultural research is published in second- and third-tier journals. This limits widespread dissemination of important works.

- Academic institutions require further refinement of cultural education. While there have been some advances, the language used to describe cultural groups and the scope of educational material require expansion and refinement.

- Ethical considerations are also important. Participant rights, such as confidentiality and informed consent, are vital if we are to increase ethnic participation in research. The introduction of Internet technology in research also requires strict adherence to ethical guidelines.

- Increasing ethnic participation in research is a continuing struggle. However, when a strengths-based approach is used, there is greater likelihood that members of ethnic groups will participate.

- Ethnic research should have, as its primary concern, an agenda of improving the social, political, emotional, and economic conditions for members of ethnic communities. To improve the lives of ethnic groups, research must address social, political, and economic factors that create and maintain disadvantage for some ethnic groups.

participation of cultural and ethnic groups in research endeavors (Brown, 2003).

Another concern is the lack of direct interaction between researchers and participants when data are collected via computer from various locations. As we saw in Chapter 11, face-to-face interaction with participants can yield more in-depth data than simple survey data (Chapter 12). When used in conjunction with more traditional approaches, Internet-administered surveys could provide additional data, thus enriching understanding of diversity. This is another area that requires addition refinement and standardization.

SUMMARY

In this chapter, we explored various issues that arise when conducting culturally sensitive research studies. As we know by now, there are many things to consider when doing cross cultural research studies. These are summarized in Box 16.2. Particular attention was given to how we conceptualize race, culture, and ethnicity in relationship to research endeavors. Also, perspectives from which we have approached social research regarding culture, race, and ethnicity were discussed. Likewise, dissemination and utilization of social research were addressed. While much research on race, ethnicity, culture, gender, and sexuality exists, there is some concern with how this research is used to enhance the quality of life for those studied. Specific suggestions and recommendations for utilization and dissemination of diversity research were also presented.

PART **V**

Data Analysis

Part V consists of two introductory data analysis

chapters: Chapter 17 discusses how to analyze

quantitative data, and Chapter 18 describes how

to do qualitative analyses.

Quantitative Data Analysis

Margaret Williams
Leslie Tutty
Richard M. Grinnell, Jr.

17

Basic Steps in the Research Process

You Are Here

After quantitative data are collected they need to be analyzed—the topic of this chapter. To be honest, a thorough understanding of quantitative statistical methods is far beyond the scope of this book. Such comprehension necessitates more in-depth study, through taking one or more statistics courses. Instead, we briefly describe a select group of basic statistical analytical methods that are used frequently in many quantitative *and* qualitative social work research studies. Our emphasis is not on providing and calculating formulas, but rather on helping the reader to understand the underlying rationale for their use.

We present two basic groups of statistical procedures. The first group is called *descriptive statistics,* which simply describe and summarize one or more variables for a sample or population. They provide information about only the group included in the study. The second group of statistical procedures is called *inferential statistics,* which determine if we can generalize findings derived from a sample to the population from which the sample was drawn. In other words, knowing what we know about a particular sample, can we infer that the rest of the population is similar to the sample that we have studied? Before we can answer this question, however, we need to know the level of measurement for each variable being analyzed. Let us now turn to a brief discussion of the four different levels of measurement that a variable can take.

LEVELS OF MEASUREMENT

The specific statistics used to analyze the data collected are dependent on the type of data that are gathered. The characteristics or qualities that describe a variable are known as its *attributes.* The variable *gender,* for example, has only two characteristics or attributes—*male* and *female*—because gender in humans is limited to male and female, and there are no other possible categories or ways of describing gender. The variable *ethnicity* has a number of possible categories: *African American, Native American, Asian, Hispanic American,* and *Caucasian* are just five examples of the many attributes of the variable ethnicity. A point to note here is that the attributes of gender differ in kind from one another—male is different from female—and, in the same way, the attributes of ethnicity are also different from one another.

Now consider the variable *income.* Income can only be described in terms of amounts of money: $15,000 per year, $288.46 per week, and so forth. In whatever terms a person's income is actually described, it still comes down to a number. Because every number has its own category, as we mentioned before, the variable income can generate as many categories as there are numbers, up to the number covering the research participant who earns the most. These numbers are all attributes of income and they are all different, but they are not different in *kind,* as male and female are, or Native American and Hispanic; they are only different in *quantity.*

In other words, the attributes of income differ in that they represent more or less of the same thing, whereas the attributes of gender differ in that they represent different kinds of things. Income will, therefore, be measured in a different way from gender. When we come to measure income, we will be looking for categories that are lower or higher than each other; when we come to measure gender, we will be looking for categories that are different in kind from each other.

Mathematically, there is not much we can do with categories that are different in kind. We cannot subtract Hispanics from Caucasians, for example, whereas we can quite easily subtract one person's annual income from another and come up with a meaningful difference. As far as mathematical computations are concerned, we are obliged to work at a lower level of complexity when we measure variables like ethnicity than when we measure variables like income. Depending on the nature of their attributes, all variables can be measured at one (or more) of four measurement levels: (1) nominal, (2) ordinal, (3) interval, or (4) ratio.

Nominal Measurement

Nominal measurement is the lowest level of measurement and is used to measure variables whose attributes are different in kind. As we have seen, gender is one variable measured at a nominal level, and ethnicity is another. *Place of birth* is a third, because "born in California," for example, is different from "born in Chicago," and we cannot add "born in California" to "born in Chicago," or subtract them or divide them, or do anything statistically interesting with them at all.

Ordinal Measurement

Ordinal measurement is a higher level of measurement than nominal and is used to measure those variables whose attributes can be rank ordered: for example, socioeconomic status, sexism, racism, client satisfaction, and the like. If we intend to measure *client satisfaction,* we must first develop a list of all the possible attributes of client satisfaction: that is, we must think of all the possible categories into which answers about client satisfaction might be placed. Some clients will be *very satisfied*—one category, at the high end of the satisfaction continuum; some will be *not at all satisfied*—a separate category, at the low end of the continuum; and others will be *generally satisfied, moderately satisfied,* or *somewhat satisfied*—three more categories, at differing points on the continuum, as illustrated in Figure 17.1.

Figure 17.1 is a 5-point scale, anchored at all 5 points with a brief description of the degree of satisfaction represented by the point. Of course, we may choose to express the anchors in different words, substituting *extremely satisfied* for *very satisfied,* or *fairly satisfied* for *generally satisfied.* We may select a 3-point scale instead, limiting the choices to *very satisfied, moderately satisfied,* and *not at all satisfied;* or we may

Figure 17.1
Scale to Measure Client Satisfaction

even use a 10-point scale if we believe that our respondents will be able to rate their satisfaction with that degree of accuracy.

Whichever particular method is selected, some sort of scale is the only measurement option available because there is no other way to categorize client satisfaction except in terms of more satisfaction or less satisfaction. As we did with nominal measurement, we might assign numbers to each of the points on the scale. If we used the 5-point scale in Figure 17.1, we might assign a 5 to *very satisfied*, a 4 to *generally satisfied*, a 3 to *moderately satisfied*, a 2 to *somewhat satisfied*, and a 1 to *not at all satisfied*.

Here, the numbers do have some mathematical meaning. Five (*very satisfied*) is in fact better than 4 (*generally satisfied*), 4 is better than 3, 3 is better than 2, and 2 is better than 1. The numbers, however, say nothing about *how much better* any category is than any other. We cannot assume that the difference in satisfaction between *very* and *generally* is the same as the difference between *generally* and *moderately*. In short, we cannot assume that the intervals between the anchored points on the scale are all the same length. Most definitely, we cannot assume that a client who rates a service at 4 (*generally satisfied*) is twice as satisfied as a client who rates the service at 2 (*somewhat satisfied*).

In fact, we cannot attempt any mathematical manipulation at all. We cannot add the numbers 1, 2, 3, 4, and 5, nor can we subtract, multiply, or divide them. As its name might suggest, all we can know from ordinal measurement is the order of the categories.

Interval Measurement

Some variables, such as client satisfaction, have attributes that can be rank ordered—from *very satisfied* to *not at all satisfied*, as we have just discussed. As we saw, however, these attributes cannot be assumed to be the same distance apart if they are placed on a scale; and, in any case, the distance they are apart has no real meaning. No one can measure the distance between *very satisfied* and *moderately satisfied*; we only know that the one is better than the other.

Conversely, for some variables, the distance, or interval, separating their attributes *does* have meaning,

and these variables can be measured at the interval level. An example in physical science is the Fahrenheit or Celsius temperature scales. The difference between 80 degrees and 90 degrees is the same as the difference between 40 and 50 degrees. Eighty degrees is not twice as hot as 40 degrees, nor does zero degrees mean no heat at all.

In social work, interval measures are most commonly used in connection with standardized measuring instruments, as presented in Chapter 5. When we look at a standardized intelligence test, for example, we can say that the difference between IQ scores of 100 and 110 is the same as the difference between IQ scores of 95 and 105, based on the scores obtained by the many thousands of people who have taken the test over the years. As with the temperature scales mentioned above, a person with an IQ score of 120 is not twice as intelligent as a person with a score of 60, nor does a score of 0 mean no intelligence at all.

Ratio Measurement

The highest level of measurement, ratio measurement, is used to measure variables whose attributes are based on a true 0 point. It may not be possible to have zero intelligence, but it is certainly possible to have zero children or zero money. Whenever a question about a particular variable might elicit the answer "none" or "never," that variable can be measured at the ratio level. The question "How many times have you seen your social worker?" might be answered "Never." Other variables commonly measured at the ratio level include length of residence in a given place, age, number of times married, number of organizations belonged to, number of antisocial behaviors, number of case reviews, number of training sessions, and number of supervisory meetings.

With a ratio level of measurement we can meaningfully interpret the comparison between two scores. A person who is 40 years of age, for example, is twice as old as a person who is 20 and half as old as a person who is 80. Children aged 2 and 5, respectively, are the same distance apart as children aged 6 and 9. Data resulting from ratio measurement can be added, subtracted, multiplied, and divided. Averages can be calculated and other statistical analyses can be performed.

It is useful to note that, although some variables *can* be measured at a higher level, they may not need to be. The variable *income,* for example, can be measured at a ratio level because it is possible to have a zero income; however, for the purposes of a particular study, we may not need to know the actual incomes of our research participants, only the range within which their incomes fall. A person who is asked how much he or she earns may be reluctant to give a figure ("mind your own business" is a perfectly legitimate response) but may not object to checking one of a number of income categories, choosing, for example, between:

1. less than $5,000 per year
2. $5,001 to $15,000 per year
3. $15,001 to $25,000 per year
4. $25,001 to $35,000 per year
5. more than $35,000 per year

Categorizing income in this way reduces the measurement from the ratio level to the ordinal level. It will now be possible to know only that a person checking Category 1 earns less than a person checking Category 2, and so on. Although we will not know *how much* less or more one person earns than another and we will not be able to perform statistical tasks such as calculating average incomes, we will be able to say, for example, that 50% of our sample falls into Category 1, 30% into Category 2, 15% into Category 3, and 5% into Category 4. If we are conducting a study to see how many people fall in each income range, this may be all we need to know.

In the same way, we might not want to know the actual ages of our sample, only the range in which they fall. For some studies, it might be enough to measure age at a nominal level—to inquire, for example, whether people were born during the depression, or whether they were born before or after 1990. In short, when studying variables that can be measured at any level, the measurement level chosen depends on what kind of data are needed, and this in turn is determined by why the data are needed, which in turn is determined by our research question.

COMPUTER APPLICATIONS

The use of computers has revolutionized the analysis of quantitative and qualitative data. Where previous generations of researchers had to rely on hand-cranked adding machines to calculate every small step in a data analysis, today we can enter raw scores into a personal computer and, with few complications, direct the computer program to execute just about any statistical test imaginable. Seconds later, the results are available. Although the process is truly miraculous, the risk is that, even though we have conducted the correct statistical analysis, we may not understand what the results mean, a factor that will almost certainly affect how we interpret the data.

We can code data from all four levels of measurement into a computer for any given data analysis. The coding of nominal data is perhaps the most complex because we have to create categories that correspond to certain possible responses for a variable. One type of nominal level data that is often gathered from research participants is *place of birth.* If, for the purposes of our study, we are interested in whether our research participants were born in either Canada or the United States, we would assign only three categories to *place of birth:*

1. Canada
2. United States
9. Other

The *other* category appears routinely at the end of lists of categories and acts as a catch-all, to cover any category that may have been omitted.

When entering nominal level data into a computer, because we do not want to enter *Canada* every time the response on the questionnaire is Canada, we may assign it the code number 1 so that all we have to enter is 1. Similarly, the United States may be assigned the number 2, and "other" may be assigned the number 9. These numbers have no mathematical meaning: We are not saying that Canada is better than the United States because it comes first, or that the United States is twice as good as Canada because the number assigned to it is twice as high. We are merely using numbers as a shorthand device to record *qualitative* differences: differences in *kind,* not in amount.

Most coding for ordinal, interval, and ratio level data is simply a matter of entering the final score, or number, from the measuring instrument that was used to measure the variable directly into the computer. If a person scored a 45 on a standardized measuring instrument, for example, the number 45 would be entered into the computer.

Although almost all data entered into computers are in the form of numbers, we need to know at what level of measurement the data exist so that we can choose the appropriate statistic(s) to describe and compare the variables. Now that we know how to measure variables at four different measurement levels, let us turn to the first group of statistics that can be helpful for the analyses of data—descriptive statistics.

DESCRIPTIVE STATISTICS

Descriptive statistics are commonly used in most quantitative and qualitative research studies. They describe and summarize a variable or variables of interest and portray how that particular variable is distributed in the sample, or population. Before looking at descriptive statistics, however, let us examine a social work research example that will be used throughout this chapter.

Thea Black is a social worker who works in a treatment foster care program. Her program focuses on children who have behavioral problems who are placed with "treatment" foster care parents. These parents are supposed to have parenting skills that will help them provide for the children with special needs who are placed with them. Thus, Thea's program also teaches parenting skills to these treatment foster care parents. She assumes that newly recruited foster parents are not likely to know much about parenting children who have behavioral problems. Therefore, she believes that they would benefit from a training program that teaches these skills to help them deal effectively with the special needs of these children who will soon be living with them.

Thea hopes that her parenting skills training program will increase the knowledge about parental management skills for the parents who attend. She assumes

that, with such training, the foster parents would be in a better position to support and provide clear limits for their foster children.

After offering the training program for several months, Thea became curious about whether the foster care providers who attended the program were, indeed, lacking in knowledge of parental management skills as she first believed (her tentative hypothesis). She was fortunate to find a valid and reliable standardized instrument that measures the knowledge of such parenting skills, the Parenting Skills Scale (PSS). Thea decided to find out for herself how much the newly recruited parents knew about parenting skills—clearly a descriptive research question.

At the beginning of one of her training sessions (before they were exposed to her skills training program), she handed out the PSS, asking the 20 individuals in attendance to complete it and also to include data about their gender, years of education, and whether they had ever participated in a parenting skills training program before. All of these three variables could be potentially extraneous ones that might influence the level of knowledge of parenting skills of the 20 participants.

For each foster care parent, Thea calculated the PSS score, called a *raw score* because it has not been sorted or analyzed in any way. The total score possible on the PSS is 100, with higher scores indicating greater knowledge of parenting skills. The scores for the PSS scale, as well as the other data collected from the 20 parents, are listed in Table 17.1.

At this point, Thea stopped to consider how she could best use the data that she had collected. She had data at three different levels of measurement. At the nominal level, Thea had collected data on gender (third column) and whether the parents had any previous parenting skills training (fourth column). Each of these variables can be categorized into two responses.

The scores on the PSS (second column) are ordinal because, although the data are sequenced from highest to lowest, the differences between units cannot be placed on an equally spaced continuum. Nevertheless, many measures in the social sciences are treated as if they are at an interval level, even though equal distances between scale points cannot be proved. This as-

TABLE 17.1

Data Collection for Four Variables From Foster Care Providers

Number	*PSS* Score	Gender	Previous Training	Years of Education
01	95	male	no	12
02	93	female	yes	15
03	93	male	no	08
04	93	female	no	12
05	90	male	yes	12
06	90	female	no	12
07	84	male	no	14
08	84	female	no	18
09	82	male	no	10
10	82	female	no	12
11	80	male	no	12
12	80	female	no	11
13	79	male	no	12
14	79	female	yes	12
15	79	female	no	16
16	79	male	no	12
17	79	female	no	11
18	72	female	no	14
19	71	male	no	15
20	55	female	yes	12

Note: PSS = Parenting Skills Scale.

sumption is important because it allows for the use of inferential statistics on such data.

Finally, the data on years of formal education (fifth column) that were collected by Thea are clearly at the ratio level of measurement, because there are equally distributed points and the scale has an absolute zero.

In sum, it seemed to Thea that the data could be used in at least two ways. First, the data collected about each variable could be described to provide a picture of the characteristics of the group of foster care parents. This would call for descriptive statistics. Secondly, she might look for relationships between some of the variables about which she had collected data, procedures that would use inferential statistics. For now let us begin by looking at how the first type of descriptive statistic can be used with Thea's data set.

Frequency Distributions

One of the simplest procedures that Thea can employ is to develop a frequency distribution of her data. Constructing a frequency distribution involves counting the occurrences of each value, or category, of the variable and ordering them in some fashion. This *absolute* or *simple frequency distribution* allows us to see quickly how certain values of a variable are distributed in our sample or population.

The *mode*, or the most commonly occurring score, can be easily spotted in a simple frequency distribution (Table 17.2). In this example, the mode is 79, a score obtained by 5 parents on the *PSS* scale. The highest and the lowest score are also quickly identifiable. The top score was 95, and the foster care parent who performed the least well on the *PSS* scored 55.

TABLE 17.2	
Frequency Distribution of Parental Skill Scores	
PSS Score	Absolute Frequency
95	1
93	3
90	2
84	2
82	2
80	2
79	5
72	1
71	1
55	1

Note: PSS = Parenting Skills Scale.

TABLE 17.3			
Cumulative Frequency and Percentage Distribution of Parental Skill Scores			
PSS Score	Absolute Frequency	Cumulative Frequency	Percentage Distribution
95	1	1	5
93	3	4	15
90	2	6	10
84	2	8	10
82	2	10	10
80	2	12	10
79	5	17	25
72	1	18	5
71	1	19	5
55	1	20	5
Total	**20**		**100**

Note: PSS = Parenting Skills Scale.

There are several other ways to present frequency data. A commonly used method that can be easily integrated into a simple frequency distribution table is the *cumulative frequency distribution,* shown in Table 17.3.

In Thea's data set, the highest *PSS* score, 95, was obtained by only one individual. The group of individuals who scored 93 or above on the *PSS* measure includes 4 foster care parents. If we want to know how many scored 80 or above, if we look at the number across from 80 in the cumulative frequency column, we can quickly see that 12 of the parents scored 80 or better.

Other tables use percentages rather than frequencies, sometimes referred to as *percentage distributions,* shown in the far right column in Table 17.3. Each of these numbers represents the percentage of participants who obtained each *PSS* value. Five individuals, for example, scored 79 on the *PSS.* Because there was a total of 20 foster care parents, 5 out of the 20, or one-quarter of the total, obtained a score of 79. This corresponds to 25% of the participants.

Finally, *grouped frequency distributions* are used to simplify a table by grouping the variable into equal-sized ranges, as is shown in Table 17.4. Both absolute and cumulative frequencies and percentages can also be displayed using this format. Each is calculated in the

same way that was previously described for nongrouped data, and the interpretation is identical.

Looking at the absolute frequency column, for example, we can quickly identify that 7 of the foster care parents scored in the 70 to 79 range on the *PSS.* By looking at the cumulative frequency column, we can see that 12 of 20 parents scored 80 or better on the *PSS.* Further, from the absolute percentage column, it is clear that 30% of the foster parents scored in the 80 to 89 range on the knowledge of parenting skills scale. Only 1 parent, or 5% of the group, had significant problems with the *PSS,* scoring in the 50 to 59 range.

Note that each of the other variables in Thea's data set could also be displayed in frequency distributions. Displaying years of education in a frequency distribution, for example, would provide a snapshot of how this variable is distributed in Thea's sample of foster care parents. With two category nominal variables, such as gender (male, female) and previous parent skills training (yes, no), however, cumulative frequencies become less meaningful and the data are better described as percentages. Thea noted that 55% of the foster care parents who attended the training workshop were women (obviously the other 45% were men) and

TABLE 17.4

Grouped Frequency Distribution of Parental Skill Scores

PSS Score	Absolute Frequency	Cumulative Frequency	Absolute Distribution
90–100	6	6	30
80–89	6	12	30
70–79	7	19	35
60–69	0	19	0
50–59	1	20	5

Note: PSS = Parenting Skills Scale.

that 20% of the parents had already received some form of parenting skills training (while a further 80% had not been trained).

Measures of Central Tendency

We can also display the values obtained on the *PSS* in the form of a graph. A *frequency polygon* is one of the simplest ways of charting frequencies. The graph in Figure 17.2 displays the data that we had previously put in Table 17.2. The *PSS* score is plotted in terms of how many of the foster care parents obtained each score.

As can be seen from Table 17.2 and Figure 17.2, most of the scores fall between 79 and 93. The one

extremely low score of 55 is also quickly noticeable in such a graph because it is so far removed from the rest of the values.

A frequency polygon allows us to make a quick analysis of how closely the distribution fits the shape of a normal curve. A *normal curve,* also known as a *bell-shaped distribution* or a *normal distribution,* is a frequency polygon in which the greatest number of responses fall in the middle of the distribution and fewer scores appear at the extremes of either very high or very low scores (Figure 17.3).

Many variables in the social sciences are assumed to be distributed in the shape of a normal curve. Low intelligence, for example, is thought to be relatively rare when compared with the number of individuals with average intelligence. On the other end of the continuum, extremely gifted individuals are also relatively uncommon.

Of course, not all variables are distributed in the shape of a normal curve. Some are such that a large number of people do very well (as Thea found in her sample of foster care parents and their parenting skill levels). Other variables, such as juggling ability, for example, would be charted showing a fairly substantial number of people performing poorly. Frequency distributions of still other variables would show that some people do well, and some people do poorly, but not many fall in between. What is important to remember about distributions is that, although all different sorts are possible, most statistical procedures assume that

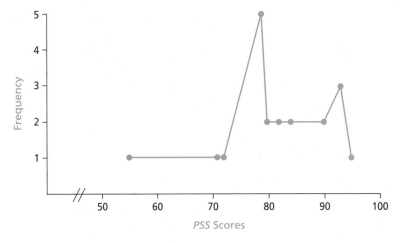

Figure 17.2
Frequency Polygon of Parental Skill Scores (From Table 17.2)

Figure 17.3
The Normal Distribution

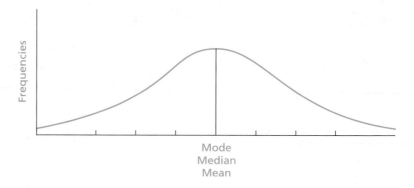

there is a normal distribution of the variable in question in the population.

When looking at how variables are distributed in samples and populations, it is common to use measures of *central tendency,* such as the mode, median, and mean, which help us to identify where the typical or the average score can be found. These measures are used so often because, not only do they provide a useful summary of the data, they also provide a common denominator for comparing groups with each other.

Mode

As mentioned earlier, the mode is the score, or value, that occurs the most often—the value with the highest frequency. In Thea's data set of parental skills scores the mode is 79, with 5 foster care parents obtaining this value. The mode is particularly useful for nominal level data. Knowing what score occurred the most often, however, provides little information about the other scores and how they are distributed in the sample or population. Because the mode is the least precise of all the measures of central tendency, the median and the mean are better descriptors of ordinal level data and above. We now turn our attention to the second measure of central tendency, the median.

Median

The median is the score that divides a distribution into two equal parts or portions. To do this, we must rank-order the scores, so at least an ordinal level of measurement is required. In Thea's sample of 20 *PSS* scores, the median would be the score above which the top 10 scores lie and below which the bottom 10 fall. As can be seen in Table 17.2, the top 10 scores finish at 82, and the bottom 10 scores start at 80. In this example, the median is 81 because it falls between 82 and 80.

Mean

The mean is the most sophisticated measure of central tendency and is useful for interval or ratio levels of measurement. It is also one of the most commonly used statistics. A mean is calculated by summing the individual values and dividing by the total number of values. The mean of Thea's sample is $95 + 93 + 93 + 93 + 90 + 90 + \ldots 72 + 71 + 55/20 = 81.95$. In this example, the obtained mean of 82 (we rounded off for the sake of clarity) is larger than the mode of 79 or the median of 81.

The mean is one of the previously mentioned statistical procedures that assumes that a variable will be distributed normally throughout a population. If this is not an accurate assumption, then the median might be a better descriptor. The mean is also best used with relatively large sample sizes where extreme scores (such as the lowest score of 55 in Thea's sample) have less influence.

Measures of Variability

Measures of central tendency provide valuable information about a set of scores, but we are also interested in knowing how the scores scatter themselves around the center. A mean does not give a sense of how widely distributed the scores may be. This is provided by measures of variability such as the range and the standard deviation.

Range

The range is simply the distance between the minimum and the maximum score. The larger the range, the greater the amount of variation of scores in the distribution. The range is calculated by subtracting the lowest score from the highest. In Thea's sample, the range is 40 (95 to 55).

The range does not necessarily assume equal intervals, so it can be used with ordinal, interval, or ratio level data. It is, like the mean, sensitive to deviant values because it depends on only the two extreme scores. We could have a group of four scores ranging from 10 to 20: 10, 14, 19, and 20, for example. The range of this sample would be 10 (20 to 10). If one additional score

that was substantially different from the first set of four scores was included, this would change the range dramatically. In this example, if a fifth score of 45 was added, the range of the sample would become 35 (45 to 10), a number that would suggest quite a different picture of the variability of the scores.

Standard Deviation

The standard deviation is the most well-used indicator of dispersion. It provides a picture of how the scores distribute themselves around the mean. Used in combination with the mean, the standard deviation provides a great deal of information about the sample or population, without our ever needing to see the raw scores. In a normal distribution of scores, described previously, there are 6 standard deviations: 3 below the mean and 3 above, as is shown in Figure 17.4.

In this perfect model, we always know that 34.13% of the scores of the sample fall within 1 standard deviation above the mean, and another 34.13%

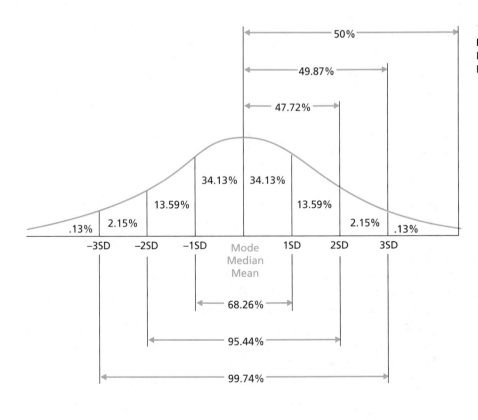

Figure 17.4
Proportions of the Normal Curve

fall within 1 standard deviation below the mean. Thus, a total of 68.26%, or about two-thirds of the scores, is between +1 standard deviation and −1 standard deviation from the mean. This leaves almost one-third of the scores to fall farther away from the mean, with 15.87% (50% to 34.13%) above +1 standard deviation, and 15.87% (50% to 34.13%) below −1 standard deviation. In total, when looking at the proportion of scores that fall between +2 and −2 standard deviations, 95.44% of scores can be expected to be found within these parameters. Furthermore, 99.74% of the scores fall between +3 standard deviations and −3 standard deviations about the mean. Thus, finding scores that fall beyond 3 standard deviations above and below the mean should be a rare occurrence.

The standard deviation has the advantage, like the mean, of taking all values into consideration in its computation. Also similar to the mean, it is used with interval or ratio levels of measurement and assumes a normal distribution of scores.

Several different samples of scores could have the same mean, but the variation around the mean, as provided by the standard deviation, could be quite different, as is shown in Figure 17.5a. Two different distributions could have unequal means and equal standard deviations, as in Figure 17.5b, or unequal means and unequal standard deviations, as in Figure 17.5c.

The standard deviation of the scores of Thea's foster care parents was calculated to be 10. Again, assuming that the variable of knowledge about parenting skills is normally distributed in the population of foster care parents, the results of the *PSS* scores from the sample of parents about whom we are making inferences can be shown in a distribution like Figure 17.6.

As can also be seen in Figure 17.6, the score that would include 2 standard deviations, 102, is beyond the total possible score of 100 on the test. This is because the distribution of the scores in Thea's sample of parents does not entirely fit a normal distribution. The one extremely low score of 55 (see Table 17.1) obtained by one foster care parent would have affected the mean, as well as the standard deviation.

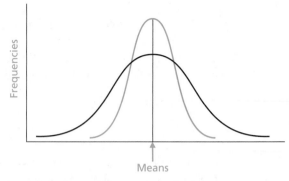

(a) Equal means, unequal standard deviations

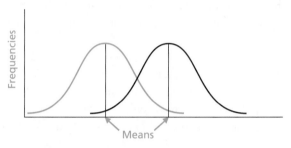

(b) Unequal means, equal standard deviations

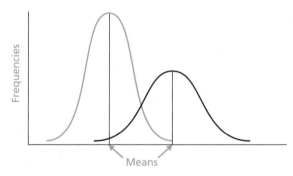

(c) Unequal means, unequal standard deviations

Figure 17.5   Variations in Normal Distributions

INFERENTIAL STATISTICS

The goal of inferential statistical tests is to rule out chance as the explanation for finding either associations between variables or differences between variables in our samples. Because we are rarely able to study an entire population, we are almost always dealing with

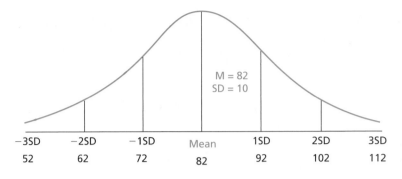

Figure 17.6
Distribution of Parental Skill Scores

samples drawn from that population. The danger is that we might make conclusions about a particular population based on a sample that is uncharacteristic of the population it is supposed to represent.

For example, perhaps the group of foster parents in Thea's training session happened to have an unusually high level of knowledge of parenting skills. If she assumed that all the rest of the foster parents that she might train in the future were as knowledgeable, she would be overestimating their knowledge, a factor that could have a negative impact on the way she conducts her training program.

To counteract the possibility that the sample is uncharacteristic of the general population, statistical tests take a conservative position as to whether we can conclude that there are relationships among the variables within our sample. The guidelines to indicate the likelihood that we have, indeed, found a relationship or difference that fits the population of interest are called *probability levels*.

The convention in most social science research is that variables are significantly associated or groups are significantly different if we are relatively certain that in 19 samples out of 20 (or 95 times out of 100) from a particular population we would find the same relationship. This corresponds to a probability level of .05, written as ($p < .05$). Probability levels are usually provided along with the results of the statistical test to demonstrate how confident we are that the results actually indicate statistically significant differences. If a probability level is greater than .05 (e.g., .06, .10), this indicates that we did not find a statistically significant difference.

Statistics That Determine Associations

There are many statistics that can determine if there is an association between two variables. We will briefly discuss two: chi-square and correlation.

Chi-Square

The *chi-square test* requires measurements of variables at only the nominal or ordinal level. Thus, it is very useful because much data in social work are gathered at these two levels of measurement. In general, the chi-square test looks at whether specific values of one variable tend to be associated with specific values of another. In short, we use it to determine if two variables are related. It cannot be used to determine if one variable *caused* another, however.

In thinking about the foster care parents who were in her training program, Thea was aware that women are more typically responsible for caring for their own children than men. Even if they are not mothers themselves, they are often in professions such as teaching and social work where they are caretakers. Thus, she wondered whether there might be a relationship between having had previous training in parenting skills and gender, such that women were less likely to have taken such training because they already felt confident in their knowledge of parenting skills. As a result, her one-tailed hypothesis was that fewer women than men would have previously taken parenting skills training courses. Thea could examine this possibility with her 20 foster care parents using a chi-square test.

TABLE 17.5			
Frequencies (and Percentages) of Gender by Previous Training (From Table 17.1)			
	Previous Training		
Gender	Yes	No	Total
Male	1 (11)	8 (89)	9
Female	3 (27)	8 (73)	11
Totals	**4 (20)**	**16 (80)**	**20**

TABLE 17.6		
Chi-Square Table for Gender by Previous Training (From Table 17.5)		
Gender	Previous Training	No Previous Training
Male	$O=1.0$	$O=8.0$
	$E=1.8$	$E=7.2$
Female	$O=3.0$	$O=8.0$
	$E=2.2$	$E=8.8$

$x^2=.8$, $df=1$, $p>.05$.
$O=$ observed frequencies (from Table 17.5).
$E=$ expected frequencies.

In terms of gender, Thea had data from the 9 (45%) men and 11 (55%) women. Of the total group, four (20%) had previous training in foster care training, and 16 (80%) had not. As shown in Table 17.5, the first task was for Thea to count the number of men and women who had had previous training and the number of men and women who had not had previous training. She put these data in one of the four categories in Table 17.5. The actual numbers are called *observed frequencies*. It is helpful to transform these raw data into percentages, making comparisons between categories much easier.

We can, however, still not tell simply by looking at the observed frequencies whether there is a statistically significant relationship between gender (male or female) and previous training (yes or no). To do this, the next step is to look at how much the observed frequencies differ from what we would expect to see if, in fact, there was no relationship. These are called *expected frequencies*. Without going through all the calculations, the chi-square table would now look like Table 17.6 for Thea's data set.

Because the probability level of the obtained chi-square value in Table 17.6 is greater than .05, Thea did not find any statistical relationship between gender and previous training in parenting skills. Thus, statistically speaking, men were no more likely than women to have received previous training in parenting skills; her research hypothesis was not supported by the data.

Correlation

Tests of correlation investigate the strength of the relationship between two variables. As with the chi-square test, correlation cannot be used to imply causation, only association. Correlation is applicable to data at the interval and ratio levels of measurement. Correlational values are always decimalized numbers, never exceeding ±1.00.

The size of the obtained correlation value indicates the strength of the association, or relationship, between the two variables. The closer a correlation is to zero, the less likely it is that a relationship exists between the two variables. The plus and minus signs indicate the direction of the relationship. Both high positive (close to +1.00) and high negative numbers (close to −1.00) signify strong relationships.

In positive correlations, though, the scores vary similarly, either increasing or decreasing. Thus, as parenting skills increase, so does self-esteem, for example. A negative correlation, in contrast, simply means that as one variable increases, the other decreases. An example would be that, as parenting skills increase, the stresses experienced by foster parents decrease.

Thea may wonder whether there is a relationship between the foster parents' years of education and score on the *PSS* knowledge test. She might reason that the more years of education completed, the more likely the parents would have greater knowledge about parenting skills. To investigate the one-tailed hypothesis that years of education are positively related to knowledge of parenting skills, Thea can correlate the *PSS* scores with each person's number of years of formal education using one of the most common correlational tests, Pearson's *r*.

The obtained correlation between *PSS* score and years of education in this example is $r = -.10$ ($p > .05$). It was in the opposite direction of what she predicted. This negative correlation is close to zero, and its probability level is greater than .05. Thus, in Thea's sample, the parents' *PSS* scores are not related to their educational levels. If the resulting correlation coefficient (r) had been positive and statistically significant ($p < .05$), it would have indicated that as the knowledge levels of the parents increased, so would their years of formal education. If the correlation coefficient had been statistically significant but negative, this would be interpreted as showing that, as years of formal education increased, knowledge scores decreased.

If a correlational analysis is misinterpreted, it is likely to be the case that the researcher implied causation rather than simply identifying an association between the two variables. If Thea were to have found a statistically significant positive correlation between knowledge and education levels and had explained this to mean that the high knowledge scores were a result of higher education levels, she would have interpreted the statistic incorrectly.

Statistics That Determine Differences

Two commonly used statistical procedures, *t* tests and analysis of variance (*ANOVA*), examine the means and variances of two or more separate groups of scores to determine if they are statistically different from one another. A *t* test is used with only two groups of scores, whereas *ANOVA* is used when there are more than two groups. Both are characterized by having a dependent variable at the interval or ratio level of measurement, and an independent, or grouping, variable at either the nominal or the ordinal level of measurement. Several assumptions underlie the use of both *t* tests and *ANOVA*.

First, it is assumed that the dependent variable is normally distributed in the population from which the samples were drawn. Second, it is assumed that the variance of the scores of the dependent variable in the different groups is roughly the same. This assumption is called *homogeneity of variance*. Third, it is assumed that the samples are randomly drawn from the population.

Nevertheless, as mentioned in Chapter 8 on group research designs, it is a common occurrence in social work that we can neither randomly select nor randomly assign individuals to either the experimental or the control group. In many cases this is because we are dealing with already preformed groups, such as Thea's foster care parents.

Breaking the assumption of randomization, however, presents a serious drawback to the interpretation of the research findings, which must be noted in the limitations and the interpretations section of the final research report. One possible difficulty that might result from nonrandomization is that the sample may be uncharacteristic of the larger population in some manner. It is important, therefore, that the results not be used inferentially; that is, the findings must not be generalized to the general population. The design of the research study is, thus, reduced to an exploratory or descriptive level, being relevant to only those individuals included in the sample.

Dependent t Test

Dependent *t* tests are used to compare two groups of scores from the same individuals. The most frequent example in social work research is looking at how a group of individuals changes from before they receive a social work intervention (pre) to afterward (post). Thea may have decided that, while knowing the knowledge levels of the foster care parents before receiving training was interesting, it did not give her any idea whether her program helped the parents to improve their skill levels. In other words, her research question became: "After being involved in the program, did parents know more about parenting skills than before they started?" Her hypothesis was that knowledge of parenting skills would improve after participation in her training program.

Thea managed to contact all of the foster care parents in the original group (Group A) 1 week after they had graduated from the program and asked them to fill out the *PSS* knowledge questionnaire once again. Because it was the same group of people who were

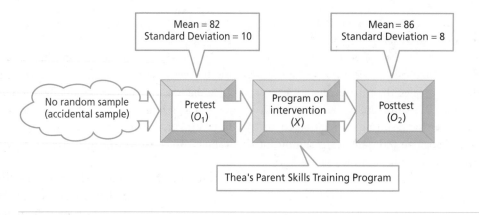

Figure 17.7   One-Group Pretest-Posttest Design Utilized in Thea's Study

responding twice to the same questionnaire, the dependent *t* test was appropriate. The research design is the one-group prettest-posttest design (Figure 17.7).

Using the same set of scores collected by Thea previously as the pretest, the mean *PSS* was 82, with a standard deviation of 10. The mean score of the foster care parents after they completed the program was calculated as 86, with a standard deviation of 8.

A *t* value of 3.9 was obtained, statistically significant at the .05 level, indicating that the levels of parenting skills significantly increased after the foster care parents participated in the skills training program.

The results suggest that the average parenting skills of this particular group of foster care parents significantly improved (from 82 to 86) after they had participated in Thea's program.

Independent t Test

Independent *t* tests are used for two groups of scores that have no relationship to each other. If Thea had *PSS* scores from one group of foster care parents and then collected more *PSS* scores from a second group of foster care parents, for example, these two groups would be considered independent, and the independent *t* test would be the appropriate statistical analysis to determine if there was a statistically significant difference between the means of the two groups' *PSS* scores.

Thea decided to compare the average *PSS* score for the first group of foster care parents (Group A) with the average *PSS* score of parents in her next training program (Group B). This would allow her to see if the first group (Group A) had been unusually talented, or conversely, were less well-versed in parenting skills than the second group (Group B). Her hypothesis was that there would be no differences in the levels of knowledge of parenting skills between the two groups.

Because Thea had *PSS* scores from two different groups of participants (Groups A and B), the correct statistical test to identify if there are any statistical differences between the means of the two groups is the independent *t* test. Let us use the same set of numbers that we previously used in the example of the dependent *t* test in this analysis, this time considering the posttest *PSS* scores as the scores of the second group of foster care parents. As can be seen from Figure 17.8, the mean *PSS* of Group A was 82 and the standard deviation was 10. Group B scored an average of 86 on the *PSS*, with a standard deviation of 8. Although the means of the two groups are 4 points apart, the standard deviations in the distribution of each are fairly large, so there is considerable overlap between the two groups. This would suggest that statistically significant differences will not be found.

The obtained *t* value to establish whether this 4-point difference (86 to 82) between the means for two groups was statistically significant was calculated to be

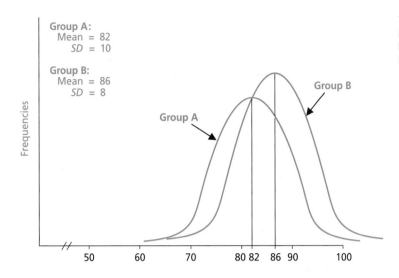

Group A:
  Mean = 82
  SD = 10

Group B:
  Mean = 86
  SD = 8

Group A

Group B

Frequencies

50   60   70   80 82 86 90   100

Figure 17.8
Frequency Distributions of *PSS* Scores
From Two Groups of Foster Care Providers

$t = 1.6$ with a $p > .05$. The two groups were, thus, not statistically different from one another, and Thea's hypothesis was supported. Note, however, that Thea's foster care parents were not randomly assigned to each group, thus breaking one of the assumptions of the t test. As discussed earlier, this is a serious limitation to the interpretation of the study's results. We must be especially careful not to generalize the findings beyond the groups included in the study.

Note that, in the previous example, when using the same set of numbers but a dependent t test, we found a statistically significant difference. This is because the dependent t test analysis is more robust than the independent t test, because having the same participant fill out the questionnaire twice, under two different conditions, controls for many extraneous variables, such as individual differences, that could negatively influence an analysis of independent samples.

One-Way Analysis of Variance

A one-way *ANOVA* is the extension of an independent t test that uses three or more groups. Each set of scores is from a different group of participants. For example, Thea might use the scores on the *PSS* test from the first group of foster care parents from whom she collected data before they participated in her program, but she might also collect data from a second and a third group

of parents before they received the training. The test for significance of an *ANOVA* is called an F test. We could actually use an *ANOVA* procedure on only two groups, and the result would be identical to the t test. Unlike the t test, however, obtaining a significant F value in a one-way *ANOVA* does not complete the analysis. Because *ANOVA* looks at differences between three or more groups, a significant F value only tells us that there is a statistically significant difference among the groups—it does not tell us between which ones.

To identify the groups, we need to do a *post hoc* test. A variety are available, such as Duncan's multiple range, Tukey's honestly significant difference test, and Newman–Keuls, and these are provided automatically by most computer statistical programs. But one caution applies: A post hoc test should be used *only after finding a significant F value,* because some of the post hoc tests are more sensitive than the F test and so might find significance when the F test does not. Generally, we should use the most conservative test first, in this case the F test.

In the example of Thea's program, let us say that she collected data on a total of three different groups of foster care parents. The first group of foster care parents scored an average of 82 on the *PSS* (standard deviation 10). The second group scored an average of 86 (standard deviation 8), while the mean score of the third group was 88 with a standard deviation of 7.

The obtained *F* value for the one-way *ANOVA* is 2.63, with a *p* >.05. Thus, we must conclude that there are no statistically significant differences between the means of the groups (i.e., 82, 86, 88). Because the *F* value was not significant, we would not conduct any post hoc tests. This finding would be interesting to Thea, because it suggests that all three groups of foster care parents started out with approximately the same knowledge levels, on the average, before receiving training.

SUMMARY

This chapter provided a beginning look at the rationale behind some of the most commonly used statistical procedures, both those that describe samples and those that analyze data from a sample in order to make inferences about the larger population.

The level of measurement of the data is key to the kind of statistical procedures that can be used. Descriptive statistics are used with data from all levels of measurement. The mode is the most appropriate mea s ure of central tendency for measurements of this level. It is only when we have data from interval and ratio levels that we can use inferential statistics—those that extend the statistical conclusions made about a sample by applying them to the larger population.

Descriptive measures of central tendency, such as the mode, median, and mean of a sample or population, all provide different kinds of information, each of which is applicable only to some levels of measurement. In addition to knowing the middle or average of a distribution of scores as provided by measures of central tendency, it is useful to know the value of the standard deviation that shows us how far away from the mean the scores are distributed. It is assumed that many variables studied in social work can be found in a normal distribution in the total population. Consequently, many descriptive and inferential statistics assume such a distribution for their tests to be valid.

Chi-square and correlation are both statistical tests that determine whether variables are associated, although they do not show causation. In contrast, *t* tests and analysis of variance (*ANOVA*) are statistical procedures for determining whether the mean and variance in one group (often a treatment group) are significantly different from those in another (often a comparison or control group).

Qualitative Data Analysis

Heather Coleman
Yvonne A. Unrau

18

Basic Steps in the Research Process

So far, this book has discussed the initial phases in designing and organizing a qualitative research study. The next important phase is to analyze the data you have collected—the topic of this chapter.

By now it should be apparent that qualitative data are typically in the form of words. According to Matthew B. Miles and Michael A. Huberman (1994), words contain both rich descriptions of situations and an understanding of their underlying meaning. Words are "fatter" than numbers and have multiple meanings, making the analysis of qualitative data quite a challenge.

We will detail the steps that one uses when doing a qualitative data analysis by referring to Leslie Tutty's (1993) qualitative research study on why women leave abusive relationships after they leave a shelter. We will use her study to illustrate how to do a qualitative data analysis in a straightforward, step-by-step process.

In contrast to quantitative studies, in which you collect your data and then analyze them using an appropriate statistical procedure, in qualitative studies it is not uncommon to conduct further and/or new interviews after you have analyzed the data collected from your previous research participants. Furthermore, the analysis is not a one-step process, but involves considering the fit of each piece of data in relationship to all the other pieces.

Thus, you must continually move back and forth between initial and later interviews, identifying units of meaning, coding, and interpreting the data as you go along. Such a blending of data collection and data analysis permits you to continue interviewing people for as long as is necessary until you truly grasp the meaning of your study's findings.

There are several ways to approach the task of analyzing interview data. One way to analyze interview data is to look for the major themes and patterns in the data, and then to break these down into subthemes and categories as such distinctions become important. In essence, you start out with a broad look at the data and then break them into smaller issues.

This chapter, in contrast, suggests that you start your analysis by looking at the smaller units. Later, you will identify similarities and differences between these to formulate how they fit together as themes and patterns. With this approach, then, you begin with the smaller units but ultimately identify the broad themes.

Both forms of analysis are appropriate, and the two can converge to yield a similar interpretation of the data. We decided to present a systematic analysis of small units in this chapter for one reason only: we believe that this approach is more likely to allow the results to emerge from the data. The process of systematically comparing and contrasting the small segments of data transcripts will keep you thinking about what each research participant is saying. There is a greater risk when you start with the broad perspective that once having identified important themes, you will apply these to segments with less attention to what is actually being said.

Nevertheless, you have the capacity to consider both broad themes and small meaning units almost simultaneously. The main point is, experiment with the best method for you, and do not be disconcerted by the existence of different approaches.

THE PURPOSE OF DATA ANALYSIS

The central purpose of analysis in qualitative studies is to sift, sort, and organize the masses of data acquired during data collection in such a way that the themes and interpretations that emerge from the process address the original research problem(s) that you have previously identified. The strength of the conclusions drawn from your study ultimately rests with the plan for *data analysis*. If you develop a research project without a systematic plan to guide the data analysis you are likely to produce biased results.

Nevertheless, as with the use of an unstructured interview where the questions unfold throughout the process instead of being fixed at the outset, the data analysis will develop differently from study to study, depending on what your research participants reveal. Rather than present a set of concrete rules and procedures about how to analyze qualitative data, we will describe the general process of such an analysis. The interaction between data collection and data analysis will allow you greater flexibility in interpreting your data and will permit greater adaptability when you draw your conclusions.

There are assumptions underlying the qualitative research approach that we discussed earlier and that are directly relevant to the analysis phase. A very brief reminder of those assumptions is therefore in order:

- The goal of your research study (and thus of the analysis) is to understand the personal realities of research participants in depth, including aspects of their experience that may be unique to them.

- You should strive to understand human experience in as much complexity as possible. This means aiming for a deep understanding of the experience and the meanings attached to it, but also of the context within which the experience is reported. The context includes the research study itself—for example, your relationship with the research participants is part of what needs to be understood when your findings are analyzed.

- Given the complexity of social behavior, there are many topics in social work that are difficult to measure in the way that you would in a quantitative study. For example, in Tutty's study, one woman was beaten to the point of needing medical treatment and another's life was threatened regularly with a gun. It would be a questionable goal to attempt to establish which woman experienced more fear. With such research topics, quantification reduces the data to trivial levels. In contrast, in a qualitative study we could describe the experience of each woman in a meaningful way. In the data analysis phase, you should organize the data in such a manner that the words, thoughts, and experiences of the research participants can be clearly communicated.

- The extent to which previous research studies and theory should influence your study is a contentious issue, and one about which you will have to exercise your own best judgment. The arguments for and against familiarity with the literature do not need repetition here, but we do need to note that the issues remain relevant. For example, you may find a literature search is relevant in the middle of the data analysis. As you are analyzing your transcripts, the concepts and relationships between the concepts that you identify may suggest more reading to discover what others have thought of similar ideas.

- In Tutty's qualitative research study, the extent to which the women expressed difficulties about going to court over custody, access to children, and divorce issues prompted her to search for literature identifying this as a problem. Similarly, when you approach the end of your analysis, a literature search comparing your conclusions with the findings of other studies is often advisable.

ESTABLISHING AN INITIAL FRAMEWORK

There are two major steps involved in establishing an initial framework for data analysis. First, you must prepare your data in transcript form, and second, you should develop a preliminary plan for proceeding with your data analysis.

Step 1: Preparing Your Data in Transcript Form

A transcript is the written record of your interviews and any other written material that you may have gathered. As the core of your analysis, it will consist of more than merely the words spoken by each person during the interview. In addition, you will include comments that reflect nonverbal interactions such as pauses, laughing, and crying.

Preparing transcripts involves five basic tasks: (1) choosing a method of analysis, (2) determining who should transcribe the data, (3) considering ethical implications in the data analysis, (4) transcribing raw data, and (5) formatting the transcript for analysis.

Task 1a: Choosing a Method of Analysis

As you know by now, the qualitative research process usually results in masses of data. A tape-recorded interview lasting an hour may result in a typed transcript of 20 to 50 pages. Interview data can be collected using a variety of aids, such as tape recordings, videotapes, and your field notes. You may gather additional data from preexisting documents, such as newspaper clip-

pings, abstracts, diaries, and letters. Throughout data collection, you will actively examine any relevant written materials and take copious notes on your reactions and ideas.

Word-processing programs have made the task of transcribing large amounts of data much simpler. Besides presenting the data in a uniform way, such programs allow you to make changes to the interviews quickly and easily, producing a clean copy of the data to analyze. Nevertheless, it is important to remember that, after being transcribed, the original sources of data must be safely stored away in case you wish to use these sources again.

Part of the reason that a qualitative analysis is considered to be a massive responsibility is that you ultimately end up comparing and sorting multiple segments from the large amount of information that you collected previously. Several methods of analysis are possible, and this choice will affect the manner in which you transcribe your data. The first option is to analyze your data using the traditional "cut-and-paste" method, whereby you use scissors to cut the typed transcript into the categories you have decided on, and to sort these into relevant groupings. Some qualitative researchers still prefer this method, remaining skeptical about the use of computers.

A second option is to use a regular word-processing program in the analysis. Even with limited knowledge of word processing, you are likely to be familiar with enough commands to sort your data into the appropriate categories for your analysis.

The third option is to use a computer program that has been developed specifically to assist in the qualitative data analysis process. Programs such as *The Ethnograph, AskSam,* NUD*IST, and ATLIS.ti are only four of the more familiar names. The software market changes so quickly that we encourage you to consult with other qualitative researchers or computer companies about what programs they recommend. Although no one has yet found a way to replace the thinking that is the critical determinant of whether an analysis truly reflects the material, a qualitative analysis has become simpler with the introduction of computer programs that are able to sort and organize segments of the text with relative ease. Computers can also assist in mechanical tasks, such as recording, editing, and formatting, leaving the analytical work to you.

One rationale for using computers in a qualitative analysis is to free up your time so you can concentrate on interpreting the meaning of the data. It is doubtful that any computer program will ever replace your role in analysis because you need to be intensely involved in the reading of the data in order to understand them.

Task 1b: Determining Who Should Transcribe the Data

The scope of a study determines the number of resources needed to complete each step and task. In smaller studies, one person is likely to have the sole responsibility for all phases, steps, and tasks from beginning to end. Although the data analysis phase may sound like a lot of work, there is a considerable benefit to you in transcribing the interviews yourself. You will become thoroughly acquainted with the content of the interviews, a critical aspect for the process of analysis, and transcribing provides an additional opportunity to review and connect with your data.

In large studies, you may have office staff support or a research assistant to help with transcribing your data. When you are fortunate enough to have the assistance of others, it is essential that all persons working on your project operate according to the same principles and procedures. It is up to you to provide some form of systematic training for them so that all data are treated according to the same decision-making rules. In this case, you might transcribe some of the interviews yourself at the beginning so that you can be clear with your assistants about what you want. For example, all transcribers should be informed about the importance of including nonverbal communication, such as laughs or pauses in conversation, in the data text. Despite the advantages of having additional assistance in transcribing, many qualitative researchers prefer to transcribe at least a portion of the data.

Task 1c: Considering Ethical Issues

As discussed in previous chapters in this book, ethics is a critical consideration throughout the research process. In the data analysis phase, confidentiality is a central ethical issue, especially when tapes and transcripts are given to research assistants or to support staff. To safeguard the research participant's confidentiality, no identifying information should be included on this material. Instead, you might assign a code name or number to identify the research participant at the beginning of the tape and then use only first names throughout the transcript. Do not use recognizable information such as birth date, social security number, or address in your code names.

In addition, you must make adequate provision to protect the privacy of your research participants by ensuring that details that might identify them are concealed. For example, if you include excerpts of interviews in your final report (see Chapter 11), a reader could potentially identify a person on the basis of his or her professional status, the names, ages, and gender of children, and the details of the unique experience. Such recognizable information should be masked in any examples.

In the study we are reporting in this chapter, the researcher had to be particularly careful to disguise identifying features because of the intensely personal nature of the situations that the women were describing. In one case, a woman's husband was being investigated as a suspect in the sexual abuse and abduction of her 10-year-old daughter. With the widespread newspaper coverage of the event, she was extremely cautious—not only did the researcher transcribe the tape herself, but no details of the family's situation were typed into the transcript or her final report.

Task 1d: Transcribing Raw Data

Transcribing data from audiotapes or videotapes is a long and arduous process, requiring careful attention and precise transcription. In most cases, transcripts should be produced *verbatim* to allow the context of the conversation to provide as much meaning as possible.

Editing and censoring during transcription can easily wipe out the context of the data and, in the process, conceal the meaning of the text.

Interviews provide context of the conversation and give flavor and texture to the data. Most important they allow you to become completely involved in the data and to view them holistically. It is, therefore, critical for you to record nonverbal interview events such as pauses, laughs, nervous moments, and excitement. You may also choose to insert notes based on your impressions or guesses about the context of the verbal comments, such as "seems reluctant to talk about what her parents thought about her going to a shelter."

Below is part of an interview from Tutty's study that includes the interviewer's notes about nonverbal communication in parentheses:

> *Interviewer:* Now that we've got the ethics forms completed, I'd like to tell you how much I appreciate you taking this time to talk about your experience after leaving Transition House.
>
> *Joy:* (enthusiastically) I have only good things to say about that place. It was so peaceful being there, you know, you don't have to worry, you don't have to be concerned. You know your children are safe and everything (pause) and you're safe. The counselors were really helpful, too. No, I really liked that place. That was my second time there (pause). Silly me (in an embarrassed tone, shifting in seat, sounds uncomfortable) I've got involved in the same relationship twice. (Sounding more solid) I decided to give it another chance because of the baby. Yeah, no . . . I liked that place a lot, it was just excellent.

Task 1e: Formatting the Transcript for Analysis

The format of the transcripts should facilitate very easy reading and allow sufficient space for writing comments. We recommend using standard-size paper and leaving the right margin as wide as 2 to 4 inches. In this way, the transcripts are structured so that you can easily write notes, codes, and line numbering alongside the corresponding text.

Numbering each line of the transcripts helps to organize data; many word-processing and computer programs that assist qualitative data analysis have a line number feature. With such numbering you can easily identify specific sections and determine where a particular word, sentence, or paragraph begins and ends, as illustrated in Box 18.1.

Step 2: Establishing a Plan for Data Analysis

Having spent a great deal of time in the initial phases of your qualitative study, you may now be feeling anxious to get the data analysis out of the way quickly. Unfortunately, given the many steps and tasks and the complex thinking involved in a qualitative analysis, you can expect to expend considerably more time and patience in processing all of the data you have collected.

One advantage of a qualitative analysis is that the researcher has freedom to consider the unique qualities of the data set. This does not mean, however, that a qualitative analysis is not systematic. It is essential that you document the rules and procedures used in your analysis in enough detail that the analytic procedures can be repeated and applied to each unit of data in the analysis.

Although a qualitative analysis is both purposeful and systematic, in the initial stages it will be guided only by *general* rules. You will develop these rules to guide you in deciding what units of data fit together in a meaningful way and how these should be coded, processes that we will discuss in more detail shortly. In subsequent stages of the analysis, you will clarify and refine the rules through reflection on and critical analysis of the situations in which each should be applied. By the end of the study, you must consistently apply the rules to all units of data.

Developing a preliminary plan for a data analysis involves two general tasks: (1) previewing the data, and (2) planning what to record in your journal.

Task 2a: Previewing the Data

Although in some cases, you will transcribe and analyze your data as you collect them, in others you will

> **BOX 18.1**
>
> 1. **Joy:** (sadly) The booze was just too much. He destroyed our house
> 2. and two apartments—things broken everywhere, holes in the wall,
> 3. doors torn off hinges, all kinds of stuff. (pause) Yeah,
> 4. after the last time at Transition House my initial thought
> 5. was to leave him and not go back, pregnant or not. And then we
> 6. got talking. (sighs) I didn't phone him for a long time
> 7. but he kept phoning me at work, trying to see me at work, you
> 8. know, saying, "I want to work this through." That was great,
> 9. I believed him, I trusted him, and then when I finally said,
> 10. "Okay, I'll come back," (pause) he kept to it for a little while.
> 11. And then he just started breaking his promises again.
> 12. And then he started sneaking drinks. It kept on increasing . . .
> 13. problems, fights kept on intensifying and that was all I could take.
> 14. The final blow was down at the fairgrounds because he wanted a
> 15. gun, a little carved gun that shoots elastics . . .
> 16.
> 17. **Interviewer:** Can you tell me more about this?

start your analysis only after you have completed data collection. Before you launch into the steps and tasks of coding and interpreting your data, it is important to become familiar with the entire data set by reading all of the available transcripts. At this point, it is important not to impose a framework or categories on the data. The meaning of the data in a qualitative analysis should emerge from the data. Thus, if categories are prematurely imposed, the interpretation of data could be colored by preconceived notions or your own particular viewpoint.

We suggest two strategies that will help you to avoid becoming focused too quickly. First, if the transcripts are extensive, do not attempt to read them all at once. When your mind starts to wander or you become impatient or start feeling uninterested, it is time to pause. Remember that a qualitative analysis takes time. If you want to produce a quality product, you must respect the process. To a large extent, the process cannot be forced.

Second, refrain from always reading notes and transcripts from the beginning of a document. When

you begin reading, you are usually in peak form. If you always confine this energy to the first section of your data, you are more likely to exclude or overlook valuable data from later sections. Reading the last third of the interview before the first portion is one technique that may help you to shed new light on each interview.

Task 2b: Using a Journal During Data Analysis

We recommend that you use a journal to record the process of the qualitative research study and your reactions to the emerging issues in your analysis. Yvonna Lincoln and Egon Guba (1985) suggest that a qualitative journal should include two key components: (1) notes on the method used in your study, and (2) notes on issues of credibility and audit trail notes (to be described later). Each component should include a section on what decisions were made during the analysis and the rationale for these.

The category scheme that you will develop will be a critical segment of the methodology section of your journal. When you unitize and initially categorize (code) your data, you will come up with numerous questions and ideas about the data. Making notes in your journal about these questions or comments with respect to identifying meaning units and categories is referred to as writing *analytical memos*. It is a useful strategy for organizing your thoughts. Although the format used for analytical memos tends to reflect the individual style of the researcher, Anselm Strauss and Juliet Corbin (1998) offer some hints about how to write useful analytical memos:

- Record the date of the memo.
- Include any references or important sources.
- Label memos with headings that describe the primary category or concept being earmarked.
- Identify the particular code(s) to which the theoretical note pertains.
- Use diagrams in memos to explain ideas.
- Keep multiple copies of all memos.
- Do not restrict the content of memos; allow for a flow of ideas.
- Note when you think that a category has been sufficiently defined.
- Keep analytical memos about your own thinking process to assist you in moving the analysis from description to interpretation.

In part, the process of writing analytical memos is what some authors refer to as leaving an *audit trail*. An audit trail is used when an outside person is called in to review what you have done, to ensure that there were no serious flaws in the conduct of your study. This individual may retrace your steps starting from collection of the raw data, carefully examining every decision you have made in the study. Because the work you do should be open to scrutiny by others, precise journal notes about your methodology are crucial.

Your journal will also help to ensure that the rules guiding the definition of categories and the assignment of units of data to those categories become universal and are consistently applied. Keeping notes about the coding process will ensure greater consistency of coding to protect rules from any whims or impulsive decisions.

You will also record the code acronym (the shortened version of the category name) that is assigned to each category, as well as the characteristics of the meaning unit that qualify it to be categorized in that particular way. Later, you may want to revise the category scheme, a point at which you again clearly record the reasons for your decision and how the characteristics of the data have changed. This process, then, will track the "evolution" of your data analysis.

As presented in Chapters 10 and 11, we recommend using a journal to record your notes about what transpired in your interviews and how you obtained your research participants. You were asked to take special note of your honest reactions to the people that you interviewed, as these comments will eventually be used to assess the credibility of the research participants in your study. If, for example, you have overrelied on one informant or developed a bias against one subset of interviewees, then your conclusions will be one-sided. Such biases will, hopefully, become more evident as you read your journal entries.

It is also essential to record other efforts at establishing the credibility of your study, such as asking others to unitize and categorize your data to provide evidence that your categorization scheme is useful and appropriate. This process, called *triangulation*, will be described in more detail later. Finally, your journal should contain a section that covers your personal reactions to your study, not unlike a personal diary. Following is an example of a comment from Tutty's journal that she used in her qualitative research study. The example shows an analytical memo that speaks to issues of both credibility and reactions to the study as a whole:

May 16, 2008. I can't help but feel that the interview with Joy went extremely well. She was surprisingly open about her story and seemed very concerned that other women who might be living with men such as her ex-partner know what options they have. She is really quite remarkable to have set up a new home with two small children, and so little income. I think her narrative really adds to the interviews we've conducted so far because she is doing so well under difficult circumstances.

FIRST- AND SECOND-LEVEL CODING

The previous two steps deal with establishing an initial framework for doing a qualitative data analysis. Steps 3 and 4 deal with first- and second-level coding.

Step 3: First-Level Coding

Once you have transcribed your data, and reviewed it in a preliminary way, you can launch into first-level coding: a combination of identifying meaning units, fitting them into categories, and assigning codes to the categories. In this section we will describe each of these tasks individually, but, once again, in practice you may find that they overlap. For example, you may be thinking about how to categorize certain meaning units as you are identifying these units in the transcripts (and will use analytical memos to make sure that you do not forget these initial ideas).

Coding begins at the point when you first notice similarities and differences between data segments or meaning units. You may also see patterns in the data that you will mentally label. As you read new data and reread old data, you will conceptually connect similar meaning units together as categories. You will use a procedure called the *constant comparison* method: Meaning units of data with the same characteristics are considered as fitting within the same category and are given the same code; meaning units that are different in important ways are put into a different category and given another code.

Coding proceeds in stages, and there are several steps involved in coding at various stages of the analysis. First-level coding is predominantly concrete, and involves identifying properties of data that are clearly evident in the text. Such content is found without combing the data for underlying meaning. Second-level coding (Step 4) is more abstract and involves interpreting the meaning underlying the more obvious ideas portrayed in the data.

By the end of the analysis phase, you will have worked with both concrete and abstract content. You will start with concrete coding at the beginning of the analysis, but work toward understanding the deeper, abstract content in the final stages of analysis. Remember, qualitative research is more than description—it takes a natural interest in the meaning underlying the words.

In summary, the primary task of coding is to identify and label relevant categories of data, first concretely (in first-level coding) and then abstractly (in second-level coding). First-level coding is a lengthy and detailed process that involves five tasks: (1) identifying meaning units, (2) assigning category names to groups of similar meaning units, (3) assigning codes to categories, (4) refining and reorganizing codings, and (5) deciding when to stop. Once again, the tasks sometimes overlap one another, and they should be viewed as absolutely essential in the first-level coding process.

Task 3a: Identifying Meaning Units

Once you have previewed the data, they need to be organized into a manageable format. To do this, you first identify the important experiences or ideas in your data. This is the process of classifying and collapsing the data into *meaning units*. You make decisions about what pieces of data fit together; ultimately, these are the segments that will be categorized, coded, sorted, and then form the patterns that will be used to summarize your interpretation of the data.

Units are the segments (or chunks) of information that are the building blocks of a classification scheme. A unit can consist of a single word, a partial or complete sentence, a paragraph, or more. It is a piece of the transcript that you consider to be meaningful by itself. At this point you are not analyzing what the data mean, you are simply identifying the important bits of what the research participants are saying.

What constitutes a meaning unit may be clear to outside readers, but this will not necessarily be the case. The developers of *The Ethnograph* computer program, for example, studied how a group of students analyzed an identical data file. While some students identified very small meaning units of 5 to 50 lines of transcript, others identified larger units, analyzing segments of between 50 and 200 lines.

Further, the category labels that the students attached to the meaning units varied considerably. Some students labeled categories in a concrete and detailed manner, but others were more impressionistic and abstract. Some students identified categories similar to those of other students, but still others identified categories that were unique. This example simply illustrates the fact that different individuals will identify and label the same meaning units differently within the same data set. The lesson is that there is no inherent "right" or "wrong" way to organize qualitative data. How one chooses to reduce data into a manageable form is an individual endeavor.

In the segment of the data set previously presented, the meaning units shown in Box 18.2 were identified (the first underlined, the next in italics) early in the first-level coding process.

In the journal, the researcher recorded that the first meaning unit related to her ex-partner's drinking (line 1), and the second is about his past destructive behavior (lines 1–3).

The third meaning unit (lines 3–10) is rather long and may need to be broken down into more than one category later on. It describes the process of reuniting with a partner after a previous shelter stay. The final meaning unit (lines 11–15) documents the experience that prompted the final shelter stay. The topics in the meaning units may become categories if the content is repeated later on in this interview or if other interviewees identify similar issues.

The first run-through to identify meaning units will always be somewhat tentative and subject to change. If you are not sure whether to break a large meaning unit into smaller ones, it may be preferable to leave it as a whole. You can always break down meaning units more finely later on in your study. This process is somewhat easier than combining units later, especially once second-level coding (Step 4) begins.

BOX 18.2

1. **Joy:** (sadly) <u>The booze was just too much</u>. *He destroyed our house*
2. *and two apartments—things broken everywhere, holes in the wall,*
3. *doors torn off hinges, all kinds of stuff. (pause)* <u>Yeah</u>,
4. <u>after the last time at Transition House my initial thought</u>
5. <u>was to leave him and not go back</u>, <u>pregnant or not</u>. <u>And then we</u>
6. <u>got talking.</u> (sighs) <u>I didn't phone him for a long time</u>
7. <u>but he kept phoning me at work</u>, <u>trying to see me at work</u>, <u>you</u>
8. <u>know</u>, <u>saying</u> "<u>I want to work this through</u>." <u>That was great,</u>
9. <u>I believed him, I trusted him, and then when I finally said,</u>
10. "<u>Okay, I'll come back,</u>" (pause) <u>he kept to it for a little while</u>.
11. *And then he just started breaking his promises again.*
12. *And then he started sneaking drinks. It kept on increasing . . .*
13. *problems, fights kept on intensifying and that was all I could take.*
14. *The final blow was down at the fairgrounds because he wanted a*
15. *gun, a little carved gun that shoots elastics . . .*
16.
17. **Interviewer:** Can you tell me more about this.

Task 3b: Identifying Categories

Once you have identified the meaning units in the transcripts, your next task is to consider which of them fit together into categories. Especially in first-level coding, the categories you identify should logically and simply relate to the data they represent. The categories may emerge from the questions you ask, or they may simply reflect the critical events that you identify in your research participants' stories.

As mentioned previously, though, while the rationale behind the categories does not have to be explained at the beginning, you must clearly explain your grounds as the data analysis proceeds and becomes more complex. The categories and their respective codes must all be defined by the end of the study.

Earlier, we introduced the method of constant comparison, which is the major technique guiding the categorization process. Constant comparison begins after the complete set of data has been examined and meaning units have been identified. Each unit is classified as either similar to or different from the others. If the first two meaning units possess somewhat similar qualities, they are tentatively placed in the same category and classified by the same code created for that category.

Remember to make notes about the characteristics of the meaning units that make them similar, and record these observations in your journal. If the first two meaning units are not similar in these identified qualities, a separate category and a new code are produced for the second one. Again, the information about what defines the second category should be recorded because the process will solidify the rules governing when to include specific meaning units in that category.

You simply repeat these steps to examine the remaining meaning units. For example, the third meaning unit is examined for similarities and differences with the first and the second category. If it differs, a third category and code are created. Constant comparison continues until all meaning units are classified into either previously described or new categories.

To illustrate how to create categories from meaning units, we will use the previous excerpt. The first meaning unit identified, "the booze was just too much" (line 1), fit with a number of Joy's other comments, as well as comments from other research participants relating to their ex-partner's abuse of substances. The category was hence labeled "Partner's Substance Abuse." The rule was that past and present substance abuse issues of the ex-partner would be included under this category.

However, issues related to any substance abuse by the interviewee herself were placed in a different category: "Research Participant's Substance Abuse." Thus, each meaning unit is considered in comparison to other similar meaning units, and the category is a way of identifying important similarities within and across individuals.

The number of categories will expand every time you identify meaning units that are dissimilar in important ways from those you have already categorized. However, you also need to attempt to keep the number of categories within manageable limits. At the beginning of constant comparison, new categories will be created quickly, and then more slowly after you have analyzed between four and five dozen data segments. Sometimes, meaning units cannot be clearly placed into any of the categories developed in the analysis and fall into the category of "miscellaneous."

These misfits should be set aside in a separate "pile" with other units that are difficult to classify. Make special note of why they do not fit. At some point, such unclassifiable meaning units may begin to resemble one another and can be placed in a category of their own. After reviewing all the categories, inspect the miscellaneous pile to decide what units might fit together in a new category or a new set of categories.

If you find that you are throwing data into the miscellaneous pile too often, you may be fatigued. This would be a good time to pause and return to the analysis when you are refreshed. The use of a miscellaneous pile will prevent you from throwing out what seem to be irrelevant meaning units. Such tossing is a risky move, because in some situations you may decide that your categorization scheme needs major revision and that you must start the whole process again from scratch. We recommend that miscellaneous units make up less than 10 percent of the total data set. More than that suggests that you have a problem with your original categorization scheme.

Occasionally, you will need to stop and reaffirm the rules that qualify the meaning units to be placed within each category. These decisions need to be justified, a factor that will later serve as the basis for tests of whether others who use your rules identify similar meaning units and categories.

The categories for your study will develop and change over time. It is natural for some categories to change or to become irrelevant (decay) in the later stages of analysis. In such instances, new categories can be created and old categories can be either revised, merged with others, or eliminated completely.

The number of categories in a study depends on the breadth and the depth you seek in your analysis of the data. Some topics require very detailed and precise analyses, with nearly every line of the transcript coded into different categories. For less detailed work, it is possible to code larger segments, for example, every 50 or even every 200 lines.

The complexity of the categorization also needs to be considered. One meaning unit may, in fact, fit into more than one category. It is also possible to code meaning units that overlap with one another. In another case called a nested code, smaller categories fit within larger, more inclusive ones. Furthermore, there can also be a complex combination of multiple, nested, and overlapping categories.

For example, in the interview with Joy, the large meaning unit talking about the couple's reconciliation (lines 3–10) could also be considered as fitting into two smaller categories, one labeled "Partner's Past Reconciliation Attempts" (lines 5–10) and another called "Reasons for Past Breakdown of Reconciliation" (lines 11–13). These may overlap with the category "Partner's Substance Abuse" (lines 1 and 12) so that substance abuse issues will sometimes be coded into the category of "Reasons for Past Breakdown of Reconciliation."

The categories must be clear enough to simplify the data and prevent the generation of unnecessary backtracking and recoding. The category labels must also reflect the substance of the meaning units. For example, in Tutty's study, many women reported having low self-esteem, which they found interfered in their ability to feel successful or to live independently from their abusive partner.

In the first round of categorization, meaning units reflecting the self-esteem issue were categorized as "Self-concept: Valueless." These words did not adequately reflect the meaning of the segments in the interviews, as not one interviewee reported that she was valueless, but many noted that they had low self-esteem. The relabeled category "Low Self-esteem" more accurately reflected what the data meant.

Task 3c: Assigning Codes to Categories

Codes are simply a form of the category name that becomes a shorthand method of identifying the categories. Codes typically take the form of strings of letters, numbers, and/or symbols. Codes are usually displayed in the margins (often the right margin) of the transcribed text.

Codes help you to navigate through many pages of text data in an efficient way. For example, one obvious issue is that some meaning units are about the woman herself, some about her partner, and some about her children. Thus, W was used as the first letter of the code name if related to the woman, P if related to her partner, and C if related to her children. A second important distinction was whether issues were past (P_a), current (C), or anticipated in the future (F).

Finally, in a list of categories about the problems encountered, the substance abuse category was labeled SA. Thus, the code that was written in the margin next to the meaning unit "The booze was just too much" was P-P_a-SA, standing for the partner's past substance abuse. As the data analysis becomes more complex, the codes become longer.

In the initial stages of second-level coding, the codes in the margins will be used to collect together all the meaning units from all of the interviews that fit within a particular category.

Task 3d: Refining and Reorganizing Coding

Before moving on from first-level coding, we suggest that you make a final sweep through the data to ensure that your analysis reflects what your research participants have said. Pause and reflect upon your analysis thus far, considering the logic of the ideas that form the basis of the rules for each category. Rather than discovering at the end of your analysis that you have made an error in judgment, now is the most appropriate time to reexamine your thinking.

You may, for example, be confused about why you created some categories, or feel uncertain about the rules of categorization for others. You may find that some categories are too complex and may be effectively split into several new categories. This is the time to clarify and confirm what qualifies each meaning unit to fit within a particular category.

You should review all the categories to see how the units "fit" with each. You can now tighten your rules to ensure that there is no vagueness about how any meaning unit is categorized. If you have conceptualized the meaning units accurately, the categories will "hang together" internally and be easily distinguished from other categories.

You might find that some categories are not completely developed or are only partially defined. Similarly, you might discover that categories that you had originally thought would emerge from the data are completely missing. You are most likely to discover missing categories while you are thinking about the underlying logic of your categorization scheme. In such a case, make a note of the missing categories, as well as of incomplete or otherwise unsatisfactory categories. You may, in fact, wish to conduct additional interviews to address any of these gaps.

This would be a good time to ask a colleague to code one or two of your interviews using the rules that you have devised. This process is a check to ensure that the categories and the rules that define them make sense. If your colleague codes meaning units in a significantly different way than yours, your categorization scheme may need to be substantially revised.

Task 3e: Deciding When to Stop

What are the indicators that signal that this may be an appropriate time to stop first-level coding? The most common indicator is that when you interview new research participants the meaning units fit easily into your current categorization scheme and no new categories emerge. This process is called "category saturation."

In essence, the data become repetitive and further analysis only confirms the ground that you have already covered. This is a good point in time to perform one final review of all the categories to ensure the thoroughness of your analysis. We will now turn our attention away from first-level coding and address the next step in the data analysis process—second-level coding.

Step 4: Second-Level Coding

When completed thoroughly, the tasks of initial coding (Step 3) produce a solid foundation from which to further refine the data analysis process. By this point, your data have been reduced and transformed in several ways. Sections from the transcribed interviews have been selected and identified as meaning units. The units have been subsequently classified as fitting into categories, with an identifying code attached.

You have read through your entire set of transcripts, coding the appropriate meaning units with the category code name. As a part of this process you have also reviewed the rules that you have developed to ensure that you can clearly explain what types of information are included in each category.

As noted earlier, second-level coding is more abstract, and involves interpreting what the first-level categories mean. Reporting on abstract content demands that you produce detailed examples of the transcript to back up each interpretation. Bruce L. Berg (2007) suggests that you need at least three independent examples to support each of these interpretations.

In second-level coding, you will pull together or "retrieve" the meaning units that fit within each category, either by computer or by cutting and pasting. This process allows you to examine the units in the categories away from any association with the person who originally stated the idea. The focus of the analysis thus shifts from the context of the interviewee to the context of the categories. In so doing, the analysis has become one level more abstract, because it is one step further removed from the original interviews.

The major task in second-level coding is to identify similarities and differences between the categories in an attempt to detect relationships. In sum, the next step of coding involves two tasks: (1) retrieving meaning units into categories, and (2) comparing categories.

Task 4a: Retrieving Meaning Units Into Categories

Earlier you identified distinct units of data and grouped and coded these based on similarities and differences. During second-level coding, you will retrieve the coded units of each category, either by cutting and pasting the typed manuscript or by using a computer program. Via this process, all the meaning units that fit within the first category are grouped together, as are the units that fit within category two, and so on.

Remember that the meaning units have been collected from a number of different research participants. Thus, this process pulls each unit away from the context of the individual's story. A drawback of the process, then, is that you might lose or misinterpret a meaning unit once it is separated from the context of each research participant's experience. The advantage is that you can consider the information in each category in a different way, across individuals. You can thus see how important it is that your rules for placing a meaning unit into a particular category were clarified during the initial coding process (Step 3).

Task 4b: Comparing Categories

Whereas previously you looked for similarities and differences between meaning units to separate them into distinct categories, the next step is to compare and contrast the categories themselves in order to discover the relationships between them. At this point in the analysis, your goal is to integrate the categories into themes and subthemes based on their properties.

Finding themes involves locating patterns that repeatedly appear in your data set. Once a theme is identified, you will develop a code for it in the same manner as you coded categories. The themes will, in most cases, form the basis of the major conclusions emerging from your analysis.

What possible types of relationships among categories might you find?

- There might be a temporal relationship, in which one category always precedes another. In cases such as this you may be able to identify a process that has some importance to the issue at hand. For example, Tutty found that, although children often initially react positively to living away from their abusive father, later they are likely to push for a reconciliation.
- There may be a causal relationship, in which one category seems to lead to another. For example, Tutty found that the women who had no further contact with their assaultive partners after leaving the shelter seemed generally able to function better. Note, though, that it is risky to assume that one category caused another when, in fact, the opposite may be true. In this example, perhaps it is the fact that the women were functioning well that led them to cease contact with their ex-partners.
- One category may be contained within another category or may be another type of the first category. In Tutty's study, she originally saw the category wherein the men beseeched and even bribed the women to return to the relationship as different from the category of threatening the women with, for example, further abuse or no support payments if they did not return. However, in this phase of analysis she shifted to seeing the "loving" pleas as related to the threats. The new theme combining these was called "Partner's Strategies to Reunite."

Obviously, you may find other types of relationships between categories, but the previous examples are commonly found. Some categories may contain enough information to be considered themes in and of themselves.

As another example of combining categories into themes, consider the study on abused women. The three categories of "Custody Issues Regarding Children," "Separation or Divorce Proceedings," and "Obtaining Restraining Orders." All involve relationships with various aspects of the legal system, including the police, lawyers, and judges.

The substance of the three categories was similar in that the women were more likely than not to have had difficulty in adequately dealing with these systems. Furthermore, the experience was likely to reignite marital issues, putting the women at risk of further abuse. The theme "Difficulties With the Legal System" was, therefore, created by combining the three categories.

LOOKING FOR MEANING AND RELATIONSHIPS

In addition to organizing the data, coding also brings meaning to the information being examined. However, once you move to the "formal" step of interpreting the data, coding at both levels is considered complete. Two important steps are involved in looking for meaning and relationships in your data. First, you will have to develop an interpretation of your data. Interpretations are sometimes descriptive, but may also suggest causal explanations of important events. Second, the research process and the conclusions must be assessed for credibility and dependability.

Step 5: Interpreting Data and Theory Building

Drawing meaning from your data is perhaps the most rewarding step of a qualitative data analysis. It involves two important tasks: (1) developing conceptual classifications systems, and (2) presenting themes or theory.

Task 5a: Developing Conceptual Classification Systems

The ultimate goal of a qualitative research study is to identify any relationships between the major themes that emerge from the data set. To do this you must develop logical interpretations of the themes that remain consistent with your earlier categorization schemes and meaning units. One idea that may help you to get a sense of the relationships between the themes and the overall nature of the data is to visually display themes and categories in a diagram. The visual representation of your themes may help you to organize the write-up of your conclusions.

It may also help you to clearly identify the interconnections between themes and categories or to identify missing categories among the data set. Matthew B. Miles and Michael A. Huberman (1994) suggest several strategies for extracting meaning from a data set.

- Draw a cluster diagram. This form of diagram helps you to think about how themes and categories may or may not be related to each other. Draw and label circles for each theme and arrange them in relation to each other. Some of the circles will overlap, others will stand alone. The circles of the themes of more importance will be larger, in comparison to themes and categories that are not as relevant to your conclusions. The process of thinking about what weight to give the themes, how they interact, and how important they will be in your final scheme will be valuable in helping you to think about the meaning of your research study.
- Make a matrix. Matrix displays may be helpful for noting relations between categories or themes. Designing a matrix involves writing a list of categories along the side of a piece of paper and then another list of categories or themes across the top. In each cell you will document how the two categories fit or do not fit together. For example, along the side you could write categories that reflect the theme "Partner's Strategies to Reunite." Across the top you could write categories from the theme of "Women's Beliefs About Leaving Their Abusive Partner." Where two categories intersect on the matrix you could note with a plus sign (+) beliefs that fit with the ex-partner's desire to live together once more, and mark with a minus sign (–) those at odds with each other. Such a matrix will give you a sense of the balance of the push to leave the abusive relationship and the pull to return.
- Count the number of times a meaning unit or category appears. Although numbers are typically associated with quantitative studies, it is acceptable to use numbers in qualitative ones to document how many of the participants expressed a particular theme. You might, for exam-

ple, be interested in finding out how many of your interviewees experienced different problems after separating from their abusive partners. You would write the code names for the women down the left side of a piece of paper and the list of problems across the top. To fill in the chart, you would simply place a check mark beside each woman's name if she experienced that particular problem.

Numbers will help to protect your analysis against bias that occurs when particularly poignant but rare examples of themes are presented. For example, in Tutty's qualitative study, one woman described the death of her daughter at the hands of her ex-partner, an event that immediately preceded their separation. Although an emotionally laden event, it was certainly not typical of the experience of most of the other women. A majority of the women, however, did express concerns about past abuse of their children by their ex-partners. Although the researcher did not discount the experience of the woman whose daughter died, that event could be better discussed in the context of the range of severity of abuse of the children.

- Create a metaphor. Developing metaphors that convey the essence of your findings is another mechanism for extracting meaning. For example, in her qualitative study of battered women who remain with their partners, Lenore Walker (1979) identified a cycle that commonly occurs whereby tension builds between a couple until the husband beats his wife. This abusive incident is followed by a calm, loving phase until the tension starts to build once again. Walker's name for this process, "the cycle of violence," is an example of a metaphor that so effectively describes this pattern that the metaphor has been extensively adopted.
- Look for missing links. If two categories or themes seem to be related, but not directly so, it may be that a third variable connects the two.
- Note contradictory evidence. Remember that contradictory evidence must be accounted for. The chain of evidence must be thorough so that

any connections between categories and themes are accounted for. Although we traditionally focus on looking for evidence to support our ideas, we must also identify themes and categories that raise questions about our conclusions. Such evidence can ultimately be very useful in providing exceptions to the process that you have described.

Task 5b: Presenting Themes or Theory

Although many qualitative researchers conclude their studies by presenting descriptions of the major themes that emerged from their data, others use the themes and their interpretations to create hypotheses or theory. In Tutty's study, for example, she simply presented the major themes that emerged from the data without any attempt to formulate these into a theory. Even so, the themes could have been reworded as questions that could then become hypotheses in future research efforts.

For example, one core theme was that the ex-partner's access to children created a situation wherein women were placed at risk of continued abuse. As a hypothesis, this could be reworded as "Women whose abusive partners visit with their children after a marital separation are more likely to experience continued abuse than women who do not see their partner under such circumstances."

In contrast, theories answer questions such as "Why does a phenomenon occur?" or "How are these two concepts related?" If theory does develop from the study, it will not be apparent at the beginning, but will grow out of the process of analysis. This is most likely to occur during the stage of classifying the categories into themes and looking for relationships between those themes.

An example of a theory that emerged from a different qualitative study of battered women is Lenore Walker's (1979) "cycle of violence," mentioned previously as an example of a metaphor. The development of theories such as Walker's involves a shift from looking at specific instances to examining general patterns. With each step of data analysis, your thinking becomes more abstract; in other words, you become further removed from the concrete examples on the original transcript.

By using the constant comparison method, you arrive at an understanding of basic patterns or ideas that connect the categories and themes developed earlier.

Step 6: Assessing the Trustworthiness of Your Results

Although developing interpretations and theory can be an exciting step in a qualitative analysis, throughout the research process you must act responsibly to ensure the trustworthiness of the conclusions that you finally draw. Qualitative researchers have identified a number of issues to think about to enhance the believability of your research findings. Approaches and emphases vary (as does the depth of detail in discussions of techniques that can be employed).

These issues will be revisited again in the following chapter, because they are relevant to report writing. At this point, we will discuss the challenges that are important to address during the analysis. The three tasks include: (1) establishing your own credibility, (2) documenting what you have done to ensure consistency, and (3) documenting what you have done to control biases and preconception.

Task 6a: Establishing Your Own Credibility

Because a qualitative study depends so much on the human judgment and discipline of the researcher, it is necessary for you to indicate why you should be believed. This is partly a matter of indicating your relevant training and experience and partly a matter of recording, in your journal, the procedures you followed, the decisions you made (with the rationale for them), and the thought processes that led you to your conclusions. Meticulous records of this sort will do much to convince those who must assess your work that they can believe in it.

Task 6b: Document What You Have Done to Ensure Consistency

Consistency (which is sometimes called dependability) is another key to establishing the believability of your study. Qualitative work is influenced by the unique events and relationships that unfold in the course of the study, but consistency in study procedures—especially in analysis—is still desirable. Hopefully, you have been rigorous in your interviewing and in developing the rules for coding, and have written detailed records of your decision making. If this is the case, another researcher should be able to follow your process and arrive at similar decisions. Also, if you yourself redo parts of the analysis at a later date, the outcome should be closely similar to that produced in your original analysis. Specific issues and procedures that you may need to address to ensure consistency include:

- Specifying the context of the interviews and how you incorporated this in your analysis. Some data collection circumstances yield more credible information than others, and you may thus choose to weight your interviews accordingly. For example, some authors claim that data collected later in the study may be more relevant than those gathered in the beginning, likely because your interviewing style will be more relaxed and less intrusive. In addition, data obtained firsthand is considered stronger than that reported by a third person. Data provided voluntarily can be assumed to be more trustworthy, as are data collected when the research participant is alone with you.

- Triangulation. This is a common method to establish the trustworthiness of qualitative data. There are several different kinds of triangulation, but the essence of the term is that multiple perspectives are compared. This might involve having a colleague use your data collection rules to see if he or she makes the same decisions about meaning units, categories, and themes; or it may consist of collecting multiple sources of data in addition to your interviews. The hope is that the different perspectives will confirm each other, adding weight to the credibility of your analysis.

- Member checking. Obtaining feedback from your research participants is an essential credibility technique that is unique to qualitative methods. Although feedback from research participants should be part of the ongoing process of the qualitative research study, it is particularly useful when your analysis and interpretations have been made and conclusions drawn. In other words, you go back to your research participants asking them to confirm or refute your interpretations.

Note that research participants may not always agree with the data, with each other, or with your interpretations. In such cases you need to decide whether to exclude the data to which the research participants object, or to record the dissenting opinion in some way and indicate your position in relation to it.

Task 6c: Document What You Have Done to Control Biases and Preconceptions

When you report your findings, it is useful to include a careful inventory of your biases and preconceptions. Cataloguing these will remind you to keep checking to ensure that your conclusions are dictated by the data rather than by your established beliefs. A list of this sort is also useful to readers, who will want to assess how successful you have been in keeping your biases under control during data collection and analysis.

Your journal recording analytical memos and a record of your decision-making process will also be valuable for this purpose. Someone who wishes to scrutinize your work especially closely will be interested in the evidence these offer regarding your attempts to be open to what your research participants had to say. Below are a few threats to the credibility of qualitative research studies, which are relevant to the question of bias, and which you may wish to think about (and address in your journal):

- Your personal bias and life view may affect your interpretation of the data. Bias is a natural human quality, and as we move from the particular to the general there is a tendency to manipulate data to fit with what we already believe.
- You may draw conclusions before the data are analyzed or before you have decided about the trustworthiness of the data collected.
- You might censor, ignore, or dismiss data as irrelevant. This may occur as a result of data overload

or because the data contradict an already established mainstream way of thinking.
- You may make unwarranted or unsupported causal statements based on your first impressions rather than on solid analysis.
- You may be too opinionated and reduce your conclusions to a limited number of choices or alternatives.

Matthew B. Miles and Michael A. Huberman (1994) have suggested strategies to deal with the above risks:

- Member checking has already been described in the above task, but is noted again here for its utility as a way of guarding against your own biases dictating your conclusions.
- In your analysis, it is easy to unthinkingly give certain events and people more consideration than others. However, this prevents you from making accurate interpretations of your data, because the people and the events selected are not sufficiently representative. You may come to the conclusion that you relied upon data that were too easily accessible or that you weighted your results toward people you liked. To compensate for such possibilities, you can deliberately search for events and people that differ markedly from those you have already interviewed, to help balance the perspective of the data that you have collected. If you detect such a bias, you can interview more people, looking especially for atypical research participants and events.
- Another source of bias is the effect that you may have on your interviewees as well as the effect that they may have on you. Such effects are particularly powerful in qualitative methods, where data collection may involve your spending long periods of time with your interviewees. It is not uncommon for the interviewer to become personally responsive to interviewees, especially when they are revealing intimate details of their experience. We we are not suggesting that you remain aloof, but if you are too responsive your interviewees may become misleading in an effort to please you.

- Looking for negative evidence resembles constant comparison, but you are looking for outliers and extreme cases. Negative evidence should be actively sought at the time when preliminary conclusions are made, to see if any data contradict or are inconsistent with your conclusion. The researcher must actively hunt for contradictory data in case they counter the preliminary conclusion and what the researcher believes.

SUMMARY

This chapter presented a systematic and purposeful approach to data analysis in qualitative research studies. The predominant steps of data analysis include transcript preparation (Step 1), establishing a preliminary plan for data analysis (Step 2), first-level coding (Step 3), second-level coding (Step 4), data interpretation and theory building (Step 5), and assessing the trustworthiness of your results (Step 6). Although these steps are presented in a linear fashion, the data analysis process is not so straightforward. You must be flexible and move back and forth between and among the steps and tasks to produce rich and meaningful findings.

Now that you have analyzed and interpreted your data, the next phase of the qualitative research process is to write up your results so that other interested social work practitioners, policy makers, educators, and re searchers have access to them. How to disseminate your findings so that they will be read is the topic of the following chapter.

Writing and Evaluating Research Reports

Part VI contains a chapter that discusses how to

write up a research report that is derived from

a research study (Chapter 19). The remaining

two chapters are geared toward evaluating

quantitatively oriented studies (Chapter 20) and

qualitatively oriented ones (Chapter 21).

Writing Reports
From Research Studies

William J. Reid

19

Basic Steps in the Research Process

Step 1 Choose a problem

2 Review the literature

3 Evaluate the literature

4 Be aware of all ethical issues

5 Be aware of all cultural issues

6 State the research question or hypothesis

7 Select the research approach

8 Determine how the variables are going to be measured

9 Select a sample

10 Select a data collection method

11 Collect and code the data

12 Analyze and interpret the data

You Are Here ▶

13 Write the report

You Are Here ▶

14 Disseminate the report

Research reports serve an important function in social work because they put new contributions to the knowledge base of the profession into a permanent written form. Without published research reports, the claim of a scientific knowledge base for social work might be difficult to substantiate.

The knowledge obtained from social work research can be reported in a variety of forms. These reports may vary in length from a brief note to a full-scale presentation several hundred pages long. They may stand by themselves or be embedded in larger works. They may be so technical that only readers with a high degree of research sophistication will understand them, or expressed in language that can be readily comprehended by any literate person. Reports can also be communicated in the form of films.

The audiences to whom reports are directed are an even more important source of variation. Reports may be read (or heard) by a handful of persons or may reach thousands. The scope of the audience reached depends largely on the medium of distribution. Reports may be circulated informally, read at a conference, distributed through mailing lists, or published as journal articles, monographs, or books, among other possibilities.

Some social work research reports are based on student projects, particularly doctoral dissertations. Both PhD and MSW candidates are encouraged to try to get reports of their studies published, provided they are of sufficient merit and interest, and some social work instructors make an effort to help students achieve this goal (see the final section of this chapter). Most of the unpublished social work literature consists of such materials as conference papers, presentations of student projects, and shorter reports to sponsoring agencies.

RESEARCH REPORTS FOR PROFESSIONAL JOURNALS

The general type of report discussed in this chapter is suitable for publication as an article in a professional social work journal. Most such reports consist of from 10 to 25 word-processed pages, including tables, figures, and references. They are usually based on single research studies and are written for a potentially wide audience. This type of report is the most common means of sharing the results of studies with other social work professionals, and it is also probably the most important, because in any field of study, articles published in journals are the principal source of additions to or modifications of the knowledge base.

Purpose of a Research Report

The main purpose of a research report is to communicate to others the knowledge that has been derived from a particular study. The researcher, taking the role of author, customarily provides a rationale for conducting the study, reviews what is already known in the problem area under investigation, and states the research question. The researcher then explains the design and methods of the study and presents the findings and the conclusions drawn from the data.

In the report, all aspects of the study should be related to the purpose of communicating the knowledge derived from it. In particular, the distinction between what has been found out and the author's use of the findings must be made clear. If this is not done, and if the findings or the means of obtaining them are distorted to advance the author's point of view, the purpose of the report will be subverted.

Writing for an Audience

Since a research report is written to be understood and utilized by a particular audience, or those who will read it, assumptions regarding the intended audience are critical. In social work, readers vary considerably in their ability to comprehend research and evaluation concepts, in their interest in technical detail, and in the criteria they use for assessing findings and conclusions. Social workers who specialize in research may desire a range and depth of information about a study's methodology. This may be of secondary concern to social workers who specialize in direct practice and are more likely to be interested in the author's speculations concerning applications of the study's findings. Professional social workers minimize such differences in audience orientations.

Authors of research reports understandably would like to satisfy both interests. There are various ways of doing this, but none is completely satisfactory. A hard-line approach taken by some authors is to write for an audience of research specialists, without a great deal of concern for other readers. In another approach, sometimes referred to as *spoon-feeding*, the author glosses over technical aspects of the study and concentrates on delivering "useful" information. A more technical version of the same study may also be prepared for an audience of researchers.

There is a satisfactory solution that avoids both of these extremes. The essential technical aspects of a study must be presented. It is impossible for readers to assess a study's findings properly with no understanding of the methods by which the findings were obtained. Researchers writing reports can help readers with the task of comprehension by providing explanations of technical procedures, and they can make an effort to enhance the relevance of a study's findings, implications, and conclusions to social work practice.

In terms of the development of the social work profession and the services it provides, the best long-run solution is to raise the level of research literacy among social workers. Professional education provides one means to this end. What students learn about research at schools of social work soon fades, however, if as professionals they are not continually exposed to research concepts by reading reports they find of interest.

ORGANIZATION AND CONTENT

This section is concerned with the "how-to" of social work report writing. The best way to get a sense of how social work research is reported is to read articles that have been published in professional social work journals. Additional resources that are useful in learning to write reports include books, articles, and manuals on writing skills and report preparation.

The general format of the article-length report usually follows a standard sequence. Within this sequence, there may be a good deal of variation in how different parts of the report are labeled, in the attention given to each part, and in the nature and internal organization of the content.

Organizational Framework

A commonly used framework for a research study report intended for publication in a professional journal consists of four parts: problem, method, findings, and discussion. The topics each part of this sequence is likely to contain are listed in Table 19.1.

This general progression of headings is followed in most reports of positivistic research studies. The example outlined in Table 19.2 shows the relation of the headings used in a hypothetical published report to these four parts. In this example, the author elicited from hospital patients critical incidents (important examples) of helpful and nonhelpful staff behavior. These incidents were then classified and analyzed to present a picture of the patients' perception of their hospital care.

The basic structure of this report follows the four-part scheme presented in Table 19.1, but the actual headings used are dictated by the particulars of the study. "Method," for example, appears under two headings, "Plan of Study" and "Classifying the Incidents." The example also illustrates a point worth noting: The first few paragraphs of a report, which present some aspects of Part 1, often have no heading.

A useful way to outline a report prior to actually writing it is to generate the major headings from the four-part structure and then break them down into subheadings applicable to the specific study. This outline is helpful in organizing divisions to be used in writing the report.

There is a significant deviation from this structure when a study is conducted in stages. For example, an evaluation of an intervention upon its termination may constitute the first stage of a study, and a follow-up of clients 6 months later may constitute the second stage. In such cases, the report could begin with a fairly standard Part 1 (statement of the problem), and then each stage could be presented as if it were a separate study, with description of the methods, presentation of findings, and discussion of findings for each stage. The report could conclude with an overall discussion and summary. This type of organization makes the most sense when the different stages of the study are sufficiently distinct in methods and findings to warrant presentation as separate units.

Statement of the Problem

The introduction to a report often proves the most difficult section to write. Although the study must be placed in some perspective, any study is potentially

TABLE 19.1

Organization of Parts in a Research Report

Parts	Contents
1. Problem	Background, rationale, and significance of the study; review of relevant research and theory; presentation and explanation of the research problem, research question, research hypothesis, and variables
2. Method	Delineation of the strategy (design) and methods of the investigation, including a description of the setting and the sampling plan; description of data collection procedures, instruments, and measurement approach
3. Findings	Presentation of findings, including data displays (tables, graphs, etc.); textual exposition of data; description of relevant analytic procedures
4. Discussion	Discussion of findings, including interpretation of data, implications for theory, practice, education, and research; limitations of study; relationship to other research; summary and conclusions

TABLE 19.2

Headings in a Published Research Report

Parts	Headings in Report	Contents
1. Problem	Unheaded introduction	Review of previous research studies
2. Method	Plan of Study	Study design; setting; sampling plan; critical incident technique
	Classifying the Incidents	Method of classifying incidents; reliability of the classifications
3. Findings	Major Findings	Frequency distribution of helpful and nonhelpful incidents; relation of patients' perceptions to different factors
4. Discussion	Discussion	Reasons why findings may differ from those of previous research studies
	Implications for Practice	Importance of patients' perceptions in shaping hospital services and staff behavior
	Implications for Training	Use of patients' questionnaires in staff monitoring and training

connected to a wide range of topics, and it is difficult to know where to begin or end. If a study evaluates a method for helping marital partners with communication problems, for example, should something be said about marital conflict as a social problem? What about theories of family communication, or other methods of marital treatment?

A pragmatic way to approach the writing of Part 1 of a report is to begin with its most essential elements—the statement of the problem area and exposition of specific research questions or hypotheses. The researcher then can ask: What do readers need to know in order to understand the problem, to place it in an appropriate context, to appreciate its significance, and to determine how its solution will contribute to existing knowledge?

The amount of attention given to these factors depends on the nature of the research question and the assumptions about the audience to whom the report is primarily directed. If the research question involves concepts or theoretical formulations that are likely to be unfamiliar to readers, some explanation of these ideas is in order. The significance of some research questions will be self-evident and need not be belabored; the importance of others has to be made clear. The relevance of the study's problem area (and result-

ing research questions) to social work practice should be articulated if it is not obvious.

The expected contribution of the report to existing knowledge can be stated through a review of literature directly related to the problem area. The review should not consist of a string of paragraphs, each presenting a capsule summary of a different study. Rather, it should organize findings pertinent to different aspects of the study, with emphasis on identifying gaps in knowledge that the report intends to fill. These preliminaries can be overdone, however. The introduction to a report is not the place for a lengthy review of the literature. It also should not be used as a vehicle for an incidental essay.

Explanation of the Research Method

Part 2 sets forth the methodology of the study, usually including descriptions of the research design, the sampling plan, data collection procedures, and measuring instruments. If an evaluation of a program or an experiment is being reported, this section should describe the setting, the nature of the program, and the independent and dependent variables.

Substantive findings (findings bearing directly on the research question or hypothesis) are not presented in this part but are deferred until Part 3. Data on the validity and reliability of the measuring instrument(s) and on characteristics of the setting may be included, however. Information concerning the sample may also be presented here rather than in Part 3, particularly if there is only a small amount of data to be reported. Aspects of methodology that may better be understood in conjunction with presentation of the findings also may be deferred until Part 3. Methods of data analysis or secondary measures obtained from manipulations of the data may best be discussed there, in the context of data presentation.

The most common shortcoming in Part 2 is insufficient or unclear presentation of the study's methods. The researcher's own intimate familiarity with these methods may breed insensitivity to the reader's ignorance of them. As a result, the study methodology may be presented in an indirect, cryptic manner. An excellent device whereby to avoid this is for researchers to put themselves in the position of unsophisticated readers.

It is particularly important to provide a clear picture of the connection between the research question and the data obtained. In order to accomplish this, some description of the study's measuring instrument, including a presentation of sample questions, is usually necessary. Ideally, the actual instrument or key portions of it should be included as an appendix, but this is usually not feasible for reports published in professional journals. In any case, the steps by which the data were obtained from the measuring instrument should be delineated. It may also be advisable to restate the research question or hypothesis in operational language, indicating the quantitative basis for measurement. For example, a hypothesis may be stated as a prediction that certain scores will be correlated or that statistically significant differences between sample groups will be found on the dependent variable.

Presentation of the Findings

The essential purpose of Part 3 is to present findings that have been anticipated by the statement of the research question or hypothesis and the explanation of the research method. While all the findings of a study need not be reported in an article-length report, all important results that bear on the research question should be shared with the audience. The two principal formats for presenting the findings are data displays and text descriptions.

Data Displays

In working on Part 3, a useful first step is to prepare the tables, graphs, figures, or other data displays that will form the core of the presentation. The narrative portion of the findings section can then be organized according to these displays, which may be in the form of tables, charts, or figures.

The first principle in displaying data is to present them in a manner that can be readily understood, given the information provided up to that point in the report. In tabular data displays, the most widely used form, this criterion is met by providing a descriptive title for the table and labels for columns and rows. In Table 19.3, hypothetical data on clients' ratings of satisfaction can be quickly grasped, even if nothing else is known about such a study. The data are reasonably complete. Percentages are given to facilitate comparisons between two groups of clients, according to whether the social workers assigned to them had MSW degrees or only BSW degrees. The number of clients giving each response to indicate their level of satisfaction—the data on which the percentages were based—is also given.

Information concerning the statistical test of significance used to test the hypothesis is given in the footnote of Table 19.3. A likely research hypothesis for this study would be that clients of social workers with MSW degrees will be more satisfied with services than clients of workers whose educations include only BSW degrees. The statistic used to test this hypothesis (or the null hypothesis, that there is no difference in level of clients' satisfaction according to workers' level of education) is chi-square (X^2), which was found to be 10.7. The number of degrees of freedom (df) is needed to perform this test with a calculator or computer, or by hand computation and the use of a published statistical table. The p is the level of statistical significance found in the chi-square test, or the probability that the

TABLE 19.3

Table Showing Client Satisfaction With Social Work Services, by Educational Level of Workers

| | Educational Level of Workers | | | | | |
| | MSW | | BSW | | Total | |
Satisfaction	Number	Percent	Number	Percent	Number	Percent
Satisfied	23	57.5	28	50.0	51	53.1
Neutral	16	40.0	13	23.2	29	30.2
Dissatisfied	1	2.5	15	26.8	16	16.7
Totals	40	100.0%	56	100.0%	96	100.0%

$X^2 = 10.7$, $df = 2$, $p < .01$.

null hypothesis can be rejected and the research hypothesis supported.

As a matter of convention, routine statistical procedures such as these are not explained in a journal report, either as part of the graphic display or in the text. This creates obvious communication difficulties for readers who lack a knowledge of statistics. Without a course in statistics, the information on statistical significance in tables appearing in professional journals can be understood only in general terms.

The data in Table 19.3 can also be displayed in more graphic forms that often are easier to grasp at a glance. The familiar bar charts (illustrated for these data in Figure 19.1) and pie charts, in which the data are shown as proportional segments of a circle, can be easily prepared with computer software programs on personal computers.

The purpose of a data display is to communicate information to the reader in a graphic manner. If a display has achieved this purpose efficiently, there should

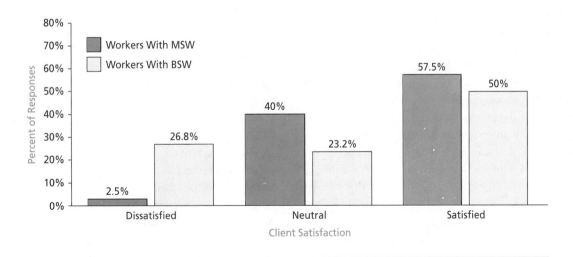

Figure 19.1 Bar Chart Showing Client Satisfaction With Social Work Services, by Educational Level of Workers

be no need to repeat the information in the text of the report. Textual commentary on data displays should be used to emphasize the main points of the data or to draw attention to characteristics of the data that might be overlooked.

Thus, in interpreting Table 19.3, the text should not plod through the obvious—"57.5% of the clients who had MSW social workers were satisfied; 40% were neutral," and so on. Rather, the text might observe that clients with MSW social workers were relatively more satisfied with service than clients with BSW social workers. In addition, it might note that dissatisfied clients accounted for the largest share of the difference.

In keeping with the purpose of data displays to enhance the reader's understanding, complex displays, such as a graph with half a dozen crisscrossing lines, should not be used. Indeed, displays should not be used at all to communicate basic information that can be expressed more simply in the text. In the example, if satisfaction data had been obtained only for clients served by MSW social workers, Table 19.3 would not be necessary.

Description in Text

The text on the findings of the report should follow a logical sequence. Data describing characteristics of research participants or respondents (demographic data) often are presented first, as a means of defining the group to which the findings relate. A convenient way to proceed with the description of findings is in the order of the research questions or hypotheses formulated from the problem area. Other findings not anticipated in this formulation can then be introduced.

It may be necessary to describe additional measurement procedures, as well as analytic methods. The amount of detail and explanation necessary to present the data analysis techniques varies. Routine data-processing procedures that are of no consequence to the study's findings certainly do not need to be reported. For example, informing readers that the data were coded, entered into the computer, and analyzed adds nothing of value to the report.

Common statistical techniques, such as standard measures of association to determine the strength of a relationship between variables, are neither explained nor referenced. It is good practice, however, to clarify their function so the essential meaning of the statistical findings can be grasped. In describing a correlation between expenditures for social work services and the patient discharge rate in mental health facilities, for example, the report might state: "The correlation coefficient between expenditures and the discharge rate was .76, which suggests a relatively high degree of association between these two variables." Specialized methods should be fully explained, however.

Presentation or Discussion of Findings

The usual practice in writing Part 3 is to present the study's findings and clarify them if necessary, but not to discuss them at length. There may be reasons to deviate from this format, however. For instance, if a study produces a number of findings, some of them may be summarized, and Part 4, the discussion section, can focus on those that are to be emphasized. If the findings and their significance are immediately apparent, the description can be brief, and Part 4 can be devoted to recommendations based on the findings.

In reports of studies using the naturalistic research approach, the presentation and discussion of the findings are often combined, and the organization follows the themes that emerge in the analysis of the data. Brief examples from the researcher's text (the notes on observations or experiments that constitute the data in naturalistic research) may be presented, often in the form of quotations from participants or observers. These extracts, which provide both illustration and documentation, also can enliven the reports of positivistic studies.

Reports based on qualitative data are not likely to contain technical information that readers will find hard to comprehend. These studies can suffer, however, from needless imprecision caused by the author's reluctance to use quantitative measures or positivistic descriptions. In summarizing the results, selected behaviors or attitudes might be described as if they were characteristic of everyone in the sample. Although excessive discriminations (one person said this, a second said that, a third said something else) should be avoided, some quantification is useful to avoid over-generalization.

Discussion of the Findings

Part 4 is primarily concerned with the meaning and importance of the findings reported in Part 3. The point for presenting data has passed; now, discussion of what the findings add up to and where they may lead is in order.

Researchers are liable to succumb to two short-comings in writing this part. One is to turn the discussion into a mere repetition of findings already presented in the report, without much commentary on their practical or theoretical significance. While it may be useful to remind readers of results that will be the focus of discussion, if the findings were adequately presented in Part 3, Part 4 should focus on further implications, general conclusions, and so on.

The second shortcoming approaches the opposite extreme. This is to ignore the findings and concentrate on an exposition of the researcher's own point of view—perhaps because the findings did not meet the researcher's expectations for the study. The findings for any study, no matter how trivial, merit some discussion, even if only to give reasons why they were not more revealing.

Explanations and Implications

The content of the discussion section varies according to the nature of the findings and what has been previously said about them. In most studies, the findings are sufficiently complex (or ambiguous) to warrant some explanation of what was in fact learned about the sample studied. Causal connections found between variables should always be discussed. For example, the length of social work treatment may be found to be positively correlated with clients' outcomes. Does this mean that greater amounts of treatment played a causative role in the outcome, or does it mean that clients who were getting better on their own tended to remain in treatment longer? Tests of rival hypotheses or other evidence or argument that can be brought to bear on this point should be presented.

In examining such relationships and determining the meaning of descriptive findings, possible sources of bias or error in data collection and measurement should be pointed out. Were the interviewers' perceptions influenced by knowledge of the study's hypothesis? Is it possible that clients were giving socially desirable responses? Inconsistencies in the findings, such as discrepancies among measures of the same phenomenon, should be identified and accounted for. The author's speculations about the reasons for unanticipated findings may also be offered. In trying to understand and explain the meaning of a study's findings, however, researchers are limited to the persons, objects, or events they actually investigated.

A rather different point concerns the importance or meaningfulness of the study's findings to other persons or situations. This is the payoff for research studies; an understanding derived from persons, objects, or events actually studied should have a broader application. Because many social work studies are not based on representative samples, however, it is not always possible to generalize within known margins of error to larger populations. Nevertheless, if some kind of generalization or implications cannot be derived from the findings, there would be little point in conducting the study.

In stating the implications, obvious statements such as "Since the sample studied was not representative, generalizations of the findings are not possible" should be avoided. Claims that the findings necessarily reflect universal truth are also needless. For most studies, it can appropriately be assumed that the findings have some implications for the field of social work. Even findings based on small, nonrepresentative samples may provide some support for, or challenge to, existing hypotheses or social work practices. They might also be used as a basis for suggesting new hypotheses or practices.

Although the findings may not "prove" or "establish" a great deal, they may "provide evidence for," "suggest the possibility that," or "raise questions about" a conclusion. With such qualified language, implications can be presented that readers will find useful but not misleading. Authors often do not push either their imaginations or their data far enough. Ultraconservative interpretations of findings may have the dubious advantage of avoiding criticism from other professionals, but they also may fail to extract useful ideas from the findings.

The conclusions of a study may be strengthened or qualified by references to related literature, using sources reviewed in Part 1 of the report or introduced in this part in order to connect the findings of the study to the results of other investigations. Introducing other authors' findings in Part 4 is also appropriate when the study's findings have been serendipitous or were not covered in the literature referred to in the introduction.

Limitations and Recommendations

The limitations of a research study, particularly major shortcomings that may affect how the findings are interpreted or applied, should be made explicit. If this is not done in a separate subsection in which specific limitations are cited, it can be made clear in interpreting the findings or developing their implications for social work. For example, a study of the needs of older people in a community may have used a sample that overrepresented the younger, healthier members of the elderly population. In discussing implications of the findings for community planning, the limiting effects of the sample bias can be pointed out.

Some authors make recommendations for further study based on the findings. These recommendations should be informative; if nothing more specific can be said than "It is important to do more research studies in this area," it is better to say nothing. To be helpful, a recommendation for further study should specify particular research questions, variables, or designs.

Recommendations for changes in policies, programs, practices, and so on are most likely to appear in reports addressed to particular decision makers (such as key agency staff members) who might be able to initiate them. In making these recommendations, the findings of the study should be synthesized with assumptions about desirable goals and some knowledge of the relevant policy or program.

SUMMARIES AND LONGER REPORTS

A final section of Part 4 sometimes is included, particularly with longer types of reports, to give a brief summary of the important findings and conclusions of the study. This may be needed if the discussion deals with a range of findings in a lengthy or discursive fashion but not if the discussion is brief, well focused, and in itself summarizes the major findings. A summary also may not be needed if an abstract of the study is furnished.

Longer reports such as master's theses, doctoral dissertations, and reports to sponsoring agencies are usually richer in detail and provide a more complete picture of the findings of a research study than article-length journal reports do. In fact, article-length reports may be based on only a portion of the findings presented in longer reports.

The length and comprehensiveness of students' course papers or reports to agencies usually make summaries necessary. A common way of studying such reports is to read only the summary and the portions that are of interest. Agency decision makers, particularly, require nontechnical summaries of studies, with emphasis on the major findings. Often such an "executive summary" is presented at the beginning of the report.

The use of footnotes and appendixes also helps unburden the text of longer reports. This suits readers who are not interested in plowing through a great deal of technical detail. At the same time, it provides valuable information for those who wish to pursue the topic further.

PUBLICATION AND DISSEMINATION

All authors are interested in communicating their work to readers who will find it of interest or potential value. The general term for exposure of a research study to an audience is *dissemination*, and the most extensive dissemination is accomplished through publication. More limited forms include distribution of copies to the staff of an organization, mailing copies to a list of prospective readers, presentations at staff meetings and conferences, and interlibrary circulation of master's theses and doctoral dissertations.

Although a simple distinction between published and unpublished reports is commonly made, there is a considerable gray area between these categories. Many reports, particularly more lengthy ones, may be "quasi published" by schools, agencies, conferences, and so forth. For example, several hundred copies of a report may be duplicated (or even printed), advertised, and sold by an agency. Because such reports lack the imprimatur of established publishers, they are sometimes referred to as "grey literature."

The most common means of large-scale dissemination of a research report is publication in a professional journal. The importance of the other forms should not be overlooked, however. With a little imagination and initiative, an unpublished report of potential interest to others can be put into circulation. For example, a state department of mental health may be able to distribute a study to its field offices, or copies might be sent to a small number of interested parties who may cite it in their own publications.

Publication in Professional Journals

Professional journals provide ready access to studies, regardless of when they were published, because present and past issues can usually be found in libraries serving the field. Searches of the professional literature in journals or periodicals can be assisted by a variety of information-retrieval tools, such as publications that print abstracts, computerized abstract services, and citation indexes. A research study reported in a periodical thus becomes part of an information network and has a better chance of being located and utilized. Moreover, because most professional journals use some form of expert review for papers submitted, there is some assurance that the articles published meet certain standards.

The number of social work journals being published changes frequently. More than 60 such journals yield a combined annual harvest of more than a thousand articles (see Table 22.1 for examples of journal titles). Most of these are geared to special-interest groups, defined by field of practice, region, auspices, social work method, and so forth. With the exception of *Social Work*, the journals have limited numbers of subscribers, and a sizable proportion is likely to be libraries.

Unsolicited reports of research studies are not received with enthusiasm by some social work journals. For one reason, editors may be concerned that the content is too technical for their readers to comprehend. Other problems may be posed by the length of the report, the cost of reproducing data displays, or difficulties in securing experts to do prepublication reviews and technical editing. If a report is accepted, the editor may want the author to revise it and perhaps to tone down technical content, eliminate tables, or reduce the length.

Submitting a Report for Publication

The surest way to get an article published in a professional journal is to write a good report based on a good research study. In writing a report for possible publication, the first step is to identify the journal to which it will be initially submitted. The report can then be written to relate to the interests of the readers of that journal and to meet its requirements concerning length, footnote style, and so forth. Information on journal policy, usually published in each issue on the journal's masthead, includes a description of the types of reports the journal is interested in and submission procedures. Various issues should be consulted for models of reports the journal has published.

If the report is rejected by the journal originally selected, it may be submitted, with whatever revisions seem advisable, to other journals. Sending copies of a report to several journals simultaneously is considered unethical and can prove embarrassing if it is accepted by more than one.

The submission of a report is simple. It is sent with the number of required photocopies (usually three or four) to the journal's editorial office, together with a brief cover letter stating that the report is being submitted for possible publication by the journal. At the journal's editorial office, a decision-making process begins that will determine whether the report will appear in the journal's pages. Key persons in this process are the editor and reviewers (referees). The reviewers are in most instances experts in the field covered by the journal and contribute their time on a voluntary basis.

The report is read independently by two or more reviewers, who are usually not informed of the author's identity. They make recommendations regarding whether the report is suitable for publication and give reasons for their decisions. Disagreements among reviewers are common, and agreement to reject a report is more usual than agreement to publish one. When reviewers disagree, the editor often makes the final decision. The position of arbitrator gives the editor a good deal of influence over which reports are published. Journal contents therefore tend to reflect the standards and biases of their editors. An editor rarely has free rein, however. Few editors would refuse to publish a report that has been endorsed by all the journal's reviewers, regardless of their own biases.

The journal's decision about using a report frequently falls somewhere between total rejection and unqualified acceptance. If the report is rejected, the author may be encouraged to revise and resubmit it, but this does not commit the journal to accept the revised report for publication. Journals tend to reject more reports than they accept. Most reports are appropriate for several journals, however, including some outside the field of social work. Since acceptance criteria vary from journal to journal, it pays to be persistent. Journals also vary concerning the feedback they supply with rejected reports. Some send out only a form letter; others include the reviewers' comments, which may be painful to read but can be enormously helpful to an author who intends to submit the report elsewhere after revision.

The author's work does not end with acceptance for publication. A copy editor then goes over the manuscript, mainly to make the report fit the style and format of the journal, though in the process questions may arise about clarity, redundancy, omissions, and the like. The author normally reviews the edited copy and makes corrections or additional changes if necessary. The author usually sees proofs of the article after the manuscript has been typeset but is discouraged from making changes at that point.

The processes of review, editing, and production take time. For authors, the clock ticks most slowly between the submission of a report and a final decision by a journal. This period of uncertainty may vary from a few weeks to several months or a year, depending on the time absorbed by the review process. There is also a time lag between acceptance and actual publication that may range from a few weeks to 2 years or more. A delay of 6 to 9 months is fairly typical for social work journals, due to such factors as the number of issues published a year; the time consumed by editing, printing, and distribution; and the backlog of accepted manuscripts.

Getting Student Work Published

For social work students who wish to submit for publication reports of studies they do in their academic work, a good first step is to consult with an instructor. If students are serious about publication, they should rewrite their course papers with that objective in mind after selecting a journal to which the finished product is to be submitted. As a rule, course papers should not be submitted as is. There is usually a great deal of distance between a first-class student paper and a report of publishable quality. In rewriting the paper, the student should be particularly sensitive to aspects of the study that may have been glossed over because of assumptions about the instructor's knowledge of those areas.

In some cases, the instructor may be willing to collaborate with the student in the rewriting and be listed as a coauthor. If the original work is a joint effort, senior authorship (the first author listed) is usually given to the one with the greatest responsibility for conducting the study and writing up the results. It is usually assumed that the senior author has made a greater contribution, but some coauthors determine the order randomly.

Students should not confine submissions to the better known social work journals, which receive numerous reports of publishable quality. They may find greater receptivity and fewer delays with some of the less well known journals, particularly those that are relatively new. And students should not be discouraged if their initial submissions are rejected. Even well-established authors must learn to live with the unpleasant reality that their work is not always welcome. If reviewers' comments are supplied, they can have considerable learning value.

SUMMARY

The purpose of conducting a social work research study is greatly enhanced by the communication of the results to others. Published reports, particularly, put new contributions to the knowledge base of the profession into a permanent, written form. The most common type of research report, and the most important in terms of dissemination of research findings, is represented by research articles published in professional social work journals.

The organization of reports published in journals follows a more or less standard format consisting of four parts: statement of the problem, explanation of the research method, presentation of the findings, and discussion of the findings. The findings are reported in the form of graphic displays such as tables and figures and in accompanying text descriptions. Explanations, implications, limitations, and recommendations of the findings are discussed in the final part of the study report.

A research report is usually written with a definite audience in mind; it may be a limited audience, such as the staff of an organization, or a more extensive audience, such as the readers of a social work journal. If the report is to be submitted to a particular journal, the author must keep in mind its requirements for such matters as article length and format. If the author is not successful with a first submission, the report can be revised, perhaps with the assistance of reviewers' comments, and submitted to another social work journal, an interdisciplinary journal, or a journal in an allied field.

The following chapter continues the discussion of social work research reports. It presents a framework for evaluating reports derived from quantitative research studies based on the contents of this chapter.

Evaluating Quantitative Research Studies

Michael J. Holosko

Basic Steps in the Research Process

You Are Here

The previous chapter presented a format for writing up the results of research studies for possible publication in professional journals. As you know from the previous chapter, when manuscripts are accepted for publication by journals, the manuscripts are now called articles. Many students routinely critique, assess, and appraise quantitative research articles for a variety of reasons (e.g., for class assignments, to appraise and acquire knowledge, and/or to develop critical and analytic thinking skills). When you develop some confidence in your ability to critically appraise research studies, you will find yourself in a more favorable position to actually conduct one. In short, such critical thinking will help you to demystify and simplify a subject that you may have found to been anxiety provoking in the past—to say the least.

In addition, and as you know from Box 1.1, the Council of Social Work Education requires you to have the ability to apply critical thinking skills within the context of your professional practice. The Council also requires you to have the ability to evaluate research studies and to apply research findings to your practice in addition to evaluating your own practice interventions. In a nutshell, you need to know how to evaluate quantitatively oriented research articles. Thus, this chapter presents the criteria you can use to evaluate quantitative research studies.

For a more detailed and extensive discussion of the contents of this chapter, see a book titled *A Primer for Critiquing Social Research: A Student Guide* (Holosko, 2006a). The most challenging part of writing this book was to simplify and distill the essence of often complicated research concepts such as sampling, statistics, limitations, and so forth into minimal critiquing criteria. As a result, please feel free to add to these as you so choose, as these criteria are deemed as the "bare bones" or minimal criteria we would need to appraise in respect to a specific part of a quantitative study.

RESEARCH VERSUS NONRESEARCH

To start an appraisal you first need to locate a published journal article that presents the results of a quantitative social work research study—either in the form of a hard copy or, more commonly, online. You are probably eager to evaluate this article (author's assumption here), but first you need to determine a rather important beginning question: Is the article I found derived from a research study or not? We can easily make the false assumption that articles published in peer-reviewed social work journals are all "research studies"; however, this is really not the case. Within the social work profession, for example, a comprehensive analyses of 13 core professional journals ($N=1,849$ articles) over a 5-year period revealed that 47% were deemed as research studies and 53% were deemed nonresearch (Rosen, Proctor, & Staudt, 1999). Similarly, in an interdisciplinary journal that a number of different professionals subscribed to (i.e., *Family Preservation Journal*), the findings indicated 41% were research and 59% were nonresearch over a 4-year period (Holosko & Holosko, 1999).

Furthermore, some social work journals are more oriented toward publishing research studies, such as *Research on Social Work Practice* and *Journal of Social Service Research*. Other journals, on the other hand, publish more nonresearch studies, such as *Affila: Journal of Women and Social Work* and *Arete*. Therefore, it would seem important at this point to define just what is meant by "research" and "social work research."

Research is the systematic investigation of phenomena. It is a process of searching, investigating, and/or discovering facts by using the scientific method. *Social work research* is social and/or behavioral research that is client-centered.

It is this applied aspect of social work research that distinguishes it from sociological, psychological, or anthropological research (cf. Holosko & Leslie, 1997, for a more detailed definition of the uniqueness of social work research and its definition). In order for the study you are critiquing to be considered as "research," then, it must include all of the five elements listed in Table 20.1. It is important to note that these elements are non–mutually exclusive (in Table 20.1); that is, all five must be present to some degree in order for the study to be classified as a "research" study.

Many published articles you read in social work journals may have started out as bona fide research studies. However, along the way, either the study itself or subsections of it were written up as nonresearch studies such as reviews of literature, or presenting a theoretical framework of some kind. These articles often require a careful rereading because the author(s) may still refer to them as research (their origin), but as published, they cannot be considered as a research study for you to critique.

Nonresearch Studies

It is important to understand what constitutes a nonresearch study. Also, you should be made aware that although, in an ideal sense, good research yields good

---

TABLE 20.1

Five Basic Elements of all Research Studies

Elements	Comments
1. A specified purpose	This may take the form of a research question, study objectives, statement of purpose, or hypothesis.
2. A rationale for the study	This is the stated reason(s) for conducting the study, a literature review, or a review of pertinent theories.
3. A specified research method	This minimally includes the study's sample and the study's procedures.
4. Analysis of the data	This may be in summarized narrative, descriptive, tabular, or graph form.
5. A conclusion	This is typically in the form of concluding remarks, a discussion of the study's findings, or implications derived from the study.

knowledge, sometimes this simply does not happen; that is, some well-written research studies produce very little in the way of "new, or even useful, knowledge." Conversely, knowledge emanating from philosophical, historical, spiritual, and nonresearch worlds has contributed immeasurably to our understanding of many important discoveries and complex phenomena, advancing our thinking considerably in the process.

A nonresearch study may have one, two, three, or four of the elements of research studies listed in Table 20.1, but not all of them (remember they are non–mutually exclusive of one another). As a result, it would be deemed a nonresearch study. Upon reviewing numerous nonresearch studies in a number of social work journals, you will notice that they generally take the forms of literature reviews, critiques, and descriptions of research methods, as listed in Table 20.2.

Sometimes you may find nonresearch studies that combine some of the three types listed in Table 20.2, such as a literature review or a critique of treatment methods. By using Tables 20.1 and 20.2 together, you may now have a way of determining a research from a nonresearch study. The assumption made is that you will be appraising quantitative research studies, so if you have a nonresearch study for this purpose, go back online and find one to critique.

CRITIQUING A FEW ISSUES

Before you start critiquing in greater depth the main components of the quantitative study you have located, some pre-issues, if you will, need to be critiqued. These are the study's (1) clarity, (2) title, (3) author's or authors' affiliation, (4) abstract, and (5) references.

Clarity

Approximately 85% of the published professional research journals used in the social science and behavioral science fields require authors to use the American Psychological Association's (APA) publication guidelines (http://www.apa.org). You should purchase the manual because it not only sets the standard for stylistic requirements but is written clearly and demonstrates how the content of a research paper can be constructively directed by using the APA format. This chapter will not go over the numerous APA stylistic requirements published in the manual but rather will distill six core elements related to research writing that can be used to critique this aspect of the study. These elements are presented in Table 20.3.

The APA manual as well as other stylistic texts specify the issues of writing more comprehensively than what this chapter presents. Research writing is not the

---

TABLE 20.2

Typical Types of Nonresearch Studies in Social and Behavioral Research Journals

Types	Comments
1. Literature reviews	These are overviews of the relevant literature, synthesis/analysis of literature, or summaries of the literature.
2. Critiques of . . .	These are critiques of laws, programs, policies, methods, cases, literature, theories, treatment methods, etc. They typically do not follow a prescribed method or procedure and are idiosyncratic to the authors' analytic perspective.
3. Descriptions of research methods	These present information about research methodologies, and they do not have a substantive research focus. They basically inform about how and why a research methodology was used and its effectiveness.

TABLE 20.3

Elements Related to Clarity of Research Writing

Writing Elements	Comments
1. Are there three core subsections evident in the study?	Can you identify minimally an introduction, method, and results?
2. Clarity of ideas, findings, and discussion	Is the tone of the article clear in expressing the author's ideas, findings, and discussion?
3. The central point is evident	As you read the article carefully, is the central point of the article evident and clearly expressed?
4. 5-cent vs. 10-cent words	When you read the study, does it have fancy 10-cent words or simpler 5-cent words? Good writers try not to use a 10-cent word when they can use a 5-cent word instead.
5. Phraseology, wordiness, redundancy, and jargon	Phraseology and wordiness refers to the author's overreliance on phrases or words that are unclear or unnecessary. Ask yourself if three pages were eliminated from this study, would it matter? Redundancy means saying the same thing over and over again, in similar or different ways. It is a writing curse that many researchers have, so watch for it. Another writing curse is the overuse of technical terminology and jargon.
6. Three reads and you're out!	Carefully reread the study three times. If after three readings you still don't know what it is about, STOP! Go and get another article to critique that is more clearly written.

same as narrative or essay writing, and it is a skill that is perfected over time. The use of APA stylistic requirements does not necessarily mean that the study is clearly written.

Title

A research report, usually in the form of a journal article, is nothing more than a summary of the findings that have been derived from a research study. Obviously, every research report has a title. In a nutshell, a title is supposed to convey briefly the contents of the report. The title should be accurately written, succinct, tell precisely what the study is about, and avoid questions. For example, the title, "Depressed Women: What About Them?", leaves too much open to interpretation, speculation, and, in this particular instance, characterization. Many students have expressed dismay over the fact that sometimes the title of a study initially captured their interest, but after they read the report, it seemed as if the content really did not materialize in the way in which the title had

promised. Table 20.4 details six features that will help an author of a research report in writing the report's title.

Author's Affiliation

Authors who publish research studies usually have their credentials and employment affiliations specified somewhere within the study—usually the first or last page. Although most professional academic journals include these in their published accounts, some do not. If the article you are critiquing publishes them, you can learn a lot from these affiliations.

You need be aware that the vast majority of authors who publish articles in professional journals are academics; that is, they work for universities and colleges. Although this can create a schism between researchers and practitioners in some professional fields like social work (Holosko & Leslie, 1997), most academics in higher education are actively engaged in research to enhance knowledge in their respective professional fields.

TABLE 20.4

Features of an Appropriate Research Title

Features	Comments
1. It should have 10–12 words.	This is the recommended length by the APA.
2. It should make sense standing alone.	It should be logical, clear, and make sense as you read it, independent of the research study.
3. It should name the important study variables or theoretical issues.	These should be cited clearly in the title.
4. Makes reference to the sample.	The title should have a reference to the that was used in the study.
5. Identifies relationships among variables.	It should identify relationships between the main study variables.
6. Avoids being cutesy, posing rhetorical questions, and using jargon.	Cutesy titles have no place in research writing. Good titles also avoid posing rhetorical questions and using jargon.

By examining the affiliation of the authors, you can determine where the authors work, their degree status, and their relationship to where the study was conducted. This may give you further insights about the study you are critiquing. If, for example, an author held the position of evaluator at a social service agency and published a research study using data from this agency, such a study is likely to be a favorable evaluation of an intervention or program at that agency. In addition, with the advance of the warp-speed World Wide Web, you can usually quickly locate where authors are employed and determine if they have conducted other studies in their respective areas to give you additional insights. Now use Table 20.5 to help you assess the authors' affiliations more fully.

TABLE 20.5

What Are the Authors' Affiliations?

Can you find out . . .
- where the authors are employed?
- their degree status
- their relationship to the study?
- any additional information about them?

Abstract

The abstract is a brief summary of the research study. Like the title, it is used for abstracting, for indexing, and for computerized search engines to retrieve articles. Without a doubt, the single most important paragraph you will read in any study is its abstract. Table 20.6 lists five attributes, or elements, of well-written abstracts.

References

One of the benefits of well-written research studies is that they typically contain extensive references. Many who critique research studies often track other studies of interest from the reference list at the back of the study or article. For the record, the citations at the end of a research study are called *references*—not bibliographies.

A simple way to critique the references used within a research study is by applying the "recency and relevancy 15-10" rule. This means that the research study should have a minimum of 15 cited references (if possible), and the references should be current, meaning most have been published in the last decade (that's where the 10 comes from). This is a general critiquing guideline, and there will be some exceptions to this, of course. Table 20.7 offers a quick and simple way to critique the references in the study you are assessing.

TABLE 20.6

Elements of Well-Written Abstracts

Elements	Comments
1. Conciseness	APA recommends not exceeding 120 words or 960 characters and spaces.
2. Clarity	Define all abbreviations (except units of measurements), acronyms, and unique terms.
3. Accuracy	Make sure that it reports accurate information that is in the body of the accompanying study.
4. Specificity	It needs a good lead sentence to catch the reader's eye. It also minimally requires the purpose, method, two to three of the major study findings, and implications.
5. Active Voice	It is written in the present (not past) tense.

MAIN SECTIONS OF A QUANTITATIVE RESEARCH ARTICLE

On a very general level, there are three main sections of quantitative research studies: (1) introduction, (2) method, and (3) results. Different journals and authors may use different titles for these three main sections, but they represent the major sections of any well-written study. Each main section usually has subheadings (specified or not):

1. Introduction Section
   Subheadings: Review of Literature, Study's Purpose
2. Methods Section
   Subheadings: Sample Selection, Research Design, Data Collection Procedures, Measuring Instruments

TABLE 20.7

Assessing the References: The "15–10" Rule

Are there . . .
- at least 15 different references cited?

In addition,
- are a majority of these recent—occurring in the past 10 years?

3. Results Section
   Subheadings: Findings, Discussion, Limitations, Implications

In fact, this chapter follows the above outline and presents ways of critiquing each of the three major sections, as well as their respective subsections. At this first level of appraising a quantitative research study, you must determine whether the three main subsections are clearly delineated and related to one another. In regard to the latter, Figure 20.1 depicts an arrow logically connecting these three main sections, as well as some basic questions to consider when appraising them both individually and in their totality.

To elaborate on Figure 20.1, if a research study is well written, these three sections will follow each other in a logical fashion. For example, the Introduction section will clearly relate to the study's purpose, which, in turn, will relate to its Methods section and then finally to the Results section. This logical research progression is called *centrality of purpose*. At this first level of critiquing the study, another way to appraise these subsections is to ask yourself upon reading each section the underpinning questions as indicated in Figure 20.1, now elaborated upon in Table 20.8.

Table 20.8 shows a simple way to begin the critique of your research study. Whether you realize it or not, your critical-thinking antennae are now up

Figure 20.1   The Relationship Between the Introduction, Method, and Results

and on as you scrutinize the quantitative study before you.

Introduction Section

The first major section of a quantitative research study is its Introduction. The actual heading "Introduction" is seldom used in the study itself; nonetheless, the first part, or beginning section, of a study is called the Introduction section. Normally, the Introduction section has two subsections (which may or may not be specified) embedded within it: (1) the Review of Literature and (2) the Purpose of the Study.

Further, the literature review generally precedes the study's purpose. Sometimes, however, the purpose is stated before the literature review or is embedded within it. As a whole, the Introduction section should answer the simple question, "Why is this study being conducted and what is its purpose?" (see Figure 20.1 and Table 20.8). If upon rereading the Introduction section you cannot assess why this study was being done or what was its purpose, you should note this as a major shortcoming of the study. You should not have to read the entire study in order to understand the answers to these two key questions.

Review of the Literature

This is the section of the study in which the majority of reviewed literature is presented. The literature section serves as corroborating evidence for the study. As such, it provides the context or backdrop for the entire study.

The actual heading "Literature Review" is used infrequently. However, the authors assemble the literature that they reviewed for the study, usually organizing their review from general or related literature to more specific literature. This means that as you read on in the Introduction section, the references cited are likely to be more closely and specifically related to the purpose of the study. In addition, if the literature review is extensive, it may be organized by using one or two subheadings.

Well-written and comprehensive literature reviews are sometimes more insightful and interesting to the novice than the actual study that follows. This is particularly true if the study was methodologically remiss and/or did not provide any meaningful findings

---

TABLE 20.8

Introduction, Method, and Results Sections of a Research Study

After reading each section of the research study, answer the following questions:

Introduction
- Why is this study being done?
- What is the purpose of this study?

Method
- With whom is this study being done?
- How is the study being done?

Results
- What was found in this study?
- Who can benefit from these findings?

or practical implications. In this regard, many students who are either critiquing or conducting research scour studies for well-written, balanced, and comprehensive literature reviews. Table 20.9 provides five criteria that can be used to critique the literature review portion within an Introduction section of a research study.

Study's Purpose

Normally at the end of the literature review, the study's purpose is clearly stated. If the study purpose is not apparent in the Introduction section, the study should not have passed peer review, and/or should not have been published in the first place. This is indeed a serious faux pas, for how can one present a study if he or she does not know what it is about? Clearly stated and easily identified study purposes are the preferred norm for any responsible researcher. As indicated in Table 20.10, the study's purpose can be stated in four ways.

Latent Purposes. Upon reading the entire study, another purpose may unfold; for example, the instruments/scales used in the study may have been tested as reliable and valid with the study's sample, and thus can be used with similar populations in the future. This is referred to as a *latent purpose*, that is, one that emerged as a result of the conduct of the study. Although this was not a central purpose stated earlier in the Introduction section, you need to be mindful of emerging latent purposes when critiquing the overall purpose of the study.

Implied Purpose, or the Purpose Behind the Purpose. Sometimes there is an implied purpose, or a purpose behind the stated purpose of the study. Examples of implied purposes can include: (1) showing that an intervention worked so a program may receive more money, prestige, credibility, and so forth; (2) negating the phenomena being studied to provide a different perspective to what we have come to know about it (for any number of reasons); (3) helping a social science academic receive

---

TABLE 20.9

Critiquing the Literature Review

Elements	Comments
1. What is the *P.O.I.* of the phenomenon being studied?	Can you determine the prevalence (*P*), occurrence (*O*), and incidence (*I*) of the phenomenon that is being studied?
2. Is this a balanced (pro and con) literature review?	Do the authors present both pro and con literature to back up their study? Although there is a natural tendency to include only pro (or supportive) literature in this section, good reviews also reflect some balance and con (or nonsupportive) studies.
3. The rationale is clear.	After reading the literature review, are the reasons for doing this study clear?
4. The literature justifies the approach.	Is the literature review, first, related to the topic of study? Second, does it clearly justify the purpose of the study?
5. Adequacy.	Is the review of the literature adequate? You may wish to revisit the "15–10" rule here in order to assess its adequacy and comprehensiveness.

TABLE 20.10

Types of Study Purposes Typically Used by Social Work Researchers

Types	Comments
1. Explicitly stated statement of purpose	This includes a sentence usually beginning with the phrase "The purpose of this study is to . . ."
2. Objectives	These are an actual listing of study objectives, which are purposes of the study. They can be serialized (e.g., 1, 2, 3) and/or listed as primary (or major) or secondary (or minor) objectives.
3. Research questions	These are a series of questions that the study is hoping to answer.
4. Hypotheses	Hypotheses are stated in one of two forms. One is directional, meaning the authors connect the variables in an applied way (e.g., those people who wear large hats are also likely to wear large shoes). The other form is the null hypothesis, in which there is no relationship implied between the variables being studied—but the authors really hope that there is (e.g., there is no relationship between hat size and shoe size among people). Hypotheses are either serialized in list form (e.g., 1, 2, 3 . . .) or listed as major or minor.

---

promotion or tenure; and (4) making a case for a stakeholder with a vested interest in a phenomenon (e.g., a larger political/government agenda behind the research). Although discerning these are difficult for the beginning research consumer, you need to be aware of their presence and acknowledge them whenever possible.

Methods Section

The Methods section is the second major section of a research study and represents its heart and soul. Above all else, this section basically answers core questions, such as, what happened? to whom? how? and why? Authors place great emphasis on detailing their methods, and for good reason. First, others may wish to replicate the study to enhance its generalizability. Second, attention to methodological detail demonstrates the authors' thinking, assumptions, and scientific rigor, and the realities and obstacles of conducting the actual study. Third, others may wish to use particular aspects of the methods they utilized in their own studies (e.g., a sampling technique, a procedure, a scale or instrument, an interview schedule). The Method section

normally includes four subareas, or subheadings: (1) sample selection, (2) research design, (3) data collection procedures, and (4) measuring instruments.

Sample Selection

This subsection can be called many things, such as Participants, Research Participants, Subjects, The Sample, Sampling, Sampling Frame, or The Sample and Population. This section, however labeled, specifies how the sample was selected. Minimally included in this description are the size of the sample, the techniques used in selecting it, the sample's relationship to the population from which it was drawn, the time lines when the sample was obtained, and any unique features of the sample. These items are elaborated upon and presented as critiquing criteria in Table 20.11.

Research Design

At this point, the authors must articulate how the study was designed. Many authors use accepted and well-established research designs (see Chapter 8). It is helpful

TABLE 20.11

Critiquing the Sample Selection

Elements of the Sample	Comments
1. Size	Statisticians define a large sample as $n > 250$, and a small sample as $n < 30$.
2. Techniques used in selection	First, is there a technique mentioned (e.g., how did the authors obtain the sample for this study?). Second, do they label the technique procedurally (e.g., random sampling, random assignment to groups, cluster sampling, snowball sampling, convenience sampling, quota sampling)?
3. Relationship to the population	Do the authors specify the sample's (n's) relationship to the population (N)? Example: its size vis-à-vis the N's size, its N generalizability, its biasness, etc.
4. Time frame for selection	How long did it take to obtain the sample?
5. Other unique features	Does the sample present any unique features (e.g., its cultural context, its relationship to treatment samples, difficulties in obtaining it, specific characteristics)?

when critiquing a study's research design to schematically draw or map out the design in an effort to critique it more clearly. These symbols will be explained in more detail in the forthcoming design parameters subsection. For the most part, these symbols are idiosyncratic to different professions. Table 20.12 describes the set of criteria that may be used to critique the first set of study design elements.

Major Research Design Classification Type. All research studies—quantitative and qualitative alike—seek the acquisition of knowledge as their overarching purpose. Quantitative studies can conceptually be classified as one of four main types: descriptive, quantitative-descriptive, experimental, or quasi-experimental. In order to classify a study, you will need to pull back a bit from the Methods section and examine—in retrospect—the overall purpose of the study. This requires for you to read and probably reread the entire study, carefully appraising its central purpose and methods used together in the investigation. Table 20.13, which provides definitions of these four major types of quantitative studies, can be used to complete this task.

TABLE 20.12

Critiquing the First Set of Study Design Elements

Design Elements	Comments
1. Time	How long did it take to complete this study?
2. Groups	How many groups or subgroups were used in the study design?
3. Replicability	Can this design be replicated?
4. Internal or external threats	Are there any internal or external threats in this study as designed? These may include issues such as history, maturation, selection, testing, experimenter expectancy, generalizability, etc.

TABLE 20.13	
Four Major Classification Types of Quantitative Social Work Research	
Types	Purpose
1. Descriptive	To describe a phenomenon for some purpose (e.g., to delineate features of it, to develop hypotheses or questions, to modify our thinking of it, or to add to our knowledge of the phenomenon).
2. Quantitative-descriptive	To describe and quantify variables and relate them to each other, For example, what variables impact on others and why?
3. Experimental	Their explicit purpose is to test the relationship between independent (treatment) and dependent (outcome) variables. In order to be classified as a true experimental study, all of the following criteria must be present: (1) randomization, (2) a manipulated treatment condition (X), (3) a comparison or control group that does not receive any treatment condition, and (4) specification of hypotheses.
4. Quasi-experimental	Having the same purpose as experimental, quasi-experimental studies require some, but not all, of the criteria in 3 (above) to be present; thus they "approximate" experimental studies.

Table 20.13 provides a way for determining the main type of the quantitative research study you are critiquing. Remember that in some studies these types may overlap (e.g., descriptive and quantitative-descriptive), but upon developing critical appraisal skills, one of these overriding classification types is prominent and can be determined.

Design Objectives.   After determining which of the major designs your study follows, you should then assess its design objective. That is, what is the overall design of this study actually trying to achieve? Table 20.14 outlines the four main objectives of quantitative research studies.

Design Parameters.   Each study is designed in a way so that the researchers may optimally collect data about the variables being studied. How they collect their data is usually determined by resources, time, convenience, opportunity or fate, and/or how the researchers mapped out or planned their study's overall design. The study plan is the researcher's "road map," which helps to systematize all data collection efforts. This ensures both the consistency of data collection and the scientific integrity of the study. In turn, this enhances the generalizability of the Methods section of the overall study.

Before describing the design parameters, it is important to acquaint yourself with some of the basic symbols or nomenclature used in mapping out the study plan or schema. Table 20.15 describes some of the more familiar symbols used in mapping out the design parameters.

Now that you have an understanding of some basic symbols, you should try to map out the design parameters in your study. Table 20.16 identifies the four design parameters used in social work research studies.

Table 20.16 refers only to the basic design parameters that delineate how study data were collected. It is important to note that any of these main design parameters can be modified by: (1) adding additional observations (O's) or treatment effects (X's), and/or (2) adding more groups to the study. In clearly mapping out your study's parameters, you will find it much easier to critique its overall method.

How Many Groups Are There?   As indicated in Tables 20.15 and 20.16, the issue of how many groups of subjects now needs to be addressed and critiqued. There

TABLE 20.14

Design Objectives of Quantitative Research Studies

Objectives	Comments
1. Exploration	To explore in-depth a phenomenon, event, population, intervention, interaction, culture, etc., in order to acquire more knowledge about it.
2. Instrument/scale development	To develop an instrument, scale, inventory, interview schedule, assessment tool, or way of measuring a phenomenon and test its utility for use others.
3. Variable relationships	To test the relationships between variables for determining how they impact, associate, predict, or influence each other.
4. Evaluation research	To assess the impact of a specific program or intervention on individuals by determining its activities and outcomes. These can be evaluations of practice or programs.

TABLE 20.15

Typical Symbols in Mapping the Design Parameters

Symbols	Description/Comments
O	The "observation" of a phenomenon. In social research this observation is usually by use of a questionnaire, survey, interview, observation, schedule, shared experience, or a secondary data source (e.g., assessment forms, census). The O is really how and where the researcher collected the data and/or observed the phenomenon. A subscripted O (O_1, O_2, O_3, etc.) means these were multiple observations of the phenomenon and therefore, multiple data collection points.
X	Capital letter X is the main treatment effect or intervention given to the sample in the study. This is almost always a planned or contrived intervention that should be defined in precise research ways. This means it should minimally have a time frame in which it was given, goals and objectives, activities, and expected outcomes. Like O, it may be offered once or repeatedly (e.g. X_1, X_2, X_3).
R	Capital letter R is the symbol for "randomness." It is typically used in two ways. One is "random" selection of a sample, meaning some form of random selection procedure was used in obtaining the sample. It may also mean "randomization," in that the sample was randomly assigned to a certain treatment condition or particular group (e.g., a comparison/control group, for study purposes).

TABLE 20.16

Four Main Design Parameters

Design Parameters	Comments
1. One-shot case study with no intervention O_1	This is when a researcher collects data at one single (and only) entry point, and there is no true intervention or treatment offered. An example would be answering a telemarketing survey over the phone, responding to a survey/interview on the street or in a classroom/hospital, or observing (and recording) who dominates meetings at work.
2. One-shot case study with an intervention $X\, O_1$	Here a defined treatment effect or intervention was given to the sample. Data were then collected about its impact (or technically its non-impact). The O_1 normally occurs after the X was administered. For example, students at a university take a statistics course (X); then they receive a final examination testing their knowledge (O_1). Sometimes, the O_1 occurs simultaneous to the X. For instance, a nurse maybe studying how patients respond to getting their flu shot from the time they enter the clinic until the time they leave the clinic. Here, the X and O_1 overlap in the study condition.
3. Pre- and posttest with an intervention $O_1\, X\, O_2$	Here data are collected before the main treatment is given (O_1). This is called the "pretest"; sometimes, it is called " the baseline." The X occurs for however long it takes to be administered (i.e., for minutes, days, weeks, months, years). Then a posttest (O_2) occurs. For most studies, O_1, and O_2 use the same data collection techniques (e.g., a battery of standardized tests, survey, observation schedule) with the same sample. For example, before a daylong stress management seminar, researchers ask respondents to fill out a survey that assesses their stress-coping skills. After the seminar, they fill out the same survey to determine if the seminar helped them by comparing pretest and posttest scores. You should note that there is publication bias among social science journals toward those studies that show the treatment (X) worked, to some extent.
4. Multiple time series design with an intervention $O_1\, X\, O_2\, O_3\, O_4$	In this design, pre- and posttests occur before and after the main treatment (X). Some time elapses after and a follow-up study is administered to the sample (O_3). More time elapses, and another follow-up study is administered to the same sample (O_4). Here the researchers are trying to determine the long-term impact of the treatment effect. For example, a sample of teenagers is mandated to take a driver's education course focusing on alcohol and drugs. They receive an alcohol and drug awareness inventory (O_1), a driver's education seminar once a week for 12 weeks (X), and then the same alcohol and drug awareness inventory (O_2). At 6 months (O_3) and 12 months (O_4), they are readministered the same inventory.

are basically four main types of groups described in Table 20.17.

By using Table 20.17, you need to determine how many groups and which type of group you have in your study. A study can include more than one type of group as outlined in Table 20.17.

Data Collection Procedures

This subsection, sometimes referred to as Procedures, instructs the reader about what was done and also how it was done. Prior to considering these requirements, it is important to first indicate where the study took place (e.g., a school, an office, an emergency room, a classroom). Also, you need to appraise whether the study collected firsthand data or secondary data (data collected for another purpose), or both. These data collection criteria, as well as others, are presented in Table 20.18.

Measuring Instruments

This area of the Method section receives much critical scrutiny because, quite simply, how you measure or assess a variable determines what you will find out about the variable. Also referred to as Materials, Measures, or both, this subsection specifies how data were collected. A variety of techniques are used to obtain data ranging from casual (Chapter 10) or structured (Chapter 9) observations of people and events (e.g., recorded in some way) to rigorously controlled clinical testing with repeated and/or multiple measures. The bottom line, though, is that somehow a phenomenon was observed, described, recorded, and/or tested, and then data were generated for research purposes.

Regardless of the materials, measures, and/or instruments used for data collection purposes, standardized measures are preferred over nonstandardized ones.

TABLE 20.17

Main Types of Research Groups

Research Group Types	Comments
1. Case studies	These are in-depth studies of single or multiple individuals, families, groups, communities, organizations, cultures, phenomena, events, policies, etc. What distinguishes these is their level of analysis, in an effort to find out particular aspects unique to the study purpose.
2. Single group	This is a singular group of persons who are observed/studied in an effort to collect information about their thinking, feelings, attitudes, knowledge, perceptions, functioning, coping, attributes, etc. What distinguishes these studies from case studies is their purpose—to find out information about the phenomena of interest (e.g., anger, depression, attitudes toward others, communication skills) as it relates to this particular group.
3. Single system research (SSR)	SSRs focus on a single group ($N=1$), which may range from an individual or case to a community. They involve the continued observation of one individual/client/system before, during, and after some from of intervention (Bloom, Fischer, & Orme, 2006). They are used frequently in the helping professions (e.g., nursing, psychology, family studies, social work, education).
4. Multiple group	These studies include more than one group of persons in their data collection. A study of a group who received some form of treatment (X) and a comparison group who were not treated would be a multiple group study of two groups.

TABLE 20.18

Critiquing Data Collection Procedures

Criteria	Comments
1. Locale	Where were the data collected?
2. What was done?	What occurred during the collection of data?
3. How were data collected?	How were data collected?
4. Primary vs. secondary	Were these primary or secondary data, or both?
5. Time	How long did it take the researchers to collect these data, first by individual case, and then by the entire sample?
6. Replicability	Could one readily replicate these data collection procedures?
7. Ethical considerations	Was there an indication of one or more of the six minimal areas of research ethics: informed consent, voluntarism, right of refusal (without prejudice), respect of dignity and privacy, risk to benefits, and specification of the purpose of the study?
8. Data collectors' relationship to study's research participants	Specify the relationship between the individuals who collected these data and the actual research participants.

As we know from Chapter 5, standardized measures/ instruments are those that have been tested for reliability and validity. Nonstandardized measures/instruments have not been scrutinized as such. Typically, social work researchers use multiple measures. Or, they can use one measure such as an inventory that has a number of measures/subscales/inventories within it (i.e., the MMPI). Table 20.19 outlines five criteria that can be used to critique the materials, measures, and/or instruments of study.

Results Section

The third, and final, main section of a research study is the Results section and typically includes subsections, such as Findings, Discussion, and Implications. These three subareas, or subsections, are often clumped under the heading of Results. For critiquing purposes, however, they need to be treated separately. The Results section represents the culmination of the research study, where the authors present what they found and what the findings mean. There are three key questions that need to be asked when critiquing the Results section of a quantitative research study:

1. What are the main findings of the study?
2. How are the findings discussed?
3. Who is this study targeted to?

Findings

The findings of a study are typically summarized in tabular, graph, or chart form. Normally, data are first presented, and then discussed. One should recall that the quantitative research study you are critiquing might have been larger and found many other things during the course of its investigation. However, in the article you are critiquing, the authors are presenting only findings they feel are important, and/or ones that suit the particular forum (e.g., a journal) in which they are presenting their study's results. As such, astute students conducting literature searches of academic research journals will recognize how the same study (or versions/parts of it) has been published in different

TABLE 20.19

Critiquing the Materials and Instruments Used

Elements	Comments
1. Instruments/scales/inventories/ observation schedules/questions	What instruments/scales/inventories/observations schedules/questions etc., were used to collect the data?
2. Materials used	In addition to the actual instruments (e.g., interview schedules, standardized tests, clinical tests), used in the study, were any other materials used during data collection (e.g., audio/ video tapes, reports, manuals, correspondence, computer records)?
3. Reliability and validity	Comment on the researchers' appraisal of the reliability and validity of the various instruments utilized in the study.
4. Replicability	Comment on the ability to replicate the use of all materials and instruments used in this study.
5. Pretesting	Do the researchers comment on whether these instruments were pretested or not?

forms across different journals for different intended audiences. This "double-dipping," as researchers call it, is not unusual.

Tables/Graphs/Charts. As indicated above, the easiest way to summarize or condense data is by placing them into tables, graphs, and/or charts. Data about the findings may also be presented in narrative form (written in the text), but the use of tables, graphs, or charts is preferred due to their simplicity and visual appeal. A general guideline is that six or fewer data points can be presented in the text, but more than that may better lend themselves to being portrayed in a table, graph, or chart. Some authors suffer from "table-itis," in that they either construct too many tables, graphs, or charts or present them in confusing ways. Table 20.20 outlines criteria for you to use in critiquing the various tables, graphs, and/or charts in your study.

Statistics. The first thing authors do when they present their data is to describe what they found. They do this with descriptive statistics as discussed in depth in Chapter 17. These are simply numerical descriptors of the data. They typically include: frequencies (f), percentages (%), the mean or arithmetic average (X), the mode or the most frequently occurring number (M_0), the median (Me) or that number in which 50% of the number set is above and 50% fall below, and the standard deviation (SD) or how far things vary from the mean in a standard way. Descriptive data are almost always presented first, before the testing of relationships within the data set.

Authors also test or analyze the relationships among the variables they have measured, via parametric and nonparametric statistical tests. The former refers to a set of statistical tests based on the assumptions of normality (i.e., the normal curve). Typical parametric tests used include: the Student t-test (t), Pearson correlation test (r), analysis of variance (ANOVA), and regression (R^2). Conversely, nonparametric statistical tests do not hold the assumptions of normality (e.g., smaller samples and/or biased samples), which are not generalizable to normal populations. Typical nonparametric tests used here include: McNemar's test, Fishers' exact test, Mann-Whitney U, Kolmogorav-Smirnov (K-S) test, and Wilcoxon sign. One test used frequently

---

TABLE 20.20

Critiquing the Study's Tables, Graphs, or Charts

Criteria	Comments
1. Number of tables, graphs, or charts	Three or fewer of any combination of tables, graphs, or charts is the general rule.
2. Titles	Are the titles of the tables, graphs, or charts "stand-alone," meaning you can understand the accompanying table, graph, or chart just by reading the title?
3. Sample size noted	Are all sample sizes noted both in the title and also within the main column and row headings of the table, graph, or chart?
4. Actual length	One-half to three-quarter of a page is the preferred length for any table, graph, or chart.
5. Clarity	Are data presented in the table, graph, or chart clearly understood?

---

by social researchers that cuts across both branches is the Chi-square test (X^2) of significance; however, different versions of it are used for both parametrics and nonparametrics. The three main issues about using any statistical test are: (1) to examine the data and their assumptions, (2) to select the correct statistical test, and (3) to then interpret what the test means.

Each parametric or nonparametric test used is presented as a test of significance. This lets you determine whether that test resulted in a statistically significant relationship between the variables (e.g., $p < .05$) or not (e.g., $p > .05$). As a result, students quickly find out that focusing on the significance levels of these inferential tests (when critiquing research studies) is far more important than the actual mathematical value of the text presented in the study (e.g., $X^2 = 14.32$). Regardless of what statistical test is being used by the researchers, if it is not significant, it is not significant. Table 20.21 provides a list of criteria that can be used to critique the statistical data and tests used in the study.

Data About the Sample.   Although data describing the sample (N) typically occur in the Results section of the research study, they are sometimes presented in the Methods section under the Sample Selection subheading. These data differ from how the sample was selected

---

TABLE 20.21

Critiquing the Statistical Data and Tests Used

Statistical Criteria	Comments
1. Presentation	In which form(s) are the statistical data presented in the study?
2. Clarity	Are the statistical data presented clearly and understandably?
3. Descriptive statistics	Which descriptive statistics are reported in the results?
4. Parametric statistics	Which parametric statistical tests are used in the study?
5. Nonparametric statistics	Which nonparametric statistical tests are used in the study?
6. Statistical significance	Are the findings of the inferential test(s) used (parametric or nonparametric) significant or not?

because they provide descriptive data about the research participants who actually took part in the study. These data usually precede other descriptive data or statistical test data because they provide a context for understanding any subsequent findings.

For instance, if the sample had an average age of 11, it would make sense that as a group, the sample scored low on the Banking Skills Inventory test. As a rule, the more detail presented about the peculiarities of the sample the better, as it assists in critiquing the findings yet to be presented. Sample data are presented either in narrative form (in the text if there is not excessive information) or in tabular form if there is more information about the sample. Table 20.22 presents the criteria for analyzing a study's sample.

Discussion

Although this subheading may not actually appear in the Results section, it is important for researchers to now discuss their study's findings and what these findings mean to social work practice, education, policy, or future research efforts. Of all the subsections of research reports, the Discussion subsection is where the researchers exercise their discretion on which "slant" to take, based on what is emphasized in this subsection. This is also deemed to be the most interpretive part of the study because, quite literally, one researcher could discuss the finding in terms of a cup that is "half empty" and render a conclusion. Yet another could discuss the same finding in terms of a cup that is "half full" and render a very different conclusion. Technically, both interpretations and their corresponding discussions would be accurate.

Authors normally discuss their results from two perspectives. One is from the perspective of the literature itself (i.e., did the findings support or refute the literature). The second is from the author's own perspective, analysis, or opinion, which is typically anchored in a point of view that is both logical (to the author) and/or "checkable." Ideally, a well-written discussion subsection presents a balanced (pro and con) and comprehensive explanation of the study's main findings. Even though we may be compelled to eventually render an overall discussion about our study's findings, they will tend to have much more credibility if they are first discussed appropriately one at a time. Table 20.23 presents a list of criteria that may be used to critique the Discussion subsection of a research study.

Limitations

Although they rarely single out limitations as a separate subsection in a research study (except for academic theses or dissertations), researchers usually cite two to three limitations of their studies, which, in a sense, will temper the studies' results and subsequent discussion of their findings. Social work research is, by

---

TABLE 20.22

Critiquing the Population (*N*) and Sample (*n*) Data

Sample Criteria	Comments
1. Size	What are the final sample sizes in this study?
2. Bias/representativeness	Would you say that this is a biased sample or a sample representative of a larger population?
3. Population (*N*) bias	Is the population (*N*) from which this sample was selected biased itself?
4. Descriptive features	What does this sample actually look like?
5. Unique features	Outside of its descriptive features noted above, does the sample have any other unique features as well (e.g., treatment contamination)?

TABLE 20.23

Critiquing the Discussion Subsection

Criteria	Comments
1. Relationship to the results	Does the discussion logically follow the previously presented results?
2. Emphasis	What findings from the results do the researchers primarily focus on in their discussion?
3. How were the results discussed?	How do the authors use literature to discuss their findings?
4. Balanced review	Does the discussion present a pro and/or con view, or differing interpretations of the results?
5. Expected or not?	Were the results discussed expected by the researchers or not?

---

its very nature, fraught with a degree of empirical uncertainty and obstacles (e.g., sampling, measurement, controlling for extraneous or confounding factors). As a result, seasoned researchers negotiate the conduct of their studies around these existing and expected obstacles. If the author fails to cite some limitations, he or she may inadvertently give the appearance to the reader that they do not exist—and this simply is not true. Table 20.24 cites the minimal criteria that should be used to assess a study's limitations.

Implications

Congratulations! You have reached the final subsection of a quantitative research study. This is where the entire study comes together, as the authors (hopefully) relate the main results of their studies, or findings, to particu-

lar groups that may benefit from knowing the findings. Prior to assessing this, you need to understand that good research ideally produces knowledge, first and foremost. So an appraisal of the types of knowledge that the study actually produced needs to be made. A method for determining this has been developed by Rosen, Proctor, and Staudt (1999). They present a hierarchy of knowledge on three levels, as indicated in Table 20.25.

As indicated previously, it is incumbent on researchers to connect or relate their studies' findings to particular groups of individuals who may potentially benefit from the findings. Normally, one or two such groups or research beneficiaries are mentioned in this context. Table 20.26 lists a selected list of such individuals, groups, or organizations that are really the study's stakeholders, or those who may have a vested interest in the findings derived from the study.

TABLE 20.24

Critiquing the Limitations Subsection

Criteria	Comments
1. What are the limitations?	What study limitations are noted by the authors? What study limitations are not noted by the authors?
2. Major or minor?	Regardless of whether the limitations are cited or not, do you consider them to be major or minor limitations?
3. Future research	What limitations need attending to in any future research studies of this nature?

TABLE 20.25

Types of Knowledge Derived From Social Work Research Studies

Knowledge Types	Definitions
1. Descriptive	Guides the classification of phenomena into meaningful conceptual categories (e.g., rates of poverty, prevalence of child abuse).
2. Exploratory	Guides the understanding of phenomena—their interrelationships, factors influencing their variability, and their consequences (e.g., relationship between depression and function, factors associated with hospital readmission).
3. Control	Identifies means of influencing events or behaviors; the direction of influence can be maintenance (prevention) or change (intervention, increasing or decreasing). Examples include studies of prevention, demonstration of the effects of interventions, etc.

TABLE 20.26

A List of Potential Individuals, Groups, or Organizations That Are Typically Targeted in Social Work Research Study Implications

Potential Stakeholders	Comments
1. Study participants	These are the individuals who provided the study data.
2. Other consumers	Clients, patients, students, or other members of a general or treatment population.
3. Practitioners	Front-line practitioners who work in social, educational, health, legal, or human service agencies. These include governmental and nongovernmental agencies.
4. Supervisors	Middle managers or supervisors working in social, educational, health, legal, and/or human service agencies.
5. Administrators	Upper-level managers working in social, educational, health, legal, and/or human service agencies
6. Policy makers	Persons involved in making policy decisions in social, educational, health, legal, and/or human service agencies.
7. Agency boards	Boards of directors of social, educational, health, legal, and/or human service agencies.
8. Communities	Members of communities, including individuals, groups, and organizations.
9. Program planners	Persons involved in planning in social, educational, health, legal, and/or human service agencies.
10. Researchers	Other social work researchers.
11. Educators	Those who may educate others about the findings of this study.
12. Funders	Individuals, groups, or organizations that provide funds for social, educational, health, legal, and/or human service agencies.
13. Providers of authority	Individuals, groups, or organizations that provide legitimacy or authority for social, educational, health, legal, and/or human service agencies.
14. Other organizations/ agencies	Other governmental or nongovernmental organizations or agencies not included in the list above.

SUMMARY

By using the information in this chapter systematically, students or consumers of quantitative research can basically pick up any such study and critique it piece by piece, section by section, subheading by subheading, from the title at the beginning to the reference list at the end. It is assumed that such critiquing skills will not only make you a better and more informed consumer of quantitative research, but will also eventually make you a better producer of it as well. In addition, the repeated use of this skill will help you to appraise social work research in a more critical way, that is, with an acknowledgment of its precise strengths and limitations, and with a more tempered skeptical—not cynical—mind's eye. It is only through developing a more open-minded and critical perspective that consumers of social work research can advance their learning of the research enterprise.

Upon using these criteria, you also have to be reminded of a few other things. One is that social work research, by its very nature, is fraught with empirical uncertainty. We constantly struggle with issues of how to better ask the right questions, how to sample more selectively, how to measure variables more precisely, how to analyze data more completely and accurately, and how to disseminate findings to groups that can best benefit from our investigations.

Such realities are viewed as the "nature of the research business," and in no way should they inhibit you from striving to conduct good research or research that is well written. It is only through our commitment to good research in social work that new facts, theories, insights, phenomena, and knowledge can be advanced. Hopefully, this chapter has provided you with an opportunity to become a better critical thinker and astute consumer of quantitatively oriented social work research. The following chapter, which parallels this one, explains how to evaluate qualitative research reports.

Evaluating Qualitative
Research Studies

James C. Raines

Basic Steps in the Research Process

Step 1   Choose a problem

2   Review the literature

You Are Here →

3   Evaluate the literature

4   Be aware of all ethical issues

5   Be aware of all cultural issues

6   State the research question or hypothesis

7   Select the research approach

8   Determine how the variables are going to be measured

9   Select a sample

10   Select a data collection method

11   Collect and code the data

12   Analyze and interpret the data

13   Write the report

14   Disseminate the report

Before we can provide evaluative criteria for qualitative studies, it is necessary to establish the justification for determining their overall "research rigor." This requires a rebuttal to the position that the question of rigor should not be applied to qualitative research (Schwandt, 1996; Shank & Villella, 2004; Wolcott, 1994). This position is untenable for philosophical, pragmatic, and ethical reasons.

On a *philosophical level*, the postmodern assertion that social reality does not exist except as it is constructed by the perceiver can lead to nihilism and absurdity (Thyer & Wodarski, 1998; Wakefield, 1995). If truth is only opinion, then we have no way to determine whether child abuse, domestic violence, and discrimination actually occur (McNeill, 2006). If they are simply different points of view with no means to determine which is correct, then societal standards will devolve into chaos and anarchy.

On a *pragmatic level*, there are at least four reasons to judge the quality of qualitative research studies:

- First, practitioners must be able to trust research enough to act upon its findings when working with clients (Lincoln, 2001).
- Second, faculty on thesis or dissertation committees must determine which student research projects are passable (Strauss & Corbin, 1998).
- Third, funding agencies and foundations must know how to evaluate the quality of qualitative research proposals (Silverman, 1997).
- Finally, journal reviewers must decide which studies deserve to be published and which do not (Raines & Massat, 2004).

On an *ethical level*, Padgett (1998) argues that since social work findings are ultimately used to inform practice and policy, rigorous criteria are also an ethical mandate. The NASW (2005) Standards for Clinical Social Work, for example, state that "clinical social workers shall seek to enhance their skills and understanding by staying abreast of research to ensure that their practice reflects the most current knowledge" (p. 21).

CRITERIA FOR EVALUATING QUALITATIVE STUDIES

This chapter addresses several criteria for evaluating qualitative research reports. Readers will be given 34 different criteria to examine the quality of each study. This is not done to promote technical essentialism or a "cookbook" approach (Barbour, 2003), but simply to remind both researchers and research consumers that there are ways to distinguish good qualitative research from bad. We will address the nine common sections contained in one form or another within qualitative research reports: (1) Introduction, (2) Review of the Literature, (3) Research Question, (4) Rationale, (5) Ethics, (6) Data Collection, (7) Research Rigor, (8) Data Analysis, and (9) Discussion.

Introduction

Every qualitative research report takes a position about two a priori issues: the nature of reality (ontology) or knowledge (epistemology). Regarding *ontology*, some researchers believe in a mind-independent reality (realists), and some believe in multiple realities (relativists). Similarly, regarding *epistemology*, some researchers believe in one best way to do research (objective empiricism), while others believe in multiple methods (subjective constructivism). Ann Hartman (1990) suggested, "These assumptions must be made explicit, because knowledge and truths can be understood and evaluated only in the context of the framing assumptions" (p. 4). Thus, it is especially important that qualitative researchers identify their philosophical assumptions up front (Anastas, 2004; Drisko, 1997; Shek, Tang, & Han, 2005).

Review of the Literature

This section will discuss seven aspects of a good literature review. An excellent literature review will be based on a sufficient search, relevant literature, and current literature; and it will possess obvious organization, demonstrate a critical evaluation, have a clear purpose, and be iterative.

Sufficient Search

To begin, a good review of the literature must be based on a sufficient search. This is even more important in qualitative research than quantitative research because it is often exploratory and interested in a diversity of viewpoints. This means the researcher searched a *sufficient* number of databases (usually at least three) and tracked down an appropriate number of leads to further sources until a point of saturation has been reached. Depending on the topic, the review may include literature from anthropology, communications, education, nursing, psychology, sociology, or theology.

Examples of Insufficient Searches

* Research on AIDS does not utilize any medical or nursing sources.
* Research on schools does not use any education or psychology sources.
* Research on religion does not use any sociological or theological sources.

Examples of Sufficient Searches

* Research on AIDS uses medical, nursing, and social work sources.
* Research on schools uses education, psychology, and social work sources.
* Research on religion uses sociological, theological, and psychological sources.

Relevant Literature

Second, the researcher should have selected the most *relevant* literature to the problem addressed. The closer the connection to the study's primary interest, the better. Most literature searches can be conceptualized as a Venn diagram. In one circle are the articles about the specific problem being researched. In the other circle are the articles about the specific population being studied. The most relevant articles address both the problem and the population.

Examples of Irrelevant Literature

* A study on adolescents with AIDS includes only studies on adults with AIDS.

- A study on children with ADHD includes only studies on adolescents with ADHD
- A study on elderly Muslims includes only studies on Islamic parenting styles

Examples of Relevant Literature

- A study on adolescents and AIDS includes studies on teens with AIDS.
- A study on children with ADHD includes studies of ADHD in elementary schools.
- A study on elderly Muslims includes studies on Islam and hospice care.

Current Literature

Third, the research unearthed must be *current*. While there is always room for classic studies, most of the material should have been published within 5 to 10 years of the acceptance date (often found at the end of the article).

Examples of Dated Literature

- More than 50% of the sources are at least 5 years old.
- More than 25% are at least 10 years old

Example of Current Literature

- More than 50% of the sources have been published within 5 years of the article's publication date
- Less than 25% will be more than 10 years old

Obvious Organization

The literature review should also be *organized* (Neuman, 2000). A good literature review has a logical progression. There are multiple ways that authors can organize their material—historically (old to recent), conceptually (general to specific), theoretically (macro to micro theories), geographically (national to local), or methodologically (quantitative, qualitative, and mixed studies). The outline should be discernible through a list of headings and subheadings.

Examples of a Disorganization

- Literature review does not include any headings or subheadings.
- Literature review mixes organizational frameworks (history, geography, method).

Examples of Obvious Organization

- Literature review utilizes headings and subheadings.
- Literature review consistently uses one organizational framework.

Critical Evaluation

Fourth, the literature review should also be *critical*. Rather than simply accepting other findings at face value, the researcher should evaluate those findings. There is no such thing as perfect research, so it is logical to assume that all research has limitations. These limitations might be the sampling plan, the data collection technique, inappropriate data analysis, and so forth. The stronger the study's method, the more weight that study ought to carry in the review. Some of the best examples of critical reviews occur in a type of research called *meta-analysis*, which uses very specific criteria to rule out weak studies in favor of strong ones (e.g., Staudt, Howard, & Drake, 2001).

Examples of Uncritical Review

- The review treats all studies equally regardless of quality.
- The review does not identify strengths or weaknesses in the studies.

Examples of a Critical Review

- The review identifies specific criteria used to locate the best studies.
- The review addresses methodological issues in the studies cited.

Clear Purpose

The literature review should be *purposeful*. In other words, the literature review should substantiate the need for the current study—perhaps there is a gap in the current literature, a qualitative method has not been used previously, or there are conflictual findings that need to be resolved. No study should be done simply because it is interesting to the researcher; its purpose and method must be driven by the literature review.

Examples of Unclear Purposes

- The literature review does not draw any conclusions.
- The conclusion is unrelated to the study question.

Examples of a Clear Purpose

- The literature review has a concluding or summary paragraph.
- The literature review provides logical support for the research question.

Iterative

Finally, as Williams, Unrau, and Grinnell (1998, 2005) emphasize, a qualitative literature search should be *iterative*, or repeated throughout the life of the study. This means that new literature is reviewed both before and after the data have been collected and may be introduced even late into the Discussion section as new insights or implications emerge.

Example of a Noniterative Review

- New literature never appears in the Discussion section.

Examples of an Iterative Review

- New literature is introduced in the Discussion section.

Research Question

One of the differences between quantitative and qualitative research is that the latter seldom formulates an explicit hypothesis. Most qualitative research then will ask an open-ended question. This section identifies two important aspects of a good research question, including clarity and key concepts.

Clarity of the Research Question

The question posed determines much of the rationale of the research design, so it is important to be *clear* from the start. There should be only one question word

Criteria	Yes	No
1. Were philosophical assumptions identified prior to the study?	____	____
2. Were the databases searched sufficient to the question?	____	____
3. Was the literature review relevant to both problem and population?	____	____
4. Was the literature current at the time it was written?	____	____
5. Did the author use headings and subheadings to organize ideas?	____	____
6. Did the author identify any differences in previous studies?	____	____
7. Did the literature review support the purpose of the study?	____	____
8. Was there evidence the literature was researched iteratively?	____	____

Figure 21.1   Criteria for Assessing the Introduction and Literature Review of a Qualitative Research Study

(e.g., *what or how*) in the question, and the question should never be double-barreled.

Examples of Poor-Clarity Questions

- How do social workers see their effectiveness and why?
- What are social workers' perceptions of their effectiveness and efficiency?

Examples of Good-Clarity Questions

- How do social workers perceive their effectiveness with clients?
- What do social work practitioners think effective practice is?

Second, good questions should also include the *key concepts* in the study. This helps readers determine the primary variables under scrutiny and avoids ambiguous language. For example, the word *good* has several connotations, including moral and ethical aspects that research cannot solve.

Examples of Missing Concepts

- How do clients get better?
- What is good social work practice?

Examples of Key Concepts

- How do clients with depression perceive improvement?
- How do social workers define effective practice?

Conceptual Definitions

Qualitative research is more interested in the subjective views of the participants than the "objective" viewpoint of the researcher and is more inductive rather than deductive (Anastas, 2004). Thus, while quantitative researchers operationally define their variables, qualitative researchers frequently offer broad conceptual definitions of their primary variables and leave the details to their respondents.

First, these constructs will ideally be *multidimensional*, including biological, psychological, sociological, and cultural dimensions. Take the term *depression*, for example. There are biological issues associated with

depression, such as disturbances in eating and sleeping. There are psychological issues, such as negative thoughts and unwanted emotions. There are social issues, such as isolation and irritability. There are even cultural issues, such as sexual and racial discrimination. If we conceptualized depression through just one lens, we could miss seeing the total picture.

Examples of Unidimensional Definitions

- Depression is defined as having negative thoughts about the future.
- Poverty is defined as having less income than the poverty line.

Examples of Multidimensional Definitions

- Depression is defined as a mixture of physiological, psychological, sociological, and cultural disturbances that lead to a state of prolonged unhappiness.
- Poverty is defined as a combination of physiological, psychological, sociological, and cultural deficits that result in a position of inferior status.

These initial definitions must also be *flexible* over the life of the study. For example, Andrews, Guadalupe, and Bolden (2003) found that they had to expand their original definition of empowerment after analyzing interviews with poor rural women from the South to include interpersonal support, intrapersonal optimism, and faith in a higher power.

Rationale

The rationale for using a qualitative method should meet two criteria. These are *logical reasons* and *goodness of fit*.

Logical Reasons

Using Unrau (2005) as a starting point, there are at least 10 logical reasons for choosing a qualitative approach.

- First, qualitative studies are most feasible when the *size* of the sample is necessarily small (30 or fewer participants).

- Second, mixed (qualitative and quantitative) studies can be justified when the *scope* of the problem is complex and a single approach may not collect all the relevant data.
- Third, qualitative studies may be required to obtain *program participation*. Some agencies have found that certain cultural groups (e.g., Native Americans) object to numerical descriptions and prefer a narrative approach (Laird, 2003; Lomawaima & McCarty, 2002).
- Fourth, *workers* may object to the additional work involved in collecting data, preferring that evaluators use existing case records, progress notes, or other narrative sources.
- Fifth, a more *intrusive* approach (e.g., in-depth face-to-face interviews) is most appropriate when the researcher wants to obtain a genuinely insider point of view. Similarly, the lack of culturally sensitive instruments may indicate that the flexibility of qualitative interviewing is preferable (Rodgers-Farmer & Potocky-Tripodi, 2005).
- Sixth, qualitative studies depend on the availability of certain *resources*: equipment such as tape recorders and a transcription machine and training on content analysis.
- Seventh, the extra *time* to conduct, transcribe, and analyze in-depth interviews is a necessity.
- Eighth, *previous research* may have neglected the qualitative focus on feelings, relationships, or natural settings (Anastas, 2004). Also finding a low level of preexisting knowledge can justify an exploratory study using a qualitative method.
- Ninth, the *clarity of variables* is a concern. Some concepts are fuzzy—they mean different things to different people. Consider the word *spirituality*, for example. Some people narrowly subsume it under Christianity, some equate it with religiosity, and some contrast it with religion altogether. Thus, the more ambiguous the concept, the more a qualitative approach to investigation should be used.
- Finally, the *stigmatization* of certain groups (e.g., gay Evangelicals) may create problems with access and require a nonprobability sampling plan

(Atkinson & Flint, 2001). Thus, there are multiple reasons for choosing a qualitative design, and the reasons should be explicitly stated by the researcher(s).

Examples of Illogical Reasons

- Qualitative method was chosen due to fear of math or computers.
- Qualitative method was chosen because it was felt to be easier.

Examples of Logical Reasons

- Qualitative method was chosen because the available sample size was small.
- Qualitative method was chosen because the primary variables were fuzzy.

Goodness of Fit

Second, there should a *goodness of fit* between the research question and the data collection techniques (Howe & Eisenhart, 1990). Qualitative research is most appropriate when the focus is on the context, feelings, interpersonal processes, and in-depth perspectives of the respondents.

Examples of Lack of Fit

- Qualitative research is chosen to determine respondents' knowledge on a survey.
- Qualitative research is chosen to determine respondents' behavior while observed.

Examples of Goodness of Fit

- Qualitative research is chosen to determine how people connected after the terrorist attacks of 9/11.
- Qualitative research is chosen to determine what people felt after 9/11.

Ethics

There are four important ethical issues to look for in qualitative research. These include value awareness, informed consent, protection of confidentiality, and doing good.

Value Awareness

Due to the subjective nature of qualitative research, it is essential that researchers demonstrate some *value awareness*. Since strongly held values have the capacity to undermine the credibility of a study, researchers should report any potential biases and how they may have affected the study (Anastas, 2004; Drisko, 1997).

Examples of Value Unawareness

* Researcher does not reveal personal connections to the participants.
* Researcher does not reveal personal reasons for doing the study.
* Researcher reveals personal connections or reasons but denies these have any effect on the conclusions drawn.

Examples of Value Awareness

* Christian researcher reveals he is a member of the congregation he is studying.
* Gay researcher reveals his sexual orientation when investigating gay bashing.
* Both researchers admit that their personal connections or reasons could affect their conclusions and identify steps they have taken to reduce this influence.

Informed Consent

Qualitative research has similar ethical requirements as quantitative research (Drisko, 1997). Research reports should at least document how voluntary informed consent was obtained (Rodwell & Woody, 1994).

Examples of Lack of Informed Consent

* Researcher who is studying children asks the kids if it is all right to ask them a few questions.
* Prison social worker asks the inmates if he can interview them about their crimes.

Examples of Informed Consent

* Researcher of children gets a signed consent from the children and their parents.

* Prison social worker gets a signed consent from prisoners, promises confidentiality, and guarantees their answers will not affect their sentence or possible parole.

Protecting Confidentiality

Since qualitative studies often use face-to-face interviews with colorful characters, it is always tempting to reveal so much that confidentiality is jeopardized. Research reports should also indicate how confidential identities were protected (Anastas, 2004). This is especially important when the research involves children or other vulnerable populations (Huber & Clandinin, 2002; Oakes, 2002).

Examples of Unprotected Confidentiality

* Researcher changes names but provides physical descriptions of people in a small town.
* Researcher changes names but provides gender and ages of people within a small association.

Examples of Protected Confidentiality

* Researcher changes names and changes descriptions to protect participants.
* Researcher changes names and omits demographic data to protect participants.

Doing Good

Finally, several qualitative researchers have suggested that research should not simply abide by the Hippocratic oath of "doing no harm," but that it should also *do good* (Lincoln, 1998; Shamai, 2003). While the standard of beneficence has been around since the Belmont Report of 1978, it was understood in a utilitarian way of producing more benefits than harm. As Christians (2005) points out, participants were often left out of this equation since the benefits accrued primarily to the researcher in the form of publications, prestige, and pay.

From a communitarian perspective, interpretivist research promotes the common good of the researched community. This includes action research that aims to liberate people from the tyrannies of racism, sexism, heterosexism, and classism (Valdivia, 2002). Denzin

(2003) describes the radical implications for research: "Participants have a co-equal say in how research should be conducted, what should be studied, which methods are acceptable, how the findings are to be implemented, and how the consequences of such actions are to be addressed" (p. 257).

Examples of Not Doing Good

- Researcher uncovers therapist's sexual abuse of clients, but does nothing about it.
- Researcher reports the therapist's sexual abuse but offers no resources for the victims.
- Researcher reports the therapist's sexual abuse and gives advice to victims but does not consider their concerns about how exposure will affect their marriages.

Examples of Doing Good

- Researcher uncovers therapist's sexual abuse of clients and discusses options with the survivors.
- Researcher documents evidence of the sexual abuse but waits until the survivors agree to make it public before reporting it.

- Researcher collaborates with the survivors about what evidence is needed, when to share it, how it will be shared, and how the consequences will be handled.

Data Collection

There are three major issues in the data collection phase of qualitative research: (1) justifying nonprobability sampling, (2) supplementing subjectivity, and (3) addressing bias.

Justifying Nonprobability Sampling

While quantitative research leans toward probability sampling, qualitative research tends toward nonprobability sampling (Padgett, 1998). Schutt (2005) discusses four common types of nonprobability sampling, but it is important for the researcher to clarify *why* this kind of sampling occurred. Availability or convenience sampling is most appropriate when the researcher is just starting to explore a phenomenon (e.g., people who sleep at rest stops) or just beginning to pilot some questions. Quota sampling is most appropriate when the researcher

Criteria	Yes	No
9. Was the research question clear?	___	___
10. Did the question include all of the major concepts?	___	___
11. Were the conceptual definitions multidimensional?	___	___
12. Did the definitions evolve as participants gave their perspective?	___	___
13. Was there a logical rationale for doing a qualitative study?	___	___
14. Was there a good fit between the research question and the method?	___	___
15. Did the study demonstrate value awareness?	___	___
16. Were informed consent procedures described?	___	___
17. Did the study describe how confidentiality was kept?	___	___
18. Did the study advance the common good of its participants?	___	___

Figure 21.2 Criteria for Assessing the Research Question, Conceptual Definitions, Rationale, and Ethics of a Qualitative Research Study

knows from the literature review which demographic characteristics (e.g., gender, age, or race) are most likely to affect the results and how often these characteristics appear in the target population. Purposive sampling is most appropriate when the researcher can find people who fit a particular profile and are knowledgeable and willing to discuss the topic.

The size of the sample is often left open until the researcher feels that the information is complete and that a point of saturation has been reached (Rubin & Rubin, 1995). Finally, snowball sampling is most useful for locating hard-to-reach participants who are part of a loosely affiliated network (e.g., married gay men) or exploring the relationships among a group (e.g., informal opinion leaders in an organization).

Examples of Nonjustification

- Researcher simply states her sample is convenient but offers no reason for it.
- Researcher states his sample is a snowball, but a random sample would be better.

Examples of Justification

- Researcher is piloting a new instrument and uses convenience sampling.
- Researcher specifies the criteria for selecting people for a purposive sample.

Supplementing Subjectivity

Another issue related to data collection regards measurement. While quantitative research tends to rely on standardized measuring instruments, qualitative studies are more likely to use semistructured or unstructured interviews, participant observation, or archival research. This means that the reliability and validity of the instruments cannot be determined in the traditional way. In fact, the chief instrument of qualitative research is the person doing the research (Franklin & Ballan, 2005). Thus, good qualitative research will take steps to supplement the *subjectivity* of the researcher by specialized measures. More will be said about this later in the section "Issues Related to Rigor."

Addressing Bias

The final issue in data collection is *bias*. We have already discussed the importance of value awareness above, and that is a prerequisite to addressing bias. Miles and Huberman (1994) discuss two sources of bias in data collection. The first involves the researcher's influence on the participants. The second involves the participants' influence on the researcher. The solution is to provide a system of checks and balances to keep biases from affecting the findings (Shek et al., 2005). Strategies for reducing the researcher's influence on participants include striving to fit into the landscape, using unobtrusive measures, being clear about your intentions with informants, and doing interviews in an informal, relaxed setting. Strategies for reducing the participants' influence on the researcher include avoiding the overuse of "elite" (articulate or attractive) respondents, avoiding "going native," seeking out "marginal" (dissident or deviant) informants, co-opting a participant to do some of the interviewing, using multiple data sources, and staying focused on the research question.

Examples of Not Addressing Bias

- The researcher asks leading questions of the participants.
- The researcher accepts the participants' version of events without scrutiny.

Examples of Addressing Bias

- The researcher dresses more like the participants to decrease social distance.
- The researcher interviews participants in familiar contexts where they feel more relaxed.
- The researcher deliberately seeks out a broad range of respondents.
- The researcher distrusts "party-line" answers and reaches for disagreement.

Research Rigor

Not surprisingly, the interpretive approach tends to use different terms for rigor than quantitative studies. Interpretivists prefer the term *trustworthiness* over *rigor*, meaning that the findings must be authentic enough to allow practitioners to act upon them with confidence (Lincoln & Guba, 2000). Instead of positivist terms like *internal* and *external validity, reliability,* or *objectivity,* interpretivists use *credibility, transferability, dependability,* and *confirmability* (Guba, 1981). Let's discuss each of these in order.

Credibility

As Williams, Unrau, and Grinnell (1998, 2005) indicate, *credibility* is the interpretivist version of internal validity. It answers the query, "Can these findings be regarded as truthful?" Credibility can be enhanced through the following measures:

- *Triangulation of data sources*—asking three different groups of people about progress (e.g., child, parent, and teacher)
- *Consulting with colleagues*—asking knowledgeable partners to check one's sampling techniques, data collection methods, or data analysis procedures
- *Negative case analysis*—purposely including contradictory data to determine the limits of the main themes or conclusions
- *Referential adequacy*—keeping an accurate account of all interviews, tapes, transcriptions, and field notes
- *Member checks*—asking the participants to give feedback on the accuracy of the information collected or the conclusions drawn by the researcher
- *Thick descriptions of verbatim statements*—providing in-depth accounts of what the participants actually said (including nonverbal and paraverbal information) so that readers can determine for themselves if they agree with the interpretation.
- *Triangulation of analysts*—using two or more coders to achieve a satisfactory level of intercoder reliability (>.80).
- *Testing for rival hypotheses*—considering other possible explanations for the observations made

in order to determine if another theory provides a better interpretation.
- *Triangulation of theories*—using different theories to understand the findings, e.g., micro, mezzo, or macro theories.
- *Prolonged engagement*—spending sufficient time with the participants to ensure that their answers are consistent over time or that they are no longer reacting to the presence of the investigator.
- *Triangulation of methods*—using different methods of collecting data, for example, through interviews, observations, or archival materials.

Examples of Poor Credibility

- Researcher conducts a single-session interview with respondents.
- Researcher collects and analyzes data without consulting colleagues or participants.
- Researcher does not provide verbatim quotes to illustrate themes.

Examples of Good Credibility

- Researcher conducts multiple interviews and occasionally repeats a question to see if the same answer is given as in the previous interview.
- Researcher repeatedly checks with colleagues and participants about the accuracy and logic of both findings and conclusions.
- Researcher provides both the context and complete sentences of verbatim quotes used to justify themes.

Transferability

Transferability is the interpretivist counterpart to external validity. While positivists tend to restrict generalizability to probability samples, interpretivists reframe the issue. As we have seen in Chapter 18, the findings may be applicable to similar populations in similar circumstances. Yin (1994) has argued that while statistical generalization is appropriate for quantitative studies, "analytic generalization" is appropriate for qualitative studies. Shadish (1995) has proposed five principles for qualitative generalization. The first principle has to do with *proximal similarity*—how alike the persons and setting are between the ones studied and the new ones in the new situation. This can be done only if the author provides a thick description of the participants and the context of the study. Miles and Huberman (1994) contrast strong and weak contexts.

Strong contexts include repeated contact, first-hand observations, a trusted investigator, an informal setting, and a private interview. Weak contexts include just a single contact, secondhand reports, a distrusted investigator, a formal setting, and a group interview. The second one has to do with *heterogeneity of irrelevancies*—how well the findings hold regardless of minor variations presumed not to be pertinent. This can be done only if the researcher has deliberately employed negative case analysis. The third rule addresses *discriminant validity*—the authenticity of the findings even in the face of alternative explanations. This can be done only if the author has tested for rival hypotheses. The fourth one is about *empirical extrapolation*—when the researcher can specify the persons or situations in which the findings hold most strongly. The fifth principle concerns *explanation*—when the researcher can predict which part of one variable is related to which part of another variable through which process. Although this is seldom done in exploratory studies, it is possible in follow-up or long-term investigations.

Examples of Poor Transferability

* Researcher claims that results can be generalized to the population without consideration of the context or characteristics of the sample.
* Researcher claims that the results can be generalized to the population without consideration of discrepant data or competing hypotheses.

Examples of Good Transferability

* Researcher cautiously applies the results to parts of the population that share similar contexts and characteristics of the sample.
* Researcher cautiously applies the results to parts of the population while making note of contradictory data or alternative hypotheses.

Dependability

Dependability is analogous to the positivist concept of reliability. It addresses the consistency or congruency of the results. Since qualitative researchers tend to believe that no one can step into the same stream twice, they do not depend on replicability to prove reliability. Dependability is improved, however, when researchers provide an *audit trail of the data collection procedures*. Dependability is also enhanced when researchers use *member checks*. Member checks can be divided into two subtypes: narrative accuracy checks and interpretive validity checks. *Narrative accuracy* can be obtained by having participants check the veracity of the transcripts, while *interpretive validity* can be obtained by having participants check the conclusions drawn from their narratives (Maxwell, 1992). Another means mentioned by Miles and Huberman (1994) is *coding checks*. These can also be divided into two subtypes: determining *intercoder reliability* (discussed above) or *intracoder reliability* by the lone researcher (Sheket al., 2005). Intracoder reliability is often done by researchers working in remote locations or by researchers who are required to work alone (e.g., doctoral students doing their dissertations). They must set aside their first set of codes and start coding the transcripts again from scratch.

Examples of Poor Dependability

* Researcher gives very limited information about the sample or the context.
* Researcher provides only a few sample questions that were asked.
* Researcher provides no descriptions of how the accuracy of the data or the conclusions were checked by others.

Examples of Good Dependability

* Researcher gives in-depth descriptions of the context and characteristics of the sample.
* Researcher gives the questions asked when providing answers from participants.
* Researcher describes in detail how the accuracy of the data and the conclusions drawn were checked by colleagues or participants.

Confirmability

Finally, *confirmability* is the interpretivist analogue for objectivity. Although qualitative studies do not aim to be objective, they must still strive to acknowledge and supplement their own subjectivity and bias. One way to track biases is through an *audit trail of the interpretive decisions* made so that readers may observe the thought processes of the investigator. Another strategy is for researchers to demonstrate reflexivity about their *bias* (see discussion above). Finally, they should indicate how their own subjectivity was supplemented by third-party confirmation, such as *consulting with colleagues, triangulation of observers*, or *member checks*. Finally, researchers may use a *process audit* by a third party to confirm the findings (Franklin & Ballan, 2005).

Examples of Poor Confirmability

- Researcher fails to describe the process of creating and revising codes.
- Researcher fails to document how the findings were checked by others.

Examples of Good Confirmability

- Researcher describes how he or she developed and revised codes.

- Researcher utilized other experts to confirm that the codes were mutually exclusive and internally consistent.

Data Analysis

As Coleman and Unrau (2005) indicate, there are a number of steps in analyzing narrative data. Each step has important implications for evaluating the quality of a qualitative study.

Transcription

The first step of transcription can utilize five strategies. The first strategy to improve accurate transcription is to use *word-processing programs* to quickly correct mistakes found by the researcher(s) or the participants. The second strategy is to *triangulate the transcribers*, using two or more persons to check the accuracy of transcription, especially the consistency in the way nonverbal and paraverbal cues are recorded. A third strategy is to *remove identifying material* so that readers cannot identify confidential sources by their revelations. Fourth, the data should be as *raw* as possible. This means that transcriptions should be as verbatim as possible and not be cleaned up to create complete sentences.

Criteria	Yes	No
19. Were reasons were given for the type of sampling?	___	___
20. Did the report address the issue of subjectivity?	___	___
21. Did the report address the issue of bias by the research or respondents?	___	___
22. Were strategies used to improve credibility?	___	___
23. Were strategies used to improve transferability?	___	___
24. Were strategies used to improve dependability?	___	___
25. Were strategies used to improve confirmability?	___	___

Figure 21.3 Criteria for Assessing the Data Collection Procedures and Issues Related to Rigor of a Qualitative Research Report

Nonverbal gestures may be recorded in parentheses; common examples include (coughs), (sneezes), and (crying). Paraverbal cues such as increased VOLUME, pauses . . . , st-st-stuttering, or *whispers* should also receive consistent treatment (Kvale, 1996). Interruptions may use brackets within a sentence [Therapist: Oh?] to indicate who interrupted the primary speaker (Mishler, 1991). Finally, transcripts should be *numbered* to make organization and retrieval of the text easier. Sometimes this is done line by line as in *Ethnograph* and sometimes done paragraph by paragraph as in *Nud*ist Nvivo* (see chapter 18).

Examples of Poor Transcription

- Minority language (e.g., Ebonics) is cleaned up so it looks like standard English.
- Spoken language is cleaned up so it is grammatically correct (e.g., no dangling participles)

Examples of Good Transcription

- Mixed language (e.g., Spanglish) is portrayed exactly as it was spoken.
- Expletives or vulgar language is left intact so that the speaker's emotions are apparent.

Data Analysis Planning

The second step of establishing a plan for data analysis has two primary strategies. First, the analyst must *preview* the data by reading over the entire narrative before trying to analyze it. Second, the analyst must create an *audit trail of interpretive decisions*. Many times a single block of text can be coded in multiple ways. Researchers should record why they made the decision to interpret as they did.

Examples of Poor Data Analysis Planning

- Researcher begins analysis before reading the entire transcript.
- Researcher fails to document the justification for questionable interpretations.

Examples of Good Data Analysis Planning

- Researcher reviews the entire transcript before making any interpretations.

- Researcher records her reasoning about the interpretation of ambiguous passages.

First-Level Coding

The third step of *first-level coding* has five strategies. First, the researcher must identify the *meaning unit*. This can usually be inferred by the verbatim quotes used in the study. Most studies will identify single statements or entire paragraphs of the participants to illustrate a particular category. Second, the investigator must assign *category names* to similar meaning units. Usually these will refer to the thoughts, feelings, or actions of the participants. Sometimes a researcher will use nested codes where smaller categories are subsumed within larger ones.

Third, the researcher will assign *codes* to the categories. Codes are simply a form of mnemonic shorthand to expedite the labeling and retrieval of categories. Next, the investigator will *revise codes*, gradually reconfiguring the categories so that some will decay while new ones will surface. This is the best time to employ *triangulation of analysts* to ensure that codes are clear and confirmed by others. Finally, the researcher will reach a point of *category saturation*, when the number and content of the categories seem complete.

Examples of Poor First-Level Coding

- Some of the categories overlap (e.g., personality disorders and mental illness).
- Some of the categories have very little support (e.g., only two quotes).

Examples of Good First-Level Coding

- All categories are mutually exclusive with no overlap (Axis I and Axis II disorders).
- All of the categories are supported by at least three quotes.

Second-Level Coding

The fourth step in analyzing qualitative data is *second-level coding*. There are two tasks in this step. First, meaning units from several sources must be *copied and pasted* into one location for analysis. *Nud*ist Nvivo* does this like a Web browser marks favorite Internet sites for future use. Second, the *patterns* between categories must be determined. Miles and Huberman (1994) identify four common patterns: themes, causal relationships, relationships between people, and theoretical constructs. Since this step of analysis is the most subjective, the strategies for *credibility* and *dependability* mentioned above must be employed to make the findings trustworthy.

Examples of Poor Second-Level Coding

- The themes or categories remain disjointed and unconnected to each other.
- The credibility or dependability issues are never addressed.

Examples of Good Second-Level Coding

- The relationships between the themes or categories are identified both horizontally and vertically (e.g., peer relationships and hierarchical relationships).
- The credibility and dependability issues are explicitly addressed.

Developing Themes and Theories

The final step in qualitative data analysis is *developing themes and theories*. There are again two tasks involved. First, researchers must develop a *conceptual scheme*. Strategies include drawing a diagram or matrix, counting the number of times a meaning unit or category appears, and creating a metaphor. Second, researchers present *theories* for why these phenomena happen. This is the time to employ *triangulation of theories* (see the definition above) to ensure a thorough understanding (Howe & Eisenhart, 1990) and to rule out *alternative hypotheses* (Shek et al., 2005).

Examples of Poorly Developed Theories

- Researcher develops theories that are just a hodgepodge of ideas.
- Researcher develops theories that consider only one perspective (e.g., micro-level practice)

Examples of Well-Developed Theories

- Researcher develops theories that are part of an integrated and coherent scheme.

- Researcher considers multiple levels of explanation for the phenomenon (e.g., micro-, mezzo-, and macro-level theories).

Discussion

After the researcher has analyzed all the data and developed some theories, it is time to place the results in context. Before this happens, however, it is necessary to describe the limitations of the current study.

Limitations

When addressing limitations, many authors of qualitative studies make the mistake of apologizing for quantitative criteria. While some of this may be due to poorly trained reviewers, qualitative researchers must take responsibility for judging their own work based on qualitative criteria (Shek et al., 2005). Only then can they discuss the implications of their work on its own terms.

Examples of Poor Discussion of Limitations

- Limitations of the study are simply not addressed at all.
- Limitations of the study are addressed in quantitative or positivist terms (e.g., not having a large random sample).

Examples of Good Discussion of Limitations

- Limitations of the study are addressed from an interpretivist point of view.
- Limitations address credibility, transferability, dependability, and confirmability.

Previous Literature

First, it is important to link what was found with the previous literature on the topic. If an exploratory study was done due to a gap in the literature, then the researchers need to say how their findings fill that hole. If a qualitative study was chosen to address the affective aspects in a well-understood area, then they need to say how their findings complement previous studies. If the study was done to resolve a debate, then they need to state the resolution of previous differences. It is not unusual for qualitative researchers to do one last literature search at this point, especially if they were doing exploratory research and discovered unexpected findings.

Examples of Poor Discussion of Previous Literature

- Researcher fails to make any connections between present and past findings.
- Researcher fails to make an iterative search of the literature.

Examples of Good Discussion of Previous Literature

- Researcher connects each finding to previous work on the subject.
- Researcher cites new literature that has a bearing on the current findings.

Professional Culture

Second, it is important to connect what was found with the professional culture. Ironically, professional communities seldom think of themselves as having a culture, but they do. They have their own values (e.g., Code of Ethics), their own rituals (e.g., graduation and licensure exams), and even their own jargon (e.g., NASW). In other words, the results should be translated into practical terms for practitioners to use (Fortune, 1999; Tsang, 2000). The results may inform future theory, practice, or policy, but the implications should be made clear.

Examples of Poor Connection to Professional Culture

- Researcher writes in language only professional researchers can understand.
- Researcher addresses only the implications for future research, not practice, theory, or policy.

Examples of Good Connection to Professional Culture

- Researcher writes in language that practitioners can understand and apply.
- Researcher addresses implications for practice, theory, or policy.

Scientific Community

Finally, it is important to link what was found with the scientific community. As Williams, Unrau, and Grinnell (1998, 2005) make clear, researchers have a responsibility to future researchers to suggest new avenues for research—continuing gaps, ongoing controversies, or

Criteria	Yes	No
26. Were strategies used to increase the accuracy of transcriptions?	⸺	⸺
27. Did the researcher employ a plan for data analysis?	⸺	⸺
28. Were clear categories developed during first-level coding?	⸺	⸺
29. Were relationships between categories clarified during second-level coding?	⸺	⸺
30. Were the themes and theories well developed?	⸺	⸺
31. Were limitations addressed from an interpretivist perspective?	⸺	⸺
32. Were the results integrated with the previous literature?	⸺	⸺
33. Were implications for theory, practice, or policy identified?	⸺	⸺
34. Were recommendations for future research made?	⸺	⸺

Figure 21.4   Criteria for Assessing the Data Analysis Procedures and the Discussion Section of a Qualitative Research Study

new ways to complement old studies. This is the reason that reports must clearly communicate both *how* they did their investigations and *what* they found. Good explorers also leave a trail for others to follow in their footsteps.

Examples of Poor Connection to Scientific Community

- Researcher does not suggest new ideas for continued research in the topic.
- Researcher does not provide sufficient detail about his or her method for others to copy.

Examples of Good Connection to Scientific Community

- Researcher provides specific ideas for continued research on the topic.

- Researcher provides sufficient detail so others can replicate the method.

SUMMARY

This chapter has briefly posited 34 distinct criteria, via four figures, for qualitative research using an interpretivist perspective. It has eschewed positivist terms, such as *reliability* and *validity*, in favor of more qualitative-friendly terms, such as *trustworthiness, credibility, transferability, dependability*, and *confirmability*. It is hoped that research instructors will use this chapter as a guide to evaluate actual qualitative research articles in their classes. It is only in the application of these principles that students really learn them.

The four chapters in Part VII provide the basic

building blocks of the evidence-based social work

practice. More specifically, Chapter 22 discusses

how to find existing information (literature); the

following chapter, Chapter 23, describes how to

evaluate the information that is found. Chapter

24 details how meta-analyses are done and how

they can be used within the evidence-based prac-

titioner model. Chapter 25, the final chapter of

this part, provides an introduction on how to do

evidence-based practice utilizing the contents

from the previous three chapters.

Finding Existing Knowledge

Lin Fang
Jennifer Manuel
Sarah E. Bledsoe
Jennifer L. Bellamy

22

Step 1	Choose a problem
2	Review the literature
3	Evaluate the literature
4	Be aware of all ethical issues
5	Be aware of all cultural issues
6	State the research question or hypothesis
7	Select the research approach
8	Determine how the variables are going to be measured
9	Select a sample
10	Select a data collection method
11	Collect and code the data
12	Analyze and interpret the data
13	Write the report
14	Disseminate the report

As you know by now after reading the previous 21 chapters, we generally explore and use available knowledge at every phase of the research and practice process. You are basically asking yourself, "What's out there that already exists to help me in my research study—or practice—so I don't have to reinvent the wheel?" This chapter answers this question by providing an overview of the sources of existing knowledge that you can utilize in addition to discussing the methods and strategies to retrieve it.

EXISTING KNOWLEDGE VERSUS LITERATURE REVIEWS

The use of existing knowledge is essential in order to do a literature review. A literature review (in a specific topic area) is a formal process undertaken before a research study is conducted. Without conducting a review of the literature, we cannot obtain a sound understanding of our topic, we cannot know what is already known, we cannot know how our topic has been previously studied, and we cannot know what the key issues are (Hart, 1998).

As you know through your university experience, an annotated bibliography is a list of knowledge sources (e.g., books, journal articles) that provides a brief description of each source. A literature review, on the other hand, involves a process of carefully assessing—and critically evaluating—the same knowledge sources that are contained in the annotated bibliography. A quality literature review has adequate breadth and depth; rigor and consistency; clarity and brevity; and an effective organization and synthesis. By utilizing existing knowledge, your literature review will justify the use of a different methodological approach to your research study, if appropriate, and demonstrate that your proposed study will provide new contributions to the field (Hart, 1998).

However, the use of existing knowledge does not take place only in the literature review phase. As mentioned earlier—and especially in qualitative studies—you use existing literature in every step of the research process, from defining research questions, selecting research participants, selecting data-gathering methods and measuring instruments, analyzing results, presenting findings, and making recommendations from those findings.

Information retrieval is a key element of any research study—quantitative and qualitative alike. Advances in computer technologies have facilitated the generation, synthesis, dissemination, and exchange of current research findings. As new assessment and intervention options are developed and studied, we have increased the opportunities to access knowledge related to social work research and practice (Jadad et al., 2000). However, without structured guidance, performing searches among the overabundance of existing resources can be time-consuming and invite anxiety and confusion to any study. The effective use of existing knowledge requires the following (Monette, Sullivan, & DeJong, 2005):

- Adequate understanding of the available resources that contain information
- Precise definition of what information is needed
- Determination of the best strategy for locating the information
- Evaluation of the information founded (the topic of the following chapter)

SOURCES OF INFORMATION

Where can the various sources of information, or existing knowledge, be found? In general, information can be found in many places. We will discuss only eight of them: (1) periodicals, (2) books and book chapters, (3) printed references, (4) grey literature, (5), government reports, (6) publications produced by nonprofit organizations, (7) the Internet, and (8) oral histories.

Periodicals

The first—and probably the most important and useful—source where existing knowledge can be found is periodicals. Periodicals are publications issued on a regular basis (e.g., weekly, monthly, quarterly, annually) and include articles written by various authors. Examples of periodicals include scholarly journals, magazines, and newspapers. Periodicals are referred to as *serials* because they are produced in series (Larsson, 1998). A journal contains scholarly articles that are directed at the professional communities and written in a specific format, whereas magazines and newspapers are intended for the general public and are usually written in a light and popular style (Monette et al., 2005).

Periodicals tend to be more up-to-date than books and book chapters, especially in reporting research findings, not only because the production process often takes longer for books than for periodicals, but also because research findings are usually first reported in scholarly journals. By presenting research findings that were derived via research studies in a concise and specific manner, journal articles offer a tremendous amount of insight into any given topic area (Monette et al., 2005).

Professional journals often include original research articles that have gone through a peer review process; a process of subjecting the author's work to the evaluation of experts in the field. As we will see in the following chapter, peer-reviewed journal articles usually meet the standards of the discipline represented by the journal. Table 22.1 provides a selective list of peer-reviewed journals relevant to our profession broken down by subject areas.

Retrieval Methods

The advances of computer technology place unlimited knowledge at our fingertips and allow us to access information, or existing knowledge, via the Internet. The Internet brings newly created and emerging research findings into our homes, offices, and classrooms. Information has become increasingly interchangeable. For example, most journal articles can be found in print, on CD-ROMs, and/or online. Because professional journal articles are available in these different formats, you should use your university's library catalog (either physically in the library or online in remote locations) and consult with a reference librarian to explore the available resources that you have access to for tapping into the various sources where existing knowledge can be found—especially in databases. Table 22.2 presents a few of the many major online multidisciplinary databases that we use in our profession.

TABLE 22.1

Social Work Journals Broken Down by Subject Areas

Child Welfare

- *Adoption Quarterly*
- *Child Abuse and Neglect: The International Journal*
- *Child Abuse Review*
- *Child and Adolescent Social Work Journal*
- *Child and Youth Services*
- *Child Maltreatment*
- *Child Welfare*
- *Children and Schools* (formerly: *Social Work in Education*)
- *Children and Youth Services Review*
- *Contemporary Issues in Early Childhood* (online journal)
- *Family Preservation Journal*
- *Journal of Adolescence*
- *Journal of Adolescent Research*
- *Journal of Aggression, Maltreatment and Trauma*
- *Journal of Applied School Psychology*
- *Journal of Child and Youth Care*
- *Journal of Early Adolescence*
- *Journal of Emotional Abuse*
- *Journal of HIV/AIDS Prevention in Children and Youth*
- *Journal of Public Child Welfare*
- *Journal of School Violence*
- *Journal of Sudden Infant Death Syndrome and Infant Mortality*
- *Journal of the American Academy of Child and Adolescent Psychiatry*
- *Journal of Youth and Adolescence*
- *Residential Treatment for Children and Youth*
- *School Social Work Journal*
- *Trauma, Violence, and Abuse*
- *Violence and Victims*

Community Practice and Policy

- *Administration and Policy in Mental Health and Mental Health Services Research*
- *Journal of Community Practice*
- *Journal of Immigrant and Refugee Services*
- *Journal of Poverty: Innovations on Social, Political and Economic Inequalities*
- *Journal of Prevention and Intervention in the Community* (Formerly: *Prevention in Human Services*)
- *Journal of Progressive Human Services*
- *Journal of Social Policy*
- *Social Policy Journal*

Education and Training

- *Journal of Social Work Education*
- *Journal of Teaching in Social Work*
- *Social Work Education*

Families

- *Child and Family Behavior Therapy*
- *Families in Society*
- *Family Journal: Counseling and Therapy for Couples and Families*
- *Journal of Family Issues*
- *Journal of Family Social Work* (Formerly: *Journal of Social Work and Human Sexuality*)
- *Journal of Feminist Family Therapy*
- *Marriage and Family Review*

Gerontology

- *Ageing and Society*
- *Clinical Gerontologist*
- *Gerontologist*
- *Gerontology and Geriatrics Education*
- *Journal of Aging and Health*
- *Journal of Aging and Social Policy*
- *Journal of Aging Studies*
- *Journal of Applied Gerontology*
- *Journal of Elder Abuse and Neglect*
- *Journal of Gerontological Social Work*
- *Journals of Gerontology: Social Sciences*
- *Journal of Intergenerational Relationships*
- *Journal of Mental Health and Aging*
- *Journal of Social Work in End-of-Life and Palliative Care*
- *Journal of Social Work in Long-Term Care*
- *Journal of Women and Aging*
- *Research on Aging*

International or Multicultural Focus

- *Asian Journal of Social Psychology*
- *Asia Pacific Journal of Social Work and Development*
- *Australian Social Work*
- *British Journal of Social Work*
- *European Journal of Social Work*
- *Hong Kong Journal of Social Work*
- *Indian Journal of Social Work*
- *International Journal of Social Welfare*
- *International Social Work*
- *Journal of Asian Studies*

(continued)

TABLE 22.1 *(continued)*

- *Journal of Black Studies*
- *Journal of Ethnic and Cultural Diversity in Social Work* (Formerly: *Multicultural Social Work*)
- *Journal of European Social Policy*
- *Journal of Immigrant and Refugee Services*
- *Journal of Social Development in Africa*
- *Social Development Issues*

Mental Health

- *American Journal of Psychiatry*
- *Archives of General Psychiatry*
- *British Journal of Psychiatry*
- *International Journal of Methods in Psychiatric Research*
- *Journal of Child Psychology and Psychiatry*
- *Journal of Clinical Psychiatry*
- *Journal of the American Academy Child and Adolescent Psychiatry*
- *Psychiatric Services*
- *Psychological Medicine*
- *Psychosomatic Medicine*
- *Schizophrenia Research*

Research

- *Journal of Applied Social Psychology*
- *Journal of Applied Social Science Studies*
- *Journal of Social Service Research*
- *Journal of Social Work Research & Evaluation*
- *Psychiatric Rehabilitation Journal* (Formerly: *Psychosocial Rehabilitation Journal and Innovations and Research*)
- *Research on Social Work Practice*
- *Social Science Information*
- *Social Science Research*
- *Social Work Research*
- *Sociological Methods & Research*

Social Work Practice (General)

- *Administration in Social Work*
- *Arête*
- *Clinical Social Work Journal*
- *Health and Social Work*
- *International Journal of Social Welfare*
- *Journal for Specialists in Group Work*
- *Journal of Applied Behavioral Science*
- *Journal of Brief Therapy*
- *Journal of Evidence-Based Social Work*

- *Journal of Health and Social Policy*
- *Journal of Human Behavior in the Social Environment*
- *Journal of Religion and Spirituality in Social Work: Social Thought*
- *Journal of Social Work*
- *Journal of Social Work Practice*
- *Journal of Sociology and Social Welfare*
- *Reflections: Narratives of Professional Helping*
- *Smith College Studies in Social Work*
- *Social Service Review*
- *Social Work*
- *Social Work in Health Care*
- *Social Work in Mental Health*
- *Social Work with Groups*

Student Journals

- *Journal of Student Social Work* (Founded by students at Columbia University School of Social Work)
- *Perspectives on Social Work* (A journal for doctoral students)
- *Social Work Perspectives* (National student submissions based on San Francisco State University School of Social Work)

Substance Abuse

- *Addiction*
- *American Journal of Addictions*
- *American Journal of Drug and Alcohol Abuse*
- *Journal of Child and Adolescent Substance Abuse*
- *Journal of Groups in Addiction and Recovery*
- *Journal of Social Work Practice in the Addictions*

Technology and Social Work

- *Computers in Human Behavior*
- *Journal of Technology in Human Services*

Women and Men's Issues

- *Affilia: Journal of Women and Social Work*
- *Clinical Supervisor*
- *Journal of Couples and Relationship Therapy*
- *Journal of Emotional Abuse*
- *Journal of Gay and Lesbian Social Services*
- *Journal of HIV/AIDS and Social Services*
- *Journal of Interpersonal Violence*
- *Signs: Journal of Women in Culture and Society*
- *Violence Against Women*

Source: Leung & Cheung (2006)

TABLE 22.2

A Sample of Multidisciplinary Electronic Databases

Database	Description	Topic or Discipline Examples	Availability
ERIC	A comprehensive, easy-to-use, searchable, Internet-based bibliographic and full-text database of education research and information that also meets the requirements of the Education Sciences Reform Act of 2002.	• Adult • Career and vocational education • Assessment and evaluation • Disabilities and gifted education • Educational management • Elementary and early childhood education • Higher education • Reading and communication • Teachers and teacher education • Urban education	Check with the library catalog or librarian for its availability. Library subscription may include access to electronic articles.
MEDLINE/ PubMed	A database from the National Library of Medicine that contains bibliographic citations and author abstracts from more than 4,600 biomedical journals published in the United States and in 70 other countries. Includes over 17 million citations dating back to the 1950s.	• Medicine • Nursing • Dentistry • Health services • Administration • Veterinary medicine • Allied health • Preclinical sciences	Access freely through www.pubmed.gov but limited to citations and abstracts. Check with the library catalog or librarian for its availability. Library subscription may include access electronic articles.
ProQuest Social Science Journals	A resource that provides a variety of scientific journals. The database includes over 510 titles, with more than 280 available in full text.	Provides information on hundreds of topics, including: • Addiction studies • Urban studies • Family studies • International relations	Check with the library catalog or librarian for its availability. Library subscription may include access to electronic articles.
PsycINFO	A comprehensive database consisting of 7.7 million cited references in citations to 156,000 journal articles, books, and book chapters, dissertations, and technical reports, all in the field of psychology and the psychological aspects of related disciplines.	• Medicine • Psychiatry • Nursing • Sociology • Education • Linguistics • Anthropology • Business • Law	Check with the library catalog or librarian for its availability. Library subscription may include access to electronic articles.
Cumulative Index to Nursing and Allied Health Literatures (CINAHL)	The authoritative source of information for the professional literature of nursing, allied health, biomedicine, and health care. Includes indexed English-language and selected foreign-language journals, books, educational software, conference proceedings, standards of professional practice, nurse practice acts, and research instruments.	• Nursing • Allied health • Biomedicine • Healthcare • Management • Behavioral medicine • Education • Consumer health	Access through library catalog. Check with the library catalog or librarian for its availability.

(continued)

Database	Description	Topic or Discipline Examples	Availability
Wilson Social Sciences Abstracts	This database provides researchers access to essential scientific journals. Users can access over 550 publications, collecting information on a variety of topics.	• Addiction studies • Community health care • Criminology • Economics • Environmental studies • Family studies • Gender studies • Gerontology • International relations • Minority studies • Planning and public administration • Political Science • Psychiatry, Psychology • Public Welfare • Social Work • Sociology • Urban Studies	Check with the library catalog or librarian for its availability. Library subscription may include access to electronic articles.

TABLE 22.2 (continued)

Books and Book Chapters

The second source where existing knowledge can be found is in books and book chapters (Yegidis & Weinbach, 2005). Generally speaking, books are secondary and tertiary resources, since most, but not all, only use the information that was derived from research studies that have been previously published in professional journals.

Printed References

The third source where existing knowledge can be found is in printed references: professional encyclopedias, yearbooks, directories, and bibliographies. These are very useful resources indeed. The abstract publications, such as *Social Work Abstracts, Sociological Abstracts,* and *Psychological Abstracts,* provide an overview on various subjects of recent journal publications. Other standard reference materials, such as *Mental Measurement Yearbook* and *Encyclopedia of Social Work,* provide information that tends to possess a high degree of credibility because they usually undergo a thorough peer review and verification process. These reference resources have the breadth but often lack the depth found in journals and books. Table 22.3 provides a list of common reference works that are useful to our profession.

Retrieval Methods

Many printed references, and books alike, can be retrieved at your university library. Most libraries have a social work reference section to facilitate your needs. For example, the University of Texas at Arlington has an annotated social work bibliography (http://library.uta.edu/guidesBibls/gbRefSocialWork.jsp). The University of North Carolina at Chapel Hill Library also provides a selected list of social work resources (http://www.lib.unc.edu/reference/socsci/socialwork.html).

Many standard-based texts and images are electronically archived. For example, the Electronic Text Center of the University of Virginia Library (http://etext.lib.virginia.edu) has a collection of approximately 70,000 online and off-line humanities texts in thirteen languages with more than 350,000 related images (e.g., book illustrations, covers, manuscripts, newspaper pages, books, museum objects) in the humanities. Many of these items are publicly accessible.

TABLE 22.3

Commonly Used Social Work References

- *American Homelessness: A Reference Handbook*
- *An Author's Guide to Social Work Journals*
- *Blackwell Encyclopedia of Social Work*
- *Encyclopedia of Adolescence*
- *Encyclopedia of Homosexuality*
- *Encyclopedia of Social Work*
- *Handbook of Empirical Social Work Practice*
- *Measures for Clinical Practice: A Sourcebook*
- *Mental Measurements Yearbook*
- *Public Welfare Directory*
- *Social Science Reference Sources: A Practical Guide*
- *Social Work Almanac*
- *Social Work Dictionary*
- *Social Work Speaks: NASW Policy Statements*
- *Statistical Abstract of the United States*
- *Statistical Handbook on the American Family*

Grey Literature

The fourth place where existing knowledge can be found is in the grey literature. Grey literature includes newsletters, technical reports, working papers, theses, dissertations, government documents, bulletins, fact sheets, conference proceedings, and other publications. Commonly, grey literature is any document or material that is published by nonprofit organizations, such as government agencies, professional organizations, research centers, universities, public institutions, and special interest groups, to name a few (Mathews, 2004). Grey literature covers a broad range of scientific disciplines and is disseminated to a wide audience, including researchers and laypersons as well.

Government Reports

Government reports are the fifth place where you can look for existing knowledge. The U.S. government, for example, sponsors many research and evaluation activities. It publishes the findings in reports, books, bulletins, and circulars. These sources can contain the research re-

sults of survey data, demonstration projects, program evaluations, needs assessments, and model social service programs (Reed & Baxter, 2003). In addition, agencies of the United Nations, such as the World Health Organizations, the Department of Economic and Social Affairs, and the Office on Drugs and Crime, also issue thousands of reports that can be valuable resources.

Retrieval Methods

Many government reports can be found in your local public and university libraries or online. Many libraries have a collection of U.S. government documents that you retrieve from the shelves. Researchers who are interested in the executive, legislative, and judicial branches of the U.S. federal government can access their information and publications through the U.S. Government Printing Office catalog (http://www.gpoaccess.gov).

The U.S. Census Bureau (http://www.census.gov) also provides bountiful resources on sociodemographic and economic characteristics of the population, such as household composition, ethnicity, and income. The National Guideline Clearinghouse (http://www.guideline.gov) provides structured summaries and full-text documents of evidence-based clinical practice guidelines. This Web site provides free access to health care providers and other stakeholder groups. It offers objective and detailed information on clinical practice guidelines and seeks to further their dissemination, implementation, and use. Users can also download and view a complete summary of each guideline. Many other U.S. government Web sites also provide useful information. Table 22.4 includes a selected list of U.S. federal government Web sites.

Publications Produced by Nonprofit Organizations

The sixth place where existing knowledge can be located is through publications published by nonprofit organizations. Some major nonprofit organizations, such as the United Way, the Robert Wood Johnson Foundation, the Robin Hood Foundation, and the RAND Corporation, produce informative research reports. These

TABLE 22.4

Federal Government Resources

Administration for Children and Families
http://www.acf.dhhs.gov

Centers for Medicare and Medicaid Services
http://www.cms.hhs.gov

Department of Health and Human Services
http://www.dhhs.gov

FedWorld Information Network (a quick way to locate government information)
http://www.fedworld.gov

The Library of Congress–THOMAS: Legislative Information
http://thomas.loc.gov

National Guideline Clearinghouse
http://www.guideline.gov/

National Institute of Mental Health
http://www.nimh.nih.gov

National Institute on Alcohol Abuse and Alcoholism
http://www.niaaa.nih.gov

National Institute on Drug Abuse
http://drugabuse.gov

Rural Empowerment Zones/ Enterprise Communities Program
http://www.ezec.gov

Social Security Online
http://www.ssa.gov

Substance Abuse and Mental Health Services Administration (SAMHSA)
http://www.samhsa.gov

U.S. Census Bureau
http://www.census.gov

U.S. Government Printing Office Catalog
http://www.gpoaccess.gov

The World Fact Book
https://www.cia.gov/cia/publications/factbook

organizations sponsor research programs and/or conduct research activities at regional, national, and international levels. They then publish the findings from their research activities.

For example, the United Way's Outcome Measurement Resource Network has a research library that offers technical reports on concepts, theories, strategies, tools, methods, and case studies relating to program outcome evaluation (United Way of America, 2006).

The RAND Corporation conducts research studies on effective interventions, national and international education, poverty, crime, population and aging, the environment, and national security issues (RAND Corporation, 2006).

Other grey literature resources include conference proceedings, doctoral dissertations, and master's theses. Professional organizations, such as the Society of Social Work Research, the Council of Social Work Education, and the American Association of Public Health, sponsor annual conferences and issue special publications, such as conference proceedings, newspapers, or fact sheets.

Retrieval Methods

Most nonprofit organizations make their publications available to the public or to members through their Web sites. In addition, you can also access these publications through databases whose collections are specifically based on grey literature via your library's online catalog. For example, ProceedingsFirst is a database that covers every published congress, symposium, conference, exposition, workshop, and meeting received by the British Library Document Supply Centre.

Doctoral dissertations and master's theses can also be accessed through ProQuest Dissertations and Theses Database. Containing citations for materials ranging from the first U.S. dissertation accepted in 1861, to those accepted as recently as the previous semester, this database provides the abstracts and full text of dissertations and theses from more than 1,000 graduate schools across North America and Europe. Many students, faculty, and other researchers use the database to search for titles and abstracts related to their respective interests. You can access the full texts of more than 1.9 million dissertations and theses on microfilm or in print. In addition, you can preview and download approximately 750,000 in the PDF format.

The Internet

The Internet is the seventh place where you can locate existing knowledge. As you know by now, many public records and statistics are available on the Internet, as

TABLE 22.5

Grey Literature Web Sources

Canadian Evaluation Society
http://www.evaluationcanada.ca
Criminology Library Grey Literature, University of Toronto
http://link.library.utoronto.ca/criminology/crimdoc/index.cfm
Fade: The North West Grey Literature Service
http://www.fade.nhs.uk
Grey Network Literature Services
http://www.greynet.org/greynethome.html
Groningen State University, Library of Behavioural Social Sciences
http://www.rug.nl/bibliotheek/collecties/bibsocwet/grijzeliteratuur
New York Academy of Medicine
http://www.nyam.org/library/grey.shtml
PsycEXTRA (a grey literature database)
http://www.apa.org/psycextra/
UNESCO (United Nations Educational, Scientific and Cultural Organization)
http://www.unesco.org/unesdi/index.php/eng/biblio/tous.116
University of Central England in Birmingham
http://library.uce.ac.uk/edgreylitres.htm

well as many journal articles and books. While it may be easier or more convenient to access materials through the Internet than by going to your public or university libraries, you should note that the quality of information on the Internet varies greatly. Though some Web sites serve as excellent resources (e.g., U.S. Census Bureau and RAND Corporation Web sites), many others, which appear to be trustworthy, may provide inaccurate or misleading information. Materials retrieved from the Internet need to be treated with great caution; the following chapter presents a few strategies for evaluating Internet sources. Nevertheless, the Internet is an important resource for brainstorming ideas and for searching social work–relevant literature.

General Search Engines

You can use general search engines and popular research Web sites to develop initial research ideas and identify potential informational resources. Popular search engines, such as Google, Lycos, AltaVista, Yahoo, MSN, and Hotpot, can easily be used as basic search tools. All these engines are highly accessible by simply pointing your mouse on the computer screen. You should familiarize yourself with a couple of these search engines and their features. In addition to the general search engines, Google Scholar is also a valuable tool of which many researchers and students alike take advantage. This search engine allows free and simple access to search for scholarly articles, books, abstracts, and citations and sometimes provides free links to full-text articles or manuscripts.

Search engines differ in the way they organize and update their materials. They also vary in the volume of material they contain. Thus, you need to use the same search phrase (discussed later in this chapter) in two or more engines in an effort to maximize the productivity of your search outcome.

Research Resource Web Sites

As discussed earlier, numerous existing sources of knowledge are available online. Many journal articles can be accessed through the journal's Web site or through electronic databases (e.g., PsycInfo). The U.S. government also maintains online databases to distribute and disseminate government reports. In addition, individual scholars' home pages and a number of professional organizational Web sites can be useful resources. Researchers often list their recent publications and presentations and may provide useful links on their own home pages. You can usually identify an individual's Web site by conducting a search using the researcher's name as the search phrase through a general search engine.

In addition, you can take advantage of some Internet Web sites for research resources. Table 22.6 provides a list of professional organizations in specific concentrations (e.g., community organization, child welfare, gerontology, rural social work). These Web sites are listed because they maintain links to researchers' home pages and links to research resources.

TABLE 22.6

Internet Resources for Social Work

Action Network for Social Work Education and Research (ANSWER)
https://www.socialworkers.org/advocacy/answer

Association for Community Organization and Social Administration (ACOSA)
http://www.acosa.org

Association for Gerontology Education in Social Work (AGE-SW)
http://www.agesocialwork.org

Association for the Advancement of Social Work with Groups (AASWG)
http://www.aaswg.org

Association on Oncology Social Work (AOSW)
http://www.aosw.org

Buros Institute of Mental Measurements
http://www.unl.edu/buros/

Child Welfare Information Gateway
http://www.childwelfare.gov

Clinical Social Work Federation (CSWF)
http://www.cswf.org

The Evidence Based Practice and Policy (EBPP) *Online Resource Training Center at Columbia University*
http://www.columbia.edu/cu/musher/Website/Website/index.htm

General Social Care Council–United Kingdom (GSCC)
http://www.gscc.org.uk

Group for the Advancement of Doctoral Education (GADE)
http://web.uconn.edu/gade

HIV InSite
http://hivinsite.ucsf.edu/InSite

Influencing State Policy (ISP)
http://www.statepolicy.org

Information for Practice from NYU (IP)
http://www.nyu.edu/socialwork/ip

Institute for Geriatric Social Work (IGSW)
http://www.bu.edu/igsw

Institute for the Advancement of Social Work Research (IASWR)
http://www.iaswresearch.org

International Association of Schools of Social Work (IASSW)
http://www.iassw-aiets.org

International Society for Prevention of Child Abuse and Neglect (ISPCAN)
http://www.ispcan.org

The Internet Public Library
http://www.ipl.org/

Inter-University Consortium for International Social Development
http://www.iucisd.org

KIDS COUNT State-Level Data Book
http://www.aecf.org/kidscount/sld/

National Association of Social Workers (NASW)
http://www.naswdc.org

National Membership Committee on Psychoanalysis in Clinical Social Work
http://www.nmcop.org

North American Association of Christians in Social Work (NACSW)
http://www.nacsw.org/index.shtml

Rural Social Work Caucus
http://www.marson-and-associates.com/rural

School Social Work Association of America (SSWAA)
http://www.sswaa.org

Society for Social Work and Research
http://www.sswr.org

The WWW Virtual Library
http://vlib.org

Oral Histories

The last source of existing evidence is oral histories. The richness and historical importance of everyday memories of ordinary people have been recognized by historians for years. Not legends, gossip, hearsay, or rumor, oral history is the systematic collection of living people's testimony about their own experiences (Moyer, 1999). In oral history projects, the interviewer records the recollections of the interviewees and develops a historical record. Because the memory and the spoken word can be presented in different forms, the collection of oral histories can vary—from taking notes by hand to elaborate electronic sound and video recordings. Moyer (1999) suggested eight steps (see Table 22.7) for conducting oral history research.

TABLE 22.7

Sequence for Oral History Research

1. Formulate a central question or issue.
2. Plan the project. Consider such things as end products, budget, publicity, evaluation, personnel, equipment, and time frames.
3. Conduct background research using non-oral sources.
4. Interview.
5. Process interviews.
6. Evaluate research and interviews and cycle back to step 1 or go on to step 7.
7. Organize and present results.
8. Store materials archivally.

Retrieval Methods

The Oral History Association (http://www.dickinson.edu/oha) has a list of oral history centers and collections. The Oral History Society in the United Kingdom (http://www.ohs.org.uk) also includes an excellent list of links to key oral history organizations, relevant journals, and other useful publications.

FINDING SOURCES OF EXISTING INFORMATION

This section outlines a basic search strategy that you can use to increase the effectiveness and efficiency of finding existing knowledge that was presented above. Finding existing knowledge is indeed exciting. However, without careful planning and a well-thought-out search strategy, searching for existing knowledge in this electronic era can easily become a daunting task.

To make the search process more enjoyable and the task more manageable, this section provides seven basic strategies that you can use to conduct an effective search: (1) identify the research topic, (2) develop a record-keeping system, (3) select search terms, (4) use more than one database or search engine, (5) use abstracts, (6) subscribe to mailing list(s) or subscribe to Really Simple Syndication (RSS; RSS is a method that uses XML to distribute the Web content on one Web

site to many other Web sites) for updates, and (7) use interlibrary loan (ILL).

Identify the Research Topic

Choosing a specific research topic or a clear research question is absolutely essential in directing and framing your search for existing knowledge. You first need to start with a general subject area that is relevant to your topic. Then you narrow your search as you develop and refine your research topic. Next, you develop some provisional research questions. While doing this, you need to remember to keep a social work perspective on the subject even though you may be searching through and identifying research studies from diverse professions.

Develop a Record-Keeping System

A good record-keeping system, though sounding trivial, will help decrease the possibility of you feeling overwhelmed by the flood of literature you will find. More important, a good record-keeping system helps create a formal bibliography and reference section for your research study. Using index cards, general computer programs (e.g., MicroSoft Access, Excel, Word), or specialized computer software (e.g., EndNote, Citation, Refworks) will help you manage the sources you eventually find. Many professional journals have a citation download function that allows you to download the complete citation information (including abstract) into a specific citation software format such as EndNote. This makes managing and storing the sources you find much easier in the long run.

Select Search Terms

To conduct a smart and targeted search, it is essential to identify the primary publications in the subject area in addition to the authors who are frequently cited. In addition, proper keywords will help you to conduct productive database searches. The reference and bibliography sections of research papers previously written in your subject area are often good starting points to identify the relevant publications and key authors. You can use a professional thesaurus to refine or broaden the search keywords. For example, to perform a search on research related to depression, you may use the keywords "mood disorders" and "dysthymia," in addition to "depression."

Construct Search Phrases Carefully

You need to be familiar with the functions of the three major Boolean operators: AND, NOT, and OR. In addition, you need to know how to use quotation marks and truncation symbols. These operators are employed in many Internet-based search engines, providing you with increased control over the type of resources that are finally identified, by either broadening or narrowing the search universe. Some examples will clarify how these operators function.

The Boolean operators AND and NOT narrow the search (see examples in Figures 22.1 and 22.2); the Boolean operator OR expands a search (see example in Figure 22.3). Boolean operators can also be combined. For example, a search for drug dependency/drug abuse/drug addiction in Vancouver can use the search phrase "drug dependency OR drug abuse OR drug addiction AND Vancouver."

To further specify or narrow a search, quotation marks can be used to enclose the phrase you use in a search engine. When quotations marks are used, only

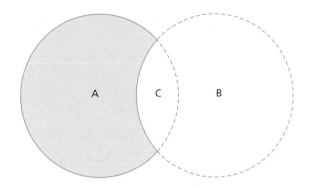

Note: A 5 Depression, B 5 Substance abuse

Figure 22.2 The Use of NOT When Performing a Search. *Example:* A student who would like to find research studies that focused on depression, but not on substance abuse, should use the search phrase: "Depression" NOT "Substance abuse". A = Area of interest

documents that have the exact phrase will be shown, narrowing the search tremendously. For example, about 39.5 million results were found in Google when using *evidence-based social work* as the search term (Figure 22.4), compared with 25,100 results when using the quote "*evidence-based social work*" (Figure 22.5).

The wildcard (*) and truncation symbol (usually #, $, ?) are helpful in expanding the search results.

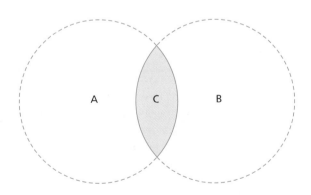

Note: A 5 Depression, B 5 Substance abuse

Figure 22.1 The Use of AND When Performing a Search. *Example:* A student who would like to find research studies that focused on both depression and substance abuse should use the search phrase: "Depression" AND "Substance abuse." C = Area of interest

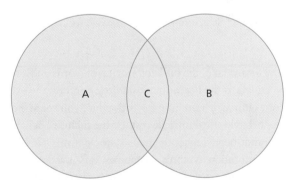

Note: A 5 Depression, B 5 Substance abuse

Figure 22.3 The Use of OR When Performing a Search. *Example:* A student who would like to find research studies that focused on either depression or substance abuse should use the search phrase "Depression" OR "Substance abuse." A, B, C = Areas of interest

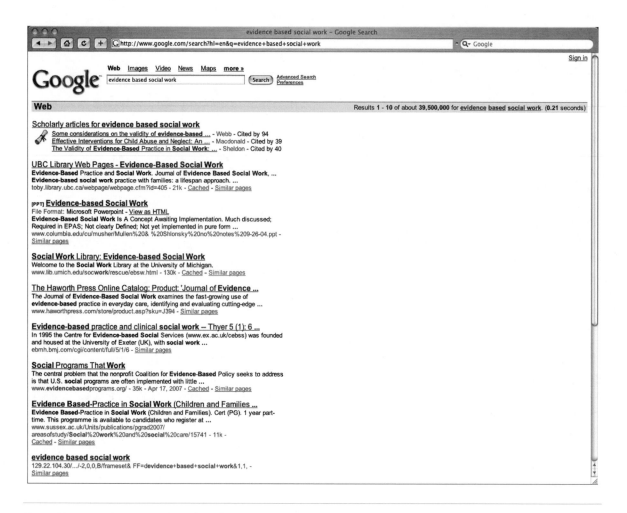

Figure 22.4 Search Term: Evidence-based social work

A wildcard takes the place of a string of words and can be added to the beginning, middle, or end of a word. For example, if searching for "behavior," you could enter "behavio∗r" to retrieve results that include "behavior" and "behaviour."

Truncation symbols sometimes vary by database. The truncation helps to search for terms beginning with a specific root word. For example, depending on the database, you may use "depress∗," or "depress$," to search for any word beginning with "depress." The database will then show results that include *depressed, depression, depressive, depressant*, and so on. Each database will have a key or a help section that defines the symbols it uses for

its wildcard and truncation symbols. It is well worth the effort to spend some time reading these sections within each database in order to tap its full potential.

Use search logic flexibility and consider the following: (1) adding truncation marks, (2) using OR, or (3) removing AND when search results are limited. Conversely, consider (1) using AND, (2) using quotation marks, (3) removing truncation marks, and (4) using NOT when the search results are overly expansive. For example, if your search results are extremely limited due to the use of AND, try searching each set of concepts again separately or using OR before connecting them by AND. Boolean operators, quotation marks,

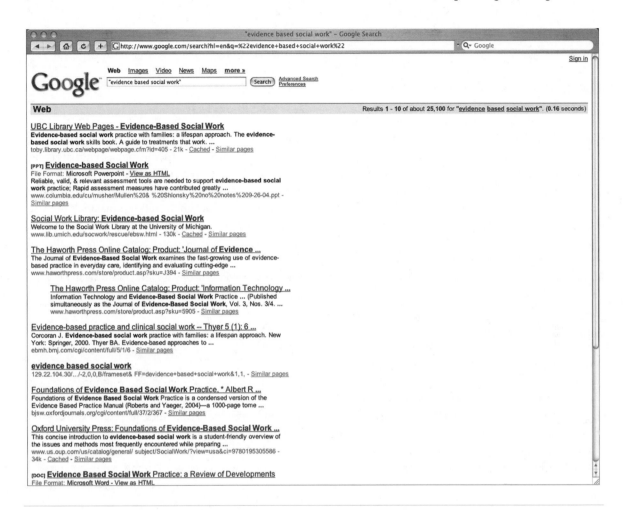

Figure 22.5   Search Term: "Evidence-based social work"

and truncation are essential tools for searching existing literature via the Internet.

Scholars have also introduced advanced search methods to facilitate knowledge retrieval in electronic databases. For example, you can use the Methodology Oriented Locaters for Evidence Searching (MOLES) as "methodologic filters" to effectively identify research evidence (Sackett, Richardson, Rosenberg, & Haynes, 1997, p. 60). MOLES are terms to identify research studies based on their type, such as effectiveness; prevention; prognosis; measurement; and exploratory, descriptive, explanatory, and syntheses studies. If you are interested in learning more about MOLES, refer to

Gibbs (2003) for further reading. The information is also available online at http://www.evidence.brookscole .com/search.html.

Use More Than One Database or Search Engine

Databases vary as to their width and breadth, their organizational systems, and the recency of the information they provide. Though databases have much in common, each covers different subjects, periodicals, and document types (e.g., conference proceedings, research reports, dissertations, book reviews, government reports). Thus, you not only must try your same search phrase using multiple search engines but also need to use multiple databases.

Use Abstracts

An abstract is a short summary of a journal article. A good one follows the flow: study purpose→research methods used→results found→conclusions and implications. The abstract information will allow you to decide whether the full article is worth obtaining to read. Browsing through abstracts can be an efficient use of time when deciding which articles should be retrieved and read, which articles need only to be noted, and which articles are not truly relevant to your research study.

Subscribe to Mailing List(s) or Subscribe to Really Simple Syndication (RSS) for Updates

Most major newspapers and magazines, and some professional journals and professional organizations as well, provide complementary electronic mailing services or RSS for users to receive information. Users are now able to have the findings from recently completed research studies constantly fed to them instead of actively searching for new knowledge in individual periodicals.

Electronic mailing service subscribers receive notice when new issues of the given periodical are available through automatic e-mail notifications that generally include the current table of contents. RSS subscribers receive the aggregated updates in a simple format on their Web browsers, desktops, or laptops. On Web pages, RSSs are typically linked with the word "Subscribe," an orange rectangle ( ), or the letters XML (XML) or RSS (RSS). You should consider uti-lizing these services to conserve effort and time when navigating complicated Web pages, which at times can become overwhelming.

Use Interlibrary Loan

Interlibrary loan (ILL) is a service that allows you to borrow books, electronic media, microfilms, journal articles, and book chapters from another library when the publication is not available in your local or university libraries. ILL allows you to obtain the full-text materials from another library without literally traveling to that library. ILL is a handy literature search resource that is often underused. Because ILL procedures vary from library to library, you need to check your local or university library's policies and procedures when utilizing this service.

SUMMARY

The pursuit of knowledge is an evolutionary process in which every increment of new knowledge generated adds to, modifies, refines, or refutes earlier findings (Subramanyam, 1981). Recent technological advancements have facilitated the availability of existing knowledge and created a rich resource for students and seasoned researchers alike. By now, you should be able to identify the various sources where existing knowledge can be found and know how to retrieve them. Mining for the treasure of knowledge is exciting and stimulating. In addition, and more important, it is a necessary task for social work practitioners and researchers alike. The following chapter discusses how to evaluate the sources you have found via the process that has been outlined in this chapter.

Evaluating Evidence

Jennifer Manuel
Lin Fang
Jennifer L. Bellamy
Sarah E. Bledsoe

23

You Are Here

The previous chapter briefly discussed where and how to search for existing evidence. Finding existing evidence, or existing literature, or existing knowledge, if you will, is only part of the battle in preparing for professional social work research and practice. Actually finding the information is only the first step. The second step is for you to evaluate the evidence you find in order to decide the most relevant, useful, and valid evidence to use to meet your research and/or practice needs. The lack of a critical evaluation of your newly found evidence may lead you to use evidence that is misinterpreted, misused, and/or biased. This chapter, along with Chapters 20 and 21, will provide you with a few tools that will enhance your ability to critically appraise the existing evidence you have found.

WHAT IS EVIDENCE?

Evidence is information that supports and guides social work practice, programming, and policy with the ultimate goal of enhancing the well-being of individuals, families, and communities. For example, you might be interested in learning about safety planning strategies for clients experiencing partner violence or the most effective way to assess their risk for suicide. Below are a few common types of evidence that are of interest to social work professionals:

- Evidence-based strategies or interventions to utilize in practice
- Prevention programs and policies that will avert a social problem
- Evidence-based methods and techniques to conduct an appropriate client assessment
- Salient factors related to a diagnosis of a disorder
- Risk and protective factors related to a problem behavior

CRITICAL APPRAISAL SKILLS

Evaluating existing evidence can be a daunting task for those of us who have multiple professional responsibilities, pressures, and deadlines. With such pressures and limited time, you can easily become tempted to use the first piece of evidence you find—especially if it is from an academic or scholarly source—without considering the evidence's relevance or validity. For example, just because an article appeared in a professional journal (see Table 22.1) does not automatically mean the information it contains is of high quality or even relevant to everyday practice settings, clients, and practitioners.

To effectively judge the quality of the existing evidence found and decide on whether a reported piece of information is good enough or appropriate to use, critical appraisal skills are absolutely a necessity. Critical appraisal is the process of systematically assessing and interpreting existing evidence. This process enhances your reading effectiveness and enables you to determine which pieces of evidence to trust and which pieces not to trust. As a result, you will have more time to concentrate on the systematic evaluation of the evidence you find and then to extract what is the most important evidence to utilize in your particular research or practice area. Using critical appraisal skills will broaden your thinking and enhance the quality of your work—in research and practice alike.

CRITICAL APPRAISAL OF SOURCES OF EVIDENCE

As described in the last chapter, there is a wide range of sources of evidence from which to choose to inform your research and practice needs. However, not all information is equally reliable or appropriate to use. It is important to view any source, regardless of whether it is a well-known journal, book, or Web source, with caution and skepticism. All research studies contain some errors and limitations. No research study is perfect!

Be careful not to accept a source based on its face value—in other words, just because a journal is well established and highly respected, or the article was published recently, does not necessarily mean the journal article contains high-quality evidence. Unless the source is examined carefully and critically, it is very easy for anyone to be misled by questionable assertions and biased perspectives.

Published Print

As you know by now, the standard sources of published print typically used in social work research and practice are peer-reviewed journal articles and books. Perhaps the least commonly used sources are popular magazines and newspapers. There are several differences between these three types of sources, including their purpose or utility, organization, and format for presenting evidence; thus, each requires different criteria in order to be evaluated. Nevertheless, some common "evaluative-type questions" (see Table 23.1) are useful to consider when searching for evidence within published print sources.

The key questions in Table 23.1 provide a general guide that you can use in determining the "trustworthiness" of a particular source. Of course, these criteria are not exhaustive and should be used in conjunction with other criteria explained not only in this chapter but in other chapters as well—especially Chapters 20 and 21. However, the questions are important to consider as you sort through the sources you find via the techniques described in the previous chapter. These questions are addressed within the sections that follow.

Journal Articles

Much of the evidence used to inform our research and practice efforts comes from journal articles. The previous chapter described a range of articles from scholarly journals, in the field of social work and in sociology, psychology, and other related fields. Prior to assessing the quality of evidence, it is important to know the types of articles you will encounter when you search the literature. For example, journals typically publish research articles based on original research studies, or *primary* research studies. These studies can be based upon observations (Chapters 9 and 10), interviews (Chapter 11), surveys (Chapter 12), secondary analyses of existing data (Chapter 13), content analyses (Chapter 14), or experimentation or randomization to treatments (Chapters 7 and 8).

Journals also publish research studies based on *secondary* research. These types of studies include reviews of published research studies (Chapter 24) or

TABLE 23.1

Key Questions for Evaluating Print Sources of Evidence

Authorship, expert, or authority	• Who is the author or expert/authority figure? • What experience do they have? • What are their credentials? • What institution or organization are they affiliated with? • What else is known about the individual (e.g., other published works)?
Purpose	• What is the purpose of the information? To inform? To sell? To persuade? • Is the purpose clear and objective, showing multiple sides of an issue? Although bias is not necessarily a reason to reject, be sure you can identify it. • Who is the intended audience? Researchers? Practitioners? Policy makers?
Content	• Is the topic covered comprehensively? Does it leave out important information? • How is the information organized? Is the approach basic or advanced? Does it provide more than one perspective? • Does the source include a bibliography or make reference to other sources? Is the bibliography detailed and accurate?
Relevancy	• Does the source cover the information or topic you need? • Is the information sufficient or is it too superficial or narrow for your purposes?
Accuracy	• Is the source well written and edited or well spoken? Are there noticeable mistakes in spelling or grammar? • Is the style of the source one that you would expect for the topic and audience? • How accurate are other references or information mentioned or referred to in the source? Is it trustworthy?
Currency	• Is the information current, dated, or outdated? Consider whether this makes a difference and what value is added for your needs?

a summary of findings from two or more primary studies. In addition, some journal articles can be more descriptive and provide general overviews (or conceptual or theoretical explanations) of a topic. The research studies journals publish range from exploratory to descriptive to explanatory.

It is also helpful to understand the process of how a manuscript is accepted for publication. It is useful at this point to distinguish between a manuscript and an article. A manuscript is what an author submits to a journal for possible publication. Once accepted by the journal for publication, and in print, the manuscript becomes an article (see Chapter 19). Before a manuscript is accepted for publication, it is reviewed by an editorial board (experts in the field). Manuscripts are generally either (1) accepted, (2) accepted with revisions, or (3) rejected. As mentioned briefly in the last chapter, this process of review made by the editorial board is referred to as *peer review*.

Most of the articles you find using ProQuest or Medline, for example, are published in peer-reviewed journals. Peer review, sometimes referred to as the "gatekeeper of science" (Campanario, 1998, p. 182), is highly accepted not only in our profession but in other professions as well. You may wish to briefly review a journal's editorial board to find out the names and credentials of its members. Journals that provide substantively relevant information, but are not peer reviewed, should be viewed with more caution than journals that have peer review boards. Articles found in non-peer-reviewed journals, however, should not be totally discounted without a critical appraisal because they can often be useful and informative.

While the peer review process is an important component to enhancing the quality and validity of publications, the process is not without criticism. First, peer review procedures and standards vary across journals. For example, some journals have two or more reviewers who accept or decline manuscripts for publication, while other journals use only one reviewer. Second, editorial boards are ideally composed of the best qualified reviewers, or experts in the field, who are well equipped to determine the quality and appropriateness of a submitted manuscript for potential publication. There is some debate, however, about whether some people who serve as peer reviewers are the most qualified and whether biases exist in their decisions (Campanario, 1998).

Journals also have different ways of selecting or choosing editorial board members. Some use specific criteria to nominate or select expert reviewers, while others allow authors to recommend potential experts, to review or exclude from reviewing the manuscript. Other concerns about the peer review process include the possibility that some journals may be partial to appoint or choose expert reviewers based on their institutional affiliation or even nationality (Campanario, 1998).

In addition, there is a potential for publication bias toward positive results, wherein journals reject manuscripts with negative findings and publish only research results that are significant or positive. Although we recognize the value of having quality control procedures in place for manuscripts prior to publication, such procedures, like the peer review system, are not problem free and should be trusted with caution.

Other Periodicals: Popular Magazines and Newspapers

Popular magazines and newspapers are usually more unreliable than journal articles because of their commercial interests. The publication process is driven by these monetary interests, rather than by a commitment to publishing scholarly or academic knowledge (Yegidis & Weinbach, 2005). There is a wide range of popular magazines and newspapers with varying degrees of credibility. Popular magazines range from highly respected publications, such as *Scientific American* and the *Atlantic Monthly*, and general public interest magazines, such as, *Newsweek* and *U.S. News & World Report*, to less reliable magazines that are geared primarily for entertaining and sensational purposes, such as *People, US,* the *Globe,* and the *Enquirer*. Newspapers also vary in quality, from the respectable to the glorified.

There are many notable differences between scholarly publications and popular magazines and newspapers. For example, articles in magazines or newspapers can be written by a member of the editorial staff, a scholar, or a freelance writer. Many of these articles, however, do not list the author in the bylines, so it is unclear who wrote them. Articles in popular magazines are more likely to be shorter than those in academic journals and may leave out crucial details about how the information described was attained. Although most magazines adhere to editorial standards, the articles they publish usually do not go through a peer review process and rarely contain bibliographic citations.

Rarely do general interest periodicals and newspapers cite sources. These periodicals can be quite attractive in appearance, although some are produced in newspaper format. Articles are often heavily illustrated, generally with color graphics, to appeal to the public's eye. Table 23.2 provides a brief review of these differences and others that distinguish popular publications from those that are scholarly.

It is important to use these sources for education or professional needs with caution. A suggested resource, located in many libraries, that provides background information to help you evaluate periodicals is *Magazines for Libraries*. This reference identifies ideological slants (e.g., left/liberal, right/conservative, neutral, alternative press, published by a political action) of more than 300 periodicals, such as popular magazines. Please note that some periodicals may not meet all of the criteria above. For example, *Scientific American*, which has

TABLE 23.2

Distinguishing Characteristics of Popular and Scholarly Publications

Popular Publications	Scholarly Publications
• Aimed at general public	• Aimed at academic or professional readers
• Often eyecatching, with glossy paper and color graphics	• Often plain cover with black-and-white graphics
• Cover a wide range of topics	• Cover a more narrowly focused topic
• Frequently available at newsstands or stores	• Usually available only by subscription
• Contain articles written by editorial staff, freelance writers, or journalists/reporters	• Often contain articles by experts in a particular field
• Author credentials may or may not be listed	• Author credentials almost always identified
• Published by commercial presses, with heavy advertising	• Frequently published by academic or association presses, with little advertising
• Generally used to inform, update, introduce, sell, or persuade	• Include original research, reviews, or essays
• Often lack bibliography or cited literature	• Articles are often peer reviewed or refereed prior to publication
	• Most often include bibliography or literature cited

glossy pages and color pictures, contains both scholarly articles and nonscholarly ones that that are geared to a more general audience. In those cases where an entire periodical cannot be put into a single category, it is important to evaluate the article itself to determine if it is scholarly or not.

Books

Scholarly books generally cover similar domains as articles. However, they are typically more comprehensive in scope, providing more extensive reviews and conceptual understandings of topics than individual journal articles do. For example, you might find a book on homelessness that contains several chapters covering multiple topics, such as the history, definitions, and health care delivery systems. Another important difference between books and scholarly journal articles is that books do not necessarily pass through the same process of peer review often used in journal publications. Editors or publishers, who may or may not be invested in the scholarly process, can influence the content of a published book.

Other competing goals, such as book sales, may drive what is included in a book.

As presented in Table 23.1, it is important to know who has written (or edited) and published the book. With this information, you will be able to ascertain their credentials and past publishing experience and whether the author (or editor) is an expert in the field. The publication information shows you whether the book is published by a commercial publisher, a university press, an institute or research center, or a government entity. It is also important to pay attention to the date of the book and whether the information is current, dated, or outdated.

Be mindful of the intended audience for the book (e.g., students, professionals, researchers) and whether the level of the book is appropriate and helpful for your understanding of the topic at hand. Does the book support or refute an argument or perspective? Does it provide examples to facilitate understanding of the material, or is it mostly theoretical or abstract? Is the information or knowledge consistent with other sources of information you have encountered? This line of questioning, in addition to the common criteria questioning, will help you judge the quality of the source and whether you think it will be useful for your research or practice purposes.

Internet Sources

Internet sources are increasingly used in searches for relevant and useful information. The Internet has a wide range of scholarly information published by university libraries and research centers, government entities, advocacy groups, and other generally known reliable sources. For example, several reputable sites with information and resources specific to social work are the National Association of Social Workers (http://www.socialworkers.org), the Social Work Access Network (http://cosw.sc.edu/swan), and the Institute for the Advancement of Social Work Research (http://www.iaswresearch.org). Produced by social work academicians and practitioners, these sites are frequently accessed and used by social work professionals and are generally accepted as reliable sources of information.

Although many Internet sources are generally reliable, many others are not, and are instead supplying misinformation. Determining which sites to trust can be challenging if you do not examine them carefully and critically. To illustrate this point, take a few moments to complete the exercise in Box 23.1. Nicholas Walliman (2005) provides seven criteria for evaluating Web sites:

BOX 23.1

Web Site Evaluation Exercise

Using a known Internet search engine, search for a social work topic, such as child abuse or mental health. Now, browse several of the Web sites, and as you compare the websites, consider these questions:

* What is the purpose of each site?
* What is each site's perspective or point of view?
* Is the information presented biased or objective?
* Is the information cited authentic and reliable?
* What are the main differences among the sites?

---

* Is the Web site accurate? Does it say what sources the data are based on? Compare the data with other sources. If they diverge greatly, is there some explanation for this?
* What authority is it based on? Find out who authored the pages—whether they are recognized experts or part of a reputable organization. Check if other publications are cited or if they provide a bibliography of other articles, reports, or books. You may need to track down the "home page" to get to the details. Also see if there is a postal address and phone number to indicate the "reality" of the organization. Web addresses that end in ".edu" (meaning education) are likely to be university or college addresses and therefore point to some intellectual credibility—no guarantee of quality but nevertheless a useful indicator.
* Is it biased? Many pressure groups and commercial organizations use the web to promote their ideas and products, and present information in a one-sided way. Can you detect a vested interest in the subject on the part of the author? Find out more about the authors, e.g. does the information about animal experiments come from an antivivisection league, a cosmetics company, or an independent research institute?
* How detailed is the information? Is the information so general that it is of little use, or so detailed and specialized that it is difficult to understand? Investigate whether it is only fragmentary and misses out on important issues in the subject, and whether the evidence is backed up by relevant data. There may be useful links to further information, other websites or printed publications.
* Is it out of date? Pages stay on the web until they are removed. Some have obviously been forgotten and are hopelessly out of date. Try to find a date of posting or updating (perhaps on the View/Page Info option on your web browser). Note that some updates might not update all the contents. Check any links provided to see if they work.

- Have you cross-checked? Compare the contents with other sources of information such as books, articles, official statistics and other websites. Does the information tally with or contradict these? If the latter, can you see why?
- Have you tried pre-evaluated "subject gateways"? The information on these sites has been vetted by experts in the relevant subjects, so can be relied upon to be of high quality. Try BUBL Link (http://www.bubl.ac.uk/link/). (p. 56)

There are some specific criteria to assist you in weighing the utility and validity of information that you find from the Internet. First, it is important to know the author or publisher of the page. URLs are often good indicators of who published the Web site. For example, is the site someone's personal home page, or is it produced by a university or professional organization? While personal home pages are not necessarily unreliable, it is important to investigate the author and any information posted because there is usually no publisher vouching for or verifying its validity.

Personal home pages are generally biased. Under most circumstances they are not considered reputable sources of evidence because more reliable and valid sources exist for most research or practice issues. In addition, domain names also may be an indication of the site's appropriateness or how it fits with your needs. For example, ".edu" is the domain name for an educational entity, and ".org" typically designates a nonprofit organization. Table 23.3 describes several examples of domain names, such as these, and their likely affiliation.

Next, examine the Web site's organization and content. Look for and investigate such links as "About Us," "Philosophy," "Background," and "Bibliography." These links provide useful information about authorship, credentials, the Web site's purpose and rationale, and possibly other works cited by the author(s) or publisher(s). Is the information in the Web site properly cited? Does the site present a particular view or perspective? Do you notice any biases? Is the information consistent with information from other sites or sources? Are the links up to date and reliable sources? Do all the links work? When was the Web site produced and last updated? Considering these questions as you browse through various Web sites will assist you in deciding which materials to trust and not to trust.

A very good online tutorial that takes you through how to evaluate online sources is "Evaluating Online Sources: A Tutorial," by Roger Munger (http://bcs.bedfordstmartins.com/techcomm/content/cat_030/evaluatingsources/index.html).

Grey Literature Sources

Grey literature sources are gaining increasing attention, primarily because of their easy access through the Internet. The meaning of grey literature varies slightly depending on the reference, but generally it is defined as nonconventional sources that are not available through traditional commercial publication channels (Weintraub, 2000). As was presented in the previous chapter, grey literature sources include, but are not limited to, scientific and technical reports, patent documents, conference papers, reports (preliminary progress or annual reports), government documents, master's theses, doctoral dissertations, newsletters, fact sheets, and memoranda. Grey literature does not include scientific or academic journals, books, or popular publications (magazines). Grey literature can be in print or electronic format (e.g., Internet, CD-ROM, audiovisual materials).

Although peer-reviewed sources are the most common venue for scholarly work, grey literature can also be an important source of information. This is particularly true for many social work practitioners who no longer have access privileges to university-system libraries or online search directories. With the advantages of the Internet, grey literature can be accessed quickly and has greater flexibility than many peer-

TABLE 23.3	
Domain Names and Affiliation	
.edu	Educational institutions
.gov	Government agencies
.org	Nonprofit organizations
.com	Commercial organizations
.net	Networking services
.ca	Canada (different for each country)

reviewed sources (Auger, 1989). Grey literature contains research summaries, facts, statistics, and other data that can offer a comprehensive view of the topic of interest (Weintraub, 2000). You can use grey literature as an introduction or overview of a particular topic prior to researching other sources.

As we discussed for standard print materials, it is important to examine grey literature for (1) the author's or publisher's experience, credentials, and affiliation; (2) the purpose of the material and particular perspective or point of view; (3) the type of information presented; (4) the utility of information to your research or practice needs; and (5) the accuracy or veracity and currency of information presented. Some grey literature sources, more than others, should especially be viewed with caution. For example, publications that have a purpose to persuade rather than inform, such as partisan political literature or editorial-type writing produced by activist groups, are less likely to offer unbiased, valid, and reliable information.

Although these resources can be used, particularly if the subject matter of your study is to observe or record popular literature, sources that are biased or inaccurate should not be used as evidence in formal literature reviews. Including questionable or unreliable sources of grey literature may be viewed negatively by the academic community.

Oral Histories

As mentioned in the previous chapter, oral histories are systematic collections of individuals' testimonies about their own experiences and background or insights and knowledge about a particular topic. Prior to using oral histories, however, it is important to understand their strengths and weaknesses. Oral histories can be a rich and contextually relevant supplement to other sources of scholarly information. Sometimes personal anecdotes incorporated into other forms of scholarly writing can provide a context that would otherwise be missing. For example, oral histories often provide background information, expert knowledge, or anecdotal information that cannot be accessed through traditional forms of published or official documents. In addition, oral histories capture and maintain archival information that might not otherwise be saved or accessible, and they often include life experiences or knowledge that is challenging to understand through quantitative research methods alone (Moyer, 1999).

If you recognize the limitations of oral histories, you will be less likely to be misled into believing that an oral history automatically yields accurate accounts or renditions of past events or knowledge. For example, it can sometimes be difficult for interviewers to conduct an oral history and write down every detail. Unless tape recorders or digital recorders are used, you must use oral histories based on the written summary and recollection of the interviewer with caution. In addition, an interviewee's memory may be in question. This is a special concern when a person is recounting traumatic events or actions that took place many years before. Therefore, it is important to understand both the context of the oral history and that it represents the perceptions of the interviewee.

As the amount of time increases between an experience and its recounting, interviewees may not remember accurately the sequence of events and omit critical actions and judgments, or may confuse events or mix unrelated information together (Moyer, 1999). Furthermore, relying solely on oral histories as sources of evidence limits your findings and conclusions to individual experiences and perspectives, potentially without consideration to external social, political, and environmental factors.

It is important to keep these limitations in mind when evaluating the quality and validity of oral histories and to know if and how the author, or interviewer, addressed these limitations. It is also important to know the methods used in conducting the oral histories. Based on suggestions by Moyer (1999), there are several questions to ask when reviewing oral histories:

- Did the author who published the oral history adequately describe the methods used?
- Was the interview conducted in a casual manner, or did it use a standard set of questions and probes?
- Were procedures put into place to elicit honest information from the interviewees?
- Did the interviewer use proper questioning techniques, record unobtrusively, and listen carefully?

- Did the interview take place in a public or private location?

Chapter 11 contains further information about this source of evidence.

CRITICAL APPRAISAL OF EVIDENCE

As mentioned at the beginning of this chapter, we frequently search for different types of evidence—from intervention programs and prevention strategies to assessment methods and diagnostic tools. This section explores different types of common evidence that you will likely encounter in your search. Because of its utility to social work practice, a considerable amount time is spent on reviewing evidence on interventions (which also encompasses prevention programs/strategies). This section concludes with some general criteria in the form of "key questions" that can be applied across the different types of evidence.

A central goal in social work is promoting and enhancing the well-being and functioning of individuals, families, organizations, and communities by implementing practices, programs, and policies. As such, it is useful to know the different types of evidence on interventions or practices and to have adequate knowledge and skills to evaluate this kind of evidence in the literature. Among research scholars in social work and other disciplines, there is debate about the types of evidence that are considered "the best." There is no agreed-upon or universal way to rate evidence, and there will not likely be consensus on this, since researchers come from a variety of disciplines with different perspectives on the types of evidence that are useful or not useful for research purposes, as well as professional practice.

One approach to evaluate evidence is a hierarchical ranking system. This system evaluates evidence based upon the research design that was used to generate the evidence. For example, when evaluating an intervention, a well-designed randomized clinical trial (RCT) is considered the "gold standard" because it minimizes the risk of confounding variables that may cloud the effect of the intervention under investigation

(Evans, 2003). Any confidence in the RCT, however, relies on the fact that the study was carried out correctly. Chapters 7, 8, and 20 provide additional information about RCT designs.

This approach, however, may underemphasize the limitations of randomized experiments and overestimate the limitations of observational studies (Concato, 2004). For instance, RCTs published in the literature more often than not contain conflicting findings. Others contend that a hierarchical approach focuses solely on measuring the efficacy of intervention research, or whether the intervention works as intended, with little attention to the appropriateness and feasibility of the interventions in the real practice world (Evans, 2003). In addition, many qualitative researchers argue that qualitative evidence is often categorized at the bottom of the hierarchy with expert opinions, when many qualitative research studies apply rigorous methodological techniques and analyses. For example, Hawker and his colleagues (2002) state that hierarchical approaches do not take into consideration the rigor that is applied to qualitative methodology; thus, the potential value of qualitative findings is lost.

Nevertheless, a hierarchical understanding of evidence is one way to organize the various types of evidence, and it is important to have this knowledge when evaluating the quality of evidence found within any given source. However, we believe that evaluating evidence is a part of a process that not only values research according to its methodological strength but also places value on the feasibility and clinical relevance of evidence and how that evidence fits with client values and preferences. The decision on what evidence to use should be placed in context with your research and practice needs.

Numerous hierarchies have been developed and used over the years (GRADE Working Group, 2004; National Health and Medical Research Council, 1995; Woolf, Battista, Anderson, Logan, & Wang, 1990). Figure 23.1 portrays one hierarchy based on a synthesis of those commonly used for ranking interventions or evidence-based practices. Because most of the methods are described in detail elsewhere in this text, here we present just a brief overview of each.

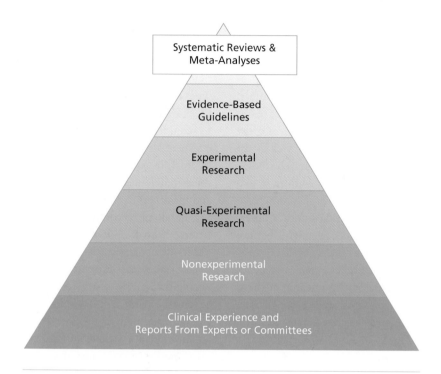

Figure 23.1   Evidence Hierarchy

Level 1: Systematic Reviews and Meta-Analyses

A *systematic review* is a comprehensive review of a body of data, or a series of studies, that uses explicit methods to locate primary studies of the "gold standard" of evidence (i.e., RCTs), appraise, and then summarize according to standard methodology (Higgins & Green, 2005). Systematic reviews can be conducted quantitatively, using meta-analysis techniques, or qualitatively, summarizing the results in narrative form (Higgins & Green, 2005). As you will see in Chapter 24, a meta-analysis is a statistical technique that combines or integrates the results of several independent RCTs that are similar enough statistically that the results can be combined and analyzed as if they were one study.

Systematic reviews, or meta-analyses, provide an efficient way to obtain evidence on a particular topic across multiple research studies. However, these reviews should still be used with caution. In addition to the same problems encountered in the literature for individual studies (i.e., poor design/methods), meta-analyses that do not account for variation across treatments, samples, measuring instruments, and analyses could lead to misleading conclusions (Bigby, 1998). For additional information about reading and evaluating systematic reviews or meta-analyses, we recommend reading Higgins and Green (2005) or Greehalgh (1997).

Level 2: Evidence-Based Guidelines

Evidence-based guidelines are sometimes referred to as *practice guidelines*. They are systematically compiled and organized statements of empirically-tested knowledge and procedures that help social workers select and implement interventions that are most effective and appropriate for attaining the desired outcomes (Rosen & Proctor, 2003a). They are typically a compendium of evidence on knowledge and the effects of interventions or approaches for a particular subject.

Most often, expert scholars in a particular area compile such guidelines based on standard review procedures. When drawing upon this body of literature, it is important to understand how the evidence base was reviewed (systematic versus expert opinion) in order to compile a compendium of evidence, as well as the methods used in the original primary research study.

For example, if you found a compendium of evidence on child abuse prevention programs, which derived from expert opinion, case studies, and/or observational studies, then the evidence might be less reliable than evidence from primarily well-designed RCTs or quasi-experimental studies. Again, it depends on the quality of the original study's research methodology: For evaluating quantitative studies, see Chapter 20; for evaluating qualitative ones, see Chapter 21.

Level 3: Experimental Research

Bias and design flaws are two primary reasons that studies conclude that an intervention is effective when really it may not be and vice versa. However, well-controlled experimental research designs are powerful methods to address these flaws. Experimental research, such as a well-controlled RCT (randomized control trial), is one in which participants are randomly assigned to either a treatment group (which is the treatment or intervention under investigation) or a control group (which receives nothing or the current standard of care). Because Chapters 7 and 8 provide a comprehensive overview of experimental designs, we will only briefly review a few of the major strengths and limitations of using this methodology.

As you know from Chapter 6, the use of random selection and assignment in experimental research studies is a powerful method to reduce such bias, which is any factor that causes the results to exaggerate or underestimate the effects of an intervention or treatment (Jadad, 1998). If random assignment is carried out correctly, there is an increased probability that differences between, or among, groups are attributed to the treatment alone. For these reasons, RCTs are considered the "gold standard" for evaluating the effectiveness of different treatments or interventions. For example, if you are searching for evidence on a school violence prevention program, you would first look for randomized controlled trials and search for other types of studies only if you do not find one. Obviously, RCTs are not the appropriate method to use for all research questions. As we saw in Chapter 2, to assess the effects of alcohol on health, for example, and for ethical reasons alone, you would not randomly assign some individuals to a group that drinks alcohol daily and the others to a second group that abstains.

Randomized controlled trials are not without limitations. If an RCT is not methodologically sound, its results are not necessarily any better than the results derived from a quasi-experimental study. Thus, when assessing the quality of evidence, it is important to look beyond the hierarchy of categories (Petticrew & Roberts, 2003). In addition, as mentioned above, various designs and methods are necessary for different types of research questions. In order to answer your research or practice question adequately and appropriately, you might need to seek out additional types of evidence.

Level 4: Quasi-Experimental Research

The next level of evidence is the *quasi-experimental design*. Unlike true experimental designs, quasi-experimental designs do not randomly assign research participants to groups. These designs usually have comparison groups rather than control groups. They do, however, tend to provide more causal support for the intervention under investigation than descriptive studies without comparison groups. Quasi-experimental designs are typically carried out when random assignment is not appropriate, feasible, or ethical. Evidence generated from quasi-experimental research designs can be very informative for your research and practice needs.

Although quasi-experimental designs attempt to achieve the internal validity of experimental designs, their evidence in terms of cause-and-effect relationships should be interpreted with caution. Evidence from these types of designs is generally less reliable than that from well-controlled randomized trials, since the two groups may differ in ways other than the treatment under investigation. In other words, the effects of the treatment may be due to other factors that were not controlled for by using random assignment. Nevertheless, quasi-experimental designs might be the most appropriate method to use to obtain evidence about a particular topic.

Level 5: Nonexperimental Research

A less preferred method for obtaining evidence is through observational studies, which may range from cross-sectional surveys to case studies (or case reports). Observational studies are exploratory or descriptive and are far less powerful than experimental and quasi-experimental designs primarily because they lack control groups or comparison groups. Thus, their results may be due to extraneous or confounding factors instead of the treatment under investigation. Because data are collected in an uncontrolled or unsystematic environment, evidence from nonexperimental research designs cannot be generalizable to the larger population; thus, it is relegated to a lower level of evidence on the hierarchy.

However, evidence from nonexperimental studies may be the most feasible ones to use under certain circumstances and may also provide additional information, which cannot be derived from higher design levels. For example, results from a nonexperimental study using client charts could reveal additional information that will help you to understand a client's symptoms or diagnosis that could not be obtained from other types of research designs.

Level 6: Clinical Experience and Reports From Experts or Committees

Knowledge from a practitioner's clinical experience and/or the opinions of experts or committees is usually considered the lowest level of evidence. This type of evidence should be used with caution because it is opinion-based, potentially biased, and at greatest risk for error. However, this should not negate the value of this kind of evidence. It can help you with understanding the process of implementing an intervention, and the barriers and facilitators of the intervention's implementation, as well as uncovering the unexpected adverse effects related to the intervention.

OTHER TYPES OF EVIDENCE

Depending on the research or practice question, you may need evidence other than on the effectiveness of various interventions to inform your work. For example, you might be interested in knowing the frequency and rates of child abuse in a particular neighborhood, city, or state. Perhaps you want to know about the common risk factors or determinants of homelessness among families, or you need information on diagnostic tools for your clients who may display mental health symptoms. Two additional categories of evidence relevant to the above issues are *evidence on assessments* and *descriptive and qualitative evidence*.

Evidence on Assessment

Assessments are used in social work practice to gather information about clients, groups, or communities regarding their situations in order to inform practice judgments and decisions about the direction or course of intervention (Gibbs, 2003). To determine whether a particular assessment is feasible, relevant, and valid, there are several considerations specific to assessments to keep in mind. These considerations are based on the work from Gibbs (2003) and Gambrill (2005). First, assess whether the assessment instrument is useful for your needs. Are the questions relevant to the specific topic or problem you are addressing? Is the assessment comprehensive in that it will provide the information you need? Second, assess the feasibility of using the assessment in practice. How difficult is it to implement? Finally, is the assessment reliable and valid? Is there information to support the reliability and validity of the assessment? Further information about assessments or diagnostic tools can be found in Chapter 6.

Descriptive or Qualitative Evidence

Descriptive or qualitative evidence is also useful to understand and use in social work research and practice situations. It provides information that may not otherwise be obtained from quantitative data. This type of evidence is typically presented in the form of narrative interviews, focus groups, case studies, and participant observations (Gambrill, 2005). Descriptive, or qualitative, evidence might be used, for example, to understand or describe your clients' perspectives or experiences about a particular service or intervention they were receiving. Some key questions to consider as you search the literature for descriptive or qualitative evidence include the following:

- Is the research question clear and answerable?
- Does the research question address a problem of clinical importance?
- Is the population or sample clearly described?
- Are the qualitative methods accurately and clearly delineated?
- Is the analytic plan described?
- Do the study findings match the conclusion?
- Are limitations discussed?

For more information about descriptive evidence, see Chapter 21. In addition, Hawker and colleagues (2002) have developed a system for critiquing qualitative evidence that you may find helpful.

GENERAL CRITERIA FOR EVALUATING EVIDENCE

There are numerous tools available for use to examine the quality and relevance of evidence. As mentioned, Gibbs (2003) and Gambrill (2005) have published several useful evaluation tools for social work students and professionals to use in practice. In addition, Greenhalgh (2001) has a series of articles in the *British Medical Journal* on reading different types of evidence, from systematic reviews, meta-analyses, and methodological quality of studies, to qualitative research and assessment tools. Many such tools are very specific to a particular kind of evidence, as we described above, and are helpful in deciding which evidence is the best and most appropriate to use for your research and practice needs.

Because various types of evidence possess unique characteristics, evaluation criteria specific to each type should be used in evaluating the quality of the evidence. However, there are common criteria that can be used across all kinds of evidence. Described below are criteria, in the form of "key questions to ask." They are compiled based on work from Hawker and his colleagues (2002), Gibbs (2003), and Gambrill (2005).

Relevance Assessment Questions

- Are the research questions clear, or are they vague or confusing?
- What types of questions are they—effectiveness, prevention, or assessment related?
- Are the questions relevant to your research or practice needs?
- What is the context of the information (e.g., population, setting, topic area, professionals involved)?
- What are the data and funding sources (e.g., professional versus client groups, private versus federal funding)? Are they clearly described?
- Are there any conflicts of interest or potential biases between the authors and the funding source?
- What is the study's research design (e.g., quantitative versus qualitative; case study versus randomized clinical trial)? Does the design fit the research question(s)?
- Is the treatment under investigation feasible in "real-world" practice settings?

Design and Analysis Rigor Questions

- Are the methods clearly described by the author? How rigorous are they?
- Does the author mention potential biases or other limitations?
- What is the sample? Are the sample selection procedures clearly delineated? How was the sample selected? Does the sample represent the larger population under study?
- Are ethical concerns described and/or addressed?
- Are the measures used reliable and valid? Are they consistent across individuals and time? Do they measure what they were designed to measure?
- What is the attrition or dropout rate? How many participants actually attended treatment sessions and follow-up interviews? How long were participants followed during the study?
- Was the follow-up short-term or long-term?
- What are the data analysis techniques used?

Do they sufficiently explain relationships? What are their weaknesses?

Accuracy and Clinical Relevance of Findings Questions

- Are conclusions accurate based on the study's findings?
- Do the findings match the methods used? For example, in uncontrolled posttest designs, which lack a control group, conclusions should not indicate that a particular treatment is effective in reducing or improving a particular behavior.
- Are the conclusions clinically relevant to a particular population? Do the risks outweigh the benefits?

Remember that not all evidence is valid and/or reliable, or presented clearly. In addition, evidence may have several unaddressed limitations, or it may not be relevant or feasible to attain. Although you may not be able to answer all of these questions for every type of evidence encountered in the literature, all the questions are important to consider in determining the evidence's potential utility for your work.

SUMMARY

This chapter has built upon the contents of Chapters 20 and 21 in that we have emphasized the need for you to use critical appraisal skills. In addition, we have provided some knowledge, skills, and tools that you can use to determine useful and relevant evidence for your research and practice needs. In critically appraising evidence, it is always important to be skeptical and consider multiple perspectives. Do not take information for granted based on its popularity or reputation. Applying critical appraisal skills in your search for evidence not only will benefit your work as a student but also will benefit your professional judgment and decision-making skills as a future social worker.

Meta-Analysis

Johnny S. Kim
Allan N. Press
Alice A. Lieberman
Thomas P. McDonald

Basic Steps in the Research Process

Step 1 Choose a problem

2 Review the literature

3 Evaluate the literature

4 Be aware of all ethical issues

5 Be aware of all cultural issues

6 State the research question or hypothesis

7 Select the research approach

8 Determine how the variables are going to be measured

9 Select a sample

10 Select a data collection method

11 Collect and code the data

12 Analyze and interpret the data

13 Write the report

14 Disseminate the report

Meta-analysis is a statistical method of collectively evaluating and quantifying a number of primary research reports based on the data and conclusions from these studies. This chapter demonstrates how to understand and interpret published meta-analyses and the basic steps in conducting a meta-analysis. Advantages and limitations of meta-analysis are discussed, along with its role in evidence-based practice.

SYSTEMATIC REVIEWS AND META-ANALYSIS

Systematic reviews synthesize the results from primary research studies addressing a specific problem by using specific strategies to minimize bias and error. These strategies involve using explicit search criteria as specified in the article and collecting all relevant studies, both published and unpublished. Furthermore, study characteristics and research designs can be evaluated and factored into the synthesized results (Cook, Mulrow, & Haynes, 1997).

Systematic reviews can be either qualitative, which summarize results from primary studies, or quantitative, which use statistical methods to combine results from primary studies (Cook et al., 1997). Systematic quantitative reviews, more commonly referred to as *meta-analysis*, integrate findings from a large collection of individual studies with similar constructs to determine the magnitude and effect (Glass, 1976).

Narrative Reviews

Another type of review more commonly found in social work research literature is narrative review, which summarizes research studies and makes recommendations for future research topics and practices in an effort to stimulate further development of knowledge. Narrative reviews differ from systematic reviews by not providing any explicit descriptions of systematic methods used to reduce bias and error. Narrative reviews tend to focus on broad topics and lack a methodology section, while systematic reviews often have a focused clinical question and detailed description of their methodology.

Narrative reviews are useful in describing the history or development of a problem, discussing data taking into account a particular theory, and describing recent developments with limited research (Cook et al., 1997). Corcoran, Miller, and Bultman (1997), however, cite several problems with narrative reviews, such as their lack of comprehensiveness in study selection (Jorgensen, Potts, & Camp, 1993), failure to synthesize the literature in a systematic way (Beck & Davies, 1987), and inability to quantitatively assess variations within studies of a program's effect on different subgroups (e.g., age, gender, ethnicity).

Systematic reviews, on the other hand, are more explicit, comprehensive, and critical than other forms of research reviews, thereby adding a unique contribution to the building of knowledge (Devine, 1997). Systematic reviews, and in particular, the statistical method of meta-analysis, have been used to identify effective practice methods developed and evaluated by social workers since the 1980s (Reid, 2002). Meta-analyses are being used increasingly to inform decision makers about the effects of a particular policy (Matt, 1997); for instance, is solution-focused brief therapy effective in reducing substance use among adolescents?

According to Cook et al. (1997), "By quantitatively combining the results of several small studies, meta-analyses can create more precise, powerful, and convincing conclusions" (p. 378). Furthermore, findings from the aggregation of multiple studies may provide a more stable and meaningful measure of the magnitude of a treatment effect than results from a single study (Perry, 1997). The larger the magnitude of the synthesized effect size, the stronger the treatment effect. A confidence interval can then be constructed as well.

ADVANTAGES OF META-ANALYSIS

Meta-analysis should not be viewed as a replacement for new primary research but rather as a complementary component useful for contributing knowledge. For example, a major advantage of meta-analysis is its triangulation of results from multiple operations of a construct. It utilizes multiple operationalizations of independent and dependent variables from primary studies

and therefore better addresses construct validity than any single primary study (Hall, Tickle-Degnen, Rosenthal, & Mosteller, 1994).

A primary research study can examine a particular intervention's effect on depression by using various validated measurement scales or behavioral observation codes. By aggregating the results from various studies that used multiple operationalizations of the construct depression, the research synthesis provides a fuller picture of the construct depression.

Lipsey and Wilson (2001) identify three major advantages a meta-analysis has over conventional narrative reviews:

* First, a meta-analysis is a structured research technique that requires each step to be documented and open to examination. Other researchers are then able to assess the meta-analyst's procedures, results, and conclusions for themselves rather than on faith that the author's conclusions are valid.
* Second, a meta-analysis can present key study findings in a more advanced manner than conventional narrative reviews. Instead of relying on qualitative summaries or "vote-counting" on statistical significance, meta-analysis involves calculations of effect sizes that estimate more precisely the magnitude and direction of each relevant statistical relationship in a collection of studies. The effect sizes are then combined with a weighted average across studies to provide a single best estimate of the effect. The precision of these point estimates is then calculated with confidence intervals around their effect size estimates.
* Third, a meta-analysis has the ability to find effects or relationships that would not be possible with narrative reviews. As Lipsey and Wilson (2001) explain, "The systematic coding of study characteristics typical in meta-analysis, on the other hand, permits an analytically precise examination of the relationships between study findings and such study features as respondent characteristics, nature of treatment, research design, and measurement procedures"

(p. 6). Additionally, the effect size estimates calculated in meta-analysis contain more statistical power than those in individual studies because meta-analysis aggregates effect size estimates across studies, giving greater weight to larger studies.

EVIDENCE-BASED PRACTICE AND META-ANALYSIS

Evidence-based practice refers to practices (accompanied with procedural manuals) that have been examined through research and shown to be effective in real-world settings (Gambrill, 1999). Evidence-based practice incorporates the clinical judgments of social workers, the needs of the clients, and the empirical studies supporting treatment interventions. Operating from this perspective requires social workers to integrate relevant scientific information with their professional judgment and include clients throughout this process (Howard, McMillen, & Pollio, 2003).

With a movement toward incorporating more evidence-based practices in social work education, social workers are trying to promote more effective practice and improve the profession's credibility. However, many popular therapeutic models and interventions, such as solution-focused brief therapy, are omitted from the list of evidence-based practice because they lack empirical support.

Evidence-based practice, however, is not without its limitations. Goldman et al. (2001) cite concerns about evidence-based practice, including its cookie-cutter approach to treatment, unrealistic expectations of its success, and lack of scientific information on working with certain problems. Not even in the field of medicine is there a one-size-fits-all approach to treatment because there is a tremendous amount of variability in humans and in each case (Jensen, Hoagwood, & Trickett, 1999). This variability among clients also leads to unsuccessful cases, even when there are similar symptoms and situations.

Goldman et al. (2001) point out that not every problem has an evidence-based practice or solution.

Other important concerns raised by various stakeholders include the following: (1) Innovative programs that have yet to acquire an evidence base could lose funding; (2) lack of time and support for clinicians to be trained in evidence-based practices; (3) high start-up cost for implementing evidence-based practices for administrators; and (4) challenges in figuring out how to finance evidence-based practices within existing insurance and Medicaid/Medicare payment systems (Goldman & Azrin, 2003).

Despite these limitations, it is clear that evidence-based practice is influencing social work education and practice. For example, according to the Council on Social Work Education Educational Policy and Accreditation Standards, the goal of social work education is to provide effective and ethical social work services through the teaching of professional skills combined with scientific inquiry (Council on Social Work Education, 2004).

Other social workers (e.g., Myers & Thyer, 1997) have raised similar ethical responsibilities as an argument for requiring social work practitioners to use therapy models that meet the criteria of evidence-based practice (Reid, 2002). Choosing among the different types of interventions has become challenging for social workers because of the wide array of choices, many of which have not been supported through empirical research. Meta-analysis can help examine the overall empirical evidence and provide more quantitative information on treatment effectiveness than p values.

Research synthesis using meta-analytic procedures is useful to examine the state of quantitative evidence that has been derived from numerous quantitatively-oriented research studies. By conducting a meta-analysis, the studies are synthesized, as a group, in order to determine their "overall effectiveness." The findings from the meta-analysis provide empirical information that can enhance our day-to-day practice activities. The meta-analyst can also test possible explanations for why treatment effects vary from study to study through predictor variables, thereby obtaining new information that is not possible in literature or narrative reviews.

THE PROCESS OF META-ANALYSIS

Meta-analysis is a systematic process that involves a set of well-thought-out steps that are open for public examination. The five steps involved in conducting a meta-analysis are (1) problem identification and definition, (2) searching the literature, (3) selecting the criteria, (4) coding the studies, and (5) computing the effect size. As mentioned earlier, each step involves critical judgments, with detailed rationales justifying those decisions. Specifying how decisions were made throughout each step helps others to examine any potential bias or inaccurate conclusions.

Step 1: Problem Identification and Definition

Any primary research study has a specific focus, and a meta-analytic study is no exception. The problem in a meta-analysis is identified in terms of the research questions or hypotheses that interest the reviewer, as specified in the dependent and independent variables contained within. The title of a published meta-analysis usually includes the independent variable and may also identify the dependent variable or variables and the outcome measures in experimental interventions.

Three types of questions are typically asked in meta-analyses:

- Taking all the studies located as a whole, is there statistical evidence for the presence of the effect of interest?
- How large is the magnitude of this effect?
- Does the magnitude of the effect size vary with other variables of interest?

An important consideration for the problem formulation is the broad nature of the research question, which allows for the inclusion of a reasonably sized sample of studies. A meta-analyst can integrate studies that investigated different research questions as long as some underlying construct unites them (Bangert-Drowns, 1997). The research question will guide which studies are included in the meta-analysis, as well as the coding structure discussed later in the chapter (Lipsey & Wilson, 2001).

For example, a meta-analysis by Tobler (1986) reports on 143 adolescent drug prevention programs that targeted adolescents in grades 6 through 12 to determine the types of programs that were most effective in preventing, decreasing, or eliminating drug use. In this analysis the independent variable is the type of drug prevention program (the intervention), which ranged from programs that only disseminated knowledge to programs that focused on altering attitudes and behavior of drug users by the use of peer pressure.

The dependent variables are the direct or indirect dimensions used to assess drug use in the studies reported. These included assessments of drug-specific knowledge; attitudes toward drug use; use of cigarettes, alcohol, soft drugs, or all drugs; and such behaviors as arrests or improvement in school grades. Many studies included more than one of these outcome measures.

Step 2: Searching the Literature

The second step involves identifying and gathering relevant studies for the meta-analysis. The reviewer's search for relevant primary research studies should encompass as broad a variety of sources as possible. The goal is to locate all studies relevant to the research problem. This can include published as well as unpublished studies such as doctoral dissertations. A common strategy in searching the literature for a meta-analytic study includes four steps. The reviewer should:

- Determine relevant descriptors or key words that will most likely flag other primary studies of interest.
- Search electronic databases for articles and journals most likely to publish primary research findings in the area of interest.
- Look through the bibliographies of research articles found for citations of additional articles of interest.
- Contact major researchers in the problem area for information on any additional studies.

Step 3: Selecting the Criteria

The third step involves selection/inclusion criteria based on the literature search. For various reasons, not all studies obtained through the literature search will be used in the meta-analysis. The meta-analyst should determine eligibility criteria to help select which primary studies will be used in the meta-analysis.

These criteria define certain characteristics of a primary study, such as sample demographics, treatments that the sample receives, research design of the study, and quantitative results provided by the study, which allows for a study to be included in the meta-analysis. A meta-analyst can exclude studies if they do not meet at least one of the inclusion criteria (Wortman, 1994).

Primary studies must also provide enough statistical information so that an effect size can be calculated. Statistical information necessary to calculate effect sizes includes sample size, mean(s), and standard deviations for both experimental and control groups. Additionally, t-test values and F-ratio results (when the degrees of freedom between groups is 1) can be used to calculate effect sizes if mean or standard deviation scores are missing.

If there is not enough information to calculate effect sizes from primary studies, then it is reasonable to exclude studies from the quantitative analysis based on this criterion. For those studies that report nonsignificant results without providing any detailed statistical information, an effect size of zero can be substituted for nonsignificant outcomes (Perry, 1997). This will lead to a more conservative pooled point estimate of the effect size.

Some meta-analysts develop a methodology rating score to help determine which studies are of the highest quality and include only those studies for the meta-analysis. As Lipsey and Wilson (2001) discuss, the advantage of using this method is that the research synthesis will yield results based on the most credible studies, but the limitations and inconclusive standards for superior methodological studies can make this criterion difficult to implement.

Additionally, the quality of methodological reporting in the social and behavioral sciences is often am-biguous and poor. A meta-analyst who uses detailed methodological criteria for study inclusion may discover it is difficult to obtain sufficient information to apply the criteria. Finally, there is a lack of agreement among researchers regarding which methods and procedures are superior in a given area of study and the seriousness if compromised (Lipsey & Wilson, 2001). Currently there are no absolute standards for this issue; however, it should be considered as a consensus on how to best deal with methodological quality assessment becomes accepted within the field of meta-analysis.

Step 4: Coding the Studies

The fourth step in conducting a meta-analysis entails developing a coding sheet that identifies which information will be extracted from each eligible study. Coding separate variables allows a meta-analyst to examine possible predictor variables to help explain any differences in studies' effect sizes.

Coding can be separated into two types: (1) by the study's characteristics, which are akin to the independent variables in a meta-analysis, and (2) by the study's findings, which are analogous to the study's dependent variable(s). Study characteristics represent factors that can influence the nature and magnitude of the effects and can include such items as methods, treatments, and sample demographics. Study findings are information about the empirical results of a study, which are necessary to calculate effect sizes. These may include items such as sample size, mean scores, and t-test statistics (Lipsey & Wilson, 2001).

Stock (1994) provides six broad coding categories to assist in this process: (1) report identification, (2) setting, (3) coding subjects, (4) methodology, (5) treatment, and (6) effect size.

- *Report identification* for a study can include noting the authors, year of publication, source of publication, reason if study was rejected, and an identification number assigned for each study.
- *Setting* involves coding based on the site of the study and can include categories such as agency, school, inpatient clinic, outpatient clinic, church, or other.

- *Coding subjects* entails noting specific characteristics of the sample such as age, gender, and ethnicity.
- *Methodology* relates to coding specific aspects of the research study and can include research design information (e.g., quasi-experimental vs. true experimental; independent groups vs. repeated measures design).
- *Treatment* involves coding type of comparison group, level of intervention (e.g., individual, group, family), number of treatment sessions, and treatment problem.
- *Effect size* coding includes sample size, outcome measures (e.g., standardized, self-report, counselor/therapist report), and statistical information necessary for calculating effect sizes (e.g., mean score, standard deviation, *t*-statistic, and *F*-ratio).

The coding process can be long and tedious, with the potential for coding error. Devine (1997) recommends that coders take frequent breaks to avoid fatigue and minimize errors. In terms of coder reliability, it is recommended that independent coders code the studies separately and then compare percentages of agreement. If there is only one coder available for the studies, Lipsey and Wilson (2001) recommend drawing a subsample of the coded studies and recoding them after sufficient time has passed since the initial coding. The results then can be compared and a percentage of agreement calculated.

Step 5: Computing the Effect Size

The principal methods for computing the effect size statistic for a study (the unit of analysis in a meta-analysis) involve the calculation of either the *d* index or the *r* (correlation coefficient) statistic as the unit of measurement. The statistic of effect size is the most commonly used index of the dependent variable. It allows a reviewer doing a meta-analysis to compute and then compare the magnitude of the results from different studies, even though in all likelihood they used different ways of operationalizing the dependent variable(s).

Thus this statistic makes it possible to convert the relevant findings from each study into a standard "yardstick" for comparison. Effect sizes for the *d* index are interpreted on classification by Cohen (1988), with .20 indicating a small effect size, .50 moderate, and .80 and above large.

Many primary studies in the field of social work use an independent-groups design whereby one group receives the treatment while the other group serves as a control, with the difference on the outcome measure representing the estimate of the treatment effect. Readers interested in effect size methods for the *r* statistic are referred to *The Handbook of Research Synthesis* by Cooper and Hedges (1994).

As we know by now, the fifth and final step involves calculating effect sizes for each of the primary studies and then pooling those effect sizes to come up with one overall estimate effect size. By calculating effect sizes, the meta-analyst converts measures in primary studies into a common metric of treatment effect or relation between variables. A common measure in primary studies is the standardized raw score difference between two group means (Bangert-Drowns, 1997).

The two most common methods for calculating an effect size for a primary study are Cohen's *d* and Hedges's *g*. Both of these effect size estimates are based on standardized mean differences between two groups, but they differ in terms of how the pooled variance is calculated. The process of calculating these statistics is far beyond the scope of this book. Readers interested in how to calculate them, however, are referred to *The Handbook of Research Synthesis* by Cooper and Hedges (1994).

CRITICISMS OF META-ANALYSIS

Meta-analysis has been found to be a valuable technique for summarizing the results of methodologically and operationally diverse but conceptually similar primary research studies, but it does have its limitations. Bangert-Drowns (1997) states that one of the main concerns about meta-analysis is that it provides an appearance of precision and comprehensiveness that can be unreal and therefore misleading.

Researcher Subjectivity and Impression

While there has been tremendous improvement in the statistical methodology of doing a meta-analysis, there is still plenty of room for researcher subjectivity and imprecision. Throughout the meta-analytic process, the researcher makes significant judgments guided by common sense and informed personal preference, which can influence the outcome (Bangert-Drowns, 1997). Some of these important decisions include what to study, the source of the data to use, the final selection criteria for studies to be included in the analysis, what to measure, who should collect and code the studies, what analyses to perform, and how to report the results (Devine, 1997).

Because a meta-analysis should involve a systematic review, each important decision made during the process should be stated up front for others to assess. As Bangert-Drowns (1997) states: "By clearly and explicitly describing search strategies and inclusion criteria, meta-analysts at least open these decisions to public scrutiny and evaluation, but such explicitness does not mitigate the effects of meta-analysts' judgments" (p. 241).

Apples and Oranges Comparison

The most common concern stated about meta-analysis involves an "apples and oranges" comparison (Bangert-Drown, 1997). Early critics were concerned with meta-analysts attempting to aggregate elements that are too dissimilar to necessitate integration and complained that meta-analysts were mixing "apples with oranges," thereby providing misleading results (Hall et al., 1994). Ultimately, the important factors include how the researcher formulates the purpose for the review and which studies are included in the research synthesis (Bangert-Drowns, 1997).

In addition, Hunter and Schmidt (1990) argue, "No matter how different the studies might be from one another, there is no logical problem in comparing numbers derived from those studies" (p. 517). They point out that meta-analysis involves an analysis of the *results* from studies, and any set of numbers can be logically compared, averaged, or analyzed. Furthermore,

Rosenthal (1984) notes that researchers think nothing of combining participants with diverse characteristics in a single primary study.

Garbage In, Garbage Out

The second criticism about meta-analysis is the garbage in, garbage out analogy. It simply involves the quality of the primary research studies used in meta-analytic reviews in the first place. Critics cite concern over researchers' willingness to accept data from poorly designed studies in an effort to be comprehensive, thereby producing misleadingly grand mean effect sizes (Bangert-Drowns, 1997). Some critics recommend including only those studies that are well designed in an effort to limit the bias that methodologically flawed studies can produce in a meta-analysis (Lipsey & Wilson, 2001).

While some researchers follow this strict guideline, others counter that it is almost impossible to find universal agreement on what constitutes "good-quality research." Furthermore, few research areas, or topics, provide enough methodologically rigorous studies to create a meaningful meta-analysis. One approach to combat this issue is to explicitly report study inclusion criteria and code methodological study characteristics (e.g., randomized vs. nonrandomized) that can be investigated as predictor variables (Bangert-Drowns, 1997; Lipsey & Wilson, 2001).

Publication Bias

Another important limitation and concern in a meta-analysis involves publication bias. Meta-analyses rely on using primary studies conducted by other researchers. Thus, obtaining all relevant studies to be included in the research synthesis is critical in presenting accurate effect size estimates. Publication bias in a meta-analysis can be caused by the biased and selective reporting of the study's results, as well as the decision to publish a study based on statistical significance (Begg, 1994).

For many decades researchers have suspected a bias toward statistically significant results appearing only in published journals (Lipsey & Wilson, 2001). Begg (1994) provided a brief overview on studies that investigated this publication bias in journals. One of the earliest studies was done by Sterling (1959), who found 286 of the 294 articles (97%) in four psychology journals reported statistically significant findings.

Additionally, Smith (1980) showed effect sizes were smaller in unpublished studies than for published ones on educational innovations. More recently, Easterbrook, Berlin, Gopalan, and Mathews (1991) found studies with statistically significant results had an increased chance of publication (odds ratio = 2.3). As these studies illustrate, if meta-analysts limit themselves only to published studies, there is a risk that the overall effect size estimates may also be upwardly biased, and therefore inaccurate. As Begg (1994) explains, "This is especially problematic in that one of the major advantages of a meta-analysis is that the aggregation of data can lead to effect size estimates with very small variance, giving the impression of conclusiveness in circumstances where the summary estimate is biased" (p. 401).

Inclusion of Grey Matter

Techniques for identifying and correcting for publication bias are still under development (Begg, 1994). One approach is to include doctoral dissertations and other unpublished research reports (often called *grey matter*), as well as published studies, in the meta-analysis. The magnitude of the effects found in dissertations and unpublished studies, such as reports "filed away" after the analysis instead of being published or studies described in papers for conferences, can then be compared with those found in the published studies to assess the extent of the file drawer problem.

Such comparisons have sometimes shown a greater rather than a lesser magnitude of effects for the unpublished studies, which suggests that the inclusion of such work is not likely to be a source of error. For example, in Tobler's (1986) study, the magnitude of the findings reported in doctoral dissertations was larger than that of those reported in published studies.

The Fail-Safe N

Another approach is the popular statistical method developed by Rosenthal (1979), which involves calculating the *fail-safe N*. This method entails calculating the number of unpublished studies with null results needed for a nonsignificant Z test statistic associated with the pooled effect size estimate. This answers the question, "How many studies finding no effect would it take to overcome the number of studies included that taken together did find an effect to justify a conclusion of no statistically significant overall effect?"

The *fail-safe N* formula provides a number ranging from a low of zero to a high in the thousands. The lower the *fail-safe N* compared with the number of studies included in the meta-analysis, the more likely is an erroneous conclusion that there is a relationship when in reality there is none. If the *fail-safe N* is only 10, for example, 10 or more sufficient studies may exist, tucked away in file cabinets or discarded, in which no relationship was found between the variables being studied. If these studies were located and included in the analysis, the conclusion about the presence of the relationship of interest would change.

Conversely if the *fail-safe N* appears to be large, then support has been found that it is unlikely that enough unpublished studies with null results exist to reverse the statistical significance found for the calculated pooled effect size estimate (Lipsey & Wilson, 2001). It should be noted that while this method does allow for a statistical calculation for examining publication bias, caution is warranted because it is based on the assumption that the results of the missing studies centers around the null hypothesis (Begg, 1994).

Tracking Down All Studies

Another common method used to offset publication bias involves trying to track down all relevant unpublished studies. Besides conducting a thorough literature search, the meta-analyst can contact experts in the field or attend relevant conferences for leads on studies known to have been conducted. However, some researchers (e.g., Chalmers et al., 1987) have criticized this method, arguing that unpublished data may be inferior in quality and therefore of questionable utility. In either case, it is important for the meta-analyst to be aware of the potential problem and attempt to correct for any possible publication bias with some of the techniques mentioned above.

SUMMARY

This chapter described the systematic quantitative review process of evaluating primary research reports to obtain effect size statistics. These statistics are then averaged to obtain a summary statistic to be used in examining the relationship between variables within a research question or hypothesis. A five-step generic problem-solving method helped introduce the concepts and computations necessary to understand and interpret published meta-analyses.

Evidence-Based Practice

Edward J. Mullen
Jennifer L. Bellamy
Sarah E. Bledsoe

You Are Here

E vidence-based social work practice is a broad framework that is used to guide decision making at all levels of social work intervention. For example, it can be used to formulate social work policy, aid in making management and supervision decisions, and help line-level social work practitioners to become more efficient and effective in their practices.

The purpose of this chapter is to introduce the fundamentals of evidence-based practice. In this spirit, and for simplification purposes, we discuss only how evidence-based practice can be used at the clinical, or direct practice, level. However, the approach can easily be adapted to other levels of intervention as well (Mullen, in press; Mullen, 2006; Gray, 2001).

WHAT IS EVIDENCE-BASED PRACTICE?

Evidence-based practice is a framework purposefully designed to help social workers operate efficiently and effectively using the technology recently developed within our new global information age. This age has already empowered us to make more rational and informed decisions about the service options we have at our disposal. It can enhance our ability, for example, to successfully navigate the mass of information that is now readily available through the Internet and other forms of media in an attempt to make our intervention choices mindfully without being overwhelmed or misled.

Evidence-based practice improves the flow of information back and forth from researchers, practitioners, and clients alike. This makes social workers better equipped to help a client system to make informed choices in the selection of the final interventions utilized. Within this framework, social work practitioners join with their clients and provide them with both empirical and practical knowledge about various treatment options. Although the final treatment decisions are made in the context of the best available evidence, clients' values and preferences ultimately drive the process.

At a basic level, evidence-based practice is nothing more than a way of doing practice—a way of assessing, intervening, and evaluating. Three highly compatible definitions of "evidence-based practice" are presented below:

- the conscientious, explicit, and judicious use of current best evidence in making decisions about the care of individual patients (Sackett et al., 1996, p. 71).
- the integration of best research evidence with clinical expertise and patient values (Sackett, Straus, Richardson, Rosenberg, & Haynes, 2000, p. 1).
- the integration of best research evidence with clinical expertise, and patient values. Where:
  - *Best research evidence* refers to clinically relevant research, often from the basic health and medical sciences, but especially from patient-centered clinical research into the accuracy and precision of diagnostic tests (including the clinical examination); the power of prognostic markers; and the efficacy and safety of therapeutic, rehabilitative, and preventive regimens.
  - *Clinical expertise* means the ability to use clinical skills and past experience to rapidly identify each patient's unique health state and diagnosis, individual risks and benefits of potential interventions, and personal values and expectations.
  - *Patient values* refers to the unique preferences, concerns, and expectations that each patient brings to a clinical encounter and that must be integrated into clinical decisions if they are to serve the patient. (Institute of Medicine, 2000, p. 147).

Figure 25.1 displays a basic diagram of how evidence-based practice is conceptualized. As can be gleaned from the three above definitions and Figure 25.1, it is simply a decision-making process in which judgments are made on a case-by-case basis using the best evidence available at the time.

As contained in Figure 25.2, it is a process that can be thought of as a cycle (Shlonsky & Wagner, 2005, as adapted from Haynes, Devereaux, & Guyatt, 2002).

As can be seen from Figure 25.2, current best evidence is the entry point wherein an actuarial (i.e.,

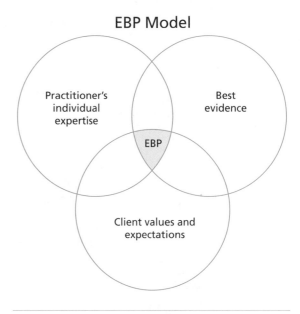

Figure 25.1   Evidence-Based Practice Model

statistically based) assessment of risk can be employed to target scarce resources. The contextual assessment (Gambrill, 1997) uses practitioner expertise to elicit key strengths and needs as well as client preferences as movement is made toward the delivery of a service, or treatment intervention.

At this point, current best evidence is again sought regarding other assessment tools (e.g., depression inventories, child behavioral indicators) and the effectiveness of various service options (e.g., multisystemic therapy, cognitive behavioral therapy for depression, parenting classes). What evidence is found is then integrated with client state/circumstances and client preferences/actions—again drawing on clinical expertise to integrate data from the various sources. In essence, research evidence supports and guides—but does not drive—the evidence-based process.

EMPIRICALLY SUPPORTED PRACTICES

Fundamentally, evidence-based practice is a process that includes finding empirical evidence regarding the effectiveness and/or efficiency of various treatment

The *Cycle* of EBP

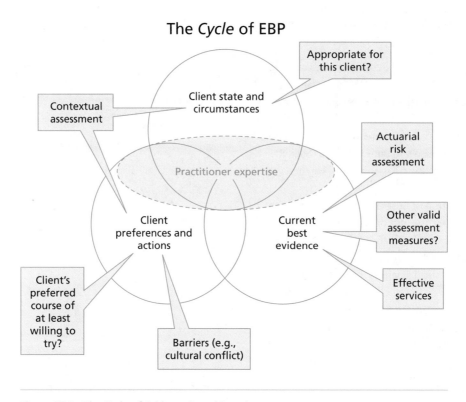

Figure 25.2   The Cycle of Evidence-Based Practice

options and then determining the relevance of those options to specific client(s). This information is then critically considered in making the final selected treatment plan. It is just as important to know that a treatment option being considered has little or no empirical support (or that the support is based on findings with a population that differs from the one you are serving) as it is to know that the practice has strong empirical support in regard to its effectiveness.

More often than not, the evidence about a diagnostic assessment instrument or the effects of a treatment intervention indicates that there are possible beneficial effects and possible harmful ones as well. In such circumstances, we and our clients alike need to weigh the possible benefits and possible harms along with other factors in making a final intervention choice. For example, while studies may show that medication in combination with psychotherapy is often most efficacious in treating mild to moderate depression in adults, there are circumstances when there are risks in-

volved in using medication. These circumstances must be discussed with clients.

The long-term effects on the children born to women taking many medications used to treat depression, for example, are unknown, whereas the negative outcomes and risks associated with depression for women, children, and families are well known. The benefits of treating with both medication and psychotherapy should be weighed against the possibility of harm for each individual woman. This would take into account other factors, such as the severity of depression and the effects the depression may have on other circumstances, such as irregular attendance at prenatal visits and attention to prenatal health care. These alone may place the client and her child at risk.

Fortunately, there are a growing number of empirically supported interventions relevant to social work practice. For example, there are now approximately 20 psychotherapies for the treatment of psychiatric disorders for which there is clear evidence of efficacy for specific problems or populations (Roth & Fonagy, 2005). There is also a range of community mental health programs that have empirical support for beneficial effects with the severely mentally ill (Drake et al, 2005). Since the early 1990s, various efforts have been made to systematically examine the empirical evidence supporting interventions and to classify the level and strength of this evidence.

These efforts have resulted in classification systems for categorizing levels of evidence that support the effectiveness of a variety of interventions. Among the earliest and most influential was the work of the American Psychological Association's Division 12 Task Forces on classification of psychological interventions or psychotherapies (Chambless et al., 1996; Chambless et al., 1998). The APA classifies interventions as:

- those that *are not empirically supported*
- those that *are empirically supported*
  - *those with well-established treatments*
  - *those with probably efficacious treatments*

Roth and Fonagy (2005) classify psychotherapies into:

- those for which there is *clear evidence of efficacy*
- those for which there is *some but limited support for efficacy*
- those for which there is *less than limited support*

A more detailed classification is used in the online digital book *Clinical Evidence,* which categorizes interventions based on a balance of benefits and harms into:

- those that are *known to be beneficial*
- those that are *likely to be beneficial*
- those where there *is a trade-off of benefits and harms depending on client circumstances and priorities*
- those of *unknown effectiveness*
- those *unlikely to be beneficial*
- those *likely to be ineffective or harmful*

Many interventions of relevance to social work practice are now known to be efficacious; that is, their effects have been found to be beneficial in controlled research studies often under specific, often optimal, conditions with careful administration to control for possible confounds. In other words, these carefully designed studies are aimed at isolating the effect of the intervention on the outcome(s) of interest. These studies are often called *efficacy studies.* This type of research study, though well suited to determining whether or not an intervention achieves its intended goal, is not necessarily well suited to testing whether or not an intervention will work under real-world conditions; that is, will it work under real day-to-day social work practice environments?

In contrast, *effectiveness studies* are carried out in everyday contexts to test the success of an intervention under more commonly experienced circumstances. Although a particular treatment may be efficacious, meaning it can achieve desired outcomes in a controlled environment, it may not be effective when it is applied on a large scale in social service agencies or provided by other social service providers. Our example (below) regarding the treatment of prenatal and postpartum depression, for example, is based on evidence coming from efficacy studies, and therefore we would need to express a degree of caution when applying this evidence to day-to-day practice situations.

EXAMPLE OF EVIDENCE-BASED PRACTICE

This section presents an example of how you—an evidence-based social work practitioner who is working within an obstetrics and gynecology (ob-gyn) clinic—would proceed using Figure 25.2 as a guide.

Background

Imagine for a moment you are a social worker in an ob-gyn clinic that provides services for low-income women in a large city. One of your responsibilities is assessing risk for psychological problems in pregnant and postpartum women. You have searched the research literature to identify common psychological problems that are risk events for low-income, urban, pregnant and postpartum women. Also, you have studied the records of the clinic and talked to experienced clinic practitioners to identify common psychological problems encountered at the clinic in the past. As a result of your searches, you have determined that the women to whom you are providing services are at an unusually high risk for depression. Your search has also shown that depressed women, and their infants, are at high risk for developing other physical and psychosocial problems.

Because of the high prevalence of depression in addition to the negative outcomes for both mothers and their infants associated with depression during pregnancy, you have begun screening your clients for depression using a standardized assessment instrument— the Edinburgh Postnatal Depression Scale (Cox, Holden, & Sagovsky, 1987). Confirming what you had previously found in your literature review, and your study of the clinic's past experiences, you have discovered that almost 20% of the pregnant women you see have symptoms that meet the criteria for "major depressive disorder" as indicated by the Edinburgh Postnatal Depression Scale. Because depression is a common and serious problem that you know you will be needing to address in your clinical practice, you are now interested in identifying and implementing an evidence-based treatment intervention in an effort to reduce depressive symptoms in this group of clients you are working with at your clinic.

You learn from your inquiries of other workers and supervisors that your clinic has typically provided a specific form of psychodynamic treatment, based on psychodynamic theory, for this type of depression. When you ask about the empirical evidence supporting the effectiveness of this form of treatment, you are told that this type of treatment, or intervention, has seemed to work in the past, but none of your colleagues are aware of any empirical studies supporting the effectiveness of this type of intervention with this particular population of clients.

The Problem

As an evidence-based practitioner, however, you are uncomfortable with your lack of knowledge about the evidence base for the psychodynamic intervention you will be providing if you follow the clinic's "traditional intervention methods" and your supervisor's recommenda-

tion. You worry that you could actually harm your clients by delivering an intervention with untested effects, or, at best, that your intervention may not be very helpful. From the last three chapters, you have developed skills for searching the literature, so you decide to use these skills to conduct a systematic search.

The Solution

You begin with an online search of the *Evidence-Based Medicine Reviews* offered by Ovid that is available to you through your university affiliation. Within the Ovid system you select the online journal *Clinical Evidence*. You have used this online journal before and have found it to be very "user-friendly." You like the way it is organized—the type of questions you ask, and how it provides clear and understandable summaries of research findings, as well as access to their specifics.

You find one relevant area within "Clinical Evidence" titled "Women's Health." Unfortunately, in this section you do not find any relevant reviews for your question. You next examine the section titled "Mental Health," and within that section you find "Depressive Disorders." You find two relevant questions in this area:

1. What are the effects of treatments in mild to moderate to severe depression?
2. What are the effects of interventions in treatment-resistant depression?

You decide to focus on the first question, since the type of depression that you will most likely be working with would not fall into the "treatment-resistant" category, at least initially. You also decide to focus on treatment interventions for "mild to moderate" rather than "severe" depression, since you think that these are likely to be the types of depression you will be seeing most frequently.

You find that there are a number of interventions listed as "Beneficial" for "mild to moderate" depression, including cognitive therapy, interpersonal psychotherapy, and a number of psychopharmacological interventions. Other interventions are listed under a category called "Likely to Be Beneficial," but since there are options in the "Beneficial" group, you decide to focus on these interventions. This review provided you with detailed information regarding these types of depression, as well as the interventions, including incidence, etiology, prognosis, and outcomes. Since the online *Clinical Evidence* journal did not include reviews specific to prenatal or postpartum depression, you decide to search further.

You then go to the Cochrane Database of Systematic Reviews within the Ovid system for your next search. In the Cochrane Database you find a category for "Depression, Anxiety, and Neurosis," and within this category you find a subcategory of reviews specific for *Depressive Disorders* containing 58 reviews. Among these you find a review article titled "Psychosocial and Psychological Interventions for Preventing Postpartum Depression" and a protocol titled "Psychosocial and Psychological Interventions for Treating Postpartum Depression." You examine the systematic review for prevention of postpartum depression and learn that 15 randomized controlled trials (RCTs) involving 7,600 women were reviewed.

You learn that the conclusion from this review is that psychosocial interventions do not reduce the numbers of women who develop postpartum depression. However, the authors note that a promising intervention is the provision of intensive, professionally based postpartum support. This review is focused on prevention rather than treatment, so you find it interesting but not specific to your search question. You are pleased to learn that there is a protocol (a prospectus for a review that is being conducted) registered with the Cochrane Collaboration, and you make note to revisit the Cochrane Database in the future to read this review when it is completed. You examine the protocol to obtain background information about what is currently known. You decide to continue your search by examining other databases within the Ovid system.

During your continuing evidence search for effective and efficient interventions that would be feasible for you to implement with your specific client population, you come across a recent review that identifies and compares research studies that have focused on the treatment of depression in pregnant and postpartum women. To your surprise, you learn from this review that based on the current best evidence, medica-

tion in combination with cognitive behavioral therapy (CBT), medication alone, group therapy, and interpersonal psychotherapy (IPT) have all been more efficacious in treating depression in postpartum women than the psychodynamic approach that your clinic has been using.

You decide that, based on the current best evidence that you have been able to find, you will consider changing your practice approach. You are cautious because the evidence comes from efficacy studies conducted in controlled settings rather than from effectiveness studies conducted in clinics like the one in which you work. Proceeding with due caution about this evidence, you first want to determine how the interventions suggested by the current best evidence fit with the state and circumstances of your clients, their preferences and actions, and your own expertise, as well as the expertise of the other social workers in the clinic who are facing similar problems with pregnant and postpartum women that utilize your clinic's services. You do not have the time or money to provide all of the potentially efficacious treatments, so you wish to identify the intervention that may fit best with the needs of the majority of your clients.

In a meeting with your colleagues you consider the options based on the current best evidence. You determine that medication is not an option that is likely to match your clients' preferences and actions. You know from past experience that many of the women who attend your clinic are reluctant to take any medication while they are pregnant, and that a recent breastfeeding initiative has increased the number of women receiving services who would be reluctant to take medication for depression in the postpartum period.

You and your colleagues are convinced when you see that your clinical expertise is also supported in the literature by studies that have been conducted with similar client populations. You determine that you should consider adopting a different course of treatment for your clients.

Group therapy has been used with some success to treat depression in studies that have focused on pregnant and postpartum women. However, after you consider the state and circumstances of your clients, you realize that this intervention may not be the best option.

Many of your clients have trouble making appointments for prenatal care due to barriers such as transportation and child care. You know that your clinic has recently expanded its hours in an effort to be available around their work schedules. You determine that group therapy may not be feasible because it would require your clients to conform to the group schedule.

So far you have now narrowed down your choice of interventions based on the best evidence, and client preferences and circumstances to two interventions: CBT and IPT. In discussing each intervention with your colleagues, you learn that, as a group, more of the social workers in your clinic are familiar with IPT than with CBT. One of the social work supervisors has received some additional training in IPT through continuing education programs and has found an experienced clinician in the outpatient mental health program at the hospital affiliated with the ob-gyn clinic who would be willing to supervise the social work staff in interpersonal psychotherapy. You determine with your colleagues that, while CBT is an evidence-based intervention that might work for your clients, given the expertise of the clinic's social work team, IPT may be the better choice.

You know you will need to monitor your clients' outcomes, since the evidence you have found does not come from effectiveness studies but is instead based on efficacy trials. Having completed this evidence-based practice process, you and your treatment team decide to review the process you have just completed in the hope that you can learn from this application of the process.

Our example so far highlights the process that might occur at the agency and practitioner levels to adopt an evidence-based practice approach. However, it is important to keep in mind that the chosen intervention, in this case IPT, may work with most of the clients, but there may be some for whom the intervention is not appropriate. Individual clients may elect other treatments. Part of evidence-based social work practice includes informing our clients completely of their treatment options (i.e., services), even if the agency or practitioner does not currently provide those services.

No single treatment, no matter how generally effective, will work well for every client. Because of the great array of service needs presented by clients and the realistic limitations inherent in day-to-day social work practice, it is unlikely that you will be able to provide the perfect intervention in every one of your cases. Therefore, to best serve your clients, you should:

1. be transparent about why you or your agency provides a particular service or service array
2. be clear regarding the outcomes that are anticipated
3. inform clients regarding what other options exist within and outside of your or your agency's purview

This process requires the synergistic combination of:

1. best evidence
2. client preferences and actions (including culture, values, attitudes, actions, and preferences)
3. assessment of client state and circumstances
4. the practitioner's individual expertise

EVIDENCE-BASED PRACTICES VERSUS EVIDENCE-BASED PROGRAMS

Sometimes distinctions are made between evidence-based *practices* and evidence-based *programs*. Evidence-based *practices* are skills, techniques, and strategies that can be used by a practitioner individually or in combination (Fixsen, Naoom, Blase, Friedman, & Wallace, 2005), such as cognitive behavior therapy, systematic desensitization, token economy motivation systems, and social skills teaching strategies.

Evidence-based *programs*, on the other hand, are groups of practices that seek to integrate a number of intervention practices within a specific service delivery setting and organizational context for a specific population, such as assertive community treatment, functional family therapy, multisystemic therapy, and supported employment.

Related to the efforts to classify practices by level and strength of empirical support is a parallel development—the publication of practice guidelines—sometimes called *best practices*. These practice guidelines are described by the Institute of Medicine as "systematically developed statements to assist practitioner and patient decisions about appropriate health care for specific clinical circumstances" (Field & Lohr, 1990).

Since the early 1990s, professional organizations and governmental agencies have formulated practice guidelines for various clinical conditions such as depression and schizophrenia (American Academy of Child and Adolescent Psychiatry, 1998; American Psychiatric Association, 1993, 1994, 1997; U.S. Preventive Services Task Force, 2002). These guidelines prescribe how practitioners should assess and treat clients. Sometimes the guidelines are based on research findings, and sometimes they are not; that is, often research studies are not available, and therefore the guidelines are based on "professional consensus." Rosen and Proctor (2003) provide a review of practice guidelines in social work.

The evidence-based social worker needs to know how to locate and critically evaluate published empirically supported practices and practice guidelines so that informed decisions can be made about their applicability to individual practice decisions. The three previous chapters provided information on how to locate and evaluate evidence, including evidence about empirically supported practices/programs and practice guidelines. Other chapters in this text provide the knowledge necessary for assessing the methodological soundness of the published evidence—the very purpose of this book.

STEPS OF EVIDENCE-BASED SOCIAL WORK PRACTICE

The example of prenatal and postpartum depression mentioned earlier in this chapter demonstrated how the evidence-based process can unfold. When learning to do evidence-based practice, it is useful to be mindful that there are six steps (Sackett et al., 2000; Straus, Richardson, Glasziou, & Haynes, 2005; Gibbs, 2003).

In the real practice world, however, these steps may not be followed in the following order:

1. Convert information needs into an answerable question. An initial assessment of the client must be done to determine what questions are important. The assessment should be used as a basis for a well-formulated question that not only must be answerable but also must be phrased in a way that a search of existing research literature can be conducted to answer the question. The question can be about assessment, description, prevention, or intervention:

- how best to reliably and validly *assess* (measure) a client problem (e.g., depression level, risk for abuse)
- how best to *describe* a client characteristic, attitude, or value (e.g., client self-identification of service needs, past feelings about service effectiveness)
- how best to *prevent* client problems (e.g., anger, violent behaviors, unsafe sexual behavior)
- how best to *intervene* to modify a client problem or to assist a client to recover from a problem (e.g., domestic violence, substance abuse, rehabilitation after medical treatment)

Example: Imagine for a moment, that you just received your MSW and are working in a small neighborhood-based agency serving predominantly low-income Latino immigrants. Your caseload includes families who have been referred to you by the local child welfare system because they have been determined to be at risk for child abuse or neglect.

A young couple that has been referred by the child welfare system to your agency, the Martinez family, presents a new challenge for you. The couple have a young child aged 30 months. Both parents report that they have been having a very difficult time managing their child on a day-to-day basis and that they feel helpless in dealing with her problematic behaviors that include uncontrollable screaming, kicking, and biting. They both feel as though their families and friends blame them for being "bad parents."

You decide it is important to intervene in order to help the Martinezes constructively address their daughter's behavioral problems. Your agency, however, does not currently espouse any standardized treatment intervention for child behavior problems.

Your coworkers tell you that the social workers within the agency are expected to use just their best judgments and intuitions and generally provide case management services. This type of intuitive-based approach makes you feel uncomfortable as an evidence-based practitioner, so you decide that you will use an evidence-based practice approach to this problem. You are wondering if a parent group intervention might be helpful, particularly since the Martinez family reports feeling isolated by their usual social support system because of their child's highly disruptive behavior. Thus, the question that you would like to answer is: "For Latino immigrant families who have a young child with behavioral problems, does parent group intervention—as compared with case management—result in better behavioral child outcomes?"

2. Track down the best evidence to answer the question.

Example: You have learned from your social work education that there are many online search engines that provide findings from research studies—or evidence. You want to be as efficient as possible in your search because you have a heavy caseload and do not have a lot of time to spend on searching. First, you attempt to find a synthesis of research studies, a systematic review, a meta-analysis, or a practice guideline, so that you do not have to sift through numerous individual research studies.

You start with the Campbell Collaboration Web site because it provides detailed and rigorous systematic reviews of intervention research studies. You are in luck! There is a systematic review available for you to download titled "Group-Based Parent-Training Programs for Improving Emotional and Behavioral Adjustment in 0–3 Year Old Children."

3. Critically appraise the evidence for its validity *(closeness to the truth)*, impact *(size of the effect)*, and applicability *(usefulness in our practice)*. Making a decision regarding the applicability of a research finding or findings to your client's specific problem area has its pitfalls. One solution is to consider the notion of "exchangeability," or the degree to which the current client matches up to the clients that participated in the research studies (i.e., age, gender, type of problem, social circumstances).

Example: You download the systematic review and read the report. You find that there is some evidence to support the use of group-based parenting programs to improve the behavior of young children. However, you have some concerns about the application of the study's results to your specific situation. First, the systematic review included only five research studies. Although the authors state that this was a sufficient number to perform a meta-analysis, they also suggest that further research studies must be added to the current evidence base in order to be more confident in the results. Also, the studies' outcomes are generally positive but are not strong in terms of clinical significance. In other words, the effect of the treatment may not translate into major or noticeable changes in targeted outcomes. Finally, although the review assessed one study that included Latino families in the United States, none of the reviewed studies' interventions were designed for, or explicitly tested with, Latino or other immigrant groups. Remember, your client system, the Martinez family, is composed of Latinos.

You know from both your research and practice experiences that cultural factors have an important impact on both parenting and intervention, so you are cautiously optimistic about the study's findings. You also seek out information about other potential interventions such as cognitive behavioral therapy and medication.

4. Integrate your critical appraisal with your practice experience and your client's strengths, values, and circumstances. You need to consider the evidence along with the values and preferences of your client.

Example: After doing your evidence search, you meet with the Martinez family again to share what you have learned. You explain to them the research studies behind each potential intervention, including the studies supporting their different options. Although your agency does not provide the interventions you found, you explain to the family that you—as their case manager—can refer them to other agencies that do provide these types of services.

In the end, the Martinezes decide that they would like to try a group parenting program. They are both hesitant to explore medication options, since their child is so young, and cognitive behavioral therapy did not seem to offer any opportunity for them to develop a social support system. After they have made their decision, you refer the family to a partner agency that has a parenting group program based on a model that was included in the Campbell Collaboration review for parents of young children with behavioral problems that is scheduled to begin next month.

5. Evaluate effectiveness and efficiency in exercising Steps 1 through 4 and seek ways to improve upon them next time.

Example: You review the process you went through in formulating your search questions, conducting your search, evaluating the evidence, and applying the evidence to your work with the Martinez family. You see some ways that you can improve this process and you make note of what you would do differently in the future.

Also, both you and your client's family are excited about the potential intervention, but you feel that it is important to monitor their progress, particularly in light of the limitations of the available research. Let us say, for example, that you decide to meet with the family every other week. During your meetings, the family completes a standardized measuring instrument that is used to monitor a child's behavior. The results from the measurements are then used to determine whether or not your intervention is successful in improving the child's behaviors. In the event that you see that no progress is being made, you can plan to consult with the family to help them find alternative treatment options.

6. Teach others to follow the same process.

Example: Your experience with this family has highlighted for you the need to share this information with other practitioners within your agency. You realize that your agency's current practice of intervening based on practitioner judgment and intuition alone could be improved by the research knowledge that you have uncovered. Further, you decide that there is a need for your agency to continually track new research findings as they become available.

You decide to present your case and your research findings to your agency at a staff meeting. Some of your fellow practitioners report that they also have struggled to work with families who have very young children with behavioral problems. Your agency decides to form a group to identify other common issues and problems in order to form other important practice questions, seek out new evidence, and synthesize these findings into their current practice frameworks.

To the extent feasible, these six steps—from problem formulation to evaluation and revision—should be collaborative; that is, they need to involve other team members and clients so as to benefit from various points of view and expertise. Furthermore, at each step in the process the practitioner's expertise, experience, and constraints (e.g., practical, financial, ethical) are considered together with practitioner and client values and preferences.

QUESTION TYPES

The questions we formulate should be questions that are important to clients and those that emerge from our daily practices. Most often they should have to do with fairly common practice problems rather than rare occurrences (more common or obvious events should be given priority over more trivial issues). The questions need to be specific enough to provide direction for an information search. Finally, they should be questions that, if answered by the evidence, will make a difference to what is done with clients. Gibbs (2003) calls these "Client Oriented Practical Evidence Search" (COPES) questions.

Five common elements are included in a well-built COPES question: (1) type of client, (2) client problem, (3) what the practitioner is considering doing with the client, (4) alternative courses of action against which the contemplated action is to be compared, and (5) what the practitioner seeks to accomplish (Gibbs, 2003):

1. Questions about how to enhance the effectiveness of an intervention
   Example: If disoriented aged persons who reside in a nursing home are given reality orientation therapy or validation therapy, which therapy will result in a client's better orientation to time, place, and person?

2. Questions about how to prevent a social problem from occurring
   Example: If sexually active high school students at high risk for pregnancy are exposed to "Baby-Think-It-Over" or to "Didactic Material on Proper Use of Birth Control Methods," which intervention will result in fewer pregnancies during an academic year, have knowledge of birth control methods, and use birth control methods?

3. Questions about how to best conduct a client assessment
   Example: If aged residents of a nursing home who may be depressed or may have Alzheimer's disease or dementia are administered a depression screening test or a short mental status examination test, which measure will be the briefest, most inexpensive, and most valid and reliable to discriminate between depression and dementia?

4. Questions about how best to describe a practice-relevant situation
   Example: If family members of children diagnosed with a learning disorder meet in a support group to receive information and support from staff and other families, what aspects of the support group will they find most helpful?

5. Questions about how to assess risk for a social problem
   Example: If crisis line callers to a battered women's shelter are administered a risk assessment scale by telephone or rely on practical judgment unaided by a risk assessment scale, then will the risk assessment scale have higher reliability and predictive validity regarding future violence?

Aaron Shlonsky and Leonard Gibbs (2004) provide examples of questions that their students created, as presented in Table 25.1. This table format contains five columns: (1) Type of Question, (2) Client Type and Problem, (3) What You Might Do, (4) Alternate Course of Action, and (5) What You Want to Accomplish.

Question Examples

This section contains example questions from the direct practice arena. They have been adapted from papers written by graduate-level social work students in a course at Columbia University School of Social Work taught by Edward Mullen. The first student (Rosario, 2003) writes:

> Evidence-based practice is a growing field in the social work arena. The essence of evidence-based practice is placing the client's benefits first by posing specific questions of importance to the client, searching objectively and efficiently for the best evidence, and then using the evidence to guide one's practice. In short, evidence-based practice is the integration of research into practice. My work as an intensive case manager for emotionally disturbed children has led me to form two COPES questions—one about *effectiveness* and one about *prevention*.

Effectiveness Question.   One of my clients is a 14-year-old African American male. He has had four arrests. His most recent arrest was for possession of drugs. Furthermore, he is a truant, does not follow household rules, may be abusing drugs, and steals. I recommended that he be referred to a residential treatment center (RTC), since his adoptive mother cannot manage him. His adoptive mother asked me if a RTC would really

TABLE 25.1

COPES Questions From Students at the University of Wisconsin–Eau Claire School of Social Work and the Columbia University School of Social Work

Name of Student	Type of Question	Client Type and Problem	What You Might Do	Alternate Course of Action	What You Want to Accomplish
Laila Salma*	Effectiveness	If African American juvenile delinquent males ages 11–15 who have committed one criminal act	become involved in an after-school tutoring mentoring and program	compared with those who do not	will they be less likely to commit a second criminal act?
Zayani Lavergne-Friedman*	Prevention	Will high-risk, very young children in urban areas	who participate in an Early Head Start program	compared with those who do not	have better literacy skills and better behavior in kindergarten?
Carilyn Imbery**	Risk/prognosis	For parents or guardians of children who have been found to have abused their child	which risk-assessment scale		would most accurately and inexpensively identify those who would reabuse their child?
Melissa Johnson**	Assessment	For elderly residents of a nursing and rehabilitation home who show signs of depression but may also have a dementia-related illness	is there a depression measure		that briefly and accurately differentiates between depression and dementia?
Tami Wilson**	Description	If patients in a hospital who are scheduled for surgery	are given discharge planning options prior to surgery	as opposed to after surgery	will patient satisfaction be higher in the former group?

Note. COPES = client-oriented, practical evidence search.
*Students at the Columbia University School of Social Work.
**Students at the University of Wisconsin–Eau Claire School of Social Work.

help her son in improving his behavior. Thus, my first COPES question is an effectiveness question:

> If delinquent youth are exposed to a residential based program, as opposed to a routine community program, will the former result in fewer delinquent behaviors?

Prevention Question: My second COPES question came from my concern for teen pregnancy. One of my clients, a 17-year-old African American female, is 3 months pregnant. I feel I could have prevented this, but it is too late now to prevent her from being a mother at an early age, so my focus should be on how I can help the other similar adolescents in my caseload from falling into the same trap. Thus, my COPES question is the following:

> Among adolescents at risk for pregnancy, will a sex education program that stresses abstinence or one that provides birth control information result in the lowest pregnancy rates?

Another graduate student wrote the following effectiveness and prevention questions (Lee, 2003):

Effectiveness Question: The first practice question stems from the population that I work with at my field placement this year. I am currently placed at a preventive service agency in which the primary target population is families at risk for losing children to foster care. In my caseload this year I have run across a number of latency aged boys with conduct problems. I have struggled all year with how best to work with these children to improve their behavior. This led me to my first COPES *effectiveness* question:

> If families of latency aged boys with conduct disorder receive parent management training or no formal training, will the former exhibit lower externalizing behavior problems?

Prevention Question: My second question was derived from a theme of violence that reoccurred in many of the conversations that I had with children and adolescents in my caseload. This led me to my first COPES *prevention* question:

> If adolescents at risk for violence receive school based violence prevention programs or no formal violence prevention training, will the former display lower rates of violence and aggression?

COPES questions also can address assessment questions, such as:

Assessment Question: This practice question derives from the fact that many of the child and adolescent clients in my agency need to be assessed for depression by the staff psychiatrist. This is a long process that involves jockeying for an appointment time as well as a fee in the form of insurance or out-of-pocket payment. This leads me to raise the COPES *assessment* question:

> If children and adolescents in my caseload are administered a computerized brief depression scale or are screened by a staff psychiatrist, will the former detect childhood depression as frequently as the latter?

COPES questions also can address descriptive issues. One student formulated the following descriptive question.

Descriptive Question: My final practice question derives from a case I have in which the mother has a history of major depression and all three children have some sort of emotional or behavioral difficulties. This yielded the following COPES *descriptive* question.

> Among children who are cared for by a primary caregiver who is diagnosed as having a depressive disorder compared with children whose caregiver has no diagnosed mental disorder, will the former children be more frequently diagnosed as having a behavioral or emotional disorder?

In summary, evidence-based practice is a process that incorporates individualized assessment by focusing on the strengths, needs, values, and preferences of clients. Specific examples of the process of formulating answerable questions and conducting efficient searches can be found in Gibbs (2003) and Shlonsky and Gibbs (2004).

DIFFERENCES BETWEEN EVIDENCE-BASED PRACTICE AND OTHER FORMS OF PRACTICE

In many ways the emergence of evidence-based practice in the 21st century can be seen as an evolution of the profession's long-standing commitment to social research and science. However, in the evidence-based practice framework there is a significant shift from the past in how practice and research are related. Previously, practice and research were seen as two separate spheres of professional activity; that is, research was conducted to add to the knowledge base that was eventually used by practitioners.

Researchers and practitioners had distinct roles and occupied separate professional worlds. In evidence-based practice these distinctions are blurred and at times even merged. Our practice questions share many of the characteristics of research questions. We search for evidence—especially research evidence—to answer our practice questions. We assess the quality of the evidence gathered using established research criteria when the evidence comes from research studies, and we collect data on the process and outcomes of our interventions.

As a consequence of the joining of practice and research, this approach to practice is qualitatively different from all previous forms of social work practice. Evidence-based social workers need new skills, including skills in assessing the quality and strength of research evidence pertaining to practice questions. Since this approach has only recently become available, it has not yet found its way into many practice settings.

EVIDENCE-BASED PRACTICE AND SOCIAL WORK VALUES

As discussed in Chapter 3, the federal standards for the ethical conduct of research with human subjects stress the centrality of three principles regarding research with humans, namely: (1) respect for persons, (2) beneficence, and (3) justice. These three principles can likewise be adapted to summarize the core benefits of evidence-based practice as follows.

Respect for Persons Including Their Autonomy

Fundamental to evidence-based practice is fostering client informed and voluntary consent in whatever service we provide. This means providing clients with relevant information about what is known regarding alternative intervention choices. We need to be prepared to share relevant information coming from research studies, as well as from other sources with our clients and their caretakers alike. For example, this could mean providing clients with information about the sensitivity and specificity of assessment procedures being considered (e.g., for detecting the presence of HIV, for detecting the presence of attention deficit and hyperactivity disorder in children). Some assessment procedures may be known to have a high instance of concluding that a disorder is present when it is not (i.e., specificity).

Similarly, for prevention and treatment choices, information about the effectiveness of alternative interventions needs to be provided to clients to the extent indicated by the principle of respect and autonomy.

Evidence-based practitioners are trained to do this, thus treating clients as autonomous individuals who voluntarily participate in intervention choices. This approach to practice honors the social work value of client self-determination. In instances where clients cannot comprehend the relevant information or are not capable of participating in decision making, we need to involve relevant caretakers or others who are responsible for our client's well-being. This approach is in sharp contrast to authoritative forms of practice wherein clients are neither provided with such information nor asked or encouraged to participate in decision making.

Evidence-based practice involves a commitment to transparency on the part of the worker—in terms of what is both known and not known about any given client problem configuration. This can be somewhat challenging not only for us but for our clients as well. Clients may want us to be *the* expert; that is, we should know the right answer and act accordingly.

Sometimes little is known about a particular client problem or treatment options that are not clearly empirically indicated. This lack of certainty can be distressing to all involved. However, it is this transparency that is absolutely necessary to uphold the principles of self-determination as well as beneficence.

Beneficence

According to the principle of beneficence, every effort should be made to maximize benefits and minimize harms to clients. Thus, we need to maximize the possible benefits to our client and minimize possible harms (e.g., see the classification system used in *Clinical Evidence*). To do this we must seek information from research studies about what is known about the possible effects of an intervention—both good and bad effects. This information is then shared with our client and the intervention team as appropriate. This typically results in weighing possible harms against possible benefits, resulting in an informed and voluntary choice. This approach to beneficence is in sharp contrast to some other approaches that make unfounded assumptions about benefits and harms or fail to take beneficence into explicit account. For example, for many years it had been assumed that so long as social work practitioners had received good social work training, then their services could be assumed to be generally effective. The training they received was typically thought by social work authorities to be appropriate and effective based on past experiences.

However, since the 1960s, research studies have disproved this belief, showing that general social work interventions typically did not result in benefits to clients. More troubling was the finding that oftentimes clients were harmed. Those of us who are developing evidence-based practice skills are learning from these experiences. We now seek out and share with our clients, as appropriate, information regarding any possible benefits and harms. Authoritative and traditional forms of practice do not pursue this principle of beneficence in a systematic and explicit way.

Justice

According to the principle of justice, we are expected to provide effective services to clients with equity. Accordingly, we are expected to strive to provide our services in a just and equitable manner. Too often in social work's history, better services were provided—knowingly or unknowingly—to more advantaged groups of individuals whether the advantage was due to race, ethnicity, gender, national origin, disability, or sexual orientation. Evidence-based practitioners deliberately seek to respect all persons and maximize beneficence. For example, this means we need to share information with all of our clients in an effort to help them to make informed and free choices to the maximum extent possible.

This also means sharing information from research studies regarding the generalizability of their findings to various day-to-day practice situations. For example, many standardized tests have been normed on middle-class white populations. In such cases, research findings regarding instrument validity, sensitivity, and specificity may be of unknown relevance to other socioeconomic or racial groups. This information needs to be shared with clients. Similarly, interventions often have been found to be effective in studies with one population (e.g., men) but of unknown effectiveness with another (e.g., women).

An increasingly troubling situation arises when expensive or complex interventions are found to be effective with one population but are thought to be too expensive or complex for another population. For example, this was the reasoning behind the decision to provide lesser antiretroviral treatment regimes to HIV-positive women during pregnancy, delivery, and postpartum in developing countries rather than the more extensive treatments found to be effective in developed countries. Evidence-based practitioners are expected to strive to familiarize themselves with such evidence and to share it with all clients (not just the advantaged group) in an equitable manner.

BENEFITS

The advocates for evidence-based practice believe that it (1) enhances the quality of decisions about care of individual clients; (2) fosters development of skills required to gather and critically appraise clients' stories, symptoms, and signs; (3) incorporates client values and expectations into the alliance between client and worker; (4) fosters generic skills in finding, appraising, and implementing evidence from the sciences; (5) provides a framework for education and self-directed life-long learning when supported by Internet information resources; (6) identifies gaps in knowledge that can then lead to new research; and (7) provides a common interdisciplinary language for treatment teams to use in practice.

Gambrill (2003) outlines a number of characteristics of evidence-based practice that support its use in social work. First, it moves the practitioner away from authoritarian practices and policies. Additionally, it enhances the opportunity to honor ethical obligations to clients and students in training by (1) informing clients and students about service effectiveness and harmfulness; (2) using effective services; (3) distributing scarce resources wisely; (4) involving clients in practice process; (5) individualizing and personalizing decisions; and (6) taking account of client differences.

Gambrill credits evidence-based practice with helping clients to develop critical appraisal skills in addition to involving them in the design and critique of practice- and policy-related research. Additionally, clients are informed participants who share in decision making, recognizing client's unique knowledge in terms of application concerns.

SYSTEMATIC REVIEWS AND META-ANALYSIS

We are sometimes faced with a formidable task when it comes to assessing the findings reported in research articles. If many research studies are found in the practitioner's literature review, the sheer amount of information may be overwhelming. In addition, findings from study to study may not be consistent (e.g., outcome measures may vary, effects may differ, sample characteristics may differ, interventions may vary). Thus, we should try to answer practice questions first by searching for synopses of the research that are prepared by high-quality reviewers, specifically for practitioners.

Chapters 22 and 23 introduced methods for locating and evaluating evidence. Systematic reviews of research evidence provide practitioners with reviews of all or nearly all of the research studies that have been conducted about a particular question such as the efficacy of an intervention. Meta-analysis (Chapter 24), a type of systematic review, is a research method that combines the data from multiple individual studies and reanalyzes the combined set to arrive at more reliable conclusions. Meta-analytic methods can control for confounding variables such as variation in sample characteristics across studies that are included in the meta-analysis.

CURRENT ISSUES

Although the current body of knowledge applicable to social work practice is growing daily, there is still a great deal that remains unknown. Certain populations, such as certain ethnic minority groups, persons with less common or particularly challenging problems, communities in rural and border regions, and immigrant or refugee groups, may find that the current evidence base is particularly lacking. Many interventions may be widely applicable to a variety of different people and issues; however, this is an untested assumption in many areas of practice and policy. There is a need for a great deal more research and the involvement of clients and practitioners in underserved groups to participate in the evidence-based practice process.

Similarly, much of the evidence-based practice focus in terms of research and application has centered on health and mental health issues. However, we can and do intervene in a much wider number of contexts. The principles of evidence-based practice can be applied to any method of practice from community organization to policy making to case management. However, information about effective approaches may not be as widely available, and the notion of evidence-based practice may be less familiar to stakeholders outside of the health and mental health environments. If evidence-based practice is to be broadly incorporated into the social work profession, research evidence in these other fields of practice will also have to be further developed.

Even in the areas of health and mental health practice, there are a great number of challenges that lie ahead as social workers move toward evidence-based practice (Mullen & Streiner, 2004; Mullen, Shlonsky, Bledsoe, & Bellamy, 2005). For example, many social workers must operate in contexts with limited resources. Engaging in evidence-based practice requires the use of technology, including computers, the Internet, and search engines (many are fee based), that are not necessarily readily accessible to practitioners. This process also requires time, especially at first, to learn the skills necessary and begin to build an evidence knowledge base from which to make practice decisions. It takes less effort to continue practice as usual than it takes to continually seek out new knowledge and test assumptions about the efficacy of one's work (Mullen, Bellamy, & Bledsoe, 2005).

Furthermore, evidence-based practice can be highly uncomfortable when one continually questions traditional practice modalities, especially when they are steeped in agency culture and tradition. However, this continued professional development is necessary to ensure ethical practice so that clients can be assured of receiving the best services possible (see Chapter 1).

SUMMARY

Evidence-based social work practice is a broad framework that can be used to guide decision making at all levels of social work intervention. This chapter described the process of evidence-based practice; what is meant by empirically supported practices; the steps of evidence-based practice; and questions that can be addressed in evidence-based practice. We have shown how it differs from other forms of social work practice, and we have stressed its ethical foundation. Finally, we have concluded with identification of current issues in evidence-based practice.

Part VIII contains one chapter, Chapter 26, on

program evaluation. Program evaluation over-

laps significantly with social work research. Since

most of the research methods contained in this

book are used in program evaluations in some

form or another, this chapter deals less with the

methods of program evaluation—methods con-

tained in the previous 25 chapters within this

book—and focuses on four simple ways a social

service program can be evaluated.

Program Evaluation

Richard M. Grinnell, Jr.
Yvonne A. Unrau
Peter A. Gabor

26

Basic Steps in the Research Process

Step 1	Choose a problem
2	Review the literature
3	Evaluate the literature
4	Be aware of all ethical issues
5	Be aware of all cultural issues
6	State the research question or hypothesis
7	Select the research approach
8	Determine how the variables are going to be measured
9	Select a sample
10	Select a data collection method
11	Collect and code the data
12	Analyze and interpret the data
13	Write the report
14	Disseminate the report

Many definitions of program evaluation exist (e.g., Ginsberg, 2001; Weinbach, 2005; Pawlak & Vinter, 2004). Overall, program evaluation is defined by a set of philosophies and methods that aim to determine "what works" in human service delivery systems. Program evaluations are always designed for a specific social service program (e.g., Rossi, Lipsey, & Freeman, 2003; Shaw, Greene, & Mark, 2006). The results of evaluation are particular to one *specific client group*, experiencing *specific conditions* of one *specific program* over a *specific time frame* in a *specific location*. In a nutshell, program evaluations utilize sound social science research principles and techniques to make judgments about programs for the purposes of improving efficiency, effectiveness, and the overall experience of services.

Accountability to various *stakeholder groups* is a central theme of program evaluation (e.g., American Physiological Society, 2002; Posavac & Carey, 2007; Preskill & Russ-Eft, 2004). For example, stakeholders such as *clients* want assurances that available services will deliver promised benefits, the *profession* is invested in knowing what works for different client groups, and *funding bodies* that provide funds for programs want to know that their dollars are committed to effective services (e.g., Bamberger, Rugh, & Mabry, 2007; Davidson, 2005; Fitzpatrick, Sanders, & Worthen, 2004). Other typical stakeholder groups include program administrators, social workers, and citizens living in a program's service area.

TYPES OF PROGRAM EVALUATIONS

There are as many different types of program evaluations (e.g., Donaldson, 2001; Fraser, Taylor, Jackson, & O'Jack, 1991; Nugent, Sieppert, & Hudson, 2001). Four types that commonly appear in social service programs are (1) needs assessments, (2) process evaluations, (3) outcome evaluations, and (4) cost-efficiency/effectiveness evaluations (Kettner, Moroney, & Martin, in press). All four types rely on the evaluator having the knowledge and skills to systematically collect and analyze data that will answer specific questions in an evaluative context—that is, for the purposes of making judgments about existing services and informing decisions about future program planning.

The far left-hand column of Table 26.1 illustrates the many approaches to evaluations. All of the approaches, however, boil down to four types of evaluations listed in the second column on the left: (1) needs assessments, (2) process evaluations, (3) outcome evaluations, and (4) cost-efficiency/effectiveness evaluations.

Needs Assessments

These evaluations aim to determine the nature, scope, and locale of a social problem (if one exists) *and* proposes feasible, useful, and relevant solution(s) to the problem(s) (Hatry, Cowan, Weiner, & Lampkin, 2003; Hatry, Wholey, & Newcomer, 2004). Needs assessments are born out of observed problems with or gaps in (or absence of) existing social services. Community leaders in response to public unrest, landmark cases, fluctuations in political and economic conditions, and changes in basic demographic trends often request needs assessments. For example, a director of a family social service agency may notice low attendance at parent support groups and may request a needs assessment to determine if the agency's group intervention is outdated or, perhaps, targeting the wrong needs (e.g., Connell, Kubisch, Schorr, & Weiss, 1995). Or, a child is abducted from a public school ground during the lunch hour, and an inquiry is undertaken to explore the general safety of children and supervision practices at all public schools.

A first step in needs assessments is to conduct an analysis of a social problem (e.g., child prostitution, drug abuse, discrimination) in a specified locale, such as an organization, neighborhood, community, and so on. However, in needs assessment it is not enough to establish the magnitude of problems; it is also necessary to identify viable strategies to address identified needs (e.g., O'Sullivan, 2004; Patton, 1997). Box 26.1 lists several published social work studies that have focused on needs assessments.

Needs Questions

Specific questions addressed by needs assessments are classified here under four general categories: (1) *Demographics:* What is the demographic profile of a community, or the people experiencing the need? (2) *History:* Have needs changed over time? Have services evolved over time? What conditions have changed in the community in the past 5 years? What types of solutions have worked in the past? (3) *Demand:* Are existing program services meeting the needs of the people being served? What are the gaps in existing services? Are there specific groups asking for services but not receiving any? and (4) *Strengths:* What are the positives in the community? What are the signs of resiliency in the community?

Process Evaluations

These evaluations describe the nature (e.g., type, frequency, duration) of *actual* program operations and client service activities. The focus is on the program's approach to client service delivery, as well as on how the program manages its day-to-day operations. In other words, the *means* of service delivery is of primary concern, while the *end* result is of secondary concern. Attention is given to how a program's services are delivered to clients and what administrative mechanisms exist to support these services (Chen, 2006).

In general, there are two major categories of processes—the client service delivery system within the program and the program's administrative support systems that sustain client service delivery. Client service delivery is composed of what workers do (e.g., interventions, activities) and what clients bring to the program (e.g., client characteristics). On the other hand, administrative support systems comprise the organizational activities that exist to support the program's client service delivery system (e.g., supervision, support staff, emergency petty cash funds, evaluation activities).

Process evaluations involve monitoring and measuring variables such as communication flow, decision-making protocols, staff workload, client record keeping, program supports, staff training, and worker-client activities. Indeed, the entire sequence of activities that a program undertakes to achieve benefits for program clients or consumers is open to the scrutiny of process evaluations. Box 26.2 lists several published social work studies that have focused on process evaluations.

TABLE 26.1

Many Types of Program Evaluations

Approach	Type	Description	Purpose	Strength	Limitation	Sample Question
Adversary oriented evaluation	Process, outcome	Balances bias through a planned effort to generate opposing points of view within an evaluation	To assure fairness and illuminate program strengths and weaknesses by incorporating both positive and negative views into the evaluation design	Diverts a great deal of subsequent criticism by addressing anticipated	Time-consuming and expensive, requiring extensive preparation and investment of human and financial resources	How effective is the Healthy Start program in reducing child abuse rates?
Black box evaluation	Outcome	Examines program output without consideration of program input	To determine program effects	Determines whether program is achieving its goals	Fails to consider why something is effective or ineffective	Do standardized test scores of high school students improve from the beginning of the term to the end?
Cluster evaluation	Process	Engages a group of projects with common funders, topics, or themes in common evaluation efforts to provide a composite overview of the success or failure of the cluster	To improve programs by identifying patterns of and lessons from the cluster	Allows multiple evaluation models, each designed for individual sites and programs based on local needs, to address collective themes or topics	Lack of standardization makes it difficult to describe how approach should be conducted	In what ways do prenatal programs for parents improve outcomes for infants?
Context evaluation	Need	Describes discrepancies between what is and what is desired	To develop a program rationale through the analysis of unrealized needs and unused opportunities	Potential for program effectiveness is enhanced when conceptual basis for program is perceived needs	Target audience may fail to recognize or articulate needs	What are the needs of low-income women in terms of prenatal health care?
Cost-effectiveness evaluation	Efficiency	Describes the relationship between program costs and outcomes for participants in substantive terms	To judge the efficiency of a program	Allows comparison and rank ordering of alternative interventions in addressing similar goals	Requires extensive technical and analytical procedures	How many dollars were expended to increase reading test scores of students?
Cost-benefit evaluation	Efficiency	Compares program costs and program	To describe the economic efficiency of a	Useful in convincing policy makers,	Difficult to quantify many outcomes in	What was the total estimated savings

		outcomes in terms of dollars	program regarding actual or anticipated costs and known or expected benefits	funders, and decision makers that dollar benefits justify the program	monetary terms and to express costs and benefits in terms of a common denominator	to society as a result of decreases in teen pregnancy rates?
Evaluation research	Outcome	Generates knowledge of program effectiveness in general rather than judging the merit of individual programs	To generate knowledge for conceptual use	Introduces objectivity and scientific rigor	Nonsignificant statistical findings do not necessarily mean that group means are equal, nor that program is ineffective	Do employers who offer on-site child care have higher staff morale than those employers who do not offer on-site child care?
Goal-free evaluation	Outcome	Gathers data directly on program effect and effectiveness without knowledge of program goals	To evaluate the actual effects free from constraints of goals and their outcome expectations	Attention to actual effects rather than alleged effects reduces tendency toward tunnel vision and increases likelihood that unanticipated side effects will be noted	Not goal-free at all but rather focuses on wider context goals instead of program-specific objectives	What are the actual effects of the mentoring program?
Goals-based evaluation	Outcome	Emphasizes the clarification of goals and the program's effectiveness in achieving goals	To measure the degree to which goals are achieved	Evaluation is sensitive to a particular program and its circumscribed goals and objectives	Fails to consider additional effects of program and neglects why it succeeds or fails	Does a parent's knowledge of child development change as a result of the program?
Impact evaluation	Outcome	Addresses impact of program on program recipient	To describe direct and indirect program effects	Tests the usefulness of a program in ameliorating a particular problem	Difficult to establish causality in social sciences	Are participants able to secure meaningful employment as a result of the job-training program?
Implementation evaluation	Process	Examines if the program is functional and operating as it is supposed to be	To determine extent to which program is properly implemented (to seek out discrepancies between program plan and reality)	Examines program operations in context as implementation strategies are neither automatic or certain	Provides no information regarding program efficiency or effectiveness	Is the program reaching the target population?

(continued)

TABLE 26.1 (continued)

Approach	Type	Description	Purpose	Strength	Limitation	Sample Question
Input evaluation	Process	Describes strong and weak points of strategies toward achieving objectives	To identify and assess program capabilities	Provides useful information to guide program strategy and design	Approach can be complex and overwhelming if priorities are not set and followed	Are home visits or group sessions more appropriate for the target population?
Outcomes evaluation	Outcome	Comparison of actual program outcomes to desired program outcomes	To determine whether program objectives have been attained	Generally is easy to understand, develop, and implement	Lacks information regarding the actual nature of the program and what is producing observed outcomes	Do patients lose weight?
Performance evaluation	Outcome	Assesses program results in terms of established performance indicators	To describe behavior changes as a result of the program	Establishes performance criteria for program recipients	Uncertainty regarding the extent to which program activities caused observed results	What study skills do youth display after participating in a tutoring program?
Process evaluation	Process	Focuses on internal dynamics and actual operations to understand strengths and weakness	To look at how an outcome is produced rather than the outcome itself	Provides feedback in development phase to improve program	Does not indicate if a program is successful or effective	How many hours of direct contact do program recipients receive?
Responsive evaluation	Process, outcome, need, efficiency	Responds to program activities and audience needs by allowing evaluation questions and methods to emerge from observation	To address the concerns and issues of the stakeholder audience	Directs the attention of the evaluator to the needs of those for whom the evaluation is being done\	Reliance on individual stakeholder perspectives may lead to subjective designs and findings	What major questions would you like the evaluation to answer?
Theory-based evaluation	Process, outcome	Evaluation based on a model, theory, or philosophy about how a program works	To identify the causal relationships that affect, operate, and influence the program	Presents rationale for choice of variables, and results can contribute to growing body of scientific knowledge	Conclusions are based on whether theory is correct or accepted	Is there a fit between the outcomes predicted by the ecological theory and the observed outcomes for families?
Utilization focused evaluation	Process, outcome, efficiency, need	Yields immediate, concrete, observable, and useful information on program decisions and activities as a result of evaluation findings	To increase the use of evaluation	Provides meaningful, relevant, and substantial information to empower users	Demands high expenditures of time, energy, and staff resources	What information is needed by stakeholders to improve future youth development programs?

BOX 26.1

Published Examples of Needs Assessments

Substantive areas are in **bold**.

Berkman, B., Chauncey, S., Holmes, W., Daniels, A., Bonander, E., Sampson, S., & Robinson, M. (1999). Standardized screening of **elderly patients'** needs for social work assessment in primary care. *Health and Social Work, 24,* 9–16.

Chen, H., & Marks, M. (1998). Assessing the needs of **inner city youth:** Beyond needs identification and prioritization. *Children and Youth Services Review, 20,* 819–838.

Davidson, B. (1997). Service needs of **relative caregivers:** A qualitative analysis. *Families in Society, 78,* 502–510.

Ford, W. E. (1997). Perspective on the integration of **substance user** needs assessment and treatment planning. *Substance Use and Misuse, 32,* 343–349.

Gillman, R. R., & Newman, B. S. (1996). Psychosocial concerns and strengths of **women with HIV infection:** An empirical study. *Families in Society, 77,* 131–141.

Hall, M., Amodeo, M., Shaffer, H., & Bilt, J. (2000). **Social workers** employed in substance abuse treatment agencies: A training needs assessment. *Social Work, 45,* 141–154.

Herdt, G., Beeler, J., & Rawls, T. (1997). Life course diversity among **older lesbians and gay men:** A study in Chicago. *Journal of Gay, Lesbian, and Bisexual Identity, 2,* 231–246.

Palmeri, D., Auld, G., Taylor, T., Kendall, P., & Anderson, A. (1998). Multiple perspectives on nutrition education needs of **low-income Hispanics**. *Journal of Community Health, 23,* 301–316.

Pisarski, A., & Gallois, C. (1996). A needs analysis of Brisbane **Lesbians:** Implications for the lesbian community, *Journal of Homosexuality, 30,* 79–95.

Safyer, A. W., Litchfield, L. C., & Leahy, B. H. (1996). **Employees with teens:** The role of EAP needs assessments. *Employee Assistance Quarterly, 11,* 47–66.

Shields, G., & Adams, J. (1996). **HIV/AIDS** among **youth:** A community needs assessment study. *Child and Adolescent Social Work Journal, 12,* 361–380.

Weaver, H. N. (1997). The challenges of research in **Native American communities:** Incorporating principles of cultural competence. *Journal of Social Service Research, 23,* 1–15.

Weiner, A. (1996). Understanding the social needs of **streetwalking prostitutes**. *Social Work, 41,* 97–105.

Zahnd, E., Klein, D., & Needell, B. (1997). **Substance use** and issues of violence among **low-income, pregnant women:** The California perinatal needs assessment. *Journal of Drug Issues, 27,* 563–584.

Process Evaluation Questions

There are many published examples in the literature of how process evaluations can help us in our professional practice. The questions they can answer can be classified under six general categories: (1) *Program Structures:* What is the program's organizational structure? What is the flow of communication? How are decisions made? What are the minimum qualifications for staff hiring? (2) *Program Supports:* What program supports exist to help workers do their jobs? Are principles of cultural competence integrated into staff training and supervision? (3) *Client Service Delivery:* What is the quality of worker activity? What do workers do? How often? (4) *Decision Making:* How are practice decisions made? How are worker activities and decision making documented? (5) *Program Integrity:* Is the program being implemented in the way that it was designed? If not, how does the program deviate from the original program "blueprint"? and (6) *Compliance:* Is the program meeting standards set by funders, accrediting bodies, or governmental agencies?

Outcome Evaluations

These evaluations determine the amount and direction of change experienced by clients during or after a program's services (e.g., Compassion Capital Fund National Resource Center, 2006; Lampkin & Hatry, 2003). More specifically, they aim to demonstrate the degree and nature of change, if any, for clients after they have received program services—that is, at program exit or some later follow-up point. The essence of an outcome evaluation is captured by the familiar phrase "begin with the end in mind." Outcome evaluations focus on the conceptual destination on a program map because

BOX 26.2

Published Examples of Process Evaluations

Substantive areas are in **bold**.

Allen, J., Philliber, S., & Hoggson, N. (1990). School-based prevention of **teen-age pregnancy and school dropout:** Process evaluation of the National Replication of the Teen Outreach Program. *American Journal of Community Psychology, 18,* 505–524.

Andersson, L. (1984). Intervention against loneliness in a group of **elderly women:** A process evaluation. *Human Relations, 37,* 295–310.

Bazemore, G., & Cruise, P. (1993). Resident adaptations in an Alcoholics Anonymous based residential program for the **urban homeless**. *Social Service Review, 67,* 599–616.

Bentelspacher, C., DeSilva, E, Goh, T., & LaRowe, K. (1996). A process evaluation of the cultural compatibility of psychoeducational family group treatment with **ethnic Asian** clients. *Social Work With Groups, 19,* 41–55.

Berkowitz, G., Halfon, N., & Klee, L. (1992). Improving access to health care: Case management for **vulnerable children**. *Social Work in Health Care, 17,* 101–123.

Blaze Temple, D., & Honig, F. (1997). Process evaluation of an Australian EAP. *Employee Assistance Quarterly, 12,* 15–35.

Cheung, K., & Canda, E. (1992). Training **Southeast Asian refugees** as social workers: Single-subject evaluation. *Social Development Issues, 14,* 88–99.

Deacon, S., & Piercy, F. (2000). Qualitative evaluation of **family therapy** programs: A participatory approach. *Journal of Marital and Family Therapy, 26,* 39–45.

Dehar, M., Casswell, S., & Duignan, P. (1993). Formative and process evaluation of health promotion and disease prevention programs. *Evaluation Review, 17,* 204–220.

Devaney, B., & Rossi, P. (1997). Thinking through evaluation design options. *Children and Youth Services Review, 19,* 587–606.

Jackson, J. (1991). The use of psychoeducational evaluations in the clinical process: **Therapists** as sympathetic advocates. *Child and Adolescent Social Work Journal, 8,* 473–487.

Jones, L., & Strandness, D. (1991). Integrating research activities, practice changes, and monitoring and evaluation: A model for academic health centers. *Quality Review Bulletin, 17,* 229–235.

Lusk, M. (1983). The psychosocial evaluation of the **hospice patient**. *Health and Social Work, 8,* 210–218.

Miller, T., Veltkamp, L., & Janson, D. (1988). Projective measures in the clinical evaluation of **sexually abused children**. *Child Psychiatry and Human Development, 18,* 47–57.

Pithers, W. (1994). Process evaluation of a group therapy component designed to enhance sex offenders' empathy for **sexual abuse survivors**. *Behavior Research and Therapy, 32,* 565–570.

Pithers, W. (1999). Empathy definition, enhancement, and relevance to the treatment of **sexual abusers**. *Journal of Interpersonal Violence, 14,* 257–284.

Rotheram, M. (1987). Evaluation of imminent danger for **suicide among youth**. *American Journal of Orthopsychiatry, 57,* 102–110.

Sieppert, J. D., Hudson, J., & Unrau, Y. A. (2000). **Family group conferencing** in child welfare: Lessons from a demonstration project. *Families in Society, 81,* 382–391.

Smith, M., Knickman, J., & Oppenheimer, L. (1992). Connecting the disconnected adult day care for **people with AIDS** in New York City. *Health and Social Work, 17,* 273–281.

they tell us where program staff and clients are headed as they work together. This focus helps to keep program administrators and workers in sync with the program's mandate (which is reflected in the program's mission or goal).

Outcome evaluations tell us *whether* programs are working, but unless experimental methodology is incorporated and program processes are carefully monitored, they are silent about *why* programs are working— or failing to work (e.g., Urban Institute, 2003). Because

experimental methodology is rarely used and program processes are often ignored, outcome evaluations have earned the name of "black box" evaluation (e.g., Brun, 2005). This label communicates the idea that clients entering the black box of the program emerge somehow changed (hopefully for the better), but it is not obvious what aspects of the program are associated with any observed client outcomes. Box 26.3 lists several published social work studies that have focused on outcome evaluations.

BOX 26.3

Published Examples of Outcome Evaluations

Substantive areas are in **bold**.

Auslander, W., Haire-Joshu, D., Houston, C., Williams, J. H., & Krebill, H. (2000). The short-term impact of a health promotion program for low-income **African American women**. *Research on Social Work Practice, 10,* 78–97.

Bacha, T., Pomeroy, E. C., & Gilbert, D. (1999). A psychoeducational group intervention for **HIV-positive children**: A pilot study. *Health and Social Work, 24,* 303–306.

Bagley, C., & Young, L. (1998). Long-term evaluation of group counseling of **women with a history of child sexual abuse:** Focus on depression, self-esteem, suicidal behaviors, and social support. *Social Work With Groups, 21,* 63–73.

Barber, J., & Gilbertson, R. (1998). Evaluation of a self-help manual for the **female partners of heavy drinkers**. *Research on Social Work Practice, 8,* 141–151.

Barker, S. B., Knisely, J. S., & Dawson, K. (1999). The evaluation of a consultation service for delivery of **substance abuse services** in a hospital setting. *Journal of Addictive Diseases, 18,* 73–82.

Burry, C. L. (1999). Evaluation of a training program for **foster parents** of infants with prenatal substance effects. *Child Welfare, 78,* 197–214.

Collins, M. E., Mowbray, C. L., & Bybee, D. (1999). Measuring coping strategies in an educational intervention for **individuals with psychiatric disabilities**. *Health and Social Work, 24,* 279–290.

Comer, E., & Fraser, M. (1998). Evaluation of six **family-support programs:** Are they effective? *Families in Society, 79,* 134–148.

Conboy, A., Auerbach, C., Schnall, D., & LaPorte, H. (2000). **MSW student** satisfaction with using single-system design computer software to evaluate social work practice. *Research on Social Work Practice, 10,* 127–138.

Deacon, S. A., & Piercy, P. P. (2000). Qualitative evaluation of **family** therapy programs: A participatory approach. *Journal of Marital and Family Therapy, 26,* 39–45.

de Anda, D. (1999). Project Peace. The evaluation of a skill-based violence prevention program for **high school adolescents**. *Social Work in Education, 21,* 137–149.

Deschenes, E., & Greenwood, P. (1998). Alternative placements for **juvenile offenders:** Results from the evaluation of the Nokomis challenge program. *Journal of Research in Crime and Delinquency, 35,* 267–294.

Ford, C. A., & Okojie, F. A. (1999). A multi-dimensional approach to evaluating **family preservation programs**. *Family Preservation Journal, 4,* 31–62.

Harrison, R. S., Boyle, S. W., Farley, W. (1999). Evaluating the outcomes of family-based intervention for **troubled children:** A pretest-posttest study. *Research on Social Work Practice, 9,* 640–655.

Hughes, R. H., & Kirby, J. (2000). Strengthening evaluation strategies for divorcing **family support services:** Perspectives of parent educators, mediators, attorneys, and judges. *Family Relations, 49,* 53–61.

Jenson, J. M., Jacobson, M., Unrau, Y. A., & Robinson, R. L., (1996). Intervention for victims of child sexual abuse: An evaluation of the children's advocacy model. *Child and Adolescent Social Work Journal, 13,* 139–156.

Jinich, S., & Litrownik, A. (1999). Coping with **sexual abuse:** Development and evaluation of a videotape intervention for nonoffending parents. *Child Abuse and Neglect, 23,* 175–190.

Mecca, W. F., Rivera, A., & Esposito, A. J. (2000). Instituting an outcomes assessment effort: Lessons from the field. *Families in Society, 81,* 85–89.

Myers, L., & Rittner, B. (1999). Family functioning and satisfaction of **former residents of a non-therapeutic residential care facility**. An exploratory study. *Journal of Family Social Work, 3,* 54–68.

Nicholson, B. C., Brenner, V., & Fox, R. A. (1999). A community-based parenting program with **low-income mothers of young children**. *Families in Society, 80,* 247–253.

Prior, V., Lynch, M. A., & Glaser, D. (1999). Responding to **child sexual abuse:** An evaluation of social work by children and their carers. *Child and Family Social Work, 4,* 131–143.

Raschick, M., & Critchley, R. (1998). Guidelines for conducting site-based evaluations of intensive **family preservation programs**. *Child Welfare, 77,* 643–660.

Salzer, M. S., Rappaport, J., & Segre, L. (1999). Professional appraisal of professionally led and **self-help groups**. *American Journal of Orthopsychiatry, 69,* 530–540.

(continued)

BOX 26.3   *(continued)*

Scriven, M. (1999). The fine line between evaluation and explanation. *Research on Social Work Practice, 9,* 521–524.

Secret, M., Jordan, A., & Ford, J. (1999). Empowerment evaluation as a social work strategy. *Health and Social Work, 24,* 120–127.

Shifflett, K., & Cummings, E. M. (1999). A program for educating parents about the effects of **divorce and conflict on children**: An initial evaluation. *Family Relations, 48,* 79–89.

Short, J. L. (1998). Evaluation of a substance abuse prevention and mental health promotion program for **children of divorce**. *Journal of Divorce and Remarriage, 28,* 139–155.

Smith, L., Riley, E., Beilenson., P., Vlahov, D., & Junge, B. (1998). A focus group evaluation of drop boxes for safe syringe disposal. *Journal of Drug Issues, 28,* 905–920.

Stone, G., McKenry, P., & Clark, K. (1999). Fathers' participation in a **divorce education program**: A qualitative evaluation. *Journal of Divorce and Remarriage, 30,* 99–113.

Welsh, W., Jenkins, P., & Harris, P. (1999). Reducing **minority** over-representation in juvenile justice: Results of community-based delinquency prevention in Harrisburg. *Journal of Research in Crime and Delinquency, 36,* 87–110.

Outcome Question

The questions that can be answered by outcome evaluations can be classified under five general categories: (1) *Program Integrity:* Is the program achieving the desired client change? To what degree is the program accomplishing its program objectives? Is the program achieving predetermined minimum standards of achievement (benchmarks)? (2) *Program Effects:* Are people who have been through the program better for it? Are they better off than others who went through similar programs? How long do client improvements last? (3) *Differential Effects:* Given the demographics of clients served, are there subgroups of clients who experience more success than others? (4) *Causality:* Is there any evidence that the program can claim responsibility for positive changes in clients? (5) *Satisfaction:* Are stakeholders satisfied with program services?

Cost-Efficiency/Effectiveness Evaluations

These evaluations demonstrate fiscal accountability and raise awareness of costs associated with providing services to specific populations (e.g., Levin & McEwan, 2000; Newmann, 2005). A program is considered cost-efficient when it is able to achieve its desired client outcomes at lower cost, compared with another program striving for the same ends. A "probation program," for example, costs less than a "jail program" simply because the probation program does not have expenses for 24-hour supervision, an institutional facility, and so on. If the probation program is successful in preventing future criminal behavior, the savings are even greater. Costs associated with prevention, however, are difficult to estimate because we cannot know for certain whether the absence of the problem was a result of the program.

Cost-efficiency/effectiveness evaluations alone provide us with data and information associated with program expenses. When combined with process and outcome evaluation, data from cost-efficiency/effectiveness evaluations can give us valuable insight into how program resources are best allocated. Because they produce dollar figures for program processes and outcomes, they have utility only when we know precisely what the program is doing (process evaluation) and precisely how much client change is produced (outcome evaluation). Box 26.4 lists several published social work studies that have focused on cost-benefit evaluations.

Cost Questions

The questions that can be answered via cost-efficiency/effectiveness evaluations can be classified under three general categories: (1) *Unit Costs:* What

BOX 26.4

Published Examples of Cost-Benefit Evaluations

Substantive areas are in **bold**.

Beshai, N. N. (1991). Providing cost efficient detoxification services to **alcoholic patients**. *Public Health Reports, 105,* 475–481.

Egger, G. M., Friedman, B., & Zimmer, J. G. (1990). Models of **intensive case management**. *Journal of Gerontological Social Work, 15,* 75–101.

Ell, K. (1996), Social work and **health care practice** and policy: A psychosocial research agenda. *Social Work, 41,* 583–592.

Essock, S. M., Frisman, L. K., & Kontos, N. J. (1998). Cost-effectiveness of assertive **community treatment teams**. *American Journal of Orthopsychiatry, 68,* 179–190.

Fahs, M. C., & Wade, K. (1996). An economic analysis of two models of hospital care for **AIDS patients**: Implications for hospital discharge planning. *Social Work in Health Care, 22,* 21–34.

Greene, V. L., Lovely, M. E., & Ondrich, J. I. (1993). The cost-effectiveness of community services in a **frail elderly population**. *The Gerontologist, 33,* 177–189.

Holosko, M. J., Dobrowolsky, J., & Feit, M. D. (1990). A proposed cost effectiveness method for use in policy for mulation in **human service organizations**. *Journal of Health and Social Policy, 1,* 55–71.

Holtgrave, D. R., & Kelly, J. A. (1998). Cost-effectiveness of an **HIV/AIDS prevention intervention for gay men**. *AIDS, and Behavior, 1,* 173–180.

Hughes, W. C. (1999). Managed care meets community support: Ten reasons to include **direct support services** in every behavioral health plan. *Health and Social Work, 4,* 103–111.

Jackson, N., Olsen, L., & Schafer, C. (1986). Evaluating the treatment of **emotionally disturbed adolescents**. *Social Work, 31,* 182–185.

Keigher, S. M. (1997). What role for social work in the **new health care practice** paradigm? *Health and Social Work, 22,* 149–155.

Knapp, M. (1988). Searching for efficiency in long-term care: De-institutionalisation and privatisation. *British Journal of Social Work, 18,* 149–171.

Levy, R. I., & Bavendam, T. G. (1995). Promoting **women's urologic self-care**: Five single-case replications. *Research on Social Work Practice, 5,* 430–441.

Pike, C. L., & Piercy, F. P. (1991). Cost effectiveness research in **family therapy**. *Journal of Marital and Family Therapy, 16,* 375–388.

Pinkerton, S. D., & Holtgrave, D. R. (1998). A method for evaluating the economic efficiency of **HIV behavioral risk reduction interventions**. *AIDS, and Behavior, 2,* 189–201.

Prentky, R., & Burgess, A. W. (1990). Rehabilitation of **child molesters**: A cost-benefit analysis. *American Journal of Orthopsychiatry, 60,* 108–117.

Robertson, E., & Knapp, M. (1988). Promoting **intermediate treatment**: A problem of excess demand or excess supply? *British Journal of Social Work, 8,* 131–147.

Segal, E. A., & Gustavsson, N. S. (1990). The high cost of neglecting **children**: The need for a preventive policy agenda. *Child and Adolescent Social Work Journal, 7,* 475–485.

Winegar, N., Bistline, J. L., & Sheridan, S. (1992). Implementing a **group therapy program** in a managed-care setting: Combining cost effectiveness and quality care. *Families in Society, 73,* 56–58.

---

is the average cost per client? What is the average cost per unit of service (e.g., intake, assessment, intervention, follow-up)? (2) *Cost Distribution:* What percentage of costs go to direct client services, administrative activities, and program development? What services were not provided due to lack of funds? and (3) *Cost Reduction/Recovery:* Is there any way in which cost could be reduced without loss of effectiveness, perhaps by offering group therapy instead of individual therapy? Are strategies for cost recovery possible?

THE FUTURE OF PROGRAM EVALUATION

The history of the social work profession tells a story that social work has long struggled with the integration research and practice methods (e.g., Adam, Zosky, & Unrau, 2004; Tripodi & Potocky-Tripodi, 2006). Much of the struggle has been focused at the practitioner level. In particular, scholars have explored the question of how social work practitioners could best embrace and incorporate research methods into their practice frameworks (e.g., Epstein, 1996; Fraser et al., 1991; Meyer, 1996; Penka & Kirk, 1991; Rosen, 1996; Rubin, Franklin, & Selber, 1992; Wakefield & Kirk, 1996; Witkin, 1996). When program-level evaluations are used in conjunction with case-level evaluations (e.g., Bloom, Fischer, & Orme, 2006), they have added benefit to understanding and applying the profession's knowledge base. Writings on program-level evaluation in social service programs date back to the 1960s (e.g., Suchman, 1967), but the impetus for human service administrators embracing program evaluation methods can be linked to the passing of the Government Performance and Results Act in 1993.

Program evaluation now serves a key function in the social work profession and is here to stay (e.g., Westerfelt & Dietz, 2005; Wholey, Hatry, & Newcomer, 2004). The National Association of Social Work and the Council on Social Work Education both recognize research and evaluation as core tools of the profession. Program evaluation has a central role in the interdisciplinary movement toward evidence-based practice (e.g., Mullen, Bellamy, & Bledsoe, 2005).

As social workers demonstrate leadership in evaluating social services and programs, the profession becomes a collaborative player with other disciplines and professions such as psychology, sociology, anthropology, and nursing in building knowledge to better understand complex human behaviors and social problems. Steeped in values of diversity and justice, social work adds a unique perspective to theory testing and other applied knowledge development efforts. Indeed, a major area yet to be developed in program evaluation of social service programs is multicultural competence—a topic that is budding in education evaluation but deserves more attention in the human service sector (see Chapter 16).

Trends in Evaluation

Hatry et al. (2004) have delineated five trends that they see will influence the evaluative enterprise over the next few years. One trend is increased emphasis on evaluation for government audits and program reviews. Faced with mounting skepticism about the effectiveness of their expenditures, public funders' demands for accountability have increased significantly in recent years. Efforts to develop evaluation templates and standard reporting forms have increased. A challenge for program administrators and staff is that externally derived evaluation requirements and standardized forms are often burdensome and seldom produce information useful to local programs. Many local organizations are becoming more proactive in program evaluation as a means of meeting accountability requirements in a manner that is compatible with operations and organizational culture and also, at the same time, produces information that is useful locally.

A second trend is continued expansion of the use of client surveys as a data collection procedure. Traditionally, clients have been looked at skeptically as sources of data, as it has been assumed that, somehow, their perspectives would be subjective, reflecting their biases. However, more and more, clients are being viewed as a key stakeholder group that possesses valuable insight about their program experiences. Client surveys can address a range of issues, including satisfaction with services, experiences with program staff and procedures, and benefits obtained.

A third trend is that new technology will speed up and enrich evaluation procedures. One set of challenges facing organizations in conducting evaluations is data collection, management, and analysis. These are not only labor-intensive activities but also require a level of technical expertise that many social service organizations lack. Computers are increasingly used in conducting program evaluations, and their use is likely to increase. One example of a comprehensive computer-assisted evaluation facility is the evaluation site operated by the Canadian Association of Family Resource Programs (http://www.frp.ca/g_evalFAQs_index.asp); this facility will carry out a variety of evaluation tasks. The system allows clients to directly complete their surveys online and also accepts surveys completed on paper, which can be scanned. The system also performs a variety of preprogrammed analyses in real time and provides reports of the results.

A fourth trend is increased use of evaluation information for improving social service programs. In addition to being a means of meeting accountability requirements, program evaluation is essential for monitoring and program improvement purposes. By collecting and analyzing data for need, process, outcome, or cost, valuable feedback is generated. When such data are collected routinely, the resulting information provides administrators and staff with feedback about how well program processes work and to what extent outcome objectives are being met. Such feedback is essential in a process of quality improvement.

A fifth trend is that university education will increasingly include evaluation material in its curricula. In recent years, there has been a renewed recognition within schools of social work of the need to ensure that evaluation content is adequately represented in the curricula. This trend is driven by an increased level of evaluation activities within organizations, which are responding to increasing demands for accountability

and also recognizing that evaluations provide valuable information for program planning and delivery. Thus, in the years to come, there is likely to be an increasing demand for social work graduates who can contribute to their organization's program evaluation activities.

SUMMARY

This chapter presented the four basic types of evaluations that can be done within a social work agency and illustrated the various questions that can be answered by each type. All types are necessary in order to carry out effective social work services. The chapter ended with five trends that the evaluative enterprise will follow over the next several years.

Glossary

Yvonne A. Unrau, Judy L. Krysik, and Richard M. Grinnell, Jr.

Abstracting indexing services Providers of specialized reference tools that make it possible to find information quickly and easily, usually through subject headings and/or author approaches.

Abstracts Reference materials consisting of citations and brief descriptive summaries from positivist and interpretive research studies.

Accountability A system of responsibility in which program administrators account for all program activities by answering to the demands of a program's stakeholders and by justifying the program's expenditures to the satisfaction of its stakeholders.

Aggregated case-level evaluation designs The collection of a number of case-level evaluations to determine the degree to which a program objective has been met.

Aggregate-level data Derived from micro-level data, aggregate-level data are grouped so that the characteristics of individual units of analysis are no longer identifiable; for example, the variable "gross national income" is an aggregation of data about individual incomes.

Alternate-forms method A method for establishing reliability of a measuring instrument by administering, in succession, equivalent forms of the same instrument to the same group of research participants.

Alternative hypothesis See *Rival hypothesis.*

Analytical memos Notes made by the researcher in reference to interpretive data that raise questions or make comments about meaning units and categories identified in a transcript.

Analytic generalization The type of generalizability associated with case studies; the research findings of case studies are not assumed to fit another case no matter how apparently similar; rather, research findings are tested to see if they do in fact fit; used as working hypotheses to test practice principles.

Annual report A detailed account or statement describing a program's processes and results over a given year, usually produced at the end of a fiscal year.

Antecedent variable A variable that precedes the introduction of one or more dependent variables.

Antiquarianism An interest in past events without reference to their importance or significance for the present; the reverse of presentism.

A Phase In case-level evaluation designs, a phase (A Phase) in which the baseline measurement of the target problem is established before the intervention (B Phase) is implemented.

Applied research approach A search for practical and applied research results that can be used in actual social work practice situations; complementary to the pure research approach.

Area probability sampling A form of cluster sampling that uses a three-stage process to provide the means to carry out a research study when no comprehensive list of the population can be compiled.

Assessment-related case study A type of case study that generates knowledge about specific clients and their situations; focuses on the perspectives of the study's participants.

Audit trail The documentation of critical steps in an interpretive research study that allows for an independent reviewer to examine and verify the steps in the research process and the conclusions of the research study.

Authority The reliance on authority figures to tell us what is true; one of the six ways of knowing.

Availability sampling See *Convenience sampling.*

Axes Straight horizontal and vertical lines in a graph upon which values of a measurement, or the corresponding frequencies, are plotted.

Back-translation The process of translating an original document into a second language, then having an independent translator conduct a subsequent translation of the first translation back into the language of origin; the second translation is then compared with the original document for equivalency.

Baseline A period of time, usually three or four data collection periods, in which the level of the client's target problem is measured while no intervention is carried out; designated as the *A* Phase in single-system designs (case-level designs).

Between research methods approach Triangulation by using different research methods available in *both* the interpretive and the positivist research approaches in a single research study.

Bias Not neutral; an inclination to some form of prejudice or preconceived position.

Biased sample A sample unintentionally selected in such a way that some members of the population are more likely than others to be picked for sample membership.

Binomial effect size display (BESD) A technique for interpreting the *r* value in a meta-analysis by converting it into a 2×2 table displaying magnitude of effect.

Biography Tells the story of one individual's life, often suggesting what the person's influence was on social, political, or intellectual developments of the times.

B Phase In case-level evaluation designs, the intervention phase, which may, or may not, include simultaneous measurements.

Case The basic unit of social work practice, whether it be an individual, a couple, a family, an agency, a community, a county, a state, or a country.

Case-level evaluation designs Designs in which data are collected about a single-client system—an individual, group, or community—in order to evaluate the outcome of an intervention for the client system; a form of appraisal that monitors change for individual clients; designs in which data are collected about a single-client system—an individual, group, or community—in order to evaluate the outcome of an intervention for the client system; also called single-system research designs.

Case study Using research approaches to investigate a research question or hypothesis relating to a specific case; used to develop theory and test hypotheses; an in-depth form of research in which data are gathered and analyzed about an individual unit of analysis, person, city, event, or society. It allows more intensive analysis of specific details; the disadvantage is that it is hard to use the results to generalize to other cases.

Categories Groupings of related meaning units that are given one name; used to organize, summarize, and interpret qualitative data. Categories in an interpretive study can change throughout the data analysis process, and the number of categories in a given study depends upon the breadth and depth the researcher aims for in the analysis.

Category In an interpretive data analysis, an aggregate of meaning units that share a common feature.

Category saturation The point in a qualitative data analysis when all identified meaning units fit easily into the existing categorization scheme and no new categories emerge; the point at which first-level coding ends.

Causality A relationship of cause and effect; the effect will invariably occur when the cause is present.

Causal relationship A relationship between two variables for which we can state that the presence of, or absence of, one variable determines the presence of, or absence of, the other variable.

CD-ROM sources Computerized retrieval systems that allow searching for indexes and abstracts stored on compact computer discs (CDs).

Census data Data from the survey of an entire population in contrast to a survey of a sample.

Citation A brief identification of a reference that includes name of author(s), title, source, page numbers, and year of publication.

Classic experimental design An explanatory research design with randomly assigned experimental and control groups in which the dependent variable is measured before and after the treatment (the independent variable) for both groups, but only the experimental group receives the treatment (the dependent variable).

Client system *An* individual client, *a* couple, *a* family, *a* group, *an* organization, or *a* community that can be studied with case- and program-level evaluation designs and with positivist and interpretive research approaches.

Closed-ended questions Items in a measuring instrument that require respondents to select one of several response categories provided; also known as fixed-alternative questions.

Cluster diagram An illustration of a conceptual classification scheme in which the researcher draws and labels circles for each theme that emerges from the data; the circles are organized in a way to depict the relationships between themes.

Cluster sampling A multistage probability sampling procedure in which the population is divided into groups (or clusters); the groups, rather than the individuals, are selected for inclusion in the sample.

Code The label assigned to a category or theme in a qualitative data analysis; shortened versions of the actual category or theme label; used as markers in a qualitative data analysis; usually no longer than eight characters in length and can use a combination of letters, symbols, and numbers.

Codebook A device used to organize qualitative data by applying labels and descriptions that draw distinctions between different parts of the data that have been collected.

Coding (1) In data analysis, translating data from respondents onto a form that can be read by a computer; (2) In interpretive research, marking the text with codes for content categories.

Coding frame A specific framework that delineates what data are to be coded and how they are to be coded in order to prepare them for analyses.

Coding sheets In a literature review, a sheet used to record for each research study the complete reference, research design, measuring instrument(s), population and sample, outcomes, and other significant features of the study.

Cohort study A longitudinal survey design that uses successive random samples to monitor how the characteristics of a specific group of people, who share certain characteristics or experiences (cohorts), change over time.

Collaterals Professionals or staff members who serve as indigenous observers in the data collection process.

Collective biographies Studies of the characteristics of groups of people who lived during a past period and had some major factor in common.

Collectivist culture Societies that stress interdependence and seek the welfare and survival of the group above that of the individual; collectivist cultures are characterized by a readiness to be influenced by others, preference for conformity, and cooperation in relationships.

Comparative rating scale A rating scale in which respondents are asked to compare an individual person, concept, or situation with others.

Comparative research design The study of more than one event, group, or society to isolate explanatory factors; there are two basic strategies in comparative research: (1) the study of elements that differ in many ways but that have some major factor in common, and (2) the study of elements that are highly similar but different in some important aspect, such as modern industrialized nations that have different health insurance systems.

Comparison group A nonexperimental group to which research participants have not been randomly assigned for purposes of comparison with the experimental group. Not to be confused with control group.

Comparison group posttest-only design A descriptive research design with two groups, experimental and comparison, in which the dependent variable is measured once for both groups, and only the experimental group receives the treatment (the independent variable).

Comparison group pretest-posttest design A descriptive research design with two groups, experimental and comparison, in which the dependent variable is measured before and after the treatment for both groups, but only the experimental group receives the treatment.

Compensation Attempts by researchers to compensate for the lack of treatment for control group members by administering it to them; a threat to internal validity.

Compensatory rivalry Motivation of control group members to compete with experimental group members; a threat to internal validity.

Completeness One of the four criteria for evaluating research hypotheses.

Complete observer A term describing one of four possible research roles on a continuum of participant observation research; the complete observer acts simply as an observer and does not participate in the events at hand.

Complete participant The complete participant is at the far end of the continuum from the complete observer in participant observation research; this research role is characterized by total involvement.

Comprehensive qualitative review A nonstatistical synthesis of representative research studies relevant to a research problem, question, or hypothesis.

Computerized retrieval systems Systems in which abstracts, indexes, and subject bibliographies are incorporated in computerized databases to facilitate information retrieval.

Concept An understanding, an idea, or a mental image; a way of viewing and categorizing objects, processes, relations, and events.

Conceptual classification system The strategy for conceiving how units of qualitative data relate to each other; the method used to depict patterns that emerge from the various coding levels in qualitative data.

Conceptual framework A frame of reference that serves to guide a research study and is developed from theories, findings from a variety of other research studies, and the author's personal experiences and values.

Conceptualization The process of selecting the specific concepts to include in positivist and interpretive research studies.

Conceptual validity See *Construct validity*.

Concurrent validity A form of criterion validity that is concerned with the ability of a measuring instrument to predict accurately an individual's status by comparing concurrent ratings (or scores) on one or more measuring instruments.

Confidentiality An ethical consideration in research whereby anonymity of research participants is safeguarded by ensuring that raw data are not seen by anyone other than the research team and that data presented have no identifying marks.

Confounding variable A variable operating in a specific situation in such a way that its effects cannot be separated; the effects of an extraneous variable thus confound the interpretation of a research study's findings.

Consistency Holding steadfast to the same principles and procedures in the qualitative data analysis process.

Constant A concept that does not vary and does not change; a characteristic that has the same value for all research participants or events in a research study.

Constant comparison A technique used to categorize qualitative data; it begins after the complete set of data has been examined and meaning units identified; each unit is classified as similar or different from the others; similar meaning units are lumped into the same category and classified by the same code.

Constant error Systematic error in measurement; error due to factors that consistently or systematically affect the variable being measured and that are concerned with the relatively stable qualities of respondents to a measuring instrument.

Construct See *Concept*.

Construct validity The degree to which a measuring instrument successfully measures a theoretical construct; the degree to which explanatory concepts account for variance in the scores of an instrument; also referred to as conceptual validity in meta-analyses.

Content analysis A data collection method in which communications are analyzed in a systematic, objective, and quantitative manner to produce new data.

Content validity The extent to which the content of a measuring instrument reflects the concept that is being measured and in fact measures that concept and not another.

Contextual detail The particulars of the environment in which the case (or unit of analysis) is embedded; provides a basis for understanding and interpreting case study data and results.

Contradictory evidence Identifying themes and categories that raise questions about the conclusions reached at the end of qualitative data analysis; outliers or extreme cases that are inconsistent or contradict the conclusions drawn from qualitative data; also called negative evidence.

Contributing partner A social work role in which the social worker joins forces with others who perform different roles in positivist and interpretive research studies.

Control group A group of randomly assigned research participants in a research study who do not receive the experimental treatment and are used for comparison purposes. Not to be confused with comparison group.

Control variable A variable, other than the independent variable(s) of primary interest, whose effects we can determine; an intervening variable that has been controlled for in the study's research design.

Convenience sampling A nonprobability sampling procedure that relies on the closest and most available research participants to constitute a sample.

Convergent validity The degree to which different measures of a construct yield similar results, or converge.

Correlated variables Variables whose values are associated; values of one variable tend to be associated in a systematic way with values in the others.

Cost-benefit analysis An analytical procedure that not only determines the costs of the program itself but also considers the monetary benefits of the program's effects.

Cost-effectiveness analysis An analytical procedure that assesses the costs of the program itself; the monetary benefits of the program's effects are not assessed.

Cover letter A letter to respondents or research participants that is written under the official letterhead of the sponsoring organization and describes the research study and its purpose.

Credibility The trustworthiness of both the steps taken in qualitative data analysis and the conclusions reached.

Criterion validity The degree to which the scores obtained on a measuring instrument are comparable with scores from an external criterion believed to measure the same concept.

Criterion variable The variable whose values are predicted from measurements of the predictor variable.

Cross-cultural comparisons Research studies that include culture as a major variable; studies that compare two or more diverse cultural groups.

Cross-sectional research design A survey research design in which data are collected to indicate characteristics of a sample or population at a particular moment in time.

Cross-tabulation table A simple table showing the joint frequency distribution of two or more nominal level variables.

Cultural encapsulation The assumption that differences between groups represent some deficit or pathology.

Culturally equivalent Similarity in the meaning of a construct between two cultures.

Cultural relativity The belief that human thought and action can be judged only from the perspective of the culture out of which they have grown.

Cut-and-paste method A method of analyzing qualitative data whereby the researcher cuts segments of the typed transcript and sorts these cuttings into relevant groupings; it can be done manually or with computer assistance.

Data The numbers, words, or scores, generated by positivist and interpretive research studies. The word *data* is plural.

Data analyses The process of turning data into information; the process of reviewing, summarizing, and organizing isolated facts (data) such that they formulate a meaningful response to a research question.

Data archive A place where many data sets are stored and from which data can be accessed.

Data coding Translating data from one language or format into another, usually to make it readable for a computer.

Data collection method Procedures specifying techniques to be employed, measuring instruments to be used, and activities to be conducted in implementing a positivist or interpretive research study.

Data set A collection of related data items, such as the answers given by respondents to all the questions in a survey.

Data source The provider of the data, whether it be primary—the original source—or secondary—an intermediary between the research participant and the researcher analyzing the data.

Datum Singular of *data*.

Decision-making rule A statement that we use (in testing a hypothesis) to choose between the null hypothesis; indicates the range(s) of values of the observed statistic that leads to the rejection of the null hypothesis.

Deduction A conclusion about a specific case(s) based on the assumption that it shares a characteristic with an entire class of similar cases.

Deductive reasoning Forming a theory, making a deduction from the theory, and testing this deduction, or hypothesis, against reality; in research, applied to theory in order to arrive at a hypothesis that can be tested; a method of reasoning whereby a conclusion about specific cases is reached based on the assumption that they share characteristics with an entire class of similar cases.

Demand needs When needs are defined by only those individuals who indicate that they feel or perceive the need themselves.

Demographic data Vital and social facts that describe a sample or a population.

Demoralization Feelings of deprivation among control group members that may cause them to drop out of a research study; a threat to internal validity.

Dependability The soundness of both the steps taken in a qualitative data analysis and the conclusions reached.

Dependent events Events that influence the probability of occurrence of each other.

Dependent variable A variable that is dependent on, or caused by, another variable; an outcome variable, which is not manipulated directly but is measured to determine if the independent variable has had an effect.

Derived scores Raw scores of research participants, or groups, converted in such a way that meaningful comparisons with other individuals, or groups, are possible.

Descriptive research Research studies undertaken to increase precision in the definition of knowledge in a problem area where less is known than at the explanatory level; situated in the middle of the knowledge continuum.

Descriptive statistics Methods used for summarizing and describing data in a clear and precise manner.

Design bias Any effect that systematically distorts the outcome of a research study so that the study's results are not representative of the phenomenon under investigation.

Determinism A contention in positivist research studies that only an event that is true over time and place and that will occur independent of beliefs about it (a predetermined event) permits the generalization of a study's findings; one of the four main limitations of the positivist research approach.

Deterministic causation When a particular effect appears, the associated cause is always present; no other variables influence the relationship between cause and effect; the link between an independent variable that brings about the occurrence of the dependent variable every time.

Dichotomous variable A variable that can take on only one of two values.

Differential scale A questionnaire-type scale in which respondents are asked to consider questions representing different positions along a continuum and to select those with which they agree.

Differential selection A potential lack of equivalency among preformed groups of research participants; a threat to internal validity.

Diffusion of treatments Problems that may occur when experimental and control group members talk to each other about a research study; a threat to internal validity.

d **index** A measure of effect size in a meta-analysis.

Directional hypothesis See *One-tailed hypotheses*.

Directional test See *One-tailed hypotheses*.

Direct observation An obtrusive data collection method in which the focus is entirely on the behaviors of a group, or persons, being observed.

Direct observation notes These are the first level of field notes, usually chronologically organized, and they contain a detailed description of what was seen and heard; they may also include summary notes made after an interview.

Direct relationship A relationship between two variables such that high values of one variable are found with high values of the second variable, and vice versa.

Discriminant validity The degree to which a construct can be empirically differentiated, or discriminated from other constructs.

Divergent validity The extent to which a measuring instrument differs from other instruments that measure unrelated constructs.

Double-barreled question A question in a measuring instrument that contains two questions in one, usually joined by an *and* or an *or*.

Duration recording A method of data collection that includes direct observation of the target problem and recording of the length of time each occurrence lasts within a specified observation period.

Ecological fallacy An error of reasoning committed by coming to conclusions about individuals based only on data about groups.

Edge coding Adding a series of blank lines on the right side of the response category in a measuring instrument to aid in processing the data.

Effect size In meta-analysis, the most widely used measure of the dependent variable; the effect size statistic provides a measure of the magnitude of the relationship found between the variables of interest and allows for the computation of summary statistics that apply to the analysis of all the studies considered as a whole.

Empirical Knowledge derived from the six ways of knowing.

Error of central tendency A measurement error due to the tendency of observers to rate respondents in the middle of a variable's value range, rather than consistently too high or too low.

Error of measurement See *Measurement error*.

Ethical research project The systematic inquiry into a problem area in an effort to discover new knowledge or test existing ideas; the research study is conducted in accordance with professional standards.

Ethics in research Positivist and interpretive data that are collected and analyzed with careful attention to their accuracy, fidelity to logic, and respect for the feelings and rights of research participants; one of the four criteria for evaluating research problem areas *and* formulating research questions out of the problem areas.

Ethnicity A term that implies a common ancestry and cultural heritage and encompasses customs, values, beliefs, and behaviors.

Ethnocentricity Assumptions about normal behavior that are based on one's own cultural framework without taking cultural relativity into account; the failure to acknowledge alternative worldviews.

Ethnograph A computer software program that is designed for qualitative data analyses.

Ethnographic A form of content analysis used to document and explain the communication of meaning, as well as to verify theoretical relationships; any of several methods of describing social or cultural life based on direct, systematic observation, such as becoming a participant in a social system.

Ethnography The systematic study of human cultures and the similarities and dissimilarities between them.

Ethnomethodology Pioneered by Harold Garfinkel, this method of research focuses on the commonsense understanding of social life held by ordinary people (the ethos), usually as discovered through participant observation; often the observer's own methods of making sense of the situation become the object of investigation.

Evaluation A form of appraisal using valid and reliable research methods; there are numerous types of evaluations geared to produce data that in turn produce information that helps in the decision-making process; data from evaluations are used to develop quality programs and services.

Evaluative research designs Case- and program-level research designs that apply various research designs and data collection methods to find out if an intervention (or treatment) worked at the case level and if the social work program worked at the program level.

Existing documents Physical records left over from the past.

Existing statistics Previously calculated numerical summaries of data that exist in the public domain.

Experience and intuition Learning what is true through personal past experiences and intuition; two of the six ways of knowing.

Experiment A research study in which we have control over the levels of the independent variable and over the assignment of research participants, or objects, to different experimental conditions.

Experimental designs (1) Explanatory research designs or "ideal experiments"; (2) Case-level research designs that examine the question, "Did the client system improve because of social work intervention?"

Experimental group In an experimental research design, the group of research participants exposed to the manipulation of the independent variable; also referred to as a treatment group.

Explanatory research "Ideal" research studies undertaken to infer cause—effect and directional relationships in areas where a number of substantial research findings are already in place; situated at the top end of the knowledge continuum.

Exploratory research Research studies undertaken to gather data in areas of inquiry where very little is already known; situated at the lowest end of the knowledge continuum. See *Nonexperimental design.*

External evaluation An evaluation that is conducted by someone who does not have any connection with the program; usually an evaluation that is requested by the agency's funding sources; this type of evaluation complements an in-house evaluation.

External validity The extent to which the findings of a research study can be generalized outside the specific research situation.

Extraneous variables See *Rival hypothesis.*

Face validity The degree to which a measurement has self-evident meaning and measures what it appears to measure.

Feasibility One of the four criteria for evaluating research problem areas *and* formulating research questions out of the problem areas.

Feedback When data and information are returned to the persons who originally provided or collected them; used for informed decision making at the case and program levels; a basic principle underlying the design of evaluations.

Field notes A record, usually written, of events observed by a researcher. The notes are taken as the study proceeds, and later they are used for analyses.

Field research Research conducted in a real-life setting, not in a laboratory. The researcher neither creates nor manipulates anything within the study, but observes it.

Field-tested The pilot of an instrument or research method in conditions equivalent to those that will be encountered in the research study.

File drawer problem (1) In literature searches or reviews, the difficulty in locating studies that have not been published or are not easily retrievable; (2) In meta-analyses, errors in effect size due to reliance on published articles showing statistical significance.

Firsthand data Data obtained from people who directly experience the problem being studied.

First-level coding A process of identifying meaning units in a transcript, organizing the meaning units into categories, and assigning names to the categories.

Flexibility The degree to which the design and procedures of a research study can be changed to adapt to contextual demands of the research setting.

Focus group interview A group of people brought together to talk about their lives and experiences in free-flowing, open-ended discussions that usually focus on a single topic.

Formative evaluation A type of evaluation that focuses on obtaining data that are helpful in planning the program and in improving its implementation and performance.

Frequency recording A method of data collection by direct observations in which each occurrence of the target problem is recorded during a specified observation period.

Fugitive data Informal information found outside regular publishing channels.

Gaining access A term used in interpretive research to describe the process of engagement and relationship development between the researcher and the research participants.

Generalizable explanation evaluation model An evaluation model whose proponents believe that many solutions are possible for any one social problem and that the effects of programs will differ under different conditions.

Generalizing results Extending or applying the findings of a research study to individuals or situations not directly involved in the original research study; the ability to extend or apply the findings of a research study to subjects or situations that were not directly investigated.

Goal Attainment Scale (GAS) A modified measurement scale used to evaluate case or program outcomes.

Government documents Printed documents issued by local, state, and federal governments; such documents include reports of legislative committee hearings and investigations, studies commissioned by legislative commissions and executive agencies, statistical compilations such as the census, the regular and special reports of executive agencies, and much more.

Grand tour questions Queries in which research participants are asked to provide wide-ranging background information; mainly used in interpretive research studies.

Graphic rating scale A rating scale that describes an attribute on a continuum from one extreme to the other, with points of the continuum ordered in equal intervals and then assigned values.

Grounded theory A final outcome of the interpretive research process that is reached when the insights are grounded on observations and the conclusions seem to be firm.

Group evaluation designs Evaluation designs that are conducted with groups of cases for the purpose of assessing to what degree program objectives have been achieved.

Group research designs Research designs conducted with two or more groups of cases, or research participants, for the purpose of answering research questions or testing hypotheses.

Halo effect A measurement error due to the tendency of an observer to be influenced by a favorable trait(s) of a research participant(s).

Hawthorne effect Effects on research participants' behaviors or attitudes attributable to their knowledge that they are taking part in a research study; a reactive effect; a threat to external validity.

Heterogeneity of respondents The extent to which a research participant differs from other research participants.

Heuristic A theory used to stimulate creative thought and scientific activity.

Historical research The process by which we study the past; a method of inquiry that attempts to explain past events based on surviving artifacts.

History in research design The possibility that events not accounted for in a research design may alter the second and subsequent measurements of the dependent variable; a threat to internal validity.

Homogeneity of respondents The extent to which a research participant is similar to other research participants.

Hypothesis A theory-based prediction of the expected results of a research study; a tentative explanation that a relationship between or among variables exists.

Hypothetico-deductive method A hypothesis-testing approach that a hypothesis is derived on the deductions based from a theory.

Ideographic research Research studies that focus on unique individuals or situations.

Implementation of a program The action of carrying out a program in the way that it was designed.

Independent variable A variable that is not dependent on another variable but is believed to cause or determine changes in the dependent variable; an antecedent variable that is directly manipulated to assess its effect on the dependent variable.

Index A group of individual measures that, when combined, are meant to indicate some more general characteristic.

Indigenous observers People who are naturally a part of the research participants' environment and who perform the data collection function; includes relevant others (e.g., family members, peers) and collaterals (e.g., social workers, staff members).

Indirect measures A substitute variable, or a collection of representative variables, used when there is no direct measurement of the variable of interest; also called a proxy variable.

Individualism A way of living that stresses independence, personal rather than group objectives, competition, and power in relationships; achievement measured through success of the individual as opposed to the group.

Individual synthesis Analysis of published studies related to the subject under study.

Inductive reasoning Building on specific observations of events, things, or processes to make inferences or more general statements; in research studies, applied to data collection and research results to make generalizations to see if they fit a theory; a method of reasoning whereby a conclusion is reached by building on specific observations of events, things, or processes to make inferences or more general statements.

Inferential statistics Statistical methods that make it possible to draw tentative conclusions about the population based on observations of a sample selected from that population and, furthermore, to make a probability statement about those conclusions to aid in their evaluation.

Information anxiety A feeling attributable to a lack of understanding of information, being overwhelmed by the amount of information to be accessed and understood, or not knowing if certain information exists.

Informed consent Signed statements obtained from research participants prior to the initiation of the research study to inform them what their participation entails and that they are free to decline participation.

In-house evaluation An evaluation that is conducted by someone who works within a program; usually an evaluation for the purpose of promoting better client services; also known as an internal evaluation. This type of evaluation complements an external evaluation.

Institutional review boards (IRBs) Boards set up by institutions to protect research participants and to ensure that ethical issues are recognized and responded to in the a study's research design.

Instrumentation Weaknesses of a measuring instrument, such as invalidity, unreliability, improper administrations, or mechanical breakdowns; a threat to internal validity.

Integration Combining evaluation and day-to-day practice activities to develop a complete approach to client service delivery; a basic principle underlying the design of evaluations.

Interaction effects Effects produced by the combination of two or more threats to internal validity.

Internal consistency The extent to which the scores on two comparable halves of the same measuring instrument are similar; inter-item consistency.

Internal validity The extent to which it can be demonstrated that the independent variable within a research study is the only cause of change in the dependent variable; overall soundness of the experimental procedures and measuring instruments.

Interpretive research approach Research studies that focus on the facts of nature as they occur under natural conditions and emphasize qualitative description and generalization; a process of discovery sensitive to holistic and ecological issues; a research approach that is complementary to the positivist research approach.

Interobserver reliability The stability or consistency of observations made by two or more observers at one point in time.

Interpretive notes Notes on the researcher's interpretations of events that are kept separate from the record of the facts noted as direct observations.

Interquartile range A number that measures the variability of a data set; the distance between the 75th and 25th percentiles.

Interrater reliability The degree to which two or more independent observers, coders, or judges produce consistent results.

Interrupted time-series design An explanatory research design in which there is only one group of research participants and the dependent variable is measured repeatedly before and after treatment; used in case- and program-evaluation designs.

Interval level of measurement The level of measurement with an arbitrarily chosen zero point that classifies its values on an equally spaced continuum.

Interval recording A method of data collection that involves a continuous direct observation of an individual during specified observation periods divided into equal time intervals.

Intervening variable See *Rival hypothesis*.

Interview data Isolated facts that are gathered when research participants respond to carefully constructed research questions; data in the form of words, recorded by transcription.

Interviewing A conversation with a purpose.

Interview schedule A measuring instrument used to collect data in face-to-face and telephone interviews.

Intraobserver reliability The stability of observations made by a single observer at several points in time.

Intrusion into lives of research participants The understanding that specific data collection methods can have negative consequences for research participants; a criterion for selecting a data collection method.

Itemized rating scales A measuring instrument that presents a series of statements that respondents or observers rank in different positions on a specific attribute.

Journal A written record of the process of an interpretive research study. Journal entries are made on an ongoing basis throughout the study and include study procedures as well as the researcher's reactions to emerging issues and concerns during the data analysis process.

Key informants A subpopulation of research participants who seem to know much more about "the situation" than other research participants.

Knowledge base A body of knowledge and skills specific to a certain discipline.

Knowledge creator and disseminator A social work role in which the social worker actually carries out and disseminates the results of a positivist and/or interpretive research study to generate knowledge for our profession.

Knowledge level continuum The range of knowledge levels, from exploratory to descriptive to explanatory, at which research studies can be conducted.

Latent content In a content analysis, the true meaning, depth, or intensity of a variable, or concept, under study.

Levels of measurement The degree to which characteristics of a data set can be modeled mathematically; the higher the level of measurement, the more statistical methods that are applicable.

Limited review An existing literature synthesis that summarizes in narrative form the findings and implications of a few research studies.

Literature review See *Literature search* and *Review of the literature.*

Literature search In a meta-analysis, scanning books and journals for basic, up-to-date research articles on studies relevant to a research question or hypothesis; sufficiently thorough to maximize the chance of including all relevant sources. See *Review of the literature.*

Logical consistency The requirement that all the steps within a positivist research study must be logically related to one another.

Logical positivism A philosophy of science holding that the scientific method of inquiry is the only source of certain knowledge; in research, focuses on testing hypotheses deduced from theory.

Logistics In evaluation, refers to getting research participants to do what they are supposed to do, getting research instruments distributed and returned; in general, the activities that ensure that procedural tasks of a research or evaluation study are carried out.

Longitudinal case study An exploratory research design in which there is only one group of research participants and the dependent variable is measured more than once.

Longitudinal design A survey research design in which a measuring instrument(s) is administered to a sample of research participants repeatedly over time; used to detect dynamic processes such as opinion change.

Magnitude recording A direct-observation method of soliciting and recording data on amount, level, or degree of the target problem during each occurrence.

Management information system (MIS) System in which computer technology is used to process, store, retrieve, and analyze data collected routinely in such processes as social service delivery.

Manifest content Content of a communication that is obvious and clearly evident.

Manipulable solution evaluation model An evaluation model whose proponents believe that the greatest priority is to serve the public interest, not the interests of stakeholders, who have vested interests in the program being evaluated; closely resembles an outcome evaluation.

Matching A random assignment technique that assigns research participants to two or more groups so that the experimental and control groups are approximately equivalent in pretest scores or other characteristics, or so that all differences except the experimental condition are eliminated.

Maturation Unplanned change in research participants due to mental, physical, or other processes operating over time; a threat to internal validity.

Meaning units In a qualitative data analysis, a discrete segment of a transcript that can stand alone as a single idea; can consist of a single word, a partial or complete sentence, a paragraph, or more; used as the basic building blocks for developing categories.

Measurement The assignment of labels or numerals to the properties or attributes of observations, events, or objects according to specific rules.

Measurement error Any variation in measurement that cannot be attributed to the variable being measured; variability in responses produced by individual differences and other extraneous variables.

Measuring instrument Any instrument used to measure a variable(s).

Media myths The content of television shows, movies, and newspaper and magazine articles; one of the six ways of knowing.

Member checking A process of obtaining feedback and comments from research participants on interpretations and conclusions made from the qualitative data they provided; asking research participants to confirm or refute the conclusions made.

Meta-analysis A research method in which mathematical procedures are applied to the positivist findings of studies located in a literature search to produce new summary statistics and to describe the findings for a meta-analysis.

Methodology The procedures and rules that detail how a single research study is conducted.

Micro-level data Data derived from individual units of analysis, whether these data sources are individuals, families, corporations, etc.; for example, age and years of formal schooling are two variables requiring micro-level data.

Missing data Data not available for a research participant about whom other data are available, such as when a respondent fails to answer one of the questions in a survey.

Missing links When two categories or themes seem to be related, but not directly so, it may be that a third variable connects the two.

Mixed research model A model combining aspects of interpretive and positivist research approaches within all (or many) of the methodological steps contained within a single research study.

Monitoring approach to evaluation Evaluation that aims to provide ongoing feedback so that a program can be improved while it is still underway; it contributes to the continuous development and improvement of a human service program; this approach complements the project approach to evaluation.

Mortality Loss of research participants through normal attrition over time in an experimental design that requires retesting; a threat to internal validity.

Multicultural research Representation of diverse cultural factors in the subjects of study; such diversity variables may include religion, race, ethnicity, language preference, gender, etc.

Multigroup posttest-only design An exploratory research design in which there is more than one group of research participants and the dependent variable is measured only once for each group.

Multiple-baseline design A case-level evaluation design with more than one baseline period and intervention phase, which allows the causal inferences regarding the relationship between a treatment intervention and its effect on clients' target problems and which helps control for extraneous variables. See *Interrupted time-series design*.

Multiple-group design An experimental research design with one control group and several experimental groups.

Multiple-treatment interference Effects of the results of a first treatment on the results of second and subsequent treatments; a threat to external validity.

Multistage probability sampling Probability sampling procedures used when a comprehensive list of the population does not exist and it is not possible to construct one.

Multivariate (1) A relationship involving two or more variables; (2) A hypothesis stating an assertion about two or more variables and how they relate to one another.

Multivariate analysis A statistical analysis of the relationship among three or more variables.

Narrowband measuring instrument Measuring instruments that focus on a single, or a few, variables.

Nationality A term that refers to country of origin.

Naturalist A person who studies the facts of nature as they occur under natural conditions.

Needs assessment Program-level evaluation activities that aim to assess the feasibility for establishing or continuing a particular social service program; an evaluation that aims to assess the need for a human service by verifying that a social problem exists within a specific client population to an extent that warrants services.

Negative case sampling Purposefully selecting research participants based on the fact that they have different characteristics than previous cases.

Nominal level of measurement The level of measurement that classifies variables by assigning names or categories that are mutually exclusive and exhaustive.

Nondirectional test See *Two-tailed hypotheses*.

Nonexperimental design A research design at the exploratory, or lowest, level of the knowledge continuum; also called preexperimental.

Nonoccurrence data In the structured-observation method of data collection, a recording of only those time intervals in which the target problem did not occur.

Nonparametric tests Refers to statistical tests of hypotheses about population probability distributions, but not about specific parameters of the distributions.

Nonprobability sampling Sampling procedures in which all of the persons, events, or objects in the sampling frame have an unknown, and usually different, probability of being included in a sample.

Nonreactive Methods of research that do not allow the research participants to know that they are being studied; thus, they do not alter their responses for the benefit of the researcher.

Nonresponse The rate of nonresponse in survey research is calculated by dividing the total number of respondents by the total number in the sample, minus any units verified as ineligible.

Nonsampling errors Errors in a research study's results that are not due to the sampling procedures.

Norm In measurement, an average or set group standard of achievement that can be used to interpret individual scores; normative data describing statistical properties of a measuring instrument such as means and standard deviations.

Normalization group The population sample to which a measuring instrument under development is administered to establish norms; also called the norm group.

Normative needs When needs are defined by comparing the objective living conditions of a target population with what society—or, at least, that segment of society concerned with helping the target population—deems acceptable or desirable from a humanitarian standpoint.

Null hypothesis A statement concerning one or more parameters that is subjected to a statistical test; a statement that there is no relationship between the two variables of interest.

Numbers The basic data unit of analysis used in positivist research studies.

Objectivity A research stance in which a study is carried out and its data are examined and interpreted without distortion by personal feelings or biases.

Observer One of four roles on a continuum of participation in participant observation research; the level of involvement of the observer participant is lower than of the complete participant and higher than of the participant observer.

Obtrusive data collection methods Direct data collection methods that can influence the variables under study or the responses of research participants; data collection methods that produce reactive effects.

Occurrence data In the structured-observation method of data collection, a recording of the first occurrence of the target problem during each time interval.

One-group posttest-only design An exploratory research design in which the dependent variable is measured only once.

One-group pretest-posttest design A descriptive research design in which the dependent variable is measured twice—before and after treatment.

One-stage probability sampling Probability sampling procedures in which the selection of a sample that is drawn from a specific population is completed in a single process.

One-tailed hypotheses Statements that predict specific relationships between independent and dependent variables.

On-line sources Computerized literary retrieval systems that provide printouts of indexes and abstracts.

Open-ended questions Unstructured questions in which the response categories are not specified or detailed.

Operational definition Explicit specification of a variable in such a way that its measurement is possible.

Operationalization The process of developing operational definitions of the variables that are contained within the concepts of a positivist and/or interpretive research study.

Ordinal level of measurement The level of measurement that classifies variables by rank-ordering them from high to low or from most to least.

Outcome The effect of the manipulation of the independent variable on the dependent variable; the end product of a treatment intervention.

Outcome measure The criterion or basis for measuring effects of the independent variable or change in the dependent variable.

Outcome-oriented case study A type of case study that investigates whether client outcomes were in fact achieved.

Outside observers Trained observers who are not a part of the research participants' environment and who are brought in to record data.

Paired observations An observation on two variables, where the intent is to examine the relationship between them.

Panel research study A longitudinal survey design in which the same group of research participants (the panel) is followed over time by surveying them on successive occasions.

Parametric tests Statistical methods for estimating parameters or testing hypotheses about population parameters.

Participant observation An obtrusive data collection method in which the researcher, or the observer, participates in the life of those being observed; both an obtrusive data collection method and a research approach, this method is characterized by the one doing the study undertaking roles that involve establishing and maintaining ongoing relationships with research participants who are often in the field settings, and observing and participating with the research participants over time.

Participant observer The participant observer is one of four roles on a continuum of participation in participant observation research; the level of involvement of the participant observer is higher than of the complete observer and lower than of the observer participant.

Permanent product recording A method of data collection in which the occurrence of the target problem is determined by observing the permanent product or record of the target problem.

Pilot study See *Pretest* (2).

Population An entire set, or universe, of people, objects, or events of concern to a research study, from which a sample is drawn.

Positivism See *Positivist research approach*.

Positivist research approach A research approach to discover relationships and facts that are generalizable; research that is "independent" of subjective beliefs, feelings, wishes, and values; a research approach that is complementary to the interpretive research approach.

Posttest Measurement of the dependent variable after the introduction of the independent variable.

Potential for testing One of the four criteria for evaluating research hypotheses.

Practitioner/researcher A social worker who guides practice through the use of research findings; collects data throughout an intervention using research methods, skills, and tools; disseminates practice findings.

Pragmatists Researchers who believe that both interpretive and positivist research approaches can be integrated in a single research study.

Predictive validity A form of criterion validity that is concerned with the ability of a measuring instrument to predict future performance or status on the basis of present performance or status.

Predictor variable The variable that, it is believed, allows us to improve our ability to predict values of the criterion variable.

Preexposure Tasks to be carried out in advance of a research study to sensitize the researcher to the culture of interest; these tasks may include participation in cultural experiences, intercultural sharing, case studies, ethnic literature reviews, value statement exercises, etc.

Preliminary plan for data analysis A strategy for analyzing qualitative data that is outlined in the beginning stages of an interpretive research study; the plan has two general steps: (1) previewing the data, and (2) outlining what to record in the researcher's journal.

Presentism Applying current thinking and concepts to interpretations of past events or intentions.

Pretest (1) Measurement of the dependent variable prior to the introduction of the independent variable; (2) Administration of a measuring instrument to a group of people who will not be included in the study to determine difficulties the research participants may have in answering questions and the general impression given by the instrument; also called a pilot study.

Pretest-treatment interaction Effects that a pretest has on the responses of research participants to the introduction of the independent variable or the experimental treatment; a threat to external validity.

Previous research Research studies that have already been completed and published, which provide information about data collection methods used to investigate research questions that are similar to our own; a criterion for selecting a data collection method.

Primary data Data in its original form, as collected from the research participants. A primary data source is one that puts as few intermediaries as possible between the production and the study of the data.

Primary language The preferred language of the research participants.

Primary reference source A report of a research study by the person who conducted the study, usually an article in a professional journal.

Probability sampling Sampling procedures in which every member of the designated population has a known probability of being selected for the sample.

Problem area In social work research, a general expressed difficulty about which something researchable is unknown; not to be confused with research question.

Problem-solving process A generic method with specified phases for solving problems; also described as the scientific method.

Process-oriented case study A type of case study that illuminates the micro-steps of intervention that lead to client outcomes; describes how programs and interventions work and gives insight into the "black box" of intervention.

Professional standards Rules for making judgments about evaluation activity that are established by a group of persons who have advanced education and usually have the same occupation.

Program An organized set of political, administrative, and clinical activities that function to fulfill some social purpose.

Program development The constant effort to improve program services to better achieve outcomes; a basic principle underlying the design of evaluations.

Program efficiency Assessment of a program's outcome in relation to the costs of obtaining the outcome.

Program evaluation A form of appraisal, using valid and reliable research methods, that examines the processes or outcomes of an organization that exists to fulfill some social purpose.

Program goal A statement defining the intent of a program that cannot be directly evaluated; it can, however, be evaluated indirectly by the program's objectives, which are derived from the program goal; not to be confused with program objectives.

Program-level evaluation A form of appraisal that monitors change for groups of clients and organizational performance.

Program objectives A statement that clearly and exactly specifies the expected change, or intended result, for individuals receiving program services; qualities of well-chosen objectives are meaningfulness, specificity, measurability, and directionality; not to be confused with program goal.

Program participation The philosophy and structure of a program that will support or supplant the successful implementation of a research study within an existing social service program; a criterion for selecting a data collection method.

Program process The coordination of administrative and clinical activities that are designed to achieve a program's goal.

Program results A report on how effective a program is at meeting its stated objectives.

Project approach to evaluation Evaluation that aims to assess a completed or finished program. This approach complements the monitoring approach.

Proxy An indirect measure of a variable that a researcher wants to study; often used when the variable of inquiry is difficult to measure or observe directly.

Pure research approach A search for theoretical results that can be used to develop theory and expand our profession's knowledge bases; complementary to the applied research approach.

Purists Researchers who believe that interpretive and positivist research approaches should never be mixed.

Purpose statement A declaration of words that clearly describes a research study's intent.

Purposive sampling A nonprobability sampling procedure in which research participants with particular characteristics are purposely selected for inclusion in a research sample; also known as judgmental or theoretical sampling.

Qualitative data Data that measure a quality or kind. When referring to variables, qualitative is another term for categorical or nominal variable values; when speaking of kinds of research, qualitative refers to studies of subjects that are hard to quantify. Interpretive research produces descriptive data based on spoken or written words and observable behaviors.

Quantification In measurement, the reduction of data to numerical form in order to analyze them by way of mathematical or statistical techniques.

Quantitative data Data that measure a quantity or amount.

Quasi-experiment A research design at the descriptive level of the knowledge continuum that resembles an "ideal" experiment but does not allow for random selection or assignment of research participants to groups and often does not control for rival hypotheses.

Questionnaire-type scale A type of measuring instrument in which multiple responses are usually combined to form a single overall score for a respondent.

Quota sampling A nonprobability sampling procedure in which the relevant characteristics of the sample are identified, the proportion of these characteristics in the population is determined, and research participants are selected from each category until the predetermined proportion (quota) has been achieved.

Race A variable based on physical attributes that can be subdivided into the Caucasoid, Negroid, and Mongoloid races.

Random assignment The process of assigning individuals to experimental or control groups so that the groups are equivalent; also referred to as randomization.

Random error Variable error in measurement; error due to unknown or uncontrolled factors that affect the variable being measured and the process of measurement in an inconsistent fashion.

Randomized cross-sectional survey design A descriptive research design in which there is only one group, the dependent variable is measured only once, the research participants are randomly selected from the population, and there is no independent variable.

Randomized longitudinal survey design A descriptive research design in which there is only one group, the dependent variable is measured more than once, and research participants are randomly selected from the population before each treatment.

Randomized one-group posttest-only design A descriptive research design in which there is only one group, the dependent variable is measured only once, and research participants are randomly selected from the population.

Randomized posttest-only control group design An explanatory research design in which there are two or more randomly assigned groups, the control group does not receive treatment, and the experimental groups receive different treatments.

Random numbers table A computer-generated or published table of numbers in which each number has an equal chance of appearing in each position in the table.

Random sampling An unbiased selection process conducted so that all members of a population have an equal chance of being selected to participate in a research study.

Rank-order scale A comparative rating scale in which the rater is asked to rank specific individuals in relation to one another on some characteristic.

Rating scale A type of measuring instrument in which responses are rated on a continuum or in an ordered set of categories, with numerical values assigned to each point or category.

Ratio level of measurement The level of measurement that has a nonarbitrary, fixed zero point and classifies the values of a variable on an equally spaced continuum.

Raw scores Scores derived from administration of a measuring instrument to research participants or groups.

Reactive effect (1) An effect on outcome measures due to the research participants' awareness that they are being observed or interviewed; a threat to external and internal validity; (2) Alteration of the variables being measured or the respondents' performance on the measuring instrument due to administration of the instrument.

Reactivity The belief that things being observed or measured are affected by the fact that they are being observed or measured; one of the four main limitations of the positivist research approach.

Reassessment A step in a qualitative data analysis in which the researcher interrupts the data analysis process to reaffirm the rules used to decide which meaning units are placed within different categories.

Recoding Developing and applying new variable value labels to a variable that has previously been coded. Usually, recoding is done to make variables from one or more data sets comparable.

Reductionism In the positivist research approach, the operationalization of concepts by reducing them to common measurable variables; one of the four main limitations of the positivist research approach.

Relevancy One of the four criteria for evaluating research problem areas *and* formulating research questions out of the problem areas.

Reliability (1) The degree of accuracy, precision, or consistency in results of a measuring instrument, including the ability to produce the same results when the same variable is measured more than once or repeated applications of the same test on the same individual produce the same measurement; (2) The degree to which individual differences on scores or in data are due either to true differences or to errors in measurement.

Replication Repetition of the same research procedures by a second researcher for the purpose of determining if earlier results can be confirmed.

Researchability The extent to which a research problem is in fact researchable and the problem can be resolved through the consideration of data derived from a research study; one of the four criteria for evaluating research problem areas *and* formulating research questions out of the problem areas.

Research attitude A way that we view the world. It is an attitude that highly values craftsmanship, with pride in creativity, high-quality standards, and hard work.

Research consumer A social work role reflecting the ethical obligation to base interventions on the most up-to-date research knowledge available.

Research design The entire plan of a positivist and/or interpretive research study from problem conceptualization to the dissemination of findings.

Researcher bias The tendency of researchers to find results they expect to find; a threat to external validity.

Research hypothesis A statement about a study's research question that predicts the existence of a particular relationship between the independent and dependent variables; can be used in both the positivist and interpretive approaches to research.

Research method The use of positivist and interpretive research approaches to find out what is true; one of the ways of knowing.

Research participants People utilized in research studies; also called subjects or cases.

Research question A specific research question that is formulated directly out of the general research problem area; answered by the interpretive and/or positivist research approach; not to be confused with problem area.

Resources The costs associated with collecting data in any given research study; includes materials and supplies, equipment rental, transportation, training staff, and staff time; a criterion for selecting a data collection method.

Response categories Possible responses assigned to each question in a standardized measuring instrument, with a lower value generally indicating a low level of the variable being measured and a larger value indicating a higher level.

Response rate The total number of responses obtained from potential research participants to a measuring instrument divided by the total number of responses requested, usually expressed in the form of a percentage.

Response set Personal style; the tendency of research participants to respond to a measuring instrument in a particular way, regardless of the questions asked, or the tendency of observers or interviewers to react in certain ways; a source of constant error.

Review of the literature (1) A search of the professional literature to provide background knowledge of what has already been examined or tested in a specific problem area; (2) Use of any information source, such as a computerized database, to locate existing data or information on a research problem, question, or hypothesis.

Rival hypothesis A hypothesis that is a plausible alternative to the research hypothesis and might explain the results as well or better; a hypothesis involving extraneous or intervening variables other than the independent variable in the research hypothesis; also referred to as an alternative hypothesis.

Rules of correspondence A characteristic of measurement stipulating that numerals or symbols are assigned to properties of individuals, objects, or events according to specified rules.

Sample A subset of a population of individuals, objects, or events chosen to participate in or to be considered in a research study.

Sampling error (1) The degree of difference that can be expected between the sample and the population from which it was drawn; (2) A mistake in a research study's results that is due to sampling procedures.

Sampling frame A listing of units (people, objects, or events) in a population from which a sample is drawn.

Sampling plan A method of selecting members of a population for inclusion in a research study, using procedures that make it possible to draw inferences about the population from the sample statistics.

Sampling theory The logic of using methods to ensure that a sample and a population are similar in all relevant characteristics.

Scale A measuring instrument composed of several items that are logically or empirically structured to measure a construct.

Scattergram A graphic representation of the relationship between two interval- or ratio-level variables.

Science Knowledge that has been obtained and tested through use of positivist and interpretive research studies.

Scientific community A group that shares the same general norms for both research activity and acceptance of scientific findings and explanations.

Scientific determinism See *Determinism*.

Scientific method A generic method with specified steps for solving problems; the principles and procedures used in the systematic pursuit of knowledge.

Scope of a study The extent to which a problem area is covered in a single research study; a criterion for selecting a data collection method.

Score A numerical value assigned to an observation; also called data.

Search statement A preliminary search statement developed by the researcher prior to a literature search and which contains terms that can be combined to elicit specific data.

Secondary analysis An unobtrusive data collection method in which available data that predate the formulation of a research study are used to answer the research question or test the hypothesis.

Secondary data Data that predate the formulation of the research study and that are used to answer the research question or test the hypothesis.

Secondary data sources A data source that provides nonoriginal, secondhand data.

Secondary reference source A source related to a primary source or sources, such as a critique of a particular source item or a literature review, bibliography, or commentary on several items.

Secondhand data Data obtained from people who are indirectly connected to the problem being studied.

Selection-treatment interaction The relationship between the manner of selecting research participants and their response to the independent variable; a threat to external validity.

Self-anchored scales A rating scale in which research participants rate themselves on a continuum of values, according to their own referents for each point.

Self-disclosure Shared communication about oneself, including one's behaviors, beliefs, and attitudes.

Semantic differential scale A modified measurement scale in which research participants rate their perceptions of the variable under study along three dimensions—evaluation, potency, and activity.

Sequential triangulation When two distinct and separate phases of a research study are conducted and the results of the first phase are considered essential for planning the second phase; research questions in Phase 1 are answered before research questions in Phase 2 are formulated.

Service recipients People who use human services—individuals, couples, families, groups, organizations, and communities; also known as clients or consumers; a stakeholder group in evaluation.

Simple random sampling A one-stage probability sampling procedure in which members of a population are selected one at a time, without a chance of being selected again, until the desired sample size is obtained.

Simultaneous triangulation When the results of a positivist and interpretive research question are answered at the same time; results to the interpretive research questions, for example, are reported separately and do not necessarily relate to, or confirm, the results from the positivist phase.

Situationalists Researchers who assert that certain research approaches (interpretive or positivist) are appropriate for specific situations.

Situation-specific variable A variable that may be observable only in certain environments and under certain circumstances, or with particular people.

Size of a study The number of people, places, or systems that are included in a single research study; a criterion for selecting a data collection method.

Snowball sampling A nonprobability sampling procedure in which individuals selected for inclusion in a sample are asked to identify other individuals from the population who might be included; useful to locate people with divergent points of view.

Social desirability (1) A response set in which research participants tend to answer questions in a way that they perceive as giving favorable impressions of themselves; (2) The inclination of data providers to report data that present a socially desirable impression of themselves or their reference groups; also referred to as impression management.

Socially acceptable response Bias in an answer that comes from research participants trying to answer questions as they think a "good" person should, rather than in a way that reveals what they actually believe or feel.

Social work research Scientific inquiry in which interpretive and positivist research approaches are used to answer research questions and create new, generally applicable knowledge in the field of social work.

Socioeconomic variables Any one of several measures of social rank, usually including income, education, and occupational prestige; abbreviated "SES."

Solomon four-group design An explanatory research design with four randomly assigned groups, two experimental and two control; the dependent variable is measured before and after treatment for one experimental and one control group, but only after treatment for the other two groups, and only experimental groups receive the treatment.

Specificity One of the four criteria for evaluating research hypotheses.

Split-half method A method for establishing the reliability of a measuring instrument by dividing it into comparable halves and comparing the scores between the two halves.

Spot-check recording A method of data collection that involves direct observation of the target problem at specified intervals rather than on a continuous basis.

Stakeholder A person or group of people having a direct or indirect interest in the results of an evaluation.

Stakeholder service evaluation model Proponents of this evaluation model believe that program evaluations will be more likely to be utilized, and thus have a greater impact on social problems, when they are tailored to the needs of stakeholders; in this model, the purpose of program evaluation is not to generalize findings to other sites, but rather to restrict the evaluation effort to a particular program.

Standardized measuring instrument A professionally developed measuring instrument that provides for uniform administration and scoring and generates normative data against which later results can be evaluated.

Statistics The branch of mathematics concerned with the collection and analysis of data using statistical techniques.

Stratified random sampling A one-stage probability sampling procedure in which a population is divided into two or more strata to be sampled separately, using simple random or systematic random sampling techniques.

Structured interview schedule A complete list of questions to be asked and spaces for recording the answers; the interview schedule is used by interviewers when questioning respondents.

Structured observation A data collection method in which people are observed in their natural environments using specified methods and measurement procedures. See *Direct observation*.

Subscale A component of a scale that measures some part or aspect of a major construct; also composed of several items that are logically or empirically structured.

Summated scale A questionnaire-type scale in which research participants are asked to indicate the degree of their agreement or disagreement with a series of questions.

Summative evaluation A type of evaluation that examines the ultimate success of a program and assists with decisions about whether a program should be continued or chosen in the first place among alternative program options.

Survey research A data collection method that uses survey-type data collection measuring instruments to obtain opinions or answers from a population or sample of research participants in order to describe or study them as a group.

Synthesis Undertaking the search for meaning in our sources of information at every step of the research process;

combining parts such as data, concepts, and theories to arrive at a higher level of understanding.

Systematic To arrange the steps of a research study in a methodical way.

Systematic random sampling A one-stage probability sampling procedure in which every person at a designated interval in a specific population is selected to be included in a research study's sample.

Systematic error Measurement error that is consistent, not random.

Target population The group about which a researcher wants to draw conclusions; another term for a population about which one aims to make inferences.

Target problem (1) In case-level evaluation designs, the problems social workers seek to solve for their clients; (2) A measurable behavior, feeling, or cognition that is either a problem in itself or symptomatic of some other problem.

Temporal research design A research study that includes time as a major variable; the purpose of this design is to investigate change in the distribution of a variable or in relationships among variables over time; there are three types of temporal research designs: cohort, panel, and trend.

Temporal stability Consistency of responses to a measuring instrument over time; reliability of an instrument across forms and across administrations.

Testing effect The effect that taking a pretest might have on posttest scores; a threat to internal validity.

Test-retest reliability Reliability of a measuring instrument established through repeated administration to the same group of individuals.

Thematic notes In observational research, thematic notes are a record of emerging ideas, hypotheses, theories, and conjectures; thematic notes provide a place for the researcher to speculate and identify themes, make linkages between ideas and events, and articulate thoughts as they emerge in the field setting.

Theme In a qualitative data analysis, a concept or idea that describes a single category or a grouping of categories; an abstract interpretation of qualitative data.

Theoretical framework A frame of reference that serves to guide a research study and is developed from theories, findings from a variety of other studies, and the researcher's personal experiences.

Theoretical sampling See *Purposive sampling*.

Theory A reasoned set of propositions, derived from and supported by established data, which serves to explain a group of phenomena; a conjectural explanation that may, or may not, be supported by data generated from interpretive and positivist research studies.

Time orientation An important cultural factor that considers whether one is future-, present-, or past-oriented; for instance, individuals who are "present-oriented" would not be as preoccupied with advance planning as those who are "future-oriented."

Time-series design See *Interrupted time-series design*.

Tradition Traditional cultural beliefs that we accept "without question" as true; one of the ways of knowing.

Transcript A written, printed, or typed copy of interview data or any other written material that have been gathered for an interpretive research study.

Transition statements Sentences used to indicate a change in direction or focus of questions in a measuring instrument.

Treatment group See *Experimental group*.

Trend study A longitudinal study design in which data from surveys carried out at periodic intervals on samples drawn from a particular population are used to reveal trends over time.

Triangulation The idea of combining different research methods in all steps associated with a single research study; assumes that any bias inherent in one particular method will be neutralized when used in conjunction with other research methods; seeks convergence of a study's results; using more than one research method and source of data to study the same phenomena and to enhance validity. There are several types of triangulation, but the essence of the term is that multiple perspectives are compared. It can involve multiple data sources or multiple data analyzers; the hope is that the different perspectives will confirm each other, adding weight to the credibility and dependability of qualitative data analysis.

Triangulation of analysts Using multiple data analyzers to code a single segment of transcript and comparing the amount of agreement between analyzers; a method used to verify coding of qualitative data.

Two-phase research model A model combining interpretive and positivist research approaches in a single study where each approach is conducted as a separate and distinct phase of the study.

Two-tailed hypotheses Statements that *do not* predict specific relationships between independent and dependent variables.

Unit of analysis A specific research participant (person, object, or event) or the sample or population relevant to the research question; the persons or things being studied. Units of analysis in research are often persons, but may be groups, political parties, newspaper editorials, unions, hospitals, schools, etc. A particular unit of analysis from which data are gathered is called a case.

Univariate A hypothesis or research design involving a single variable.

Universe See *Population*.

Unobtrusive methods Data collection methods that do not influence the variable under study or the responses of research participants; methods that avoid reactive effects.

Unstructured interviews A series of questions that allow flexibility for both the research participant and the interviewer to make changes during the process.

Validity (1) The extent to which a measuring instrument measures the variable it is supposed to measure and measures it accurately; (2) The degree to which an instrument is able to do what it is intended to do, in terms of both experimental procedures and measuring instruments (internal validity) and generalizability of results (external validity); (3) The degree to which scores on a measuring instrument correlate with measures of performance on some other criterion.

Variable A concept with characteristics that can take on different values.

Verbatim recording Recording interview data word-for-word and including significant gestures, pauses, and expressions of persons in the interview.

Wideband measuring instrument An instrument that measures more than one variable.

Within-methods research approach Triangulation by using different research methods available in *either* the interpretive *or* the positivist research approaches in a single research study.

Words The basic data unit of analysis used in interpretive research studies.

Worker cooperation The actions and attitudes of program personnel when carrying out a research study within an existing social service program; a criterion for selecting a data collection method.

Working hypothesis An assertion about a relationship between two or more variables that may not be true but is plausible and worth examining.

References

Abudabbeh, N. (2005). Arab families: An overview. In M. McGoldrick, J. Giordano, & L. Garcia-Preto (Eds.), *Ethnicity and family therapy* (3rd ed., pp. 423–436). New York: Guilford.

Adam, N., Zosky, D., & Unrau, Y. (2004). Improving the research climate in social work curricula: Clarifying learning expectations across BSW and MSW research courses. *Journal of Teaching in Social Work, 24*(3), 1–18.

Alexander, C. (2006). Writing race: Ethnography and difference. *Race and Ethnic Relations, 29*, 397–410.

Almeida, R. (2005). Asian Indian families: An overview. In M. McGoldrick, J. Giordano, & L. Garcia-Preto (Eds.), *Ethnicity and family therapy* (3rd ed., pp. 377–394). New York: Guilford.

Alston, R. J., & Turner, W. (1994). A family strengths model of adjustment to disability for African American clients. *Journal of Counseling and Development, 72*, 378–383.

American Academy of Child and Adolescent Psychiatry. (1998). Practice parameter for the assessment and treatment of children and adolescents with depressive disorders. *Journal of the American Academy of Child Adolescent Psychiatry 37*, 63–83.

American Physiological Society. (2002). *Planning and effective program evaluation: A short course for project directors*. Bethesda, MD: Author.

American Psychiatric Association. (1993). Practice guideline for major depressive disorder in adults. *American Journal of Psychiatry, 150*, 1–26.

American Psychiatric Association. (1994). Practice guideline for the treatment of patients with bipolar disorder. *American Journal of Psychiatry, 151*, 1–36.

American Psychiatric Association. (1997). Practice guideline for the treatment of patients with schizophrenia. *American Journal of Psychiatry 154*, 1–63.

American Psychological Association. (2000). *Style helper*. Washington, DC: Author. http://www.apa.org/apa-style.

American Psychological Association. (2001). *Publication manual of the American Psychological Association* (5th ed.). Washington, DC: Author.

American Psychological Association. (2005a) *Report of the 2005 Presidential Task Force on Evidence-Based Practice*. Washington, DC: Author

American Psychological Association. (2005b, July 1). *APA 2005 report: Best available research evidence*. Washington, DC: Author.

Anastas, J. W. (2004). Quality in qualitative evaluation: Issues and possible answers. *Research in Social Work Practice, 14*(1), 57–65.

Anderson, C. (2003). The diversity, strength, and challenges of single-parent households. In F. Walsh (Ed.), *Normal family processes* (3rd ed., pp. 121–152). New York: Guilford.

Andrews, A. B., Guadalupe, J. L., & Bolden, E. (2003). Faith, hope, and mutual support: Paths to empowerment as perceived by women in poverty. *Journal of Social Work Research and Evaluation, 4*(1), 518–522.

Andrews, L. (1984). Informed consent statutes and the decision-making process. *Journal of Legal Medicine, 1*, 163–217.

Appelbaum, P., & Roth, L. (1982). Competency to consent to research: A psychiatric overview. *Archives of General Psychiatry, 39*, 951–958.

Atkinson, R., & Flint, J. (2001, Summer). Accessing hidden and hard-to-reach populations: Snowball research strategies. *Social Research Update, 33*. Retrieved May 19, 2005, from http://www.soc.surrey.ac.uk/sru/SRU33.html

Auger, C. P. (1989). *Information sources in grey literature* (2nd ed.). London: Bowker-Saur.

Axinn, W., Pearce, L., & Ghimire, D. (1999). Innovations in life history calendar applications. *Social Science Research, 28*, 243–264.

Baer, J. (1999). Family relationships, parenting behavior, and adolescent deviance in three ethnic groups. *Families in Society, 78,* 279–285.

Bailey, K. D. (1994). *Methods of social research* (4th ed.). New York: Free Press.

Bainbridge, W. (1989). *Survey research: A computer-assisted introduction.* Belmont, CA: Wadsworth.

Bales, R. F. (1950). *Interaction process analysis.* Reading, MA: Addison-Wesley.

Bamberger, M. J., Rugh, J., & Mabry, L. (2007). *Real world evaluation: Working under budget, time, data, and political constraints.* Thousand Oaks, CA: Sage.

Bangert-Drowns, R. L. (1997). Some limiting factors in meta-analysis. In W. J. Bukoski (Ed.), *Meta-analysis of drug abuse prevention programs* (NIDA Report No. 170, pp. 234–252). Rockville, MD: National Institute on Drug Abuse.

Bangs, R., Kerchis, C. Z., & Weldon, S. L. (1997). *Basic living cost and living wage estimates for Pittsburgh and Allegheny County.* Pittsburgh: University of Pittsburgh and UCSUR.

Barbee, E. L. (1992). African American women and depression: A review and critique of the literature. *Archives of Psychiatric Nursing, 6,* 257–265.

Barbour, R. S. (2003). The newfound credibility of qualitative research? Tales of technical essentialism and co-option. *Qualitative Health Research, 13*(7), 1019–1027.

Barlow, J., & Parsons, J. (2005). Group based parent-training programs for improving emotional and behavioral adjustment in 0–3 year old children. The Campbell Collaboration. Retrieved August 22, 2006, from http://www.campbellcollaboration.org/index.asp

Beck, J. G., & Davies, D. K. (1987). Teen contraception: A review of perspectives on compliance. *Archives of Sexual Behavior, 16,* 337–376.

Begg, C. B. (1994). Publication bias. In H. Cooper & L. V. Hedges (Eds.), *The handbook of research synthesis* (pp. 399–409). New York: Russell Sage Foundation.

Benney, M., Riesman, D., & Starr, S. (1956). Age and sex with the interview. *American Journal of Sociology, 62,* 143–152.

Berg, B. L. (2007). *Qualitative research methods for the social sciences* (6th ed.). Boston: Allyn & Bacon.

Berger, R. (2002). Gay stepfamilies: A triple-stigmatized group. *Families in Society, 81,* 504–516.

Berkman, C. S., & Zinberg, G. (1997). Homophobia and heterosexism in social workers. *Social Work, 42,* 319–332.

Bettelheim, B. (1982, March 1). Reflections: Freud and the soul. *New Yorker,* 52.

Bigby, M. (1998). Evidence-based medicine in a nutshell. *Archives of Dermatology, 134,* 1609–1618.

Billups, J. O., & Julia, M. C. (1987). Changing profile of social work practice: A content analysis. *Social Work Research and Abstracts, 23,* 17–22.

Black, D. J. (Ed.). (1984). *Toward a general theory of social control* (Vol. 1). Orlando, FL: Academic Press.

Blau, P. M. (1964). *Exchange and power in social life.* New York: Wiley.

Bloom, M., Fischer, J., & Orme, J. (2006). *Evaluating practice: Guidelines for the accountable professional* (5th ed.). Englewood Cliffs, NJ: Prentice-Hall.

Blythe, B. J., & Tripodi, T. (1989). *Measurement in direct practice.* Thousand Oaks, CA: Sage.

Boruch, R. F. (1989). Resolving privacy problems in AIDS research: A primer. In L. Sechrest, H. Freeman, & A. Mulley (Eds.), *Health services and research methodology: A focus on AIDS* (DHHS Publication No. PHS 89–3439, pp. 165–180). Rockville, MD: U.S. Government Printing Office.

Bossert, S. T. (1979). *Tasks and social relationships in classrooms.* New York: Cambridge University Press.

Bourgois, P., Lettiere, M., & Quesada, J. (1997). Social misery and the sanctions of substance abuse: Confronting HIV risk among homeless heroin addicts in San Francisco. *Social Problems, 44,* 155–173.

Bowman, P. J. (1983). Significant involvement and functional relevance: Challenges to survey research. *Social Work Research and Abstracts, 19,* 21–26.

Boyd-Franklin, N. (1989). *Black families in therapy.* New York: Guilford.

Boyd-Franklin, N. (2003). Race, class and poverty. In F. Walsh (Ed.), *Normal family processes* (3rd ed., pp. 260–279). New York: Guilford.

Brady, S., & Busse, W. J. (1994). The Gay Identity Questionnaire: A brief measure of homosexual identity formation. *Journal of Homosexuality, 26,* 1–22.

Brett, D., & Cantor, J. (1988). The portrayal of men and women in U.S. television commercials: A recent content analysis and trends over 15 years. *Sex Roles, 18,* 595–609.

Brewer, J., & Hunter, A. (1989). *Multimethod research: A synthesis of styles.* Thousand Oaks, CA: Sage.

Bronfenbrenner, U. (1989). Ecological systems theory. *Annals of Child Development, 6,* 187–249.

Bronfenbrenner, U., & Ceci, S. (1994). Nature-nurture reconceptualized in developmental perspective: A bioecological model. *Psychological Review, 101,* 568–586.

Brown, T. (2003). Internet based research: Is it a viable strategy for increasing the representation of ethnic minorities in psychological research? *Individual Differences Research, 1,* 211–229.

Broxmeyer, N. (1979). Practitioner-research in treating a borderline child. *Social Work Research and Abstracts, 14,* 5–10.

Brun, C. F. (2005). *A practical guide to social service evaluation.* Chicago: Lyceum.

Bryant, A. S., & Demian, S. (1994). Relationship characteristics of American gay and lesbian couples: Findings from a national survey. *Journal of Gay and Lesbian Social Services, 1,* 101–117.

Burt, M. (1996). Homelessness: Definitions and counts. In J. Baumohl (Ed.), *Homelessness in America* (pp. 15–23). Phoenix, AZ: Oryx Press.

Cain, D., & Combs-Orme, T. (2005). Family structure effects on parenting stress and practices in the African American family. *Journal of Sociology and Social Welfare, 32,* 19–40.

Cain, R. (1996). Heterosexism and self-disclosure in the social work classroom. *Journal of Social Work Education, 21,* 65–76.

Caldwell, C., Zimmerman, A., Bernat, D., Sellers, R., & Notaro, P. (2002). Racial identity, maternal support, and psychological distress among African American adolescents. *Child Development, 73,* 1322–1336.

Campanario, J. M. (1998). Peer review of journals as it stands today: Part 1. *Science Communication, 19,* 181–211.

Campbell, D., & Stanley, J. (1963). *Experimental and quasi-experimental designs for research.* Chicago: Rand McNally.

Caspi, A., Moffitt, T., Thornton, A., Freedman, D., Amell, J., Harrington, H., Smeijers, J., & Silva, P. A. (1996). The life history calendar: A research and clinical assessment method for collecting retrospective event-history data. *International Journal of Methods in Psychiatric Research, 6,* 101–114.

Catania, J., McDermott, L., & Pollack, L. (1986). Questionnaire response bias and face-to-face interview sample bias in sexuality research. *Journal of Sex Research, 22,* 52–72.

Chalmers, T. C., Lein, H., Sacks, H. S., Reitman, D., Berrier, J., & Nagalingam, R. (1987). Meta-analysis of clinical trials as a scientific discipline, I: Control of bias and comparison with large co-operative trials. *Statistical Medicine, 6,* 315.

Chambless, D. L., Baker, M. J., Baucom, D. H., Beutler, L. E., Calhoun, K. S., Crits-Christoph, P., Daiuto, A., DeRubeis, R., Detweiler, J., Haaga, D. A. F., Johnson, S. B., McCurry, S., Mueser, K. T., Pope, K. S., Sanderson, W. C., Shoham, V., Stickle, T., Williams, D. A., & Woody, S. R. (1998). Update on empirically validated therapies, II. *Clinical Psychologist, 51,* 3–16.

Chambless, D. L., Sanderson, W. C., Shoham, V., Bennett Johnson, S., Pope, K. S., Crits-Christoph, P., Baker, M., Johnson, B., Woody, S. R., Sue, S., Beutler, L., Williams, D. A., & McCurry, S. (1996). Update on empirically validated therapies. *Clinical Psychologist, 49,* 5–18.

Chauncey, G. (1994). *Gay New York: Gender, urban culture, and the making of the gay male world, 1890–1940.* New York: Basic Books.

Chen, H. T. (2006). *Practical program evaluation: Assessing and improving planning, implementation, and effectiveness.* Thousand Oaks, CA: Sage.

Christians, C. (2005). Ethics and politics in qualitative research. In N. K. Denzin & Y. S. Lincoln (Eds.), *Handbook of qualitative research* (3rd ed., pp. 139–164). Thousand Oaks, CA: Sage.

Cohen, J. (1988). *Statistical power analysis for the behavioral sciences* (2nd ed.). Hillsdale, NJ: Erlbaum.

Coleman, H., & Unrau, Y. A. (2005). Analyzing qualitative data. In R. M. Grinnell, Jr., & Y. A. Unrau (Eds.), *Social work research and evaluation: Quantitative and qualitative approaches* (7th ed., pp. 403–420). New York: Oxford University Press.

Compassion Capital Fund National Resource Center. (2006). *Measuring outcomes.* Washington, DC: Author.

Concato, J. (2004). Observational versus experimental studies: What's the evidence for a hierarchy? *Journal of the American Society for Experimental Neuro-therapeutics, 1,* 341–347.

Cone, J., & Foster, S. (1995). *Dissertations from start to finish: Psychology and related fields.* Hyattsville, MD: APA Publications.

Connell, P. J., Kubisch, A. C., Schorr, L. B., & Weiss, C. H. (1995). *New approaches to evaluating community initiatives: Concepts, methods, and contexts.* Washington, DC: Aspen Institute.

Constantine, M., & Blackmon, S. (2002). Black adolescents' racial socialization experiences, their relations to home, school, and peer self-esteem. *Journal of Black Studies, 32,* 322–335.

Converse, J. M. (1984). Attitude measurement in psychology and sociology: The early years. In C. F. Turner & E. Martin (Eds.), *Surveying subjective phenomena* (Vol. 2, pp. 3–40). New York: Russell Sage Foundation.

Cook, B. W. (1977). Female support networks and political activism. *Chrysalis, 3,* 43–61.

Cook, D. J., Mulrow, C. D., & Haynes, R. B. (1997). Systematic reviews: Synthesis of best evidence for clinical decisions. *Annals of Internal Medicine, 126,* 376–380.

Cooper, H., & Hedges, L. V. (1994). *The handbook of research synthesis.* New York: Russell Sage Foundation.

Corcoran, J., Miller, P., & Bultman, L. (1997). Effectiveness of prevention programs for adolescent pregnancy: A meta-analysis. *Journal of Marriage and the Family, 59,* 551–567.

Core Institute. (1994). *Core alcohol and drug survey: Long form.* Carbondale, IL: Southern Illinois University, APSE Core Analysis Grantee Group, Core Institute, Student Health Programs.

Council of National Psychological Associations for the Advancement of Ethnic Minority Interests. (2000). *Guidelines for Research in Ethnic Minority Communities.* Washington, DC: Author.

Council on Social Work Education. (2004a). *Educational and policy accreditation standards.* Washington, DC: Author. Retrieved March 6, 2004, from http://www.cswe.org

Council on Social Work Education. (2004b). *Preamble.* Washington, DC: Author. Retrieved March 6, 2004, from http://www.cswe.org

Couper, M. P., Baker, R. P., Bethlehem, J., Clark, C. Z. F., Martin, J., Nicholls, W. L., & O'Reilly, J. M. (Eds.). (1998). *Computer assisted survey information collection.* New York: Wiley.

Cox, J. L., Holden, J. M., & Sagovsky, R. (1987). Detection of postnatal depression: Development of the 10-item Edinburgh Postnatal Depression Scale (EPDS). *British Journal of Psychiatry 150,* 782–786.

Crosbie-Burnett, M., & Lewis, E. (1993). Use of African American family structures and functioning to address the challenges of European American post-divorce families. *Family Relations, 43,* 243–248.

Cross, T., Bazron, B., Dennis, K., & Isaacs, M. (1989). *Towards a culturally competent system of care* (Vol. 1). Washington, DC: Georgetown University Child Development Center.

Cumberbatch, G., Jones, I., & Lee, M. (1988). Measuring violence on television. *Current Psychological Research and Review, 7,* 10–25.

Curry, H., Clifford, D., & Hertz, F. (2002). *A legal guide for lesbian and gay couples* (11th ed.). Berkley, CA: Nolo.

Czaja, R., & Blair, B. (1995). *Survey research.* Thousand Oaks, CA: Pine Forge Press.

Davidson, E. J. (2005). *Evaluation methodology basics: The nuts and bolts of sound evaluation.* Thousand Oaks, CA: Sage.

Davis, J. A., & Smith, T. W. (1992). *The NORC general social survey: A user's guide.* Thousand Oaks, CA: Sage.

Deenen, A. A., Gijs, L., & van Naerssen, A. X. (1994). Intimacy and sexuality in gay male couples. *Archives of Sexual Behavior 23,* 421–431.

DeMaria, W. (1981). Empiricism: An impoverished philosophy for social work research. *Australian Social Work, 34,* 3–8.

Denenberg, R. (1994). *Report on lesbian health.* Washington, DC: National Gay and Lesbian Task Force Policy Institute.

Denzin, N. K. (2003). *Performance ethnography: Critical pedagogy and the politics of culture.* Thousand Oaks, CA: Sage.

Denzin, N. K., & Lincoln, Y. (1994). Introduction: Entering the field of qualitative research. In N. K. Denzin & Y. Lincoln (Eds.), *Handbook of qualitative research* (pp. 1–17). Thousand Oaks, CA: Sage.

Derezotes, D. (1995). Evaluation of the Late Nite Basketball Project. *Child and Adolescent Social Work Journal, 12,* 33–50.

Devine, E. C. (1997). Issues and challenges in coding interventions for meta-analysis of prevention research. In W. J. Bukoski (Ed.), *Meta-analysis of drug abuse* (NIDA Report No. 170, pp. 130–146). Rockville, MD: National Institute on Drug Abuse.

Dewhurst, A. (2005). Computer and Internet based research guidance. New York: Columbia University Morningside Institutional Review Board.

Dietel, R., Herman, J., & Kruth, T. (1991). *What does research say about assessment?* Oak Brook, IL: North Central Regional Educational Library (NCREL).

Dillman, D. A. (1978). *Mail and telephone surveys: The total design method.* New York: Wiley.

Dillman, D. A. (1982). Mail and other self-administered questionnaires. In P. Rossi, J. Wright, & A. Anderson (Eds.), *Handbook of survey research* (pp. 346–355). New York: Academic Press

Dillman, D. A. (2000). *Mail and Internet surveys: The tailored design method* (2nd ed.). New York: Wiley.

Dillman, D. A., Christenson, J. A., Carpenter, E. H., & Brooks, R. M. (1974). Increasing mail questionnaire response: A four-state comparison. *American Sociological Review 39,* 744–756.

Dodd, D. K., Foerch, B. J., & Anderson, H. T. (1988). Content analysis of women and racial minorities as news magazine cover persons. *Journal of Social Behavior and Personality, 3,* 231–236.

Dodson, J. (1997). Conceptualization of black families. In H. McAdoo (Ed.), *Black families* (3rd ed., pp. 67–82). Thousand Oaks, CA: Sage.

Dohrenwend, B. P., & Dohrenwend, B. S. (1982). Perspectives on the past and future of psychiatric epidemiology. *American Journal of Public Health, 72*, 1271–1279.

Dohrenwend, B. S., Colombatos, J., & Dohrenwend, B. P. (1968). Social distance and interview effects. *Public Opinion Quarterly, 32*, 410–422.

Dollard, J., & Mowrer, O. H. (1947). A method of measuring tension in written documents. *Journal of Abnormal and Social Psychology, 42*, 3–22.

Dolnick, E. (1984, July 16). Why have the pollsters been missing the mark? *Boston Globe*, pp. 27–28.

Donaldson, S. I. (2001). Overcoming our negative reputation: Evaluation becomes known as a helping profession. *American Journal of Evaluation, 22*, 355–361.

Drake, R. E., Goldman, H. H., Leff, H. S., Lehman, A. F., Dixon, L., Mueser, K. T., & Torrey, W. C. (2001). Implementing evidence-based practices in routine mental health service settings. *Psychiatric Services, 52*, 179–182.

Drake, R. E., McHugo, G. J., & Biesanz, J. C. (1995). The test-retest reliability of standardized instruments among homeless persons with substance use disorders. *Journal of Studies on Alcohol, 56*, 161–167.

Drisko, J. W. (1997). Strengthening qualitative studies and reports: Standards to promote academic integrity. *Journal of Social Work Education, 33*, 185–197.

Duehn, W. D. (1985). Practice and research. In R. M. Grinnell, Jr. (Ed.), *Social work research and evaluation* (2nd ed., pp. 19–48). Itasca, IL: Peacock.

Duncan, G., Brooks-Gunn, J., & Klebanov, P. (1994). Economic deprivation and early childhood development. *Child Development, 65*, 296–318.

Dunn, C. M., & Chadwick, G. L. (2002). *Protecting study volunteers in research: A manual for investigative sites*. Boston: CenterWatch.

Easterbrook, P. J., Berlin, J. A., Gopalan, R., & Mathews, D. R. (1991). Publication bias in clinical research. *Lancet, 337*, 867–872.

Eichler, M. (1988). *Nonsexist research methods: A practical guide*. Boston: Allen & Unwin.

Engel, R. J. (1988). *The dynamics of poverty for the elderly*. Unpublished doctoral dissertation, School of Social Work, University of Wisconsin, Madison.

Engel, R. J., Welsh, R., & Lewis, L. (2000). An evaluation of orientation and mobility training and rehabilitation teaching: Improving the well-being of vision-impaired older adults. *Re:View, 32*, 67–76.

Engram, E. (1982). Methodological problems in the study of the Black family. In E. Engram (Ed.), *Science, myth, and reality: The Black family in one-half century of research* (pp. 78–87). Westport, CT: Greenwood.

Ensel, W., Peek, K., Lin, N., & Lai, G. (1996). Stress in the life course: A life history approach. *Journal of Aging and Health, 8*, 389–416.

Epstein, I. (1996). In quest of a research-based model for clinical practice: Or, why can't a social worker be more like a researcher? *Social Work Research, 20*, 97–100.

Erikson, E. (1980). Identity and the life cycle. New York: Norton.

Esterberg, K. (1994). Being lesbian and being in love: Constructing identity through relationships. *Journal of Gay and Lesbian Social Services, 1*, 57–82.

Ettelbrick, P. L. (1996). Legal issues in health care for lesbians and gays. *Journal of Gay and Lesbian Social Services, 5*, 93–109.

Eyberg, S., & Pincus, D. (1999). *Eyberg Child Behavior Inventory and Sutter-Eyberg Student Behavior Inventory: Revised*. Odessa, FL: Psychological Assessment Resources.

Fabricant, M. (1982). *Juveniles in the family courts*. Lexington, MA: Lexington.

Federal Policy for the Protection of Human Subjects, 55 *Federal Register* 28,003 (June 18, 1991). (codified at 54 C.F.R. pt. 46).

Field, M., & Lohr, K. (Eds.). (1990). *Clinical practice guidelines*. Washington, DC: National Academy Press.

Fischer, J., & Corcoran, K. (2007). *Measures for clinical practice and research: A sourcebook* (4th ed., 2 vols.). New York: Oxford University Press.

Fisher, L., Goldschmidt, R. H., Hays, R. B., & Catania, J. A. (1993). Families of homosexual men: Their knowledge and support regarding sexual orientation and HIV disease. *Journal of the American Board of Family Practice, 6*, 25–32.

Fitzpatrick, J. L., Sanders, J. R., & Worthen, B. R. (2004). *Program evaluation: Alternative approaches and practical guidelines* (3rd ed.). White Plains, NY: Longman.

Fixsen, D. L., Naoom, S. F., Blase, K. A., Friedman, R. M., & Wallace, F. (2005). *Implementation research: A synthesis of the literature*. University of South Florida, Louis de la Parte Florida Mental Health Institute, the National Implementation Research Network (FMHI Publication No. 231). Florida Mental Health Institute: Tampa, FL.

Folkman, S., Chesney, Pollack, L., & Phillips, C. (1992). Stress, coping, and high-risk sexual behavior. *Health Psychology, 11*, 218–222.

Forero, J. (2000a, July 28). Census takers say supervisors fostered filing of false data. *New York Times*, p. A21.

Forero, J. (2000b, June 12). Census takers top '90 efforts in New York City, with more to go. *New York Times*, p. A29.

Fortune, A. E. (1999). Intervention research [Editorial]. *Social Work Research, 23*, 2–3.

Fowler, F. J. (1988). *Survey research methods* (Rev. ed.). Thousand Oaks, CA: Sage.

Fowler, F. J. (1995). *Improving survey questions: Design and evaluation.* Thousand Oaks, CA: Sage.

Franklin, C., & Ballan, M. (2005). Reliability and validity in qualitative research. In R. M. Grinnell, Jr., & Y. A. Unrau (Eds.), *Social work research and evaluation: Quantitative and qualitative approaches* (7th ed., pp. 438–449). New York: Oxford University Press.

Franklin, C., & Jordan, C. (1997). Qualitative approaches to the generation of knowledge. In R. M. Grinnell, Jr. (Ed.), *Social work research and evaluation: Quantitative and qualitative approaches* (5th ed., pp. 106–140). Itasca, IL: Peacock.

Fraser, M. (1996). Aggressive behavior in childhood and early adolescence: An ecological-developmental perspective on youth violence, *Social Work, 41*, 347–361.

Fraser, M., Taylor, M. J., Jackson, R., & O'Jack, J. (1991). Social work and science: Many ways of knowing? *Social Work Research and Abstracts, 27*(4), 5–15.

Gambrill, E. (1997). *Social work practice: A critical thinker's guide.* New York: Oxford University Press.

Gambrill, E. (1999). Evidence-based practice: An alternative to authority-based practice. *Families in Society, 80*, 341–350.

Gambrill, E. (2001). Social work: An authority-based profession. *Research on Social Work Practice, 11*, 166–175.

Gambrill, E. (2003). Evidence-based practice: Sea change or the emperor's new clothes? *Journal of Social Work Education, 39*, 3–23.

Gambrill, E. (2005). *Critical thinking in clinical practice.* Hoboken, NJ: Wiley.

Garcia-Preto, N. (2005). Latino families: An overview. In M. McGoldrick, J. Giordano, & L. Garcia-Preto (Eds.), *Ethnicity and family therapy* (3rd ed., pp. 153–165). New York: Guilford.

Garnets, L. D., & Kimmel, D. C. (1993). Introduction: Lesbian and gay male dimensions in the psychological study of human diversity. In L. D. Garnets & D. C. Kimmel (Eds.), *Psychological perspectives on lesbian and gay male experiences* (pp. 1–51). New York: Columbia University Press.

Garrett, G., & Schutt, R. (1990). Homelessness in Massachusetts: Description and analysis. In J. Momeni (Ed.), *Homeless in the United States: State surveys* (pp. 73–90). New York: Greenwood.

Geismar, L. L., & Wood, K. M. (1982). Evaluating practice: Science as faith. *Social Casework, 63*, 266–272.

Gelfund, H., & Walker, C. (2000). *Mastering APA style: Student's workbook and training guide* (2nd ed.). Hyattsville, MD: APA Publications.

Gibbs, L. E. (2003). *Evidence based practice for the helping professions: A practical guide with integrated multimedia.* Pacific Grove, CA: Brooks/Cole-Thompson Learning.

Gibbs, L. E., & Gambrill, E. (2002). Evidence-based practice: Counterarguments to objections. *Research on Social Work Practice, 12*, 452–476.

Gilbert, J. M. (2003*). Principles and recommended standards for cultural competence education of health care professionals.* Los Angeles: California Endowment.

Ginsberg, L. H. (2001). *Social work evaluation: Principles and methods.* Boston: Allyn & Bacon.

Glass, G. V. (1976). Primary, secondary, and meta-analysis. *Educational Researcher, 5*, 3–8.

Gleick, J. (1990, July 15). The census: Why we can't count. *New York Times Magazine*, pp. 22–26, 54.

Gochros, H. L. (1978). Counseling gay husbands. *Journal of Sex Education and Therapy, 4*, 6–10.

Goicoechea-Balbona, A., Barnaby, C., Ellis, I., & Foxworth, V. (2000). AIDS: The development of a gender appropriate research intervention. *Social Work in Health Care, 30*(3), 19–37.

Golden, C. (1996). What's in a name? Sexual self-identification among women. In R. C. Savin-Williams & K. A. Cohen (Eds.), *The lives of lesbians, gays, and bisexuals: Children to adults* (pp. 229–249). Ft. Worth, TX: Harcourt Brace.

Goldfinger, S. M., & Schutt, R. K. (1996). Comparisons of clinicians' housing recommendations and preferences of homeless mentally ill persons. *Psychiatric Services, 47*, 412–421.

Goldman, H. H., & Azrin, S. T. (2003). Public policy and evidence-based practice. *Psychiatric Clinics of North America, 26*, 899–917.

Goldman, H. H., Ganju, V., Drake, R. E., Gorman, P., Hogan, M., Hyde, P. S., & Morgan, O. (2001). Policy implications for implementing evidence-based practices. *Psychiatric Services, 52*, 1591–1597.

Goleman, D. (1993, September 7). Pollsters enlist psychologists in quest for unbiased results. *New York Times*, pp. C1, C11.

Gordon, R. (1992). *Basic interviewing skills.* Itasca, IL: Peacock.

Gottman, J. M. (1979). *Marital interaction*. New York: Academic Press.

Gouldner, A. W. (1970). *The coming crisis of Western sociology*. New York: Basic Books.

GRADE Working Group. (2004). Grading quality of evidence and strength of recommendations. *British Medical Journal, 328*, 1490–1498.

Gray, J. A. (2001). *Evidence-based healthcare* (2nd ed.). New York: Churchill Livingstone.

Greene, B. (1994). Ethnic-minority lesbians and gays: Mental health and treatment issues. *Journal of Consulting and Clinical Psychology, 62*, 243–251.

Greenhalgh, R. (2001). *How to read a paper: The basics of evidence based medicine (systematic reviews and meta-analyses)*. London: BMJ Books.

Grinnell, F. (1987). *The scientific attitude*. Boulder, CO: Westview.

Grinnell, R. M., Jr., & Williams, M. (1990). *Research in social work: A primer*. Itasca, IL: Peacock.

Grinnell, R. M., Jr., Williams, M., & Tutty, L. M. (1997). Case-level evaluation. In R. M. Grinnell, Jr. (Ed.), *Social work research and evaluation: Quantitative and qualitative approaches* (5th ed., pp. 529–559). Itasca, IL: Peacock.

Grisso, T. (1996). Voluntary consent to research participation in the institutional context. In B. H. Stanley, J. E. Seiber, & G. B. Melton (Eds.), *Research ethics: A psychological approach* (pp. 203–224). Lincoln: University of Nebraska Press.

Groves, R. M. (1989). *Survey errors and survey costs*. New York: Wiley.

Groves, R. M., & Couper, M. P. (1998). *Nonresponse in household interview surveys*. New York: Wiley.

Groves, R. M, & Kahn, R. L. (1979). *Surveys by telephone: A national comparison with personal interviews*. New York: Academic Press.

Gruenewald, P. J., Treno, A. J., Taff, G., & Klitzner, M. (1997). *Measuring community indicators: A systems approach to drug and alcohol problems*. Thousand Oaks, CA: Sage.

Guba, E. G. (1981). Criteria for assessing the trustworthiness of naturalistic studies. *Educational Communication and Technology Journal, 29*(2), 75–91.

Guilford, W. P. (2001). The origins of informed consent: The International Scientific Commission on Medical War Crimes, and the Nuremberg Code. *Bulletin of the History of Medicine, 75*, 37–71.

Hall, J. A., Tickle-Degnen, L., Rosenthal, R., & Mosteller, F. (1994). Hypotheses and problems in research synthesis. In H. Cooper & L. V. Hedges (Eds.), *The handbook of research synthesis* (pp. 17–28). New York: Russell Sage Foundation.

Hann, D., Winter, K., & Jacobsen, P. (1999). Measurement of depressive symptoms in cancer patients: Evaluation of the Center for Epidemiological Studies depression scale (CES-D). *Journal of Psychosomatic Research, 46*, 4387–4443.

Hare, J. (1994). Concerns and issues faced by families headed by a lesbian couple. *Families in Society, 75*, 27–35.

Harry, J. (1990). A probability sample of gay males. *Journal of Homosexuality, 19*, 89–104.

Hart, C. (1998). *Doing a literature review*. Thousands Oaks, CA: Sage.

Hartman, A. (1990). Many ways of knowing [Editorial]. *Social Work, 35*, 3–4.

Haslam, N. (1997). Evidence that male sexual orientation is a matter of degree. *Journal of Personality and Social Psychology, 73*, 862–870.

Hatry, H. P., Cowan, J., Weiner, K., & Lampkin, L. M. (2003). *Developing community-wide outcome indicators for specific services*. Washington, DC: Urban Institute.

Hatry, H. P., Wholey, J. S., & Newcomer, K. E. (2004). Other issues and trends in evaluation. In J. S. Wholey, H. P. Hatry, & K. E. Newcomer (Eds.), *Handbook of practical program evaluation* (2nd ed., pp. 670–684). San Francisco: Wiley.

Hauser, D. *Five years of abstinence-only-until-marriage education: Assessing the impact*. Washington, DC: Advocates for Youth.

Hawker, S., Payne, S., Kerr, C., Hardey, M., & Powell, J. (2002). Appraising the evidence: Reviewing disparate data systematically. *Qualitative Health Research, 12*, 1284–1299.

Haynes, B., Devereaux, P., & Guyatt, G. (2002). Clinical expertise in the era of evidence-based medicine and patient choice. *APC Journal Club, 136*, A11–A14.

Hays, D., & Samuels, A. (1989). Heterosexual women's perceptions of their marriages to bisexual or homosexual men. *Journal of Homosexuality, 18*, 81–100.

Heckathorn, D. (1997). Respondent-driven sampling: A new approach to the study of hidden populations. *Social Problems, 44*, 174–199.

Hedges, L. V. (1994). Fixed effects model. In C. Harris & H. Larry (Eds.), *The handbook of research synthesis* (pp. 285–299). New York: Russell Sage Foundation.

Hedges, L. V., & Olkin, I. (1985). *Statistical models for meta-analysis*. New York: Academic Press.

Heineman, M. B. (1981). The obsolete scientific imperative in social work research. *Social Service Review, 55*, 371–397.

Herek, G. M. (1993). Documenting prejudice against lesbians and gays on campus: The Yale Sexual Orientation Survey. *Journal of Homosexuality, 25*, 15–30.

Herek, G. M., Gillis, J. R., Cogan, J. C., & Glunt, E. K. (1997). Hate crime victimization among lesbian, gay, and bisexual adults: Prevalence, psychological correlates, and methodological issues. *Journal of Interpersonal Violence, 12*, 195–215.

Herek, G. M., Kimmel, D. C., Amaro, H., & Melton, G. G. (1993). Avoiding heterosexist bias in psychological research. *American Psychologist, 46*, 957–963.

Higgins, J. P. T., & Green, S. (Eds.). (2005). Cochrane handbook for systematic reviews of interventions 4.2.5 [updated May 2005]. In *The Cochrane Library, Issue 3*. Chichester, UK: Wiley.

Holmes, S. A. (1994, May 16). Census officials plan big changes in gathering data. *New York Times*, pp. A1, A13.

Holmes, S. A. (1996, February 29). In a first, 2000 census is to use sampling. *New York Times*, p. A18.

Holmes, S. A. (2000, May 4). Stronger response by minorities helps improve census reply rate. *New York Times*, pp. A1, A22.

Holosko, M. J. (2001). An overview of qualitative methods. In B. Thyer (Ed.), *Handbook of social work research methods* (pp. 263–273). Thousand Oaks, CA: Sage.

Holosko, M. J. (2006a). *A primer for critiquing social research: A student guide*. Belmont, CA: Thomson/Nelson, Brooks/Cole.

Holosko, M. J. (2006b). A suggested authors' checklist for submitting manuscripts to *Research on Social Work Practice. Research on Social Work Practice, 16*, 449–454.

Holosko, M. J., & Holosko, D. A. (1999). What have we learned from articles published in the *Family Preservation Journal? Family Preservation Journal, 4*, 1–12.

Holosko, M. J., & Leslie, D. (1997). Obstacles to conducting empirically-based practice. In J. Wodarski & B. Thyer (Eds.), *Handbook of empirical social work practice: Vol. 2. Social problems and practice issues* (pp. 433–451). New York: Wiley.

Holsti, O. (1969). *Content analysis for the social sciences and humanities*. Reading, MA: Addison-Wesley.

Howard, M. O., McMillen, C. J., & Pollio, D. E. (2003). Teaching evidence-based practice: Toward a new paradigm for social work education. *Research on Social Work Practice, 13*, 234–259.

Howe, K., & Eisenhart, M. (1990). Standards for qualitative (and quantitative) research: A prolegomenon. *Educational Researcher, 19*(4), 2–9.

Hox, J. (2002). *Multilevel analysis: Techniques and applications*. Mahwah, NJ: Erlbaum.

Huber, J., & Clandinin, D. J. (2002). Ethical dilemmas in relational narrative inquiry with children. *Qualitative Inquiry, 8*, 785–803.

Hudson, W. W. (1978). First axioms of treatment. *Social Work, 23*, 65–66.

Hunter, J. E., & Schmidt, F. L. (1990). General criticisms of meta-analysis. In J. E. Hunter & F. L. Schmidt (Eds.), *Methods of meta-analysis: Correcting error and bias in research findings* (pp. 506–534). Thousand Oaks, CA: Sage.

Hunter, S., Shannon, C., Knox, J., & Martin, J. (1998). *Lesbian, gay, and bisexual youths and adults: Knowledge for human services practice*. Thousand Oaks, CA: Sage.

Hussain-Gambles, M., Atkin, K., & Leese, B. (2004). Why ethnic minority groups are under-represented in clinical trials: A review of the literature. *Health and Social Care in the Community, 12*, 382–388.

Hyman, H. H. (1954). *Interviewing in social research*. Chicago: University of Chicago Press.

Institute of Medicine. (2000). *Crossing the quality chasm: A new health system for the 21st century*. Washington, DC: National Academy Press.

Jadad, A. (1998). *Randomized controlled trials: A user's guide*. London: BMJ Publishing.

Jadad, A. R., Haynes, R. B., Hunt, D., & Browman, G. P. (2000). The Internet and evidence-based decision-making: A needed synergy for efficient knowledge management in health care. *Canadian Medical Association Journal, 162*, 362–365.

Jenkins, S. (1975). Collecting data by questionnaire and interview. In N. A. Polansky (Ed.), *Social work research: Methods for the helping professions* (Rev. ed., pp. 140–155). Chicago: University of Chicago Press.

Jensen, P. S., Hoagwood, K., & Trickett, E. J. (1999). Ivory towers or earthen trenches? Community collaborations to foster real-world research. *Applied Developmental Science, 3*, 206–213.

Johnson, L. (1997). Three decades of black family empirical research: Challenges for the 21st century. In H. McAdoo (Ed.), *Black families* (3rd ed., pp. 94–114). Thousand Oaks, CA: Sage.

Jones, J. H. (1993). *Bad blood: The Tuskegee syphilis experiment*. New York: Free Press.

Jorgensen, D. L. (1989). *Participant observation: A methodology for human studies*. Thousand Oaks, CA: Sage.

Jorgensen, S. R., Potts, V., & Camp, B. (1993). Project Taking Charge: Six-month follow-up of a pregnancy prevention program for early adolescents. *Family Relations, 42,* 401–406.

Kadushin, A., & Kadushin, G. (1997). *The social work interview: A guide for human service professionals* (4th ed.). New York: Columbia University Press.

Kagawa-Singer, M. (2000). Improving the validity and generalizability of studies with underserved U.S. populations expanding the research paradigm. *Annals of Epidemiology, 10,* 92–103.

Kagawa-Singer, M. (2001). From genes to social science: Impact of the simplistic interpretation of race, ethnicity, and culture on cancer outcome. *Cancer, 91,* 226–232.

Kagawa-Singer, M., & Chung, R. C. Y. (2002). Cultural relevance of diagnostic categories: A conceptual discussion. In K. S. Kurasaki, S. Okazaki, & S. Sue (Eds.), *Asian American mental health: Assessment theories and methods* (pp. 87–96). San Francisco: Jossey-Bass.

Kagawa-Singer, M., & Kassim-Lakha, S. (2003). A strategy to reduce cross-cultural miscommunication and increase the likelihood of improving health outcomes. *Academic Medicine, 78,* 577–587.

Kagay, M. R., & Elder, J. (1992, October 9). Numbers are no problem for pollsters. Words are. *New York Times,* p. E5.

Katz, D. (1942). Do interviewers bias polls? *Public Opinion Quarterly, 6,* 248–268.

Kelaher, M., Ross, M. W., Rohrsheim, R., Drury, M., & Clarkson, A. (1994). Dominant situational determinants of sexual risk behavior in gays. *AIDS, 8,* 101–105.

Kenney, C. (1987, August 30). They've got your number. *Boston Globe Magazine,* pp. 12, 46–56, 60.

Kettner, P. K., Moroney, R. K., & Martin, L. L. (in press). *Designing and managing programs: An effectiveness-based approach* (3rd ed.). Thousand Oaks, CA: Sage.

Khin-Maung-Gyi. F. A., & Whalen, M. D. (2002). Recruitment of research subjects. In R. Amdur & E. Bankert (Eds.), *Institutional review board: Management and function* (pp. 176–179). Sudbury, MA: Jones & Bartlett.

Kifner, J. (1994, May 20). Pollster finds error on Holocaust doubts. *New York Times,* p. A12.

Klein, F., Sepekoff, B., & Wolf, T. J. (1985). Sexual orientation: A multi-variable dynamic process. *Journal of Homosexuality, 11,* 35–49.

Koeske, G. (1994). Some recommendations for improving measurement validation in social work research. *Journal of Social Service Research, 18,* 43–72.

Kohut, A. (1988). Polling: Does more information lead to better understanding? *American Sociological Review, 52,* 713–731.

Kraemer, H., & Thiemann, S. (1987). *How many subjects? Statistical power analysis in research.* Thousand Oaks, CA: Sage.

Krout, J. A. (1985). Service awareness among the elderly. *Journal of Gerontological Social Work, 9,* 7–19.

Kvale, S. (1996). *Inter Views: An introduction to qualitative research interviewing.* Thousand Oaks, CA: Sage.

• Labaw, P. J. (1980). *Advanced questionnaire design.* Cambridge, MA: ABT Books.

Laird, J. (2003). Lesbian and gay families. In F. Walsh. (Ed.), *Normal family processes* (3rd ed., pp. 176–209). New York: Guilford.

Laird, S. E. (2003). Evaluating social work outcomes in sub-Saharan Africa. *Qualitative Social Work, 2,* 251–270.

Lampkin, L. M., & Hatry, H. P. (2003). *Key steps in outcome management.* Washington, DC: Urban Institute.

Larsson, L. C. (1998). Glossary of library and database terms. *Creating a serials database in Access: A primer for resource center managers.* Retrieved August 20, 2006, from http://faculty.washington.edu/~larsson/conf/aiha98/primer/glossary.htm

LaSalla, M. (2001). Monogamous or not: Understanding and counseling gay male couples. *Families in Society, 82,* 605–611.

LaVeist, T. A. (2000). On the study of race, racism, and health: A shift from description to explanation. *International Journal of Health Services, 30,* 217–219.

Lavrakas, P. J. (1987). *Telephone survey methods: Sampling, selection, and supervision.* Thousand Oaks, CA: Sage.

LeCroy, C. W., & Goodwin, C. (1988). New directions in teaching social work methods: A content analysis of course outlines. *Journal of Social Work Education, 19,* 43–49.

Lee, J., & Twaite, J. A. (1997). Open adoption and adoptive mothers: Attitudes toward birthmothers, adopted children, and parenting. *American Journal of Orthopsychiatry, 67,* 576–584.

Lee, W. (2003). *Evidence-based practice: Efforts to integrate research into practice.* Unpublished manuscript, Columbia University School of Social Work, New York.

Leung, P., & Cheung, M. (2006). *Journals in social work and related disciplines.* Houston, TX: Graduate College of Social Work, University of Houston.

Levin, H. M., & McEwan, P. J. (2000). *Cost-effectiveness analysis: Methods and applications* (2nd ed.). Thousand Oaks, CA: Sage.

Levy, P. S., & Lemeshow, S. (1999). *Sampling of populations: Methods and applications* (3rd ed.). New York: Wiley.

Lewis, O. (1966). *La vida: A Puerto Rican family in the culture of poverty.* New York: Random House.

Liang, J., Tran, T. V., Krause, N., & Markides, K. S. (1989). Generational differences in the structure of the CES-D scale in Mexican Americans. *Journal of Gerontology, 44*, 110–120.

Lincoln, Y. S. (1998). From understanding to action: New imperatives, new criteria, new methods for interpretive researchers. *Theory and Research in Education, 26*(1), 12–29.

Lincoln, Y. S. (2001). Varieties of validity: Quality in qualitative research. In J. C. Smart & W. G. Tierney (Eds.), *Higher education: Handbook of theory and research* (Vol. 16, pp. 25–72). New York: Agathon Press.

Lincoln, Y. S., & Guba, E. G. (1985). *Naturalistic inquiry.* Thousand Oaks, CA: Sage.

Lincoln, Y. S., & Guba, E. G. (2000). Paradigmatic controversies, contradictions, and emerging confluences. In N. K. Denzin & Y. S. Lincoln (Eds.), *Handbook of qualitative research* (2nd ed., pp. 163–188). Thousand Oaks, CA: Sage.

Link, B., Phelan, J., Stueve, A., Moore, R., Brenahan, M., & Struening, E. (1996). Public attitudes and beliefs about homeless people. In J. Baumohl (Ed.), *Homelessness in America* (pp. 143–148). Phoenix, AZ: Oryx Press.

Lipsey, M. W., & Wilson, D. B. (2001). *Practical meta-analysis.* Thousand Oaks, CA: Sage.

Litwin, M. S. (1995). *How to measure survey reliability and validity.* Thousand Oaks, CA: Sage.

Lomawaima, K. T., & McCarty, T. L. (2002). *Reliability, validity, and authenticity in American Indian and Alaska native research. ERIC Digest* (ERIC Document Reproduction Service No. ED470951). Charleston, WV: ERIC Clearinghouse on Rural Education and Small Schools.

Loth, R. (1992, October 25). Bush may be too far back, history of polls suggests. *Boston Globe*, p. 19.

Luna, I., Torres de Ardon, E., Lim, Y. M., Cromwell, S., Phillips, L., & Russell, C. (1996). The relevance of familism in cross-cultural studies of family caregiving. *Journal of Nursing Research, 18*, 267–283.

Luster, T., & McAdoo, H. (1994). Factors related to the achievement and adjustment of young African American children. *Child Development, 65*, 1080–1094.

Macgowan, M. J. (2004). Psychosocial treatment of youth suicide: A systematic review of the research. *Research on Social Work Practice, 14*, 147–162.

Mackelprang, R. W., Ray, J. A., & Hernandez-Peck, M. (1996). Social work education and sexual orientation: Faculty, student, and curriculum issues. *Journal of Gay and Lesbian Social Services, 5*, 17–31.

Mallon, G. P. (1997). Knowledge for practice with gay and lesbian persons. In G. P. Mallon (Ed.), *Foundations of social work practice with lesbian and gay persons* (pp. 1–30). Binghamton, NY: Harrington Park Press.

Maluccio, A. N. (1979). *Learning from clients.* New York: Free Press.

Mandara, J., & Murray, C. (2000). Effects of marital status, income, and family functioning on African American adolescent self-esteem. *Journal of Family Psychology, 14*, 475–490.

Mangione, T. W. (1995). *Mail surveys: Improving the quality.* Thousand Oaks, CA: Sage.

Manuel, R. (2000). *The conceptualization and measurement of race: Confusion and beyond.* Ann Arbor: University of Michigan Institute for Social Research.

Marin, G., & Marin, B. V. (1991). *Research with Hispanic populations.* Thousand Oaks, CA: Sage.

Martin, A., & Hetrick, E. (1988). The stigmatization of the gay and lesbian adolescent. In M. Ross (Ed.), *The treatment of homosexuals with mental health disorders* (pp. 163–184). New York: Harrington Park Press.

Martin, J. (1997). Political aspects of mental health treatment. In T. R. Watkins & J. W. Callicutt (Eds.), *Mental health policy and practice today* (pp. 32–48). Thousand Oaks, CA: Sage.

Martin, J., & Knox, J. (1997). Loneliness and sexual risk behavior in gays. *Psychological Reports, 81*, 815–825.

Mathews, B. S. (2004). Gray literature: Resources for locating unpublished research [Electronic version]. *College and Research Libraries News*, 65. Retrieved August 20, 2006, from http://www.ala.org/ala/acrl/acrlpubs/crlnews/backissues2004/march04/graylit.htm

Matt, G. E. (1997). Drawing generalized causal inferences based on meta-analysis. In W. J. Bukoski (Ed.), *Meta-analysis of drug abuse prevention programs* (NIDA Report No. 170, pp. 165–182). Rockville, MD: National Institute on Drug Abuse.

Maxwell, J. A. (1992). Understanding and validity in qualitative research. *Harvard Educational Review, 62*, 279–300.

McAdoo, H. (1997a). The roles of African American fathers in the socialization of their children. In H. McAdoo (Ed.), *Black families* (3rd ed., pp. 183–197). Thousand Oaks, CA: Sage.

McAdoo, H. (1997b). Upward mobility across generations in African American families. In H. McAdoo (Ed.), *Black families* (3rd ed., pp. 139–162). Thousand Oaks, CA: Sage.

McClelland, D. C. (1961). *The achieving society.* New York: Free Press.

McKee, M., Britton, A., Black, N., McPherson, K., Sanderson, C., & Bain, C. (1999). Interpreting the evidence: Choosing between randomized and non-randomized studies. *British Medical Journal, 319*, 312–315.

McLoyd, V., Cauce, A., Takeuchi, D., & Wilson, L. (2000). Marital processes and parental socialization in families of color: A decade review of research. *Journal of Marriage and the Family, 62*, 1070–1093.

McNeill, T. (2006). Evidence-based practice in an age of relativism: Toward a model for practice. *Social Work, 51*, 147–156.

Merton, R., Fiske, M., & Kendall, P. (1956). *The focused interview*. Glencoe, IL: Free Press.

Messinger, L., & Topal, M. (1997). Are you married? Two sexual-minority students' perspectives on field placement. *Affilia, 12*, 106–113.

Meyer, C. H. (1996). My son the scientist. *Social Work Research, 20*, 101–104.

Miles, M. B., & Huberman, A. M. (1994). *Qualitative data analysis: An expanded sourcebook* (2nd ed.). Thousand Oaks, CA: Sage.

Milgram, S. (1965). Some conditions of obedience and disobedience to authority. *Human Relations, 18*, 57–75.

Milgram, S. (1974). *Obedience to authority: An experimental view*. New York: HarperCollins.

Miller, D. C. (1991). *Handbook of research design and social measurement* (5th ed.). Thousand Oaks, CA: Sage.

Mirowsky, J. (1995). Age and the sense of control. *Social Psychology Quarterly, 58*, 31–43.

Mirowsky, J., & Hu, P. N. (1996). Physical impairment and the diminishing effects of income. *Social Forces, 74*, 1073–1096.

Mirowsky, J., & Ross, C. E. (1991). Eliminating defense and agreement bias from measures of the sense of control: A 2 X 2 index. *Social Psychology Quarterly, 54*, 127–145.

Mirowsky, J., & Ross, C. E. (1992). Age and depression. *Journal of Health and Social Behavior, 33*, 187–205.

Mirowsky, J., & Ross, C. E. (1999). Economic hardship across the life course. *American Sociological Review, 64*, 548–569.

Mishler, E. G. (1991). *Research interviewing: Context and narrative*. Cambridge, MA: Harvard University Press.

Mitchell, C. G. (1999). Treating anxiety in a managed care setting: A controlled comparison of medication alone versus medication plus. *Research on Social Work Practice, 9*, 188–200.

Monette, D. R., Sullivan, T. J., & DeJong, C. R. (2005). *Applied social research: A tool for human services*. Belmont, CA: Brooks/Cole-Thompson Learning.

Moran, M. R. (1992). Effects of sexual orientation similarity and counselor experience level of gays' and lesbians' perceptions of counselors. *Journal of Counseling Psychology, 39*, 247–251.

Morell, C. (2000). Saying no: Women's experiences with reproductive refusal. *Feminism and Psychology, 10*, 313–322.

Morris, S. B., & DeShon, R. P. (2002). Combining effect size estimates in meta-analysis with repeated measures and independent-groups designs. *Psychological Methods, 7*, 105–125.

Morrow, D. F. (1996). Heterosexism: Hidden dimension in social work education. *Journal of Gay and Lesbian Social Services, 5*, 1–16.

Mosteller, F., & Colditz, G.A. (1996). Understanding research synthesis (meta-analysis). *Annual Review of Public Health, 17*, 1–23.

Moyer, J. (1993, 1999). Step-by-step guide to oral history. Retrieved August 20, 2006, from http://www.dohistory.org/on_your_own/toolkit/oralHistory.html

Mueser, K. T., Yamold, P. R., Levinson, D. F., Singhy, H., Bellack, A. S., Kee, K., Morrison, R. L., & Yadalam, K. G. (1990). Prevalence of substance abuse in schizophrenia: Demographic and clinical correlates. *Schizophrenia Bulletin, 16*, 31–56.

Mufson, L., Dorta, K. P., Wickramaratne, P., Nomura, Y., Olfson, M., & Weissman, M. M. (2004). A randomized effectiveness trial of interpersonal psychotherapy for depressed adolescents. *Archives of General Psychiatry, 61*, 577–584.

Mullen, E. J. (2006). Facilitating practitioner use of evidence-based practice. In A. R. Roberts & K. Yeager (Eds.), *Foundations of evidence-based social work practice* (pp. 152–159). New York: Oxford University Press.

Mullen, E. J. (in press). Evidence-based policy and social work in healthcare. *Social Work in Mental Health (special issue: Social Work and Mental Health, a Global Research and Practice Perspective), 6*(2, 3, & 4).

Mullen, E. J., Bellamy, J. L., & Bledsoe, S. E. (2005). Implementing evidence-based social work practice. In P. Sommerfeld (Ed.), *Evidence-based social work: Towards a new professionalism?* (pp. 149–172). Berlin: Peter Lang.

Mullen, E. J., Shlonsky, A., Bledsoe, S. E., & Bellamy, J. L. (2005). From concept to implementation: Challenges facing evidence based social work. *Evidence and Policy: A Journal of Debate, Research, and Practice, 1*, 61–84.

Mullen, E. J., & Streiner, D. L. (2004). The evidence for and against evidence based practice. *Brief Treatment and Crisis Intervention, 4,* 111–121.

Myers, L. L., & Thyer, B. A. (1997). Should social work clients have the right to effective treatment? *Social Work, 42,* 288–299.

Nardi, P. M., & Sherrod, D. (1994). Friendship in the lives of gays and lesbians. *Journal of Social and Personal Relationships, 11,* 185–199.

National Association of Social Workers. (1999). Code of Ethics *of the National Association of Social Workers.* Washington, DC: Author.

National Association of Social Workers. (2005). *NASW standards for clinical social work in social work practice.* Washington, DC: Author.

National Commission for the Protection of Human Subjects of Biomedical and Behavioral Research. (1978). *The Belmont Report: Ethical principles and guidelines for the protection of human subjects of research.* DHEW Publication No. (OS) 78–0013 and (OS) 78–0014.4, 18 Apr 1979. Retrieved October 10, 2006, from http://ohst.od .nih.gov/mpa/belmont.php3

National Geographic Society. (2000). *Survey 2000.* Retrieved January 21, 2005, from http://survey2000. nationalgeographic.com

National Health and Medical Research Council. (1995). *Guidelines for the development and implementation of clinical guidelines.* Canberra: Australian Government Publishing Service.

National Institute of Alcohol Abuse and Alcoholism. (1995). College students and drinking. *Alcohol Alert, 29,* 1–6.

National Opinion Research Center. (1992). *The NORC general social survey: Questions and answers* (National Data Program for the Social Sciences). Chicago: Author.

Navarro, M. (1990, March 25). Census questionnaire: Link to democracy and source of data. *New York Times,* p. 36.

Neuman, W. L. (2000). *Social research methods: Qualitative and quantitative approaches* (5th ed.). Boston: Allyn & Bacon.

Neuman, W. L. (2006). *Social research methods: Qualitative and quantitative approaches* (6th ed.). Needham Heights, MA: Allyn & Bacon.

Neuman, W. L. (2007). *Basics of social research: Qualitative and quantitative approaches* (2nd ed.). Boston: Allyn & Bacon.

Newmann, J. P. (1987). Gender differences in vulnerability to depression. *Social Service Review, 61,* 447–468.

Newmann, J. P. (1989). Aging and depression. *Psychology and Aging, 4,* 150–65.

Newmann, J. P. (2005). *Using cost-effectiveness analysis to improve health care.* New York: Oxford University Press.

Nie, N. H., & Erbring, L. (2000). *Internet and society: A preliminary report.* Palo Alto, CA: Stanford Institute for the Quantitative Study of Society.

Nugent, W. R., Sieppert, J. D., & Hudson, W. W. (2001). *Practice evaluation for the 21st century.* Belmont, CA: Brooks/Cole.

Oakes, J. M. (2002). Risks and wrongs in social science research: An evaluator's guide to the IRB. *Evaluation Review, 26,* 443–479.

O'Brien, K. (1993). Improving survey questionnaires through focus groups. In D. L. Morgan (Ed.), *Successful focus groups: Advancing the state-of-the-art* (pp. 105–117). Thousand Oaks, CA: Sage.

Ogbu, J. (1997). African American education: A cultural-ecological perspective. In H. McAdoo (Ed.), *Black families* (3rd ed., pp. 234–250). Thousand Oaks, CA: Sage.

Orshansky, M. (1977). Memorandum for Daniel P. Moynihan. Subject: History of the poverty line. In M. Orshansky (Ed.), *Measure of poverty: Technical paper I: Documentation of background information and rationale for current poverty matrix* (pp. 232–237). Washington, DC: U.S. Department of Health, Education, and Welfare.

Ortega, D. M., & Richey, C. A. (1998). Methodological issues in social work research with depressed women of color. *Journal of Social Service Research, 23,* 47–68.

O'Sullivan, R. G. (2004). *Practicing evaluation: A collaborative approach.* Thousand Oaks, CA: Sage.

Padgett, D. K. (1998). *Qualitative methods in social work research: Challenges and rewards.* Thousand Oaks, CA: Sage.

Patterson, O. (1969). *The sociology of slavery.* Rutherford, NJ: Fairleigh Dickinson University Press.

Patton, M. Q. (1997). *Utilization-focused evaluation.* Thousand Oaks, CA: Sage.

Pawlak, E. J., & Vinter, R. D. (2004). *Designing and planning programs for nonprofit and government organizations.* San Francisco: Wiley.

Pawson, R. (2002). Evidence-based policy: In search of a method. *Evaluation, 8,* 157–181.

Penderhughes, E., Dodege, K., Bates, J., Pettit, G., & Zelli, A. (2000). Discipline responses: Influence of parents' socioeconomic status, ethnicity, beliefs about parenting, stress, and cognitive-emotional processes. *Journal of Family Psychology, 14,* 380–400.

Penka, C. E., & Kirk, S. A. (1991). Practitioner involvement in clinical evaluation. *Social Work, 36,* 513–518.

Perry, P. D. (1997). Realities of the effect size calculation process: Considerations for beginning meta-analysts. In W. J. Bukoski (Ed.), *Meta-analysis of drug abuse preven-*

tion programs (NIDA Report No. 170, pp. 120–128). Rockville, MD: National Institute on Drug Abuse.

Petticrew, M., & Roberts, H. (2003). Evidence, hierarchies, and typologies: Horses for courses. *Journal of Epidemiology of Community Health, 57*, 527–529.

Pinderhuse, D. (2000). Foreword. In Y. A. Assensoh & L. Hanks (Eds.), *Black and multicultural politics in America* (pp. xi–xii). New York: New York University Press.

Pivin, F. F., & Cloward, R. A. (1971). *Regulating the poor: The functions of public welfare.* New York: Vintage Books.

Pollner, M., & Adams, R. E. (1994). The interpersonal context of mental health interviews. *Journal of Health and Social Behavior, 35*, 283–290.

Posavac, E. J., & Carey, R. G. (2007). *Program evaluation: Methods and case studies* (7th ed.). Englewood Cliffs, NJ: Prentice-Hall.

Preskill, H., & Russ-Eft, D. (2004). *Building evaluation capacity.* Thousand Oaks, CA: Sage.

Presser, S., & Blair, J. (1994). Survey pretesting: Do different methods produce different results? *Sociological Methodology, 24*, 73–104.

Purdy, M. (1994, March 12). Bronx mystery: 3rd-rate service for 1st-class mail. *New York Times*, pp. 1, 3.

Putnam, I. (1977). Poverty thresholds: Their history and future development. In M. Orshansky (Ed.), *The measure of poverty: Technical paper I: Documentation of background information and rationale for current poverty matrix* (pp. 272–283). Washington, DC: U.S. Department of Health, Education, and Welfare.

Radloff, L. (1977). The CES-D scale: A self-report depression scale for research in the general population. *Applied Psychological Measurement, 1*, 385–401.

Raines, J. C. (2003). Social workers' countertransference issues with spiritually-similar clients. *Social Work and Christianity, 30*, 256–276.

Raines, J. C., & Massat, C. (2004). Getting published: A guide for the aspiring practitioner. *School Social Work Journal, 29*(1), 1–17.

RAND Corporation. (2006, August 9). History and mission. Retrieved August 20, 2006, from http://www.rand.org/pubs/

Rankin, B., & Quaine, J. (2000). Neighborhood poverty and social isolation of inner-city African American families. *Social Forces, 79*, 139–164.

Reed, J. G., & Baxter, P. M. (2003). *Library use: Handbook for psychology* (3rd ed.). Washington, DC: American Psychological Association.

Reid, W. J. (2002). Knowledge for direct social work practice: An analysis of trends. *Social Service Review, 70*, 6–33.

Reid, W. J., & Shyne, A. (1969). *Brief and extended casework.* New York: Columbia University Press.

Reid, W. J., & Smith, A. D. (1989). *Research in social work* (2nd ed.). New York: Columbia University Press.

Resnicow, K., Braithwaite, R. L., Dilorio, C., & Glanz, K. (2002). Applying theory to culturally diverse and unique populations. In K. Glanz, B. K. Rimer, & F. M. Lewis (Eds.), *Health behavior and health education* (pp. 485–509). San Francisco: Jossey-Bass.

Resnicow, K. T., Baranowski, T., Ahluwalia, J. S., & Braithwaite, R. L. (1999). Cultural sensitivity in public health: Defined and demystified. *Ethnicity and Disease, 9*, 10–21.

Ricciutti, H. (1999). Single parenthood and school readiness in white, black, and Hispanic 6- and 7-year olds. *Journal of Family Psychology, 13*, 450–465.

Ridley, C. R., Mendoza, W., Kanitz, B. E., Angermeier, L., & Zenk, R. (1994). Cultural sensitivity in multicultural counseling: A perceptual schema model. *Journal of Counseling Psychology, 41*, 125–136.

Riedel, M. (2000). *Research strategies for secondary data: A perspective for criminology and criminal justice.* Thousand Oaks, CA: Sage.

Robinson, C. (1998). Blaxploitation and the misrepresentation of liberation. *Race and Class, 40*, 1–12.

Robinson, D., & Rhodes, S. (1946). Two experiments with an anti-Semitism poll. *Journal of Abnormal and Social Psychology, 41*, 136–144.

Rodgers-Farmer, A., & Potocky-Tripodi, M. (2005). Gender, ethnicity, and race matters. In R. M. Grinnell, Jr., & Y. Unrau (Eds.), *Social work research and evaluation: Quantitative and qualitative approaches* (7th. ed., pp. 89–94). New York: Oxford University Press.

Rodney, H., Tachia, H., & Rodney, L. (1999). The home environment and delinquency: A study of African American adolescents. *Families in Society, 80*, 551–559.

Rodwell, M. K., & Woody, D., III (1994). Constructivist evaluation: The policy/practice context. In E. Sherman & W. J. Reid (Eds.), *Qualitative research in social work* (pp. 315–327). New York: Columbia University Press.

Rogers, G., & Bouey, E. (1996). Phase two: Collecting your data. In L. M. Tutty, M. A. Rothery, & R. M. Grinnell, Jr. (Eds.), *Qualitative research for social workers: Phases, steps, and tasks* (pp. 50–87). Boston: Allyn & Bacon.

Rosario, C. M. (2003). *Evidence-based practice: Efforts to integrate research into practice.* Unpublished manuscript, Columbia University School of Social Work. New York.

Rosen, A. (1996). The scientific practitioner revisited: Some obstacles and prerequisites for fuller implementation in practice. *Social Work Research, 20,* 105–111.

Rosen, A., & Proctor, E. K. (2003). Practice guidelines and the challenge of effective practice. In A. Rosen & E. K. Proctor (Eds.), *Developing practice guidelines for social work intervention* (pp. 1–14). New York: Columbia University Press.

Rosen, A., Proctor, E., & Staudt, M. (1999). Social work research and the quest for effective practice. *Social Work Research, 23,* 4–14.

Rosenberg, M. (1965). *Society and the adolescent self-image.* Princeton, NJ: Princeton University Press.

Rosenthal, R. (1979). The "file drawer problem" and tolerance for null results. *Psychological Bulletin, 86,* 638–641.

Rosenthal, R. (1984). *Meta-analytic procedures for social research.* Thousand Oaks, CA: Sage.

Rosenthal, R. (1994). *Homeless in paradise: A map of the terrain.* Philadelphia: Temple University Press.

Rosenthal, R. (1994). Parametric measures of effect size. In C. Harris & H. Larry (Eds.), *The handbook of research synthesis* (pp. 97–109). New York: Russell Sage Foundation.

Ross, C. E. (1990). Work, family, and the sense of control: Implications for the psychological well-being of women and men. Proposal submitted to the National Science Foundation, University of Illinois at Urbana.

Ross, C. E., & Bird, C. E. (1994). Sex stratification and health lifestyle: Consequences for men's and women's perceived health. *Journal of Health and Social Behavior, 35,* 161–178.

Ross, C. E., & Van Willigen, M. (1996). Gender, parenthood, and anger. *Journal of Marriage and the Family, 58,* 572–584.

Ross, C. E., & Wu, C. (1995). The links between education and health. *American Sociological Review, 60,* 719–745.

Ross, C. E., & Wu, C. (1996). Education, age, and the cumulative advantage in health. *Journal of Health and Social Behavior, 37,* 104–120.

Rossi, P. H. (1989). *Down and out in America: The origins of homelessness.* Chicago: University of Chicago Press.

Rossi, P. H., Lipsey, M., & Freeman, H. E. (2003). *Evaluation: A systematic approach* (7th ed.). Thousand Oaks, CA: Sage.

Roth, A., & Fonagy, P. (2005) *What works for whom? A critical review of psychotherapy research.* New York: Guilford.

Roth, D. (1990). Homelessness in Ohio: A statewide epidemiological study. In J. Momeni (Ed.), *Homeless in the United States* (Vol. 1, pp. 145–163). New York: Greenwood.

Royce, D., Thyer, B., Padgett, D., & Logan, T. K. (2001). *Program evaluation: An introduction* (3rd ed.). Belmont, CA: Wadsworth.

Rubin, A., & Babbie, E. (2006). *Research methods for social work* (5th ed.). Pacific Grove, CA: Wadsworth.

Rubin, A., Conway, P. G., Patterson, J. K., & Spence, R. T. (1983). Sources of variation in rate of decline of applications to MSW programs. *Journal of Education for Social Work, 19,* 48–58.

Rubin, A., Franklin, C., & Selber, K. (1992). Integrating research and practice into an interviewing skills project: An evaluation. *Journal of Social Work Education, 28,* 141–152.

Rubin, H., & Rubin, I. (1995). *Qualitative interviewing: The art of hearing data.* Thousand Oaks, CA: Sage.

Ruggles, P. (1990). *Drawing the line: Alternative poverty measures and their implications for public policy.* Washington, DC: Urban Institute.

Sackett, D. L., Richardson, W. S., Rosenberg, W., & Haynes, R. B. (1997). *Evidence-based medicine: How to practice and teach EBM.* New York: Churchill Livingstone.

Sackett, D. L., Rosenberg, W. M. C., Muir Gray, J. A., Haynes, R. B., & Richardson, W. S. (1996). Evidence based medicine: What it is and what it isn't: It's about integrating individual clinical expertise and the best external evidence. *British Medical Journal, 31,* 71–72.

Sackett, D. L., Straus, S. E., Richardson, W. S., Rosenberg, W., & Haynes, R. B. (2000). *Evidence based medicine: How to practice and teach EBM* (2nd ed.). New York: Churchill Livingstone.

Schneidman, E. (1985). At the point of no return. *Psychology Today, 19,* 55–58.

Schober, M. F. (1999). Making sense of survey questions. In M. G. Sirken, D. J. Herrmann, S. Schechter, N. Schwartz, J. M. Tanur, & R. Tourangeau (Eds.), *Cognition and survey research* (pp. 77–94). New York: Wiley.

Schulberg, H. C., Saul, M., McClelland, M., Ganguli, W., & Frank, R. (1985). Assessing depression in primary medical and psychiatric practices. *Archives of General Psychiatry, 42,* 1164–1170.

Schuman, H., & Converse, J. M. (1970). The effects of black and white interviewers on black responses. *Public Opinion Quarterly, 35,* 44–68.

Schuman, H., & Presser, S. (1981). *Questions and answers in attitude surveys: Experiments on question form, wording, and context.* New York: Academic Press.

Schutt, R. K. (1992). *The perspectives of DMH shelter staff: Their clients, their jobs, their shelters, and the service system.* Unpublished report to the Metro Boston Region of the Massachusetts Department of Mental Health, University of Massachusetts at Boston.

Schutt, R. K. (2005). Sampling. In R. M. Grinnell, Jr., & Y. A. Unrau (Eds.), *Social work research and evaluation: Quantitative and qualitative approaches* (7th ed., pp. 149–169). New York: Oxford University Press.

Schutt, R. K., Goldfinger, S. M., & Penk, W. E. (1992). The structure and sources of residential preferences among seriously mentally ill homeless adults. *Sociological Practice Review, 3*, 148–156.

Schutt, R. K., Gunston, S., & O'Brien, J. (1992). The impact of AIDS prevention efforts on AIDS knowledge and behavior among sheltered homeless adults. *Sociological Practice Review, 3*, 1–7.

Schwandt, T. A. (1996). Farewell to criteriology. *Qualitative Inquiry, 2*(1), 58–72.

Seligman, M. E. (1975). *Helplessness*. San Francisco: Freeman.

Shadish, W. R. (1995). The logic of generalization: Five principles common to experiments and ethnographies. *American Journal of Community Psychology, 23*, 419–428.

Shadish, W. R., & Haddock, C. K. (1994). Combining estimates of effect size. In C. Harris & H. Larry (Eds.), *The handbook of research synthesis* (pp. 97–109). New York: Russell Sage Foundation.

Shamai, M. (2003). Therapeutic effects of qualitative research: Reconstructing the experience of treatment as a by-product of qualitative evaluation. *Social Service Review, 7*, 455–467.

Shank, G., & Villella, O. (2004). Building on new foundations: Core principles and new directions for qualitative research. *Journal of Educational Research, 98*, 46–55.

Shapiro, J. R., & Mangelsdorf, S. C. (1994). The determinants of parenting competence in adolescent mothers. *Journal of Youth and Adolescence, 23*, 621–641.

Shaw, I. F., Greene, J. C., & Mark, M. M. (Eds.). (2006). *The SAGE handbook of evaluation*. Thousand Oaks, CA: Sage.

Shek, D. T., Tang, V. M., & Han, X. Y. (2005). Evaluation of evaluation studies using qualitative research methods in the social work literature (1990–2003). *Research on Social Work Practice, 15*, 180–194.

Shepherd, J., Hill, D., Bristor, J., & Montalvan, P. (1996). Converting an ongoing health study to CAPI: Findings from the National Health and Nutrition Study. In R. B. Warnecke (Ed.), *Health survey research methods conference proceedings* (pp. 159–164). Hyattsville, MD: U.S. Department of Health and Human Services.

Shlonsky, A., & Gibbs, L. (2004). Will the real evidence-based practice please stand up? Teaching the process of evidence-based practice to the helping professions. *Brief Treatment and Crisis Intervention, 4*, 137–153.

Shlonsky, A., & Wagner, D. (2005). The next step: Integrating actuarial risk assessment and clinical judgment into an evidence-based practice framework in CPS case management. *Children and Youth Services Review, 27*, 409–427.

Silverman, D. (1997). The logics of qualitative research. In G. Miller & R. Dingwall (Eds.), *Context and method in qualitative research* (pp. 12–25). London: Sage.

Skinner, H. A., & Sheu, W. (1982). Reliability of alcohol use indices: The lifetime drinking history and the MAST. *Journal of Studies on Alcohol, 43*, 1157–1170.

Slone, L., & Hull, J. (2002). Deception of research subjects. In R. Amdur & E. Bankert (Eds.), *Institutional review board: Management and function* (pp. 244–249). Sudbury, MA: Jones & Bartlett.

Smith, M. L. (1980). Publication bias and meta-analysis. *Evaluation in Education, 4*, 18–21.

Smith, T. W. (1984). Nonattitudes: A review and evaluation. In C. F. Turner & E. Martin (Eds.), *Surveying subjective phenomena* (pp. 215–255). New York: Russell Sage Foundation.

Sosin, M., Colson, P., & Grossman, S. (1988). *Homelessness in Chicago: Poverty and pathology, social institutions and social change*. Chicago: Chicago Community Trust.

Staudt, M., Howard, M. O., & Drake, B. (2001). The operationalization, implementation, and effectiveness of the strengths perspective: A review of empirical studies. *Journal of Social Service Research, 27*(3), 1–21.

Sterling, T. D. (1959). Publication decisions and their possible effects on inferences drawn from tests of significance—or vice versa. *Journal of the American Statistical Association, 54*, 30–34.

Stewart, A. L., & Napoles-Springer, A. (2000). Health-related quality of life assessments in diverse population groups in the United States. *Medical Care, 38*, 102–124.

Stewart, D. W. (1984). *Secondary research: Information sources and methods*. Thousand Oaks, CA: Sage.

Stille, A. (2000, May 20). A happiness index with a long reach: Beyond G.N.P. to subtler measures. *New York Times*, pp. A17, A19.

Stock, W. A. (1994). Systematic coding for research synthesis. In H. Cooper & L. V. Hedges (Eds.), *The handbook of research synthesis* (pp. 125–138). New York: Russell Sage Foundation.

Stout, D. (1997a, March 23). Officials are starting early in their defense of the 2000 census. *New York Times*, p. 37.

Stout, D. (1997b, May 4). Senate panel opposes use of sampling in next census. *New York Times*, p. 31.

Straus, S. E., & McAlister, F. A. (2000). Evidence-based medicine: A commentary on common criticisms. *Canadian Medical Association Journal, 163*, 837–841.

Straus, S. E., Richardson, W. S., Glasziou, P., & Haynes, R. B. (2005). *Evidence-based medicine: How to practice and teach EBM* (3rd ed.). New York: Elsevier/Churchill Livingstone.

Strauss, A., & Corbin, J. (1998). *Basics of qualitative research: Techniques and procedures for developing grounded theory*. Thousand Oaks, CA: Sage.

Subramanyam, K. (1981). *Scientific and technical information resources*. New York: Marcel Dekker.

Suchman, E. (1967). *Evaluative research: Principles and practice in public service and social action programs*. New York: Russell Sage Foundation.

Sudarkasa, N. (1997). Interpreting the African heritage in Afro-American family organization. In H. McAdoo (Ed.), *Black families* (3rd ed., pp. 9–40). Thousand Oaks, CA: Sage.

Sudman, S. (1976). *Applied sampling*. New York: Academic Press.

Survey on Adultery: "'I Do' Means 'I Don't.'" (1993, October 19). *New York Times*, pp. A19, A20.

Sutton, C., & Broken Nose, M. (2005). American Indian families: An overview. In M. McGoldrick, J. Giordano, & L. Garcia-Preto (Eds.), *Ethnicity and family therapy* (3rd ed., pp. 43–54). New York: Guilford.

Swarns, R. (1996, October 15). Moscow sends homeless to faraway hometowns. *New York Times*, pp. A1, A12.

Tatum, B. (1997). Out there stranded? Black families in white communities. In H. McAdoo (Ed.), *Black families* (3rd ed., pp. 214–233), Thousand Oaks, CA: Sage.

Taylor, J. (1977). Toward alternative forms of social work research: The case for naturalistic methods. *Journal of Social Welfare, 4*, 119–126.

Thompson, P. (1988). *The voice of the past: Oral history* (2nd ed.). New York: Oxford University Press.

Thyer, B. A. (2005). A comprehensive listing of social work journals. *Research on Social Work Practice, 15*, 310–311.

Thyer, B. A., & Wodarski, J. S. (1998). First principles of empirical social work practice. In B. A. Thyer & J. S. Wodarski (Eds.), *Handbook of empirical social work practice: Vol. 1. Mental Disorders* (pp. 1–21). New York: Wiley.

Tickle, J. J., & Heatherton, T. F. (2002). Research involving college students. In R. Amdur & E. Bankert (Eds.), *Institutional review board: Management and function* (pp. 399–400). Sudbury, MA: Jones & Bartlett.

Timmer, D., Eitzen, S., & Talley, K. (1993). *Paths to homelessness: Extreme poverty and the urban housing crisis*. Boulder, CO: Westview.

Tobler, N. S. (1986). Meta-analysis of 143 adolescent drug prevention programs: Quantitative outcome results of program participants compared to a control or comparison group. *Journal of Drug Issues, 16*, 537–567.

Tourangeau, R. (1999). Context effects. In M. G. Sirken, D. J. Herrmann, S. Schechter, N. Schwartz, J. M. Tanur, & R. Tourangeau (Eds.), *Cognition and survey research* (pp. 111–132). New York: Wiley.

Tripodi, T., & Epstein, I. (1978). Incorporating knowledge of research methodology into social work practice. *Journal of Social Service Research, 2*, 11–23.

Tripodi, T., Fellin, P., & Meyer, H. (1983). *The assessment of social research* (2nd ed.). Itasca, IL: Peacock.

Tripodi, T., & Potocky-Tripodi, M. (2006). *International social work research: Issues and prospects*. New York: Oxford University Press.

Tsang, A. K. T. (2000). Bridging the gap between clinical practice and research: An integrated practice-oriented model. *Journal of Social Service Research, 26*, 69–90.

Tucker, W. (1994). *The science and politics of racial research*. Champaign: University of Illinois Press.

Turner, C. F., & Martin, E. (Eds.). (1984). *Surveying subjective phenomena* (Vols. 1 and 2). New York: Russell Sage Foundation.

Tutty, L. M. (1993). After the shelter: Critical issues for women who leave assaultive relationships. *Canadian Social Work Review, 10*, 183–201.

Tutty, L. M., Rothery, M. L., & Grinnell, R. M., Jr. (Eds.). (1996). *Qualitative research for social workers: Phases, steps, and tasks*. Boston: Allyn & Bacon.

Tzavaras-Catsambas, T., & Preskill, H. S. (2006). *Reframing evaluation through appreciative inquiry*. Thousand Oaks, CA: Sage.

United Way of America. (2006). Outcome Measurement Resource Network *Research Library*. Retrieved August 20, 2006, from http://national.unitedway.org/outcomes/library/pgmomres.cfm

Unrau, Y. A. (2005). Selecting a data collection method and data source. In R. M. Grinnell, Jr., & Y. A. Unrau (Eds.), *Social work research and evaluation: Quantitative and qualitative approaches* (7th ed., pp. 339–349). New York: Oxford University Press.

Unrau, Y. A., Gabor, P. A. & Grinnell, R. M. (2007). *Evaluation in social work: The art and science of practice* (4th ed.). New York: Oxford University Press.

Urban Institute. (2003). *Surveying clients about outcomes.* Washington, DC: Author.

U.S. Bureau of the Census. (2003). *Survey abstracts.* Retrieved July 12, 2004, from http://www.census.gov/mainlwww/ dsabstraccJan03.pdf

U.S. Preventive Services Task Force. (2002). Screening for depression: Recommendations and rationale. *Annals of Internal Medicine, 136,* 760–764.

Valdivia, A. N. (2002). Bell hooks: Ethics from the margins. *Qualitative Inquiry, 8,* 429–447.

Valentine, C. A. (1971). The culture of poverty: Its scientific significance and its implications for action. In E. B. Leacock (Ed.), *The culture of poverty: A critique* (pp. 193–225). New York: Simon & Schuster.

van Wormer, K., Wells, J., & Boes, M. (2000). *Social work with lesbians, gays, and bisexuals: A strengths perspective.* Boston: Allyn & Bacon.

Villeneuve, M., & Maranda, S. (2005). Preparing entry-level practitioners for evidence-based practice. *Journal of the Canadian Health Libraries Association, 26,* 13–21.

W. K. Kellogg Foundation. (1998). *Evaluation handbook.* Battle Creek, MI: Author.

W. K. Kellogg Foundation. (2004). *Logic model development guide.* Battle Creek, MI: Author.

Wakefield, J. C. (1995). When an irresistible epistemology meets an immovable ontology. *Social Work Research, 19,* 9–17.

Wakefield, J. C., & Kirk, S. A. (1996). Unscientific thinking about scientific practice: Evaluating the scientist-practitioner model. *Social Work Research, 20,* 83–95.

Walker, L. (1979). *The battered woman.* New York: Harper & Row.

Walliman, N. S. R. (2005). *Your research project.* Thousand Oaks, CA: Sage.

Ward, L. (2004). Wading through the stereotypes: Positive and negative associations between media use and black adolescents' concepts of self. *Developmental Psychology, 40,* 284–294.

Webb, E. I., Campbell, D. T., Schwartz, R. D., & Sechrest, L. (2000). *Unobtrusive measures* (Rev. ed.). Thousand Oaks, CA: Sage.

Webb, S. A. (2001). Some considerations on the validity of evidence based practice in social work. *British Journal of Social Work, 31,* 57–79.

Weber, R. P. (1984). Computer-aided content analysis: A short primer. *Qualitative Sociology, 7,* 126–147.

Wechsler, H., Lee, J. E., Kuo, M., & Lee, H. (2000). College binge drinking in the 1990s: A continuing problem. Results of the Harvard School of Public Health 1999 College Alcohol Study. Retrieved December 1, 2006, from http://www.hsph.harvard.edu/cas/rpt2000/CAS2000rpt2 .html

Wechsler, H., Nelson, T., & Weitzman, E. (2000). From knowledge to action: How Harvard's college alcohol study can help your campus design a campaign against student alcohol abuse. *Change, 32,* 38–43.

Weinbach, R. W. (2005). *Evaluating social work services and programs.* Boston: Allyn & Bacon.

Weinbach, R. W., & Grinnell, R. M., Jr. (2007). *Statistics for social workers* (7th ed.). Boston: Allyn & Bacon.

Weintraub, I. (2000). *The role of grey literature in the sciences.* Retrieved August 18, 2006, from http://library.brooklyn .cuny.edu/access/greyliter.htm

Weiss, C. H. (1998). *Evaluation* (2nd ed.). Upper Saddle River, NJ: Prentice-Hall.

Weiss, I. K., Nagel, C. L., & Aronson, M. K. (1986). Applicability of depression scales to the old old person. *Journal of the American Geriatrics Society, 34,* 215–218.

Weisz, J. R., McCarty, C. A., & Valeri, S. M. (2006). Effects of psychotherapy for depression in children and adolescents: A meta-analysis. *Psychological Bulletin, 132,* 132–149.

Weitzman, E. A., & Miles, M. B. (1995). *Computer programs for qualitative data analysis: A software sourcebook.* Thousand Oaks, CA: Sage.

Wendler, D., Kington, R., Madans, J., Wye, G. V., Christ-Schmidt, H., et al. (2006). Are racial and ethnic minorities less willing to participate in health research? *PLoS Med 3,* e19.

Westerfelt, A., & Dietz, T. J. (2005). *Planning and conducting agency-based research: A workbook for social work students in field placements* (2nd ed.). Boston: Allyn & Bacon.

Wholey, J. S., Hatry, H. P., & Newcomer, K. E. (Eds.). (2004). *Handbook of practical program evaluation* (2nd ed.). San Francisco: Wiley.

Williams, M., Tutty, L. M., & Grinnell, R. M., Jr. (1995). *Research in social work: An introduction* (2nd ed.). Itasca, IL: Peacock.

Williams, M., Unrau, Y. A., & Grinnell, R. M., Jr. (1998). *Introduction to social work research.* Itasca, IL: Peacock.

Williams, M., Unrau, Y. A., & Grinnell, R. M., Jr (2005). Writing qualitative proposals and reports. In R. M. Grinnell, Jr., & Y. A. Unrau (Eds.), *Social work research and evaluation: Quantitative and qualitative approaches* (7th ed., pp. 421–435). New York, Oxford University Press.

Williamson, J. B., Karp, D. A., Dalphin, J. R., & Gray, P. S. (1982). *The research craft.* Boston: Little, Brown.

Witkin, S. L. (1996). If empirical practice is the answer, then what is the question? *Social Work Research, 20,* 69–75.

Wolcott, H. F. (1994). On seeking—and rejecting—validity in qualitative research. In H. Wolcott (Ed.), *Transforming qualitative data: Description, analysis, and interpretation* (pp. 337–373). Thousand Oaks, CA: Sage.

Woodrum, E. (1984). Mainstreaming content analysis in social science: Methodological advantages, obstacles, and solutions. *Social Science Research, 13,* 1–19.

Woolf, S. H., Battista, R. N., Anderson, G. M., Logan, A. G., & Wang, E. (1990). Assessing the clinical effectiveness of preventive maneuvers: Analytic principles and systematic methods in reviewing evidence and developing clinical practice recommendations. *Journal of Clinical Epidemiology, 43,* 891–905.

Wortman, P. M. (1994). Judging research quality. In C. Harris & H. Larry (Eds.), *The handbook of research synthesis* (pp. 97–109). New York: Russell Sage Foundation.

Wright, J., & Weber, E. (1987). *Homelessness and health.* New York: McGraw-Hill.

Yegidis, B. L., & Weinbach, R. W. (2005). Using existing knowledge. In R. M. Grinnell, Jr., & Y. A. Unrau (Eds.), *Social work research and evaluation: Quantitative and qualitative approaches* (7th ed., pp. 45–57). New York: Oxford University Press.

Yin, R. K. (1994). *Case study research: Design and methods* (2nd ed.). Thousand Oaks, CA: Sage.

Youngblut, J., & Brooten, D. (1999). Alternate child care history of hospitalization and preschool child behavior. *Nursing Research, 48,* 29–34.

Zakour, M. (1994). Measuring career-development volunteerism: Guttman scale analysis using Red Cross volunteers. *Journal of Social Service Research, 19,* 103–120.

Zastrow, C., & Kirst-Ashman, K. (2007). *Understanding human behavior and the social environment* (7th ed.). Chicago: Nelson-Hall.

Credits

CA: Wadsworth. © 2007 by Wadsworth Publishing. Reprinted with permission.

Figure 5.3 Adapted from: "Assessment of Client-Patient Satisfaction: Development of a General Scale," by Daniel L. Larsen, C. Clifford Attkisson, William A. Hargreaves, and Than D. Nguyen, *Evaluation and Program Planning, 2* (1979): 197–207. Used with permission.

Figure 5.4 Adapted from: *Diagnostic and Statistical Manual of Mental Disorders* (4th ed.), by the American Psychiatric Association. Washington, DC: Author, 1994.

Figures 7.1–7.10 Adapted from: *Research in Social Work: A Primer*, by Richard M. Grinnell, Jr., and Margaret Williams. Copyright © 1990 by F. E. Peacock Publishers; *Research in Social Work: An Introduction* (2nd ed.), by Margaret Williams, Leslie M. Tutty, and Richard M. Grinnell, Jr. Copyright © 1995 by F. E. Peacock Publishers; and *Introduction to Social Work Research*, by Margaret Williams, Yvonne A. Unrau, and Richard M. Grinnell, Jr. Copyright © 1998 by F. E. Peacock Publishers.

Figure 10.1 Adapted from: *Research in Social Work: A Primer*, by Richard M. Grinnell, Jr., and Margaret Williams. Copyright © 1990 by F. E. Peacock Publishers.

Figure 10.2 Adapted from: *Social Research Methods: Qualitative and Quantitative Approaches* (6th ed.), by W. Lawrence Neuman. Copyright © 2006 by Allyn & Bacon.

Figure 11.1 Adapted from: *Filial Deprivation and Foster Care*, by Shirley Jenkins and Elaine Norman. Copyright © 1972 by Columbia University Press.

Figure 12.2 Adapted from: *Questions and Answers in Attitude Surveys: Experiments on Question Form, Wording, and Context*, by H. Schuman and S. Presser. Copyright © 1981 by Academic Press.

Figures 12.3, 12.4, and 12.8 Adapted from: "Work, Family, and the Sense of Control: Implications for the Psychological Well-being of Women and Men," by C. E. Ross. Proposal submitted to the National Science Foundation, University of Illinois at Urbana, 1990. Used with permission.

Figure 12.6 Adapted from: *The Perspectives of DMH Shelter Staff: Their Clients, Their Jobs, Their Shelters, and the Service System*, by R. K. Schutt. Unpublished report to the Metro Boston Region of the Massachusetts Department of Mental Health, University of Massachusetts at Boston, 1992.

Figure 12.7 Adapted from: Metro Social Services, Nashville-Davidson County, TN, 1987, Path Community Survey.

Figure 12.9 Adapted from: *The NORC General Social Survey: A User's Guide*, by J. A. Davis and T. W. Smith. Copyright © 1992 by Sage Publications.

Figure 12.10 Adapted from: *Mail and Telephone Surveys: The Total Design Method* (pp. 74–75), by D. A. Dillman. Copyright © 1978 by John Wiley. Reprinted with permission.

Figures 17.3, 17.5, and 17.8 Adapted from: "Univariate Analysis," by Donald W. Beless, in *Social Work Research and Evaluation*, edited by Richard M. Grinnell, Jr. Copyright © 1981 by F. E. Peacock Publishers.

Figure 25.1 Adapted from: "Will the Real Evidence-Based Practice Please Stand Up? Teaching the Process of Evidence-Based Practice to the Helping Professions," by A. Shlonsky and L. Gibbs, *Brief Treatment and Crisis Intervention, 4* (2004): 137–153.

Figure 25.2 Adapted from: "The Next Step: Integrating Actuarial Risk Assessment and Clinical Judgment into an Evidence-Based Practice Framework in CPS Case Management," by A. Shlonsky and D. Wagner, *Children and Youth Services Review, 27* (2005): 409–427.

TABLES

Table 5.1 Adapted from: "The *CES-D* Scale: A Self-Report Depression Scale for Research in the General Population," by L. Radloff, *Applied Psychological Measurement, 1* (1977): 385–401. © 1977. Reprinted with permission of Sage Publications, Inc.

Table 15.2 "But Does It Work? Improving Evaluations of Sexuality Education," by Debra W. Haffner and Eva S. Goldfarb, *SIECUS Report*, Vol. 25, No. 6 (August/September 1997). Retrieved January 6, 2007, from: http://www.siecus.org/pubs/evals/ButDoesItWork.pdf

Table 16.1 Adapted from: *Research Design for Social Work and the Human Services* (2nd ed.), by Jeane W. Anastas. Copyright © 1999 by Columbia University Press. Used with the permission of the publisher.

Table 20.25 Adapted from: "Social Work Research and the Quest for Effective Practice," by A. Rosen, E. Proctor, and M. Staudt, *Social Work Research, 23* (1999): 4–14.

Table 25.1 Adopted from: "Will the Real Evidence-Based Practice Please Stand Up? Teaching the Process of Evidence-Based Practice to the Helping Professions," by A. Shlonsky and L. Gibbs, *Brief Treatment and Crisis Intervention, 4* (2004): 137–153.

Table 26.1 Dawn C. Koger, Ph.D., Early Childhood Consultant, Oakland Schools, 2111 Pontiac Lake Road, Waterford, Michigan 48328. Used with permission.

CHAPTERS

Chapter 1 Adapted and modified from: "Chapter 1: Introduction to Social Work Research," by Margaret Williams, Yvonne Unrau, and Richard M. Grinnell, Jr., in *Research Methods for Social Workers* (5th ed., pp. 2–31), by Margaret Williams, Yvonne Unrau, and Richard M. Grinnell, Jr. Copyright © 2005 by Eddie Bowers Publishing. Also adapted from: *Research in Social Work: A Primer*, by Richard M. Grinnell, Jr., and Margaret Williams. Copyright © 1990 by F. E. Peacock Publishers; *Research in Social Work: An Introduction* (2nd ed.), by Margaret Williams, Leslie M. Tutty, and Richard M. Grinnell, Jr. Copyright © 1995 by F. E. Peacock Publishers; and Margaret Williams, Yvonne A. Unrau, and Richard M. Grinnell, Jr., *Introduction to Social Work Research*. Copyright © 1998 by F. E. Peacock Publishers.

Chapter 3 Adapted from: "Chapter 2: The Quantitative Research Approach," by Margaret Williams, Yvonne Unrau, and Richard M. Grinnell, Jr., in *Research Methods for Social Workers* (5th ed., pp. 32–55), by Margaret Williams, Yvonne Unrau, and Richard M. Grinnell, Jr. Copyright © 2005 by Eddie Bowers Publishing.

Chapter 4 Adapted from: "Chapter 3: The Qualitative Research Approach," by Margaret Williams, Yvonne Unrau, and Richard M. Grinnell, Jr., in *Research Methods for Social Workers* (5th ed., pp. 56–76), by Margaret Williams, Yvonne Unrau, and Richard M. Grinnell, Jr. Copyright © 2005 by Eddie Bowers Publishing.

Chapter 5 Adapted and modified from: "Chapter 3: Conceptualization and Measurement," by Rafael Engel and Russell K. Schutt, in *The Practice of Research in Social Work* (pp. 63–100). Copyright © 2005 by Sage Publications, Inc. Reprinted by permission of Sage Publications.

Chapter 6 Adapted from: "Chapter 4: Sampling," in *Investigating the Social World: The Process and Practice of Research* (4th ed., pp. 127–164), by Russell K. Schutt. Copyright © 2004 by Pine Forge Press. Reprinted by permission of Pine Forge Press.

Chapter 7 Adapted and modified from: "Chapter 8: Case-Level Designs," by Margaret Williams, Yvonne Unrau, and Richard M. Grinnell, Jr., in *Research Methods for Social Workers* (5th ed., pp. 146–165), by Margaret Williams, Yvonne Unrau, and Richard M. Grinnell, Jr. Copyright © 2005 by Eddie Bowers Publishing.

Chapter 8 Adapted and modified from: "Chapter 9: Group-Level Designs," by Margaret Williams, Yvonne Unrau, and Richard M. Grinnell, Jr., in *Research Methods for*

Social Workers (5th ed., pp. 166–210), by Margaret Williams, Yvonne Unrau, and Richard M. Grinnell, Jr. Copyright © 2005 by Eddie Bowers Publishing.

Chapter 12 Adapted from: "Chapter 8: Survey Research," by Rafael Engel and Russell K. Schutt, in *The Practice of Research in Social Work* (pp. 221–272). Copyright © 2005 by Sage Publications, Inc. Reprinted by permission of Sage Publications.

Chapter 17 Adapted from: "Chapter 15: Data Analysis," in *Research in Social Work: An Introduction* (pp. 277–303), by Margaret Williams, Leslie M. Tutty, and Richard M. Grinnell, Jr. Copyright © 1995 by F. E. Peacock Publishers.

Chapter 18 Adapted from: "Phase Three: Analyzing Your Data," by Heather Coleman and Yvonne Unrau, in *Qualitative Research for Social Workers: Phases, Steps, and Tasks* (pp. 88–119), edited by Leslie M. Tutty, Michael A. Rothery, and Richard M. Grinnell, Jr. Copyright © 1996 by Allyn & Bacon. Reprinted by permission. Example used in Chapter 18 adapted and modified from: "After the Shelter: Critical Issues for Women Who Leave Assaultive Relationships," by Leslie M. Tutty, *Canadian Social Work Review, 10* (1993): 183–201. Copyright © 1993 by *Canadian Social Work Review.* Used by permission.

Chapter 26 Adapted and modified from: *Evaluation in Social Work: The Art and Science of Practice*, by Yvonne A. Unrau, Peter A. Gabor, and Richard M. Grinnell, Jr. Copyright © 2007 by Oxford University Press.

Glossary Some of the terms in the glossary may have been adapted and modified from: "Glossary," by Yvonne A. Unrau, in *Evaluation and Quality Improvement in the Human Services*, by Peter A. Gabor and Richard M. Grinnell, Jr. Copyright © 1994 by Allyn & Bacon; *Evaluation for Social Workers: A Quality Improvement Approach for the Social Services* (2nd ed.), by Peter A. Gabor, Yvonne A. Unrau, and Richard M. Grinnell, Jr. Copyright © 1998 by Allyn & Bacon; *Research in Social Work: A Primer*, by Richard M. Grinnell, Jr., and Margaret Williams. Copyright © 1990 by F. E. Peacock Publishers; *Student Study Guide for the Fourth Edition of* Social Work Research and Evaluation, by Judy Krysik, Irene Hoffart, and Richard M. Grinnell, Jr. Copyright © 1993 by F. E. Peacock Publishers; *Student Study Guide for the Fifth Edition of* Social Work Research and Evaluation: Quantitative and Qualitative Approaches, by Yvonne A. Unrau, Judy L. Krysik, and Richard M. Grinnell, Jr. Copyright © 1997 by F. E. Peacock Publishers; *Student Study Guide for the Sixth Edition of* Social Work Research and Evaluation: Quanti-

Index

Page numbers in *italics* indicate figures or tables.